Adolescent Development
and Behavior

Adolescent Development and Behavior
THIRD EDITION

JEROME B. DUSEK
Syracuse University

Prentice Hall Upper Saddle River, New Jersey 07458

Library of Congress Cataloging-in-Publication Data

Dusek, Jerome B.
    Adolescent development and behavior / Jerome B. Dusek.—3rd ed.
      p.   cm.
    Includes bibliographical references and index.
    ISBN 0-13-362922-8
    1. Adolescent psychology.   I. Title.
BF724.D84   1996   95-20434
155.5—dc20   CIP

Acquisitions editor: Pete Janzow
Production supervisor: Andrew Roney
Manufacturing buyer: Tricia Kenny
Cover design: Bruce Kenselaar
Photo research: Page Poore
Cover illustration: Robert Zimmerman

Printed in the United States of America
10 9 8 7 6 5 4 3 2 1

ISBN 0-13-362922-8

Prentice-Hall International (UK) Limited, *London*
Prentice-Hall of Australia Pty. Limited, *Sydney*
Prentice-Hall Canada Inc., *Toronto*
Prentice-Hall Hispanoamericana, S.A., *Mexico*
Prentice-Hall of India Private Limited, *New Delhi*
Prentice-Hall of Japan, Inc., *Tokyo*
Simon & Schuster Asia Pte. Ltd., *Singapore*
Editora Prentice-Hall do Brasil, Ltda., *Rio de Janeiro*

Dedication

To Herbert Bilford, a scholar, teacher, and scientist who was dedicated, unassuming, and involved in making others' lives better. I am proud to have known him. I hope he would be proud of this work.

Preface

At the time the first edition of *Adolescent Development and Behavior* was published, college and university courses dealing exclusively with adolescent development were somewhat rare. In most cases adolescence was discussed in the last few weeks of a course on child development or in the context of a course on human development. Only a few archival journals were devoted to disseminating information specifically about adolescence, there were few texts devoted solely to describing development during the adolescent years, the Society for Research on Adolescence did not exist—those interested in adolescence were members of the Society for Research in Child Development—and those few who saw the importance of making the distinction of transitions during the early and late adolescent years were ignored.

In the intervening period all this has changed. Courses dealing with educating students about the unique aspects of adolescent development are common, a large number of journals provide forums for those who conduct research and advance our knowledge about the adolescent years, the number of texts in the field has grown substantially, several societies are devoted exclusively to disseminating knowledge about the adolescent years, and many more scholars are now being trained specifically in the study of adolescent development. All of this is very exciting. The study of adolescence is growing up.

One of the more important aspects of this growth is the burgeoning amount of knowledge about the importance of ethnic background and minority group membership in the adolescent experience. Although noting cross-cultural differences in the adolescent experience, research on the impact of ethnicity was not a force in the field. Today, it is a major concern of many researchers. It is arguably most notable in the area of identity development—Phinney's research has been seminal in pointing out the importance of ethnic identity development. But it also is evidenced in virtually every other aspect of importance to understanding adolescence as a transition to adulthood. This is a logical extension of realizing that adolescence takes place within cultural contexts.

In the earlier editions we described adolescence as virtually all who write about it or teach it do: a transition between childhood and adulthood. This definition is based on the view that adolescence is only one part of a life of development—life-span developmental psychology. The growing research literature allows for expanding the ways in which we can relate adolescent development to both childhood precursors and adulthood outcomes. Examples include identity development, psychological adjustment, and the importance of peer relations.

A goal of previous editions was to attempt to dispel some of the myths about adolescence—*Sturm und Drang* comes to mind. I remain delighted when I observe students gain insight and realize that a single or even several difficult episodes does not necessarily mean adolescence is an especially stressful period of time, for example. Because the large majority of those reading this text will be at the end of their adolescence in some ways and young adults in other ways it is important to allow them to use their own experiences as they read and study the material. Several changes in this edition are aimed at helping students draw on their personal experiences as they explore the study of adolescence. It is hoped this will help them capture the excitement that researchers in the field feel and understand that although the myths have some truth, they are nothing more than stereotypes born from a lack of understanding.

THE CURRENT EDITION

We have retained many aspects of earlier editions of *Adolescent Development and Behavior* in the current edition. Several new features have been incorporated to facilitate student learning.

Life-Span Context.   Adolescence continues to be presented within a life-span context, with the transition from childhood roles into adulthood roles strengthened in this edition. This is evident in our discussion of adaptation to parental divorce, the impact of peer groups and friendships, the emergence of a sense of self, the impact of the school, and the learning of adulthood roles. It also is exemplified in the discussion of the impact of parental rearing practices not only on the child but also on the adolescent. In order to help students understand the importance of considering adolescence within the context of a life-span view of development, Chapter 2 contains a discussion of the special features of developmental theories.

Uniqueness of Adolescence. The emphasis on adolescence within the life span is not done at the cost of the fact that adolescence is in some ways unique—some developmental events occur for the first time during adolescence. Just as childhood—learning to walk, starting school, developing friendships—and adulthood—taking a full-time job, marrying, becoming a parent—have unique experiences, adolescence also entails first-time encounters: The initiation of intimate friendships, career selection, entrance into the sexual sphere, and coming to grips with identity issues are just a few examples.

Cultural Diversity. As we noted, researchers have increased their emphasis on the importance of ethnic group membership in the study of adolescence. This is reflected in the much expanded discussion of ethnicity and minority group membership in this edition. Although some texts contain an entire chapter devoted to discussions of ethnic and minority group membership, I chose not to place the material in a separate chapter. Discussions of ethnic and minority group membership are integrated into the discussions of the various topics. The salience of ethnicity for identity development is discussed in the presentation of material dealing with general identity development, for example. I chose this approach for two reasons. First, my experience teaching undergraduates, and especially freshmen and sophomores, at several universities has demonstrated that students too often treat material in separate chapters as independent and in some ways separate. By integrating the material within the discussion of a topic I hope to decrease students' tendencies to view ethnicity as somehow separate. Second, integrating information on the importance of ethnicity and minority group membership into topical discussions highlights its importance.

Special Emphasis Boxes. As in previous editions, each chapter contains boxes that highlight new areas of research, provide further elaboration of some point discussed in the text, or urge the student to think beyond the material presented.

Chapter Vignettes and Analogies. Users of previous editions will note two changes aimed both at facilitating student learning and placing the material into real-life contexts. First, each chapter opens with a vignette drawn from my experiences in raising an adolescent son. Each is true and occurred just as I describe. The vignettes were chosen to illustrate some aspect of the material presented in the chapter. Second, in each chapter students are encouraged in the text to draw on their own experiences and relate them to the material. For example, students are urged to reflect on their own physical growth rate and how they reacted to those who were early or later maturers, how they dealt with school transitions, including becoming a college freshman, and the peer groups to which they belonged.

Similarly, the use of analogies to illustrate concepts has been increased. In discussing identity statuses, for example, the process of identity development is likened to the process of selecting a college major: Identity achievement is like having selected a major; trying to decide what the major will be is similar to the moratorium status. The discussion questions that end each chapter further allow the student to relate the material to personal experiences. Some encourage the student to survey friends or roommates to gather data about their experiences and relate the findings to the material in the text. Others are more reflective in nature. They require the student to integrate information.

Eclectic Approach.   An eclectic approach is taken throughout. No single perspective is imposed on the student or the material included. The emphasis remains on integrating research findings into a coherent whole and drawing on the best means of explanation available.

Research Design and Statistics.   The appendix dealing with research design and basic statistical concepts is retained for those who wish their students to have exposure to this material. A new section on the special problems of studying minority group adolescents has been added.

Pedagogical Aids.   Each chapter contains an outline of the contents, a listing of the major issues addressed, a comprehensive summary, and a glossary of the key terms that appear in bold print.

ACKNOWLEDGMENTS

Writing a new edition of a text is an involved endeavor that is accomplished best with advice and input from knowledgable others. Their suggestions for topical inclusion or exclusion, editorial suggestions, and critical review are greatly appreciated.

Jerome B. Dusek

Contents

6 Self-Concept, Self-Esteem, and Identity 140

7 Sex-Role Socialization 170

8 Adolescent Sexuality 196

9   **Adolescents and Work   236**

10   **Parent and Family Influences   269**

11   **Peer Group Influences on Adolescent Development   306**

Introduction to Adolescence

1

Major Issues Addressed

The Size of the Adolescent Population
Definition of Important Terms in the Study of Adolescence
How Adolescence Evolved
Adolescence as a Transition Period and a Stage of Development
Alternative Views of the Nature of Adolescence
The Developmental Tasks of Adolescence
Cultural Diversity and Understanding Adolescence
The Research Approach to Understanding Adolescence

I walked into the house to find a neatly folded pile of clothes in the middle of the living room. He came out of his room and announced he would not "wear those clothes anymore" and that I "had better get used to having an adolescent around the house." He was 11 and I was just preparing to help him realize he was becoming an adolescent. He beat me to it!

◆   ◆   ◆

In our culture, as in all others, children grow into adolescents, whatever that may mean in their culture or subculture. They don't necessarily understand it, and don't care if they do. The same is true of most parents. It seems just to happen, but does it? In some ways yes; in others no. These are the issues we explore in this text. In this chapter we learn that the stage of life we call adolescence didn't just happen; social/cultural factors made it happen. And they are the same forces that cause it to constantly change in many ways, and to be different at different social times, for various ethnic groups, and in rural versus urban areas.

INTRODUCTION

As a student in a course about adolescent psychology, you are in a unique position: You have lived, and in some ways still are living, in the period of development you are studying. During your earlier adolescent years you experienced the physical growth changes that made you a physically mature adult. You had a transition to a junior high or middle school, your relationships with your parents began to change, and how teachers, peers, and others expected you to behave also changed. During your later adolescent years you began to think seriously about becoming an adult, were forced to make important long-term decisions about the future (for example, with respect to the curriculum you would complete in high school), and began to experience pressures to decide what you would do upon completing high school.

Much of what you will study is "average" or "typical" adolescent development, because that is what researchers describe. But such descriptions ignore your unique, individual developmental experiences. Therefore, you should fill in the individual component by drawing on your own experiences. If you were an early or late maturer, did your experiences match those of your friends and those reported by the researchers who have studied it? How old were you when you went on your first date? If you are a member of an ethnic minority group, have those who have written about identity development, for example, captured the essence of your experiences? You likely will find that drawing on your own personal experiences leads to greater knowledge, insight, and understanding than simply reading this text.

Cultural and Generational Differences in Adolescent Development

Adolescence is not only a "stage" of development, it is an experience. The experience of adolescence takes place within a specific historical time frame, cultural context, and subculture defined by gender, ethnicity, or area of the country. This means we must be sensitive to considering how adolescence is different from one generation to another due to the historical, economic, and technological times, from country to country as a result of broad cultural differences, for those of different ethnic groups, and from subculture to subculture within the broader society.

Your adolescence, that of your parents, and that of future generations, such as your children, will share certain commonalities, such as biological growth to physical maturity, but were or will be unique in other respects, such as specific music likes and dislikes and modes of dress. In all likelihood you will have your own adolescents around the year 2015. What music will they listen to; will you "understand" it? How will they dress? What technological advances will make their adolescent experience different from yours? Differences in these components of the adolescent experience mean there will be a "generation gap" in how you and your children understand what it means to be an adolescent.

Adolescence also differs between cultures. Adolescence in the United States is different from that in England, Australia, the countries making up the former Soviet Union, China, and other industrialized and nonindustrialized nations. Institutional and societal values and mores impact on the meaning of the various transitions during adolescence, making the experience of adolescence peculiar to the broader social order. Moreover, as the culture changes so, too, does the nature of adolescence (Kett, 1977). Those who were adolescents during the Great Depression had a different adolescence than yours, for example (Elder, 1974).

Of course, there is not *one* American culture; there are many variations linked to social class, ethnic group, religious group, gender, and the like. All adolescents share certain common experiences, but they also have unique **individual differences**, characteristics that are important to the particular adolescence they experience. Adolescents who grow up in poverty have a different adolescence than those who grow up in middle- or upper-class families, regardless of other individual difference characteristics. Similarly, each of us has an ethnic background and value system that impacts on our adolescent experience. African American, Asian, Hispanic or Latino, Native American, and White adolescents do not live identical experiences. The current trend toward valuing the cultural diversity of those who compose the general and adolescent population, as opposed to the melting pot notion, means we need to pay close attention to how that diversity tempers the nature of the adolescent experience.

Estimating the Size of the Adolescent Population

Although we cannot determine precise numbers of adolescents because census data are reported by age groupings and not developmental epoch, we can estimate the size of the adolescent population by looking at the numbers of individuals in various age ranges.

The total population of the United States in 1990 was approximately 249 million (U.S. Bureau of the Census, 1992c). In the age range 10 to 19, roughly those we would label adolescents, there were approximately 34.8 million people. The adolescent portion of the population, then, represented about 14% (1 in every 7 people) of the total population of the United States. There are about 17.1 million early adolescents (ages 10 to 14) and 17.7 million late adolescents (ages 15 to 19). There are about 5.25 million African American adolescents and 26.2 million White adolescents, the remainder being largely Asian and Hispanic/Latino adolescents. About half of the adolescent population is male and half female, regardless of racial/ethnic group. Clearly, adolescents form a very large segment of the population.

DEFINITION OF CRITICAL TERMS
IN ADOLESCENT PSYCHOLOGY

The term *adolescence* comes from the Latin verb *adolescere*, which means "to grow up" or "to grow to maturity." As it is commonly defined, then, **adolescence** is seen as a biological bridge between childhood and adulthood. We also view it as the stage in which the individual is required to adapt and adjust childhood *behaviors* to culturally acceptable adult forms. Adolescence is more than a transition; it is a stage of development in its own right, just like childhood or adulthood.

Puberty is the term used to denote the point in time when an individual reaches sexual maturity and becomes capable of bearing offspring and reproducing the species. Puberty, then, is a much more specific term than adolescence.

Pubescence refers to the approximately 2-year period that precedes puberty; it is the period when the physiological changes that cause development of both the primary and secondary sex characteristics that make the individual a biologically mature adult begin. Pubescence occurs during late childhood and early adolescence, with puberty occurring somewhat later, as we discuss in Chapter 3.

In addition to the highly individualistic physiological and physical correlates of adolescence, there are also important social and cultural determinants. For example, in some societies adolescence as we understand it does not even occur. Instead, a *puberty rite ceremony,* or *rite of passage,* marks the end of childhood and the beginning of adulthood. In these societies, adolescence is an extremely short period of time, virtually the time from the beginning to the end of the puberty rite.

Defining adolescence, then, is a difficult task. Identifying the start of adolescence presents no particular problem: It is generally agreed that adolescence starts with the physical changes that occur during pubescence. However, it is more difficult to define the end of adolescence, *adulthood.* The term *adulthood* usually refers to the stage of life when a person is fully developed physically, is emotionally and socially mature, and is economically independent. However, because people do not mature in all these areas at the same rate, adulthood is a very inadequate scientific term.

To help clarify, we usually assume that adulthood is reached when one is engaging in the socially defined roles of typical adults in the society. In the United States, these include voting, economic independence, completing education, and perhaps marrying and parenting, among others. Although this definition of adulthood also presents problems (for example, how to classify college students—see Box 1-1), it is a reasonable set of bases on which to define the end of adolescence.

For our purposes, then, adolescence is that span in time bounded at the lower end by the beginnings of the physiological changes accompanying pubescence and bounded at the upper end by the assumption of various adulthood

Adolescents from different cultural and ethnic backgrounds share common experiences but also find unique aspects to their adolescence. (*Laima E. Druskis*)

BOX 1–1　Are College Students Adolescents?

As we explained in the text, adolescence is a difficult stage of development to define. This is especially true for the end point of adolescence: the entrance into adulthood. It is the defining characteristics of adulthood that lead to the interesting question of college students being adolescents. Adults, in a general sense, are viewed as being economically, emotionally, and socially independent of their original family and parents. In addition, adults often are viewed as better able than adolescents to accept responsibility, plan for the future, and behave in a mature manner. All of these characteristics are nebulous and difficult to define.

Consider the circumstances of a typical 14- or 15-year-old. This person is in a school setting, economically dependent on the family, likely not emotionally mature, perhaps not able to accept complete responsibility for all of his or her actions, and not employed full time. These characteristics are reminiscent of those that describe children. A major difference between adolescents and children, however, is the level of physical development. Adolescents' physical development is much closer to adults' than to children's. And, on the other dimensions mentioned here, adolescents are more advanced toward adulthood than are children.

Now consider a typical adult. This adult probably is economically independent of his or her parents, relatively emotionally mature, able to plan for the future, capable of accepting responsibility, and usually employed. To be sure, not all adults fit this mold, and those who do may not fit it all the time. Nonetheless, these distinctions differentiate adults and adolescents.

Now consider the typical high school student who has recently become a college student. Although many may participate in a work study program as part of a financial aid package to pay their expenses, they likely depend on their parents for some economic support. They need not, or do not, accept many responsibilities with which adults must deal. Responsibility for providing food, clothing, and shelter for a family are some examples. Although most college students are emotionally and socially much more mature than children or younger adolescents, they are likely less so than many adults.

This example raises several interesting points. First, it demonstrates what Erikson (1968) called the rolelessness of adolescence: The adolescent is neither child nor adult. Second, it suggests that many college students are very similar to adolescents, and, indeed, might well be considered adolescents. At the same time, however, they are very similar to adults. They are physically, socially, and intellectually more like adults than children.

No doubt some of these students object to being described as adolescents, even though certain adolescent characteristics may aptly describe them. Perhaps their concerns can be allayed by our pointing out that we must consider transitions into adulthood individually. The first transition is biological; other transitions are completed, in no as yet identified order, throughout the adolescent years. Hence one may indeed be economically independent, socially or emotionally mature, or able to accept and deal with adult-type responsibilities. However, because we do not achieve all these competencies at the same time, we exhibit characteristics of adulthood and adolescence at the same time.

A variety of individual differences make the adolescent experience unique for each of us. Whether we are male or female, early or late maturing, or members of an ethnic minority influences the nature of our adolescence. These individual difference characteristics are important to understanding how one experiences adolescence.

Are college students adolescents? In some ways, yes. Economic dependence on parents, for example, is a characteristic of adolescence, not adulthood. Because most college students are economically dependent, they are in that way adolescents. In some ways, such as biological maturity, ability to make long-range decisions, and ability to plan for the future, no. And, of course, some college students are more, or less, advanced toward adulthood than others. Where do you stand?

roles. Because we acquire these roles at different ages we become adults in stages; we lose our adolescence gradually. And our own individual circumstances are important in determining how soon we must take on some adultlike roles.

For example, adolescents in single-parent families may have to assume responsibilities for others, such as a younger sibling, at a relatively young age. Latchkey children (those who come home after school and must fend for themselves until a parent gets home) must learn more adultlike behaviors sooner than those who have an adult at home when school lets out. Earlier maturers are expected to behave more like older adolescents than are average or late maturers; they are expected to assume more adult roles sooner than their average or late maturing peers.

Age does not define adolescence.   There are several reasons why we have not used age (e.g., the teen years) to define adolescence. First, considerable variation exists (approximately 4 years) in the age of onset of pubescence. This variability is not recognized in an age-related definition. In addition, the 18-year-old is still likely to be in school and hence not engaged in full-time adulthood roles. Second, age is not a psychological variable. It is simply a measure of time and only a very rough index of the experiences one encounters that are critical to psychological development. Finally, to restrict adolescence to the teenage years, for example, is to ignore the fact that many individuals (for example, college students) play some "adolescent" roles into their early 20s (see Box 1–1).

HOW DID ADOLESCENCE DEVELOP?

We did not always have a developmental period of adolescence *as we know it*; it came into being during the mid-1800s, and since then has grown in length. Prior to that time, children were considered to be simply miniature adults, not people who fundamentally were somehow different. Just look at paintings of families or children from that and earlier times. Children often were depicted in staid poses and adult dress, for example. The many social and cultural changes that have occurred since the mid-1800s not only created adolescence, but continue to cause it to evolve and change (Kett, 1977). Adolescence is a product of social evolution, including codified laws, social institutions, and cultural expectations, and it changes as the culture evolves.

The Evolution of Adolescence

A number of social conditions created the American form of adolescence. One important influence was the urbanization and industrialization of the nation. During the rural/agricultural years children were considered to be merely minia-ture adults (Kessen, 1965; Kett, 1977). They were expected to work on the farm or take apprenticeships, for example. In comparison to current-day stan-dards, children and adolescents often were taken advantage of. They worked in mines, factories, and sweatshops for long hours and very little pay. A predomi-nant aspect of the rearing philosophy was to prepare the child for an adult job through work experiences. Formal schooling was available for the elite but not the masses. Adolescence as we know it did not exist.

With increasing urbanization during the late 1800s and throughout the 1900s, increasing numbers of youth grew up in urban areas (about 76% of Amer-icans live in or near urban areas today). As a result, a number of social and legal events occurred that impacted dramatically on the nature of adolescence. Child labor laws initiated in the mid-1800s took children and adolescents out of the factories, mines, and sweatshops in order to protect jobs for adults. Refinements of the laws defined working conditions that attempted to ensure safe and hu-mane working conditions for older adolescents. Other laws (for example, crimi-nal) defined special conditions for youngsters up to the age of 16 or 18. These laws were enacted to allow the courts to treat youth and adults differently. Youth did not have to suffer the same punishment as adults.

During the late 1800s and early 1900s a major factor in the evolution of adolescence occurred: mandated public education for those between the ages of 6 and 18. Placing large numbers of youth in schools contributed to the forma-tion of adolescence in several ways. First, it established a formal separation of youth from adults. It gave youth a role standing of their own. As age grading in schools increased—the one-room multigrade school really did exist—schooling separated those we call children from those we now call adolescents. Second, schooling forced increased contact and time with peers. Perhaps more than any other single factor, required schooling formalized adolescence, not only through the setting and peer contact, but also because of youth activities associ-ated with the school setting (J.S. Coleman, 1961).

As detailed by Kett (1977), then, adolescence is a developmental period that was created by a variety of changes in the society. Although the biological changes associated with adolescence are universal—except for severe depriva-tion or some physical pathology condition, all humans mature biologically—the nature of adolescence depends on cultural and subcultural factors, changes within a culture as the culture evolves, ethnic group membership, and the other sociocultural circumstances within which one is living.

Adolescence as a Special Stage and Transition

Although adolescence represents a transition to adulthood, much as childhood represents a transition to adolescence, adolescence is a unique period in devel-opment of its own right. First, with the exception of infancy, biological changes occur more rapidly than at any other point in the life span. These changes are relatively obvious signals that the individual is approaching adulthood. As a result of these biological changes, others' expectations for the individual's behavior change, and the individual's views of the self change. Understanding adolescence means more than viewing it as a transition; it means understanding an individual who is living a particular stage of development, much like childhood or adulthood.

Second, adolescence presents the opportunity to study the impact of the joint influence of biological and social change on development. The rapid biological growth interacts with (influences) changing social and personal expectations for behavior that impact on the individual's behavior. By studying how each contributes to explaining the adolescent's behavior, we gain a more clear perspective of adolescence as a transition as well as an important developmental stage in its own right. In this regard, consider the concerns of those who are very early or very late maturers (Chapter 3). The nature of their adolescence is very different from that of the average maturer because of both their own views of their growth and the views of the others, such as peers and parents, with whom they interact.

Finally, a number of important qualitative changes, changes in kind as opposed to amount, occur during the adolescent years. The adolescent becomes capable of reproduction. Changes in thinking skills (abstract thinking ability), peer relations (developing friendships that help one explore one's own individuality), and moral thinking (new views about right and wrong) occur. In each instance, the result is a growth toward similarity to adulthood roles or perspectives. The qualitative transitions that occur are significant indicators of adulthood. Understanding these transitions helps us understand how adulthood emerges.

The transitions of adolescence involve virtually every sphere of development into adulthood. They occur as a result of continually changing and developing roles and tasks. And they take place over an extended period of time. Havighurst (1951; see Box 1–2) detailed these transitions in his discussion of developmental tasks. As he pointed out, we do not experience all these transitions at the same time; we enter "adulthood" in bits and pieces, first this way and then that. And the tasks are different for early and late adolescents.

PERSPECTIVES ON ADOLESCENCE

The Social View of Adolescence

From a societal perspective, adolescence is a period of development during which children acquire the skills and attitudes that will help them become adults who contribute to society in meaningful ways. Adolescents are given the time to learn to be adults. Today's adolescents are not required to play an adult-like role in society. For the most part, they are not needed or wanted in the job market (Campbell, 1969), for example. By keeping adolescents out of the job

BOX 1–2   Developmental Tasks of Adolescence

Robert Havighurst (1951) coined the term **developmental task** to describe the individual's accomplishment of certain social abilities or attitudes related to development. Developmental tasks are skills, knowledge, functions, or attitudes that individuals must acquire at various stages during their lifetime in order to adjust successfully to the more difficult roles and tasks that lie before them. Developmental tasks are acquired through physical maturation, social fulfillment, and personal effort. Successful mastery of developmental tasks produces a well-adjusted individual who should be competent and capable of dealing with future levels of development. Failure to acquire these developmental skills can often result in maladjustment, increased anxiety, and an inability to deal with the more difficult tasks to come. Finally, Havighurst believes the developmental tasks of any given stage are sequential in nature; that is, each task is a prerequisite for each succeeding task.

The optimal time for each task to be mastered is, to some degree, biologically determined. Havighurst believes there is a critical period of time during which the individual should master each of the various developmental tasks for that particular age and stage of development. Although Havighurst points out that the kinds of developmental tasks through which the individual must proceed may differ from culture to culture, he notes that biologically determined tasks are more likely to be culturally universal than are tasks that have a strong cultural component. With respect to adolescence, Havighurst has noted nine major tasks:

1. Accepting one's physical makeup and acquiring a masculine or feminine sex role.
2. Developing appropriate relations with age-mates of both sexes.
3. Becoming emotionally independent of parents and other adults.
4. Achieving the assurance that one will become economically independent.
5. Determining and preparing for a career and entering the job market.
6. Developing the cognitive skills and concepts necessary for social competence.
7. Understanding and achieving socially responsible behavior.
8. Preparing for marriage and family.
9. Acquiring values that are harmonious with an appropriate scientific world picture.

As you can see, tasks 1, 2, and 8 have a strong biological basis and should be relatively universal. Because they also entail social behaviors, how one resolves these tasks will depend on cultural standards. Tasks 3, 5, and 6 are somewhat biological, but their basis in biology is less obvious. Again, however, these tasks should be relatively universal. Tasks 4, 7, and 9 have no obvious biological basis and might be characteristic of some cultures but not others.

Thornburg (1970–1971) reexamined Havighurst's tasks in an attempt to relate resolving them to changes in cultural, physical, and personal development that have occurred. He discerned that some tasks are now more difficult to master. For example, preparing for and entering the job market is more difficult now than 45 years ago. There are fewer lower skill jobs; more jobs require advanced training. As a result, adolescence is now longer and more complex than it used to be. In turn, this may mean that today's parents have more problems in understanding the nature of adolescence than did their own parents, which may contribute to intergenerational (parent–adolescent) conflict. It also means that socializing adolescents, teaching them to become responsible adults, may be more difficult.

market, society guarantees a greater number of jobs for its adults and protects children and adolescents from exploitation.

Second, it takes a good deal of time to acquire the training and skills necessary to function in our complex adult society. For example, of the occupations available in our society only about 5% are for unskilled labor. Adolescence, then, is a period of time during which the individual may obtain the skills and training necessary to prepare for a vocation in a society in which those without marketable skills are at a disadvantage.

Finally, adolescence gives the person time to learn other, non-work-related adult activities and skills. Society suffers unless its adult members are well prepared for their marital, parental, and civic roles. Because our society is becoming increasingly complex, the learning of these roles is more difficult than in previous generations. The lengthening of the period of adolescence in modern times is in part a response to these complexities. However, just as the individual needs time to learn complex and changing adulthood roles, so too must society provide the supporting structure for these new roles. Today's adolescents, both male and female, are told they should try to reach their greatest possible potential. Yet society has not provided all of the necessary supports for that achievement, such as access to technical training programs or a college education. Hence the development of society and the development of the individual are somewhat out of synchrony. This can produce frustration for both the individual and society, and can make adolescence a difficult transition.

Developmental Psychology Viewpoint of Adolescence

From a developmental perspective, adolescence is a period of time for experimenting with adulthood roles and determining a realistic sense of self. One may decide to be a leader or follower, an active athlete or passive observer, and experiment with a host of other roles that relate to how one views oneself (for example, intelligent, valuable, sickly). Because adolescents do not have to accept the degree of responsibility that adults do when they take on various roles, the long-term consequences of trying out a role and having it fail are not as great as they are for adults. Adolescents can determine the degree to which various social roles and situations are comfortable. It is a time when one may ask the question "Who am I?" and begin to answer it meaningfully.

Biological Perspective of Adolescence

The biological changes that accompany adolescence occur earlier than either the intellectual or social changes. Gender differences in the rate of biological growth may be responsible for differences in adult expectations for the behavior of adolescent females and males. During early adolescence, for example, girls often are expected to behave more like adults than are boys of the same age. Similarly, timing of maturation—whether one is an early or late maturer—is related to social interactions with parents, other adults such as teachers, and peers. Early physical maturers often are treated as more socially and emotionally

Adolescence is a time for asking and answering
the question, "Who am I?" (*Ken Karp*)

mature than they are, or than their age-mates, which may result in unreasonable
expectations being imposed on them. As discussed later in Chapter 3, this may
have lasting effects on one's personality.

These biological influences are intimately related to the social and developmental factors just discussed (M. Richards & Petersen, 1987). The adolescent period gives the individual time to learn the social behaviors and to acquire and
become comfortable with the psychological characteristics that are appropriate
to a biologically mature person. By having this time period to catch up, the individual can better integrate the social behaviors with the biological changes that
influence the behaviors and expectations of others toward her or him.

The Intellectual-Competency View of Adolescence

Adolescents, unlike children, are capable of abstract thinking (formal operations), which allows them to view the social environment in ways not previously possible (see Chapter 4). Adolescents become capable of understanding
the thought processes of others and of interacting with the environment in new

and different ways. Changes in moral thinking (Chapter 5) and in views of the self (Chapter 6) also occur as a result of these cognitive advances. The increased cognitive competence of adolescents also changes the way they feel about the biological and developmental changes they experience. From this perspective, then, adolescence is a time during which the individual learns to cope with abstract thinking, and the consequences of that thinking, as related to self-views, social development, and to interactions with parents, teachers, peers, and others who have a significant impact on the socialization process.

RESEARCHING ADOLESCENCE

It is through research that we describe development in an objective manner, relatively free of subjective opinion. Unlike the early philosophers, who based their views of development on personal experiences (Muuss, 1988), modern-day scholars of adolescence base their views on the scientific approach.

For example, suppose we are interested in studying how being an early versus late maturer is related to interactions with peers. We could ask a group of adolescents if they were or were not early maturers and obtain a measure of their peer popularity. Or, we could observe fifth-grade students on the playground, and infer their maturity status and peer popularity. Finally, we could bring groups of fifth graders into the laboratory, have them rate their physical maturity with reference to a standard set of photographs, and have them interact in some predetermined situation while we observe them. Each method has its virtues and drawbacks. However, the important point is that our conclusions about any relation between early or late maturity and peer relations would be based not on our subjective opinions, but on objective observation. Hence what we find is more likely to be a good representation of the truth and not simply our own opinion.

The evaluation of our observations and the methods by which they are made involve statistics and research design. These concerns are discussed in the appendix. Throughout the text we draw on examples of research to support the statements of general trends in adolescent development. That is why you will see citations to the researchers who have done the observations. Differences in techniques of observation, differences in measurement of the behavior under study—for example, asking people if they were early maturers versus measuring maturity level through X rays of bones—may lead to somewhat different conclusions. That should *not* distress you. We have attempted to present the most consistent evidence available.

Finally, some of the research you will read about is very recent; other research was conducted 20, 30, or more years ago. In part, this reflects the changing interests of researchers. New topics of interest and importance arise—such as studying the impact on development of being an adolescent with a depressed mother. Other topics become resolved—for example, adolescent conformity to peers. In order to provide a sound and thorough treatment we draw on both the newer and the older research, and we give credit to those who conducted it.

SUMMARY

Adolescence is a transition period between childhood and adulthood, a time when the child acquires the social, emotional, and personal skills necessary to enter the adult world. Although all stages of life may be considered transitions, adolescence is a special transition. It is when we become capable of reproducing the species. We begin to think seriously about our future vocational roles. We acquire more adultlike peer and other social relations.

Adolescence begins with the biological changes preceding the growth spurt and ends when the individual becomes an adult. Confusion about entering adulthood results from not attaining adult status in all spheres of development at the same time. Hence adolescence has been described as a period of rolelessness, and adolescents as being neither child nor adult.

Adolescence evolves within a cultural setting because the nature of the transition depends on the natures of childhood and adulthood, which vary across cultures, subcultures, and ethnic groups. Moreover, as a culture changes, the nature of adolescence changes. In the United States, several of the major factors that have influenced the type of adolescence experienced are industrialization, urbanization, child labor laws, and universal public education. Each contributed to segregating young people from adults and adulthood roles, and each contributed to the development of what we call adolescence.

The nature of adolescence also depends on one's own special circumstances. The adolescent experience is different for males and females, for those from various racial/ethnic group backgrounds, and for those from other cultures. Although all adolescents experience some common events, such as the growth spurt, the meaning of these changes depends on one's particular circumstances.

Despite the importance of individual differences in the adolescent experience, adolescence entails mastering a set of developmental tasks as one prepares for adulthood. To the degree the adolescent deals with these tasks successfully, he or she should emerge from adolescence as a well-adjusted and well-socialized adult. This requires a well-integrated view of the various roles we play. Adolescence is a time during which we begin to integrate various roles in meaningful and constructive ways.

Given the complex nature of the various influences on adolescent development, it is clear that when we study adolescent development we are really studying interactions between parents, peers, teachers, the social structure, and the developing individual characteristics of the adolescent. Obviously, this is an arduous and difficult task and no single theory, or perhaps even any set of theories, can detail all the facets of the developmental changes that occur in adolescence. To accommodate this complexity, we detail development in a series of chapters that deal with various important influences on the adolescent's development. We discuss adolescent social development with respect to parents, peers, the school, and other social institutions, and from the perspective of the adolescent with respect to moral development, self views, and vocational development. In addition, biological and intellectual changes are discussed, both in their own right and as they relate to other aspects of adolescent development.

GLOSSARY

adolescence: Developmental period between childhood and adulthood that begins with the biological changes of pubescence. It gradually ends as we slowly take on various adult roles.

developmental task: In Havighurst's view, a psychological or social milestone in development, the successful mastery of which prepares the individual for future development.

individual differences: Characteristics that vary among individuals and may relate to differences in developmental experiences.

puberty: Ability to reproduce the species. A specific biological event.

pubescence: Several-year period prior to puberty when hormonal changes are beginning and the growth spurt is starting.

DISCUSSION QUESTIONS

1. In what ways was your parents' and your adolescence similar and different? Why did the similarities and differences occur?

2. Although age may not be a sound means of defining adolescence, could it be a useful way to describe some other developmental epoch? Why or why not?

3. How might your children's adolescence be different from yours? What factors might cause these differences?

4. In what ways do individual difference characteristics make the adolescent experience different? What are the most important of such characteristics?

2

Explaining Adolescent Behavior

Major Issues Addressed

The Nature of Theories in Explaining Development
The Role of Research in Testing Theories
Theories of Adolescent Development
The Emergence of Adolescence in Cultural Contexts
The Importance of Culture in Defining Adolescence
The Special Nature of Developmental Theories
The Relation Between Theory and Research
Research Designs to Test Theories of Development

Stereotypes of adolescents abound. They are moody. They are going through "that stage." They think they know it all. It is an exceptionally stressful time. Just look at media depictions, and the adolescent you are confronted with is someone who is confused and troubled. Media presentations often exaggerate the degree to which adolescents have difficulties, and often capitalize on adolescent independence strivings and common stereotypes in their portrayals. Although this treatment may entertain, it does not depict the typical adolescent's experience.

◆   ◆   ◆

I never thought he was particularly stressed, and he didn't either. Sure, on occasion he believed life was difficult, but don't we all. In contrast, our neighbors thought their children were going through "that stage," often commenting they were "having trouble" with their adolescents, but everything would be fine in a year or two. They had bought into the stereotype; they truly believed adolescence was an especially stressful period of life, a time to be endured and lived through.

◆   ◆   ◆

Is adolescence really a time of heightened stress, a period when one becomes troubled and confused? Some think so, but others don't. Was your adolescence an especially troubling time, or did you just experience some ups and downs? How about that of your friends? In this chapter we look at alternative views of how to explain why adolescents behave as they do. And we address specifically the question of adolescence as an especially stressful period of life.

INTRODUCTION

In this chapter, we discuss the nature and role of theories in explaining adolescent development. In so doing, we review a number of important theories formulated to explain aspects of adolescent development. We also examine the relation between theories and research, and the importance of research as an aid to our understanding of adolescent development.

DEFINITION OF THEORY

A **theory** is simply a statement, or a group of statements, that attempts to explain some event. A theory is a model of why some particular behavior, as opposed to some other behavior, occurs; a theory describes the factors that cause some piece of behavior.

Our interest, of course, is in understanding adolescence and adolescent behavior. Questions we address include the following:

- Is adolescence really an especially stressful period of life?
- When does adolescence start and when does it end?
- Why do independence strivings increase during adolescence?
- What is the cause of changes in parent–adolescent relations and how can we make adjustments easier?
- Does being an early or late maturer affect personality development?

The theoretical perspectives discussed in this chapter all attempt to explain questions such as these and to spell out the important influences on adolescent development.

The Functions of Theories

Theories have two major functions (P.H. Miller, 1993):

1. Integrate information.
2. Predict new events and explain behavior.

Most theories are relatively narrow in scope and deal only with very specific forms of behavior, such as the effects of various rearing techniques on dependency and self-esteem. By looking at a number of theories, we can put together a more complete picture of the factors that exert an important influence on the developing adolescent.

By deriving **hypotheses**—best guesses as to the causes of behavior—from a theory, one can predict that given a certain set of circumstances a certain behavior should occur. Hence theories predict what conditions will cause some behavior and in this way explain why that behavior occurs.

Although this is very abstract, in reality, using theories—integrating information and discovering the causes of behavior—is something we all do in many common activities (see Box 2-1). We all have expectations (hypotheses) about what causes some adolescents to become delinquents, how different types of child rearing may relate to self-esteem, and how we expect others to behave, such as professors in the classroom, for example. What differentiates our commonsense theory building from that of the scientist lies more in the level of sophistication than in the nature of the theory building.

BOX 2–1   Theory Building and Hypothesis Testing in Everyday Situations

Building theories, formulating hypotheses, and collecting data to test the hypotheses often seems to belong only to the world of the scientist, or perhaps to your chemistry or physics laboratory. However, we all engage in such activities almost daily, and almost every time we encounter a new situation. We may not do so with the sophistication of the scientist or ask questions as complex, but the processes in which we engage are closely allied to those of the research scientist.

As a college student you have a "theory" about how your classes will be conducted. This theory allows you to integrate information concerning the number of class meetings, types of assignments, the work you must do, and how these will vary with the type of class—laboratory, large lecture section, recitation section, seminar. In addition, as you start each new class you have hypotheses about how you, the instructor, and your fellow students will behave. As the class progresses, you gather information (data) that allows you to test your hypotheses and, if necessary, modify your theory in order to better explain your behavior and that of the instructor and the other students. For example, your hypotheses about the conduct of a large lecture section will be altered if the instructor conducts it more like a recitation section. You have "tested" the hypotheses drawn from your theory, and found you may have to alter them.

Other common examples of our everyday use of the scientific method are easy to identify. One that is particularly salient for our understanding of adolescence deals with dating. Try to recall your first date—few of us ever forget it. What were your assumptions about the event? These include what you would be doing, how you would get there, who else would be there, and how the date would end. What expectations (hypotheses) did you have for your behavior and that of your date? These would include circumstances about being picked up at your residence (or picking someone up), no doubt what you would talk about, how you would act, and how the date would progress. Finally, think about how you tested (collected data about) your "best guesses," or hypotheses. Did you match your date's apparel? Did he or she act as you expected? Did you feel like a "good" date? Was it a success?

Whereas we conduct research in an informal manner, the scientist must do so more objectively and rigorously in order to provide the best possible means of explaining behavior. Scientists use sophisticated research designs and statistical analysis to evaluate their theories and hypotheses. But the general processes we use in our everyday lives is not very different from the scientific approach.

In this text we emphasize the scientific approach to the study of adolescence. The major reason is so we can draw on objective evidence about why adolescents develop as they do. In doing so, we draw on each of the different types of theories discussed in this chapter. This eclectic approach will allow us to come to understand adolescent development and behavior in the best possible ways we can.

Developmental theories are aimed specifically at describing changes in behavior over time. In doing this, they must accomplish three tasks (P. H. Miller, 1993):

1. *Describe* changes within a behavior over time.
2. *Describe* changes in relations among several behaviors over time.
3. *Explain* the developmental patterns described.

Examples of each of these tasks are found throughout this text. You will study how the self-concept changes over time (e.g., it becomes more abstract), how peer relationships change during adolescence (e.g., they become more intense), and the timing of physical growth sequences (e.g., some are earlier maturers and others are late maturers), for example. These descriptions are a necessary first step in theory development; they provide the basic information about what is to be explained.

By describing how the self-concept is related to peer relationships and physical growth and how these associations change over time, one is providing the descriptions required by the second task. You will read, for example, that less popular adolescents have poorer self-concepts than more popular adolescents, and that earlier maturers have a more positive self-concept than later maturers.

The third task involves explaining the changes described in the first two. That is, it entails explaining the developmental sequences, or the course of development, for the relationships observed. For our current example, this would involve explaining why one's popularity develops as it does, why one's self-esteem develops as it does, and why popularity is related to self-esteem in the manner it is. As you might surmise, this is a very difficult task because both popularity and self-concept are affected by many other factors (e.g., parental rearing techniques, school performance) that one might or might not have measured. This complexity in part is responsible for our having mini-theories, theories that attempt to explain narrowly defined relations.

The Relation of Theory to Research

An important aspect of any theory is that it must be testable. A theory that cannot be tested is useless because its validity, that is, its accuracy as a model for describing development, can never be ascertained. Each time a set of hypotheses from a particular theory is supported by research we have more confidence that the theory is a reasonable explanation of the behavior of interest. If a theory generates hypotheses that are not supported by research, we lose confidence in it. In such cases, we may either alter the theory or completely abandon it in favor of an alternative theory. It is through the generation of testable hypotheses that theories guide the research effort.

The most widely utilized research designs to test developmental theories are cross-sectional or longitudinal. Each allows us to measure development of behavior over time. In a **cross-sectional study,** individuals of different ages are tested one time. For example, we might hypothesize that older adolescents will have less stereotyped ideas about sex roles than younger adolescents because they are more advanced cognitively. To test this hypothesis, we might give a questionnaire to adolescents aged 12, 14, 16, and 18, and then compare sex-role stereotypes for different age levels. Any *age differences* would either substantiate our hypothesis or indicate it is incorrect. As an alternative, we could conduct a **longitudinal study**, in which we repeatedly survey the same group of adolescents as they mature. Hence we could have adolescents complete the questionnaire when they are 12, 14, 16, and 18. In a longitudinal study we measure *age changes* because we have the same people involved in the research at each time period.

The study of change (age difference or age change) is central to developmental psychology. As detailed in the appendix, the study of age differences, although relatively easy and inexpensive, may result in **developmental trends** (differences in behavior related to age) very different from the age change obtained with longitudinal research. For example, we might find through cross-sectional research that younger adolescents (ages 12 and 14) have less rigid views of sex roles than do older adolescents (ages 16 and 18). A longitudinal study might reveal that older adolescents have less rigid views of sex roles. Which set of findings reveals the "true" developmental trend? To determine the answer is not simple. As we note in the appendix, it may be that cohort and time-of-measurement differences account for the discrepant findings.

A **cohort** is a group of people born about the same time. In a cross-sectional study those in the different age groups are in different cohorts and had different developmental experiences that could cause them to hold different views because they grew up at different times. In 1995, 12-year-olds (born in 1983) had a different set of school, social, and family influences than average 18-year-olds (born in 1977), due to changes in educational philosophy, the economic and social climate, and changes in the family experience (e.g., increases in single-parent families and maternal employment). Age differences might reflect differences in experiences, not development. This is not true in a longitudinal study because all individuals of the same age were born in the same year. Age differences cannot reflect cohort differences, but only changes in behavior that reflect development.

Time of measurement is the term developmental psychologists use to indicate when some behavior, value, or attitude was assessed. For example, attitudes about premarital sexual intercourse might well be expected to change with new trends in the social climate (time). Consider the well-publicized sexual freedom of today's adolescents. As discussed in Chapter 8, we find that prevailing attitudes of adolescents about sexuality are different now than they were a generation ago because of changing social standards. Adolescents who grew up a generation ago have different views about sexuality than those of the current generation. That tells us we must exercise caution in interpreting developmental trends because we must consider the degree to which the topic under study is susceptible to the social times.

THEORIES OF ADOLESCENT DEVELOPMENT

Theories of adolescent development are formulated (1) to describe the biological changes that accompany adolescence and how they affect adolescent development, and (2) to explain the cultural-psychological factors that relate to the adolescent period of development. The complexity of integrating these various influences is in part responsible for the lack of a well-articulated and unified theory of adolescent development. Obviously, explaining the impact of biological hormonal changes on behavior, and integrating that with the impact of psychological and social changes in behavior, is an extremely difficult task. For convenience, we have grouped the theories into those that take a biological, psychodynamic, cognitive-developmental, anthropological, social-learning, or historical perspective of development.

Biological Theories

Because the first obvious signs of emerging adolescence are biological, a number of theorists have stressed the importance of biology in explaining adolescent development. The first to do so was G. Stanley Hall, called the father of developmental psychology. He began the scientific study of adolescence, which was marked by the publication of his pioneering work, entitled *Adolescence,* in 1904. Being significantly influenced by Charles Darwin's *On the Origin of Species* (1859), Hall formulated his notion of **recapitulation**, which states that the experiential history of the species becomes part of the genetic material of the individual, and thereby is passed on from generation to generation (see Table 2–1). Hall postulated the development of the organism mirrors the development of the species; the individual develops in a series of stages that correspond to the stages passed through by humans in their evolution. He believed **ontogeny** (the development of the individual) **recapitulates phylogeny** (the development of the species). Because he believed humans develop in stages, he formulated a *stage theory* of development.

Infancy (birth to age 4) reflects the animal stage of human development, when the species was walking on four legs. The infant acquires the sensorimotor skills necessary for survival. The years 4 to 8 represent the childhood stage and recapitulate the hunting/fishing ancestry of humans. Vestiges of this stage, he claimed, are seen in such children's games as hide-and-seek, and in building hiding places reminiscent of human's cave-dwelling history. The next stage, youth (ages 8 to 12), reflects the life of savagery, in which rote-learned behav-

Table 2–1   Hall's Theory of Human Development

Inherited History of Species	Developmental Stage	Behavior Related to Stage
1. Ontogeny recapitulates phylogeny	1. Infancy (0–4)	Learn survival skills
2. Recapitulation theory	2. Childhood (4–8)	Hunting/gathering
	3. Youth (8–12)	Rote survival skills
	4. Adolescence (12 to mid-20s)	Storm and stress
	5. Maturity	Adult roles

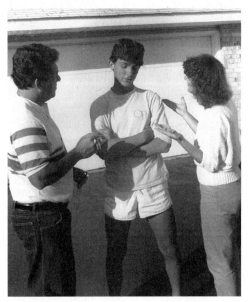

Hall believed adolescence was a time of storm and stress. Popular stereotypes often depict adolescents in conflict with their parents, a vestige of Hall's thinking. Coleman's research showed this not to be the case. (*Cleo Freelance Photo*)

iors were necessary for survival. Adolescence (age 12 through the early to mid-20s) corresponds to a time when the human race was in a period of rapid transition. Adolescence is followed by the stage of maturity, reflecting the current social order.

Although a number of Hall's notions have now been disproven by research in genetics and developmental psychology, his thinking shaped and focused the study of adolescence for many years. The most influential of Hall's concepts was his view of adolescence as a period of storm and stress *(Sturm und Drang)*. For Hall, adolescence corresponded to a period when the human race was in a turbulent and transitional stage, reminiscent of Rousseau's (1762/1911) views of adolescence. Rousseau "warned" parents that hormonal changes signal the coming of a "tumultous change" and that they should be wary and guide the "ship" with a sturdy hand on the helm.

Even today the storm-and-stress view of adolescence is highly prevalent, but the scientific evidence that adolescence is such a period is not convincing. For example, no strong evidence supports the idea of emotional instability during adolescence, and research does not indicate dramatic changes in personality or social relations. Rather, adolescence seems to represent a series of smoothly evolving changes in development. For some adolescents there may indeed be periods of storm and stress, as there are for some individuals at any point in the life span. On the whole, however, storm and stress is not an apt or appropriate description of adolescence.

Why, then, does this notion persist? First, many parents view adolescence as a period of storm and stress because it is difficult for them to let go of their adolescents, to permit them to become independent. Hence they may become defensive in their reactions to, and views of, adolescence, projecting their own feelings of conflict and confusion onto the adolescent rather than themselves. They may view the adolescent as the one who is going through a period of storm and stress when in fact it is they who are doing so. Second, the media does much to promote the storm-and-stress view of adolescence. Think of the number of television programs that deal with runaways, juvenile gangs, drug addicts, and teenage prostitutes. It is no wonder many are tempted to generalize from these specific instances to the adolescent population as a whole. Obviously, this is both unfair and unrealistic. Perhaps it reflects the fact that adults are writing about adolescent development. Were adolescents writing about themselves, such views might not appear.

J. C. Coleman (1978) helped clarify the storm-and-stress view of adolescence by noting that the various stresses on the adolescent do not all occur at the same time. The adolescent deals with one or two stressful events, which lessens the stress, then deals with other stresses. No adolescent wakes up in the morning and has a first date, takes the SATs, deals with breaking up with a boy- or girlfriend, gets a driver's license, and then has lunch. Coleman's focal theory, which is detailed in Box 2–2, reminds us that adolescence occurs over a number of years. Because we tend to compress the time frame of adolescence we may view all the changes as occurring over a very short period of time, which is not the case.

Coleman also notes that children, adults, and the elderly also face stressors. Some of these are unique to their period of life. For example, young children face the stress of toilet training, starting school, and coping with a sibling. Adults deal with the stresses of getting a job, adapting to marriage, and child rearing. Early and late adolescents must face changing schools. Older adults must grapple with the stresses of retirement, health concerns, and monetary issues. Similarly, other stressors may be experienced by those of any age. Children, adolescents, and adults may have to struggle with divorce, death of a parent or friend, or moving to a new residence, for example. At present, there is no means to determine if the total stress faced differs for children, adolescents, adults, or the elderly. Nor is there any generally agreed on way to compare the coping skills of children, adolescents, or adults to various stressors. As we conclude in Box 2–2, then, it is inappropriate to argue that adolescence is a more stressful period in the life span than any other developmental epoch.

Ausubel (1954), another theorist who stressed the importance of the adolescent biological changes, noted two important changes that influence adolescent development (see Table 2–2). **Psychobiological** change refers to psychological change that results from biological change, for example, the psychological reactions to the increase in the sex drive. Psychobiological changes are

BOX 2–2   Is Adolescence an Especially Stressful Time?

Undoubtedly adolescence is a time of many changes, the most obvious being biological. But changes in peer, parent, and social roles also occur. Parents, peers, teachers, and society in general exert considerable pressure on the adolescent to grow up. It is no wonder a popular stereotype of adolescence is that it is a time of extreme stress.

J.C. Coleman (1978), however, points out that research on adolescent development leads to the conclusion that adolescence is not an *especially* stressful time in the life span. He shows that evidence from research on the generation gap, conformity, and other areas contradicts the storm-and-stress concept. Although some adolescents may experience extreme stress, most of the time most adolescents do not. During much of the adolescent years, most adolescents get along well with parents, cope with school demands, and adjust well to changing social demands.

Coleman suggests a *focal theory* that can help resolve the controversy between the research findings and the common-sense view of adolescence. According to his theory, the peak age of concern for various stressful situations differs. Although there is some overlap, it is unlikely that several peak at the same time. The process of adaptation involves dealing basically with one or two issues at a time, resolving them, and then facing the next issues. Only rarely are there concentrations of many issues at one time.

One implication of Coleman's view is that we must avoid the tendency to collapse the time frame of adolescence. Our retrospective views will lead us to perceive adolescence as occurring over a relatively short period of time. We must continually realize that adolescence lasts 6, 7, 10, or more years for some people. The stresses and decisions we face occur over this entire period. They are not lumped into a year or two, as they may in retrospect appear to be.

A second implication is that all of life has stressors and that there is no reason to believe adolescence is any more or less stressful than any other developmental epoch. You can demonstrate this yourself. Have several of your friends write down what they see as the particularly stressful events they face today, in late adolescence. Then have them indicate those events that were especially stressful during their adolescent years. What are the stressors faced by infants (toilet training, language development), children (starting school, arrival of a sibling), adults (becoming a worker, getting married), and the elderly (money, health)? You will discover that all phases of development entail stressful events. Some are common—changing schools, moving, perhaps dealing with parental divorce. Some are unique—such as toilet training, having your first date, starting school, having your first job, getting married, and retiring.

Although each stage of development has stress, it is not possible to demonstrate that one stage is more stressful than any other. There is no evidence that adolescence is especially stressful in a normative sense. Although some adolescents may in fact have a very difficult and stressful experience, most do not.

universal because they are based in biology and occur in all cultures. However, cultural factors determine the manner in which psychobiological changes shape adolescence. The increase in the sex drive is socialized differently in different societies, for example.

Psychosocial change refers to personal and social changes that are due to

Table 2–2   Ausubel's Theory of Adolescent Development

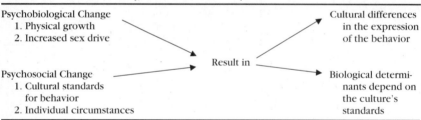

Psychobiological Change
1. Physical growth
2. Increased sex drive

Psychosocial Change
1. Cultural standards
   for behavior
2. Individual circumstances

Result in

Cultural differences
in the expression
of the behavior

Biological determi-
nants depend on
the culture's
standards

cultural factors. Psychosocial changes are culturally specific in nature, such as cultural differences in socializing pre- and postadolescent sexual behavior. Hence, for Ausubel, important biological changes occur in adolescence, particularly the emergence of the new sex drive, but culturally determined psychosocial changes related to the biological changes also occur. Both types of change are important in the expression (culturally based) of sexual behavior (due in part to the increased sex drive). Another example of the interaction of biological and sociocultural influences on development may be found in independence strivings. The adolescent grows bigger, more experienced, and more competent and knows it, and others must learn to adapt and react to these changes and the adolescent's demands for independence.

Certain important focuses in the study of adolescence originated with these maturational theorists. For example, they strongly emphasized the study of the relation between physiological development and behavior, which is a major consideration in current studies of adolescence. In Chapter 3 we deal exclusively with the biological changes that occur in adolescence and the relation of these changes to behavior.

Psychodynamic Theories

The psychodynamic view of development rests on several fundamental principles (Adelson & Doehrman, 1980). First, we can understand the adolescent's current behavior only through reference to his or her past experiences and personal history. By knowing something of the adolescent's developmental history (for example, how he or she was reared), we can gain a better understanding of current behavior.

Second, psychodynamic theories emphasize biological drives. During adolescence, this emphasis has been translated into a focus on the increase in the sex drive. This perspective of adolescence is well illustrated in the writings of Anna Freud (1948, 1958).

Anna Freud, the daughter of Sigmund Freud, believed the behavior of adolescents is caused by a sudden upsurge of sexuality (increase in the sex drive) that results from the biological changes of pubescence. She believed maturational factors (biological change) directly influence psychological functioning. The increase in sexuality brings about a recurrence of the Oedipal situation, which once again must be resolved. However, this time the resolution is through attraction to opposite-sex peers instead of identification with the same-sex parent. The increase in the sex drive creates stress and anxiety, which may call into play one or more defense mechanisms (see Table 2–3).

Defense mechanisms restore equilibrium and protect the individual from experiencing anxiety. Defense mechanisms represent useful and adaptive means of coping with stress. The most important defense mechanisms for understanding adolescence are asceticism and intellectualism. The former refers to attempts to deny completely the existence of instinctual drives, such as the sex drive, in order not to give in to them. Carried to extremes this may include the eating, sleeping, and other basic drives related to physical needs. Intellectualism refers to an abstract, impersonal evaluation of important issues in a manner implying they are not conflictual. Discussions of whether premarital sex is right or wrong and the existence of God, for example, may represent the adolescent's way of dealing with deep-seated personal conflicts.

A simple example may help illustrate how defense mechanisms work. One defense mechanism associated with the increase in sexuality is to avoid contact with opposite-sex individuals. Of course, this is maladaptive because it cuts off meaningful social relationships. An alternative to denial is to develop appropriate relations with opposite-sex peers, what many consider a desirable outcome for adolescents.

Defense mechanisms reduce the anxiety associated with the drive and satisfy immediate needs. However, their frequent use may result in unsatisfactory interpersonal relationships because they stunt personal growth and increase social distance between the individual and others.

Peter Blos (1962, 1967, 1972, 1974), another psychodynamic theorist, views adolescence in the context of adjustment to sexual and biological maturation. He divides adolescence into five stages: latency, early adolescent, adolescent, late adolescent, and postadolescent, each with a unique major emphasis (see Table 2–4).

During the latency phase, sexual inhibition is prevalent as the ego and superego control the instincts. This phase ends with puberty and the concomitant increase in the sex drive. It is in this phase that defenses against the instincts come to the fore. In early adolescence there is an emphasis on same-sex friendships and the peer group, and an adoption of values that oppose those of

Table 2–3 Anna Freud's Theory of Adolescence

Biological Changes		Anxiety		Use Defense Mechanisms		Behavior that Reduces Anxiety
1. Hormones related to the sex drive 2. Physical growth	cause →	1. Fear of opposite sex 2. Fear of feeling sexual	invoking →	1. Asceticism (deny instincts) 2. Intellectualism (make drive seem nonconflictual)	resulting in →	1. Avoid opposite sex 2. Have only platonic relationships 3. Don't date

Table 2–4   Blos's View of Adolescence

Stage	Major Emphasis
1. Latency	Inhibition of instincts, e.g., sex drive
2. Early Adolescent	Peer group relations are strengthened
3. Adolescent	Love relationships develop
4. Late Adolescent	Identity: "Who am I?"
5. Postadolescent	Begins to adopt adulthood roles

the parents. Because parental values are no longer seen as absolutely correct and right, the superego and ego are weakened and, in extreme cases, delinquency behaviors may emerge. During adolescence, heterosexual love relationships emerge, and there is an increased interest in the self. The major focus of late adolescence is the "Who am I?" question. Self-esteem becomes stable and one's sex-role identity is established. The end result is the emergence of a stable personality in the young adulthood years. Finally, postadolescence involves completing the goals set for the self, including entrance into the adulthood roles of marriage and parenthood. Each sex further develops a sex-role image, including that of being a mother or father.

In his best known work, *Childhood and Society* (1963), Erik Erikson shifted the emphasis of psychoanalytic theories of adolescence from the sexual nature of the stage to the psychosocial realm. He emphasized the acquisition of ego identity, the sense of who and what one is. Because culture determines to some degree how ego identity is established, Erikson emphasized cultural determinants of development much more than earlier psychodynamic theorists.

Erikson views development as occurring within a series of psychosocial stages that are in part biologically determined (Table 2–5). Associated with each stage is a crisis, which is simply a psychosocial task that is encountered. Each crisis involves conflict and has two possible outcomes. If the more positive and healthy resolution is worked out, that quality becomes part of the ego and further healthy development is facilitated. If the less desirable outcome occurs, that quality is incorporated into the ego and interferes with further healthy development. Less optimal development of a given crisis may result in psychopathology and less optimal resolution of subsequent crises. Each crisis is continually present, and could recur, but is most pronounced at a particular age.

Table 2–5   Erikson's Eight Stages of Development

Developmental Period	Basic Crisis
1. Infancy	Trust vs. mistrust
2. Early childhood	Autonomy vs. shame and doubt
3. Preschool age	Initiative vs. guilt
4. School age	Industry vs. inferiority
5. Adolescence	Identity vs. identity confusion
6. Young adulthood	Intimacy vs. isolation
7. Adulthood	Generativity vs. stagnation
8. Senescence	Ego integrity vs. despair

Source: Adapted from Erikson, E. (1963). *Childhood and society* (2nd ed.). New York: Norton.

For example, the identity crisis is most pronounced during middle adolescence, but is revisited with changing life roles, when one becomes a worker, a spouse, a parent, or retiree. Identity development is a lifelong process, with the identity crisis recurring as major life changes are encountered.

Erikson views adolescence as a time of marginal self-identity. The adolescent is seen as being in a poorly defined role, neither child nor adult, which leads to a disruption of identity (the identity vs. identity confusion crisis; Table 2-6). This is a result of both physical—entrance into the growth spurt—and social factors—increasing emphasis on making educational decisions and beginning to consider future occupations—that force the adolescent to consider alternatives (P.H. Miller, 1993). Assuming the crisis is successfully resolved during adolescence, the individual moves into the adult stages of development and the corresponding crises with a sense of who one has been, who one is, and who one wishes to become. If the adolescent does not resolve the identity crisis successfully, the ego is damaged and a sense of role diffusion and identity diffusion may result, making resolution of the adulthood crises more difficult and perhaps less successful. For example, those who resolve this crisis less optimally likely will have difficulty with the next crisis—intimacy vs. isolation. It is difficult to develop intimate relations with others when one does not know who one is.

In identity formation, Erikson stresses the importance of developing a vocational identity and a personal philosophy of life. Formation of the former requires adolescents to come to grips with their own talents, abilities, and opportunities (for example, the likelihood of attending college or some other postsecondary training). Developing a philosophy of life, including religious (personal) and political (social) beliefs, provides the adolescent with a frame of reference for evaluating and coping with life events. If the adolescent is not capable of forming a coherent and acceptable identity, self-doubt, role diffusion, and indulgence in self-destructive activities may result. In turn, these poor images of the self may result in juvenile delinquency or personality aberrations.

A well-developed identity has two components: continuity of the self over time and integration of the self. The former refers to seeing the self as remaining relatively the same from day to day—there is a "you" that does not change each time you wake up in the morning. Think about your basic values, beliefs, ideals, and goals. Were they the same yesterday? Will they be tomorrow? How about last week, last month, last year, or 5 years ago? The further into the past, the less similar, of course—identity does change, but slowly and gradually. We are not a new person every day.

Integration of the self refers to the various roles we play. You are a son or

Table 2-6 Erikson's Theory of Adolescence

Biological Change	Identity Crisis	Identity
1. Physical growth 2. Sexual maturity $\longrightarrow$	"Who am I?" What do I believe; what are my values? $\longrightarrow$	Values, beliefs to guide behavior

Erikson, E. (1963). *Childhood and society* (2nd ed.). New York: Norton.

daughter, a student, perhaps someone's boyfriend or girlfriend, perhaps a worker. You play many roles, and the "you" that is portrayed in part depends on the role you currently are playing. But the various "yous" you play are integrated—you can switch from one to the other with relative ease. The "you" with your parents is not the same "you" portrayed when you are a worker. But there are substantial similarities, making it easy for you to switch from one to the other. Your identity is integrated.

In refining Erikson's view of identity, James Marcia (1980) defined it as a continually changing organization of one's attitudes, values, and beliefs. The process of identity formation involves facing a crisis and making a commitment with respect to vocation, religion, and politics. For Marcia, a crisis is a period of questioning, information gathering, and reflection. By commitment, Marcia means the individual has adopted a set of values. In essence, Marcia is describing the process you use when making any important decision, such as your choice of a major. In choosing your major you faced some tension and you sorted through possibilities. You gathered information, perhaps by talking with parents and friends, and perhaps by taking certain courses to learn more about the particular major. Finally, you made a commitment—you chose a major.

Marcia argues that identity development proceeds in much the same manner. More specifically, identity development involves crises with regard to occupational and ideological (religious and political beliefs) concerns. As one wrestles with these concerns and finally resolves them, one achieves an identity. Marcia has identified four basic types of people, each having a unique identity status (see Table 2–7).

Identity achievers have experienced a period of decision making and are now committed to an occupation and set of ideological values, all of which are *self-chosen*. That is, the person has worked through his or her concerns in these areas and has made certain choices. These people have strength in their convictions and are adaptive and well adjusted. They accept both their strengths and weaknesses, and they have realistic goals. **Foreclosures** also have made a commitment, but their choices have been made by others. For example, parents

---

Table 2–7   Marcia's View of Identity Development

Development involves both the facing of a crisis (a period of questioning and thinking) and a commitment (adoption) to a set of values and beliefs that guides behavior. Marcia chose the realms of religion (personal philosophy of life), politics (social philosophy of life), and vocation (personality) as the areas most indicative of identity formation. By examining whether one has faced a crisis and made a commitment Marcia identified four identity statuses.

		CRISIS	
		Yes	No
COMMITMENT	Yes	Identity Achieved	Foreclosed
	No	Moratorium	Identity Diffuse

who push their children into entering a vocation they themselves may have desired run the risk of rearing offspring who will have a foreclosed identity status, resulting perhaps in the child being rigid, dogmatic, and conforming. Those who immerse themselves too strongly in a peer group also run the risk of becoming foreclosed because they too strongly adopt their perception of what the group wants or believes. Adolescents who try to "become" what they believe someone they want to like them desires, may adopt a foreclosed identity. **Identity diffusions** evidence no commitment to an occupation or ideological stance, although they may have experienced a decision-making period. They may appear to be carefree, charming people, or they may appear psychopathic. They may be younger adolescents who have yet to face the crises, or they may simply have no concern with ideological matters. **Moratoriums** are those who are *in a crisis* about occupational or ideological decisions. They are wrestling with the decisions that lead to a commitment. This stage is a prerequisite to identity achievement; it represents the period of questioning. The moratoriums may seem confused and unstable because they have yet to make a commitment. The college environment fosters this form of identity because occupational choices and values get challenged and the student is encouraged to think about, or rethink, these concerns.

The normative developmental course is from the identity diffuse to moratorium to identity achiever status. Those who go from an identity diffuse to foreclosed status have short-circuited the process, and may not experience optimal development. We do not achieve an identity that remains with us forever. As we encounter new roles and experiences (e.g., getting married, having children, taking a full-time job), our identity may change; the identity crisis is continually present and subject to new resolution. You may have chosen a major only to find it was not what you thought it would be. You were forced to think about occupational goals again—you "lost" your identity achiever status and became moratorium.

In these psychodynamic views of adolescence, we see an emphasis on personality development in general, and identity issues in particular. All point to the importance of biological factors interacting with social factors in explaining adolescence, and view adolescence as a period of adjustment, or perhaps maladjustment, leading the individual into adulthood. All emphasize the importance of adolescence as a period of developing a sense of self and purpose.

Cognitive-Developmental Theory

Several times we have already noted that adolescents *evaluate* some event, *make* some decision, or *consider* some experience, and that they do so differently than children. Of course, such terms connote thinking and point to the importance of cognition in explaining adolescent development. Although there is no cognitive-developmental theorist who has focused exclusively on the adolescent years, the writings of Jean Piaget are highly pertinent to our understanding of adolescent development.

Jean Piaget (1952) proposed that intelligence develops in a series of stages and that it reflects the emergence of biological predispositions as well as cultural influences. Because we detail Piaget's theory in depth in Chapter 4, we just describe it briefly here (see Table 2–8).

The preadolescent is capable of concrete operational thinking, that is, thinking about what is real, the "here and now." In contrast, the adolescent is able to think in the abstract, about what is possible and what could be. The adolescent can think about how he or she might be, not just about how he or she is. These abstract thinking skills allow adolescents to consider identity issues, such as the "Who am I?" question, on an abstract level; they can answer in more than concrete terms such as age, name, and various likes and dislikes (see Chapter 6). Indeed, one is tempted to argue that the adolescent identity crisis occurs simply "because it can." The adolescent has the thinking skills to weigh alternatives and make long-term plans and commitments.

The abstract nature of adolescent thinking competencies also relates to how the adolescent perceives the external environment, including the society and its relation to the individual. How we think about others and our relation to them, about the relation between people and the society, and infer others' intentions and feelings is called **social cognition**. Robert Selman (1980) has attempted to spell out how one's perspective taking changes as one's cognitive competencies change. His theory is spelled out in Chapter 4, but a glimpse of it here will help clarify the importance of cognitive development in explaining adolescent development.

Think about your best friend for a moment. How does this person feel about sports? Do you feel the same way? If not, can you take his or her viewpoint? If this person were to describe you, what would he or she say about you? As you engage in this exercise, you are using the social cognitive skills Selman calls social role taking. Selman has described how these skills develop and change from the early childhood years through the adolescent years. With the ability to think abstractly, the adolescent comes to understand that one's motives and actions are in part shaped by psychological factors. Adolescents, unlike children, have the ability to consider not only their own perspective but that of others. For example, how are your views of yourself similar and different from what your best friend might say?

These social role-taking skills relate to adolescents' views of the nature of friendships and to their view of the social system—laws, morality, and the importance of mutual consensus. They develop in conjunction with the kinds of

Table 2–8   Piaget's Theory of Intellectual Development

Biological Factors	Alter $\longrightarrow$	Forms of thinking	Allowing $\longrightarrow$	Result
1. Inherited growth patterns		1. Preadolescent = concrete 2. Adolescent = abstract		Concrete self views Abstract views of self

Social cognitive theorists such as Selman point
out that during adolescence we develop the ability
to take and understand another person's point of
view, even if we do not agree with it. (*PH Archives*)

cognitive skills Piaget has described, and are another illustration of how understanding the emergence of cognitive skills during adolescence is important not
only in its own right but also with regard to understanding adolescent social behavior.

During adolescence, then, cognitive competence reaches a peak, and this
relates to how one views the self and others, as well as the relation between the
self and others. By examining the relationships between cognitive development
and other behaviors, we gain insight into adolescent peer relations, personality
development, and views of the social order.

Anthropological Theories

Adolescence takes place within cultural contexts that define expected and allowable behavior and exert a very significant impact on the nature of adolescence, a
point brought home most directly by the cultural anthropologists. The writings
of the cultural anthropologists challenged those of Hall, Freud, and others who
emphasized the preeminence of biological bases for adolescent development.

The cultural anthropologists pointed out that the nature of adolescence—its length, the roles played, its function—depends on the culture in which one is growing up. (*Doranne Jacobson/ United Nations*)

They demonstrated that the developmental patterns found in Western cultures were not necessarily found in all cultures. For example, the psychological and social importance of physiological change is largely determined by the cultural context within which it occurs. In different cultures the changes are associated with different behavioral expectations and different sanctioned behaviors.

The two most influential cultural anthropologists who have written about adolescent development are Margaret Mead and Ruth Benedict. Mead's *Coming of Age in Samoa* (1950) and *Growing Up in New Guinea* (1953) are two field studies of the effects of culture on adolescent development. Mead was among the first to point out that in order to understand the development and unfolding of human behavior, one must look at the role of cultural institutions. Her research in cultures with religious, economic, and social institutions quite different from ours supported the notion of *cultural relativism*. Cultural institutions do not entirely determine how one will develop; individual and biological factors play a role. Development will differ from one culture to another because of differences in cultural institutions.

As an example of cultural relativism, Mead (1950) noted that the Samoan culture, unlike ours, was characterized by a patience and gentleness that did not pressure individuals with regard to sexual or religious conflicts. She wrote that adolescents and their parents did not experience serious disagreements, and underscored the sharp contrast in these patterns and those found in American culture. As a result, Mead argued that cultural norms dictated an easygoing, smooth transition through adolescence and into adulthood, even with regard to such concerns as sexual behavior; the experimentation with and expression of sexual behavior, Mead noted, met with no guilt, shame, or social sanction. She further argued that cultural conditioning was the key to explaining diversity in the adolescent experience. Cultural standards are taught to children and adolescents. Because these differ between cultures, and because they change as cultures evolve, the adolescent experience continually changes.

The cultural relativism of adolescence is easily demonstrated. Write a brief description of what it was like for you to be an adolescent. What were your experiences with drugs and alcohol, dating, relations with parents, school experiences, and concerns for safety? How do those compare with the experiences of a fellow student from a foreign country? Why are the similarities and differences present? What aspects of the culture related to the differences? To see how changes within a culture impact on the adolescent experience, compare your adolescence with that of your parents. What were the similarities and differences? What important cultural changes occurred between your generation and theirs that may have caused the differences?

Ruth Benedict (1938) spelled out specific ways in which culture affects the adolescent experience. She argued that the differences and similarities in the roles children and adults are expected to play were the important factor (see Table 2-9). In some cultures, the roles played by children and adults are very similar. In others, such as ours, the expectations are quite different. Her point was that cultures vary in the degree of *continuity* in child–adult roles and, hence, in the nature of the transition from childhood to adulthood. If the transition occurs in a socially and legally defined *discontinuous* manner, the developmental patterns underlying transitions from childhood to adulthood will differ from those found in cultures in which such transitions are relatively continuous. Benedict notes that in Western cultures there are a number of discontinuities in child and adult behaviors. Children must learn new behaviors and must unlearn childhood behaviors in order to become adults. In other cultures, the roles played by children and adults are not very different; the child need not unlearn childhood behaviors to assume adult roles or status.

Benedict's major point is that discontinuity in adolescent and adulthood

Table 2–9   Benedict's Theory of the Adolescent Transition to Adulthood

Culturally defined continuities and discontinuities	Result in →	Different adult and adolescent roles	Influencing →	Ease of transition from adulthood to adolescence

roles produces emotional strain which, in turn, produces conflict. Cultural continuity, in contrast, results in a smooth and gradual growth from childhood to adulthood with relatively little conflict. Those cultures with a greater number of discontinuities have an adolescence that is more difficult to traverse because the individual is expected to assume new responsibilities. In contrast, in cultures where there is greater continuity adolescents will not be expected to acquire as many new roles, and the development from childhood to adulthood will be smoother.

A number of examples make Benedict's point clear. In our culture, children—and to a large extent most adolescents—are not expected to work or to contribute to the welfare of the community or family. In other cultures, however, children are expected to contribute to the community or family with "worklike" behavior. The role of sexuality in childhood, adolescence, and adulthood is another important area of transition. In our culture the "official" view is that one must wait until marriage to learn and engage in sexual behavior, whereas in other cultures, children as well as adolescents are allowed to engage in sexual behaviors and, indeed, may be encouraged to do so. The many discontinuities in our culture may contribute to the stresses adolescents experience.

Benedict (1938) identified three dimensions of continuity versus discontinuity that are important for understanding adolescent development:

1. Responsible versus nonresponsible role status;
2. Dominance versus submission;
3. Contrasted sexual roles.

The *responsible versus nonresponsible* dimension is illustrated by children and adolescents not being expected to work and contribute to the family's welfare, whereas such contributions are expected after graduation from high school, trade school, or college. In earlier times, when we lived in an agricultural society, for example, the transition from nonresponsible to responsible roles was smoother because both children and adolescents were expected to contribute to family welfare according to their ability (e.g., by doing various tasks on the farm, from feeding animals to helping with cooking). As a result, the transition to adulthood was easier.

The independence strivings of adolescents are one illustration of the *dominance versus submission* dimension. In general, training adolescents to be independent or to engage in appropriately dominant behavior is difficult. Therefore, adolescents in our society may experience ambivalence and at times difficulty learning to be independent and assertive in appropriate ways. As a result, the transition to being an appropriately dominant and assertive adult, as when supervising the work of others or rearing a child, is a more difficult transition than it need be.

Perhaps one of the most personal discontinuities for all of us is that involving *contrasting sexual roles.* In our culture, sexual experimentation is discouraged, and even illegal. The official stance is that one is not to engage in sexual behavior until one is married. Hence one must "unlearn" adolescent values, attitudes, and roles—or experience a degree of guilt—and learn new adulthood roles upon marriage, a clear discontinuity that may be very stressful.

The examples just cited illustrate Benedict's major point: Discontinuities experienced during development can cause emotional strain and stress that make adolescence and the transition to adulthood roles and behaviors difficult. The greater the number of discontinuities, the more difficult the transition to adulthood. We have not only social-role discontinuities, but also legal ones defined by age—for drinking, voting, dropping out of school, and getting married, for example. These discontinuities add to the stress of the transition to adulthood and emphasize the role of societal factors in the evolution and nature of adolescence.

You can identify some of these continuities and discontinuities in your own adolescent experience. Think about the roles you play now. Are you expected to contribute to the economic welfare of your family or to support yourself? Were your parents or grandparents? If you are under the age of 21, how do you perceive laws regulating alcohol use? Do they make you feel "disenfranchised"? Would you want things to be different?

In sum, cultural anthropologists emphasize the importance of cultural diversity in describing and explaining the adolescent experience. This diversity comes in the form of differing societal standards, alternative ethnic patterns of values and experiences within a culture, and broad subcultural patterns that define the specific nature of adolescence.

Social-Learning Theory

Social learning theorists also emphasize the importance of the environment in fostering the nature of development, and provide a theoretical description of development based on concepts from learning theory and theories of imitation and modeling (see Table 2–10). Environmental agents (e.g., parents, teachers, peers) shape (teach) behavior both by directly reinforcing desired behaviors and by providing models of socially appropriate behavior.

Albert Bandura's theory will serve as our example. Bandura outlined the basis for social-learning theory in several works (1969, 1973) and, in conjunction with Richard Walters (1959, 1963), discussed social-learning theory as it relates to adolescent development.

According to Bandura, observation of a model may have several effects on

Table 2–10   Social-Learning Theory of Adolescence

Type of Learning		Behavior
1. S-R	Teach →	Repeat positively reinforced acts.
		Don't repeat punished behaviors.
2. Observation of a model	Effect →	Learn new behaviors
		Don't do what models are punished for doing.
		Do what successful models do.

the observer. By observing a model the adolescent may learn an entirely new behavior, which Bandura calls a **modeling effect**. An adolescent may learn delinquent behavior (e.g., how to hot-wire a car) by observing someone else do it, for example. Parents and other family members are significant models for most adolescents, as are others outside the family—ministers, teachers, neighbors. As adolescence progresses, peers become more influential models, as witnessed by the increase in peer conformity during adolescence. By observing peers or older siblings adolescents may "learn" how to be an adolescent. That is, they learn the mannerisms, slang language, acceptable dress codes, and other aspects of the adolescent culture.

A second function of observing a model is called an **inhibition/disinhibition effect** due to the observer seeing the consequences of a model's behavior. A punished behavior is less likely to be imitated than one that is sanctioned. Observing a punished behavior inhibits the adolescent from doing it; observing a rewarded behavior disinhibits the adolescent from doing it. An example of an inhibition effect might be not doing drugs after seeing someone have a bad trip. An example of a disinhibition effect is going along with the crowd when others do so.

Finally, the observation of a model may have a **response-facilitation effect.** The response of the model acts as a cue to the observer to demonstrate a similar behavior already in his or her repertoire. For example, watching how a friend behaves toward the opposite sex may lead you to use the same tactics in getting a date.

Rather than assuming the unfolding of behavior in some predetermined developmental (maturational) pattern, social-learning theorists propose that adolescent development is due to cultural conditioning (much as the cultural anthropologists argue) and social expectations for certain kinds of behaviors (Bandura, 1964; Bandura & Walters, 1959). The notion is that adolescents will exhibit behaviors which are in relative harmony with the kinds of behaviors they learned in childhood, and that the best way to explain development is by looking at the impact of models and the reinforcement contingencies the adolescent experiences. This thinking simply echoes the notion that there is continuity in human growth patterns and at no particular age level are there sweeping changes in behavior that might be due to what we would call maturational development. Unlike the cognitive theorists, the social-learning theorists do not believe development occurs in a sequence of stages.

Deviant development that emerges during the adolescent years is seen as a failure of socialization processes that were begun in childhood. Children who are taught to behave adversely in stressful situations, who are taught to exhibit deviant behavior, or who do not learn to deal adequately with reality will exhibit similar kinds of behaviors in adolescence.

One practical emphasis of the social-learning theorists has been on parental child-rearing practices. Parents not only are models, but they are teachers because they use discipline in rearing their children and adolescents. We discuss the impact of child rearing in detail later, but it is worthwhile to note here that parental disciplinary techniques are important to adolescent identity development, feelings of competence, and general psychological adjustment. For example, using physical punishment to discipline an aggressive adolescent may teach the adolescent you can get along in the world by using physical means for getting what you want, the opposite of the desired effect.

Like the psychodynamic theorists, the social-learning theorists would have us view adolescence as part of a lifelong developmental history, including aspects of child-rearing patterns of parents, subcultural impacts on development, and peer modeling and reinforcement contingencies.

Historical Theories

Researchers (Dragastin & Elder, 1975; Elder, 1980; J. Hill & Monks, 1977; Kett, 1977) also have examined adolescence within the context of social history. Although this perspective is more a description than a theory, it provides valuable insight into the evolution of adolescence.

At the most basic level, researchers have examined how societal changes impact on the nature of adolescence (see Table 2–11). By looking at how changes in length of formal education, occurrences such as the Great Depression, and transfer of socialization from parents to societal institutions (e.g., the school) relate to generational differences in the nature of adolescence, these researchers study transitions in the nature of adolescence. In a very real sense, this theorizing relates development to "real-life" events and studies development in naturally occurring environmental circumstances.

An example will help make the virtue of this approach more clear. Elder (1980) studied the change in socialization influences of the post–World War II family. Prior to the war, the family was the major influence on socialization. Following it, the school and the peer group became more salient. The major impetus was the increase in average school size, which doubled between the 1930s and 1960s. This larger school size resulted in the increased influence of peers. In addition, the division of schools into elementary (K–6), junior high (7–9), and high school (10–12) helped establish lower boundaries for adolescence through age segregation. These and other changes in schooling resulted in a shifting of

Table 2–11 Historical Perspective of Adolescence

Conditions		Influence

Historical events
  1. economic trends
  2. political climate
  3. job opportunities
	Impact
	⟶
		Cause changes in the nature
		  of adolescence across generations.

Changes in social institutions
  1. school structure
  2. family structure
    a. nuclear
    b. maternal employment
    c. single parent
		Shape the nature of adolescence
		  in specific ways across and
		  within generations.

Theorists who emphasize historical contexts note that changes in the culture, such as technological advances, have changed the nature of the adolescent experience. (*Laima E. Druskis*)

socialization away from parents and toward peers. The school increasingly became the private domain of the adolescent. Imagine your own dinner table conversation. "How was school today?" your parent might ask. "Fine," was likely your reply. "What did you do?" "Nothing much." You, and adolescents in general, view the school as a private domain, one of the reasons J.S. Coleman (1961) has suggested there may be an adolescent culture.

As another example of this approach, Elder (1974) describes the effects of growing up during the Great Depression. The individuals Elder studied were in their late childhood and early adolescence during the Great Depression; he was interested in determining the impact of that experience on later life. He found that the effects of the Depression were moderated by the social status of the family in which the youngster grew up. As adults, middle-class boys from families that suffered serious financial setbacks were psychologically more healthy, had stronger drive, and were employed in more prestigious jobs than their counterparts whose families did not suffer such serious hardships. In contrast, among boys from lower socioeconomic status, economic hardship was a detriment; boys whose families suffered greatly obtained less education and held lower status jobs as adults. Girls from middle-class families that suffered economic hardship were more likely to assume household roles, to get less education, and to prefer more the homemaker role than was the case for their counterparts.

This type of analysis has the advantage of allowing us to place aspects of adolescent development into a historical perspective. This historical approach is well illustrated in Kett's (1977) work tracing the social evolution of adolescence (Box 2-3). Research of this type points to the critical importance of the histori-

BOX 2–3   The Social Evolution of Adolescence

In his work *Rites of Passage*, Kett (1977) traced the relationship among social, religious, political, and economic events and changes since the late 1700s in conceptualizations of children and their place in society. Although we cannot summarize his entire treatise here, a few examples not only will point out the richness to be found in his work, but will illustrate the importance of considering cultural/historical events in the discussion of adolescence.

One interesting perspective is the social role played by children in the late 1700s and early 1800s. Until about age 7, both boys and girls basically were in the care of women and were viewed in some ways as a hindrance. This care involved education, such as it was, for women taught the schools. Once the farming season began, however, the male children no longer attended school because they were needed to work on the farm. In other words, male children were expected at an early age to contribute to the family's welfare by working; they were expected to "pay their way." Thereafter, school was attended only in winter months. Relatively permanent entrance into the work force was often achieved by age 11 or 12. Contrast this pattern with your own experience. In all likelihood, you have been attending school since you were 5 or 6 years old, working for the most part in the summer only. And for most of you, this work was for your own spending money. Few of you were expected to work for your keep, as were children in the 19th century.

Leaving home was also a different experience in those times. Although some children left home for formal schooling, this was a rare occurrence. Much more frequent was the "farming out" of a child as early as age 12 or 13. In these instances, the father might farm out a son and receive a small amount of money. The son would be bound to work, for example at farming, in a factory, in a store, or at a trade, for room and board. After completing an agreed on length of time, often until he was 21, the son was free to return to the family and might receive some money from his master. In general, the concept was twofold. First, the son's family had one fewer child to feed and clothe. Assuming there were sufficient children for the family's needs, the family benefited from this arrangement. Second, the child might learn a trade or become an apprentice, both of which were of benefit to the child.

This treatment of children is no doubt foreign to you, but this is because it reflects a view of children very different from the current dominant perspective. A hint of this can be gained from looking at definitions of age groups during these times. "Infancy," unlike today, included those aged 6 or 7 or less, "childhood" referred to those up to age 16 or so, and "youth" to those up to ages in the mid-20s. These terms carried with them much more than simple age meaning, including work responsibilities, training for vocations, and expectations for schooling. So, when did the era of adolescence akin to the way we know it begin?

Kett cites information indicating that adolescence began to occur in Europe and America between 1900 and 1920. The lower boundary, or entrance into the stage of adolescence, was indexed by biological change. Biological processes became indicators for social transitions. The upper boundary, entrance into adulthood roles, increasingly stretched as adolescents remained in school longer and as other social factors delayed entrance into adulthood roles.

In part, the evolution of adolescence was a result of industrialization and urbanization. These events kept youth out of the job market, contributed to the formalization of increasing lengths of time in schooling, and segregated youth from adult roles.

In part, adolescence emerged as a result of changes in the nature of the family. The modal family unit was extended, not nuclear. Moreover, trends toward having fewer children spaced more closely meant all children in a family might be teens at the same time. This trend contributed to generational distance, specifically between parent and offspring. Finally, social institutions of a secular nature (the Boy Scouts or YMCA), the emergence of child labor laws, and the availability of mass education contributed to the identification of a separate group within the society. Adolescence, then, was the (unintentional) product of a host of social, economic, political, and legal changes in the society.

The importance of Kett's work is that it shows how changes in the society at many levels—religious, social, economic, academic, vocational—coalesced to change perceptions of, and opportunities for, youngsters. The lesson of this message lies in our understanding that, perhaps more than any other stage in development, adolescence is subject to change. Adolescence is a social evolutionary phenomenon. Part of the difficulties you may have had with your parents stems from the different nature of adolescence for your parents and for you. In turn, as social changes occur over the years, your children, who will be adolescents sometime around the year 2010, will have an adolescent experience different from yours.

cal times within which adolescence occurs. In order to understand adolescence, we must also look at the role of cultural institutions, such as the school, and events, such as the Depression, that may influence it.

AN ECLECTIC APPROACH

The explanation of adolescent development clearly is complex. None of the theories discussed here explains all or even most of adolescence. However, each contributes something to our understanding of, and ability to explain, adolescent behavior.

The key to integrating the various theories is understanding that adolescence is on the one hand a personal experience and on the other hand a cultural phenomenon. The individual experiences and interprets the biological changes on a personal level. Similarly, others, such as parents and peers, react to the changes and expect corresponding changes in behavior. The personal meaning of the changes experienced, and the expectations for behavioral changes, depend on the nature of the culture. As the culture changes, so too does the meaning of the changes and the expected behaviors.

In addition, adolescence is part of the life span; although it is a transition out of childhood and into adulthood, it also is a stage of development in its own right, just like childhood or adulthood. Although we can understand adolescence only within a developmental context that includes understanding the person's individual history and the nature of development in general, we also must consider the unique nature of adolescence.

The cognitive changes of adolescence allow the individual to interpret the biological and social changes in new and different ways. In turn, societal conditions temper what the individual perceives to be the "adolescent role." Only by considering both the individual and cultural factors that impact on the person can we understand adolescence.

SUMMARY

Theories are statements of the factors that cause some form of behavior to occur. As such, they are critical to our understanding of the causes of development. In order to determine the accuracy of a theory, that theory must produce hypotheses that can be tested by research. If a theory is supported by the findings of the research we can use it to integrate information about behavior and to predict when and under what conditions new behaviors should occur. These are the major functions of any theory. For adolescence, this translates into explaining the importance and impact of the biological and social changes that occur.

Five major theoretical orientations contribute to our understanding of adolescence. From the biological approach we gain an understanding of the importance of physical change as related to adolescent behavior. The biological theorists emphasize the changes in drive level that occur as a result of pubescence.

The psychodynamic theorists also emphasize drive changes. Anna Freud focuses on maldevelopment resulting from defenses against drive increases. However, more current theorists stress aspects of personality organization and identity development. In all instances, the focus is on individual adjustment during a time of significant change.

The cognitive-developmental theorists study the nature of thinking processes as they evolve during the adolescent years. From this perspective it is clear that adolescent perceptions of the self and society change as cognition changes.

The social-learning and anthropological theorists stress the importance of cultural factors in the shaping of adolescence. They note that cultural standards determine both the nature and importance of the changes that signal the introduction of adolescence. Hence they help us understand how and why adolescence differs from culture to culture.

The historical approach plays the important role of explaining the evolution of adolescence both across societies and within a single society over time. By examining the historical basis of adolescence we can better understand how and why it occurs as it does.

Although no theory can explain all of adolescent development, each perspective provides insight into why adolescents behave the way they do. Only by looking at its personal and social context within a life-span perspective can we begin to explain adolescent development.

GLOSSARY

cohort: Group of people born about the same time.

cross-sectional study: Assessment of different aged individuals at about the same time. Allows the study of age differences in development.

developmental trend: Difference in behavior that is associated with age.

disinhibition effect: In social-learning theory, the reinforcement experienced by a model that may cause an observer to exhibit a behavior he or she might otherwise not perform.

foreclosure: In Marcia's theory, the identity type in which a commitment has been made but without a period of questioning.

hypothesis: Best guess as to the causes of some event; tested through research.

identity achiever: In Marcia's theory, an individual who has had a period of questioning and then made a commitment to the factors defining an identity.

identity diffusion: In Marcia's theory, an individual who has not faced a period of questioning or made a commitment.

inhibition effect: In social-learning theory, the reinforcement consequences experienced by a model that may cause an observer not to exhibit a behavior he or she might otherwise perform.

longitudinal study: Assessment of the same group of individuals at different times (ages).

Allows the study of age changes in development.

modeling effect: In social-learning theory, learning a new and novel behavior or behavioral sequence through observation of a model.

moratorium: In Marcia's theory, a state of being in a period of questioning or crisis with regard to issues defining identity.

ontogeny recapitulates phylogeny: In Hall's theory, the idea that the development of the individual goes through a sequence mirroring the evolution of the species.

psychobiological: Impact of biological factors on psychological behaviors.

psychosocial: In Erikson's theory, a crisis involving the individual's development with respect to social roles.

recapitulation: In Hall's theory, the notion that social experiences are encoded into the genetic material passed on to the next generation.

response-facilitation effect: In social-learning theory, the idea that observation of a model acts as a cue to the observer to emit a similar behavior already in the observer's repertoire.

social cognition: Process of thinking about other people and the self in relation to others.

theory: Statement or group of statements that attempts to explain some event and predict new events.

DISCUSSION QUESTIONS

1. Which stressors are similar and which are different across the life span? On the basis of this information, what can you conclude about adolescence being an especially stressful period of life?

2. What discontinuities can you identify as important during the adolescent years? Are these equally important for all or most adolescents? How might they vary for those with different backgrounds?

3. Of the variety of social conditions that have led to the evolution of adolescence in the United States, which were most important for you and why?

4. In what ways are stereotypes of adolescence today the same as they were a generation ago? In what ways different? Why do the differences exist?

5. In what ways are the popular stereotypes of adolescents useful, or not, for our understanding of adolescence?

6. How are the theories of the cultural anthropologists and the social-learning theorists similar and different?

7. What anxieties might adolescents face and how might they cope with them?

Biological Change and Adolescent Development

3

Major Issues Addressed

The Hormonal Basis of Pubertal Changes
Individual Differences in Rates of Physical Growth
Sex Differences in Rates of Physical Growth
Major Physical Changes During the Growth Spurt
Secular Trends in Physical Growth Rates
Psychological Effects of Early vs. Late Maturity
Psychological Effects of Menarche and First Ejaculation
Psychological Effects of Body Type
The Biosocial View of Development

He was "growing like a weed." He couldn't wait to get taller than me. But more important psychological changes came with the physical growth changes. He seemed more confident and sure of himself, and he seemed like he wanted "to grow up" not just physically but in other ways as well. It was as though physical growth held many meanings for him, private and important. He wouldn't or couldn't share them with me, but it was obvious he was beginning to see himself in new and different ways.

◆   ◆   ◆

The physical growth we experience during our early adolescent years signals to us, and to others, that we are changing. And the changes we feel are more than physical. They relate to how others view us and to how we view ourselves. This can cause us at times to feel unsure of who we are. We may feel awkward, gangly, and uncoordinated, or we may be especially conscious of our height—or lack of it. We explore the physical changes and their psychological impact in this chapter.

INTRODUCTION

We have defined adolescence as that life epoch beginning with the physical changes leading to the growth spurt and ending when one assumes adulthood roles. In this context, the growth to adult stature and physique and the attainment of reproductive capability represent developmental markers signaling entrance into a new stage of development. Collectively, these changes, called **puberty,** are especially important for our understanding of adolescent development and behavior.

First, the biological changes themselves, and particularly the changes in hormone balances, exert a relatively direct influence on behavior. Mood fluctuations and other psychological states are directly related to biological functioning (Petersen, 1988; Simmons, Blyth, & McKinney, 1983).

Second, the growing person reacts to the biological changes. Self-views are affected by one's assessment of physical growth. Moreover, the adolescent must adapt to the fact that others expect different behavior, and because physical growth signals the entrance into adulthood new responsibilities must be accepted. Parents may treat the adolescent as more grown-up, may expect more adultlike behavior, and indeed may perceive the person very differently. Peers also react to the adolescent's physical growth, and the adolescent must interpret these reactions and respond to peers differently.

Finally, changes in expected behavior come from the broader culture. Adolescents must learn new roles as defined by the larger society in which they grow up. More mature social behavior is expected of the more physically mature adolescent—regardless of the age of attainment of physical maturity (Clausen, 1975). This may be a difficulty for some adolescents who mature very early because they may be much younger psychologically than they appear physically.

The first part of this chapter briefly describes the nature of the biological changes that occur during the early adolescent years. We discuss the psychological impact of these changes in the second portion.

THE INTERNAL CLOCK

Human physical growth and development occur in an orderly sequential fashion. Each cell is predetermined to divide a certain number of times. A woman's menstrual cycle begins when a hormonal signal announces her body is ready; she achieves a highly individualized regularity of hormonal release; and then another signal announces the end of her fertility. Even death comes as the expected culmination of the organism's growth cycle. This regularity in the sequence of growth is highly individualistic because each of us has our own biological clock. Some will mature earlier than others. Some will experience a more rapid growth spurt and others a slower growth into physical adulthood.

The Biological Clock in Humans

We all are controlled by internal biological clocks, even though we are largely unaware of this control. Consider the example of jet lag: The body literally revolts because time on an outside clock dictates we should engage in one set of behaviors, for example, eating dinner, and time on an inside clock dictates another behavior, perhaps sleeping. Many a traveler from the East to the West Coast has experienced this difference between inner and outer clocks.

In humans, this biological clock begins ticking at conception. Physical development unfolds in a predetermined sequence beginning with a fertilized egg and ending approximately 9 months later with a new human whose life systems can function independently of its mother's. However, even prenatal development is subject to environmental influences: The fertilized egg develops not only according to a genetic plan but also is subject to environmental influences, especially negative ones called **teratogens** (Dudgeon, 1973). Teratogens usually exert an effect only if an embryo or fetus is exposed to them at a critical period in its development or if they are present during labor and delivery (such as anesthetics taken by the mother). If rubella (German measles) is present during the first 3 months after conception when body structures are in the process of forming, it can cause malformations. Once some organ or limb is formed, it is less likely a teratogen can result in malformation, although it may result in malfunction of an organ. Drug use, alcohol consumption, smoking, and a poor diet are examples of common teratogens that can adversely affect the developing embryo and fetus, which is why they should be avoided by pregnant women. Prenatal growth involves biological events that occur in an environment: the healthier the environment, the healthier the prenatal growth.

Physical growth during the adolescent years also reflects both biological and environmental factors. At some point the biological clock activates the growth processes that result in the individual attaining adult physical status. This growth is influenced by a variety of environmental factors. Poor nutrition, severe living conditions, and prolonged illness are just a few examples of environmental circumstances that can impact on physical development during the growth spurt as well as during the childhood years.

Onset and Termination of the Growth Spurt

The reasons for the onset of the biological events leading to puberty and the growth spurt remain unknown (Grumbach, Grave, & Mayer, 1974; Katchadourian, 1977). One factor that may be responsible is a critical weight (Frish, 1974, 1983). Frish reports that pubertal onset in girls occurs at about 67 pounds (30 kg), peak velocity of weight gain at about 87 pounds (39 kg), and menarche at about 105 pounds (47 kg), regardless of age. In other words, pubertal events are related more closely to body weight than to age. The reason for this relationship, Frish suggests, lies in changes in metabolic rate, which decrease the sensitivity of the hypothalamus to estrogen. The decreased sensitivity results in an increase in "normal" estrogen levels sufficiently high to result in increased growth rates and sexual maturation. Similar procedures may operate in males.

Our lack of knowledge about the onset of puberty is far surpassed by our inability to explain its termination. Although it may appear obvious that growth should stop, it is unclear why hormone levels stabilize and other aspects of the growth spurt cease.

GLANDS AND HORMONES

The physical changes that we see, and the growth to mature reproductive capability, are the result of the influence of hormones. Hormones are chemical substances that influence cells. They are secreted by endocrine (ductless) glands directly into the bloodstream. Hormones are produced in one part of the body and are carried by the bloodstream to another part of the body where they exert their effect on target tissues. For example, gonadotropic (gonad-seeking) hormones are produced in the pituitary gland and travel through the bloodstream to act on the gonads, the ovaries and testes.

It is through the actions of hormones that we enter the growth spurt and change into physically mature adults. The influence of hormones also causes our reproductive systems to mature, allowing us to become capable of reproducing the species. The growth changes at the start of adolescence—height, weight, body shape, maturation of the reproductive system—are simply continuations of the earlier growth of the individual. No new biological systems are created during adolescence.

Endocrine Glands

The **endocrine glands** that play the major role in adolescent growth are depicted in Figure 3-1. The rate of secretion of their hormones is controlled by a complicated negative feedback system that *turns off* production of a hormone when a specific level is reached (Katchadourian, 1977). When a hormonal deficiency is detected, the **hypothalamus** secretes releasing factors that initiate secretion of particular hormones. These releasing factors travel the bloodstream and stimulate the pituitary to produce a variety of hormones, each of which has a target organ it is programmed to activate. Activation of the target organ results in the production of the hormone detected to be at a low level. When the level of the hormone becomes optimal, the pituitary, through the hypothalamus, maintains that level.

Hormones serve several major functons (Grumbach et al., 1974). The one most important for our purposes is known as morphogenesis, the determination of organ shape and structure (morphology) . The action of hormones on specific components of the body causes changes in overall body shape and structure. Specific examples are the development of the gonads and the primary and secondary sex characteristics, and bone and skeletal growth. This influence of hormones affects not only the physical characteristics we see—height and body shape—but also those we do not observe, such as internal organ structure.

Major Hormones Causing the Growth Spurt

Some two dozen hormones exert various influences on us (Katchadourian, 1977). Those that are particularly important to the growth spurt and our understanding of adolescent development are human growth hormone, testosterone, estrogen, and progesterone.

Human growth hormone (HGH).   Produced by the anterior (front) portion of the pituitary gland, **human growth hormone** (HGH) is a tropic hormone that stimulates a target organ to respond in some way. HGH fosters the development of protoplasm and skeletal growth, plays a vital role in glucose and fat metabolism, and generally fosters growth. Its specific role in pubertal growth remains something of a mystery, however. That it is critical may be seen from studies of its underproduction, which results in dwarfism, and its overproduction, which

Figure 3–1   The Endocrine System

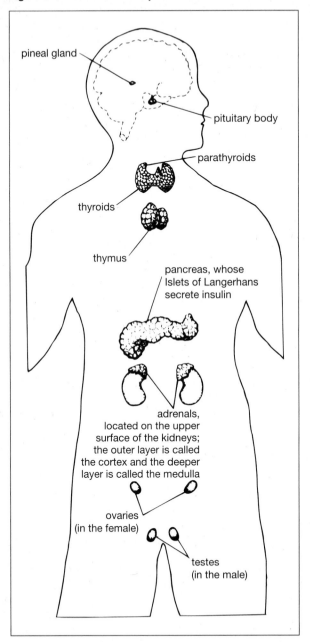

results in giantism (Connell, Davis, Goldzieher, & Wallace, 1971; Grumbach et al., 1974). Although we do not know of any specific effect it has during the growth spurt, we do know it must be present for normative growth to occur.

Synthetic growth hormones, those made in a laboratory, are used in several ways. One is as a therapy for arrested development. In some instances growth does not proceed as it should, and the use of growth hormone is necessary to allow the person to grow in a normative manner. Growth hormones also are used to increase the rate of growth of animals and stimulate milk production, for example. Bovine somatotropin (bovine growth hormone) injected into cows increase their milk production by about 10%.

Other major hormones affecting the development during the growth spurt are the **steroids**. Steroids are sex hormones produced by the gonads. The three major steroids pertinent to our discussion are **testosterone, estrogen,** and **progesterone.** These three hormones are present in all of us; we all have both male and female hormones because these three hormones are also produced by the adrenal cortex, the outer part of the adrenal gland (Katchadourian, 1977). Where the two sexes differ is in the concentration of each hormone. These hormones are known as "sex hormones" not only because they are produced primarily by the gonads but also because they strongly affect primary and secondary sex characteristic development. The male hormones are called **androgens**. There is no comparable term to describe the collection of female hormones.

Testosterone.   Testosterone, and other androgens, are produced in the male by the interstitial, or Leydig, cells in the testes. In females, testosterone is produced mainly by the adrenal cortex (Katchadourian, 1977). The low concentration of testosterone in boys increases dramatically during pubescence, the blood level amount increasing between 10- and 20-fold. The major effect of testosterone is to promote growth of the reproductive system and the muscles. Hence it is both a sex hormone and a growth hormone, and the major cause of the pubertal changes in males. It is responsible for the change in voice (due to enlargement of the larynx), the development of secondary sex characteristics (beard and other body hair), increases in the sex drive (see Box 3–1), and for making the skin susceptible to acne. It also increases height growth and hastens completion of bone growth, that is, reaching full adult growth. In girls, the androgens contribute to the growth of body hair.

Estrogen.   Estrogen is produced by the ovarian follicles (Graafian follicles). Its level increases in both males and females during the growth spurt, but the increase is much greater in females. In many ways it functions in females much as testosterone does in males: It contributes to muscle growth and growth in height, development of the secondary sex characteristics, increases in the sex drive, completion of bone growth, and body fat distribution. Its function in males is unclear (Katchadourian, 1977).

BOX 3–1   Hormonal and Social Influences on Adolescent Behavior

During adolescence we all experience very large increases in hormones. But we do not all experience them at the same time (age). Hence adolescence presents a unique opportunity to study the interacting influences of biological and social influences on behavior.

Considerable research has been conducted on the role of testosterone in males' behavior (Halpern & Udry, 1992). Those with higher testosterone levels have been shown to engage in more verbal and physical aggression, delinquency, and other problem behaviors. In addition, higher testosterone levels are related to increased sexual ideation, noncoital (for example, petting) sexual behavior, and sexual intercourse.

In considering such findings, it is tempting to conclude that sexual behavior or behaving aggressively is caused by the elevated hormone levels. However, simple observation and reflection on your own experiences shows this is not the case. Most people, including adolescent boys with very elevated testosterone levels, do not behave aggressively, and those who do don't behave aggressively all the time. Social conditions—peer pressure, institutionalized expectations for how one will behave, and social maturity—play a role in determining our behavior.

This biosocial perspective was clearly shown by Dornbusch et al. (1981) in their study of the biological and social factors that were related to starting to date. In a study of over 6,700 adolescents, they found that for both males and females age was a better predictor of starting dating than were measures of physical maturity. Dating is determined more by peer group norms and societal expectations for when one will start dating than by biological factors, such as increases in hormones related to the increased sex drive.

In general, then, we may view hormones as predisposing an individual toward certain behavior rather than causing the person to engage in it. Social/cultural factors play a somewhat stronger role in determining whether or not the individual will in fact engage in the behavior.

Progesterone.   Although progesterone is secreted by the ovarian follicles, it is mainly produced by the remains of the follicle, called the **corpus luteum,** after the egg cell is released. Each follicle has an ovum (egg cell). When the ovum is released, the tissue that remains behind (the corpus luteum) increases the production of progesterone. This accounts for the increase in progesterone level after ovulation, and is the direct cause of the increase in body temperature following ovulation. If the egg cell is fertilized, the corpus luteum is retained and the progesterone level remains high in order to prepare the uterus for the implantation of a fertilized egg cell and to facilitate lactation. If no pregnancy occurs, the corpus luteum dies away and progesterone production declines.

During puberty, the production of estrogen and progesterone takes on a cyclic pattern, resulting in the menstrual cycle. The cycles are generally quite irregular during puberty, and can be quite variable in length even in adulthood. As a result, it is very difficult to predict when ovulation will occur, which is one reason using the rhythm method of birth control is especially unreliable during the adolescent years.

PHYSICAL GROWTH DURING ADOLESCENCE

Boys and girls are born about the same size, and during the first 10 years of life grow at about the same rate (Katchadourian, 1977). At birth, boys are about 29% and girls 31% of final mature height. At age 10, boys are about 78% and girls 84% of final adult height. Girls reach final adult height about age 17, and boys at about age 19. These age differences in percentage of final adult height are largely due to the fact that boys enter the growth spurt later than girls. Because boys have a longer period of slow, regular growth they end up taller than girls, much as later maturers—who also have a longer period of slow growth—on average end up taller than earlier maturers.

Sex differences in growth rates are evident throughout the childhood and adolescent years. Starting at birth, a general maturity factor favors girls in motor, cognitive, and sexual development. This difference begins as early as fetal life and probably is due to the mother's immunological system acting against the boy's Y chromosome, or the relative smallness of the boy's Y compared to the girl's X chromosome. At birth boys are approximately 4 weeks behind girls in

During the early and middle adolescent years, girls are physically more mature than boys because they enter the growth spurt sooner. (*Larry Kolvoord/The Image Works*)

physical and motor development, and until adulthood they remain behind: In maturational age, a boy is 20% behind a girl of the same chronological age (Tanner, 1970; see also Faust, 1977). As a result, girls enter the growth spurt about 2 1/2 years ahead of boys.

The Growth Spurt

The growth spurt (see Figure 3-2) may be characterized as an acceleration and then deceleration of skeletal growth. There are very substantial individual differences in entrance into the growth spurt, its length, and when it is completed. Girls may enter the growth spurt as early as $9\frac{1}{2}$ or as late as 15 years of age. The average girl enters the growth spurt at about $10\frac{1}{2}$, reaches the peak year of growth at about age 12, and completes the growth spurt by age 14. The average girl reaches **menarche** (first menstrual cycle) at about 12.8 years (Faust, 1977). Boys may enter the growth spurt as early as $10\frac{1}{2}$ or as late as 16. The average boy starts the growth spurt at about $12\frac{1}{2}$ years, reaches the peak year of

Figure 3–2 Average Annual Increments in Height of Boys and Girls

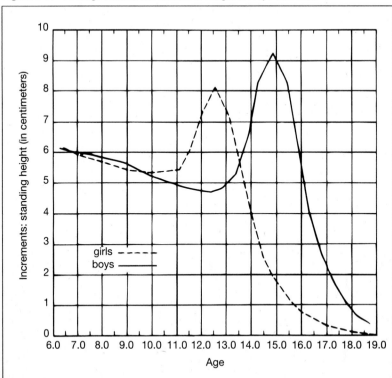

Source: Adapted from Shuttleworth, F.K. (1939). The physical and mental growth of girls and boys age six to nineteen in relation to age at maximum growth. *Monographs of the Society for Research in Child Development, 4* (Serial No. 22), 16.

growth at about age 14, and completes the growth spurt by age 16 (Tanner, 1970). Boys gain more height (average 21.1 cm or 8.3 in) during the growth spurt years than girls (average 19.6 cm or 7.7 in), and grow more during the peak year (average 10.4 cm or 4.1 in) than girls (average 9 cm or 3.5 in).

Despite these gender differences, there are a number of similarities in growth patterns for the two sexes (Faust, 1977). For each sex, the average duration of the growth spurt is about 2.8 years. The shortest duration for the growth spurt is about 1.9 years for boys and 1.5 years for girls; the longest duration is about 4 years for both sexes. Sequencing of growth trends, specifically for pubertal growth, is the same for the two sexes (Table 3-1; Faust, 1977; Tanner, 1970). These are *species-specific* patterns of growth—the patterns of boys' and girls' growth is similar because we all are humans.

Katchadourian (1977) interprets the sex differences in growth in a historical/evolutional manner. Males have been selected for certain traits (for example, physical strength and prowess) and females for others (for example, increased childbearing years). Later entrance by males into the growth spurt contributes in part to their greater size—they have a longer period of slow growth enabling them to grow bigger. Entering the growth spurt relatively early optimizes the length of females' childbearing years. Given that the years are limited by the biological clock, the earlier a girl enters them the longer time period she may reproduce. In the hunting culture of our early years as a species, both trends may have been adaptive and contributed to survival of the species. Although these biological differences contributed to sex-role differentiation (L. Hoffman, 1977), they no longer apply, which has contributed to the impetus to change sex roles. In industrialized nations, strength no longer is an advantage with regard to providing for a family and longevity of childbearing years is not an issue with regard to reproduction.

Table 3–1   Chronology of Pubertal Growth Changes

Age	Female	Age	Male
10-12	Critical phase in internal organ structural growth; equivocal morphology	12-13	Critical phase in internal organ structural growth; equivocal morphology
11-12	Initial development of breast and pelvis	13-14	Initial pubic hair growth, juvenile type
12-13	Initial pubic hair growth; juvenile type	14-15	Intensification of thoracic and muscular development
13-14	Initial axillary hair growth	14-15	Initial axillary growth
13-14	Menarche	14-16	Increase in size of genital organs
15-18	Completion of definitive female shape and psyche	16-18	Beginning of frank facial hair growth
		19-22	Completion of definitive male shape and psyche

Source: Botella-Llusia, J. (1973). *Endocrinology of women* (p. 342). Philadelphia: Saunders. Reprinted by permission of W.B. Saunders and the author.

Physical Changes During the Growth Spurt

The entire body, external and internal, undergoes considerable change during the growth spurt years. Because the external aspects of growth—height, body shape—are most important for the adolescent's social and psychological development we emphasize those aspects of growth.

Height.   Growth in height (see Figure 3-2) is one of the more dramatic and observable changes that occur during the growth spurt. The rate of gain in height is very rapid, approximating that of the late infancy years (about age 2). The phrase "growing like a weed" is an apt description of growth for many adolescents. The author grew 6 inches in the summer between the sixth and seventh grades!

Much of the growth in height is in the long bones of the legs and in trunk length (Katchadourian, 1977). The accelerated growth in the legs contributes to the stereotype of the gangling adolescent. For some who grow especially quickly this awkwardness can be real—they are prone to spilling the glass of milk at the table because they must get used to arms and fingers that are longer than they are accustomed to.

Growth in height ceases when the skeleton matures. This maturation is illustrated in Figure 3-3, which details bone growth in the hand, an index of physical maturation used in the Berkeley Growth Studies (discussed later). As the figure shows, bones grow not only longer, due to cartilage growth, but closer together. The **epiphyses,** which are the cartilage tips of the longer bones such as those found in the fingers and legs, grow closer together as skeletal maturity is achieved. As long as cartilage is present the bones grow longer and the person grows taller. As estrogen or testosterone exerts its influence to hasten bone growth over cartilage growth (which is called bone ossification), the cessation of growth draws nearer; when the cartilage tips, called end plates, are completely ossified, growth ceases. Indeed, the longer time males have for slow growth at the epiphyses prior to entering the growth spurt is in part why they are on average taller than females.

Weight.   Gains in weight are due largely to nonskeletal growth, mainly muscle and fat growth. Boys have gained about 55%, and girls 59%, of their adult weight by age 10 (Katchadourian, 1977). The growth curve for gain in weight is similar in shape to that for height, but gain in weight is much more variable because of its reliance on diet and exercise.

Muscle growth.   Peak growth in musculature occurs about 3 months after the peak growth in stature (Katchadourian, 1977). Related to increases in muscle size are increases in strength. It is in this area that sex differences present at birth—for example, hand grip—become magnified. Male's muscle cells increase by a factor of 14, female's by a factor of 10, between ages 5 and 16.

Body fat.   Subcutaneous fat, which is fat deposited directly under the skin, helps define body shape. At the onset of the growth spurt, there is a progressive loss of body fat, especially in boys, who generally experience a negative fat bal-

Figure 3–3   Age and Sex Differences on Ossification of the Hand and Wrist

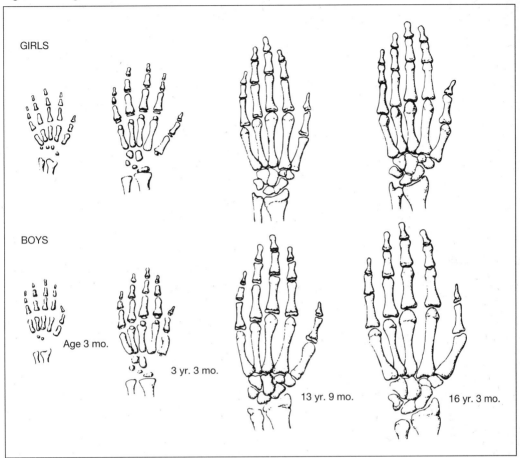

GIRLS

BOYS

Age 3 mo.

3 yr. 3 mo.

13 yr. 9 mo.

16 yr. 3 mo.

Source: Redrawn from an illustration in Shuttleworth, F. K., (1949). The adolescent period: A pictorial atlas. *Monographs of the Society for Research in Child Development, 14* (Serial No. 49). The original illustration was based on unpublished material of Nancy Bayley.

ance (they burn up more fat than is produced) that contributes to their "string bean" look. The loss of existing body subcutaneous fat is not as great among girls, which results in their entering adulthood with more body fat than boys. Moreover, females tend to "collect" subcutaneous fat in the region of the pelvis, breasts, upper back, upper arms, hips, and buttocks, which causes them to be more rounded. This sex difference in amount and distribution of body fat is responsible, in part, for the more muscular look of males. The fat layers of females cover the muscles, making their definition harder to see.

Internal changes.   Virtually all internal organs increase in size and weight during the growth spurt. The heart doubles in size, lungs and respiratory capacity increase, exercise tolerance—the ability of the body to function under physical

stress—increases. Brain growth, which is about 95% of adult weight by age 10, is minimal.

Sexual development.   Sexual development includes development of both the primary and secondary sexual characteristics. Although this aspect of development parallels the other growth trends just discussed, it is unique in that it signals the emergence of reproductive maturity. The age ranges and relative developmental aspects ot sexual maturity are illustrated in Figure 3-4.

In girls, the first visible sign of entrance into the growth spurt is growth of the breasts. In the average girl this starts àt about age 11 and is completed about age 15, the range of onset of growth being between 8 and 13 years, and the range of completion being between 13 and 18 years (Katchadourian, 1977). Although size and shape of the breasts have nothing to do with their capacity to nurse infants or respond to erotic stimulation, considerable psychological importance is attached to their development. It is not uncommon for a young woman to be concerned about whether her breasts will be the right size and shape, and a certain amount of self consciousness and preoccupation is common. Largely this is a result of social stereotyping concerning the size and importance of breasts.

The appearance of pubic hair is usually the second sign of puberty in girls. It begins to grow between ages 11 and 12 and the adult pattern is achieved by about age 14.

The internal sexual organs—the ovaries, uterus, vagina, fallopian tubes— all grow larger and increase in weight. The uterine wall becomes more muscular, as does the vagina. The ovaries, which are nearly completely developed at birth, do not undergo dramatic change. A female is born with about 500,000 immature ova (egg cells). During the course of her reproductive years about 500 will mature.

Menarche (the first menstrual period) usually occurs two years after the start of breast development and after the peak growth spurt in height. The average age of menarche in the United States is 12.8 years, the range being between 9 and 18 years. Although there usually is a short period of sterility during the growth spurt, this is not an effective contraceptive technique (Katchadourian, 1977).

In boys, pubertal onset is indicated by enlargement of the testes. This starts between the ages of 10 and $13\frac{1}{2}$, and is accomplished between the ages of $14\frac{1}{2}$ and 18. Testes produce sperm cells when the seminiferous tubules increase in size and their lining matures. Sperm cells are produced throughout the male's life.

The prostate gland increases considerably in size during the growth spurt. Its secretions account for much of the volume of semen during ejaculation. Some researchers (e.g., Katchadourian, 1977) have equated ejaculation in males psychologically with menarche in females, for it may be just as startling or unsettling. Also, it signifies achievement of sexual maturity.

The penis and scrotum grow markedly about a year after the onset of tes-

Figure 3–4   Schematic Sequence of Events at Puberty.   An average girl (upper) and boy (lower) are represented. The range of ages within which each event charted may begin and end is given by the figures placed directly below its start and finish.

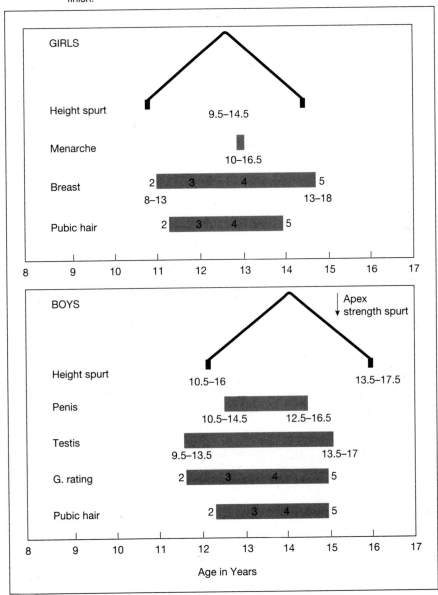

Source: Tanner, J. M. (1974). Sequence and tempo in the somatic changes in puberty. In M. M. Grumbach, G. D. Grave, & F. E. Mayor (Eds.), *Control of the Onset of Puberty.* New York: Wiley.

ticular growth and the first appearance of pubic hair (between ages 10 and 15). Growth is completed between ages $13\frac{1}{2}$ and $16\frac{1}{2}$. The size and shape of the penis are unrelated to physique, race, or sexual pleasure (Katchadourian, 1977).

A common pubertal event in males is a cracking of the voice. This results from a deepening of the voice due to enlargement of the larynx. Similarly, the appearance of facial and other body hair signals entrance into physical adulthood.

About 40% of boys experience some transient but normal breast enlargement (Katchadourian, 1977) for a short time during the growth spurt. In extremely rare cases, this breast enlargement may be pathological (gynecomastia) and require medical treatment.

In reading about typical or normative growth trends it is difficult to not compare one's own growth to the averages. When did you grow the most? When did you stop growing—or have you? How does your individual growth compare to the averages? In all likelihood the various aspects of your growth fell in the normative age ranges, but probably were not at the averages. This is simply a reflection of the substantial variability in normative growth that results from our unique genetic makeup and environment.

The Secular Trend

The term **secular trend** refers to generational differences in direction and magnitude of somatic (body) change (Frish, 1983; Meredith, 1963; Roche, 1979). Over recent generations, there has been an increase in final adult height of about a half an inch or so for each generation, more recent generations being taller (Roche, 1979). Other secular trends exist for body weight, age at entrance into the growth spurt, and age at maturity, for example. Your generation of adolescents not only is taller than your parents' generation, but you entered the growth spurt earlier, grew more, grew more quickly, and reached final adult physical growth sooner.

The secular trend in height is evidenced from ages 1 to 20 (Figure 3-5), with the largest generational difference occurring during the adolescent years because more recent generations of adolescents enter the growth spurt earlier, making them taller than previous generations at the same age. In other words, your generation of adolescents is more physically mature—in terms of height, weight, body build, age of menarche, and the like—than your parents were at a comparable age. This difference in rate and timing of growth may contribute to intergenerational (parent–adolescent) conflict because it may temper what it means to be an adolescent. Parents may be out of touch with the nature of adolescence, in part because of differences in rates of physical growth. Because physical growth characteristics are related to social behaviors, the social adolescent experience of parents and their adolescents may be very different.

It is important to stress that the secular trend refers to growth for generations of people and not individuals. You may or may not be taller than your parents. If you are taller, you may be much more than a half inch taller. These dif-

Figure 3–5   Schematic Curves of Mean Stature for 1880 and 1960.   Inset shows differences between the curves at selected ages.

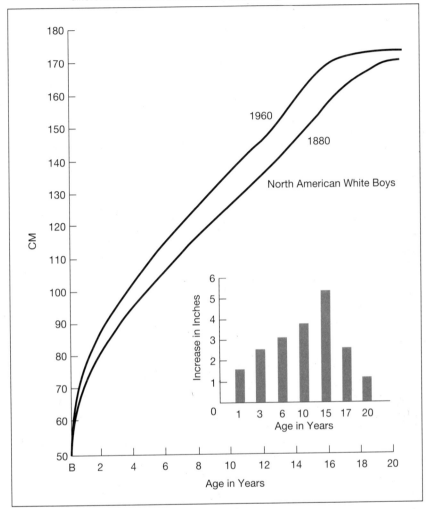

Source: Meredith, H. (1963). Change in the stature and body weight of North American boys during the last 80 years. In L. P. Lipsitt & C. C. Spiker (Eds.), *Advances in Child Development and Behavior* (Vol. 1). New York: Academic Press.

ferences reflect individual differences in genetics and environment. Check with your friends—admittedly not a random sample of your generation—for their height and that of their same-sex parent. You no doubt will find some who are taller and others who are shorter. Now calculate the average height for your male and female friends and their parent. If you have a reasonable sample size you likely will discover that the average difference is smaller than the largest difference for a single person. This is an illustration of the difference between individual growth and generational growth.

Some evidence indicates the secular trend has ended in England, the United States, Japan, and other developed countries (Roche, 1979). The secular trend largely is a result of improvements in nutrition and health care that impact favorably on the more recent generation. Despite the continued existence of poor nutrition and health care, the proportion of children and adolescents receiving adequate nutrition and health care is high enough that further increases will not result in a continued secular trend.

Could a secular trend the reverse of what we have experienced occur? The answer is yes. If environmental conditions were to change sufficiently to alter the nutritional and health-care status of large numbers of children and adolescents, we could find that entrance into the growth spurt occurs later, final adult height is shorter, and attaining full growth takes longer. It is not difficult to imagine the conditions that could bring about this reverse secular trend. Just study the conditions that existed in Iraq after the Gulf War. It is often claimed that the Iraqis were "bombed back to the Stone Age." Similar conditions exist in other countries experiencing different types of war. Although it is unlikely these events will occur in the United States, consider what might happen if the greenhouse effect turned our vast farmlands of the Midwest to dust bowls. Could the impact on the nutrition of the nation result in a reverse secular trend?

Influences on the Growth Spurt

The individual differences in age at entrance into the growth spurt and progression through it are due to both genetic and environmental factors. The species-specific growth patterns just noted are one example. We grow in part the way we do because we all are humans. Additional evidence for biological control during the growth spurt comes from research showing that identical twins enter the growth spurt at nearly identical ages, and that there is an increasing discrepancy in entrance into the growth spurt as genetic similarity decreases (Katchadourian, 1977).

Nutrition is an important environmental factor influencing pubertal growth. Malnutrition stunts growth and delays entrance into the growth spurt. Males are generally more susceptible than females to this negative influence. It should come as no surprise that less privileged adolescents enter puberty later and do not grow as much, probably because of nutritional deficits (Katchadourian, 1977).

Eveleth and Tanner (1976) studied average age of menarche (1) in different countries, (2) in different socioeconomic groups within the same country, and (3) within a country at different times—the secular trend. They reported that in countries where nutrition and health care were generally better, average age of menarche was lower. Hence it was lower in industrialized countries such as the United States, France, England, and Japan. It was generally higher in less well-industrialized countries, such as many of the African nations and

India. Adolescent females from more affluent backgrounds experienced menarche sooner than those from less well-off families. Since the mid-1800s the average age of menarche has been declining in industrialized nations (Bullough, 1981).

Several other environmental influences affect pubertal growth. Illness may retard growth, but after the illness is over a catch-up occurs, resulting in no permanent deficit. Although climate does not affect puberty, season of the year does. Height increases most in spring, weight in autumn. The mechanisms responsible for these effects are unknown at present. Finally, extreme physical exercise, as experienced by those in training for gymnastics, ballet, or other physically strenuous activities, retards menarche and may cause exercise amenorrhea (skipping of periods), which reverses quickly once the extreme exercise is stopped (Stager, Ritchie, & Robertshaw, 1984).

Genetic potential and environmental factors are interacting influences on our physical growth. Each of us has a genetic inheritance that, if met optimally, will lead to an earlier entrance into the growth spurt, and if met less than optimally, will lead to a later entrance into the growth spurt. If we are healthy and well nourished we will grow more optimally and reach our genetic potential sooner than if we are not (Frish, 1983).

PSYCHOLOGICAL ADJUSTMENT
TO PHYSICAL GROWTH

Two aspects of physical change during the growth spurt years are of special potential importance in explaining psychological functioning. Pubertal status refers to how physically mature or developed we are regardless of age (see Box 3-2). Pubertal timing refers to the degree to which the pubertal changes coincide with the norm, the degree to which we are ahead of or lag behind our agemates. Each of these influences how we view ourselves and how others react to us. Biological factors affect intrapersonal (within the individual) and interpersonal (between individuals) aspects of psychological functioning.

Psychologists use two models to explain the relation between physical change and psychological functioning: the direct-effects model and the mediated-effects model (Petersen & Taylor, 1980; M. Richards & Petersen, 1987; see Figure 3-6).

Direct-Effects Model

According to the **direct-effects** model, biological change directly results in psychological effects. Direct causal linkages are hypothesized between biological factors and psychological development.

Although scant evidence supports a direct-effects model (Petersen & Taylor, 1980; M. Richards & Petersen, 1987) one area of support comes from the study of hormone effects on behavior. Research on premenstrual tension indi-

BOX 3–2 Pubertal Status and Adolescent–Parent Relations

One of the stereotypic beliefs about adolescence is that it is accompanied by an increase in autonomy and in conflict with parents. Researchers (e.g., J. Hill, Holmbeck, Marlow, Green, & Lynch, 1985a, 1985b; Kracke & Silbereisen, 1992; Savin-Williams & Small, 1986; Steinberg, 1989) have begun to study the relation between the adolescent's pubertal status and adolescent–parent interactions. The findings of these studies indicate that pubertal status, independent of age, is indeed related to parent–adolescent conflict and to increased adolescent autonomy. More specifically, with increasing physical maturation, adolescents feel less close to their parents, and their feelings of emotional autonomy from parents increases. There also is an increase in feelings of dissatisfaction and conflict in offspring-parent relations. These feelings are stronger with respect to associations with mother than they are with respect to interactions with father. They are also more prevalent during the early to mid-adolescent years than later.

In discussing how we might explain the role of pubertal status, and not age, in these distancing behaviors, Steinberg (1989) proposes an evolutionary perspective that draws on research into social interactions in nonhuman primates and on anthropological evidence. Numerous examples exist of increased hostility in nonhuman primates between parents and offspring as the offspring enter puberty. These conflicts, in effect, drive the offspring away from the natal (family) group. Especially among monogamous species, this ensures mating outside the natal group.

Steinberg (1989) outlines the possible role of evolutionary factors in the increasing distance between adolescents and their parents. First, he notes that in humans the increased distancing during early adolescence, and the subsequent decline in such distancing during later adolescence, is consistent with findings for nonhumans. Second, he notes that historically we have had cultural institutions for separating adolescents and their parents. Hence in the 1850s the practice of "placing out" adolescents at puberty (Kett, 1977), and the practice of extrusion—sending adolescents away from the family unit at puberty—which occurs in a variety of cultures, are formalized means of separating the adolescent from the family unit.

Applying this line of reasoning to human adolescence, Steinberg suggests that the ultimate cause of increased adolescent–parent conflict during early adolescence may reflect the need to ensure that adolescents find mates outside the natal unit. With industrialization, improved health care and nutrition, and the like, we have seen adolescence lengthen because we mature at an earlier age and remain economically dependent on parents longer than previously. Hence the amount of time sexually mature adolescents remain in the family unit has increased substantially, which may contribute to prolonged periods of adolescent–parent conflict.

As we noted in the text, however, it is plausible that as adolescents mature, parents simply give more leeway because they expect their adolescents to begin to engage in more autonomous behavior. From this perspective, increases in conflicts may simply reflect honest differences in opinion regarding autonomy issues.

The interdisciplinary approach to explaining adolescent behavior may prove useful in helping us gain insights. When further such research is done, we will be better able to judge the contribution. As Sandra Scarr (1992) noted in her presidential address before the Society for Research in Child Development, the study of species-typical genes and environments and individual variations in them may show how they affect personality, social, and intellectual development. By studying interactions between them, we should be able to explain developmental variations better and identify children in need of specific types of interventions.

Figure 3–6 The Direct- and Mediated-Effects Models of the Influences of Biology on Psychological Functioning

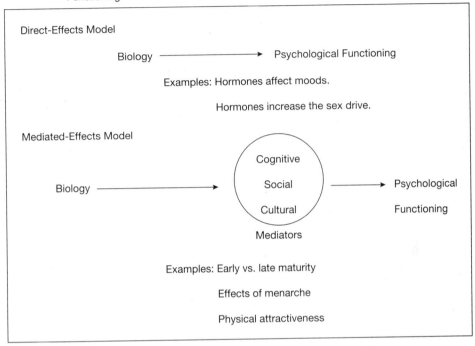

cates it has in part a hormonal basis (Delaney, Lupton, & Toth, 1988; Melges & Hamburg, 1977). About the 22nd day of the menstrual cycle, when the levels of both estrogen and progesterone are increasing, about 40% of women experience an increased degree of moodiness, irritability, lowered self-esteem, anxiety, and depression. These negative emotions and self-feelings generally are not as strong during the earlier days of the cycle. Keeping in mind that all of us at times are moody or feel poorly about ourselves, the important point is the dramatic and substantial nature of the changes. These findings have led some investigators to argue that, along with sociocultural factors, hormone balances directly affect psychological behavior (Melges & Hamburg, 1977).

In searching the literature, however, it is difficult to find very many clear demonstrations of direct biological effects on aspects of psychological development during adolescence. This has led many researchers to consider mediational factors in explaining links between biological changes and behavior (M. Richards & Petersen, 1987).

Mediated-Effects Models

In **mediated-effects** models, it is assumed biological changes affect psychological events through both individualistic and sociocultural (contextual) factors. In other words, the effects of biological change on psychological development and behavior are indirect; they are mediated by other factors (Petersen & Taylor, 1980).

Consider pubertal timing—being an early, average, or late maturer. In and of itself it matters only that you mature and become capable of reproducing the species. It makes no difference if you do that early, on average, or later. But we all know that it *is* important. Why? First, we all have some feelings about growing up—we may be excited or we may not want to accept the responsibility we perceive will be thrust on us. Second, we evaluate how we are growing relative to our friends and we don't want to be out of sync. Third, others—friends, parents, teachers—begin to treat us differently as we grow, and if we are particularly early or late we may get treated differently than those who are perceived as average maturers. You need consider only your own growth if you were an early or late maturer. How did others react to you, and how did you feel about that? If you were an average maturer, did you make fun of those who were early or late? Were you more or less pleased that you were maturing at the same rate as most of your friends?

According to the mediated-effects model, the adolescent's cognitions are one mediator for understanding the effects of biological change. Adolescents interpret the meaning and importance of the biological changes, the reactions of others to them—before and after the change—and how the change fits sociocultural norms (Clausen, 1975). In other words, being an early, average, or late maturer does not directly affect the adolescent. Rather, it is the adolescent's interpretation of the timing of entrance into pubertal changes that is important.

A second important mediator is social. Late maturers may be treated as less grown-up than their age-mates and, therefore, may develop poorer self-esteem and feelings about their body. Early maturers may be expected to take responsibilities for which they are not prepared just because they are more physically mature. The early maturing fifth-grade girl who continually is asked to watch the class when the teacher leaves the room may not want that responsibility, and may feel embarrassed.

The third major mediator is sociocultural standards for normative physical growth. Those who are extremely early or extremely late maturers, and those whose body builds do not match culturally determined standards for physical attractiveness, may suffer as they develop through the growth spurt.

An advantage of the mediated-effects model over the direct-effects model is that it allows understanding of individual differences in the effects of biological change on psychological development. Adolescents growing up in different cultures or subcultures may react differently to the same biological change. And adolescents within the same sociocultural context may react differently as a result of different rearing experiences, different interpretations of the biological event, or different interpretations of the behavior of others. Some examples of the use of this model to explain adolescent development are found in studies of the effects of early versus late maturity, reactions to menarche, and the influence of body build.

Peer reactions to differences in physical growth rates are important mediators of the effects of being an early or late maturer. (*Ken Karp*)

Early vs. Late Maturity

The initial research on the effects of adolescent physical growth on personality development came from the Berkeley Growth Studies. The researchers examined groups of adolescents of the same age and selected for study those who were either very early or extremely late maturers, usually the upper and lower 20% of the sample. **Skeletal age,** the degree to which bone ossification was complete as shown in X rays of the hand and knee, was used as the method of assessing maturity. The participants completed personality measures, and measures of social, emotional, and intellectual adjustment were obtained from peers, parents, and teachers. The data for the early and late maturers then were compared. Because the results are different for males and females we discuss them separately.

Early/late maturity in males. During the early and midadolescent years, male early maturers are taller, heavier, more muscular, more advanced in pubic and axillary hair growth, and more sexually mature than late maturers. Late maturers, on the contrary, are characteristically long legged, of slender build, and physically weaker than their same-age peers.

Because of their precocious sexual and physical maturity, early maturers have the advantage of size, strength, and greater masculinity over late maturers. In our culture, which values physical attractiveness and competency, early maturers definitely have the edge over average and late-maturing adolescents purely on the basis of body build. For example, in most high schools early maturers are the most popular and desirable boyfriends and leaders. These favorings by both peers and adults in the social sphere during the crucial adolescent years of identity formation have widespread psychological effects. Many early-maturing boys have advantages in athletic competition, which can facilitate social relationships through popularity and enhance self-esteem.

Behavioral differences were also readily apparent in comparisons between these two groups (Clausen, 1975). Adult ratings of male adolescents found that late maturers were consistently rated as less physically attractive, less masculine, less well groomed, more childish, more attention seeking, more tense, and less mature than early maturers (Jones & Bayley, 1950). Peer ratings of late maturers found them viewed as more restless, talkative, bossy, less self-assured, and less popular than their early-maturing classmates (Mussen & Jones, 1957). Moreover, early-maturing boys were seen as having more positive social attributes than late maturers by both adults and peers. Finally, early-maturing boys perceived themselves as more attractive because they were closer to physical maturity (Petersen, Leffert, & Graham, 1994; Tobin-Richards, Boxer, & Petersen, 1983). From these adult and peer ratings it can be seen that the extent of physical maturity readily elicits personality judgments from all the people with whom an individual comes into contact.

These social and personality judgments by others inevitably influence the adolescent's self-esteem (Clausen, 1975). The researchers from the Berkeley Growth Studies found that late maturers consistently perceived themselves as imbeciles or weaklings who were scorned by their parents or authorities. On projective tests they saw heroes as incapable of solving their own problems and needing the help of others for an answer. The early maturers' themes, however, centered around potency, aggression, and positive self-attributions (Mussen & Jones, 1957). The late maturers were more likely to hold negative or derogatory self-attributions than were the early maturers, a factor that was probably due to frustration of their strivings to be potent or strong.

The late-maturing boy has negative experiences because he is usually treated like a child longer than others by being denied leadership and other adultlike responsibilities, which may seriously damage his self-esteem (Clausen, 1975). His lack of development may hinder him in the classroom, in the locker room, and in the sports arena. Teachers may hesitate to attribute mature thoughts to him because of his immature physique. He may be singled out as a troublemaker because of his attention-seeking behavior, whether real or imaginary. His generally younger looking stature, less mature muscle growth, and lower exercise tolerance and strength may prevent him from competing successfully with others in physical contact sports, and indeed may hinder the development of social relationships with peers, particularly in the heterosexual sphere. The male late maturer may perform poorly in the classroom because he may come to feel he just can't measure up to anyone's standards.

More recent research (e.g., Duncan, Ritter, Dornbusch, Gross, & Carlsmith, 1985; Petersen, 1985, 1988) extended the study of early vs. late maturity into new realms. Duncan and colleagues (1985) reported that early-maturing boys were more likely to have behavioral problems at school, to be truants, and to engage in delinquent behavior, suggesting there may be detriments to being an early maturer. Others (Andersson & Magnusson, 1990) have reported that early maturers may be more prone to substance use and abuse than later maturers. These seemingly detrimental effects of early maturity may result from early-maturing boys forming friendships with older peers who engage in behavior that is difficult for those who are younger.

Peskin (1967, 1973; Livson & Peskin, 1980) has paid special attention to these concerns. He notes that early maturers may not have a sufficient amount of time to develop values and views about themselves prior to coping with the biological changes of puberty. Hence their pubertal experience may be more anxiety provoking. Peskin also reports that during the initial stage of pubertal growth early maturers were more anxious, less intellectually curious, more somber, more submissive, less exploratory, and less active than their later maturing counterparts. Later maturers have more time to ready themselves for the pubertal changes and develop skills to cope with peer pressure and other facets of social interaction that may help them avoid some of the negatives of growing up. Early maturity not only has advantages, then, but also may carry some disadvantages.

Early/late maturity in females.   The situation is much different for early-maturing girls (Jones & Mussen, 1958). They not only mature earlier than their sisters, but very much earlier than their male counterparts. They are at the absolute lower extreme of entrance into the growth spurt—potentially a very lonely position in which to find oneself. The early-maturing girl is faced with physical changes that her peers are not as yet experiencing. This may intensify the effects of menarche, for example, or may bring added discipline, restrictions, and confusion that are burdens to the early-maturing girl (Bardwick, 1971). She may even be socially ostracized by her own age-mates, who may view being "in phase" as important for social acceptance (Frisk, Tenhunen, Widholm, & Hortling, 1966; Petersen, 1988).

The early-maturing girl faces overall adjustment problems, not only with adults but also with her peers. She may seek the companionship of older individuals whose interests and problems are more similar to hers than are those of her prepubescent age-mates. She may come to see school as a childish waste of time because of her inability to interact emotionally with her age-mates. The early-maturing girl may be as much as 5 to 6 years ahead of average-maturing boys and as much as 2 to 3 years ahead of her same-sex peers. She therefore finds herself with few peers with whom she can share her growth experiences.

The early-maturing girl must also deal with physical development and the hormonal aspects of her mature femininity without relatively close contact from peers having similar experiences (Clausen, 1975). The negative feelings many female adolescents have about menarche, for example, may further increase tenseness and discomfort. Girls of normal or late maturation levels may share their insecurities and questions with each other. Parents may greet her confidences with increased worrying and added restrictions; peers simply don't know what she is talking about.

In addition to these difficulties, the early-maturing girl is more prone to engage in delinquency, use drugs and alcohol, and have problems in school, perhaps because she associates with older boys who introduce her to these activities (Aro & Taipale, 1987; Magnusson, Sattin, & Allen, 1986; Petersen, 1988). Whether a male or female, then, early maturity carries some detriments.

Current research shows a link between being an early maturing girl and the emergence of pathology. Compared to their later maturing sisters, early maturing girls are more likely to exhibit signs of depression and eating disorder symptoms (Hayward, Killen, & Taylor, 1994; Koff & Rierdan, 1993). In addition, although early maturing girls are more popular and begin to date earlier, they also do less well in school, have more behavior problems in school, and have a poorer body image (Koff, 1993; Koff & Rierdan, 1993; Petersen et al., 1994). As was the case for males, early maturity in females has both advantages and disadvantages. Whether the disadvantages continue in adulthood, or whether the later maturing girls will subsequently exhibit similar levels of pathological symptoms, must await future research (Hayward et al., 1994).

The late-maturing girl does not appear to be so handicapped, probably because girls enter pubescence approximately 2 years ahead of boys of the same age. She may even appear to have the best of both worlds because she enjoys a prolonged girlhood and emerges from puberty at the same time as her same-age male peers. She may have endured doubts about her female identity (Jones & Mussen, 1958), but they are relatively successfully resolved in the reality of a first date or when members of the opposite sex find her attractive. She will also have the advantage of newness to the dating routine at a time when her early-maturing sisters may have tired of the "immature" activities of the newly matured males their own age.

Any adolescent who experiences any sort of a developmental deviation may experience not only the psychosocial problems detailed here, but also other psychosomatic disturbances, which may include tics, nail biting, sleep and digestive problems, motor deficits, and unusual fatigue. These symptoms strongly suggest that perceived asynchrony in development may be a determining factor in physical as well as psychological problems (Frisk et al., 1966). In this regard, Petersen, Graber, and Sullivan, (1990) have noted the importance of adolescents' perceptions of pubertal timing as related to their feeling ready to engage in adult-type behaviors. Those who perceive themselves to be earlier maturers feel they are ready to engage in more adult behaviors—drinking, smoking, drug use. The perception of being an earlier maturing adolescent may be as important to understanding behavioral changes as the fact of being an earlier maturer.

Long-term effects.   There are several studies of the long term consequences of having been an early or late maturer. The initial studies again come from the Berkeley Growth Studies. At age 38, early-maturing males rated themselves as more responsible, cooperative, warm, persistent, and as being looked on to play a leadership role. But they also rated themselves as more rigid and conforming

(Jones & Mussen, 1958). Late maturers rated themselves as more rebellious, self-indulgent, impulsive, and childish, but also as more insightful and creative. These self-descriptions are very similar to the adult and peer ratings of these individuals during their adolescence. In addition, the late maturers held fewer jobs of responsibility (executive) and leadership, but they had happier and more successful marriages (Jones, 1965; Mussen & Jones, 1957).

Similar findings have been reported for 30-year-old females. The early-maturing females, who were under stress during adolescence, as adults saw themselves as more self-directed, self-assured, and competent than did the late-maturing girls (Peskin, 1973). Although some evidence (Magnusson et al., 1986) shows deleterious longterm effects of being an early-maturing girl—for example, developing negative attitudes toward school and completing less education—it seems the early-maturing female profits socially and intellectually.

The evidence suggests that degree of physical maturity to a large extent determines societal expectations for the adolescent's behavior. For example, adults generally expect more mature and adultlike behavior from an early maturer than from a late maturer, likely because early maturers more closely resemble adults (Clausen, 1975). However, even the early-maturing postpubertal adolescent lacks the cognitive and social maturity of an adult, and therefore may not be able to live up to these expectations. Conflicts between what is expected and what is possible may cause serious harm to the early maturer's self-esteem. An early-maturing boy who is president of his high school class may bear the onus for class pranks the rest of his life because school authorities expected more from him than his younger appearing classmates.

On the other hand, late maturers are expected to behave more like children. An example is the 14-year-old whose parents force her to wear "little girl" clothes when she wants to dress like her more developed age-mates. Again, expectations exist that are not necessarily congruent with the capacities of the individual; adult expectations that are inappropriate and out of step with the adolescent's developmental level and associated competencies may result in conflict between adolescent and parent.

Go back in time to your freshman year in high school. Who were the class leaders; who the most popular students? Who was listed in the yearbook as the most likely to succeed? Who were the star athletes? These likely are the individuals that most thought would be successful and happy. If you have seen any of them recently, did the expectations come true? How are they different now than then? Such differences reflect judgments based in part on physical development, not the individual's psychological characteristics.

Psychological Reactions to Menarche and First Ejaculation

Menarche and first ejaculation are concrete signs that one has become capable of reproducing the species (Brooks-Gunn & Reiter, 1990). These events occur only once and may be viewed as milestones in development. Each may have a profound impact on how the adolescent experiences physical growth and its behavioral and psychological consequences.

Menarche, the onset of the menstrual cycle, is a signal of female sexual maturity and fertility. As such, it is an important event in the lives of adolescent females. It would be surprising, indeed, if menarche did not have associated with it important psychological concomitants. Contrary to both theoretical and popular beliefs, menarche is apparently not an overly traumatic event for most adolescent girls. Ruble and Brooks-Gunn (1982) report that adolescent girls indicate both positive and negative feelings about menarche. And, for postmenarcheal girls, the negative aspects of menarche, particularly the physical symptoms, were not as severe as expected. Brooks-Gunn and Ruble (1982) suggest that premenarcheal girls may attend more selectively to negative information, or may receive more negative than positive information from parents or peers, about menstruation and, hence, expect it to be more debilitating than in reality it is. Once the girl experiences menstruation firsthand, she is in a better position to understand both the positive and negative aspects of menstruation and develops a more balanced perspective about it.

An important aspect of the adolescent girl's feelings about menstruation is the information the girl has had about it. Brooks-Gunn and Ruble (1982) questioned girls about the sources from which they gained information about menstruation. The major sources of information, as you might expect, were other females, particularly the girl's mother, and doctors. Males were not seen by the girls as a particularly useful source of information, and they were viewed as having negative perspectives on menstruation. It is interesting to note that those girls who indicated they had gained significant amounts of information from males reported more debilitating and negative effects of menstruation than girls who learned less from males. Moreover, girls who know little of what to expect, that is, those who are not prepared for understanding menstruation, have a more unpleasant and difficult experience (Rierdan, Kobb, & Stubbs, 1989).

Postmenarcheal girls are somewhat more interested in their femininity than are premenarcheal girls (Greif & Ulman, 1982). They have a heightened awareness of their physical appearance and of cross-sex relationships. Postmenarcheal girls also are more psychologically mature than premenarcheal girls, as assessed by measures of figure drawing, general adjustment, and self-concept.

We can conclude that menarche and menstruation are very significant negative events for some girls; fortunately, the percentage of girls for whom this is the case is small. In general, it appears that menstruation may initially be disconcerting and an inconvenience for many girls, but this is not a long-lived effect. As the girl has personal experience with menstruation she is able to develop a balanced view of the positive and negative aspects of it. As a result, it is not as negative as some popular conceptualizations may suggest.

Much less is known about males' reactions to their first ejaculation. Indeed, boys are likely to be more well informed about the menstrual period than they are about male ejaculation, for which the most common source of information is peers or literature. The available evidence indicates that unlike girls, who tell their mothers and soon thereafter their girlfriends about menarche, boys remain relatively silent about ejaculation (Gaddis & Brooks-Gunn, 1985). Some boys' first ejaculation occurs as a nocturnal emission (wet dream), for others it is through masturbation, and for some a result of sexual intercourse. The scant evidence indicates it is not a cause of embarrassment or fear, but rather is seen as a positive event signifying growing up and entering adulthood.

Both male and female adolescents experience an entrance into adulthood sexuality, but it is different in important ways. For girls there is greater preparation and more discussion of the meaning and physical feelings associated with the event than there is for boys. For boys, secrecy seems to prevail, and there is little open discussion of the event. And menarche and first ejaculation may be experienced under very different circumstances—first ejaculation may occur under a wider variety of circumstances (masturbation, intercourse) than menarche, which is much more a biologically determined event. Although it is tempting to consider them similar experiences, then, the important differences in the manner they are experienced likely make them psychologically quite different.

Body Type

As we noted earlier, personality depends to some degree on the body shape and type of the individual, that is, adolescents' internal reactions to their external physical changes. Sheldon (1940), a psychologist interested in the relationship between psychological characteristics and body type, categorized three distinct body types, each postulated to have a corresponding personality or temperament associated with it. **Endomorphs** are soft, flabby individuals with underdeveloped bones and muscles and a tendency toward fat. **Mesomorphs** have a highly developed bone and muscle structure, a hard firm physique, and a tendency toward an athletic build. **Ectomorphs** have linear and fragile bodies characterized by a flatness of chest and delicacy of bone structure; they are thin and slightly muscled, with a great deal of energy and a high metabolic rate but little strength.

Although it has some appeal, there are a number of problems with this approach to personality development. It is simplistic and there are few pure body types. However, Lindzey (1965) writes that Sheldon's notion of a relationship between somatotype and personality has some merit because behavior and body structure each may be jointly determined by genetic and environmental factors. For example, family and environmental factors, such as nutrition, that affect physical growth may influence personality in the same manner as they do sexuality and general growth. Lindzey also points out that physical handicaps such as diabetes and obesity produce personality types, and that although these are extreme cases, they do suggest that physical characteristics affect person-

The importance of one's body build lies in the reactions of others and cultural stereotypes regarding physical appearance. (*Shirley Zeiberg*)

ality and emotions. Finally, Lindzey acknowledges society's role in forcing personality–physique interactions by its tendency to typecast individuals based on physical aspects such as skin color, size, physique, and the like.

Researchers have examined the relationship between body build (somatotype) and other aspects of development. By age 7 there is a clear preference for an athletic (mesomorphic) type of body build. Children and adolescents view the mesomorph as having leadership and athletic ability, and as being psychologically stable. There were fewer positive traits and views of endomorphs and ectomorphs. In turn, evidence indicates that, in peer relations, mesomorphs tend to be more dominant and the other types of children more submissive and timid. In other words, the expectations of peers are, in one way or another, translated in the behavior of the group's members, some assuming dominant, and others more passive, roles within the group. Finally, some evidence (Clausen, 1975) indicates that adolescent body build is related to personality ratings by adults when the individual was a child. Males who were ectomorphic at maturity were rated as shy, not very active, and not very happy as infants. Mature mesomorphs were rated just the opposite during their infancy years.

During adolescence, peer relations were the most strongly related to body build. The ectomorphs were viewed as seeking attention by nearly any means available, as less knowledgeable about peer group functioning, not being selective in making friends, and as the butt of jokes. Although there are apparently some social-class differences that temper these findings, for example, the effects just reported are much less strong in the middle social-class levels, it appears that adolescents engage in a kind of self-fulfilling prophecy based on sociocultural standards for preferences in body build.

The importance of body type and maturity rate lies in the social behavior of others toward the adolescent and in the adolescent's self-esteem, the mediators listed in Figure 3–5. Because body type and maturity rate are by and large genetically and hormonally controlled, there is little, if anything, the individual can do in the normal course of events to alter these biological aspects of development. Because social structure (a mediator) provides advantages to early-maturing individuals, biological factors have profound influences on psychological development. If perceptions of infants determine how one reacts toward the infant and then child and adolescent, it would be consistent with a mediated-effects model of how physical characteristics influence personality development.

Body Image

Body image refers to how the adolescent perceives his or her body within the context of cultural standards of attractiveness. How satisfied adolescents are with their bodies depends to a great extent on their perceptions of how others view them—few can be objective about their body image. In turn, adolescents' self-esteem rests in part on their body image (Stiles, Gibbons, Hardardottir, & Schnellmann, 1987; Tobin-Richards et al., 1983). Those who perceive a more positive body image have higher self-esteem.

What constitutes a "good" body image differs for males and females. For males, and especially for early maturers, it is the appearance of a beard (Tobin-Richards et al., 1983). The appearance of facial hair seems to be a more important signal of entrance into adulthood than pubertal timing, and facial hair is obvious to the boy and others even if he is destined to be shorter than others because of his genetic makeup. Body size takes second place to a specific observable index of maturity.

For girls the matter is more complex. Generally speaking, later maturers have a more positive body image than earlier maturers, perhaps because they retain the thin, long-legged physique that is associated in our culture with an ideal body type for females (Petersen et al., 1994). Once puberty and its concomitant gains in subcutaneous fat occur, however, the body image of girls decreases, resulting in the lowered body image of postpubertal girls (Brooks-Gunn & Warren, 1989; Tobin-Richards et al., 1983). Tobin-Richards et al. (1983) do note an exception to this general rule, however. Breast development is a specific event related to body image. Girls who develop breasts sooner, or who have more well-developed breasts, have better body images. Breast development in girls may be akin to facial hair development for boys. Each is a "public" indicator that one is entering adulthood.

Increases in eating disturbances are related to body image in females, particularly if they are early maturers. Koff (1993; Koff & Rierdan, 1993) suggests that eating concerns initially may be triggered by increases in body fat and weight, but that the psychological response to these increases, in the form of an increasingly negative body image, is more important in the development of eating disorders. Earlier maturing girls have a poorer body image and elevated eating-related concerns. Koff (1993) argues that initial concerns about weight may result in dieting and over time may generalize to concerns with overall appearance (body image). Ultimately, the initial concern with body fat and weight becomes less important in predicting eating-related concerns and body image becomes more important. Body image, a psychological reaction to physical appearance, becomes a cognitive mediator of eating disturbance.

SUMMARY

The biological changes that occur during the early to mid-adolescent years are a result of the complex influences of hormones. The hormones are secreted by the endocrine glands, ductless glands that send their secretions directly into the bloodstream. Testosterone, estrogen, and progesterone are the most important. Their levels increase considerably during adolescence and cause the growth spurt, resulting in final adult physique and sexual maturity.

Girls enter the growth spurt about $2\frac{1}{2}$ years ahead of boys, and complete the spurt earlier. But boys grow more during the growth spurt years, partly because they have a longer period of slow growth prior to entering the growth spurt. Despite these sex differences, there are many similarities in growth spurt development, including the duration of the spurt and the sequence of biological changes. More recent generations of adolescents evidence a secular trend; they enter the growth spurt earlier, grow bigger, reach maturity sooner, and have an increased adult size relative to earlier generations. This secular trend, which seems to be ending in Western industrialized nations such as the United States, England, and Japan, is primarily due to increased health care and nutritional advances.

The biological changes of puberty influence psychological development primarily through personal cognitions and sociocultural mediators. Hence the negative effects of being a late maturer or an ectomorph reflect the adolescent's evaluations and attributions to both the self and the behavior of others toward the self. Of primary importance in this regard is the peer group. Adolescents, especially boys, who are late maturers or who deviate considerably from the preferred mesomorphic body build, tend to be viewed as more childish and are somewhat less accepted in the peer group. In addition, their own behavior may include more childish modes of interacting with both peers and adults. Some evidence suggests these differences in the perceptions of others, and the actual behavior of the individual may even be evident in the infancy and childhood years. Whatever the mechanisms, it is clear that biologically determined physical growth plays an important role in aspects of psychological development such as personality. This is most evidenced in studies of body image. Those who show obvious signs of entrance into adulthood—boys growing beards and girls developing breasts—have better body images than those showing these characteristics later.

GLOSSARY

androgen: General term meaning male sex hormone.

corpus luteum: Temporary body organ formed when the egg cell separates from the ovary.

direct-effects model: Model or theory that explains how biological factors directly influence psychological development and behavior.

ectomorph: Body type characterized by a thin build, slight muscles, and a high metabolic rate.

endocrine glands: Glands that secrete hormones directly into the bloodstream.

endomorph: Body type characterized by softness, flabbiness, and underdeveloped bones and muscles.

epiphyses: Cartilage tips of long bones.

estrogen: Major female hormone responsible for growth.

human growth hormone: General growth facilitating hormone; no specific function during the growth spurt.

hypothalamus: Part of the brain which secretes hormones that affect the anterior pituitary and trigger the start of the growth spurt.

mediated-effects model: Attempts to explain the effect of biological factors on psychological development through reference to intermediary factors, such as cognitive, social, and cultural factors.

menarche: First menstrual period.

mesomorph: Body type characterized by highly developed bones and muscles and a tendency toward an athletic physique.

progesterone: Female hormone especially involved in preparing the uterus for a fertilized egg cell.

puberty: Term used to refer to the physical growth, including sexual maturation, that occurs during the growth spurt years.

secular trend: Intergenerational differences in direction and magnitude of somatic growth.

skeletal age: Age determined on the basis of degree of bone ossification.

steroids: Term referring to sex hormones.

teratogen: Environmental influence that is harmful to the developing fetus.

testosterone: The major male growth hormone.

DISCUSSION QUESTIONS

1. Think about how you physically grew up. Was it an even and smooth growth or did some parts of your body complete growth before other parts? How did this affect your self-esteem?

2. How old were you when you started the growth spurt? How old when you completed the period of relatively rapid growth? Were you "on time" or early or late?

3. The startle reflex is caused in part by very rapid increases in certain hormones. What are they? What function of hormones is reflected in this reflex? What model of the effects of biology on behavior best explains this reflex?

4. What might be some of the behavioral manifestations of adolescent "distancing"? Did you experience any of them while you were growing up?

5. How did others react to you as you were growing up? How did you treat early- or late-maturing peers? Why?

6. In what ways is body build related to psychological development? What is your body build? Do you think others treat you in certain ways because of your body build? If so, how?

7. What were your initial reactions upon learning about menstruation? Why did you have those reactions?

4

Intellectual and Cognitive Development in Adolescence

Major Issues Addressed

Alternative Ways to View the Nature of Intelligence
Intelligence as Problem-Solving Ability
Developmental Trends in IQ Scores
Intelligence as Ways of Thinking
Piaget's Theory of Intelligence
Intelligence and Explaining Adolescent Behavior
Social Cognition and Adolescent Development
Creativity and the Adolescent

He won; I lost. How could that happen? He wanted to stay up until 11 o'clock to watch a television news program dealing with drug use among adolescents, but it was a school night. I "knew" he would be tired the next day, and might not be ready for school. But no matter what argument I made, he had an answer that seemed logical and made sense. I had to give in and gamble he would be right. He was; I wasn't.

◆　　　　◆　　　　◆

During adolescence we gain the ability to think in an abstract and logical manner. We can consider alternatives, as in "if–then" thinking. We can see future consequences of our behavior, and begin to make complex logical arguments. In this chapter we examine how adolescent thought processes develop and how this development impacts on the adolescent in other than intellectual ways.

INTRODUCTION

During adolescence the ability of the individual to learn, think, and make use of knowledge peaks. IQ scores peak and stabilize during the adolescent years, and the ability to think abstractly, consider multiple possibilities, and understand the long-range consequences of decisions increases. These changes are related to resolution of the identity crisis, the development of political views, and the adolescent's understanding of the nature of social interactions. We first explore various views of the nature of intellect and then discuss some relations between intellectual development and other aspects of adolescence.

WHAT IS INTELLIGENCE?

There is no simple definition of intelligence; there is not even a generally accepted one. For the purposes of our discussion, we need concern ourselves only with the fact that **intelligence** is usually defined in one of two ways: quantitatively (psychometrically) or qualitatively (structurally).

The quantitative approach typically views intelligence as learning or problem-solving ability. People are seen as having greater or lesser amounts of these particular abilities. Although there are alternatives to assessing these abilities, the typical way is with an intelligence, or IQ, test. The IQ test produces a number (a score) representing the individual's relative standing in the population. Because IQ is a number we call it a quantitative measure of intelligence. The quantitative approach is nondevelopmental; that is, it assumes the meaning of an IQ score is the same at all ages.

An alternative approach is to view intelligence as modes of "thinking," that is, to see it as reflecting how the individual processes information from the environment. It is assumed the individual processes environmental information differently during the various stages of intellectual development because each stage reflects a different way of thinking. An emphasis on different means of thinking, as opposed to different amounts of ability, typifies the developmental approach to understanding intellect.

THE QUANTITATIVE APPROACH TO INTELLIGENCE

The quantitative approach to the study of intelligence dates back to the pioneering work of Alfred Binet, father of the intelligence test. In 1904 the French government commissioned Dr. Binet (a physician) to develop a test that would identify those students who might need special help in their education. In collaboration with his colleague Theofile Simon, Binet developed a test that would pick out the students who would have difficulty with the general curriculum.

Because Binet's intent was to develop a test that would predict school performance, he chose to sample behaviors from a number of areas related to school performance, such as perceptual-motor (hand-eye) coordination, memory, perception, verbal ability, and logical reasoning. He assumed performance on these types of tasks would reflect something of the child's general learning abilities as related to the skills used in school learning.

Binet's first test was published in 1905. In 1916 Lewis Terman, a psychologist at Stanford University, adapted Binet's test for use in the United States. This adapted test became known as the Stanford-Binet intelligence test, after the university and the original test constructor. It was Terman who devised the original formula for the **intelligence quotient:** IQ equals MA/CA × 100. In this formulation, IQ is a rate measure; it reflects the child's rate of acquisition of presumably universally taught information and skills—the test content just mentioned. **CA** is the child's chronological age. **MA** is the child's performance on the test measured as mental age units. It is a measure of developmental level, or how far the person has come intellectually. Today, IQ is not determined this way. Rather, test scores are converted to IQ scores by comparing them to population norms determined in a more complex manner. Retention of the term *IQ* is simply for convenience. Nonetheless, it is assumed that people with higher IQs learn things more quickly than those with lower IQs. In the same vein, people with high IQs are capable of demonstrating test performance well above their age;

people with low IQs perform below their age level. The classification system that often is used to describe IQ levels is listed in Table 4–1.

Types of IQ Tests

There are two types of IQ tests. *Group tests* are of the paper-and-pencil variety. Although they are easy and cheap to administer they tap only limited behavior and are not particularly accurate. If you took the IOWA Achievement Tests in high school you also probably took the Cognitive Abilities Test, a form of group IQ test. *Individually administered* tests, such as the Stanford-Binet and the Wechsler Intelligence Scale for Children–Revised (WISC–R), are more time consuming and costly to administer (a trained examiner must give the test), but they are more accurate and sample a wider variety of behavior.

As an analogy, think about the types of tests you take in your college courses. In some classes your grade (score) is determined only by your performance on multiple-choice examinations. In other classes your grade is determined by multiple-choice items, short answer or matching questions, and perhaps by essay questions. The former assessment is like a group IQ test—a single method of assessment that has limitations is used. The answers can be scored by an optical scanner. Although the scores are accurate, the method of assessment is limited. The more varied method of testing is similar to an individual IQ test: Although some scoring is very straightforward (e.g., matching), to completely determine the score requires a "trained examiner" (the essays) who has expertise and invests more time. The multiple methods of assessment allow greater insight into what the student "knows" or doesn't.

Cautions in Interpreting IQ Scores

Several cautions must be taken when interpreting IQ scores. First, an IQ score represents a range of scores that allows only a rough estimate of ability. For example, an adolescent with an IQ of 95 can be considered within the normal range of intelligence, but the adolescent's actual IQ may be much higher or

Table 4–1 Classifications of Intelligence

IQ	Classification	Percent Included
130 and above	Very superior	2.2
120–129	Superior	6.7
110–119	Bright normal	16.1
90–109	Average	50.0
80–89	Dull normal	16.1
70–79	Borderline	6.7
69 and below	Mental defective	2.2

Source: Wechsler, D. (1955). *Manual of the Wechsler Adult Intelligence Scale.* New York: Psychological Corporation. Reproduced by permission from the *Wechsler Adult Intelligence Scale Revised.* Copyright © 1955, 1981 by The Psychological Corporation. All rights reserved.

lower because the test is not a perfect measure and his or her performance is affected by a number of factors (fatigue, attention span, attitude when taking the test, etc.).

Second, IQ scores are not "real" in the sense of physical characteristics. IQ is what psychologists call a hypothetical construct that is useful in understanding behavior. Too often teachers, parents, and the general public assume IQ is real, like curly hair or long earlobes.

Finally, as we discuss in Box 4–1, there is not unanimous agreement on how many "intelligences" there are. In interpreting an IQ score one must know the "kind" of IQ score one is dealing with. As noted in Box 4–1, an IQ test results in three scores: overall IQ, verbal IQ, and quantitative IQ. Although you likely don't know your three IQ scores, consider your SAT scores. You had one score for quantitative ability, another for verbal skills, and a total score. Unless you had an extremely high or very low score, a large number of combinations of quantitative and verbal scores could result in your total score. For some, the two scores are very similar; for others, they are quite different. Which is most representative of your abilities? In order to make use of SAT scores, one needs to know which score is being used. The same applies to IQ scores.

The Nature/Nurture Controversy

Perhaps the most heated controversy concerning IQ scores has revolved around attempts to determine the degree to which intelligence is inherited versus learned. This debate has a long history, dating back to the initial studies of Galton (1883) in England and continuing up to modern-day investigations (Herrnstein & Murray, 1994).

The study of the relative contributions of genetics and environment to the development of intelligence is pursued by those interested in the field of developmental behavioral genetics, the study of individual differences in development through the use of behavioral genetic techniques of research (Crnic & Pennington, 1987). Developmental behavioral geneticists attempt to answer the question of how genetic endowments and environmental contexts interact during development. Early research (reviewed by Scarr, 1992) was based on a very simplistic approach; researchers simply correlated the IQs of individuals with differing degrees of genetic relationship. (We explain statistical correlations in the appendix.) They found that identical twins have more highly correlated IQs ($r = .86$) than do fraternal twins ($r = .55$), whose IQs were more similar than those of siblings ($r = .47$). Because fraternal twins are no more genetically similar than siblings, these findings indicate that environmental factors also play a role in IQ test performance.

Contemporary approaches are much more sophisticated. The extensive research of Scarr (1992, 1993) and her colleagues has utilized the *adoption model* to assess the impact of environment on intellectual functioning and personality development. Studying the development of adopted adolescents allows researchers to assess environmental impacts without the contaminating influences

BOX 4–1   How Many Kinds of Intelligence Are There?

Historically, in the psychometric approach intelligence has been viewed as a general learning or problem-solving ability. Spearman (1927) expressed this general learning ability as **g** for general intelligence. Because we must measure g through some test that has content (numbers, words, perceptual skills), we get inexact estimates of g due to what he called specific aspects of intelligence (**s** factors). Hence, although he believed there was a general intellectual ability, he also identified specific skills that one has, which he treated as nuisances to measuring g.

Horn (1968) and Cattell (1941, 1963) speak of crystallized and fluid intelligence. Crystallized intelligence involves those intellectual skills that are acquired through cultural means, including formal education. Examples include number skills and vocabulary. Fluid intelligence is assessed by memory, flexibility in modes of thinking, and relation-perceiving abilities that are not culturally taught, but rather seem to reflect the means by which the central nervous system operates. The individually administered IQ tests include both types of measures.

Robert Sternberg (1988) proposed a *triarchic theory of intelligence*; he suggests that in order to examine one's intelligence we need to measure three types of intelligence. *Componential intelligence* involves memory and information processing. It is the type of intelligence assessed by IQ tests. *Contextual intelligence* entails thinking in a practical manner and adapting to the various contexts in which we live. It is the ability to draw on our history of experiences in a variety of situations. *Experiential intelligence* includes our ability to use insight and creativity to solve new problems. It is akin to what we might call creativity. Sternberg argues that all three types of intelligence are important and that any of us might be high in one or the other—

we all might be intelligent in different ways.

Others postulate even more types of intelligence. Gardner (1983; Walters & Gardner, 1986) postulates seven forms of intelligence: musical, bodily-kinesthetic, logical-mathematical, linguistic, spatial, interpersonal (understanding others), and intrapersonal (understanding the self). Each form has its own signal system. Musical intelligence involves the ability to create in the realm of pitch and rhythm; interpersonal intelligence is evidenced in a heightened ability to understand how others feel and what motivates them; bodily-kinesthetic intelligence reflects the ability to control one's body in space. Each form of intelligence may be associated with some specific vocational outcome—those high in musical ability may become composers or orchestra directors; those high in interpersonal intelligence may become therapists or politicians; those high in bodily-kinesthetic intelligence may become dancers or surgeons. Gardner believes each is a legitimate form of intelligence and feels that by expanding our notion of what intelligence is we will avoid the stereotyping of intelligence as mathematical and linguistic abilities, which are highly favored by our culture and are the ones typically measured by standardized intelligence tests.

Perhaps the extreme of this perspective is offered by Guilford (1988), who has postulated there are 180 identifiable types of intellectual abilities. He identified six types of mental operations (e.g., memory, creativity), five types of content (e.g., auditory, verbal), and six types of products (e.g., words, relations)—the product of these three dimensions of intelligence is 180. He believes that by examining the pattern of scores on a variety of intelligence tests one will gain a more precise understanding of the adolescent's abilities.

The typical IQ test administered today

provides three scores: an overall IQ score, a score for verbal IQ, and a score for performance IQ. Verbal IQ includes measures such as digit span (ability to repeat back a random string of digits), vocabulary, information (answering questions about things one learns simply by living in our culture, such as colors or the number of days in a week), and other culturally acquired information. Performance IQ includes measures such as object assembly (putting together puzzles of pictures of common objects), block design (using cubes of different colors to reproduce a design seen in a picture), and picture completion (arranging pictures so a story results). By examining scores on the verbal and performance subscales, a school psychologist, for example, can help design a curriculum for those who are having difficulty with the standard one.

How many intelligences are there? Is musical ability intelligence or "talent"? It depends on what one means by intelligence and how one distinguishes that from talent. Do we really need to consider more than two types of intelligence? Do we need to consider 180? Perhaps the answer depends on our purposes. If we wish to predict school performance we likely need only one or two measures. If we are interested in vocational guidance we may need more. In any event, we must keep in mind that whenever we use tests to identify people for any purpose there is the likelihood of error because the tests are not perfectly reliable. Tests should be only one means of helping us determine the adolescent's abilities.

of genetics because the adopted adolescent has no genetic similarity to the adoptive parents or siblings.

In one of the studies, Scarr and her colleagues (Grotevant, Scarr, & Weinberg, 1977; Scarr, 1992, 1993; Scarr, Webber, Weinberg, & Wittig, 1981) studied environmental effects on adolescents' IQs, school achievements, personalities, and interests. Research with children showed similarities between adopted children's IQs and those of their adoptive parents, and between adopted children's lQs and those of their siblings in the adoptive family (Scarr, 1992). The purpose of the adolescent adoption study was to determine if these similarities, which indicated a relatively important influence of environment, continued through the adolescent years.

A total of 194 adolescents and young adults (age range 16 to 22) composed the adoptive sample; all were placed in adoptive families during their first year of life. Unlike the findings for the childhood study, the lQs of the adoptees during their adolescence were not correlated with the IQs of their siblings, with whom they were raised for minimally 18 years. Moreover, their IQs were only minimally related to the educational level of the adoptive parents but were moderately related to the educational level of their biological parents, this correlation being as high as that between the adoptive parents and their own children. Similar findings occurred in the domains of vocational interests, personalities, and attitudes. These latter results are consistent with the idea that biological factors are important to IQ test performance.

Scarr (1992) offers the following explanation. Unlike young children, adolescents grow away from the influence of their families and have greater freedom in pursuing their own interests, likes, and choices. As siblings enter and grow through the adolescent years, they become less and less alike, in part because of biological factors. The adopted children build a world related to their own genotype (genetic makeup). Because the genotype is different from that of their adopted siblings, they come to resemble them less and less. Biologically related siblings, however, build similar niches, in part because of their shared genotype.

Although these findings appear to indicate that environment has little if any impact on development, Scarr (1992, 1993; Scarr & Weinberg, 1983) cautions that this is not the case, pointing out that studies such as these help define environmental impacts to which various genotypes will respond. By identifying environmental influences that affect genotypes, we can develop better intervention programs to alleviate deficits in development. For example, it is now known that adolescents who as children were placed in Head Start classes were less likely to be recommended for special classes or be retained in a grade level, performed better in school, and had better attitudes toward school than control students who did not have preschool experiences (Lazar & Darlington, 1982).

What may we conclude with respect to the nature/nurture issue and intelligence, then? The work of the developmental behavioral geneticists suggests the important question is not how much genetics and environment contribute to intelligence but rather simply how each contributes to intellectual develop-

Growing up in poverty may affect IQ test performance because of poor nutrition and health care, poorer schools, and other factors related to learning. (*Marc Anderson*)

Children who attend preschool programs such as Head Start have better self-esteem, do better in school, and have higher standardized test scores during adolescence than those who did not attend preschool. (*Ken Karp*)

ment (Scarr, 1992; Scarr & Weinberg, 1983), because it is clear that each does. Accepting the proposition that both heredity and environment are important leads to questions of how to structure environments to best suit various genotypes and promote optimal development.

IQ AND ADOLESCENT DEVELOPMENT

The information just presented tells us a good deal about one view of the nature of intelligence. What does it tell us about the adolescent and adolescent development?

IQ and School Performance

Most psychologists today would probably agree that the most valuable aspect of the intelligence test is its usefulness as a predictor of school performance. This is not surprising because the test was devised to do just that and it does it moderately well—partly because the skills, knowledge, and motives necessary to do well on an IQ test are those that are also necessary to do well in school. We can use the IQ score as one diagnostic tool to help determine the adolescent's ability to deal with the school curriculum (Slavin, 1994). But, we must remember that school performance is affected by many other factors. Simply think of all the factors that affect your test scores and grades on papers and other assignments. How hard you study and the quality of your study techniques, the atmosphere in which you do your assignments, whether or not you enjoy a particular course, and a host of environmental factors all have an impact on the grades you receive.

IQ Changes During Development

The IQ score does not remain stable throughout the individual's life; it changes, although not necessarily in predictable ways. One way to measure change in IQ is by examining correlations between IQ scores from tests administered at different age levels. The higher the correlation, the more similar (less change) the IQ scores. A number of investigators have employed this strategy, and we can draw several general conclusions.

First, year-to-year IQ scores are highly similar, ranging from about .7 during the childhood years (for example, age 6 to age 7) to about .9 during adolescence (for example, age 12 to age 14), indicating that IQ scores change less during adolescence than during childhood (Sameroff, Seifer, Baldwin, & Baldwin, 1993). Adolescence seems to be the time when IQ scores peak and remain relatively stable, not declining until the middle (for performance IQ) or late (for verbal IQ) adulthood years (Aiken, 1987). Nonetheless, there is change, and for some individuals it can be rather substantial, for example, as much as 20 or 30 points.

Several research teams have examined the reasons for change in IQ scores from the childhood through the adolescent years. In an extensive study, McCall, Applebaum, and Hogarty (1973) reported information for 80 subjects tested 17 times between the ages of $2^{1}/_{2}$ and 17. Factors associated with declines in IQ scores during the childhood and adolescent years included parents who did not attempt to promote mature behavior, particularly mental and motor skills related to those tapped by IQ tests, and who used either the most lenient or most severe parental punishment. The researchers suggest that modes of parenting may be a "risk factor" with regard to change in adolescent's IQ test performance.

The family and social risk factors associated with IQ from preschool to the adolescent years was the subject of a study by Sameroff et al. (1993). They measured various risk factors (for example, mother's anxiety and mental health, family social support, major stressful life events, and minority status) and related these to the child's and adolescent's IQ score. Regardless of the specific risk factors present, the greater the number of risk factors the lower the child's or adolescent's IQ. For both White and Black adolescents, as the number of risk factors increased the IQ score decreased. For example, after taking into account the mother's IQ (a means of adjusting for genetic contributions to IQ scores), the mean IQ score of each group was about 115 when the number of risk factors was 0 or 1, but was just over 90 when the number of risk factors was 4 or more during very early childhood. During adolescence, those with 0 to 2 risk factors had IQs between 107 and 115; those with 4 risk factors had IQs of just above 90. These same trends were present even when social class and race were statistically controlled; that is, the relation between risk factors and IQ is not due to social-class factors or ethnic group membership.

Other environmental factors have been demonstrated to affect one's IQ test score. Poor nutrition in infancy, a critical period for brain growth, is associated with reduced IQ and academic performance (Lozoff, 1989). Similarly, it is well documented that exposure to lead (through paint, for example) is associated with reduced IQ test scores. Finally, simply entering school later than one's peer group can detrimentally affect IQ scores (Ceci, 1991).

IQ and Understanding the Adolescent

How does this information from the psychometric approach help us better understand adolescents and their development? The answer lies primarily in our knowing that adolescence is a time during which IQ test performance reaches a peak. We learn something about the development of intelligence by studying IQ test performance of adolescents.

However, the IQ approach does not tell us much about the *thought processes* of adolescents and how they may differ from those of children because the psychometric approach is nondevelopmental; it presumes that IQ (intelligence) means the same thing at all ages. Hence changes in IQ scores are presumed to reflect motivational states of the individual and errors of measurement within the test or testing situation and not some underlying and fundamental difference in thought processes. Using IQ tests as an exclusive measure also ignores other intellectual traits of adolescents, such as creativity (Box 4–2), that may be very important for understanding adolescent behavior and performance in school.

THE QUALITATIVE DEVELOPMENT
OF ADOLESCENT INTELLIGENCE

The qualitative study of intelligence is based on the notion that the individual continually undergoes transitions in development that may be characterized as stages reflecting different types of thought processes. Further, it is assumed that people change from one stage to another in an orderly sequence; intelligence is viewed as reflecting the emergence of qualitatively different modes of thinking. That is, the way a child thinks can be distinguished from how a preadolescent thinks, which in turn is different from the thinking of an adolescent. These differences cannot be quantified because the changes are in the way one thinks, not in the amount of intelligence one has. Thus this approach focuses on describing the qualities of the different modes of thinking that occur throughout development.

Several aspects of stage theory are important. First, stage theory does not imply that behavior develops in a steplike fashion. The transitions between stages are gradual. Second, age is not a good representation of stage. Individuals progress through the various stages of development at different rates; therefore, one might find two individuals of the same chronological age whose competencies indicate they are in different stages of development. Finally, stage theory implies that all individuals progress through the same sequence of stages in the same order. In other words, everyone must pass through stage A before stage B, stage B before stage C, and so on.

BOX 4–2   Creativity and the Adolescent

Intellective skills often have been divided into two types: convergent thinking and divergent thinking. **Convergent thinking** involves attempting to derive the one correct solution to some problem. **Divergent thinking** involves generating multiple solutions to a problem that does not necessarily have a single best solution. Divergent thinking is involved in acting creatively; creativity is the ability to devise novel solutions to problems.

This is the basic premise underlying tests of creative thinking, such as those devised by Torrance (1966). On the Uses subtest, subjects are asked to think of all the uses they can for an object (e.g., a brick). Many uses will be thought of by most people: to build a building, to prop open a window, to keep a door from closing, for use as a paperweight. Others will be thought of very infrequently, for example, using the holes as a candleholder. These infrequent responses are labeled "creative" because only a few would think of them.

Creativity is viewed as an intellectual skill unrelated to intelligence. Some creative individuals have high and others low IQ scores; and some low creative individuals have high and others low IQ scores. The idea is that creativity is an intellectual skill we all possess to varying degrees, just as is the case with IQ, and that creativity and IQ are not synonymous skills.

Highly creative adolescents enjoy freedom in problem solving and do not have difficulty when a problem is ambiguous (Dacey, 1989). They enjoy working with problems that have few if any rules that might too highly structure their thought processes, and they do not fear being wrong—they enjoy taking risks in their thinking.

It appears that parental rearing techniques are related to the development of creative thinking by adolescents. Parents of creative adolescents set relatively few rules for their behavior, choosing instead to set expectations they model for their children. They encourage curiosity and independence, and encourage experimenting even though the experiment might fail (Dacey, 1989). By behaving this way, the parents encourage the adolescent to think independently, to not fear failure, and to ruminate about their mistakes and learn from them. The adolescents are not afraid to try new and novel approaches to activities and problems.

The study of creativity, although not as extensive as the study of IQ, is also based on the psychometric approach to the study of intellective functioning. For example, various tests of creativity have been developed. It is a skill that is included in one form or another by virtually all those who suggest there are more than one or two forms of intelligence.

Piaget's Theory of Cognitive Development

Piaget's (1952) theory is an example of a qualitative view of intellectual development. He views intelligence as developing in a series of stages, each of which entails a qualitatively different mode of thinking.

The three major theoretical concepts in Piaget's theory are illustrated in Table 4-2. One is *content,* by which Piaget means behavior, either as action, as verbal explanation of thought processes, or as thought itself. The second is *structure,* which is simply a set of cognitive operations for behaving in certain

The qualitative approach to intellect is focused on the nature of thought processes and how they change with development. (*Ken Karp*)

ways. Finally, there is *function*, which refers to adaptation and organization, the broad characteristics of intelligence that are the essence of intelligent behavior. Adaptation consists of two components: assimilation and accommodation. *Assimilation* is the incorporation of sensory information into existing cognitive structures. Something new is related to what we already know. This changes our structure (what we know). *Accommodation* is the change in cognitive structures due to this new information. *Organization* means every intelligent act occurs within the child's existing cognitive competencies. According to Piaget, we function intellectually the way we do because we biologically are "built" to do so. In other words, Piaget believes our central nervous system is constructed in a way that causes us to processes sensory input in the way he describes.

As you can see in Table 4–2, functions produce structures that in turn re-

Table 4–2   Basic Concepts in Piaget's Theory of Intellectual Development

Concepts	Components
Function	... Organization Adaptation assimilation accommodation (age invariant)
produces	
Structures	... Cognitive rules. They change with level of development; the structures themselves (and thereby the individual's level of development) are revealed by the content (behavior) they produce.
resulting in	
Content	... Overt or covert (thinking) behavior that reflects structural development. It changes with age.

According to Piaget, regardless of age we function intellectually in the same way and pass through four stages of cognitive development. (*Bachmann/The Image Works*)

sult in content. Function refers to the broad aspects of intelligence that are the same for all people and remain constant across the life span. Hence, in Piaget's theory, infants, children, adolescents, and adults all function intellectually in the same way, through the processes of assimilation and accommodation. Assimilation and accommodation work together. In order for assimilation of environmental information to occur, the cognitive structures must accommodate to the new information. Accommodation, in turn, allows for further assimilation. Accommodatory acts are continually being extended to new and different features of the environment. These newly accommodated-to events are then assimilated into the cognitive structures of the organism, thereby changing those structures to some degree and making further accommodatory acts possible.

Through the assimilation and accommodation mechanisms the individual forms *schemas,* or cognitive structures (Flavell, 1985). Structures refer to our understanding of how our world operates. They have reference to a particular action sequence or behavior. Cognitive structures are in continual states of change as a result of the effects of assimilation and accommodation. New information is taken in (assimilation), it changes the structure (accommodation), which allows further assimilation.

To illustrate the processes, answer the following question: Assuming you are not there now, does the place you slept last night still exist? (If you are there, select a different location—the room for your next class.) Unless you have learned it burned down or was otherwise destroyed, you surely will answer yes. For Piaget, the interesting point is not your answer, but what thought processes allowed you to make the answer. How do you know it still exists? The answer lies in the concept of object permanence: In our world, objects have permanence apart from our interactions with them. Object permanence is learned; we are not born knowing it. During much of infancy "out of sight is out of mind." We must learn that even though an object is not in our sight or hand, it can still exist. How do we do that? We see our parents, the family pet, baby-sitters, and others come and go out of sight. We hear a voice we recognize coming from another room. We might be playing with a toy that drops from the crib. Initially, we react as though it no longer exists. Although much oversimplified, this example illustrates Piaget's notions; we acquire cognitive structures by simply living and experiencing our world. If you have ever baby-sat for a 12-month-old or so infant, you no doubt have had to retrieve a toy the infant threw out of the crib or play pen, only upon returning it to the infant to discover it was thrown out yet again, the infant crying until you bring it back. Why does the infant do this? Perhaps it is "mental play," the infant learning that objects can go away but still exist.

Assimilation and accommodation are prompted by the mechanisms of equilibrium and disequilibrium. **Equilibrium** is a homeostasis (balance) between the individual's structures and the sensory demands of the environment. If the individual's cognitive structures match environmental demands, a state of equilibrium exists between the individual and the environment. When environmental information does not match the individual's cognitive structures, as when new problems are encountered, a state of disequilibrium exists. **Disequilibrium,** then, is a mismatch between existing structures and environmental stimulation. This disequilibrium initiates the assimilation/accommodation mechanism as the individual tries to assimilate the new information and accommodate existing structures to it. Through the continous process of equilibrium and disequilibrium, structures are changed and become more complex. This is how cognitive development progresses (Piaget, 1970). Moving from a state of structural disequilibrium to a new and higher state of equilibrium is what Piaget means by cognitive development. Because of the higher state of equilibrium, the individual is able to solve more complex problems, view experiences in new and different ways, and advance higher order generalizations. In other words, the individual is more cognitively sophisticated.

Piaget has identified four stages of cognitive development: *sensorimotor* (birth to 2 years), *preoperational* (2 to 7 years), *concrete operational* (7 to 11 years), and *formal operational* (11 and up). Although these age norms are only rough indicators of developmental level, the periods of concrete and formal operational thinking span the adolescent years.

Sensorimotor and preoperational thinking. To gain a firm and clear understanding of adolescent cognitive processes as described by Piaget, it is necessary to review briefly the thinking processes of the infant and the child. The nonoperational (illogical) thinking of the infant and child provide an informative contrast to the adolescent's more advanced thought processes.

The basis of all intellectual behavior lies in the infant's sensorimotor intelligence. The infant lacks symbolic functions; thinking is through senses and actions. Thinking initially is in terms of simple and then increasingly complex action-structures, moving from actions based on reflexive behavior to habits (of action) to intelligent behavior such as that exhibited by movements causing desired effects—for example, kicking a crib to make a mobile shake. Coordination of arms, legs, hands, eyes, mouth, and so forth, reflect sensorimotor assimilation as the infant builds increasingly complex sensorimotor cognitive structures. Infants' thought processes are action oriented and egocentric—they are based on one's own body and actions. Sensorimotor intelligence, then, organizes actions in terms of objects, space, time, and causality. However, this form of **cognition** is very much tied to the here and now, to immediately present objects and actions. As infants slowly decenter—come to realize objects exist apart from actions on them (the concept of object permanence we discussed earlier)—thought processes slowly develop representational capabilities.

It is difficult for us to imagine what Piaget means by sensorimotor intelligence. It has not been our primary mode of thought for a long time. To illustrate, think about how you would define an infant's rattle. You would likely say it is something the infant shakes, it makes noise, and is a toy. How would an infant define it? Certainly not in a verbal way—the infant does not have language. Assuming the infant could understand our request for a definition, the infant would define it with sensorimotor actions, shaking the fist in which it is held or chewing on it. The infant thinks in a sensorimotor manner.

During the preoperational period, two important developments occur. In the *preconceptual* substage (roughly ages 2 to 4), the child acquires the ability to symbolize the external environment by means of internal "signifiers." The rapid development of language during this time is both a result of this symbolization ability as well as a contributor to it.

The *intuitive* substage (roughly ages 4 to 7) is so named because, although the child begins to use mental "operations," the principle behind the operations escapes the child. For example, the child may be able to sort pictures of objects into groups but may not understand the principles underlying the classification. During this stage, the child may well define an infant's rattle in much the same manner we do.

Operational thinking.   The use of logical thought processes, operational thinking, begins to emerge when the child is 7 to 8 years old. It is epitomized by an integrated cognitive system by which children organize and cognitively manipulate the world around them. There are two stages of operational thinking: concrete and formal. The former covers the later childhood and preadolescent years and the latter the adolescent years.

During the concrete operational period (roughly ages 7 to 11), the child develops logical operations, that is, logical thought processes, that can be applied to concrete problems. **Concrete operations** refer to thinking that is tied to reality, to the way things are, and to things that exist. The major limitation of concrete thinking is the inability of the individual to think in the abstract or to think about the possible as well as the real. The concrete operational preadolescent is bound to the reality of the here and now as personally experienced and has difficulty dealing with hypothetical situations.

One way this limitation may be seen is in studies of the self-concept. If asked to describe the self, for example by completing the sentence "I am . . . " a number of times, the concrete operational child is likely to list physical characteristics (a redhead, tall, strong), gender, grade in school, likes such as dancing or sports, moods (happy or sad), and address. Few if any responses will be what we could term abstract qualities. In one study the author used this technique with a group of fifth graders. One boy crossed out the "I am" stem, substituted the stem "I like," and listed 20 sports! The concrete operational child does not think of the self in terms of abstract personal qualities. Those who are formal operational may still complete the stem with concrete responses (after the first few weeks of classes a favorite of college students is "I am tired"), but for most a higher percentage of their answers will be abstract—political views, personality traits, and indications of a future orientation as in a vocational choice. This is a result of the qualities of thinking that formal operations allows.

It is in the area of formal operational thinking (ages 11 and up) that Piaget has most directly addressed the adolescent period of development. A major theme is that the adolescent is capable of imagining the many possibilities inherent in a particular situation. The adolescent is not bound by the here and now, but is able to compensate mentally for transformations in reality and to develop the capability of dealing with abstract problem-solving situations. Because this form of thinking is important to understanding aspects of adolescent development other than intellectual functioning, we discuss it in detail.

Formal Operations and Adolescent Thinking

The period of **formal operations** is characterized by the ability to use abstract thinking skills (Inhelder & Piaget, 1958). As adolescence progresses our facility with abstract thinking skills allows us to formulate complex and logical theories of social, political, and moral philosophy—views of what could be, or should be. Adolescents are able to conceptualize the possible as well as the real—they can think about what may be as well as what is (Keating, 1980; Piaget, 1980). Formal operations allow the adolescent to combine propositions in order to confirm or disprove hypotheses through the isolation of the variables that cause some event. This form of thinking is called hypothetico deductive (if–then), and it is very much like the kind of thinking employed in science.

The emergence of this form of thinking is illustrated in Piaget's experiment designed to allow children and adolescents to discover the factor(s) that affect the oscillation of a pendulum (Inhelder & Piaget, 1958). A pendulum was constructed by hanging a weight on a string. The subject was shown how to change the length of the string, the weight, and how to release the object from different heights with different degrees of force. The subject was asked to discover which of the four factors (string length, object weight, height of the drop, force of the drop), or combinations of them, affected the rate of oscillation of the pendulum, and was allowed to experiment with the materials in any way desired. Try this experiment yourself. Take a shoelace and measure 1-inch lengths. Tie the lace to the arm of your study lamp and hang a pencil, a pen, and a marker from it and let each drop from the same height. Now, change the length of the lace and repeat the experiment. Repeat each with a different "push" as you let it go. What can you conclude?

The behavior of the preoperational child is extremely haphazard and ineffectual. There is no real overall plan or pattern to the manipulations the child performs. For example, some children try to determine if weight is a factor by using a long string with a heavy weight and a short string with a light weight, which cannot tell anything of the role of either variable because both are being manipulated simultaneously. Due to such procedures, the preoperational child rarely comes to the correct conclusion that it is the length of the string that makes the difference. The child's inability to devise appropriate experiments precludes obtaining the correct solution.

The "experiments" of the concrete operational child are considerably more accurate and reflect a much higher level of intellectual ability. In fact, some even come up with the correct answer. However, most concrete operational children do not design the procedures of their "experiments" in such a way as to come to the correct conclusion. For example, Inhelder and Piaget report that one subject observed that a short but heavy pendulum swung more rapidly than a light but long one, and concluded that both length and weight were determining factors in the oscillation of the pendulum. Obviously, this is an incorrect conclusion because it is based on an incorrect procedure. Nevertheless, the logic the child used to arrive at the conclusion was consistent with what he observed.

The behavior of the formal operational adolescent is qualitatively quite different from the behavior of children in earlier stages of cognitive development. The "experiments" are adequately designed, the results accurately observed, and proper logical conclusions are drawn from the observations. Formal operational acdolescents are aware immediately that there are several possible determinants of the frequency of oscillation of the pendulum. They realize, furthermore, that any one, or combination, of them may be critical to determining the frequency. This type of realization is what Piaget refers to when he says that formal operations allow the imagining of purely hypothetical results. Before engaging in any experimentation, the adolescent is capable of conceiving all possible outcomes of the experiment. An example might be testing a long string with light and heavy weights and testing a short string wlth the same light and heavy weights. In this way it is possible to see if string length makes a difference, if weight makes a difference, or if some combination of the two is the determinant. In other words, the adolescent begins with a hypothetical set of determinants, conducts experiments that are designed to test the hypotheses, and is capable of accurately observing, reporting, and drawing conclusions from the results of the experiments. Because the experiments are well conceived, the results accurately observed, and appropriate logical thinking applied to them, the adolescent is able to come to the correct conclusion.

This behavior demonstrates the hypothetico-deductive (if–then) nature of formal operational thinking. The adolescent is able to discover that the length of the string is the important varlable: *If* the short string is used and the swing is fast, *then* a long string will swing more slowly, assuming weight and force are the same.

What, then, have we learned about adolescent thought processes from the foregoing discussion? First, we know the adolescent is capable of dealing with the possible as well as the real. In fact, the real is only one particular instance of the possible. Second, adolescent thinking also reveals that the structures of formal operational thinking can be applied to a variety of novel situations because they are content-free thinking structures. Formal operational thinking is a process or means of thinking about anything. This makes the adolescent's thought processes extremely flexible, much more so than those of the concrete operational or preoperational child. Because adolescents can conceive of a number of possible alternatives to a problem before investigating the situation, they are less likely to be surprised or confused by outcomes that are unusual.

We must stress again that adolescent thought processes are *qualitatively* different from those of younger children. They are better simply because they can be applied successfully to a greater variety of problems than can the thought processes of the concrete or preoperational child. They are not better because the adolescent has "more" intelligence.

Implications of Piaget's Theory for Adolescent Development

Piaget's theory of cognitive development has a number of implications for helping us understand and explain adolescent development. Each of the examples here is discussed in detail in a later chapter.

Moral development.   Kohlberg (1976) has formulated a stage theory of moral development that is related to and parallels the levels of cognition defined by Piaget (it is discussed fully in Chapter 5). Kohlberg believes that as cognitive competencies increase, the individual's capability for understanding increasingly complex and subtle moral issues also increases. The highest levels of moral thinking are reached when the individual becomes capable of formal operational thinking. In all likelihood, this is a result of the adolescent's newly found abilities to reason about various alternatives and to see different perspectives of an issue. The content-free formal operational structures and the logical abstract thinking processes reflected in them are applied to moral judgments and result in increasing capabilities to deal with intricate moral issues.

Although the concrete operational preadolescent may hold very strong views about abortion or physician-assisted suicide, the rationale for the view is likely to be very concrete and rigid: Killing fetuses and people is wrong or women should have control of their bodies and the very sick should have the right to die with dignity and as little suffering as possible. Adolescents may hold views at either pole, but have the ability to understand the alternative view, argue logically against it, and support their own view in a logically consistent manner.

Relations with parents.   Elkind (1970) notes that understanding the dynamics of formal operational thinking allows us to gain insight into a number of adolescent social behaviors, including parent–child conflict. Adolescents' ability to formulate hypotheses makes it possible for them to respond to parental demands with a list of possible alternatives. The rebelliousness of adolescence may in part be due to an awareness of the difference between the possible and the real. Because adolescents often perceive a gap between the "ideal" and the "real" world, they may come to feel parents are hypocrites, professing one set of ideals and living by another.

As the adolescent enters the job market and joins the adult world with its various roles and responsiblities, the relatively pure cognitive approach to understanding society is replaced by a more realistic perspective. More than one individual has observed that as he or she grew older (and out of adolescence) his or her parents grew smarter.

Self-concept and identity.   Current theorizing suggests a link between self-concept and identity development and cognition (Dusek, Carter, & Levy, 1986). As our earlier example illustrated, formal operational adolescents are able to conceive of the self in abstract ways that are unavailable to the concrete operational child or preadolescent. Suppose you described yourself as "friendly." What does that mean? How do you know you are friendly? Friendly is an abstract quality that encompases a variety of cognitions (e.g., I like people) and behaviors (e.g., I try to help people when I can). Formal operations allows the adolescent to combine the individual characteristics into higher order abstract traits.

The qualities of formal operational thinking also apply to the resolution of Erikson's identity crisis. In order to have an identity crisis one must realize that one could be different; one must be able to see the possible as well as the real. One must be able to project the self into the future. These forms of thinking are not possible without some of the aspects of formal operational thinking. Indeed, one is tempted to argue that we have an identity crisis because we can: Our newfound thinking skills open up new ways to think about the self.

Egocentrism.   Adolescents are not only capable of thinking about their own thoughts, but also of conceptualizing the thoughts of others—thinking about what others are thinking. According to Elkind (1967b, 1978a, 1978b), it is this latter ability that is the foundation of adolescent **egocentrism.** Egocentrism results from the adolescent's inability to separate his or her own thoughts—and the events to which they are directed—from the thoughts of others. Because the adolescent is absorbed with thoughts about the self, he or she feels others must be too.

One consequence of this egocentrism is that adolescents feel they are on stage, playing to an *imaginary audience,* with attention continually focused on them. It is an imaginary audience because seldom is the adolescent's perception veridical; it results from a failure to separate the objective and subjective effects of reality. One need only observe a group of adolescents walking down a school

Egocentrism leads adolescents to believe that everyone is as interested in their thoughts and feelings as they are. (*Ken Karp*)

hallway or in a mall, all talking and none listening to the other, to observe the imaginary audience phenomenon. All think the others are as interested in their thoughts as they are because what they are thinking about must be important. Because adolescents feel on stage and therefore important, they begin to view their own thoughts and feelings as special and unique, as something no one else has ever experienced. Elkind (1967b, 1978a, 1978b) calls this the *personal fable.* The personal fable arises from the failure to differentiate the universal and particular aspects of reality (Elkind, 1978a). If you have ever done anything that made you feel especially guilty you may have experienced thoughts similar to the personal fable—everyone must know what I did!

Research to date (Elkind, 1967b; Elkind & Bowen, 1979; Enright, Lapsley, & Shukla, 1979; Enright & Sutterfield, 1980; Goossens, 1994) has centered on the imaginary audience aspect of adolescent egocentrism. Elkind and Bowen (1979) hypothesized that one effect of the imaginary audience would be to increase the adolescent's feelings of self-consciousness (because of the tendency to view the self as being on stage). Consistent with predictions, scores on the Imaginary Audience Scale (a measure of willingness to reveal aspects of the self) increased (unwillingness to reveal the self) from 4th, to 6th, to 8th grade and declined by 12th grade. Similar findings were reported by Enright and his colleagues.

The developmental trend for egocentrism matches that for adolescent conformity to peers, and is consistent with other research (Hudson & Gray, 1986) showing that younger adolescents are more shy and self-conscious than older adolescents. It may be that adolescents conform in order not to stick out—to not reveal the self—and to reduce feelings of self-consciousness. As the identity becomes more firm and developed, egocentrism and shyness decline, which may result in the lower conformity to peers that occurs during the later high school years.

Idealism, Hypocrisy, and Pseudostupidity

Because adolescents are able to see not only what exists but also what could be, there is a tendency for an idealistic view of society—what exists is not ideal and therefore should be changed (Elkind, 1967b). They may take the side of the underdog, politically and economically, become excessively critical of the adult world, and develop utopian views of what society should be. During early adolescence the "rebellion" of the adolescent is primarily verbal (Elkind, 1967b). During later adolescence, as egocentrism (an emphasis on self) declines and a more sociocentric (emphasis on the social system) view is developed, adolescents may translate their verbal idealism to actions aimed at dealing with the faults they see (Elkind, 1967b; Enright & Sutterfield, 1980). They may become activists.

Hypocrisy refers to pretending to be what one is not or behaving in ways one is not. Some researchers (e.g., Elkind, 1978b) have pointed out links between adolescent cognitive development and hypocritical behavior. It is not uncommon for adolescents to espouse one set of views, such as the importance of eating healthy food, and yet behave in ways antithetical to the belief—eating high-salt, high-fat fast food. They may believe strongly in openness and honesty, yet not behave that way with parents or friends. Elkind suggests the discrepancies between what is believed and how one behaves may result from the development of the ability to formulate and understand the value of the ideal, a cognitive process, but an inability to link the belief to specific applications, a behavioral process. He suggests that especially during the earlier adolescent years the ability to formulate an ideal that generally is seen as good is equated with having achieved that ideal. In later adolescence, Elkind notes, there is a convergence between ideals and behavior and some of what we may view as hypocritical behavior declines. Adolescents may join organizations that actively promote the ideals they hold.

The term *pseudostupidity* refers to the failure to successfully solve a basically simple problem because one has applied too complex a solution (Elkind, 1978b). The "newness" of formal operational thinking skills allows the generation of multiple solutions to a problem, but the lack of experience in sorting through possible solutions results in failure. The adolescent who has recently moved to a new school may go through contortions to make new friends, when simply being one's self is likely the best route to follow.

The idealism, hypocrisy, and pseudostupidity of which Elkind speaks are related to the emergence of, and learning to deal with, formal operational thinking skills. They are experienced by most adolescents, but to widely differing degrees. And they don't disappear during adulthood. Many adults are idealistic, but few join organizations such as Green Peace or the World Wildlife Fund. On occasion adults behave hypocritically, and often are chastised by their adolescents for doing so. Adults, too, sometimes attempt to apply solutions that are too complex for the problem. The point is that these are normative aspects of development and do not indicate abnormal development. They also are part of the stereotype of the confused and troubled adolescent, because one whom adults see as idealistic and yet hypocritical may well be described as confused.

Beyond Formal Operations

Some researchers (e.g., Arlin, 1975; Commons, Richards, & Armen, 1982) have suggested that during late adolescence and adulthood there may be at least a fifth stage in the qualitative development of intellect. Arlin calls this fifth stage *problem-finding*. Commons and colleagues call it *structural analytical thinking*. Although there are some differences, a central concept is that the new stage of thought allows one to look at problems in new ways. Formal operational thinking allows one to consider a problem, or group of similar problems, and apply a general problem-solving strategy—a method or system—to solve the problem. The fifth stage expands one's approach to problems in significant ways.

Arlin emphasizes the point that we develop problem-finding skills: We become more capable of recognizing when a problem exists and identifying it and the important questions that must be dealt with in solving the problem. Commons stresses our increased ability to view problems from different perspectives or systems, a kind of stepping back for a third-person look at the situation. Doing so may allow one to reconcile apparently distinct views of a situation.

If you ever have done less well than you thought you ought to in a course, you may have experienced these forms of thinking. One approach you might have taken is to analyze the problem within the existing system, which is a characteristic of the formal operational thinking stage. From this perspective you might conclude you need to study harder, the professor really isn't very good and so is not allowing you to learn as well as you might, and the tests simply are not fair. Although there is little you can do about the professor or the tests, you could spend more time studying, or perhaps even study with others, in an attempt to improve your performance. You would be viewing the problem within a single system.

Alternatively, you might sit down and step out of the situation (structural analytical thinking) to view the situation from a variety of perspectives—yours, the professor's, or that of other students in the course. In so doing, you might identify specific aspects of the problem that had not occurred to you previously (problem-finding) and generate possible solutions. Although you might indeed conclude you need to spend more time studying, you might also decide you need to regularly meet with the professor to ensure you are learning the appropriate material. You might conclude your notes are incomplete because the professor talks rather rapidly, and decide to tape the lectures. By examining the situation "outside" of it, you were able to identify problems you had not previously seen and apply solutions that may have worked for you in other situations.

Like the research on intelligence based on the psychometric approach, that based on the qualitative approach provides insights into our understanding of intelligence. Adolescence is a time when we attain the advanced ability to think abstractly and all that implies. Later adolescence and adulthood seem to be times when we may reach further advances in thinking competencies. By considering each perspective on intelligence we gain a more complete understanding and appreciation for the complexity of what we call intellect.

Unlike the psychometric approach, however, the qualitative approach allows us to begin to understand other aspects of adolescent development. We gain insights into adolescent personality, understanding of the society in which we all live, parent–adolescent relations, and adolescents' interactions with peers. In this sense, then, the qualitative approach is more valuable to our understanding of adolescence.

SOCIAL COGNITION

The study of how the person comes to know, understand, and conceptualize the social world, and particularly the self in relation to other people, is termed **social-cognition** (S. J. Sherman, Judd, & Park, 1989). Social cognition involves psychological processes such as memory, attention, information processing (Box 4–3), and role taking (S. J. Sherman et al., 1989).

Selman's Model of Social Cognition

Selman (1976, 1980) proposed a stage theory of social cognition based on structural views of intelligence; it focuses specifically on aspects of role taking (Selman & Byrne, 1974). To assess the stage of role taking, Selman developed a series of social dilemmas concerning four social domains: individual, friendship, peer group, and parent–child. After reading the dilemma, the subject answers a series of questions aimed at assessing understanding of the domain. For example, in the area of friendships, the respondents answer questions aimed at assessing their views of how and why friendships are formed, intimacy in friendships, reciprocity between friends, jealousy in friendships, resolving conflicts with friends, and how and why friendships break up. In the individual realm, issues assessed include understanding of the private (for example, thoughts) aspects of others, ability to comprehend the self, personality traits, and how people change. Issues assessed in the peer group realm are how and why groups form, group cohesion, conformity to the group, understanding of group norms, working within a group, the functions of the group leader, and why groups disband. In the parent–child relations area, issues addressed are why parents have children, emotional bonds between parent and child, obedience to the parents, the child's and parent's views of punishment, and conflict resolution between parent and child.

Selman (1976) emphasized the adolescent's differentiation of the self from others and the ability to coordinate the self-perspective and the perspectives of others. This allowed him to determine the degree of *social understanding* (as opposed to knowledge) the adolescent has acquired. There are five stages in the development of role taking and social understanding.

BOX 4–3 Information Processing and Adolescent Intelligence

Information processing approaches to the study of intellect are concerned with the ways (processes) by which we incorporate, interpret, store, and retrieve the information that comes to us through our sensory system (Flavell, 1985; P. H. Miller, 1993). Therefore, it is concerned with the study of memory processes, strategies used in problem solving, attention, and other means by which we incorporate, store, and retrieve experiences we have had. In many ways, this approach views the human mind as operating in a manner analogous to a computer. The study of developmental trends in the various abilities involved in information processing provide insight into how and why adolescents' intellectual competence differs from children's.

Those who research adolescent information processing note that adolescents not only remember more information, for example, but they use different processes than children in order to do so. Adolescents given a list of items to memorize are much more likely than children to rehearse each item in the list along with several newly encountered items, and so forth through the list, which is a strategy that facilitates memory and retrieval of information.

Adolescents also know more about how memory works and about strategies for memorizing information. Consider how you study for multiple-choice exams. What strategies do you use? In contrast to children, adolescents "know" how much they can remember and develop strategies to help them maximize the amount of information they can store in memory.

Adolescents also can attend to more information at a given point in time than can children because they have acquired more information than children—they simply "know more." This earlier acquired knowledge allows the adolescent a skeleton on which to build new information, and makes it easier to learn (remember) new information. For example, consider your experience in taking psychology courses and that of your classmates. Those with more background in psychology will find the information in this text easier to comprehend, learn, and remember than those with less background. The previous experience and information learned facilitates learning the new information.

The information processing approach to intelligence focuses on the processes by which intelligence operates. The emphasis is on identifying the rules individuals use for solving problems, remembering information, and learning to store information. This approach allows us to investigate individual differences in how individuals function intellectually, and to identify the means by which they do so.

Information is received through the senses—visual, auditory, tactual, olfactory, and taste. We selectively attend to this information, until it is mentioned you likely don't attend to (feel) the chair you may be sitting on. Information that is attended to also is interpreted: A comment you and a friend hear may be interpreted in very different ways depending on experience. If you have more background in studying psychology the term *S-R* means more—has a different interpretation—than if you have less. The information must be remembered, entered into memory. Rehearsal, what you do when you study, allows information to be entered into long-term memory, which has a virtually infinite capacity. You can retrieve the information either through recall or recognition. By recalling the information you can use it to solve problems, be they questions on an examination or some practical concern. Adolescents are more facile in these processes than are children: They receive more information, retain more information, think about it more logically, and are able to apply it to more situations than are children. Hence they are better problem solvers. The information processing approach helps us understand better how and why adolescents "think" better than children.

The first stage is labeled *Egocentric Undifferentiated* (ages 3 or 4 to 6) because the child is unable to distinguish a personal perspective from another's point of view. The second stage, *Subjective Perspective Taking* (ages 6 to 9), is characterized by the ability to understand that the self and others may have different perspectives of a social situation, which may result in their thinking and feeling differently. In this stage we see the beginnings of social perspective taking. It is in the third stage, *Reciprocal Perspective Taking* (ages 8 or 9 to 12), that preadolescents become capable of making inferences about the perspectives of others, and come to realize how others may view them and their behavior.

The early adolescent is in the fourth stage, *Mutual Role Taking* (ages 10 or 11 to 15). These individuals can "step out of the situation" and take a holistic perspective of a social situation, a perspective such as might be taken by a third party. The early adolescent can coordinate his or her own perspective and that of others. Hence early adolescents can understand the mutual nature of social relationships.

The final stage, characteristic of later adolescence and adulthood, is called *In-Depth and Societal Perspective Taking.* The individual understands the shared social system perspective of social situations, and comes to appreciate the importance of group consensus, a consensus derived from many possible

Social cognition involves understanding the various roles we all play (*Steve & Mary Skjold/The Image Works*)

multiple mutual perspectives. As a result, the adolescent and adult understand there are many levels of social perspectives, and that one's psychological characteristics determine, in part, one's perspective.

An example taken from Selman will help clarify the development of social role taking. Consider the child's understanding of punishment by the parent. In the first stage, children know that punishment follows misbehaving, but they cannot infer their parents' motives for punishing. In the second stage, children understand that parents punish to teach the child what is wrong and at times to protect the child ("Don't touch the hot stove!"). The child infers motives for punishment. During the third stage the preadolescent comes to realize that punishment at times instills fear (anxiety) which, when internalized, controls behavior. Preadolescents also realize that punishment is a form of communicating parental concern for their well-being. Early adolescents, in the fourth stage, begin to view punishment as only one way, and probably not the best for them, of controlling behavior. But they also understand that parents have needs and personalities that must be expressed, and that punishment may serve such a need. Finally, during the last stage, the older adolescent realizes that punishment may reflect an unconscious attempt on the part of the parent to control others psychologically. The increasingly sophisticated understanding of the function of punishment reflects both the development of social understanding and cognitive competence.

Social Cognition and the Adolescent

More socially competent adolescents are more facile in thinking about social situations, better able to assess the consequences of their behavior for themselves and others, and better able to devise strategies for dealing with social conflict (M. Ford, 1982). In addition, those adolescents who are better able to behave effectively in challenging social situations score high in wanting to help others, wanting to get socially involved, and wanting to get along with peers and parents. Ford concluded, on the basis of these findings, that social cognition and social behavior were related.

Drawing on social cognitive theorizing, Lapsley (1985; Lapsley, Jackson, Rice, & Shadid, 1988; Lapsley, Milstead, Quintana, Flannery, & Buss, 1986) has suggested that the imaginary audience phenomenon (discussed earlier) is best explained by the immature understanding characteristic of Selman's stage 3 perspective-taking skills. This stage involves the ability to self-reflect, which results in an awareness of self-awareness and in a distorted view of one's own individuality and importance. As adolescents enter Selman's stage 4, they gain the ability to see the self in relation to others and realize the self can be part of the background, resulting in a decline in the imaginary audience.

Understanding how cognitive development is related to the adolescent's views of social relations also contributes to our ability to explain other aspects of adolescent development, such as sibling relations and political views. It helps us relate advances in cognitive development to adolescent social behavior.

SUMMARY

There are two prevailing views of the nature of intelligence. One, the quantitative, or psychometric, views intelligence as an ability people are assumed to have more or less of. This perspective has emphasized identifying individual differences in this ability. A second emphasis has been that of the developmental behavioral geneticists, who have focused on identifying how genetic and environmental factors contribute to intelligence. The result of these efforts has shown that both environment and heredity are important contributors to intelligence, and has resulted in the identification of a number of "risk" factors (ranging from diet to parental rearing practices) related to IQ test performance.

It is now well established that IQ peaks during the adolescent years and remains stable through the adulthood years, declining only slightly during the aging years. There is, however, considerable change in IQ, with a minority of children and adolescents having an IQ that remains relatively constant from early childhood through adolescence.

The greatest utility of IQ scores seems to be for educational purposes. IQ scores correlate moderately with performance on achievement tests and are a good predictor of ability to perform well in the traditional school curriculum. However, lQ scores tell us very little about adolescent development. This is because the quantitative approach is not a developmental perspective of intelligence.

The second perspective is the qualitative, or cognitive developmental, view of intelligence. Theorists of this persuasion view intelligence as changing in nature as development progresses. Piaget, for example, has identified four stages of cognitive development. The highest stage, formal operations, is reached during the adolescent years. The adolescent is able to think abstractly, to consider the possible (what could be) as well as the real (what is), and to use if–then thinking. Research based on this perspective has focused on identifying the competencies (cognitive skills) that emerge with development. One such skill is social cognitive in nature. The field of social cognition is concerned with examining the importance of changing cognitive skills for aspects of social development, including the ability to take another person's point of view. Researchers have demonstrated that this ability changes from childhood to adolescence, with adolescents having a much more flexible and broad understanding of social interactions.

Another line of research is aimed at explaining how cognitive advances relate to adolescent personality development, including self-concept, idealism, hypocrisy, pseudostupidity, and egocentrism. With development, self-concept is viewed more abstractly, idealistic views of the society are emphasized but one's behavior may not coincide with these perspectives, and there is a tendency to apply overly complex solutions to simple problems. In addition, the type of egocentrism associated with adolescence reveals that the adolescent has hesitancies about revealing aspects of the self. This hesitancy is related to peer group conformity. In all these instances, evidence indicates that the emergence of abstract thinking skills impacts on development.

In contrast to the quantitative approach, the qualitative approach contributes substantially to our understanding of adolescent development and behavior. We gain insights into adolescent relations with parents and peers, adolescent views of society, and adolescent personality development when we consider cognitive gains during adolescence. This is a direct result of the view that the way individuals think and understand the world around them changes in important ways as they develop.

Thus the two perspectives of intelligence are not contradictory, but are complementary. Each tells us something different about intelligence because each has a different definition and emphasis on the issues involved in studying the intellect. It also is clear that the qualitative view allows us to gain greater insights into other aspects of adolescent development than does the quantitative view.

GLOSSARY

CA (chronological age):   Time since birth.

cognition: Processes of knowing, perceiving, and evaluating events.

concrete operations: In Piaget's theory, mental operations applied to real, as opposed to possible, events.

convergent thinking: Problem-solving thinking in an attempt to derive the one correct answer to a problem.

disequilibrium: In Piaget's theory, a motivational mechanism resulting from an imbalance between how the individual interprets events and emerging new ways of understanding events.

divergent thinking: Deriving a variety of solutions to a problem that has no one correct solution.

egocentrism: Extreme concern and interest in the self, often to the exclusion of interest in others.

equilibrium: In Piaget's theory, a balance between the individual's cognitive competencies and the demands of the environment.

formal operations: Abstract, logical thinking skills that can be applied to the real as well as the possible; if-then thinking.

g: In Spearman's terms, overall general intelligence.

intelligence: Intellectual ability.

intelligence quotient (IQ):   Measure of intellectual capability derived from performance on a standardized test of intelligence (IQ = $MA/CA \times 100$).

MA (mental age):   Developmental marker based on performance on an intelligence test.

operational thinking: In Piaget's theory, logical thinking, either concrete or formal.

s: According to Spearman, a specific factor (such as mathematical ability) involved in intelligence.

social cognition: Cognitive skills applied to social situations.

DISCUSSION QUESTIONS

1. In what ways are the quantitative and qualitative approaches to intellect the same? In what ways different?

2. What might you do to improve the adolescent's IQ test performance? Is this a worthwhile thing to try to do? Why or why not?

3. Is IQ a useful measure for understanding how we get along in everyday life? Why or why not?

4. Given the properties of formal operational thinking skills, what might be the contribution of formal operational thinking to Erikson's identity vs. identity diffusion crisis?

5. At times, adolescents take very idealistic views of social problems and ills. How can knowledge about the nature of intelligence help us explain this behavior?

6. As noted in the text, some have postulated there is more than one kind of "intelligence." What are the advantages of having more information than a single IQ score; what are the disadvantages?

7. Cattell and Horn argue for two types of intelligence, crystallized and fluid ability. How might these be relevant to the education of adolescents?

8. How is creativity distinguished from intelligence? Is it a useful distinction to make?

5

Moral Development in Adolescence

Major Issues Addressed

Theoretical Perspectives on Moral Development
Socialization Influences on Moral Development
Moral Thinking and Moral Behavior
Masculinity/Femininity and Moral Development
Moral Education
The Development of Religious Views
The Development of Political Views

"How could you envy him," I asked. "He had to pay a multi-million dollar fine and serve prison time for cheating on the stock market." The reply simply was, "Well, he had the money to pay it! He just got caught doing what a lot of other people do." The end seemed to justify the means.

◆   ◆   ◆

It is not until mid to late adolescence that an understanding of the importance of the social system and shared rules for behavior becomes an emphasis in moral thinking. Once that is achieved, the importance of avoiding the breakdown of the system "if everyone did it" becomes an important part of moral understanding. In this chapter we explore the changing nature of the adolescent's understanding of rules, morality, and the social order.

INTRODUCTION

During adolescence we construct a set of values that will help us function successfully as adult members of society. The development of these values begins during childhood and becomes a major developmental task of adolescence (Havighurst, 1951). This broad-ranging task, which involves understanding the importance of rules and of the relation of the person to the society, is referred to as *moral development*. As the values of childhood are surrendered, adult values slowly emerge. The study of moral development focuses on several aspects of the transition between childhood and adulthood values. Some theorists, such as Freud, have focused on moral character and behavior. Others such as Piaget, Kohlberg, and Gilligan have focused on moral reasoning and judgment. Finally, a number of researchers have focused on the socialization processes related to moral judgments and moral behavior. The role of parental rearing practices and of school programs focused on values clarification are examples.

ADOLESCENCE AND MORAL DEVELOPMENT

There are several reasons for studying moral development during adolescence. Adolescents' ability to think abstractly allows them to take new views of right and wrong, good and bad. In so doing, adolescents act as moral philosophers.

They continually redefine their value system as they wrestle with the moral dilemmas they personally face or see through the media. Should I engage in pre-marital sex? Is physician-aided suicide ever "right"? How do you feel about these types of issues? *Why* do you feel this way? As you will learn here, your rationale for your views reflects what researchers call moral judgment. As we grow through the adolescent years there is a change in how we make moral judgments.

Adolescents are concerned with behaving in "right" ways as opposed to the child's concern with not behaving in the "wrong" way. For adolescents the right way to behave is defined by their values and beliefs. For example, adolescents are much more likely than children to protest school-imposed rules they feel are wrong or the failure to renew a well-liked teacher's contract by skipping school or walking out. During adolescence we may begin behaving in accord with moral codes we hold important, even though we know we might be "punished."

Finally, as adolescents wrestle with the identity crisis (Chapter 2)—defining who and what they are—they become concerned with personal and social moral codes. The development of these moral views influences how the adolescent views the society, politics, and religion. What should society do about the homeless? Should we have welfare programs that support the able bodied who do not work? Is it necessary to attend formal religious services in order to be religious?

WHAT IS MORALITY?

Early writing in the area of moral development was left to philosophers, who evolved three major doctrines of morality, each of which is represented in contemporary psychological theorizing (M. L. Hoffman, 1970). The **doctrine of original sin** assumed parental intervention is necessary to save the child's soul. Current-day vestiges of this viewpoint may be found in Freud's view of the conscience, or superego, which is the internalization of parental standards of right and wrong.

The **doctrine of innate purity** argued that the child is basically moral, or pure, and that society, and especially adults, are corrupting influences. This view is represented in the theorizing of Piaget (1932), who argues that morality develops from the acquisition of autonomy emerging from the need to get along with peers. Because parent–child relationships are basically heteronomous—the child is ruled by the parents—the child does not have the opportunity to engage in the give-and-take that allows the learning of social rules.

The third philosophical doctrine is the **tabula rasa** (blank slate) notion, which assumes the child is neither innately pure nor corrupt but rather the product of environmental influences. One's experiences are "written" on the slate. The current-day representatives of this position are the social-learning theorists.

Psychologists make a distinction between morality and moral behavior.

Morality refers to the rules that guide social and interpersonal behavior, and include rules that are written down (e.g., laws) as well as those that are not, such as treating people courteously. **Moral behaviors** are those behaviors that are consistent with rules of morality. Hence moral behaviors include social behaviors of all types. In order to have successful peer and adult relationships, the adolescent must learn the rules (morality) of the society and act in accordance with these rules (moral behavior or conduct).

THEORIES OF MORAL DEVELOPMENT

Among psychologists, the psychoanalytic, social-learning, and cognitive-developmental theorists have had the greatest impact on the understanding of moral development. Because each perspective has a different emphasis, we need to discuss all three in order to gain a rounded picure of moral development.

Psychoanalytic Theory

According to the principles of psychodynamic theory, morality is part of the individual's superego, or conscience, which results from resolution of the Oedipal complex and identification with the same-sex parent (Freud, 1924). Identification refers to the internalization of the values and behaviors of the same-sex parent. Society ensures its survival through this identification by imposing its cultural standards, as represented by the parents' behaviors, attitudes, and aspirations, on the individual. Freud's theorizing has stimulated considerable research into the effects of parental behavior on the child's moral development. The major research has centered on the consistency of moral behavior across situations and the role of parental disciplinary techniques in shaping moral behavior.

Consistency in adolescents' moral behavior.   One implication of Freudian theory is that identification with a single individual should result in personality types that result in consistency in moral behavior across situations. Research has centered on questions such as whether or not adolescents could be classified as "cheaters" or "noncheaters" and whether or not there is a general trait of "honesty," with some adolescents behaving honestly all the time and others not.

By examining adolescents' cheating in a variety of situations it has been shown there is a general trait of honesty (Burton, 1963): Some adolescents tend to be cheaters and others not. Hence an adolescent who is likely to cheat in one situation is likely to cheat in other similar situations. Moreover, some adolescents consistently follow rules and regulations and others do not (Peck & Havighurst, 1960). The adolescent's rule-following orientation seems to remain stable from ages 10 to 17.

This is not to say that situational (contextual) factors play no role in the adolescent's moral behavior. Adolescents are more likely to violate moral standards when the odds of getting caught are low (M. Ford, Wentzel, Wood,

Research suggests that some adolescents violate
rules—cheat on tests, defy authority, become
delinquent—due to a general trait of cheating.
(*Ken Karp*)

Stevens, & Siesfeld, 1989). And cheating is likely to increase if the benefits of
doing so are high, that is, when the incentives are large. College students are
more likely to cheat as the term progresses and they become more concerned
with their final grades (Gardner, Roper, Gonzalez, & Simpson, 1988). They also
are more likely to cheat if they are not doing well in their courses. Although
moral character is important to explaining behavior, situational factors also play
a significant role. Under the right circumstances, any of us might be tempted to
cheat, and if the stakes are high enough we might do so.

   These studies provide evidence that by the time children enter the adolescent years, they have developed a moral character that provides a general orientation toward moral behaviors. Research on how this orientation is learned has
focused largely on parental discipline techniques.

Discipline and adolescent morality.   Researchers have examined how parental discipline is related to a variety of measures of the adolescent's internalization of
moral standards: *resistance to temptation,* a measure of resistance to violating a

standard when the chances of getting caught are remote or nonexistent; *guilt,* the intensity of the internal emotional response following transgression; *reactions to transgression,* which are **moral judgments** about a transgression; and *confession,* admitting a transgression.

Several types of parental discipline have been studied. *Induction discipline* involves explaining why what was done was wrong and providing examples of alternative ways to behave. *Power-assertive discipline* refers to the use, or threat of use, of physical punishment or withdrawal of privileges. It rests on the fact that the parent is more powerful than the child. *Love withdrawal discipline* involves ignoring the adolescent, isolating him or her, or expressing dislike or disappointment toward the adolescent.

Research (e.g., Olejnik, 1980; Parikh, 1980) shows that for adolescents and college students, mothers' frequent use of power-assertive discipline is related to weak moral development, whereas maternal induction and affection are associated with moral growth. It seems that induction techniques facilitate moral development because their cognitive component allows discipline to be a learning experience. This is missing in the other disciplinary techniques.

Although fathers' disciplinary techniques have not been shown to be related to moral development, fathers' presence apparently is especially important for boys. Boys from father-absent homes score lower on indexes of moral development than boys from father-present homes (M. L. Hoffman, 1970). There are two possible explanations for this finding. First, fathers may provide direct in-

Power assertive discipline emphasizes the parent's control over the adolescent and relates negatively to moral development. Inductive discipline involves using a disciplinary situation as a teaching opportunity. It relates positively to moral development. *(Left: Bob Daemmrich/The Image Works. Right: Shirley Zeiberg)*

struction for moral standards in nondisciplinary situations. Second, it may be that the father's disciplinary role is critical only in exceptional circumstances, for example, delinquency, because mothers handle most disciplinary situations. In either event, the role of the father in moral development is apparently not as important as that of the mother.

These investigations lend credence to the psychoanalytic interpretation of moral development. Induction discipline helps the child identify with and internalize parental moral values, as demonstrated in the relation between adolescent moral behavior and earlier parental child-rearing techniques. Parental disciplinary techniques seem to be important in the development of a general moral orientation. The reason adolescents behave differently in "moral" situations—cheating, concerns about social moral issues, and views of right and wrong—is due in part to parental disciplinary techniques. In this regard, it has been shown that consistent inductive discipline is the preferred mode (Zelkowitz, 1987) for promoting moral development.

Social-Learning Theory

Social-learning theorists believe moral behavior is acquired through the same mechanisms as any other behavior, namely, the processes of direct teaching and generalized imitation (Kurtiness & Gewirtz, 1987). Hence, to explain why adolescents do or do not behave in a manner considered morally correct, social-learning theorists examine the adolescent's reinforcement history and important models, including parents and peers. In keeping with our cheating example, if you cheat to get better grades and do not get caught, you are more likely to continue to cheat—it has paid off and you have been positively reinforced. Similarly, observing classmates cheating and not getting caught may result in your cheating. Your successful peers have modeled behavior you might emulate.

An important implication of this approach is that children's and adolescents' moral orientations should be susceptible to change in the face of models who exhibit an orientation different from theirs. This implicaiton was tested in research with children and adolescents (e.g., Bandura & MacDonald, 1963; LeFurgy & Woloshin, 1969). Some children and adolescents have primarily an objective and others primarily a subjective moral orientation. The former make moral judgments on the basis of the consequences of an act, for example, the cost of a vase that gets broken; the latter make judgments on the basis of intent—whether or not the individual intended to break the vase. By exposing subjects to models with the opposite orientation, and by reinforcing the subjects for imitating the models, it has been shown that the child's or adolescent's moral orientation can be changed. And the changes in orientation last for at least a few months; they are not just temporary changes that occur in the experimental situation.

Studies such as these demonstrate that an important factor in moral development is the behavior of those we observe around us. Because we are more likely to imitate those who are very important to us, such as our peers, parents, or favorite teachers, or those who are like us, such as very close friends, these people become important to our moral development and behavior. Parents who primarily use power-assertive discipline may teach the adolescent it is all right to deal with others in the same manner. Similarly, admired peers may model and reinforce the adolescent for behaving in immoral ways, such as delinquency, and contribute to the adolescent becoming a delinquent. In this case, the rewards, tangible and otherwise, of successful delinquent behavior reinforce the adolescent for behaving that way. How many times did you do something you might not otherwise have done just because "everyone else was doing it"? You wanted to be accepted by others. We all have done that to a greater or lesser degree because we have seen it pay off for us.

The importance of observational learning in the socialization process is at the heart of concerns about the impact of the mass media, and especially television, on the adolescent (Fine, Mortimer, & Roberts, 1990). In general, the argument is that viewing violence, sex (in the guise of love), or unbridled autonomy encourages adolescents to behave in violent ways, engage in promiscuous sex, and be extremely rebellious. Although it no doubt is true that some adolescents' values are strongly shaped by what they see, hear, and read in the media, it is very difficult if not impossible to draw sweeping generalizations for the adolescent population as a whole. Indeed, one group of reviewers (Fine et al., 1990) have argued there is no scientific evidence that adolescents' behavior is *systematically* impacted by media presentations.

Think about your own contact with the media—MTV, cable TV, music, video games—you will be able to identify them. Do you especially seek out violence or sex in your media contact? Does it encourage you to behave in a similar manner? Do you, or would you, behave like the alienated adolescent so often portrayed in the media? Just how much does the music you listen to, the TV

Media portrayals of adolescents exaggerate typical adolescent behaviors. (*David Young-Wolfe/Photo Edit*)

programs you watch, and the movies or videos you see influence how you behave? It appears that for most adolescents the answer is "not much."

One difficulty in confirming a direct link between media portrayals of adolescents and adolescent behavior is the problem of establishing cause and effect.
Does watching violence or listening to "sexy" music cause the adolescent to behave in a similar manner? Or do those who are more violent, or who are more
prone to seeking out indiscriminate sex, actively choose the same in their contact with the media? Does the media *cause* the adolescent to behave in a particular way, or do those with particular predispositions seek out certain types of
media contact?

A second difficulty stems from the fact that it is adults who are concerned
with and write about the negative impact of the media on the adolescent. Adults
and adolescents who view the same TV program or listen to the same music do
so with different perspectives (Prinsky & Rosenbaum, 1987). Where adults may
see a modeling of violence or defiance of authority, adolescents may see com-
edy because they have a different set of perspectives and beliefs that influence
how they interpret what they perceive. Because they have different perspectives, expectations, and backgrounds, adolescents and adults may come away
with very different interpretations of a particular piece of music or a MTV video
(Prinsky & Rosenbaum, 1987).

Finally, although criticisms of what is presented on television hold some
truth, we must remember that media portrayals are not all bad. And adolescents
are influenced by many other models and exposed daily to others like themselves who do not behave in the stereotypic ways portrayed in the media. Is the
media, and especially television, getting a bad rap? Probably not entirely. But as
your own experience will lead you to conclude, the impact of violence or sex
on television likely has a much more limited impact on adolescent behavior
than some claim.

The Cognitive-Developmental Approach
to Moral Development

The emphasis of the cognitive-developmental approach is on moral judgments
and their related thought processes, which are seen as emerging in a sequence
of stages much in the same manner as the stages of intellectual development. As
development progresses, the moral thinking processes in each stage are integrated into those in the next higher stage, the emerging stage being an integration of the old and the new. The stages of development are passed through in
an invariant sequence, and age is not equivalent to stage.

Piaget's theory.   Piaget (1932) studied the development of two aspects of morality: (1) the development of the understanding of rules, and (2) conceptualizations of justice. By studying these two aspects of morality, Piaget was able to discover both how the understanding of rules developed from childhood through

adolescence and how notions of justice changed. After considering the development of each, Piaget formulated a model of how morality develops.

Piaget suggested two broad stages of moral development. In the first stage, variously termed *morality of constraint* or *moral realism,* one obeys rules because they are viewed as rigid and unalterable. Behaviors are viewed as either right or wrong, depending on the extent to which the behavior follows established social rules, particularly as stated by the parents. The young child does not take into account the intentions of the person who breaks a rule or misbehaves. Thus younger children believe in what Piaget has termed *immanent justice*, the notion that misdeeds will be punished simply because they are wrong. Morality is equated with following rules because they are the rules.

The adolescent, in contrast, operates according to a *morality of cooperation.* At this second stage of moral development, rules are viewed as being determined by reciprocal agreements depending on the social circumstances. To illustrate, simply think about the times you have played various games and altered the rules because of special circumstances. The adolescent realizes rules are not absolute—they can be altered by mutual agreement. Notions of justice include considerations of the intentions of others. Following moral rules is viewed as being essential to the functioning of society. Punishment is viewed as being suited to the misdeed (punishment by reciprocity) rather than simply being dished out by authority (expiatory punishment).

M. L. Hoffman (1980) summarized Piaget's view that experience with peers is the primary influence on the individual's progressing from the earlier to later stage of moral reasoning. Peer interactions involve the kind of give-and-take that is necessary for moral development in two ways. First, by sharing in decision making with peers, the child gains confidence in his or her ability to apply rules to specific situations and make decisions about changing rules. Thus rules come to be viewed as flexible rather than rigid, and as the result of agreement and cooperation between individuals sharing a common goal as opposed to being set down in concrete by some "higher" authority. Second, through various role-taking experiences with peers, the child learns that he or she thinks and feels about experiences in a way similar to peers, who in turn think and feel about things in a way similar to the child. This realization helps the youngster learn that rules are useful because they benefit the group. It also helps the child understand the motives behind the actions of others, and thereby allows the child to base moral judgments on intention rather than simply on overt behavior. As we noted earlier, because child–parent interactions do not contain this sort of give-and-take they do not promote moral development as well. Finally, some research with college students (Thoma & Ladewig, 1993) points out that close friends foster higher levels of moral thinking. College students with multiple friendships and supportive close college friends have higher levels of moral development, presumably because such friendships help one formulate values more clearly.

The development from concrete to formal operational thinking skills also facilitates moral development. Abstract thinking skills allow the adolescent to take the other's perspective and see the "morality" in the various sides of an argument. Abstract thinking also allows the adolescent to better understand the arbitrariness of rules—including those in our established legal code. This is necessary for understanding that rules are flexible and formulated through common agreement.

An important limitation of Piaget's theorizing about moral development was his focus on children as opposed to adolescents and adults. Lawrence Kohlberg based his notions in part on Piaget's views and discussed moral development not only in children but also in adolescents and adults.

Kohlberg's theory of moral development.   Like Piaget, Kohlberg (1963, 1976, 1984) believed morality develops in a series of stages related to the stages through which cognitive development proceeds. Further, he assumed children have a morality that is distinct and different from adult morality. His interest was in trying to understand moral thinking—the thought processes underlying moral judgments.

In his research, Kohlberg interviewed a large number of boys ranging from 6 to 16 years of age. During the interviews the children and adolescents heard 10 stories (Table 5-1 has examples) in which a moral dilemma was posed. After reading the story, the participants were asked a series of questions (e.g., Should Heinz have stolen the drug? Why or why not? Did the druggist have the right to charge such high prices? Why or why not?). Kohlberg was not particularly interested in the specific alternatives selected, but rather in the reasons given for the choices because they reflect the subject's way of thinking about the situation and, therefore, reveal the thought processes underlying moral judgment. Although stories such as that of Heinz may seem artificial and contrived, they represent moral dilemmas, and adolescents face a number of such dilemmas in real life when they consider issues such as whether or not to take a job during the school year, whether it is right to engage in sex or use drugs, should they sneak a drive in the family car even though they don't have a license. Understanding

---

Table 5–1   Examples of the Moral Dilemma Stories Used by Kohlberg

1. Joe's father promised Joe that he could go to camp if he earned the $50 for it, and then changed his mind and asked Joe to give him the money he had earned. Joe lied and said he had earned only $10 and went to camp using the other $40 he had made. Before he went he told his younger brother Alex about the money and about lying to their father. Should Alex tell their father?
2. In Europe, a woman was near death from a special kind of cancer. There was one drug that the doctors thought might save her. It was a form of radium that a druggist in the same town had recently discovered. The drug was expensive to make, but the druggist was charging 10 times what the drug cost him to make. He paid $200 for the radium and charged $2000 for a small dose of the drug. The sick woman's husband, Heinz, went to everyone he knew to borrow money, but he could only get together about $1000, which is half of what it cost. He told the druggist that his wife was dying and asked him to sell it cheaper or let him pay later. But the druggist said: "No, I discovered the drug and I'm going to make money from it." So Heinz got desperate and broke into the man's store to steal the drug for his wife. Should the husband have done that?

Source: From Kohlberg, L. (1963). The development of children's orientations toward a moral order: I. Sequence in the development of moral thought. *Vita Humana, 6,* 11-33.

how adolescents react to moral dilemmas as represented in the Heinz story gives us clues about how adolescents resolve their own dilemmas.

On the basis of responses to the questions about the dilemmas, Kohlberg postulated three levels of moral development each with two levels of moral reasoning, for a total of six stages. Column 1 in Table 5–2 lists the stages in the developmental sequence, columns 2 and 3 reflect the cognitive organization concerning morality for each stage, and the last column describes the social perspective of the stage.

At the *preconventional level* the child's concepts of good and bad, right and wrong, are determined by the physical consequences resulting from actions, that is, by rewards and punishments for specific behaviors, or by the perceived power of those in authority. In *stage 1* the physical consequences of an act completely determine its goodness or badness. There is an unquestioning deference to authority motivated by a desire to avoid punishment. In *stage 2* acts are defined as right if they are satisfying to the self or to others. There is some indication of a concept of fairness and egalitarianism of a reciprocal nature, but it is of the naive "you do for me and I'll do for you" sort.

At the *conventional level,* the immediate physical consequences of an act become secondary to maintaining the accepted social order and living up to the expectations of others. Behavior at this level differs from that at the preceding level because the child not only behaves in a manner consistent with the expectations of others, but also identifies with and incorporates the rules of others and respects their judgment. *Stage 3,* characteristic of adolescents, is composed of a "good boy" "nice girl" morality. Good and bad are defined by what pleases others. The adolescent may well conform to the cultural stereotype of what is good and bad behavior, but begins to judge the behavior of others on the basis of their intentions to mean well. *Stage 4* may be characterized by a "law and order" orientation toward authority, rules, and maintenance of the social order. "Right" behavior is defined as doing one's duty, showing respect for authority, and maintaining the social order for its own sake. Although similar to stage 1, the stage 4 orientation differs in that it includes a respect for an underlying moral order that is maintained by reward and punishment. At this stage, the individual also is able to understand that others have rights.

At the *postconventional* or *principled* level, moral values and principles are defined according to equitable standards or rights, and the possibility of inconsistencies between several socially accepted standards is realized. There is an effort to define morality in a manner distinct from the authority of groups and from the individual's identification with various groups. *Stage 5* is characterized by defining morality in terms of mutually agreed upon standards, such as contracts. There is an emphasis on the legal point of view, but with the knowledge that laws are formed on some rational basis and can be changed to fit changing social situations. This latter characteristic is an important distinction between stages 4 and 5. There is also an awareness that personal opinions are relative and that conflict can be resolved through a set of agreed upon procedures. *Stage 6* is characterized by defining *right* according to a set of abstract

Table 5–2   The Six Moral Stages Identified by Kohlberg

Level and Stage	CONTENT OF STAGE		
	What Is Right	Reasons for Doing Right	Social Perspective of Stage

Level 1, Preconventional
Stage 1:
  Heteronomous
  Morality
	To avoid breaking rules backed by punishment, obedience for its own sake, and avoiding physical damage to persons and property.	Avoidance of punishment, and the superior power of authorities.	*Egocentric point of view.* Doesn't consider the interests of others or recognize that they differ from the actor's; doesn't relate two points of view. Actions are considered physically rather than in terms of psychological interests of others. Confusion of authority's perspective with one's own.

Stage 2:
  Individualism,
  Instrumental
  Purpose, and
  Exchange
	Following rules only when it is to someone's immediate interest; acting to meet one's own interests and needs and letting others do the same. Right is also what's fair, what's an equal exchange, a deal, an agreement.	To serve one's own needs or interests in a world where you have to recognize that other people have their interests, too.	*Concrete individualistic perspective.* Aware that everybody has his or her own interest to pursue and these conflict, so that right is relative (in the concrete individualistic sense).

Level II, Conventional
Stage 3: Mutual
  Interpersonal
  Expectations,
  Relationships, and
  Interpersonal
  Conformity
	Living up to what is expected by people close to you or what people generally expect of people in your role as child, sibling, friend, etc. "Being good" is important and means having good motives, showing concern about others. It also means keeping mutual relationships, such as trust, loyalty, respect, and gratitude.	The need to be a good person in your own eyes and those of others. Your caring for others. Belief in the Golden Rule. Desire to maintain rules and authority that support stereotypical good behavior.	*Perspective of the individual in relationships with other individuals.* Aware of shared feelings, agreements, and expectations which take primacy over individual interests. Relates points of view through the concrete Golden Rule, putting yourself in the other guy's shoes. Does not yet consider generalized system perspective.

Stage 4: Social System and Conscience	Fulfilling the actual duties to which you have agreed. Laws are to be upheld except in extreme cases where they conflict with other fixed social duties. Right is also contributing to society, the group, or institution.	To keep the institution going as a whole, to avoid the breakdown in the system "if everyone did it," or the imperative of conscience to meet one's defined obligations.	*Differentiates societal point of view from interpersonal agreement or motives.* Takes the point of view of the system that defines roles and rules. Considers individual relations in terms of place in the system.

Table 5–2   *Continued*

	CONTENT OF STAGE		
Level and Stage	What Is Right	Reasons for Doing Right	Social Perspective of Stage
Level III, Postconventional, or Principled			
Stage 5: Social Contract or Utility and Individual Rights	Being aware that people hold a variety of values and opinions, that most values and rules are relative to your group. These relative rules should usually be upheld, however, in the interest of impartiality and because they are the social contract. Some nonrelative values and rights like *life* and *liberty,* however, must be upheld in any society and regardless of majority opinion.	A sense of obligation to law because of one's social contract to make and abide by laws for the welfare of all and for the protection of all people's rights. A feeling of contractual commitment, freely entered upon, to family, friendship, trust, and work obligations. Concern that laws and duties be based on rational calculation of overall utility, "the greatest good for the greatest number."	*Prior-to-society perspective.* Perspective of a rational individual aware of values and rights prior to social attachments and contracts. Integrates perspectives by formal mechanisms of agreement, contract, objective impartiality, and due process. Considers moral and legal points of view; recognizes that they sometimes conflict and finds it difficult to integrate them.
Stage 6: Universal Ethical Principles	Following self-chosen ethical principles. Particular laws or social agreements are usually valid because they rest on such principles. When laws violate these principles, one acts in accordance with the principle. Principles are universal principles of justice: the equality of human rights and respect for the dignity of human beings as individual persons.	The belief as a rational person in the validity of universal moral principles, and a sense of personal commitment to them.	*Perspective of a moral point of view* from which social arrangements derive. Perspective is that of any rational individual recognizing the nature of morality or the fact that persons are ends in themselves and must be treated as such.

Source: Adapted from Kohlberg, L. (1976). Moral stages and moralization: The cognitive developmental approach. In T. Lickona (Ed.), *Moral development and behavior: Theory, research, and social issues.* New York: Holt, Rinehart & Winston.

universal ethical principles, for example, the Golden Rule or the greatest good for the greatest number. The basic notion is that universal principles of justice, equality, and human rights exist and that these may be in conflict with existing law. When such a conflict exists, the law must be challenged, which may occur through civil disobedience. Individuals such as Dr. Martin Luther King, Jr., and some of those who protested the Vietnam War by refusing the draft, were operating at this level. They protested what they felt were unjust laws or practices that were in conflict with strongly held moral values and accepted the penalty for their actions.

Kohlberg's theorizing has generated considerable discussion, debate, and research about issues in moral development. One focus has been on Kohlberg's claim that the stages of moral development are *universal* (Perlmutter & Shapiro, 1987), that they occur in all cultures.

Kohlberg (1969) reported data for 10-, 13-, and 16-year-olds in the United States, Taiwan, Mexico, Turkey, and the Yucatán. At age 10 in each region, the order of the stages is the same as the order in which they occur. That is, judgments are based on stage 1 most often, stage 2 next most often, and so forth. In the United States, the trend is toward judgments increasingly based on stages 3, 4, and 5. Stage 6 is used relatively infrequently. In all the other cultures, both stages 5 and 6 are used relatively infrequently, but the order of use is as Kohlberg predicted.

Some other research lends credence to Kohlberg's claim of universality in the stages of moral judgment. Parikh (1980) compared moral development in U.S. and Indian adolescents; C. B. White (1975) examined moral development in Bahamian children and early adolescents; Snarey, Reimer, and Kohlberg (1985) surveyed Israeli kibbutzim adolescents; and Ma (1988) investigated moral judgments in groups from Hong Kong, mainland China, and England. In all these studies the clear finding is that moral judgments and reasoning develop in the sequence described by Kohlberg (Boyes & Walker, 1988; Walker, DeVries, & Trevethan, 1987). Adolescence is the time when moral reasoning at more advanced stages emerges, and this occurs in an orderly fashion.

The findings of longitudinal studies provide even stronger support for Kohlberg's claim of stage sequentiality. The most extensive longitudinal study of moral reasoning levels was reported by Colby, Kohlberg, Gibbs, and Lieberman (1983), who retested subjects in Kohlberg's original sample six times over a 20-year interval. Over the course of the 20 years, no subject skipped a stage or reverted to the use of a prior stage. More recently Walker (1989) reported the results of a 2-year longitudinal study of moral reasoning in children (grades 1 and 4), adolescents (grades 7 and 10), and their parents. Again, the findings supported the stage sequence postulated by Kohlberg, with higher stages of moral reasoning emerging with increasing age level.

Taken in total, the evidence supports the view that moral reasoning and judgment develop in an identifiable sequence with adolescence being the time when more advanced stages of moral thinking begin to emerge. Apparently, there are no important gender differences in this finding, either with respect to its sequence or ultimate stage of moral reasoning attained.

Other researchers have focused on Kohlberg's claim that level of cognitive development underlies level of moral reasoning. L. C. Lee (1971) demonstrated what is perhaps the clearest relationship between cognition and moral development. The subjects of her study were 195 middle-class boys, 15 from each grade level from kindergarten through 12. She determined the subjects' levels of both cognitive and moral development and then related them. She found that cognitive development level, independent of age, correlated highly with the level of moral reasoning. For example, concrete operational thinking predicted a decrease in level 1 (authority) moral reasoning, and formal operational thinking predicted an increase in level 4 (societal) moral reasoning. Other researchers have provided evidence relating stages of cognitive development to level of moral reasoning in preadolescents and adolescents (Krebs & Gillmore, 1982; Lutwak, 1984; Tomlinson-Keasey & Keasey, 1974; Walker, 1980) and adults (Rowe & Marcia, 1980). All these researchers reported that higher levels of moral development were related to higher levels of cognitive development.

The relationship between level of cognitive development and level of moral development probably has two bases. First, cognitive development is related to perspective taking about moral issues (for example, Colby et al., 1983). As you can see in Table 5-2, different social perspectives are associated with the different levels of moral development. It is likely that, as cognitive skills develop, perspective taking along moral lines changes, these changes being in part responsible for the relationship between cognitive and moral development. Some evidence suggests that discussions of moral issues with parents (Parikh, 1980) and peers (Damon & Killen, 1982; Niles, 1986) facilitate changes in social perspective taking, likely by producing cognitive conflict (disequilibrium) resulting in structural change and thereby change in moral reasoning (Walker, 1983; Walker & Taylor, 1991).

Second, formal operational thinking allows the individual to consider the possible as well as the real, and to think abstractly (Chapter 4). Examination of Table 5-2 shows that increases in moral development are associated with increasingly abstract concepts of justice (what is right and the reasons for doing right). Adolescence is the time when we begin to understand the rules of society in more flexible ways.

This theorizing is important to our understanding of adolescents because it helps explain their idealism, particularly with regard to their views of the nature of the social system, politics, and the "rules" of social interaction. Formal operational thinking allows the adolescent to consider the possibility that the society might be different with different political systems because of the hypothetico-deductive (if-then) thinking that accompanies formal operational competence. Adolescents might argue that all countries should dispense with all nuclear (and other) weapons, thereby eliminating the threat of nuclear war. The adolescent might well not consider the possibility that some nation might cheat, however.

These are real-life types of issues. With the demise of the Cold War era we hear much about determining how and when the United States should "project its influence" in the world. Should we have fought the Gulf War? Should we have had troops in Somalia? What about Bosnia? Should Dr. Kevorkian be allowed to assist the incurably ill commit suicide? What do you think? Why do you think that? Are there other reasonable perspectives? Understanding your perspectives, how you think about moral issues, is what Kohlberg tried to do and describe.

A final area in which Kohlberg's theory has been challenged is its basis in a male-oriented view of the social system, a view that rewards achievement and competition, and the fact that it is based only on initial interviews with males. Carol Gilligan has been the most outspoken researcher to have suggested that Kohlberg's male-oriented perspective may make it seem that females have a lower moral development because the dominant cultural standards are not consistent with the traditional feminine sex role (see Box 5-1). Gilligan has formulated an alternative basis for a theory of moral development based on interviews with females.

Gilligan's theory of moral development.   Carol Gilligan (1982) suggests that males and females have different orientations toward moral issues. Males tend to take a *justice* orientation toward moral concerns; the important question is whether or not people are treated "fairly" and according to accepted rules. Gilligan proposes that females have a *caring* orientation toward moral concerns; responsiveness to human needs is emphasized. Whereas the justice orientation is based on the perspective that moral decisions should be made from a detached and objective perspective (perhaps because of Piaget's emphasis on rules in his seminal research), the caring orientation is based on the premise that moral decisions should be made on the basis of responsiveness to others.

Consider the Heinz example in Table 5-1. The justice orientation emphasizes rules, the right of the druggist to charge whatever he wished, and the fact that Heinz acted illegally by stealing someone else's property. The caring orientation emphasizes the lack of the druggist's concern for others—Heinz's frustration and poor economic circumstances and Heinz's wife's illness. How one decides to score the responses to the moral dilemmas determines which orientation receives emphasis and thereby who—those emphasizing justice or those emphasizing caring—scores higher in moral reasoning. Should Heinz have stolen the drug? If you stress the law orientation your score will be high if the scoring scheme emphasizes Kohlberg's system and low if it emphasizes Gilligan's. The reverse also will be true—if your answer emphasizes concern for others and the idea we all are responsible for others, you will score higher under Gilligan's system than under Kohlberg's.

Which orientation—justice or caring—is the correct one? Gilligan (Gilligan & Attanucci, 1988) suggests the two approaches are complementary; neither is "correct." Rather, it seems the orientation one employs in moral dilemma situations reflects one's orientation and involvement in the dilemma (Lonky, Roodin, & Rybasch, 1988). When asked to imagine the moral dilemma is one's own, people are more likely to take a caring as opposed to justice orientation. When viewing a dilemma from the perspective of an outside observer, one is more likely to take a justice orientation. As we noted in Box 5-1, both males and females are able to take either orientation; the orientation one adopts depends on one's own involvement in the moral dilemma. Would your stance about physician-assisted suicide change if you had a relative or friend who was suffering from cancer with no hope of a cure?

BOX 5-1   Are There Gender Differences in Moral Reasoning?

Carol Gilligan, in her book *In a Different Voice* (1982), suggests that current theories of moral development are biased toward male perspectives of morality. She points out that contemporary as well as more historical perspectives of morality are based on the writings of men, not women. As a result, she suggests that females may seem to score lower on tests of moral judgment because they view moral concerns through a different perspective. In addition, she points out that although in contemporary culture one particular perspective—that emphasizing achievement, competition, and detached individualism—is considered more mentally healthy and appropriate, there may be another equally valid perspective to approaching moral concerns.

In the *justice* orientation, as represented in the writings of Piaget and Kohlberg, the emphasis in moral reasoning is on individual rights and whether or not individuals are treated fairly. In the *care* perspective, the emphasis is on attention to others' needs, with moral judgments based on attachments to others. Drawing on conceptualizations of existing sex roles, Gilligan points out that the former perspective is "male oriented" and the latter "female oriented." Current tests of moral reasoning give greater weight to the male-oriented perspectives of morality, those most consistent with the male sex role. As a result, Gilligan argues, females as a group may seem to have lower levels of moral thinking than males because females tend to look at the world differently.

Gilligan's critique of theories of moral development stirred considerable debate and research (see Baumrind, 1986; Donenberg & Hoffman, 1988; Friedman, Robinson, & Friedman, 1987; Gilligan & At-tanucci, 1988; Walker, 1986, 1989). The general findings of these studies are that there are no sex differences in moral judgment, whether the scoring scheme is based on Kohlberg's model or on an alternative one assessing moral judgments on both the justice and care dimensions. In other words, it does not appear that current methods of assessing moral reasoning are biased against females. In addition, it appears that both males and females are capable of making moral judgments on both the justice and care dimensions, although females may be more likely to use the latter dimension.

An interesting finding is that educational level is related to level of moral development, but perhaps not in the same way for males and females (Baumrind, 1986; Boldizar, Wilson, & Deemer, 1989). For males, both involvement in and dedication to educational goals were indirectly related to moral development. For females, they were directly related. Boldizar and colleagues suggest that institutional settings that are male oriented as opposed to female oriented account for this sex difference. Males see the opportunity to advance in a male-dominated culture. For females, this is less likely.

Although the research does not bear out Gilligan's initial assertion of bias in assessments of moral judgment, her critique has led to important research on the bases of moral judgments that tie these judgments to broad-based cultural concerns such as sex roles. Her thinking has inspired studies that clarify the very complex nature of examining moral thinking and link moral thinking to other major research domains, such as sex roles.

Role Taking and Moral Development

Piaget suggested that role playing, particularly in the context of peer interactions, is important in moral development. The relationship between role taking and moral development was described by Robert Selman (1976) and Lawrence Kohlberg (1969). Selman suggested that role-taking ability, which develops in a series of stages parallel to Piaget's stages of cognitive development, influences the child's understanding of the social world and how conflicts should be resolved. Moral judgments reflect the application of role taking to the moral domain. Kohlberg (1969, 1976; Colby et al., 1983) noted that progression through the stages of moral development may be enhanced by role-taking opportunities because role taking allows the child to learn to take someone else's point of view. As we noted earlier, discussions about moral issues, which are in effect role-playing opportunities, enhance moral development. Some researchers (e.g., Arbuthnot, 1975; Krebs & Gilmore, 1982; Moir, 1974; Walker, 1980) have shown that the opportunity to engage in role playing in moral dilemma situations increases adolescents' level of moral reasoning, and that involvement in social participation is an important aspect of moral development (Keasey, 1971). This seems to be due to enhanced ability to understand others' views and reduced egocentrism (Rest, 1976; Selman, 1976).

Moral Judgment and Moral Behavior

Very little research·has been done to determine if moral judgments are, in fact, related to moral behavior. Some evidence indicates that the relationship may depend on the individual's involvement in the moral issue (Weiss, 1982) and the

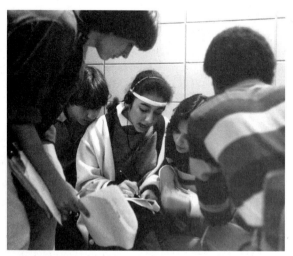

Playing different roles, such as being a leader, not only teaches accepting responsibility, but according to social cognitive theorists, it also promotes moral development. (*Ken Karp*)

individual's general level of moral reasoning (Coady & Sawyer, 1986). Adolescents hold higher moral standards for others than they do for themselves. For example, when adolescents were asked whether a transgression should be reported to parents they used lower level moral reasoning when they were to presume they, as opposed to someone else, performed the act; they held higher moral standards for others than for the self. Other evidence (e.g., Coady & Sawyer, 1986; Rest, 1983) indicates that those with higher levels of moral development are less likely to cheat or engage in antisocial behavior. Finally, delinquents have lower levels of moral development than their nondelinquent agemates (see Box 5–2).

Some researchers (e.g., Kupfersmid & Wonderly, 1980; Sobesky, 1983) have suggested that in order to accurately assess the relation between moral judgment and moral behavior one must deal with real-life situations such as those found in the workplace, in preparing income tax, and in returning of found money. How we think about moral issues seems to be relatively distinct from how we behave in moral situations.

It is not surprising that adolescents do not *always* behave at the moral level of which they are capable; virtually no one does. Adolescents engage in delinquency for a variety of reasons—feeling they will not get caught or needs for believing they belong to a group. Although they may morally "know better," adolescents engage in unsafe sexual intercourse. What these examples illustrate is simply that behavior is a result of both personal and situational factors. We should not expect that level of moral thinking is the sole determinant, or even the strongest, of the adolescent's behavior.

By studying both moral behaviors, such as shoplifting, and moral judgments, such as knowing the difference between right and wrong, cognitive developmental theorists have shown that the two do not necessarily go hand-in-hand. (*Mike Kagan/Monkmeyer Press*)

BOX 5–2   Morality and Delinquency

As detailed in the text, the study of morality and behavior is fraught with difficult problems. One line of investigation that researchers have pursued is the study of differences in moral judgments between delinquent and nondelinquent groups. These research endeavors were undertaken to examine the possibility that delinquents are delayed in their moral reasoning judgments, this immaturity leading to their engaging in behaviors normally considered immoral.

Jurkovič (1980) reviewed the literature on the relationship between moral reasoning and delinquent behavior. In one set of studies the moral reasoning of delinquents and nondelinquents was compared. In general, it was found that delinquents had a less mature level of moral reasoning than nondelinquents. In addition, it was found that the moral development of delinquents evidenced a developmental lag compared to the moral development of nondelinquents; that is, although the older delinquents had higher levels of moral reasoning than the younger delinquents, those levels were only comparable to nondelinquents who were chronologically younger. Hence immature moral reasoning, in itself, cannot be considered the sole cause of delinquency.

Although adolescents who do not give up their premoral orientation while their peers are progressing in moral reasoning may be at risk for engaging in behaviors considered delinquent, progressing to higher levels of moral thinking does not insulate the adolescent from engaging in delinquent behaviors.

Jurkovič (1980) suggested that moral thinking is only one of a complex of factors that determines the behavior in which we engage. Temperamental, biological, and personality factors are also important in delinquency. In addition, situational contexts are important in determining behavior. Finally, Jurkovič noted that delinquents may well rationalize their behavior with age-appropriate stage 3 or 4 moral judgments, thereby making it seem to them that what they are doing is acceptable.

A study of Petronio (1980) is interesting in this light. He investigated the possibility that repeater delinquents of 13 to 17 years of age might have lower levels of moral reasoning than nonrepeaters. This possibility was based on the notion that repeat offenders may have an arrested moral development, making them more prone to engage in delinquent acts. Surprisingly, however, he found that the repeater delinquents had a *higher* level of moral reasoning (stage 3) than the nonrepeaters (stage 2). Just as Jurkovič (1980) suggested, the repeater delinquents rationalized their behavior with age-appropriate moral standards. Petronio suggests they did this in an attempt to reduce their feelings and appearances of "badness."

Jurkovič (1980) drew several conclusions on the basis of the existing evidence. First, he concluded that the link between delinquency and low levels of moral thinking has not been shown to be very strong. Delinquents are as heterogeneous in their moral thinking as others. Second, he noted that, just as moral thinking is complexly related to other behaviors, the links between moral judgments and delinquency are also complex. Few, if any, behaviors, including delinquency, are determined by a single factor. Indeed, that is in part what makes predicting human behavior so difficult. Hence attempts to increase the level of moral thinking ability of delinquents, which can be done (Niles, 1986), may not translate to reductions in delinquency.

MORAL EDUCATION

A continuing debate centers on the degree to which the school system should be involved in the teaching of morals. On the one hand, it seems almost impossible for schools to not teach moral values—the system emphasizes concern for others, following rules, and working for the common good. On the other hand, questions center on what values should be taught, how they are best taught, and who should decide what should be taught (Perlmutter & Shapiro, 1987).

Regardless of how one feels about these issues, a bit of reflection reveals that the school system is a setting in which moral values are taught. Teachers set examples of fairness and honesty, consideration for others, and the importance of behaving in a manner consistent with rules and regulations designed to benefit the whole. Classmates present other value systems that must be considered in addition to one's own. From the time students arrive at school until they leave, they are exposed to a host of values and ideals that fall in the moral realm, even if there is no specific curriculum focused on the development of moral thinking and moral behavior.

Curricula and methods schools use specifically to teach morality fall into three broad categories, each consistent with the theoretical perspectives of moral development already discussed: values clarification, behavior modification, and cognitive-developmental.

Values Clarification Curricula

The essential aspect of values clarification curricula is the determination of the **values** one holds dear and would be willing to stand up for (see Box 5-3). Adolescents ponder many issues that have a value orientation: When, if ever, should there be war? What sexual values should I hold? Why can't wealth be distributed more evenly so there would be no poor people? Since many of my friends use drugs why shouldn't I? What kind of person do I want to be?

The procedures used in values clarification do not focus on what the correct answer to these questions should be (Minuchin & Shapiro, 1983; Perlmutter & Shapiro, 1987)—the answers are subjective and individual decisions. Rather, values clarification aims to help students learn the process of valuing and become aware of the values they hold. Students learn to weigh pros and cons and to consider the implications of making various choices. It is hoped they will become more adept at thinking about the values they hold and at thinking about values in general. Through teaching directed at how to analyze and refine one's values, and through the indirect learning that all of us experience, we come to hold personal values and to realize there are individual differences we should appreciate. Values clarification curricula help make adolescents more aware of their values and provide mechanisms for thinking about values.

A variety of techniques are used in values clarification classes. One re-

BOX 5–3   Adolescent Values

The importance of value clarification lies in the establishment of a system of values. As adolescents develop formal operational cognitive skills, these skills are applied to concerns of personal beliefs, as we dis- cussed in Chapter 4. The value system re- sulting from these introspections is impor- tant for resolving moral conflicts because it provides a basis for decision making (Feather, 1980).

Four Most Important and Four Least Important Values in Five Groups of Male Students

			TERMINAL VALUES		
Rank of Value	United States	Canada	Australia	Israel	Papua New Guinea
1	Freedom	Freedom	Wisdom	A world at peace	A world at peace
2	Happiness	Happiness	True friendship	National security	Equality
3	Wisdom	Mature love	Freedom	Happiness	Freedom
4	Self-respect	Self-respect	A sense of accomplishment	Freedom	True friendship
15	Pleasure	A world of beauty	A world of beauty	A comfortable life	A sense of accomplishment
16	Salvation	Social recognition	Social recognition	Social recognition	Pleasure
17	National security	National security	National security	A world of beauty	Mature love
18	A world of beauty	Salvation	Salvation	Salvation	A world of beauty

			INSTRUMENTAL VALUES		
Rank of Value	United States	Canada	Australia	Israel	Papua New Guinea
1	Honest	Honest	Honest	Honest	Honest
2	Responsible	Responsible	Broad-minded	Responsible	Helpful
3	Ambitious	Loving	Responsible	Logical	Responsible
4	Broad-minded	Broad-minded	Loving	Capable	Ambitious
15	Cheerful	Imaginative	Imaginative	Clean	Independent
16	Polite	Polite	Polite	Imaginative	Clean
17	Clean	Clean	Clean	Obedient	Logical
18	Obedient	Obedient	Obedient	Forgiving	Imaginative

Source: Feather, N.T. (1980). Values in adolescence. In J. Adelson (Ed.), *Handbook of adolescent psychology*. New York: Wiley.

Rokeach (1973) divides values into two types: terminal, which reflect end states of our existence, and instrumental, which re- late to ways of behaving. He goes on to note that, although there likely are many more instrumental than terminal values, the numbers of each likely are much smaller than the number of other more spe- cific beliefs and attitudes we hold. The dis- tinction between terminal and instrumental values and our other beliefs and attitudes is that the former two types of values are cen- tral to our belief system—our other beliefs and attitudes reflecting the more general core values. Changes in core values, then, will have widespread effects on our general belief system.

In one of the more extensive studies of the development of adolescent value systems, Feather (1975, 1980) examined college students' values by using Rokeach's (1973) Value Survey. The survey lists 18 terminal and 18 instrumental values. The respondents are asked to rank each set of values in regard to the self.

Feather (1975, 1980) had male college students in five countries complete the survey, in order to examine cultural differences in value systems. Three countries (United States, Canada, Australia) were relatively affluent and two (Israel, Papua New Guinea) were not. The surveys were conducted in the late 1960s and early 1970s. The results of the survey are presented here for the four most important and four least important terminal and instrumental values, that is, for the values deemed most and least important on the basis of the responses to the survey.

Examination of the table shows similarities in the values of students from the three affluent countries. Nonetheless, there are differences reflecting the varying emphases of each country. For example, the high stress in the United States on achievement is present. The values of the Israeli students reflect the political climate of the Middle East. Finally, the Papua New Guinea students' values reflect the emergence into nationhood at the time the data were collected.

Because values are so closely tied to national perspectives and issues, it should not be surprising to find that as national tides change, so, too, do adolescent value structures. For example, it has been noted among college professors that students seem more task oriented now than in the 1960s and 1970s, and that students seem to be more attuned to academics. Indeed, later data on adolescent interests (Bachman, Johnston, & O'Malley, 1980) showed this is the case.

quires students to make forced choices of what they would rather be, for example, a loner or a person in lots of groups. Another procedure asks students to rank-order world issues, such as poverty, national defense, the environment. By discussing the reasoning underlying the choices, students become more aware of how they think about issues and how they make choices about values. The teachers in values clarification classes act as moderators, probing the students for reasons for choices while at the same time avoiding criticism or evaluation of the students' choices.

The values clarification curricula have been criticized on several grounds. One is that by not taking a stand on *any* values, the approach may teach students to tolerate all values or become unsure if they should hold any values firmly. A second is that the approach teaches there are no values central to the society and that all should hold. A third is that clarifying values is not necessarily related to improved morality. Finally, by sharing values in a public forum such as the classroom, the adolescent may come into serious and open conflict with those who hold different values. It is one thing to discuss differences in values with close friends; it is another to do so in the classroom situation.

Behavior Modification and Moral Behaviors

As the name implies, behavior modification, which is based on the social-learning perspective of moral development, has as its aim the training of moral behaviors. As opposed to teaching processes of value determination or moral judgment, the emphasis is on teaching children and adolescents to behave in what are considered morally correct ways (Perlmutter & Shapiro, 1987).

One method used is to reward or punish specific behaviors directly. In effect, this is the practice parents use with children but also with adolescents to get them to behave in ways the parents wish. Hence, when parents withdraw a privilege because the adolescent has engaged in behaviors deemed undesirable, such as staying out too late, or allow special privileges because the adolescent has exhibited appropriate behavior, they are using behavior modification techniques to alter the adolescent's behavior along the lines they deem appropriate. Teachers, too, use such techniques to control the behavior of their students in the classroom—violation of school rules can have severe consequences.

Second, adults act as models for moral behavior. Parental behavior can set examples for how one should behave in a variety of circumstances. Similarly, teachers are models for fairness, rule following, and responsibility. In this way, both parents and teachers are teaching moral behaviors—and at times they are at odds with each other.

Although behavior modification and modeling clearly are effective means of altering behavior, there are some criticisms of this way of teaching morality. First, inconsistencies in reinforcement teach conflicting messages. Second, there may well be differences in the behaviors deemed moral by parents and those deemed moral by teachers. Third, the behaviors taught as moral reflect the individualistic perspectives of those doing the teaching. As some critics have noted, there are few generally accepted moral behaviors, and many of those reflect very middle-class values that may not be applicable to everyone. Finally, behavior modification, in itself, does not teach why certain behaviors are preferable to others. Critics argue that adolescents need to be taught why certain behaviors are more moral than others so they can rely on this knowledge when moral choices must be made. This task is the forte of the final perspective on moral education.

Teaching Moral Reasoning

Curricula aimed at teaching the principles of moral reasoning are derived from Kohlberg's theory. The exemplary program was established by Kohlberg in 1974 and emphasizes discussing realistic issues that arise in the school environment, with a focus on the importance of give-and-take, mutual caring, and group commitment (Kohlberg, 1980). In this system, the teacher facilitates discussion of moral issues, bringing out the importance of various alternatives for the larger community (the school). The aim is to persuade the students to feel a stronger sense of responsibility to the community, as in Kohlberg's stage 4 moral thinking. There is no attempt to get the students to begin to make moral judgments at stages 5 and 6, in part because it is apparent that relatively few people reason about moral issues at these levels. By discussing rules for conduct, the students not only became more aware of the reasons for rules but also begin to follow the rules more closely.

The question of which technique of teaching morality is better is very difficult. At present, no strong evidence indicates that one or the other approach has a long-term impact on the adolescent's behavior (Damon, 1988). One must, of necessity, opt for the procedure that not only teaches whatever is considered appropriate behavior, but also teaches the cognitive skills that allow for internalization of moral rules that can be applied to circumstances outside the realm of specifically taught behavior. In this regard, it appears that Kohlberg's scheme may in the long run prove most beneficial.

THE DEVELOPMENT OF RELIGIOUS AND POLITICAL THINKING

Discussions of morality must include considerations of religion and politics. Moral reasoning and moral behavior are intimately related to religious values. All religions have teachings about moral values to which children and adolescents are exposed. How do adolescents view religion and its importance in their lives? Morality also involves laws, social interaction, and one's views of the relation between the person and the social system, particularly as represented by government. One's developing political views reflect in part one's ideas about the relation between the political system and the individual.

The Adolescent and Religion

The cognitive changes of adolescence trigger a questioning about the role of religion in the individual's life. Questions center on issues such as the role that religion should play in one's life, what it means to be religious, does one need to attend religious services to be a religious person. Although some adolescents experience what might be called a religious crisis (McAdams, Booth, & Selvik, 1981), most do not. Rather, for most adolescents, there is simply a renewed interest in religion as it takes on a more serious and personal meaning.

Adolescents' views of religion.   During adolescence views of religion change. As adolescents grow older, religion tends to become more a matter of personal conviction than external circumstance (Fowler, 1981; Gallup & Poling, 1980). Although no evidence indicates a repudiation of religious beliefs during the adolescent years, adolescents come to view religion in a more personal and less dogmatic manner.

This was shown dramatically in a survey by Gallup and Poling (1980). The adolescent subjects had little confidence in organized religion, and about 40% rated the honesty and ethical standards of the clergy as only average or less.

During adolescence, views of the role of religion in one's life become more personal. (*Shirley Zeiberg*)

Gallup and Poling suggest their results reflect a lack of confidence in organized religion, perhaps because it is viewed as not changing with the times.

The notion that views of religion are tied to the "social times" received considerable credence in a study conducted by Caplow and Bahr (1979). They surveyed the attitudes of adolescents in "Middletown," a community first surveyed 50 years earlier. Although views on the purpose of religion, namely, to prepare one for the hereafter, changed little over the course of 50 years, a number of other opinions did. For example, far fewer adolescents believed the Bible is a sufficient guide for dealing with modern problems, that it is wrong to go to the movies on Sunday, and that Christianity is the one true religion. In turn, many more believed evolution is a more accurate explanation for the origin of the human species than the biblical account.

Conceptualizations of God also change during adolescence. Young children view God in a very concrete way—as a person with a physical form like theirs (Fowler, 1981). Their approach to religion also is very concrete: To be religious you must attend a house of worship. With the onset of formal operational thinking skills, conceptions of God and religious beliefs change and become more abstract. Adolescents do not see God as a physical being. They wrestle with apparent inconsistencies in religious presentations of God (such as God being good) and conditions in the world, for example, poverty and suffering.

Religious behavior.   The changing views of adolescents are reflected in attendance at religious services and in the view that religion is important in the lives of people. Data from the mid-1970s through the mid-1980s (Youth Indicators, 1988) showed a decline in the percentage of high school seniors who attend religious services weekly, from about 41% to about 35%. There were few changes for those who attended less regularly. Younger adolescents are more likely to attend services regularly than are older adolescents (Johnston, Bachman, & O'Malley, 1986).

Typically, adolescent females attend services more frequently than adolescent males, and better educated adolescents attend more frequently than less well-educated adolescents. Attending services also is related to parental behavior. If parents attend services regularly, their adolescents also do. This seems particularly true for Catholics, who have the highest rate of church attendance, and somewhat less true for Jews, who have the lowest attendance rates. African American adolescents view religion as more important in their lives and attend services more than do White youth.

Some changes in religious behavior have been noted. Religion is losing its influence on the daily lives of the American people. The percentage of students feeling that religion is becoming less important in their daily lives has increased during recent years. This is in direct contrast to the increases in the percentage of those who viewed religion as important between the Depression and the World War II years. Concurrent with this view is an increasing tendency to view religion more as a part of a philosophy of life and less as a means of personal salvation. Should this trend continue, it will become difficult to separate religious notions from notions of morality.

Cognition and religious views.   The age changes in various views of religion lead to the possibility that religious views are subject to reinterpretation as one develops cognitively. Some evidence, indeed, points in this direction.

Using an open-ended set of questions, Elkind (1978a) asked 5- to 14-year-olds about their views of religion. He compared the answers of those who were concrete operational and those who were formal operational. The concrete operational students were much less reflective and personal in their views of religion. For example, they viewed going to a place of worship as a sign of one's religiosity, whereas the formal operational students argued religiosity was signified by one's ideological perspectives and personal beliefs about religious practices. In general, the data are consistent with the notion that, as one matures cognitively, the perspective of religion becomes both more personal and more abstract.

The Adolescent's Political Thinking

The study of political socialization is extremely complex, encompassing issues in political behavior (voting, political activism); the acquisition of political values (liberal versus conservative viewpoints); interpersonal relations (the role of compromise in political decision making); and the understanding of the nature of the social order (the roles of government and laws, community versus individual rights). We focus on evidence on the link between moral development and political thinking, that is, the adolescent's perception of political issues and understanding of the social order.

Although moral and political development are closely related, moral development is seen as being more general, as relating to both public and private thinking concerning interpersonal issues (E. V. Sullivan, 1970). Political thinking is more specific; it relates to thinking about the relationship between individuals and public institutions. Hence it concerns the types of issues raised earlier. From the developmental perspective, however, both are related to general progressions in cognitive development, which provide the underlying basis for examining their relationship in this chapter. In this regard, an important question is the degree to which changing cognitive competencies are related to political thinking.

If the cognitive-developmental perspective on understanding of the social order is a fair approximation of reality, there should be a relationship between political thinking and moral development. This was the subject of an investigation conducted by Lonky, Reihman, and Serlin (1981). They had students in grades 8, 10, and 12 complete the Defining Issues Test (DIT; a measure of moral development) and answer questions concerning aspects of political thinking, values, and beliefs (for example, the nature of minority rights, equality of opportunity, and social welfare). Subjects were then divided into low and high groups on the basis of their answers on the DIT. Those evidencing more advanced moral thinking scored higher on all questions concerning political thinking than those with lower levels of moral development. The authors concluded that more mature and abstract political thinking was associated with higher levels of moral thinking, which in turn were associated with higher levels of cognitive development.

Other research shows a link between moral and political thinking. Conservative, liberal, and egalitarian political views correspond, respectively, to Kohlberg's last three stages of moral development (E. Simpson, 1987). Understanding the reasons for having government and laws and political organizations increases between ages 6 and 15 (Berti, 1988). This research indicates that moral and political thinking are intertwined, reflecting a common underlying basis, likely cognitive development.

In middle or late adolescence, political views take on a different and more mature tone. Older adolescents view political agencies as existing to protect the rights of people. Political and social problems can be solved by the mutual cooperation of individuals and social institutions. Perhaps most importantly, older adolescents have cognitive capabilities that allow them to think of the ramifications and implications of various kinds of decisions; they can see beyond the immediate consequences of social rules. Older adolescents demonstrate a reasoned and rational view of the development, nature, and function of existing political systems. Notions such as political compromise (Berti, 1988; Furth & McConville, 1981), the rights of the individual, the rights of the community, and the guarantees that political systems owe to individuals become important criteria for making political and social decisions. By 15 to 18 years of age, adolescent political views are representative of those in the adult world. It seems it is no accident that 18 years of age represents the lower limit for voting rights. It is at this time that the individual's political thinking has matured in terms of realizing both short-term as well as long-term consequences of decisions, and can take into account the variety of circumstances that might legitimately influence, and be affected by, a given political decision.

An example from the research of Adelson (1971) illustrates these changes. The ingeniously devised cross-cultural research asked adolescents in the United States, England, and West Germany to set up a political and legal system for an imaginary group of 1,000 people who ventured to an island in the Pacific. This approach avoided contamination of differing existing political systems. The responses of the adolescents were scored for views about the purpose of government, the utility of law, and the emergence of political entities such as political parties and offices. Views about the nature of justice and crime, individual and community rights and freedom, and the function of politicians and political entities were also examined.

Twelve-year-old adolescents viewed laws as ways to prevent people from engaging in illegal activities, a form of circular argument relating to punishment-obedience (if you are disobedient you get punished; if you got punished you must have been disobedient). The older adolescents viewed laws as ways to enforce the rights of the individual within the social order. Younger adolescents viewed fear of punishment as a primary motive for obeying the law. As you might expect from our discussion of Kohlberg's notions about the development of morality, the younger adolescents viewed situations or individuals as either right or wrong, good or bad. The older adolescents, however, were more likely to recommend remediation rather than punishment for lawbreakers. In addition, older adolescents understood the relativity of laws to particular times and circumstances. In this sense, they viewed laws as being made by people for the good of people.

The emergence of political ideology parallels closely both Piaget's stages of cognitive development (see Chapter 4) and Kohlberg's notions of reciprocity of justice and contracts. As such, the development of political thinking represents another aspect of applied moral thinking.

SUMMARY

Early writing concerning morality was left to the philosophers, who developed three general perspectives. The doctrine of original sin led to the current psycho-analytic view, the doctrine of innate purity was the precursor of the cognitive-developmental perspective, and the tabula rasa (blank slate) notion was the basis for the learning-theory view of moral development.

The focus of the psychodynamic theorists is on the development of the superego, which is viewed as the internalization of societal standards of right and wrong. From this perspective, one develops a moral "character" through identification with the same-sex parent. Social-learning theorists focus on moral behavior, which they view as resulting from both imitation and direct training. This perspective has led to considerable research on the importance of child-rearing practices and the importance of models in the development of morality. The cognitive-developmental perspective, in which it is assumed morality develops in a sequence of stages that are universal, is focused on moral judgments as opposed to moral behavior. As a result, the research emphasis is on the relationship between cognitive development and moral thinking. With increases in cognitive development, moral decision making becomes less concrete and self-centered and indicates an increased understanding of the individual living in a social system in which moral concerns are resolved in ways deemed appropriate for the common good.

Each perspective has something to contribute to our understanding of moral development during the adolescent years, a critical time for transitions in moral behavior and judgment. Moral behavior is impacted by a variety of factors, including major socializing agents and cognitive development. To predict moral behavior requires information gleaned from all three perspectives. In this regard, social perspective taking seems to be an important factor. Cognitive development is related to an increasingly abstract view of the nature of social interactions, including the reasons for behaving in ways consistent with what is considered the best for the common good. These changes in social perspective taking are related to changes in moral thinking.

One concern in the study of moral thinking has centered on the bases used to measure it. Kohlberg's scheme rests heavily on the view that morality reflects issues of law, contracts, and the view of individual rights. Gilligan has proposed an alternative based on a caring perspective. From this view, which may be more prominent for females, concern for others is at the core of moral judgments. A second concern has centered on the role of the school system in promoting moral development. The various curricula developed for moral education have not yet been shown to impact in a long-term way on adolescents' moral behavior. A third emphasis is centered on the role of the media—TV, music, video games—in moral development. In this regard, it is unclear whether those who are more violent are more prone to engage in more violent media, or if violent media make one more violent.

Moral development is related in a general way to other realms of development such as religious and political thinking. As adolescents mature, their religious and political views become more personalized. They develop new views of the social order and social institutions that shape their views of religion and politics. Religious views become more abstract, as do perspectives of what a religious person is. Attendance at religious services declines, doubting of religious doctrine increases, and the role of religion becomes more personalized with development through the adolescent years.

A similar phenomenon occurs with respect to political thinking. Unlike children, adolescents have more mature views of the reasons for laws, come to understand that the rights of the individual must be viewed within the context of the larger community, and begin to understand the complex interplay between political institutions and the individual.

Developments in these latter two realms, as in moral thinking generally, rest on advances in cognitive functioning. As the adolescent develops formal operational skills, he or she comes to view aspects of the social order in a more mature adultlike fashion. Wrestling with both personal and social issues represents a maturing process adolescents experience as they grow into adulthood.

GLOSSARY

doctrine of innate purity: Notion that the child is basically moral and pure and society is a corrupting influence.

doctrine of original sin: Notion that parental intervention is necessary in order to save the child's moral soul.

guilt: Internal feeling that one experiences when breaking a rule or doing something one should not do.

induction discipline: Form of discipline involving explaining why a behavior was wrong and suggesting alternative ways to behave.

love withdrawal discipline: Form of discipline that uses ignoring and expressing displeasure to punish.

moral behavior: Those behaviors that are consistent with rules of morality.

morality: The rules that guide social and interpersonal behavior.

moral judgment: An individual's judgment of why some behavior should or should not be done.

power-assertive discipline: Form of discipline that involves physical punishment, or the threat of it, and the withdrawal of privileges to punish the adolescent.

tabula rasa: Concept that the child is born neither innately pure nor innately corrupt and is a product of environmental influence.

values: Ideals and moral beliefs one holds about the proper way to behave.

DISCUSSION QUESTIONS

1. Freud argued that morality is obtained by identification with the same-sex parent. What did Freud mean by identification? How does it take place?

2. In what ways are the psychoanalytic and social-learning theories of moral development alike? In what ways are they different?

3. Which type of parental disciplinary technique seems best for rearing adolescents? Why?

4. What is the most recent moral judgment you had to make? How did you resolve it? On what basis did you make your decision?

5. How might adolescents in various stages of moral development reason about the moral dilemma of whether or not premarital sex is appropriate?

6. How do most adolescents acquire their religious and political affiliations? Why?

7. Are there some values that are so central to our society everyone should hold them? What are they?

8. How are religious and political views similar? How are they different?

6

Self-Concept, Self-Esteem, and Identity

Major Issues Addressed

The Distinction Between Self-Concept, Self-Esteem, and Identity
Parental Influences on the Development of Self-Views
Developmental Changes in Self-Views
The Role of Possible Selves
Social Class and Self-Views
Delinquency and Self-Esteem
Ethnic Influences on Self-Views
The Self and Psychological Adjustment
Gender Differences in Identity Development
Identity Development in Biracial Adolescents

He came home from school in a "funny" mood that day. He was about 13 and had seemed moody for a few weeks. He would not talk about it, but I knew something was bothering him. After some small talk about school, he announced, "I'm no longer David, I'm Dave. That's how I want to be known!" He was redefining himself—or perhaps really defining himself for the first time in ways important for the long term.

I then understood his moodiness, or at least part of it. He was changing physically and mentally, and these changes led to his reconsidering who he was.

During adolescence we undergo a redefinition of self as we attempt to understand who and what we are. We begin to define ourselves in new and different ways. In this chapter we explore the development of self-views and why adolescence is a time of self-redefinition.

INTRODUCTION

Perhaps no other psychological construct has received the theoretical and empirical attention that has been directed toward the self. Over 100 years ago, William James (1890) devoted an entire chapter of his *Principles of Psychology* to a description of the development of views of the self. Since that time, thousands of articles in the scientific literature and in the popular press have been devoted to issues concerning the self.

Major concerns have centered on issues related to the development of self-views, how self-views change as we mature, how we acquire concepts of self, and important influences on self-development. More than any other single aspect of adolescent development, the self-concept, and related constructs such as self-esteem and identity, have been topics of study. No doubt this attention is in large part a result of Erik Erikson's (1959, 1963, 1968) view of adolescence as a time when the individual faces a crisis (a period of questioning and exploration) with regard to self-development. Peter Blos (1979) also contributed substantially to our understanding of identity. Among his many contributions was the notion that the adolescent must separate the self from the parents in order to develop a mature ego. As Adams (1992) has noted, these two psychoanalytic theorists pointed the way for much of the research that has been done on identity, specifically, and other self-views more generally.

SELF-CONCEPT, SELF-ESTEEM, AND IDENTITY

There are nearly as many different definitions of the self as there are individuals who have studied it. For William James (1890) the self was simply an object like any other—the self was whatever the individual felt belonged to the self, including the material self and the social self. James's *material self* referred to the individual's possessions, including the body. He referred to this as the "Me" aspect of the self. James's *social self* was concerned with the views the individual felt others held about that person. This aspect of the self he referred to as the "I" self. There was also an affective component associated with the self, the individual's evaluation of the self.

Others (for example, Cooley, 1902; G.H. Mead, 1934) have defined the self as that meant by the pronouns *I, me,* and *mine.* From this perspective, the self is all those feelings the individual has about the self. These feelings arise and develop from social interactions with others and from concerns about how others view us. By learning to view the self as others do, we learn to predict how others will react to us; the self comes to regulate our behavior, especially our social behavior.

Defining the Multiple Self-Views

Current-day psychologists believe there are multiple selves (Box 6-1). **Self-concept** may be defined as the *ways* in which we view ourselves, the *dimensions* along which we describe our self. In this sense, it contains perspectives of our physical self, ourself in various roles such as son or daughter, friend, relative, and other dimensions that are important to us, such as our academic or athletic self.

Self-esteem is our evaluation of our self. Global self-esteem is our overall evaluation of our self, how we generally feel about our self. Each of our specific self-concepts also has an associated self-esteem. For example, you have an academic self-concept and an academic self-esteem: good, average, or poor student. It now is generally accepted that there is more than one self-concept and more than one self-esteem (e.g., Harter, 1989; Wylie, 1979). Although it is possible to measure global self-concept—your general view of yourself—researchers have found it more productive to view self-concept as multifaceted. Hence they study

---

BOX 6–1   Conceptualizing the Self

Psychologists have identified a number of different means by which people characterize the self. As an exercise to illustrate these different self-views, follow these directions:

1. Take a sheet of paper and number the rows from 1 to 20. For each row complete the sentence "I am _____."
2. Go back and read each statement. Using the following rating scale, write down a number indicating how you *generally* feel about the statement: 1 = Very Bad, 2 = Bad, 3 = OK, neither bad nor good, 4 = Good, 5 = Very Good.
3. Using the same scale, read each statement again and write down a number indicating how you feel about it *right now*.
4. On another sheet of paper, write a brief statement about your basic values and beliefs, those characteristics you feel are basic to you.
5. Write a brief paragraph about what you very much wish to become, and another about what you very much fear becoming, or wish to avoid becoming.

The 20 statements you used to complete the sentence "I am _____" represent your self-concept. The self-concept is measured by the ways in which we view the self. If you examine your statements, you probably will find you can group them into several dimensions, such as physical characteristics, academic performance, and social roles. And you no doubt will find that some of your statements are very concrete (age, physical descriptions, gender) whereas others are quite abstract (good friend, athletic). Changes in self-concept from childhood to adolescence reflect continuities

(sameness) and discontinuities (changes) in the ways along which we view the self.

The use of the rating scale to make evaluations about the self-concept is a measure of self-esteem. Self-esteem refers to how you feel about your self, both in general (baseline self-esteem) and at any given moment in time (barometric self-esteem). As we note in the text, baseline self-esteem is relatively stable (unchanging) across the adolescent years; barometric self-esteem is subject to moment-to-moment fluctuations (instability).

The paragraph you wrote about your values and beliefs reflects your identity. Your identity guides and directs your behavior.

The last two paragraphs you wrote represent your *possible selves*. In each instance, the possible self represents a cognitive appraisal of a potential self. By striving to become a particular possible self, we influence our own future development (Markus & Nurius, 1986). For example, aspiring to a given vocation may cause you to study more diligently and work harder to achieve that goal.

Each form of self-assessment allows important information about how people view the self and provides a unique way for us to examine how self-views change as we pass from childhood through adolescence and into adulthood. The self-concept allows qualitative measures of change (continuity vs. discontinuity) and the self-esteem quantitative measures (stability vs. instability). The identity allows us to determine how values change as we adopt new social roles.

---

social or academic self-concept, or even mathematic and verbal self-concept as components of academic self-concept (Marsh, Byrne, & Shavelson, 1988).

Identity refers to the values, beliefs, and ideals that direct our behavior (Dusek et al., 1986; Erikson, 1959, 1963; Grotevant, 1986, 1987, 1992; Marcia, 1980). It is a self-developed, internal, and ever-changing organization of our attitudes and beliefs. It helps us identify our strengths and weaknesses, and our uniqueness as well as similarity to others. Identity provides a sense of continuity (sameness) of the self over time and a sense of integration of the self.

Identity development reflects a life-span process of exploration (Dusek, 1987a; Grotevant, 1987, 1992), and it undergoes continual changes as we encounter new and different roles, such as worker, spouse, parent, and retiree. With each new role we explore our identity further and make adjustments dependent on the new role. Think about your freshman year at college. You were in a new environment, living with a group of strangers, and perhaps away from home for an extended period of time for the first time. You also were playing a number of new roles. How did this substantial change in your environment affect how you viewed yourself? Was your self-confidence changed? Did you feel as socially adept as when you left home? After your first few tests and papers, did you feel you needed to adjust your view of yourself as a student? No doubt some aspects of your identity changed. Identity exists within a context that includes not only the external environment with its demands and expectations but also one's personal characteristics such as general psychological adjustment (A.S. Waterman, 1992).

Until quite recently the notion that identity development involved making a choice was generally accepted. Hence one may choose a vocation, the role religion will play in one's life, and one's political affiliation. Current researchers have criticized this perspective, noting that identity also involves characteristics over which we have no choice: gender (Archer, 1992; Patterson, Sochting, & Marcia, 1992); ethnic background (Phinney & Rosenthal, 1992; Phinney, Devich-Navarro, DuPont, & Estrada, 1994); and being adopted (Grotevant, 1992). These *assigned* characteristics influence the nature of identity formation and are critical to it, perhaps by placing constraints—real or imagined—on the choices the individual feels may be made. Sexism and racism in the workplace may cause one to limit occupational choices, potentially making one's assigned aspects of identity limit consideration of choices for a vocation.

Although identity continually changes across the life span (Grotevant, 1992), psychologists have emphasized identity development during adolescence because it is the first time the individual has the cognitive skills to address identity questions meaningfully. Adolescents' formal operational thinking skills allow them to understand they can be different and can choose the kind of person they wish to be (they can see the possible as well as the real, what they could be as well as what they are). Hence adolescence is when we first seriously begin to deal with questions such as "Who am I?", "What will I become?", and "How do I wish to be?"

Self-Views as Self-Understanding

Self-understanding refers to how we come to know the self and how that knowledge changes with development. By examining the particular attributes (contents) used to describe the self, Damon and Hart (1988) proposed four levels of self-descriptions, each level reflecting differing understandings of the self and being incorporated into the next level. Earlier views of the self are not lost, but they wane in importance. In early childhood (level 1), the self is conceived as a group of separate categories and is described by reference to momentary emotional states, preferences, and physical descriptions. There is no particular sense of integration of the various aspects of the self. In middle to late childhood (level 2), the self is defined in relation to others and with regard to normative standards. At this level, for example, children may describe their skills as being better than, or not as good as, those of their friends. We see the beginnings of viewing the self in social contexts. Level 3 (early adolescence) descriptions reflect the emerging importance placed on social interactions and contexts, as adolescents come to understand they live in a highly social world. There is a preponderance of self-descriptions reflecting self-appeal and characteristics that are important in social interactions. During late adolescence (level 4), the self is described in terms of a system of beliefs, moral standards, and a philosophy of life. This level reflects the late adolescent's understanding of the self in a social order, or social system (society), consisting of mutually accepted and agreed on codes of conduct.

Self-Understanding and Cognitive Development

Thus the development of self-descriptions is influenced by emerging cognitive competencies. Harter (1986, 1989) summarized the relation between self-views and Piaget's theory of cognitive development. The preoperational child's self-descriptions refer largely to the child's immediate experience (e.g., physical characteristics, likes and dislikes, possessions). Young children cannot make reference to inner psychological states because their thinking skills are bound to observable and often momentary events. Hence the self is described in similar terms.

The emergence of concrete thinking skills allows the child to group individual modes of behaving (e.g., liking sports, being strong, and being able to run fast) into higher order generalizations, or traits (e.g., athletic). During middle childhood, then, trait descriptions of the self emerge.

Formal operational thinking allows the individual to consider the possible as well as the real, and to understand the unobservable as well as the observable. By mid to late adolescence the individual is able to think abstractly about the self, including the psychological, or inner, self, and the individual can integrate trait labels into higher order descriptions that are more abstract and further removed from specific behaviors. For example, the traits *likable, outgoing, concerned about others,* and *enjoys doing things for others* might be grouped into the much more abstract category of *friendly.* On the one hand, abstract trait descriptions allow us to conceive of the self in new and important ways. On the other hand, abstract trait descriptions are more open to distortion and may be less realistic (Harter, 1986, 1989). During adolescence one might see the self in very different ways than others do.

Self-descriptions and self-understanding are clearly related to cognitive skills. Changes in these skills allow us to view the self in new and different ways. Indeed, it is very tempting to suggest that we experience an Eriksonian-like self-crisis during adolescence simply because we are able to do so: Abstract thinking allows us to see the possible as well as the real; we are able to view what we might be as well as what we are. This can result in confusion, a crisis, because we begin to understand we have choices and can be many things. As we have new experiences and make choices we slowly develop a more firm self and the crisis subsides.

DEVELOPMENTAL TRENDS IN SELF-CONCEPT, SELF-ESTEEM, AND IDENTITY

Describing developmental trends in the various self-views has been a major concern of researchers. In part, this emphasis stems from theoretical concerns, as we describe next. But the concerns are also of a more practical nature, because self-views are related to many other aspects of the adolescent's life, such as school performance, psychological adjustment, and social relations.

Theoretical Underpinnings

A number of psychologists have suggested that self-views undergo significant change during the adolescent years. For Erikson, this aspect of development was represented by the identity versus identity diffusion crisis. For Anna Freud (1948, 1958), it was represented by a recurrence of the Oedipal situation following the latency period. However conceptualized, the general perspective is that adolescence represents a time when our views of the self change substantially.

The physical changes of the growth spurt years are suggested as one cause of changes in self-views. Because our bodies change physically, we are forced to reevaluate our "self." Our cognitive competencies change too, causing us to evaluate ourselves differently. Changes in peer relations and interactions wlth parents, increases in independence strivings, and the new roles we play also cause us to reevaluate our self.

Types of Change in Self-Views

Because there are different types of self-views, it is necessary to measure the development of self-views in multiple ways. One cannot measure changes in identity on the same metric that one uses to measure development in self-esteem. Each type of change is associated with one of the measures of self-views: qualitative change with self-concept, quantitative change with self-esteem, and stage change with identity.

Qualitative change refers to change in type or kind, not amount. When assessing changes in self-concept—the ways in which we view the self—we are assessing qualitative change. If the dimensions (ways) in which we view the self remain much the same as we mature, we can conclude that self-concept is *con-*

tinuous. If the ways in which we view the self are very different at different parts of the life cycle, we must conclude the self-concept is *discontinuous*.

Quantitative change refers to change in amount. If self-esteem for some aspect of self-concept remains relatively the same from year to year we conclude that self-esteem is *stable*. If it changes, we conclude it is *instable*. The most widely used measure of stability versus instability in self-esteem is the correlation coefficient (see appendix). High positive correlations between measures of self-esteem taken at different points in time indicate stability; low correlations indicate instability.

Studies of identity development typically have focused on whether or not individuals change in their stage of identity status (see Chapter 2). For example, does becoming identity achieved mean one never changes? What is the typical progression through the four stages of identity development?

Each type of change tells us something different about how self-views develop. Qualitative change informs us about differences in the manner in which we view the self. Quantitative change enlightens us as to how we evaluate our various aspects of self. Change in identity status allows us to relate self-views to changing life roles, such as graduating from high school or becoming a parent.

Change in Self-Concept

Studies of change in self-concept have focused on how the ways in which we view the self are different in childhood and adolescence. It is now well established that self-descriptions shift from being predominantly concrete during childhood to being predominantly abstract during later adolescence and adulthood (Montemayor & Eisen, 1977; M. Rosenberg, 1986). Children primarily describe the self with reference to physical characteristics, likes and dislikes, and possessions (Damon & Hart, 1988). Adolescents are more likely to describe the self in terms of emotions, moods, motives, and beliefs that are not always overtly observable.

A study conducted by Bernstein (1980) showed that the progression from concrete to abstract self-descriptions is a gradual process. He found that adolescents not only used more abstract means to describe the self but also were better able to justify inconsistencies in their self, for example, being willing to help one sibling with homework while not being willing to help another. He also reported that older adolescents are better able than children or younger adolescents to integrate aspects of self-descriptions into more abstract belief systems. During adolescence we develop more abstract views of the self and become able to justify apparent inconsistencies in the self.

Finally, Dusek and Flaherty (1981) administered a self-concept scale to students in grades 5 through 12 and reported that for each grade level the same four aspects of self-concept were present (see Table 6–1). Subjects were asked to read each of the bipolar adjective pairs and put a check mark on a line separating them indicating how they viewed themselves. (Try this by writing each adjective pair in Table 6–1 at the left and right end of a sheet of paper and then

Table 6–1   Adjectives Describing Each Self-Concept Factor

Achievement/ Leadership	Congeniality/Sociability	Adjustment	Sex Appropriateness of Self-Concept
confident-unsure	friendly-unfriendly	happy-sad	hard-soft
leader-follower	good-bad	healthy-sick	rugged-delicate
sharp-dull	kind-cruel	refreshed-tired	strong-weak
smart-dumb	nice-awful	relaxed-nervous	
success-failure		satisfied-dissatisfied	
superior-inferior		stable-unstable	
valuable-worthless		steady-shaky	

Source: Derived from Dusek, J. (1978). *The development of the self-concept in adolescents* (Final Report, Grant No. RO1-HD-09094). Washington, DC: National Institute of Education.

drawing a line between them; separate the line into 7 equal segments and make your check marks. You can score your views by giving the line segment nearest the positive pole—confident, friendly, happy, hard—a score of 7 and decreasing the value from 6 to 5 to 1 toward the less desirable pole—unsure, unfriendly, sad, soft. Keep in mind that the Sex Appropriateness of the Self-Concept is a measure of masculinity and femininity—there is no desirable end point—so score either end 7.)

Achievement/Leadership reflects the individual's feelings of competence and sense of being a striving, achieving person. Congeniality/Sociability reflects the person's view of the self as a sociable, outgoing, and warm person. Adjustment is viewing the self in a homeostatic balance with the environment. Sex role is the perspective of sex typing of the self. Because the same four aspects of self-concept were present at all age levels, Dusek and Flaherty concluded that self-concept is continuous across the adolescent years. No new dimensions were added.

Think about how you view yourself. You have an academic, social, and family self-concept. You have had these for a long period of time. You also have some view of your sex role. Although how you perceive these (your self esteem) may change—as we discuss next—the dimensions (ways) on which you see yourself do not change much.

Change in Self-Esteem

Because self-esteem is a quantitative measure of how one views some aspect of self-concept, self-esteem development has been measured through numerical means, such as illustrated in Box 6-1. The stability of the self-esteem (how much it stays the same or changes) is assessed by administering a self-esteem measure at different points in time and then determining if the scores are highly similar or different. The lower the difference between two scores from different testings, the more stable the self-esteem.

In general, the results of these studies indicate that self-esteem is very stable across the adolescent years. Engel (1959) reported a correlation of .78 for measures of self-esteem obtained from 172 students tested in grade 8 and again in grade 10. Similar findings have been found for high school students (R. Carlson, 1965), middle school students (McCarthy & Hoge, 1982), and college students (Constantinople, 1969). Dusek and Flaherty (1981) reported correlations for four measures of self-esteem (see Table 6–1) for 330 students in grades 5 through 10 tested each year for 3 years. The correlations indicated a moderate to high degree of stability in self-esteem across the adolescent years. In a 2 1/2-year longitudinal study of approximately 2,400 Norwegian students, Alsaker and Olweus (1992) reported that for intervals of up to 1 year stability correlations were high, but that for longer time intervals the magnitude of the correlations decreased substantially.

The most extensive studies of self-esteem development have been conducted by Bachman and his associates (Bachman & O'Malley, 1977, 1986; O'Malley & Bachman, 1983). These studies are exceptional because of the large sample sizes and the testing of individuals after they left school.

O'Malley and Bachman (1983) have summarized the data from their own large-scale study and data from five other investigations. Although their analyses indicate small and consistent increases in self-esteem across the age range from 13 to 23 years, they suggest that self-esteem is best viewed as stable—the changes are not very large.

Contrary to the suggestions of a number of theorists, then, there is no evidence to indicate an upheaval or drastic change in self-esteem during the adolescent years. As Dusek and Flaherty (1981) indicated, the person who enters adolescence is virtually the same as the person who emerges from it in terms of self-esteem. We can expect adolescents' self-esteem to change to a degree, but they will not become different people during the adolescent years.

A word of caution is in order. The data reported here are for groups of adolescents. That is, change was assessed not for individuals, but for groups of adolescents of the same age. It may well be that some individual adolescents undergo significant and dramatic change—upward or downward—in self-esteem during the course of the adolescent years.

The issue of *individual* change in self-esteem was the focus of a study by Block and Robins (1993). They examined self-esteem in a group of 44 males and 47 females tested in the freshman and senior years of high school and 5 years after graduation (about age 23). As in the research we reported earlier, they found that self-esteem *for the group* was highly stable across the high school years and into young adulthood. In this consistency they also found very substantial change. About a third of the males and nearly 60% of the females decreased in self-esteem across the 9-year period, the remainder increasing.

The finding of relative stability of self-esteem during adolescence may seem at odds with your own experiences. No doubt, you have at one time or another felt either highly pleased or displeased with yourself; your view of yourself changed, perhaps dramatically and substantially. To reconcile these common experiences with the conclusions from the research cited here, we draw on M. Rosenberg's (1986) notion that there are two types of self-esteem (see Box 6–1).

Barometric self-esteem reflects the fact that self-esteem is subject to 154 moment-to-moment fluctuations, which may occur rapidly. For example, if you receive a poor test grade you may feel bad and your academic self-esteem may be lowered. However, after some time, your academic self-esteem will increase to its former level. What you have experienced is an alteration of your barometric self-esteem. M. Rosenberg (1986) has suggested that early adolescence is a time of increased volatility of the barometric self-esteem, which may account for the commonsense perspective that adolescence is a time of rapid fluctuations in self-perceptions and is a time of confusion.

Baseline self-esteem is not subject to moment-to-moment fluctuations. It is stable over time and is not influenced by immediate experiences. Hence if you receive a poor test score your baseline self-esteem will not be affected very much if at all. Indeed, your barometric self-esteem will recover to its former level in part because your baseline self-esteem is at odds with the momentary experience and will help you reassess it. You know you are a better student than your poor score shows you to be, and the reason you know that is partly due to your baseline academic self-esteem. Can the baseline self-esteem change?

Barometric self-esteem fluctuates as we have elating or unhappy experiences. Our baseline self-esteem allows our barometric self-esteem to come back to a typical level. (*Left: Michael Newman/Photo Edit. Right: Tony Freeman/Photo Edit.*)

Of course. Some students who enter college do poorly over extended periods of time and their academic baseline self-esteem declines. A student athlete who stars on her high school basketball team but cannot compete as successfully at the college level may experience a lowering of her athletic baseline self-esteem. Changes for the better also can occur, as in the student who had a mediocre academic record in high school but excelled at college.

The longitudinal studies of self-esteem stability assessed baseline self-esteem. The general stability of baseline self-esteem is a result of the stability of its determinants. Parental child-rearing practices, overall school performance, and social interactions with peers—all of which are important to baseline self-esteem development—are unlikely to fluctuate widely or rapidly. Hence it is not surprising that baseline self-esteem remains relatively stable for most adolescents.

Change in Identity

According to Erikson (see Chapter 2), the major crisis adolescents face is identity versus identity diffusion. Optimal solution of this crisis is an important precursor to entering the adulthood years and their crises. Successful resolution of this crisis allows the individual to face the intimacy versus isolation crisis of the early adulthood years in good stead (see Box 6–2), making the study of how **identity status** develops and changes over time important not only to understanding adolescence but also adulthood.

It may be helpful to our discussion to use an analogy to identity status development, namely, your choice of an academic major. Those who have selected a major and begun studies to meet the requirements of that major are similar to those who are identity achieved. They have given thought to what they wish to do, have taken courses and spoken with others about their choice. They have faced a period of questioning, which is akin to what Erikson calls a crisis. Those who are deciding are collecting information, weighing alternatives, taking courses, and making choices. They are similar to those in the moratorium stage. Those who have not yet begun to think about their major are similar to the identity diffuse individual. Finally, those who are majoring in a program of study someone else wants them to follow—I want to study music but my parents want me to go into business—are acting in a foreclosed manner. Just as any of us might change our mind about a major (the author was going to be a high school mathematics teacher until he took introductory psychology), we might change some values related to identity. To keep to our analogy, many of you will have selected a major (identity achievement) and then found it was not what you expected or wanted, resulting in your reconsidering what your major should be (moratorium). You changed "stages" of the process of deciding on a major. The same occurs in identity development.

Marcia (1976) reported longitudinal data of identity development in 30 males he first tested as college students in 1966 (Marcia, 1966). Forty-seven percent changed identity status over the 6-year time span between testings. Only 3

BOX 6–2   Identity as Preparation for Intimacy

According to Erikson (e.g., 1963), the initial crisis of adulthood is intimacy versus isolation. By intimacy Erikson meant acquiring the ability to commit oneself to intimate relationships with others. His emphasis was not so much on physical intimacy as it was on psychological intimacy—revealing the true self, including one's aspirations, fears, and most deep feelings, to others. Isolation is evidenced by an alienation of oneself from others, perhaps by harming those people who encroach on one's tenuous relations with others.

In order to establish intimate relations with others, one must first know who and what one is. This is why Erikson notes that the identity crisis occurs prior to the intimacy versus isolation crisis. If order to reveal the inner self to others, one must know what that inner self is and have self-acceptance. How could others accept you if you do not know who you are and accept yourself? Those who have not resolved the identity crisis within the optimal range have trouble developing intimate relationships, for they continually fear they will reveal they have no firm sense of self. Although these adolescents may exhibit socially approved behaviors consistent with a sense of identity, they cannot develop intimate relations involving revealing the true inner self (Dyke & Adams, 1987). Josselson (1988) goes so far as to suggest that for females the concept of self including relations to others may be critical to identity development.

Some research has focused on the sequentiality of the identity and intimacy crises. Orlofsky, Marcia, and Lesser (1973) developed an intimacy status interview and identified five intimacy statuses. *Isolates* have few relationships and none are intimate. *Stereotyped* individuals have friends but the relationships are superficial and tend to be self-serving. *Pseudointimates* appear to be committed to a single heterosexual relationship, but it does not involve genuine openness and mutuality of expression of feelings. *Preintimates* have a few truly intimate relationships involving openness and reciprocal acceptance but they are not committed to long-term relationships. *Intimates* are self-aware and relate to others in open and reciprocal relationships of some length. These relationships are mutually satisfying, not self-serving.

Research (e.g., Marcia, 1976; Orlofsky et al., 1973) has shown that those in the intimate group were identity achieved. Preintimates were in the moratorium identity category—although they had not yet completed their identity formation they had progressed sufficiently to be able to develop some intimate friends. Those in the stereotyped and pseudointimate groups evidenced a foreclosed identity. Having adopted an identity that satisfies others they were unable to develop intimate relationships. Isolates were identity diffuse. These findings indicated a correspondence between identity development and the formation of intimate friendships such that with increasing resolution of the identity crisis there was an increase in intimate relationships with peers (Kacerguis & Adams, 1980).

Females generally score higher in intimacy than do males, perhaps because of differences in resolution of the identity crisis (Hodgson & Fischer, 1979; Josselson, 1988). These researchers note that for females an important aspect of the identity crisis involves the interpersonal realm, whereas for males issues concerning competence and vocational concerns predominate. The gender differences in intimacy may result from the fact that interpersonal concerns are more closely linked than vocational issues to intimate relationships.

Findings such as those reported here support Erikson's theorizing of the relationship between identity and intimacy and show the importance of the crises faced by adolescents as they prepare for adulthood. In this sense, then, adolescence clearly is a transition to adulthood.

of the 16 subjects in the foreclosure and identity diffusion statuses changed to a higher status; 8 of the 14 identity achiever and moratorium subjects moved to a lower status. Marcia suggests that achieving an identity during the college years may not result in continued identity achievement, but that not having achieved an identity during the college years is predictive of not having achieved one 6 years later.

Although Marcia studied only males, Adams and Fitch (1982) reported changes in identity statuses for both male and female freshman, sophomore, and junior college students over a 1-year period. They found that the patterns of change in identity status were very similar for both genders, but that males had a more accelerated rate of growth—they changed earlier than the females. This is an important finding in light of the suggestion (Marcia, 1980) that Erikson's theorizing may be a more appropriate description of male than female identity development (Box 6-3).

One of the more extensive studies of identity development across the adolescent years was conducted by Archer (1982). Twenty males and 20 females at each of the grades 6, 8, 10, and 12 completed a modified version of Marcia's (1966) identity status interview. Archer noted that the identity diffusion and foreclosure statuses were relatively developmentally immature, in the former case, because the individual has not made a commitment to an identity and is not in the process of making one, and in the latter case, because the commitment to an identity is premature and made without appropriate exploration. She further suggested that the moratorium and identity achiever statuses were developmentally mature. Moratorium individuals are looking to make a commitment, obtaining information about possible choices, and selecting among choices. The identity achiever status is developmentally mature because these individuals have experienced a crisis and have made a commitment to an identity. Archer expected to find an increase in the proportion of students in the more developmentally advanced statuses with increases in grade level.

The results were generally in line with the predictions. With increasing grade level, there were increases in achiever status. More of the older adolescents than younger adolescents were in the more developmentally mature identity statuses. However, the developmentally mature statuses accounted for relatively few individuals. Those in the moratorium and identity achiever status groups accounted for only 11% of the 6th graders, 13% of the 8th and 10th graders, and 19% of the 12th graders. During the early to mid adolescent years, identity status is best characterized as developmentally immature. Apparently, a mature identity develops during the very late adolescent and early adulthood years. Some evidence in support of this suggestion comes from Meilman (1979), who studied 25 males each at ages 12, 15, 18, 21, and 24. He reported increases in achiever status and decreases in the diffusion and foreclosure statuses with increases in age. The transition to achiever status occurred mostly in the 18- to 24-year-old age range.

The considerable body of research on identity development during the college years, which cover the 18- to 24-year-old age range, bears directly on this

BOX 6–3   Gender and Identity Development

Much has been written about gender differences in identity development during the late adolescent and early adulthood years. Theoretical advances in the areas of identity development (Adams & Jones, 1983; Archer, 1992; Grotevant & Thornbecke, 1982; Marcia, 1980; S. J. Patterson et al., 1992; A. S. Waterman, 1982) and sex-role acquisition related to identity development (Hodgson & Fischer, 1979; A. S. Waterman, 1982) have fueled these concerns. In general, these researchers note that the traditional masculine and feminine sex roles have different emphases, with the masculine role stressing more heavily the instrumentality and achievement (vocational choice) associated in Erikson's theory with the formation of an identity.

Some impetus for investigating the possibility of gender differences in identity achievement also comes from methodological concerns (Grotevant & Thornbecke, 1982; Marcia, 1980; A. S. Waterman, 1982). One criticism is aimed directly at Marcia's (1966) instrument for measuring identity status, which was developed with men. It is noted that the interview assesses crisis and commitment in occupational, political, and religious areas, and that especially the first may be more related to the traditional masculine sex role. Some evidence (Grotevant & Thornbecke, 1982; Kacerguis & Adams, 1980) indicates that occupational identity achievement may be more central to successful resolution of the identity crisis. As a result, males may be more likely than females to appear identity achieved on the identity status interview. These criticisms have resulted in an expansion of Marcia's interview by including assessment of crisis and commitment in areas central to the traditional female sex role (S. J. Patterson et al., 1992). Grotevant and his co-workers (Grotevant & Thornbecke, 1982; Grotevant, Thornbecke, & Meyer, 1982) have assessed identity development not only in the occupational, political, and religious realms but also in the domains of dating, friendship, and sex roles in an attempt to develop an instrument that is more appropriate for assessing female identity development.

A. S. Waterman (1982) and S. J. Patterson et al. (1992) have reviewed the research findings on sex differences in identity status. The general conclusion is that sex differences are relatively rare; males and females evidence similar patterns of identity development in the various interview topic areas. However, the identity statuses may have different psychological implications for males and females. Specifically, for both males and females the identity achiever status reflects good adjustment and the identity diffusion status indicates poor adjustment. Moratorium status males appear like identity-achieved males and show better adjustment than males in the foreclosure and diffusion statuses. For females, the distinctions between the various identity status groups are not as clear; in some instances, identity achievers and moratoriums are similar and in some instances identity achievers and foreclosures are similar.

Although both males and females traverse the identity crisis in a similar fashion, it may be that the areas assessed have differential importance to males and females. S. J. Patterson et al. (1992) note that the most recent research indicates occupational concerns are of equal importance to males and females, but that interpersonal concerns (sexuality, sex roles) and a balancing of career and marriage plans were more important issues for females.

It is important, in this regard, to consider identity development in a historical context. Although it may be true that a generation or so ago female identity development might have been properly linked to intimacy issues because of the stereotype of the traditional female sex role (S. J. Patterson et al., 1992), that may be much less the case now. Changes in sex roles and what society considers appropriate, particularly career orientations for females, seem to have made vocational identity development more similar than different for contemporary males and females. As we have stressed throughout the text, development takes place within a social context, and as that context changes so, too, do various aspects of development. Nonetheless, the stronger concern of females with balancing both career and interpersonal (marriage) concerns means they face a more complex task in forming an identity than do males (S. J. Patterson et al., 1992).

Considerations such as these have led Josselson (1988) to suggest that for women identity involves not only the processes of exploring alternatives and then making a commitment but also a process of "connectedness." For women, identity involves a concern for relatedness to others and for interpersonal relationships to a larger degree than it does for males.

point (Montemayor, Brown, & Adams, 1985; A. S. Waterman, Geary, & Waterman, 1974; A. S. Waterman & Goldman, 1976; A. S. Waterman & Waterman, 1971). The general procedure in these studies was to have the students complete the identity status interview in the beginning of their freshman year and then at some later point, such as the end of the freshman year or the end of the senior year. Identity statuses were determined for the areas of occupation, religion, and politics in accord with Marcia's formulation. As one might expect on the basis of the vocational emphasis of college and of college students, there was an increase in identity achievers for the vocational area. Although there was some evidence of an increase in identity achievers in the political area, there was no evidence of an increase in identity achievers in the religious area. Hence it appears that college attendance does influence identity in the vocational area. Change in the ideological areas, namely religion and politics, however, occurs later, perhaps because the experiences—marriage, child rearing—needed to solidify an identity do not occur until the young adulthood years.

Adams and Fitch (1982) suggest the college atmosphere presents the individual with a milieu that prompts identity crises. Hence it is reasonable to expect that some who are identity achieved will change during the course of their college years to a moratorium status. Moreover, it is very possible that identity achievement during the college years is in some ways specific to the peculiar environment of college life. College students eat with, attend class with, socialize with, and live with many others their own age. Contact with adults outside the classroom, or with those younger, is rare in college life. Upon entering the noncollege world, the young adult may well demonstrate some regression in identity status as a reconceptualization of identity within the noncollege atmosphere occurs. Some evidence (Munro & Adams, 1977) indicates that at the same age more noncollege than college youths are identity achieved. Such evidence is consistent with the notion that identity continually develops (Erikson, 1963),

Some argue that attending college promotes the development of a "college student" identity. When students leave college they likely will change their identity status. (*University of California*)

perhaps changing with different contextual (role) demands (Grotevant, 1992). We should expect the regression reported by Marcia (1976) for identity-achieved college students because of the substantial change in life contexts when college is completed.

Several conclusions may be derived from the research about changes in identity development. First, adolescence is a time of relatively immature identity development; few adolescents are identity achieved. Second, attending college seems to promote a type of identity achievement perhaps best labeled as "college student." Finally, once identity-achieved status has been reached it does not mean identity never changes. It is best to view identity development as a continuous process of achievement, loss, and reachievement as we take on new roles, such as worker, spouse, parent, or retiree. Each new major role requires that we rethink our identity—face a new crisis—and come to a new resolution of identity issues.

As we have seen here, self-views change, albeit not dramatically or in a manner consistent with Hall's view that adolescence is a time of storm and stress. The changes, quantitative (self-esteem), qualitative (self-concept), and in identity statuses, are gradual and reflect the changing circumstances encountered as development progresses. We turn next to some of the major influences on the development of self-views.

INFLUENCES ON THE DEVELOPMENT
OF SELF-VIEWS

We all grow up in a family and are subject to the rearing influences of our parents or parent and the family structure—single parent or two parent, large or small. We come from a particular social and economic background that influences the opportunities we have, where we grow up, the schools we attend. We belong to an ethnic group, physically mature, attend school, and live in a social environment. All these circumstances influence our self-views.

Parental Influences

One of the earliest studies of the impact of parental rearing practices on the development of self-views was done by Coopersmith (1967), who studied self-esteem in fifth- and sixth-grade boys. High-self-esteem boys were reared by parents who were highly accepting and warm, and who provided a home atmosphere that was understanding and tolerant. There were clear rules and definite limits for acceptable behavior, and when the adolescent was punished the punishment was appropriate but not harsh. The home atmosphere was one of mutual respect; when disagreements between parent and adolescent occurred they were occasions for mutual growth and understanding, not situations that resulted in hostility. In contrast, low-self-esteem boys were reared by parents who were too permissive—some to the point of being neglecting—or who were very harsh in their discipline.

Litovsky and Dusek (1985) reported similar findings for junior high school (grades 7–9) males and females. Those who had higher self-esteem viewed their parents as more warm and accepting, as being low in the use of guilt and intrusiveness, and as being fair in rule making and enforcement.

Recently, researchers have begun to focus efforts on understanding the role of parental rearing in self-esteem development of minority adolescents. Leiderman, Meldman, and Ritter (1989) studied relations between child-rearing practices and self-esteem in African American, Asian, and Hispanic adolescents. Regardless of ethnic group membership, those with higher self-esteem had parents who were more warm, accepting, and understanding of their adolescents. The fact that African American adolescents' self-esteem is comparable to that of adolescents in the other ethnic groups may seem surprising, given the racism and general disadvantages experienced by most African American adolescents (Harter, 1990). However, the research shows that parents, African American, Asian, Hispanic, or White, who employ positive rearing practices will rear adolescents who have high self-esteem (Felson & Zielinski, 1989). They teach their adolescents to value themselves, allow them to learn their competencies, and provide a home atmosphere that is supportive and conducive to personal growth.

Parental rearing practices also are related to identity development (Adams & Jones, 1983; Litovsky & Dusek, 1988; Williams, 1993). Adolescents who say their parents encourage their freedom, do not use guilt to a high degree, and who are not too controlling and regulating have a more well-developed identity. Adolescents who say their parents are intrusive (e.g., always snooping into their private lives) and not very warm or accepting do not have well-developed identities.

Feeling wanted provides a sense of worth and value that is translated into a positive view of the self. Perceiving the parents are neither too intrusive nor too regulating allows one to feel free to engage the environment, to do new and different things without the fear of punishment, which helps build confidence and competence. Having parents who are close monitors but flexible in rule making and enforcement allows the adolescent to learn competencies and feel in control of his or her own life, an important aspect of self-esteem and identity. Parental rearing practices that promote autonomy and the learning of one's unique individuality also foster identity development (Adams & Jones, 1983; Williams, 1993). Adolescents who are able to explore their competencies in an

Regardless of ethnic background, parental acceptance is an important factor in adolescent's developing a sound self-esteem and identity (*Kathy McLaughlin/The Image Works*)

atmosphere that is free of the fear of rejection and severe punishment in the event one makes a mistake are better able to learn their competencies and explore their identity. Of course, that is what optimal resolution of the identity crisis is all about. Stifling the exploration of the self may lead to a foreclosed identity.

Adolescents not only have parents who rear them, but also grow up in a family structure. Does living in a single parent or blended family influence the adolescent's self-views? Research findings indicate the answer is yes. Rosenberg (1985) studied self-esteem in a group of adolescents living with their mother (it still is rare for a father to have child custody). Although it was common for most of these adolescents to have lowered self-esteem, those who were younger, or who had mothers who were younger, had even lower self-esteem. M. Rosenberg suggested that mothers somewhat older than the average mother with adolescents of the same age may better cope with becoming a single parent, and that older adolescents may better cope with parental divorce and living in a single-parent family. He also reported that parental remarriage had a negative influence on the adolescent's self-esteem, perhaps because of the changes in family structure and rules that occur when a stranger enters the household.

The most comprehensive studies of family structure and adolescents' self-esteem were conducted by Parish and his associates (Nunn & Parish, 1987; Parish & Taylor, 1979; Young & Parish, 1977), who studied school-age and college students in intact, blended (the mother remarried), and single-parent (mother custody) families. They reported that college students who came from divorced families had lower self-esteem than those who came from intact families, suggesting the negative impact of parental divorce on the adolescent's self-esteem may be long lasting. Although they hypothesized that those from blended families would have elevated self-esteem, that was not the case. Those in intact families had the highest self-esteem and those in divorced families the lowest; those in blended families had self-esteem closer to that of those in the divorced group.

These studies point out that self-esteem is adversely affected by parental divorce and that the negative effects of parental divorce and living in a single-parent family may last for some time. Moreover, maternal remarriage does not moderate these detriments.

Social-Class Influences

The relation between self-esteem and social class (usually determined by some measure of parental income, education, occupation, or a combination of these) has been the subject of a number of investigations. Some evidence suggests that adolescents who come from poorer families have less positive self-esteem than those whose families are relatively well off. Some researchers (e.g., Demo & Savin-Williams, 1983) have suggested this is a result of middle-class students doing better in school, their higher performance leading to higher self-esteem (Bachman & O'Malley, 1986; see Box 6–4). Other evidence (e.g., Soares &

Soares, 1972; Trowbridge, 1972) suggests that whether adolescents come from an economically middle- or lower-class background, or are advantaged or disadvantaged, may not be as strong an influence on self-esteem as some have suggested. This is not very surprising when one considers that home atmosphere is a critical factor in self-development. A poor home atmosphere and a poor relationship with parents are likely to produce a lower self-esteem regardless of social status or the degree to which one is advantaged. Material possessions or quality of neighborhood are less likely to be a factor, especially if the home atmosphere is one conducive to self-growth. Low self-esteem may emerge in either middle- or lower-class homes.

Filsinger (1980) has elaborated this contextual analysis of the relation between self-views and social class. He focused on the concept of self-efficacy, the feeling that one is capable of achieving some desired goal. Self-efficacy theory predicts that individuals interacting in social-class contexts higher than their own are more likely to have higher self-esteem and those interacting largely in social-class contexts lower than their own are likely to have lower self-esteem. Those whose best friends are of a higher as opposed to lower social class should have higher self-esteem than those whose best friends are of a lower social background. To test these notions, Filsinger and Anderson (1982) correlated self-esteem and (1) one's own social class, (2) best friend's social class, and (3) the difference between own and best friend's social class. The correlation between own social class and self-esteem was not statistically significant, but that between self-esteem and best friend's social class was statistically reliable. Filsinger and Anderson suggest that college students gain a sense of social status and a feeling of competence from associating with close friends of higher social status, perhaps because they have greater confidence in themselves. Unfortunately, the converse—associating with best friends of lower social classes—may be detrimental to feelings of self-competence.

Maturational Influences

Mussen and Jones (1957) studied self-esteem in early- and late-maturing boys. They hypothesized that the slower rate of physical growth and the concomitant social disadvantages that late-maturing boys experience would have detrimental effects on their self-esteem. Their hypothesis was borne out. Late-maturing boys indicated more feelings of inadequacy than early-maturing boys, and they showed a generally negative self-esteem. Of course, physical maturation in and of itself cannot cause this difference. Mussen and Jones suggested that social influences (in the form of differential expectations and behaviors), not biology, were the critical factor. The late maturers may have felt rejected by their parents and other authority figures, may have been less likely to try to assert independence, may have had stronger underlying dependency needs, and may have been more sensitive about their personal feelings than early maturers.

Jones and Mussen (1958) studied self-esteem in early- and late-maturing girls. They reported that the early-maturing girls were somewhat better adjusted

BOX 6–4   Self-Esteem and School Achievement

In general, measures of self-esteem are positively correlated with grades earned in school and with achievement test performance. Those who have higher self-esteem get higher grades and do better on achievement tests than do children with lower self-esteem (Marsh, 1987). Moreover, high- and low-self-esteem children behave differently in the classroom (Shiffler, Lynch-Sauer, & Nadelman, 1977). High-self-esteem students evidence more task-oriented behavior (doing classroom work) and low-self-esteem students show more nontask behavior (such as looking around and watching others).

Observations such as these have led to the investigation of the causal direction in the relationship between self-esteem and school achievement. Self-enhancement theorists argue that the predominant causal sequence is from self-esteem to school achievement. In other words, they believe high self-esteem causes good school achievement. From this perspective, the initial responsibility of the school system should be to build strong, positive self-esteem in students. Then, it is argued, school achievement will be respectable. The reverse view is espoused by the skill-development theorists, who believe that doing well in school results in self-esteem enhancement and that doing poorly results in a lowering of self-esteem. With regard to educational philosophy, they would argue the major role of the school system initially should be to develop solid educational skills, including academic and social skills, that will ensure adequate achievement and thereby promote a positive self-esteem (Calsyn & Kenny, 1977).

Evidence in support of each position is available. Shavelson and Bolus (1982), for example, reported that for a sample of seventh and eighth graders, self-esteem was causally predominant over measures of school achievement. Calsyn and Kenny (1977), however, reported that for students in grades 8 through 12, academic achievement was causally predominant over self-esteem. Finally, it appears that attempts to increase school achievement via programs aimed at self-esteem enhancement have typically failed, perhaps because the self-esteem enhancement procedures were faulty.

At the present time, it appears best to consider the causal relationship between self-esteem and school achievement as reciprocal. Undoubtedly, feeling competent is important to school success. One need only listen to the reasons students give for not wishing to take certain types of courses. Often the major reason is "I don't do well in that (subject)." Clearly, this is an expression indicative of the causal importance of self-esteem. In turn, doing well in a subject area promotes interest in the topic and the feeling one can do well. To keep to the analogy, we can look at the reasons for wishing to enroll in courses in some area, including the often heard "I want to take (subject) because I like it and do well in it."

So how should this information be used? Should teachers tell all students they are good? Should they simply stress overall academic achievement? One answer to these questions may be what is termed the *multidimensional classroom* (Slavin, 1994). In such a classroom teachers emphasize that there are many pathways to success; some students do well in math, others in music, and others in art. There is no one way to succeed. Teachers also avoid unnecessary distinctions between students that highlight individual skills. Finally, there is an increased emphasis on putting forth maximum effort. In such an atmosphere all students can succeed and reap the personal benefits of their success.

than the late-maturing girls. They scored higher on total adjustment, family adjustment, and feelings of personal adequacy. Simmons and Blyth (1987) reported that early-maturing girls' self-esteem may suffer because of their perceptions of their physical appearance. Because they are somewhat heavier and do
not see themselves as having an ideal culturally stereotyped female figure, they
tend to be the most dissatisfied with their body image. This might contribute to
a poorer self-image.

These findings suggest that adolescents' views of their physical attractiveness and not just maturity rate is important to self-esteem. Indeed, some research
indicates that physical appearance is the single most important component of
general self-esteem, especially for females, who report greater difficulty adjusting to pubertal changes than do males (Simmons & Blyth, 1987; Zumpf, 1989).

Ethnicity

We live in a pluralistic society. Although the majority of the American population is White, the proportion of African American, Asian, and Hispanic Americans is growing as is the number of biracial adolescents (L.I. Phillips, 1992; Phinney et al., 1994; see Box 6–5). Growing up in a multiethnic society has been the
norm for a number of generations, but only recently have social scientists begun
to examine questions about self-development and how it may differ for those
not of the dominant ethnic group(s). The most extensive writing on these concerns has been done by Phinney and her colleagues (Phinney, 1989, 1990; Phinney & Alipuria, 1987; Phinney & Rosenthal, 1992). Her research shows that although there are similarities in identity development among adolescents from
various ethnic groups, there also are differences.

A major difference between identity formation for those in the dominant
culture and those from different ethnic groups is that the latter have an added
dimension to their identity—**ethnic identity**. Ethnic identity refers to the degree to which one feels he or she belongs to a particular ethnic group and how
that influences one's feelings, perceptions, and behavior. Aspects of ethnic identity include feelings of belonging to a particular group, identifying the self as a
member of the group, holding shared values and attitudes with others who belong to the group and to the group's traditions and history, and positive or negative attitudes toward the group. It is important to note that the term *ethnic* is
not equated with the term *race* in this research: Ethnic refers to an identifiable
group such as African American, Italian, Jewish, Catholic, Japanese. Researching
how ethnic identity influences self-views is one way of studying individual differences in identity development. How does being a member of a minority religious group, a second-generation immigrant, or someone who speaks with an
accent impact on your self-views? If it does not, are you one of the majority ethnic group? Can you understand how these factors influence those who are not
of your group and how they view the self and develop an ethnic identity?

Phinney (Phinney & Rosenthal, 1992) has observed that the establishment
of ethnic identity progresses through a sequence of stages paralleling those pro-

BOX 6–5 The Special Case of Biracial Adolescents

The numbers of biracial (African American/Anglo-American) adolescents is estimated to be between 300,000 and 500,000, and increasing (Hiraga, Cauce, Mason, & Ordonez, 1993) due to increases in the number of biracial marriages. Just as the African American adolescent faces some special tasks in the development of self-views, it has been suggested that biracial adolescents may experience a unique set of tasks in the development of their self-views.

In order to investigate this possibility, Hiraga and colleagues surveyed a group of 17 biracial adolescents (African American and White) and compared their responses to a group of 17 monoracial (African American) adolescents. The two groups were matched in age, year in school, gender, family income, and family composition. The measures included family relationships, peer relations, self-development, psychological adjustment, and ethnic identity.

Although differences on the measures of family and peer relations, self-views, and psychological adjustment were minimal and generally not statistically significant, the differences between the groups for ethnic identity were large and consistently different. The monoracial adolescents identified much more with the African American cultural heritage than did the biracial adolescents. For example, compared to the biracial sample the monoracial adolescents rated themselves as more African American, believed the African American heritage was more a part of them, and felt their cultural history was more important to them. The biracial adolescents felt they fit better into the white culture and identified more with it than did the monoracial adolescents.

It appears, then, that although biracial adolescents may face some stresses within the extended family, in general they feel about their peer relations no differently than do the monoracial adolescents. Hiraga et al. go on to note, however, that biracial adolescents are in the unique position of not having one ethnic group with which to identify. This is reflected in their lower identification with the African American heritage. Because the reasons for this difference are not known, and because the long-term consequences have not been explored—there are no lengthy longitudinal studies of development among biracial adolescents—it is unclear whether or not biracial adolescents will face identity or interpersonal difficulties as they grow through the adolescent years.

posed by Marcia for general identity development. Initially, there is no questioning of one's ethnic identity. Attitudes at this stage are analogous to a foreclosed identity—they are the result of others such as parents or the larger society. This is followed by a crisis specifically involving ethnic identity—a kind of ethnic moratorium—during which the adolescent may feel a sense of difference and conflict between his or her values and those of the dominant culture. Adolescents must explore how their group is viewed by society, concerns of prejudice and discrimination, and how their ethnic group is similar to and different from that of the dominant society. This is followed by the development of an achieved ethnic identity—the individual achieves a sense of belonging and identifying with his or her ethnic group. For minority adolescents, developing an achieved ethnic identification is associated with higher self-esteem; this is not

Ethnic identity—be it racial, religious, or country of origin—
begins at home and follows a course of development similar
to that which Erikson described for general identity. (*PH
Archives*)

the case for majority group adolescents, perhaps because ethnic identity is less
important for them (Phinney & Rosenthal, 1992).

Ethnic identity begins at home in the family context. Parents and other significant family members introduce the child to the ethnic group rites, beliefs,
and values in an attempt to inspire ethnic pride and provide feelings of belongingness. Another important influence is the ethnic community, which is a subculture that provides settings for learning and practicing components of ethnic
identity. A more cohesive, organized, and larger ethnic community contributes
to greater ethnic identity (Phinney & Rosenthal, 1992).

Some researchers (e.g., Spencer & Dornbusch, 1990) have tried to determine if the development of a coherent identity is more difficult for minority
adolescents. Although the *process* of identity formation seems to be the same,
the achievement of a coherent identity seems to be different. Minority youth
grow up in a culture dominated by those who are different, and grow up in a
culture in which racial stereotypes provide a different context for exploring
identity issues than it does for those in the dominant culture. As Phinney points
out, this difference in contexts results in the minority adolescent facing somewhat different identity crises with different potential outcomes.

Some minority youth assimilate, that is, they attempt to adopt the values
and norms of the majority culture and become a part of it. However, because
they have a different physical appearance, or talk with an accent, or have religious beliefs that are not those of the dominant culture, they may face discrimination and feelings of alienation for failure to meet the standards of the dominant
culture. Others may deal with the ethnic identity issue through alienation—they
live the life of the majority culture but have feelings of not fitting in, feeling estranged and alienated. Those who adopt a separation type of identity reject the

majority culture and values and take on the perspectives of their ethnic group. Finally, some adolescents attempt to adopt a bicultural identity, in which they take on the values and ideals of both the majority and minority cultures and attempt to balance them. This latter resolution to the ethnic identity crisis may lead to a feeling of marginality—the individual attempts to be accepted by the majority but does not quite make it. He or she is rejected by both cultures.

Psychologists do not know as much about how identity development is impacted by ethnic group membership as they would like because it has been little studied (Phinney & Rosenthal, 1992; Phinney et al. 1994). There is no doubt, however, that whereas the *process* of identity development may well be the same for those adolescents in majority and minority groups, the *content* of identity development differs. Only when we have more fully explored the importance of ethnic group membership will we be able to detail better how being in an ethnic minority impacts on identity development.

IMPORTANCE OF STRONG SELF-VIEWS

Quite aside from theoretical concerns about describing the development of self-views and determining factors that influence that development, the exploration of adolescent self-views is important to understanding everyday aspects of adolescent behavior.

Self-Esteem and Adjustment

People with low self-esteem exhibit more symptoms of unhealthy emotional development (e.g., nervousness, insomnia, psychosomatic illness) than do individuals with high self-esteem (Harter, 1989). Adolescents with low self-esteem are especially vulnerable to criticism and rejection because these reinforce their feelings of low self-worth. Low-self-esteem adolescents tend to avoid social activities, including heterosexual relationships, that might result in rejection or failure. As a result, they often feel they cannot succeed in social situations. The vicious circle is then developed.

In this vein, researchers (e.g., Harter, 1989; Pfeffer, 1986; M. Rosenberg, 1986) have explored the role of self-esteem in adolescent depression and suicide. Adolescents with low self-esteem are prone to a depressive mood. In addition, they are less likely than their high-self-esteem counterparts to do well in activities that are important to them and their parents, such as school, which may lead them to feelings of helplessness—they can't satisfy themselves or their parents. These feelings of depression and helplessness are highly predictive of them considering suicide as their only answer to their problems.

The Self and Delinquency

Generally speaking, researchers have found that delinquents tend to be more socially assertive, hostile, destructive, and lacking in self-control than nondelinquents. It has been suggested that this behavioral pattern represents a defense against a negative or inadequate self-esteem resulting from frustration due to rejection (Ahlström & Havighurst, 1971; J. J. Conger & Miller, 1966). Delinquents perceive themselves in much the same way they are perceived by others—lazy, bad, and ignorant. They do not see themselves as desirable people, and they have relatively little respect for themselves. These differences begin early in life with more serious behavioral manifestations appearing during adolescence.

The issue of causal direction in the relation between self-esteem and delinquency is very complicated (Bynner, O'Malley, & Bachman, 1981; Harter, 1989). One view is that engaging in delinquency causes one to have a lower self-esteem because the delinquent comes to see the self negatively (F. Rosenberg & Rosenberg, 1978). The delinquent begins to see the self through the eyes of others and internalizes their negative feelings and attitudes toward him or her. From this view delinquency is seen as the cause of lower self-concept.

An alternative hypothesis is that having a low self-esteem causes one to engage in delinquent behavior. Kaplan (1975) suggests that a buildup of negative feelings about the self due to inability to measure up to the standards of others causes some adolescents to seek the company of those who reject traditional standards in favor of alternatives, often involving delinquency. By living up to the alternative standards the individual gains the prestige that is unavailable in other contexts.

Bynner et al. (1981) suggest a third hypothesis, that engaging in delinquent behavior acts to increase self-esteem for those with an initially low, not high, self-esteem. The difference between this and the previous hypothesis rests on the emphasis on an initial low self-esteem. The positive relation between self-esteem and delinquency reported in some studies should be evident only for those with low self-concepts.

Bynner et al. (1981) tested these hypotheses in a longitudinal study involving nearly 1,500 boys tested in grades 10, 11, and 12, and 1 year after leaving school. For the high-self-esteem group there was no evidence that reductions in self-esteem caused the boy to engage in delinquency. Indeed, some evidence showed that engaging in delinquency might have reduced self-esteem. For the low-self-esteem group, the evidence indicated that engaging in delinquency increased self-esteem. For low-self-esteem adolescents, delinquency offers a way to gain self-regard.

Changing Self-Views

It is clear that having a positive self-esteem is advantageous and healthy. Yet it also is evident that many adolescents do not have adequate self-views, which may contribute to emotional, educational, and behavioral problems. This makes it important to investigate methods for improving poor self-views.

Some clues about how one might change self-views come from our earlier discussions of significant influences on self-view development. Parents who create a warm, accepting, and appropriately controlling home atmosphere in which the adolescent feels wanted can help improve the adolescent's self-esteem. Parents of adolescents with poor self-esteem would do well to provide this type of home atmosphere in order to increase their child's chances of adapting well to adult life.

Some researchers have attempted to improve self-esteem through changes in school programs aimed at improving school performance. Although some effects in the desired direction were observed, the preponderance of the evidence is on the negative side. To date, it has not been unequivocally demonstrated that alterations in the school environment significantly improve self-views.

SUMMARY

Early conceptualizations of the self viewed it in a trait perspective. More contemporary psychologists see self-views as theories of the self or in the context of self-understanding. As a result, views of the self are seen in a developmental context stressing progressive changes with development, and especially development in cognitive skills and one's view of the self living in a society.

There are a variety of ways in which we view the self. Self-concept refers to the dimensions along which we view the self—physical, academic, and social. Self-esteem refers to our evaluations of the self, how positively or negatively we view our various self-concepts. Our baseline self-esteem is our general evaluation of our self-conept; barometric self-esteem refers to our evaluation of the self at any given point in time. Baseline self-esteem is relatively stable; barometric self-esteem is subject to momentary fluctuations due to immediate circumstances. Our identity is revealed in the values and ideals we hold; identity acts as a guide to our behavior. We also hold possible selves: hoped for and feared.

Because there are different types of selves, we must assess change in self-views in different ways. Change in self-concept is measured by examining changes in the dimensions (ways) in which we view the self. The evidence is that although we add new ways to describe the self as we develop, we do not lose earlier ways to view the self. Hence self-concept is said to be continuous rather than discontinuous. Baseline self-esteem is assessed through quantitative, as opposed to qualitative, means. The evidence is that although barometric self-esteem fluctuates as a function of momentary events, baseline self-esteem is relatively stable across the adolescent years. Changes in identity status categories occur as we acquire new roles (e.g., worker, spouse, parent, retiree), but the changes are slow and gradual, not sudden and abrupt.

Self-views are influenced by a variety of factors. Parental child-rearing techniques that are warm, firm but not strict, and make the adolescent feel wanted promote good self-esteem and identity. Being overindulgent, too strict, and making the adolescent feel unwanted foster poor self-views. Lower-social-class children and adolescents have poorer self-esteem than their middle-class peers. This seems to reflect differences in parental child-rearing techniques as well as more general effects associated with the social relations of those in the lower economic strata. Early maturers, and particularly males, tend to have more positive self-images than later maturers. This difference apparently is a result of different treatment by adults and peers, the advantages associated with being an early maturer, and the confidence early maturers gain by virtue of their relatively larger physique vis-à-vis peers. The development of an ethnic identity among African American, Asian, and Hispanic youth involves the same processes as identity development in the adolescents in the dominant culture, but the end result may be different. This is a result of the minority adolescent having an added aspect to identity—ethnic identity. Finally, self-conceptions are related to aspects of cognitive development. With increasing cognitive competence, self-views become more abstract and complex.

Having positive self-views is important in many ways. Adolescents with higher self-esteem are better adjusted psychologically, have higher career aspirations, and conform more appropriately to generally accepted social standards. Hence they fare more successfully in the real world. The development of means to alter poor self-esteem might be useful for helping the adolescent become better adjusted, but other factors also must be taken into account if one wishes to alter the behavior of poor-self-esteem adolescents, because views are only one factor determining behavior.

GLOSSARY

barometric self-esteem: Self-esteem that is subject to moment-to-moment fluctuations as a result of immediate experiences.

baseline self-esteem: More permanent perspective of the self that is not subject to moment-to-moment fluctuations.

cross-sectional study: Assessment of different aged individuals at about the same time. Allows the study of age differences in development.

ethnic identity: Sense of belonging to an ethnic group, including how that influences one's perceptions, feelings, and behaviors.

identity: Constellation of one's values, morals, and beliefs that guides one's behavior.

identity status: In Marcia's theory, one's state of identity development: achieved, diffuse, moratorium, or foreclosed.

longitudinal study: Assessment of the same group of individuals at different points in time (ages). Allows the study of age changes in development.

qualitative change: Change in type or kind. The self-concept changes in kind because we add new dimensions to our views of the self as we develop.

quantitative change: Change in amount or evaluation. Our self-esteem changes quantitatively.

self-concept: One's perception of the self.

self-esteem: One's evaluation, from positive to negative, of the self-concept.

DISCUSSION QUESTIONS

1. Keeping in mind that ethnic identity means more than racial identity, what ethnic identity do you have? What role did your parents, friends, and social institutions play in your developing ethnic identity?

2. What possible selves do you have? In what ways do possible selves influence what you do?

3. Which parental rearing techniques are most highly associated with high self-esteem? Why? What are some specific examples of parents behaving in this way?

4. In what ways are the various self-views we hold similar and in what ways different? Why do we have so many different ways of viewing the self?

5. Why does self-esteem generally decline when adolescents change schools? What factors are related to a recovery of self-esteem?

6. Think of some examples when your barometric self-esteem changed a lot. How do these changes relate to your base-line self-esteem?

7. How are identity and cognitive development related? How do psychologists explain these relations?

8. How might we account for siblings having different identities or self-esteem even though their parents use the same general rearing practices with them?

9. What do researchers mean when they state that self-views are theories of the self? In what ways is this theory of the self similar to and different from other theories about which you have read?

10. How are social roles and identity related? How do the various social roles you play impact on your identity? What future roles will you play and how might they change your identity?

7

Sex-Role Socialization

Major Issues Addressed

Biological Contributions to Sex Differences in Behavior
Historical Basis of Sex Differences
The Nature of Psychological Androgyny
Current Changes in Sex-Role Stereotypes
Theories of Sex-Role Development
The Nature of Socialization
Cognitive Development and Adolescents' Sex Roles

When he was 4 or 5 all of a sudden there were "boy things" and "girl things," with little in between. I suppose he learned these distinctions at school and from friends. He had learned the differences in behaviors that were associated with the genders, even though I had tried to emphasize similarities and avoid stereotyping. But I was just one of many he was exposed to. As he got older, the shades of gray emerged and got larger; he began to understand that sex roles were arbitrary.

Sex roles are learned through a variety of means. All of us know what the traditional sex differences in behavior are, although few of us likely can tell exactly how or when we learned them. In this chapter we explore sex roles and the social and biological bases for gender differences in behavior.

INTRODUCTION

One of the most important aspects of our self-views is our sex-role identity, our view of our self within the context of societally defined gender roles. Sex roles affect not only our perspective of our self, but also our vocational decision making, our views of the nature of marriage and parenting, how we perceive others, and virtually all other aspects of our identity. Sex roles are in part learned, beginning in infancy and developing continually throughout life (Eccles, 1987; Fagot & Leinbach, 1987). They are learned through the processes of socialization, just like other social behaviors. One purpose of this chapter is to describe the socialization processes involved in sex-role development.

A second purpose of this chapter is to describe sex-role development and its consequences during the adolescent years. During adolescence many existing sex differences in behavior emerge (Eccles, 1987; Unger, 1979) and sex roles begin to stabilize (Absi-Semaan, Crombie, & Freeman, 1993). Adolescence, then, presents a unique opportunity to study the multifaceted socialization agents that affect sex-role development.

THE NATURE OF SOCIALIZATION

Definition of Socialization

Socialization is a difficult term to define because it is used to describe *what, why,* and *how* the individual comes to behave in ways deemed appropriate by society. Because all human beings live in social systems that have rules and norms for behavior, everyone must learn to behave in ways deemed "appropriate" by the society. Although various cultures and subcultures differ with respect to the specific behaviors seen as appropriate, all have standards for what will and will not be tolerated. Members of a society learn these social rules, as well as how far they may be stretched. Socialized behavior is evidenced in all aspects of our lives, from relations with parents, siblings, and others to how to behave in school, on a job interview, or on a date. Socialization, then, may be defined as the study of how individuals learn the knowledge and skills required for effective participation in the society.

From this perspective it is clear that although **sex roles**—the prevailing societal stereotypes for male and female behavior (Rabin, 1987)—may partly be biologically based (Box 7–1), they largely involve learning societal stereotypes. The stereotypes are taught by parents, peers, and other social agents and institutions, and are reinforced by each of these. The task of those interested in studying sex-role socialization is to explain how the individual acquires knowledge about sex roles and the nature of the influence exerted by cultural agents, institutions, and biological factors.

Adolescents are active in their socialization, for example, as in teaching their parents current adolescent clothes preferences. (*Leo De Wys, Inc.*)

Box 7–1 The Biological, Cognitive, and Social Determinants of Masculinity and Femininity

Historically, the study of sex roles and the learning of preferences for masculine and feminine sex roles has focused on social processes. Hence the emphasis of researchers has been on explaining the transmission of sex-role stereotypes from one generation to another, with the emphasis on the *learning* of sex-typed behaviors.

More recent perspectives have come to view sex-role acquisition as involving more than learning. More specifically, Mitchell, Baker, and Jacklin (1989) have suggested that, as is the case with many personality traits, masculinity and femininity may have a biological basis as well. In order to investigate this possibility they examined the development of masculinity and femininity in identical, or monozygotic (the same genetic makeup) and fraternal, or dizygotic (50% of genes shared) twin pairs, the latter including both same-sex and opposite-sex individuals, who were children or early adolescents (ages 5–12). They reported that, depending on the measure of masculinity or femininity used, between 20% and 40% of the masculinity and femininity scores was due to genotype (genetic makeup). In other words, identical (monozygotic) twins had masculinity and femininity scores that were more similar than nonidentical (dizygotic) twins. The differences that existed (the remaining 60% to 80%) were accounted for by individual experiences the individuals had—such as different interactions with adults, different teachers, different friends, having different accidents, and the like. They concluded that in order to explain children's and preadolescents' views about sex roles one needs to consider both biological predispositions as well as the teaching/modeling influences of sociocultural factors.

In their study of sex typing in children and early adolescents (ages 5–12), Serbin, Powlishta, and Gulko (1993) investigated the cognitive-developmental, gender schema, and social-learning factors involved in sex-role learning and flexibility. They concluded that in order to adequately explain sex-role learning we need to consider the contributions of all three approaches to the study of sex roles. For example, sex-role flexibility (nonstereotyping of occupations and activities) and knowledge (knowing what the sex-role stereotypes are) were related to cognitive development—those with more advanced cognitive development were more flexible and less stereotyped. The importance of social factors in sex-role learning was shown by the fact that those with mothers who frequently exhibited "reversed" sex-role behaviors (for example, traditionally masculine behaviors) around the house had lower scores on measures of sex-typed preferences.

Research such as this suggests that sex typing is a very complex process that involves biological factors, cognitive development, and individual social experiences. No single approach can hope to explain how or why individuals develop the sex roles they possess. This suggests that sex typing, or masculinity and femininity, are multidimensional traits, including personality characteristics, occupational decision making and choices, and social behaviors. Each involves cognitive, affective, and behavioral aspects that are critical to how we acquire, evaluate, and exhibit the behaviors we call sex roles.

Socialization and Adolescent Development

There are several important implications of our definition of socialization. First, socialization involves learning. It is important to identify those who are the primary teachers with respect to the adolescent's socialization. Second, socialization reflects cultural expectations and stereotypes. We expect children, adolescents, and adults to behave in different ways. We expect more mature behavior from adolescents than from children; when adolescents engage in "childish" or immature ways we express displeasure. Third, socialization, is a two-way street; it involves an interaction between the individual and the behavior expected of that person by socializing agents—parents, peers, social institutions. This is a dynamic interaction, with the role of socializer (teacher) and socializee (learner) continually interchanging (R. Q. Bell, 1968; Rheingold, 1969). Just as parents socialize adolescents, adolescents socialize parents. As a general example, consider how you gained greater independence from your parents. It no doubt was a give-and-take process. As you grew in maturity and responsibility you showed your parents you could act in a responsible manner and deserved greater independence; they learned. You "taught" them, but not without them also teaching you, as in giving you advice. Role learning and role teaching go hand in hand. It is this give-and-take process that may be at the heart of much parent–adolescent conflict. When one party, in either the role of socializer or socializee, violates too strongly the expectations of the other, conflict can result.

In the realm of sex-role learning the same interchanging of socialization roles occurs. As social expectations for sex-role-appropriate behavior change—for example, an adolescent girl calling a boy for a date—adolescents must teach their parents the new norms. In turn, parents must learn the more "modern-day" norms for adolescent behavior. Because parents and their offspring experienced adolescence in different generations (cohorts) some aspects of sex-typed behavior will be different. The same process occurs in other interpersonal relations, such as those involving boyfriend–girlfriend interactions. Each member of the couple "teaches" the other how he or she wishes to be treated.

The last important implication of our definition of socialization deals with the processes through which it occurs. Although the particular behaviors socialized may change from generation to generation, the psychological processes and mechanisms involved in explaining socialization remain the same across generations. During the past 15 to 20 years there have been changes in sex roles. As a result, the sex roles learned by today's adolescents are different from those learned by their parents when they were adolescents. But the manner in which the sex roles were learned—from parents, peers, social institutions—remains the same. Although you and your parents learned somewhat different sex roles, the manner in which you learned them (the processes of learning them) was the same.

In sum, socialization is a very complex phenomenon. Consider yourself as an example. You are either a male or a female, a son or daughter, probably a college student, from a particular social background, of a particular ethnic group, growing up in a particular social climate and time, with a particular set of beliefs. Psychologists who study socialization try to explain how you became what you are by reference to your gender, the social roles you play, your personal background, and the prevailing sociocultural factors that impinged on you.

SEX TYPING

The term **sex typing** refers to the acquisition of the motives, attitudes, values, and behaviors regarded by a society as masculine or feminine, as appropriate for males and females. Sex typing begins in infancy when children are labeled male or female and are treated differently because of the label. Parents and others begin to shape the child's behavior in accord with societal expectations for acceptable and expected behavior for males and females. Sex role learning begins.

In most cultures, the **masculine role** is viewed as an instrumental one. Males are viewed as controlling, independent, assertive, competitive, aggressive, and manipulators of the environment. The **feminine role** is seen as involving passivity, dependence, nurturance, nonaggressiveness, and warmth. The fact that these roles are reversed in some cultures (Block, 1973) points to the importance of the cultural context within which the roles are defined. What is considered masculine in one culture may not coincide with what is seen as masculine in another. Moreover, as cultural expectations regarding the roles of males and females change, sex roles change. What is considered appropriate masculine and feminine behavior today is different from what it was during your parents' adolescence because of broader changes in the social system. The women's movement in the United States is an attempt to move sex roles away from their historical context and relate them to broader cultural changes (see Box 7-2)—greater acceptance of women working outside the home and having long-term career opportunities, the ability to plan for the number and spacing of children, and the increase in single-parent families.

In considering the cultural definition of sex roles, it is important to keep in mind that subcultural influences impact on the broader definition of sex roles (Cunningham & Swanson, 1993; Jessor, 1993). A variety of social and historical circumstances, such as racism and slavery, have resulted in African American females having a greater sense of independence in their sex roles than is the case for White females (Gibbs, 1988; McAdoo, 1981). The very high death rate of young African American males (Gibbs, 1988), their poor educational and economic futures (Gibbs, 1988; McAdoo, 1981) relative to White males, and overall discrimination all have historically contributed to the "traditional" African American female sex role involving a greater acceptance of economic and personal independence than that of White females.

Evidence also shows that at least some sex differences in behavior have a biological basis (Quadagno, Briscoe, & Quadagno, 1977). This research, which we review later, reveals that there are biological (hormonal) influences on some sex-typed behaviors (e.g., aggressiveness). However, the prevailing view is that

BOX 7–2   The Historical Basis of Sex Differences

There can be little doubt that sex differences in behavior, which form the foundation of sex roles, have a historical basis in biological sex differences (e.g., L. Hoffman, 1977; Unger, 1979). The biological ability of females to bear and nurse infants is at the heart of the basis of the female sex role: child caretaker, nurturer, homemaker. In turn, the greater physical strength and endurance of males is the foundation of the male sex role: provider, aggressor, protector. Early in the history of humans, this division of roles likely served a useful function and aided survival of the species. As humans evolved and developed increasingly complex social institutions and as technology advanced, the need for the historical division of sex roles eroded. Today, in contemporary American society, the initial bases for the historical differences in sex roles no longer exist. Hence there has been considerable social and political pressure to break down barriers created by sex roles.

In an interesting paper, Lois Hoffman (1977) provided an insightful perspective of how technological and medical advances in American society have influenced family roles, and thereby in part eliminated the necessity for a number of differences in sex-typed roles. In particular, she noted that women are spending much less of their adult lives in mothering functions. In part, this is a result of increased use of contraception to prevent unwanted pregnancies and to allow the planning of desired pregnancies. In part, it is due to increased acceptance of female employment. And, in part, it reflects increases in life expectancy. Moreover, technological advances have made it possible for women to cast off the traditional homemaker role and pursue activities outside the home because of freed-up time. Few of you grew up in families in which someone had to shop every day, bake bread, or do laundry daily. We have refrigerators and freezers, buy bread at the grocery store, and have appliances that make doing laundry and cooking much easier now. It no longer is necessary to have someone at home all day to run the household. One of Hoffman's major points is that with "freed-up time" women may engage in other than traditional sex-role activities.

Rabin (1987) has taken a more pessimistic view. She notes, for example, that the time now saved because of technological advances is used up in other, different household chores, such as driving children to medical appointments (because doctors no longer make house calls), standing in line at supermarkets, putting away groceries, and chauffeuring offspring to various after-school and out-of-school activities. In other words, Rabin argues, even in two-earner families the basic running of the household and its ancillary responsibilities falls on the female. Some of the time savings noted by Hoffman simply are not there. In support of Rabin's views, surveys of college students (e.g., O'Connell et al., 1989) show that college females remain committed to the traditional motherhood role. Why? Perhaps because other social changes (greater opportunities for students to participate in extracurricular opportunities, the reduction in the number of us who grow up in extended families with built-in child caretakers) have replaced the earlier ones that took up time. Perhaps also because the masculine sex role has not changed or not changed as much, leaving earlier sex-role inequities intact.

One important implication of these perspectives is that existing sex differences reflect the socialization of sex roles to a greater degree than they do biological differences (see Box 7–1). Historically, girls have been socialized for the motherhood role. That still seems to be the case, despite their increased socialization for instrumental roles. It still is expected that the wife will be responsible for the bulk of the routine operation of the household and of child care, even if she is employed outside the home. This state of affairs reflects the fact that although attitudes about female employment, for example, may have changed, behaviors have not, likely due to the long history of sociocultural conditioning of these sex differences.

This perspective of the evolution of sex roles does not deny that biological factors may be important contributors to sex differences. Rather, it is based on the notion of the interaction between biological and social factors in the evolution of sex differences and similarities. Sex differences and sex roles, then, may be seen to reflect not only biological differences, but also the evolution of culture.

socializing influences interact with biological influences in the expression of sex-typed behaviors. Hence it appears most wise not to take either extreme position—both biology and socialization are important to sex roles and sex differences in behavior.

Sex-Role Stereotypes

At one time traditional sex-role stereotypes—males being competitive, assertive, and masters of the environment and females being dependent, nurturant, passive, and nonaggressive—may have been adaptive (Box 7-1). However, relatively recent changes in the culture have led many to challenge the traditional sex roles as both "obsolete" and unnecessarily restrictive.

Have sex-role stereotypes changed during your lifetime? The answer is both yes and no. Although contributions to family income and achievement strivings (as in getting an advanced education and working outside the home) no longer are as sex typed as previously (S. Albrecht, Bahr, & Chadwick, 1979; Urberg, 1979), college females remain committed to the motherhood role and plan to stay home with their children for some length of time (Baber & Monaghan, 1988; O'Connell, Betz, & Kurth, 1989; Box 7-3) to a much greater degree than do college males. College males and females maintain the view that child care and daily household management remain the province of females.

On the basis of these studies, we must conclude that the adolescents' sex-role stereotypes have undergone relatively little substantive change. The few documented changes—less stereotyping of achievement motivation and an increased desire for long-term careers—are important, however. These changes reveal a broadening of the female sex role into areas traditionally considered not only masculine but desirable. Therefore, they represent a convergence of sex-role stereotypes. Whether additional changes will occur, of course, remains for the future to answer. Changing strongly entrenched stereotypes is a difficult and long-term process. In this context, it is important to note that despite the greater acceptance of women having full-time careers there is a continued feeling that women still should have the primary, and historically feminine, responsibility for child care and the day-to-day operations of the household. In other

---

BOX 7–3   Career and Motherhood Expectations of College Women

With the increasing opportunities for outside-the-home employment of women, researchers have begun to explore the expectations of college women with regard to career and motherhood plans (Baber & Monaghan, 1988; O'Connell et al., 1989). In each instance, these researchers asked college women in either traditional (e.g., nursing) and nontraditional (e.g., engineering) career programs about their plans regarding balancing working outside the home and their role as mother. Nearly all the women reported they planned to work full time until their first child was born. This was true for both those entering traditional as well as nontraditional careers. Following the birth of their first child, however, only a minority, albeit a sizable one (from 25% to 46%), said they planned to go back to work full time. Although a slightly greater percentage of women in nontraditional career paths planned to return to work full time by the time their first child was 1 year old, the difference was not large. Again, we see that sex-role behaviors, although changing somewhat for women, remain substantially in the traditional mold.

Baber and Monaghan note that a substantial percentage of these women argue they will take rather long maternity leaves, including some who state they will do so for a full year or more. However, these women seemed to have failed to consider that they may not have a job to return to. Laws limit the amount of time one may take a maternity leave and still have the employer hold the job open, and most businesses have a maternity leave of only 6 weeks. As a result, the careers of these women are at risk. After 6 weeks their employers may have no jobs for them.

The findings of both these studies point out another interesting phenomenon. Although the percentage of women training to enter nontraditional careers has increased, no doubt due in part to changing sex-role stereotypes, these changes have not been translated into changing family plans. Even those women who have sufficiently overcome traditional sex-role stereotypes to train for nontraditional careers plan to play a rather traditional family role, at least for some period of time.

These studies point out the complexity of sex-role stereotypes and the degree to which changing them is complex. Measures of career training and planning show changes. But with regard to family life, changes have been minimal and slower in coming.

---

words, when women go to work they are more likely than men to have two jobs.

It is interesting to speculate about the importance of other cultural changes in the etiology of the documented changes in sex roles. The greater achievement strivings of females and acceptability of careers outside the home for them may reflect the increase in the proportion of working mothers (see Chapter 10 for a complete discussion of maternal employment). Evidence shows that the daughters of working mothers have more flexible sex-role stereotypes and are more career oriented. Moreover, they are more approving of mothers working than are daughters of mothers who do not work. The working mother provides an alternative model for her daughter. Adolescent female high school seniors who talk with their mothers a good deal about their future plans hold less traditional gender-role beliefs and future career plans. Changes in traditional sex-role stereotypes, then, are fostered by broad cultural and interpersonal factors, such as the necessity of two incomes in the household, a social climate that allows consideration of changes, and personal circumstances that allow the possibility of change.

Sex Differences in Behavior

Sex-role stereotypes concern expected differences in behavior associated with the sex of the individual. The most extensive study of sex differences in behavior was published by Maccoby and Jacklin (1974). They reviewed research investigating sex differences in a variety of areas, including school learning, memory, perception, personality, and the like. They then summarized their findings by listing areas in which (1) stereotypes were not supported by experimental evidence, (2) real sex differences existed, and (3) questionable sex differences existed. Nonsupported beliefs included girls being more social and suggestible and boys being more analytic. Real sex differences existed for girls having greater verbal ability and boys excelling in visual-spatial ability. Questionable sex differences were found for activity level, dominance, and competitiveness. More recent research has documented further some of these sex differences. For example, differences in spatial ability are well documented (e.g., Linn & Petersen, 1985; Tracy, 1987), as are sex differences in mathematics achievement (e.g., Feingold, 1988; Wentzel, 1988), although the basis of these differences is not well understood (see Box 7-4). No doubt the reasons for these sex differences are complex and involve both biological and social factors.

PSYCHOLOGICAL ANDROGYNY

Historically, the study of sex-role stereotypes and sex differences in behavior has been based on the notion that masculinity and femininity are polar opposites. In other words, it has been assumed the more feminine an individual perceived the self to be, the less masculine the self was perceived to be. Draw a line and label one end masculine and the other feminine. Now put a check mark on the line to indicate how you view yourself. The closer you marked to the masculine or feminine end, the more you see yourself in that way and the less you see yourself in the opposite way.

Research and theorizing by Sandra Bem (1981) and Janet Spence (Spence & Helmreich, 1981) focused on the concept of psychological androgyny. Underlying this perspective is the view that masculinity and femininity are not polar opposites, but rather are relatively independent dimensions along which our behavior may differ. Each of us may see ourselves as having greater or lesser degrees of traditionally masculine *and* feminine characteristics. Draw two lines, labeling one feminine and the other masculine. Assume each goes from low to high. Now put a check mark on each line to indicate how feminine and how masculine you perceive yourself to be.

BOX 7–4   Sex Differences, Sex Roles, and Mathematics Achievement

Sex differences in mathematical ability are well documented (Feingold, 1988; Wentzel, 1988). Boys are more likely than girls to choose mathematics courses as electives (J. Sherman & Fennema, 1977) and, although classroom performance of boys and girls in mathematics courses remains consistent across the high school years, standardized test score performance of females declines across the high school years, dropping below that of boys by grade 11 (Feingold, 1988; Wentzel, 1988). Although some evidence (Feingold, 1988) indicates that sex differences in standardized test performance are diminishing in the earlier grade levels, the difference favoring boys in the later grade levels has remained constant for over the past 30 years.

In attempting to determine the complex reasons for sex differences in mathematics achievement, some researchers (e.g., Eccles et al., 1993; Eccles & Wigfield, 1985) have examined the role played by teacher–student interactions in the classroom and its impact on student expectancy for success in the study of mathematics. More specifically, they have focused on sex differences in the teacher's use of praise and criticism in the classroom.

Heller and Parsons (1981) observed teacher–student interactions in junior high school (grades 7 and 9) mathematics classes. Teachers were asked to indicate how well they thought the students would do in an advanced mathematics course, and students were asked how well they thought they would do in both familiar and unfamiliar mathematics tasks. The researchers reported no sex differences in teacher use of praise and criticism and no sex differences in teacher expectancies for performance. However, girls had lower expectancies for success on unfamiliar mathematics tasks, which might be related to their hesitancy to enroll in mathematics when it is an elective.

Parsons, Kaczala, and Meece (1982) replicated these findings in their study of teacher–student interactions in grades 5 to 9. However, they reported that girls had lower expectancies (self-concept of ability) when teachers praised high-expectancy boys (those they felt would do well in advanced math) but not girls. Parsons and her colleagues also reported that praising high-expectancy girls had a positive effect on all girls. It seems that distributing praise and criticism similarly for both sexes and for both high- and low-expectancy children attenuates sex differences in student expectancies for mathematics success.

That teachers' use of praise and criticism plays some role in sex differences in mathematics achievement and student expectancies for success in mathematics seems clear on the basis of these studies. Equally clear is the fact that this is not a simple relationship. For example, the influence of the teacher may be different for children than for adolescents. Nonetheless, the data reveal that sex differences in mathematics achievement and self-concept of mathematics ability are determined in part by sex differences in student–teacher interaction.

Another line of research has focused on the role of parents (Eccles, Jacobs, Harold-Goldsmith, Jayaratne, & Yee, 1989; Jovanovič, 1993; Raymond & Benbow, 1986; Yee & Eccles, 1988). The aim of this line of inquiry has been to investigate whether or not parents differentially encourage their adolescent males and females to excel in mathematics, and whether or not parents have differential expectations for males and females in mathematics. Although some evidence (Raymond & Benbow, 1986) indicates that parental encouragement and assessment of adolescents' performance in math is not differential for males and females, other evidence (Eccles, Jacobs, et al., 1989; Jovanovič, 1993; Yee & Eccles, 1988) indicates that parents hold differential expectations for young children's mathematics performance that are sex typed in favor of boys. In addition, parents attribute boys' performance to ability and girls' performance to effort (Eccles et al., 1989).

The effort to identify the causes of sex differences in mathematics achievement seems to indicate that there are important socialization factors, reflecting prevailing sex-role stereotypes, which contribute to boys doing better than girls. In studying this literature it may seem that boys and girls are at opposite ends of mathematics achievement. This is not the case. Many girls have high levels of mathematics achievement, and a substantial percentage of boys have difficulty in mathematics. In the study of sex differences in achievement it is important to keep in mind the large degree of overlap in the distributions of achievement. Any individual girl or boy may be very successful or not. Group differences such as those studied by the researchers do not allow us to note the substantial individual differences within the genders.

Psychological **androgyny** refers to sex-role flexibility and adaptability. The major underlying assumption is that the individual may act in either a traditionally masculine or traditionally feminine manner, depending on situational constraints and needs, and do so comfortably. One example Bem (1977) uses is the firing of an employee (which involves the stereotypical masculine traits of assertiveness and dominance) with sensitivity and understanding (which involves the stereotypical feminine traits of empathy and compassion). Both Bem and Spence have argued that the androgynous sex role is the most adaptive because it allows the greatest behavioral flexibility. Androgynous individuals are those who are able to demonstrate either masculine or feminine behaviors in accord with situational demands.

In order to measure psychological androgyny, Bem (1974) developed the **Bem Sex Role Inventory (BSRI),** and Spence (Spence, Helmreich, & Stapp, 1974) developed the **Personal Attributes Questionnaire (PAQ).** Each instrument is composed of several scales, one measuring masculine traits and one feminine traits. Those completing the scales indicate the degree to which each trait is characteristic of them. Scores for masculine and feminine self-attributions are then calculated. By dividing the subjects at the median masculinity and femininity scores (see appendix), four classifications of individuals are obtained. *Androgynous* individuals rate themselves high (above the median score) in both masculine and feminine traits. *Masculine* individuals rate themselves high on masculine traits and low (below the median) on feminine traits. *Feminine* individuals rate themselves low on the masculine traits and high on the feminine traits. **Undifferentiated** individuals rate themselves low on both the masculine and feminine traits. The masculine and feminine individuals have a sex-role "preference" in that they view themselves more strongly on one of the scales than the other. Androgynous and undifferentiated individuals do not have a sex-role "preference." They differ in that the androgynous view the self high on both masculinity and femininity whereas the undifferentiated view the self low on both masculinity and femininity.

Two types of evidence have been collected to test the hypothesis that an androgynous sex role is preferable to the others. One focuses on behavior: Do androgynous individuals *behave* differently than others? The second centers on psychological adjustment: Are androgynous individuals *better adjusted psychologically?*

Androgyny and Behavior

Behavioral evidence in support of the claim that an androgynous sex role leads to greater flexibility is relatively scarce. In her initial study, Bem (1975) reported that androgynous college students exhibited masculine independence and feminine playfulness in appropriate situations but sex-typed individuals displayed traditionally sex-typed behavior in each situation. G. Russell (1978) reported that both androgynous and feminine fathers engaged in more day-to-day care of their children and played with their children more than did fathers who were in the masculine or undifferentiated sex-role categories. No differences were found for mothers in the four sex-role categories. Androgynous and feminine fathers, both of whom viewed themselves high in traditional feminine traits, were more nurturant and sensitive toward their children.

Behavioral evidence linking sex roles and adolescent behavior is limited to sexual behavior. Researchers (Leary & Snell, 1988; Whitley, 1988) have examined the relation between college students' sex roles and their sexual experience (whether or not they had engaged in sexual intercourse, number of sexual partners). For males, level of masculinity was positively related to sexual experience—those with higher masculinity scores had higher scores on the sexual experiences questionnaires. Level of femininity was unrelated to sexual experience for males. For females the findings were more complex. Masculinity was related positively to sexual experience, but this was true only for females with low femininity scores. High femininity acted as a deterrent to sexual behavior for females. Of course, these findings are consistent with sex-role stereotypes, with masculine individuals of both sexes, and androgynous males, but not females, having the greater sexual experience.

Until further behavioral evidence is available, any conclusions concerning the advantage of an androgynous sex role with regard to daily behaviors, child rearing, working, and day-to-day household chores must be tentative, particularly as it relates to the adolescent years. However, the scant available evidence is consistent with the suggestion that an androgynous sex role is related to greater behavioral flexibility.

Androgyny and Psychological Adjustment

A correlate of the behavioral flexibility hypothesis is that an androgynous sex role should be psychologically more healthy than sex-typed sex roles because the latter restrict psychological growth. To investigate this hypothesis, researchers have examined the relation between sex roles and various measures of psychological adjustment (see Dusek, 1987b), primarily in college students.

Some researchers have shown that androgynous individuals have higher self-esteem than masculine, feminine, or undifferentiated individuals. They argue that this is the case because of the more wide-ranging self-views, feelings of competence, and comfort with different situations that androgyny allows. Other researchers (see Dusek, 1987b) have argued it is not the balance between high levels of masculinity and femininity that results in a more positive self-esteem, but rather it is simply high masculinity. The basis of this suggestion is that masculine traits are more valued in our culture. These researchers provide evidence that androgynous and masculine subjects score equally high on measures of self-esteem. Because the masculine individuals have relatively low femininity scores, whereas both groups have relatively high masculinity scores, the argument goes, it is high masculinity and not a balance of high masculinity and high femininity that is important to adjustment.

It is conceivable that the nature of the relationship between sex-role orientations and self-esteem depends on the specific aspect of self-esteem that is measured. To test this hypothesis, Flaherty and Dusek (1980) had college males and females complete the BSRI and a measure assessing four aspects of self-esteem: Achievement/Leadership (a measure of the traditional masculine/instrumental role); Congeniality/Sociability (a measure of the traditional feminine/expressive role); Adjustment (a measure of psychological adjustment); and Masculinity/Femininity. The androgynous and masculine subjects scored highest on the instrumental scale, the androgynous and feminine subjects scored highest on the expressive aspect of the self, the androgynous subjects had slightly (but not significantly) higher scores on the adjustment aspect of the self, and the masculine subjects had the highest and the feminine subjects the lowest scores on Masculinity/Femininity, with the androgynous subjects having a middle score.

Ziegler, Dusek, and Carter (1984) used the same instruments and procedures to test adolescents in grades 6, 8, 10, and 12. They found relationships between self-esteem and sex-role orientation similar to those reported by Flaherty and Dusek. Of interest, there were no grade-level differences in these relationships. During the adolescent years, then, an androgynous sex role is associated with higher levels of several aspects of self-esteem. These data support the suggestion that an androgynous sex role is associated with better psychological adjustment.

Other researchers have examined the relation between sex roles and resolution of Erikson's developmental crises. The general perspective has been that because some of Erikson's crises are largely masculine oriented, for example, the industry versus inferiority crisis, and because others, for example, the identity versus identity diffusion crisis, entail core components of sex roles, the relation between sex roles and crisis resolution may provide important insights into psychological adjustment. In order to test these possibilities, Della Selva and Dusek (1984) had college students complete the BSRI and a measure of resolution of the identity versus identity diffusion and industry versus inferiority crises. They found that the androgynous subjects scored highest, the masculine and feminine subjects next highest, and the undifferentiated subjects lowest on resolution of the crises. Further, they demonstrated it was the possession of high levels of masculinity *and* femininity that related to more successful resolution of the crises. Similar results were reported by A. S. Waterman and Whitbourne (1982) and by Glazer and Dusek (1985). In addition, in these latter two studies, it was demonstrated that the advantage of the androgynous sex role extended across all six of Erikson's crises. These studies provide clear evidence that an androgynous sex role is associated with more successful resolution of various crises faced in the course of childhood and adolescent development.

The results of the research reported in this section leave little doubt that an androgynous sex role is associated with higher self-esteem and more optimal psychosocial crisis resolution. However, it should also be pointed out that a sex-typed sex role is associated with better adjustment than an undifferentiated sex role. In studies of self-esteem (e.g., Flaherty & Dusek, 1980) and resolution of developmental crises (for example, Della Selva & Dusek, 1984; A. S. Waterman & Whitbourne, 1982), undifferentiated subjects had by far the poorest scores. As Flaherty and Dusek (1980) noted, then, it may be best to be androgynous, but it is better to be sex typed than undifferentiated. Although sex-typed roles have their disadvantages, it is important for a balanced perspective to realize they are better than the undifferentiated sex role.

Developmental Trends in Androgyny

An interesting question concerns developmental trends in sex typing and androgyny. Hyde and Phillis (1979) had subjects aged 13 to 85 complete the BSRI in order to examine age differences in sex-role orientations. They reported that the proportion of androgynous males increased with age and the proportion of androgynous females decreased with age. Ziegler and colleagues (1984) found a similar trend for adolescents in grades 6, 8, 10, and 12. For males, there was a trend toward androgyny; for females, there was a shift away from androgyny and toward a feminine sex role. They suggested it is difficult for women to acquire masculine traits as they get older because those traits have a "youthful" tenor. Males, however, could acquire feminine traits relatively readily. For example, as males mature, acquiring the traditionally female traits of nurturance, caring for the feelings of others, and being sensitive to others' needs will stand them in good stead in their roles of boyfriend, husband, and father. Males who score high in femininity tend to have happier marriages than males who do not score as high (Antill, 1983). Hence an increase in the proportion of androgynous males should be expected because it is adaptive.

The most extensive investigation of age differences in sex-role orientation was undertaken by Spence and Helmreich (1979). They had high school students, college students and their parents, and a group of parents of first and second graders complete the Personal Attributes Questionnaire (PAQ). Males had higher masculine scores, and females, higher feminine scores. The *adult* males had higher masculinity scores than the younger males (whose scores were like those reported by Ziegler and others). There were no age trends on the feminin-

The percentage of androgynous males increases during adolescence partly because such individuals acquire adaptive traditionally-feminine nurturant behaviors. The proportion of feminine females increases, probably because of attempts to match social stereotypes. (*Left: Charles Gatewood. Right: James Carroll*)

ity scale. Spence and Helmreich suggested it may be adaptive for all people to become more instrumental with increasing age because of responsibilities for schooling, work, and other instrumental tasks that are faced with increasing independence. Males may find this easier because of the traditional masculine role. Females may not become more instrumental because the traditional feminine role holds them back.

THE BIOLOGICAL BASES OF SEX DIFFERENCES

Interest in biological influences on sex differences stems in part from our knowledge of prenatal and postnatal differences between the sexes. Males tend to be miscarried more often and are more susceptible to diseases throughout their lives. Female infants tend to be physically more mature at birth than male infants—females walk and talk earlier and enter the growth spurt several years earlier than boys. These biological differences suggest the possibility that sex differences in behavior may have a biological link.

Research on the biological bases of human sex differences is not extensive. Some researchers (e.g., Ehrhardt & Baker, 1973) have examined the relationship between hormones and sex-typed behavior, such as aggression (Maccoby & Jacklin, 1980; Tieger, 1980). A second approach (e.g., Money & Ehrhardt, 1972; Money, Hampson, & Hampson, 1955) has been to examine how hereditary influences may be modified by social factors.

Hormones and Sex Differences

Some biological research on sexrole behaviors has focused on the effects of hormones—estrogen, progesterone, and testosterone. The general notion has been to examine the activating function of the hormones; the presence or absence of the hormone may exert some influence on current behavior (Tieger, 1980). One specific hypothesis is that hormones absorbed prenatally may contribute to gender differences in behavior. For example, injecting pregnant monkeys with testosterone (a male hormone) results in hermaphroditic female offspring who exhibit not only physiological alterations, but also show behavior patterns more similar to those of males than to those of females (Quadagno et al., 1977). Injecting male hormones into an infant female monkey after birth does not alter physical attributes but can result in changed behavioral patterns, including dominance and aggressive behavior (Tieger, 1980). The research with animals demonstrates a link between hormones and behavior that in humans is called sex typed (Quadagno et al., 1977; Tieger, 1980).

Research with humans is much less conclusive (Maccoby & Jacklin, 1980; Tieger, 1980), in part because of the important and appropriate ethical issues involved in research on hormonal reactions. We cannot in good conscience just randomly select pregnant women or children to be injected with hormones so we can observe the impact on offspring behavior. As a result, research has focused on accidental occurrences of hormone abnormalities.

Research with humans shows that male hormones masculinize the prenatal development of girls. Ehrhardt and Baker (1973) studied 17 fetally androgynized girls and their sisters, who served as a control group. The androgynized girls, who were exposed to excessive prenatal androgens because of genetic anomalies or because the mother took hormone therapy to help prevent possible miscarriage, exhibited masculinized behavior. They had a preference for outdoor sports, preferred to play with boys, and showed little interest in doll play or other so-called girlish activities. Both mothers and children rated these girls as having masculinized behaviors. It is important to note, however, that Ehrhardt and Baker (1973) found no evidence of increased fighting or aggressive attacking in these girls. Hence they suggested that aggressiveness may be the wrong variable on which to try to measure biological influences on sex differences.

Ehrhardt and Baker (1974) replicated these findings for girls but also found that boys experiencing similar circumstances were more energetic and active than a matched control group of boys. However, they again found no evidence indicating the androgynized boys were more prone to fighting or engaging in other aggressive activities. It seems reasonable to conclude that prenatal exposure to androgens increases activity levels and perhaps some aspects of sex-typed behaviors, but does not relate to aggressiveness, at least as measured in these studies.

Some research has been conducted on the effects of prenatal exposure to estrogen or progesterone (both are female hormones). Yalom, Green, and Fisk (1973) showed that teacher ratings of boys exposed to very high levels of estrogen or progesterone (their mothers were being treated for diabetes and the drugs contained these hormones) indicated lower assertiveness at age 6 relative to a control group. These differences continued through age 16, perhaps because being less assertive causes others to treat one less assertively; in other words, it may not be solely a hormonal influence. Girls exposed to excesses of progesterone under similar circumstances tend to be less tomboyish and show increased preferences for feminine clothes.

A direct assessment of the relation between testosterone levels and females' sex roles was reported by Baucom, Besch, and Callahan (1985). They found that androgynous and masculine females, those with higher masculinity scores, had higher levels of testosterone than did feminine females. Those with higher testosterone levels also saw themselves as being more instrumental (self-directed, action oriented). Those with lower testosterone levels saw themselves as more expressive (nurturing, moody, caring).

The information reviewed here points to the interactive influences of biological predispositions and social factors in determining sex-typed behaviors (Quadagno et al., 1977; Tieger, 1980). Social influences, for example reacting to boys' greater physical size, responding to sex differences in activity level, or behaving toward children in accord with social stereotypes, mediate biological influences on sex-typed behavior, as we discussed in Chapter 3.

Social Factors, Biology, and Sex Differences

The most extensive demonstration of the interactive influence of biological factors and social influences on sex-typed behavior comes from the research of John Money and his colleagues at Johns Hopkins University. In one set of studies (Money & Ehrhardt, 1972; Money et al., 1955) they examined behavior in androgynized females. These girls had normal internal reproductive systems but abnormal external genitalia. Although they showed an interest in marriage and having children and dated like other girls, they also behaved in ways typically considered more masculine, as in aggressive play and games. They learned through cultural and social forces to overcome the biological anomalies and play the feminine role.

In other research Money and Ehrhardt (1972) studied children who were assigned the incorrect sex at birth because of deceptive external genital anomalies. Babies with male chromosomal patterns were raised as girls, and babies with female chromosomal patterns were raised as boys. In all 19 cases, the child learned to behave in a manner consistent with the assigned sex, which was opposite to the chromosomal sex. Thus socialization influences overrode biological attributes.

These data reinforce the view that although there may be biological predispositions for certain sex differences in behavior, we cannot ignore the role played by social factors. As Maccoby and Jacklin (1980) point out, in examining sex differences in behavior we must consider a variety of influences, including biological, social, and societal/cultural. This point is brought home forcefully when we consider the topic of sex differences in aggression. Although more males than females tend to be highly aggressive, the overlap in the distributions of male and female aggressiveness is very substantial. If there is a biological predisposition toward aggressiveness in males, most males do not behave in aggressive ways most of the time. Biological agents, such as hormones, may predispose us to behave in certain ways, but social factors (socialization) are a more important determinant of our behavior. Again, then, we see the two sexes are more similar than different.

THEORIES OF SEX-ROLE DEVELOPMENT

We noted earlier that hormones may predispose the individual to certain behaviors but that environmental factors are more important determinants of our behavior. It is the culture (environment) that determines the criteria for sex-typed behaviors—masculinity and femininity. And it is through the environment that sex-typed behaviors are learned. We are socialized to behave in ways consistent with broadly defined cultural standards. Three major theories attempt to explain how socialization, including sex-role learning, occurs: psychodynamic, social-learning, and cognitive.

Psychodynamic Theory of Socialization

The first broad-ranging developmental theory of socialization was formulated by Sigmund Freud (1924; see also Chapter 2). Freud believed sex-role acquisition occurs through identification with the same-sex parent as a result of resolution of the Oedipal complex. By **identification,** Freud meant the child takes on the characteristics (values, attitudes, personality traits, behaviors, likes and dislikes) of the same sex parent (see Figure 7–1). As a result, Freud believed boys learn how to be males and girls learn how to be females by identifying with their fathers or mothers, respectively. Put simply, Freud believed identification results in the development of a firm superego (conscience), which is the internal (mental) representation of societal standards of behavior, including sex-role behavior. Because the parents' values represent, to a greater or lesser degree, the values deemed acceptable by society in general, identification with the parent is critical to socialization. Some children may see parents play very different roles: Mother stays home, cooks, is gentle and caring; father goes to work, is not as involved in child care, and does house repairs. Others may see parents play highly

Figure 7–1   Theoretical Sequences in Psychosexual Identification

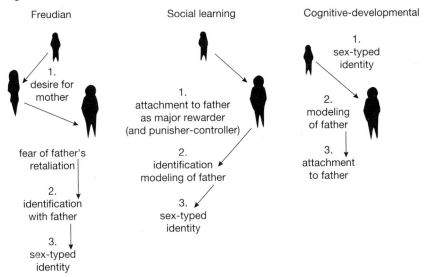

overlapping roles: Both go to work, both prepare meals, both mow the lawn. The process of identification (socialization) is the same, however. The child sees and hears how mothers/fathers, men/women behave and learns that role.

Because Freud assumed primary sex-role identification takes place in early childhood, his theory had little to say about adolescent sex typing. The implications of Freudian theory for adolescent socialization rest on the importance it places on early childhood experiences. If these have long-term effects on personality development, they will affect the adolescent's behavior.

One problem with this approach is it suggests a lack of flexibility in sex roles because of the emphasis placed on early sex-role learning. From this perspective, there is no means of understanding how an adolescent with a traditionally masculine or feminine sex role might change and develop a less stereotyped sex role. In addition, Freud did not clearly spell out what the psychological mechanisms of identification were—it seems almost magical. This difficulty led the social-learning theorists to reformulate many of Freud's concepts and place them within more directly observable behaviors.

Social-Learning Theories of Socialization

The work of Robert Sears (1950) was the first attempt to describe social behavior within a learning-theory framework. Sears's primary emphasis was on parental child-rearing practices. He was strongly influenced by Freud's theorizing and tried to translate Freudian theory into learning-theory terms. His basic thesis was that personality development in children is determined by the ways in which the child is raised, a tenet clearly taken from Freudian theory.

Sears's writings allow us to pick out several basic assumptions about the causes of behavior that fit not only his conceptualizations but also those of other social-learning theorists. One is that behavior is at once both the cause and the result of other behavior. For example, it is well known that individual differences in children, such as gender or temperament, cause parents to react differently toward the child from the first few days of life. Of course, the child's behavior is a response to adult behavior. Hence socialization is a two-way process in which the behavior of the individual depends on the behavior of other people and in which the individual's behavior acts to elicit specific behaviors from others.

Sears's second basic notion is that behavior is learned by reinforcement from others. Because the child is reinforced for some behaviors and not reinforced, or perhaps even punished, for others, the child learns socially approved behaviors. If the same contingencies exist in the adolescent's world, similar behaviors will be exhibited in adolescence and adulthood.

Humans are conditioned from infancy through childhood and even through adolescence to respond to environmental cues. Fagot and Leinbach (1989), for example, found that parents who reinforced sex-typed behavior in their 18-month-olds reared children who learned sex-role labeling earlier (by age 27 months) and who at age 4 were more aware of sex-role discriminations. The parents of the early labelers "taught" their infants and young children to attend to and learn about sex roles.

A second way social behaviors are learned is through the process of imitation. Imitative learning occurs when people match their behavior to the behavior of some other person (model). Imitative learning is itself a learned behavior.

Social learning theorists emphasize the importance of imitating same-sex parents in the learning of sex-typed behaviors and sex roles. (*Ken Karp*)

Gewirtz (1969) speaks of generalized imitation, which is a learned tendency to imitate models, particularly if they are adults. By being reinforced for imitating, the child learns to imitate adults. These adults are primarily the parents during the child's early life. As the social world expands, however, the child and adolescent come to imitate other adults, for example, friends of their parents or teachers. Imitative learning becomes generalized and is applied to a variety of models in a variety of circumstances. Identification with parents occurs, then, because of generalized imitation. It is no surprise that there are similarities in parent and offspring personality and behavior because offspring imitate their parents.

The many social models to which the adolescent is exposed highlight the importance of imitative learning for adolescent social development. Parents are important models for children and remain important for adolescents. Adolescents can learn how to behave in different social situations, such as weddings and formal parties, by observing their parents in these kinds of situations. In addition, parents provide models for appropriate behaviors in a number of other social spheres, such as moral thinking and sex-role-specific behaviors. Generally speaking, too, parents are the models for the adult social behaviors the adolescent is expected to acquire.

Other members of the family unit are also models for the adolescent. Older brothers and sisters, particularly, are important in introducing the young adolescent to the social world of the peer group. Although virtually no research exists on this issue, older siblings are highly important models for the adolescent because they engage in social activities and behaviors that are more similar to the adolescent's own than are those of the parent. This similarity facilitates observational learning.

From the social-learning perspective, sex-role learning is the result of direct training and observational learning (see Figure 7–1). Parental stereotypes of sex-appropriate behaviors may be reinforced as well as modeled by parents. As a result, boys and girls learn to behave in different ways because they are taught to behave in those ways and because they see their parents behaving in sex-typed ways. Of equal importance, too, is the role played by other models and reinforcing agents, such as teachers, peers, other immediate and extended family members, and the media (Carter, 1987; Eron, Huesmann, Brice, Fischer, & Mermelstein, 1983; Fagot & Leinbach, 1987; Monique, 1994). Some researchers (Monique, 1994; Truglio, 1993) have noted that the very high rate of sexually oriented and sex-role stereotyped interactions (average 25%) in the popular TV programs watched by adolescents is a major contributor to continued sex-role stereotyping.

Cognitive-Developmental Theories of Socialization

The cognitive perspectives of sex-role learning emphasize the child's comprehension of and attention to the importance of gender and sex-role socialization. Drawing on Piaget's theory (see Chapter 4), Lawrence Kohlberg attempted to describe the role of cognitive development in sex-role learning. Kohlberg contended that the child's cognitive representation of the external social world determines the child's basic sex-role learning. This view is predicated on Piaget's suggestion that intellectual development involves redefinitions of the world that, in turn, demand new ways of adapting and coping. Therefore, intellectual development is both an initiating force in social development and a facilitator of it (Kohlberg & Zigler, 1967). Kohlberg suggests that sex-role learning starts early in life with the child's self-categorization as a boy or girl. Sex-typed preferences in children's activities and relationships are viewed as resulting from these initial judgments of gender identity. Boys value masculine things and girls value feminine things because these are consistent with their conceived identities (Kohlberg & Zigler, 1967). A young girl engages in sex-appropriate behavior because she knows she's a girl and finds it rewarding to act like one (see Figure 7-1). Sex-role learning for adolescents follows the same pattern. Adolescents organize their sex-role learning according to gender identity.

Other cognitive attempts to explain sex-role development emphasize what Bem (1981) called *gender schema* (see also C.L. Martin & Halverson, 1981, 1987). A gender schema is a theory, a cognitive representation, of the two sexes, sex differences in behavior, and sex roles. Gender schemas function to regulate behavior (for example, by influencing goal setting), influence the information to which we attend (by highlighting the sex appropriateness of the behaviors to which we attend), and influence how we perceive our social world (through sex-typed lenses; Bem, 1981; C.L. Martin & Halverson, 1987). The general notion is that as we grow we develop expectations and rules about the nature of the social world much the same way we do about the physical world (e.g., Carter & Patterson, 1982; Levy & Carter, 1989). For example, from childhood through early adolescence we increasingly understand that sex roles involve rules for behavior that are culturally determined and flexible. Gender schemas, then, act to filter the information we perceive from the external world (C.L. Martin & Halverson, 1987). Sex-typed individuals are assumed to have gender schemas that emphasize examining incoming information in that manner, and that guide the individual to engage in opposite-sex behavior at low levels. Gender schemas also relate to our stereotypes of others (Hudak, 1993). Androgynous males have a stereotype of women that is much more androgynous than is the stereotype of masculine men, who see women as much more feminine than masculine.

Eccles (1987) has formulated a life-span cognitive theory of sex-role development. One basic assumption of this model is that sex-role transcendence—overcoming sex-role stereotyping—is the most developmentally mature sex-role perspective. Eccles views adolescence as an especially important time in the development of perspectives of sex roles. The cognitive changes that occur during early adolescence allow the individual to perceive sex roles in new and more flexible ways. Peer groups become more heterosexual in composition, and the identity crisis causes the individual to consider a number of critical issues—

career plans, role as mother or father, being a spouse, rearing children—that need to be resolved. According to Eccles, if the environment provides androgynous models the adolescent will progress toward sex-role transcendence. If the environment provides more traditional models the adolescent will develop a more traditional sex role. Sex-role transcendence does not mean the absence of sex roles but rather the knowledge that they are arbitrary. Further, it means understanding that processing information and making judgments on the basis of gender schemata is limiting.

Comparison of the Psychodynamic, Social-Learning, and Cognitive-Developmental Theories

Figure 7-1 depicts the psychodynamic, social-learning, and cognitive-developmental views of sex-role development. As you can see, the cognitive-developmental view is very nearly the opposite of the social-learning view, and both differ considerably from the Freudian view. The cognitive view contrasts with the psychoanalytic view in that identification with respect to sex is not fixed and established early in the child's life, but rather is a concept that changes with development. In addition, the social-learning view and the cognitive view agree that imitation is an important part of sex-role theory.

If you consider the nature of the cognitive changes that occur during the adolescent period (Chapter 4), it is not difficult to see that changes in perception of sex roles are quite possible from a cognitive-developmental view. The development of formal operations allows the adolescent to restructure his or her former perceptions of an appropriate sex role. Formal operational thinking allows us to imagine hypothetical alternatives to traditional sex roles (for example, androgyny). As a result, cognitive development allows new ways to consider socialization phenomena, including changes in, and alternatives to, traditional sex-role conceptualizations, and points to the importance of the cognitive dimensions in socialization. Of course, these possibilities exist only after entering adolescence.

SUMMARY

Socialization refers to the acquisition of those behaviors considered appropriate by the society. An important aspect of adolescent socialization is the learning of sex-role stereotypes. Traditionally, the masculine role has been viewed as instrumental, and the feminine role has been viewed as expressive. Hence the male sex role includes the traits of assertiveness, mastery, achievement, and aggressiveness. The female sex role includes the characteristics of passivity, warmth, and gentleness. Although these different roles may at one time have been adaptive, they no longer are considered essential to survival of the species. As a result, there have been considerable pressures toward sex-role convergence, that is, toward males acquiring some of the traditionally feminine traits and females acquiring some of the traditionally masculine traits. Some evidence indicates that such changes in the traditional stereotypes are occurring, but the norm is still largely in the direction of the historical sex differences in behavior.

Current conceptualizations of sex roles do not consider masculinity and femininity to be polar opposites. Rather, the prevalent perspective is that any individual possesses both masculine and feminine traits, although to greater or lesser degrees. Hence some individuals are sex typed in the traditional vein, but others are considered androgynous: They view the self as being capable of expressing masculine or feminine traits to a high degree depending on situational demands. Some theorists argue that the androgynous sex role leads to better psychological adjustment, for example, as measured by self-esteem or other aspects of adjustment. Available evidence indicates this is the case, although behavioral evidence showing greater adaptability for androgynous individuals is very scant.

An important area in the study of sex roles is concerned with biological predispositions toward differences in behavior between the sexes. Research on biological influences on sex differences in behavior is scarce. Some evidence reveals hormonal influences on sex-typed behavior, such as aggression. However, the preponderant conclusion is that although there may be biological differences between the sexes that predispose them to behave differently, social factors are more important determinants of behavior than are biological predispositions. Hence, although some evidence links aggression to the hormone testosterone, socialization influences cause most people, male and female, not to behave aggressively most of the time.

There are three major theoretical approaches to the explanation of sex differences. Psychodynamic theory focuses on identification with the same-sex parent, from whom sex-typed behaviors are learned. Social-learning theorists note the importance of direct training and the effects of models for the learning of sex-typed behavior. Cognitive-developmental theorists argue that sex differences in behavior result from the abstraction of social rules about sex differences—how males and females behave. By observing these differences we learn the rules for "acceptable" behavior. Each perspective has something to offer in the explanation of sex-role learning, and no one theory is preferred over the others.

The adolescent years represent an important time for the transition to adulthood. The adolescent is exposed to a number of important socializing influences from which both sex-typed behavior and more general social behavior are learned. Parents are the most important agents of socialization, in part because they have reared the individual for a long period of time. However, peers and other adults are also important to the adolescent's socialization. Finally, social institutions, such as the school and the media, influence to a significant degree the socialization of the adolescent. Because sex-role stereotypes are present in each instance, the adolescent is continually exposed to sex-typing situations.

GLOSSARY

androgyny: Perception of the self as having both masculine and feminine psychological characteristics to a large degree.

Bem Sex Role Inventory (BSRI): Questionnaire used to assess one's perception of the self as possessing traditional masculine and feminine sex-role characteristics.

femininity (feminine role): In terms of sex roles, the sex role characterized by passivity, expressivity, and nonaggressiveness.

identification: In Freud's theory, taking on the characteristics and values of the same-sex parent.

masculinity (masculine role): In terms of sex roles, the sex role characterized by assertiveness, achievement, and independence.

Personal Attributes Questionnaire (PAQ): Questionnaire to assess sex roles.

sex role: Cultural ascriptions of behaviors differentially by gender.

sex typing: Acquisition of sex-role hehaviors.

socialization: Term referring to what, why, and how an individual comes to behave in the manners deemed appropriate by the society in which he or she lives.

undifferentiated: With regard to sex roles, the perception of the self as not possessing traditionally masculine or traditionally feminine sex roles to a large degree.

DISCUSSION QUESTIONS

1. Have a friend or roommate write down what he or she thinks your sex role is, and you do the same for the other person. How accurate do each of you feel the other was? Why did the differences exist?

2. How do sex roles limit the vocations one considers entering? What are the personal, social, interpersonal, and cultural reasons for these limitations?

3. How is the development of sex roles related to the adolescent's identity? How might changes in how one views one's sex role change one's identity status (according to Marcia)?

4. How do teachers and other school personnel impact on the child's and adolescent's sex-role development?

5. In what ways does the media impact on the adolescent's sex-role development? What type of sex roles are ascribed to adolescents in films and on television?

6. In what ways do you think sex roles have changed during your adolescence? How else should they change? Why?

7. What specific parental behaviors and attitudes might impact on the sex role the adolescent develops? How did your parents affect your sex role?

8. How is your sex role different from that of your same-sex parent? Why do the differences exist?

8

Adolescent Sexuality

Major Issues Addressed

Sexuality and Other Adolescent Interests
Sex Differences in Attitudes About Sex
Premarital Sexual Experiences
Generational Differences in Sexual Behavior
Date Rape and Courtship Violence
Adolescent Contraceptive Use
Parent and Peer Influences on Adolescent Sexuality
Sexually Transmitted Diseases
The Function and Effectiveness of Sex Education
Adolescents and Homosexuality
The Adolescent Mother and the Adolescent Father
The Nature of Adolescent Romantic Relationships

I was concerned he might be sexually active. Not because of sex per se, but because of safe sex. These are the days of AIDS and other epidemic levels of sexually transmitted diseases. I wanted to be a "good" parent and try to "do the right thing." We had talked about contraception and a variety of other aspects of sexuality in an impersonal manner. But I didn't know if he was sexually active, so I asked him. He responded, "That's too personal." The conversation ended.

◆   ◆   ◆

Adolescents are sexual. More than at any previous time, more adolescents are engaging in more sexual intercourse. And many are not engaging in "safe" sexual practices. Yet sex is a matter most adolescents, or parents, find they cannot discuss with each other. In this chapter we explore adolescent sexuality, its emergence, its psychological impact, and its consequences.

INTRODUCTION

Perhaps no single event during the adolescent years has as dramatic or widespread effects as the realization of sexuality. In part, this is a result of physical changes—growth to adult physical maturity, development of secondary sexual characteristics, and the increase in the sex drive. In part, it is a result of social factors, including peer and parent influences, pressures involved in dating, and cultural stereotypes involving adolescents and sexuality. The biological changes and social influences cause the adolescent to begin to integrate sexuality into the identity (Box 8-1). In a sense, a whole new dimension is added to the self, which requires considerable adjustment. It is not surprising the adjustments might be problematic for some.

BOX 8–1   The Meaning of Sex in Adolescents' Lives

Although researchers have learned a good deal about adolescent sexual behavior and attitudes about sexuality, little is known about why adolescents engage in sexual relationships that can put them at risk for social, emotional, and health difficulties. Does engaging in sex enhance self-esteem, reduce depression, facilitate identity development? Do adolescents engage in sex to learn about someone else, to get back at someone with whom they are angry, to gain a sense of power or achievement? These were the types of questions in an investigation conducted by Turner and Feldman (1994) with a group of 18- to 26-year-old adolescents and young adults from African American, White, and Latino backgrounds.

Some of the interview responses indicated that adolescents and young adults engage in sex in order to explore identity development. They do this in several ways. One involved "playing a role" as might occur in casual sex and trying to play the role they believed their partner wanted. Another was using sex to learn their limits about sexuality—under what conditions and with whom they will engage in sex. Turner and Feldman liken these explorations to the types of identity and autonomy seeking the adolescent experiences in family relationships—learning how they feel about being sexual, about sexual relationships, and integrating sexuality into the identity in a way that will preserve the relationship.

The interviews also revealed that becoming sexual impacted on the respondents' self-esteem and emotional well-being. Some participants indicated they used sex to release anger or to enhance their feelings of well-being when they were lonely or sad. Others indicated they engaged in sex in the context of a friendly relationship they knew would not lead to increased involvement, which they did not want. Still others indicated just the reverse: When they had sex they did it with someone with whom they wanted to develop a more romantic relationship.

Turner and Feldman note that because sex plays so many different roles in the everyday lives of adolescents, it is important that we socialize it in the broader context of interpersonal relations. Although sex education classes teach many facts about sexuality, they generally focus on the biology of reproduction, the mechanics of sex, and contraception. Perhaps socializing sexuality within the context of interpersonal relating, Turner and Feldman suggest, may have beneficial influences on adolescents' safe sex practices beyond those gained through other means.

A variety of concerns center on adolescent sexual behavior. Parents worry not only about their adolescents engaging in sex and perhaps becoming involved in a pregnancy or contracting a sexually transmitted disease, but also about their ability to deal with the emotional aspects of becoming sexual. From a societal perspective, health-related problems, and the implications of large numbers of children being born and reared by adolescent mothers, are major concerns. From the adolescent's perspective, attention also focuses on how to be a "good" sexual partner and how to communicate with a partner about what one desires.

It is important to note at the outset of our discussion that sexuality begins in childhood. Children are curious about the physical differences between boys and girls. They experience sexual arousal, play "doctor" or "nurse" in attempts to learn about the other sex, and at times upset adults when they do so. As a result, children also learn that sexual behavior is something secret, not to be shared with their parents or other adults. The sexual behavior of adolescents, then, is simply a continuation of that of childhood. It is another example of how adolescence is a transition from childhood to adulthood forms of behavior.

ADOLESCENCE AND SEXUALITY

Both professional views, such as psychological and psychiatric perspectives of adolescence, and common stereotypes link the adolescent years and sexuality. Theoretical conceptualizations as well as everyday common concerns have focused on many aspects of adolescent sexuality and on the effects of adolescents becoming sexual.

Adolescent Interest in Sex

One stereotype is that sex is a very consuming interest of adolescents. Certainly your own experience demonstrates that was not the case as you were growing up. You no doubt had a variety of interests, and sex may have been one of them. But it likely did not consume you. It is this stereotype that is at the center of much of the media's portrayal of adolescents.

The most extensive study of the relationship of interest in sexuality to other adolescent interests was conducted by Dusek and his colleagues (Dusek, Kermis, & Monge, 1979; Dusek & Monge, 1974). They investigated adolescent interests in 14 different areas, including 5 directly related to sexuality (see Table 8-1). Although interest in sexual relations was listed as a topic of interest by over a third of seventh graders, the percentage of respondents in other grade levels indicating an interest in sexuality was substantially lower. Across the adolescent years, a variety of other topics, such as interest in others and wondering what one will become are of importance to more adolescents.

Examination of Table 8-1 reveals another important aspect of adolescent interest in sexuality: Interest in sexual intercourse apparently is one thing and interest in consequences of sex, such as sexually transmitted diseases and contraception, is another. Apparently adolescents and college students view sex as

Table 8–1   Percentage of Males and Females in Five Grade Levels Listing a Topic Related to Sexuality

Topic	MALES					FEMALES				
	5	7	9	11	College	5	7	9	11	College
Social diseases	0	0	0	0	3	0	0	3	6	1
Birth control	0	0	0	1	10	0	0	3	6	20
Sexual relations	5	35	19	13	13	2	39	9	6	18
Dating	0	4	2	3	3	2	18	3	9	0
Love and marriage	0	0	0	3	3	0	9	9	6	8

Source: Adapted from Dusek, J., & Monge, R. (1974). *Communicating population control facts to adolescents* (Final Report, Grant No. RO1-HD 06724). Submitted to the National Institute of Child Health and Human Development, National Institutes of Health, U.S. Department of Health, Education, and Welfare.

in some sense independent of some of its potential consequences, perhaps because these have not been personally experienced. This is consistent with Elkind's views of adolescent egocentrism (Chapter 4)—being infected with a sexually transmitted disease or becoming pregnant is something that happens to others, not you.

The Sex Drive

In order to explain adolescent sexual behavior, one must take a **biosocial perspective**. According to this perspective, biological factors are important due to the increase in hormones that occurs during adolescence. The surge in hormones increases the sex drive and is the cause of our more general physical maturity, including sexual appeal. Social factors operate through the encouragement or discouragement of having sexual involvement. Hence social norms, peer expectations and experiences, sex-role socialization, religious views, and a host of other social influences are important mediators (the mediated-effects model discussed in Chapter 2) of the adolescent's sexual experiences.

The research of Richard Udry and his colleagues shows how biological factors and social influences codetermine the adolescent's sexual experience. During the adolescent years there is an increase in the sex drive, a relatively universal physiological phenomenon related to hormonal development (Udry, 1987). In males, the rapid rise in testosterone levels that occurs between ages 12 and

The sex drive is related to different sexual values, attitudes, and behaviors in males and females.
(*Shirley Zeiberg*)

14 is associated with increases in the sex drive as measured by nocturnal emissions and masturbation (Higham, 1980).

In addition, research (Smith, Udry, & Morris, 1985; Udry, Talbert, & Morris, 1986) has shown that boys with increased androgen (e.g., testosterone) levels are more likely to be sexually active than boys with lower androgen levels. More biologically mature younger boys are more likely to be sexually active than less mature but older boys. Some evidence (Halpern, Udry, Campbell, & Suchindran, 1992) indicates that the relation between testosterone and sexual behavior for boys may hold only for earlier maturers. For later maturing boys, sexual behavior seems more under the control of social factors; despite their physical immaturity they do engage in sexual behaviors. The relationships reported for boys did not hold for girls. Although increased androgen levels in females were associated with a greater interest in sex, social factors, such as an environment discouraging premarital sexual intercourse for females, exerted a stronger influence on females' decision to engage in sex.

Although one must be cautious in ascribing causal influences to hormones—more mature males are more physically attractive to females—it does appear that hormones exert a rather direct and strong influence on the sexual behavior of boys, at least if they are earlier maturers. In girls, the influence of hormones is less direct, and social contexts are more important. Hence to understand the causes of adolescent sexual behavior, we must consider both biological and sociocultural factors—that is, how the sex drive is socialized.

There is a sex difference in how male and female adolescents deal with the socialization of the sex drive as well as in how the sex drive affects the individual. The basis of this sex difference no doubt lies in cultural conditioning. The evidence indicates that adolescent males require relatively direct expressions of the sex drive. Adolescent males engage in greater amounts of sexual activity, such as sexual intercourse or masturbation, than do females, and males' attitudes about sexual behavior are more liberal than females' (P. Miller & Simon, 1980). For example, males are more likely than females to agree that sex outside of a strong emotional involvement is acceptable (Haas, 1979). Adolescent males also are aroused more than adolescent females by a wider variety of stimuli, such as erotic art or films (P. Miller & Simon, 1980).

The sex drive for girls is more diffuse and may be displaced into other areas and dealt with more indirectly. Aspects of the quality of the relationship between the girl and her partner are very important for most expressions of her sexuality (Haas, 1979). A majority of adolescent females would agree that sexual intercourse is acceptable if the two people are in love and is not acceptable if the two people are not in a romantic relationship. Females are less likely than males to list pleasure, pleasing their partner, and relieving sexual tension as reasons for having sex (Leigh, 1989). Males are more likely to list lust or pleasure, and females love or emotional involvement, as reasons for having sex (Whitley, 1989). As a result, sexual impulses are more likely to be integrated with other aspects of social-emotional development for girls, particularly within the context of overall heterosexual relationships.

These sex differences in integration of the sex drive are related to differences in actual sexual behavior. P. Miller and Simon (1980) suggest that for males the rewards intrinsic to sex are more important than the relationship with the girl for the initial partner. In part, they believe this translates into feelings of achievement, noting that a third of the college males had sex with their initial partner only one time and another third five or fewer times. This would not be expected if the relationship was one involving strong attachment. In addition, substantial percentages of males immediately talk with someone other than their partner about their experience (Kallen & Stephenson, 1982). Other intrinsic rewards for males include feelings of power and control, a sense of masculinity, and a sense of becoming more grown up.

P. Miller and Simon (1980) suggest that for the adolescent female the partner rather than an audience or sense of achievement is critical in understanding sexual intercourse—29% of their college sample were still engaging in sexual intercourse with their initial partner and another third had sex with their initial partner between 6 and 20 times. In addition, a smaller percentage (14%) of females immediately discussed their sexual experience with someone other than their partner, although the percentage discussing their experience within a month (65%) was similar to the percentage of males doing so (71%) (Kallen & Stephenson, 1982).

The importance for females of being in an involved, serious relationship when considering their first sexual intercourse crosses cultural boundaries. In a comparison of American and Swedish adolescent females, I.M. Schwartz (1993) reported that very high percentages of each group felt a "strong" involvement with their initial partner (86% of Americans, 79% of Swedes) and believed they were in a "serious" relationship with him (Americans 82%, Swedes 75%). Moreover, relatively few (13% of Americans and 20% of Swedes) had sex with their initial partner only once (no evidence was presented as to whether this was by her choice or by the choice of her partner). About 50% of each group had sex with her initial partner 20 or more times.

Although both males' and females' initial sexual experience is likely to occur prior to marriage, the circumstances are different. The modal male will engage in his initial sexual intercourse with someone with whom he has no particular emotional attachment. He will have sex with her a few times and then never again. The modal female will be in love with her initial partner and may be planning to marry him. Some evidence (Kallen & Stephenson, 1982) indicates that these differences are getting smaller—there is a convergence between the sexes with females now holding somewhat more liberal views and males increasingly becoming concerned with relationship quality. These differences in adolescent sexuality are probably in part due to differences in the biological and hormonal makeup of the sexes and in part due to the different ways boys and girls are socialized about sex. These teachings affect not only actual sexual behavior, but also attitudes toward sexuality, the integration of sexuality with other components of the personality, and the development of romantic relationships (Box 8–2).

BOX 8–2   Adolescent Romantic Relationships

Although much research has centered on describing and understanding adolescent sexual behavior, very little theorizing or research has focused on elucidating the nature and development of adolescent romantic relationships. The nature of the early adolescent views of romantic relationships likely is important to identity development and to the development of intimacy during later adolescence. Moreover, early experiences in romantic relationships may be important to the development of later romantic relationships.

The most comprehensive theory of how adolescents view romantic relationships has been proposed by Furman and Wehner (in press; also Wehner, 1993). Drawing on the writings of H. S. Sullivan (1953), who believed the development of romantic relationships involved learning to coordinate security, intimacy, and lustful needs, they have proposed a behavioral systems view of heterosexual romantic relationships (to date, it appears no one has formulated a comparable theory of homosexual romantic relationships). According to Furman and Wehner, romantic views refer to global perceptions of the romantic self, possible romantic partners, and the nature of romantic relationships. Romantic views consist of conscious behavioral patterns and unconscious working models of how things are/ought to be. Although views of romantic relationships are thought to be influenced by one's other interpersonal relationships (for example, with parents and with peers), they are not identical with the views one holds for these other interpersonal relationships because romantic relationships involve different types of interactions than the other relationships. They go on to note that, over time, the adolescent's views of romantic relationships evolve and change into the adult form, which is characterized by the integration of attachment, caregiving, affiliative, and sexual/reproductive needs.

Furman and Wehner have tested hypotheses derived from this perspective in several studies involving adolescents (as young as age 14) and young adults (as old as 24). They found that the four characteristics of views differed for different types of interpersonal relationships. For example, although the meeting of attachment and affiliative needs was present in views of parental, peer, and romantic relationships, the overlap in views was not very great. They suggest these needs develop from infancy onward and that some overlap should be expected—part of romantic relationships involves affiliation and attachment and when developing romantic relationships one will draw on previous experiences in these areas from other relationships. For example, if one has learned not to turn to parents or peers as a "secure base" he or she may not do so in romantic relationships. The reverse also is the case. However, because romantic relationships are different from other relationships, the person's views of the relationship with a romantic partner will differ somewhat from that with parents or peers.

The nature of romantic relationships also changes with development (Feiring, 1993). During mid-adolescence (age 15) personality traits and physical attractiveness are more important than interpersonal qualities in romantic relationships. Girls have a more psychoaffectional and boys a more psychobiological view of romantic relationships. By late adolescence (age 18) intimacy, friendship, compatibility, and other affiliative qualities are common descriptors of romantic relationships for both females and males. Both sexes now have a predominantly psychoaffectional view of romantic relationships.

What can we learn from the little that is known about the development of adolescents' views of romantic relationships? It appears that previous experiences in parental and peer relationships influence to some degree our development of styles of interaction with romantic partners. However, because the individual with whom we are romantically involved is different, the overlap in our behaviors and views of the relationship are different. Moreover, evidence (e.g., Turner & Feldman, 1993) indicates that as the romantic partner changes, the nature and style of the views of the ro-

mantic relationship change. Findings such as this point to the fact that our views of interpersonal relationships depend to a high degree on the person with whom we are relating. They also depend on our experience in such relationships—with increasing experience adolescents develop models of romantic relationships similar to those of adults.

SEXUAL ATTITUDES OF ADOLESCENTS

Attitudes about sexuality, including when it is considered appropriate and when it is expected, are shaped by social influences. We should expect different standards in different cultures, and different standards in the same culture at different times. In addition, sexuality is socialized differently in different social classes and ethnic groups within a culture.

Cultural Differences in Sexual Socialization

Cultures differ widely in how sexuality is socialized during the childhood and adolescent years (Herdt, 1990). In some, sexual development is *sequential.* For some period of time, children and adolescents are expected to not engage in sex. Then, for example, when they get married, there is an abrupt change in what is expected. In these cultures, sexual behavior represents what Benedict (1938) called a *discontinuity.* Herdt labeled a second form of socializing sexuality *emergent.* In these societies, sexual behavior is semidiscontinuous—the "official" standard, for example, may be to prohibit premarital sexual intercourse but the restrictions may not be very serious and may not be enforced with any vigor. This form of sexual socialization is more common in rapidly changing societies and characterizes the contemporary American scene since about the 1960s. A third form of sexual socialization is called *linear.* Sexual behavior not only may be allowed but may even be encouraged in children and adolescents; and there are few restrictions. In these societies, sexual behavior is *continuous* (in Benedict's terminology).

Within a culture there are wide variations in sexual attitudes and beliefs. For example, males in our culture hold more liberal attitudes and engage in more sexual behavior than do females. And, even within the gender groupings, there are wide individual differences in attitudes and behaviors. Some adolescents have monogamous sexual relationships; others have multiple sex partners.

In addition, there are substantial ethnic group differences in adolescents' sexual behavior. White, Black, and Hispanic adolescents are exposed to different socialization influences that impact on their sexual behavior and values. Where it is possible to do so, we explore these differences in order to spell out important individual differences in sexual socialization.

Adolescent Attitudes Toward Sexuality

One generalization that emerges from studies (Leigh, 1989; Whitley, 1988) of adolescent attitudes about sex is that the permissibility of various sexual behaviors is related to the intensity and nature of the relationship between the individuals. In general, both male and female adolescents, and especially older ones, believe sexual intercourse is more permissible if the partners are engaged or have a strong emotional commitment to each other. Similarly, both male and female adolescents believe the quality of the relationship is an important factor in the decision to have sexual intercourse, although males tend to be somewhat more liberal than females in this matter. Moreover, it is very clear that both males and females agree sex with someone you know only casually is not appropriate. A second generalization is adolescents agree that the older the individuals, the more reasonable it is for them to engage in various sexual behaviors.

These trends reflect, in part, changing cultural standards about sexuality

Changes in adolescent attitudes about sex reflect the broad changes in societal views of sexuality as expressed, for example, in a variety of media depictions of sex. (*Left: PH Archives. Right: Anita Duncan*)

(Chilman, 1986). Just as adolescents have developed more liberal attitudes about premarital sexuality, so, too, have adults. The changes in adolescents' attitudes are part of more general attitudinal changes in the broader social order. One can see such changes in movies, television (HBO, MTV), song lyrics, and changing attitudes about adolescent pregnancy and childbearing. Similarly, societal changes in views of the double standard with regard to sexuality no doubt contributed to the liberalizing of adolescent female attitudes about sexuality. Most male and female adolescents feel there should not be a double standard for premarital sex. What seems to exist today is a single standard of permissiveness in the context of an affectionate relationship (Koch, 1988). It is important to note, however, that these changes in attitudes do not mean adolescents are promiscuous. Most adolescents who engage in sexual intercourse are monogamists. The stereotype of the "oversexed" adolescent describes relatively few individuals.

SEXUAL BEHAVIOR DURING ADOLESCENCE

One question concerns gender differences in sexual behavior. Do the traditional sex differences, with more male than female adolescents engaging in sex, still exist? A second concern is generational differences in the percentage of adolescents engaging in sexual intercourse. Is there a sexual revolution, and if so for whom? A third matter of interest is the age at which adolescents begin to engage in sexual intercourse. Are adolescents experiencing sex sooner now than in previous generations? Finally, investigators are looking more directly at individual differences, such as ethnic group membership, and how they relate to sexual behavior.

The Development of Sexual Behavior

When the typical person thinks about adolescence and sexuality it likely is in the context of sexual intercourse. We usually do not consider the fact that sexual intercourse is an end point that results from a developmental progression involving a variety of other sexual experiences.

One means of examining the development of sexual behavior is to look at the change from **autoerotic behavior** to **sociosexual behavior** (Katchadourian, 1990). Autoerotic sexual behavior is that which is experienced alone, such as fantasies about having various sexual experiences, or masturbation. Sociosexual behavior is that involving another person, and includes necking, petting, and sexual intercourse. Adolescents generally experience a progression from autoerotic to sociosexual experiences.

Some researchers have examined the developmental progression in sociosexual behavior (e.g., Hyde, 1990). This research has focused on heterosexual behavior; we know virtually nothing about the progression for homosexual behavior. The typical progression is from kissing, to French kissing, to petting, including the woman's breasts or either partner's genitals, to sexual intercourse, and for some to oral sex. In general, one's attitudes about the acceptability of a specific sexual behavior are more liberal than one's actual experience at any given age level. For example, although about 90% of males and 70% of females believe oral sex is OK, only about a third have ever practiced it (Haas, 1979). And boys' attitudes and behaviors about a given sexual behavior are more liberal than girls of the same age. Although these gender differences exist, the progression of sexual activity is very similar for boys and girls.

Premarital Sexual Intercourse Experiences of Adolescents

No one today can doubt that significant percentages of adolescents engage in premarital intercourse. Although adolescent sex always has existed, the percentage doing so now is greater than in previous generations because there have been substantial cultural shifts in how we view and socialize sexuality. A number of interesting issues about adolescent premarital sexual intercourse have been researched.

Sex Differences.   Over the years there have been substantial changes in adolescent sexual behavior. Specifically, the gap in gender differences in sexual intercourse, although still present, is now much more narrow. For example, Hayes reports that by age 18, roughly the age of graduation from high school, about 64% of adolescent males and 44% of adolescent females have engaged in sexual intercourse at least one time. By age 20, 83% of males and 74% of females have engaged in premarital sexual intercourse. Adolescent females, then, still lag adolescent males by about a year in their engaging in sexual intercourse, but the difference is much less now than it was nearly two generations ago. The largest changes in adolescent premarital sexual intercourse have occurred for females, and especially for White females (Zelnick, Kantner, & Ford, 1981), who as a group showed about a 50% increase in premarital sexual intercourse between 1971 and 1982.

What do these statistics mean? First, there has been a convergence in the sexual behavior of adolescent males and females. The large gender differences no longer exist. Second, the changes for females seem to reflect changing perspectives of when sex is appropriate. Historically, females have had stronger feelings that sex is appropriate only in a romantic context; sex reflected an emotional commitment. These feelings are less strong now (Koch, 1988). Fewer females expect to marry their first sexual partner and more males report being in love with theirs.

Changes over Time.   Current-day adolescents are engaging in sexual intercourse at earlier ages than was true in previous generations. This trend is much more prominent for females than for males. If we have experienced a so-called sexual revolution, it has been for adolescent females, not males. For example, in 1972, about a generation ago, Eastman reported that by age 17 about 50% of males had engaged in premarital sexual intercourse. The comparable percentage was not reached for females until about age 19 or 20. Other research (e.g., Hayes,

1987; Katchadourian, 1990) indicates a lowering in the age of first sexual intercourse for females, but not much of a change for males (Hofferth, Kahn, & Baldwin, 1987). As you can see in Table 8–2, the percentage of 15- to 19-year-old females who have engaged in premarital sexual intercourse has risen steadily since 1971. By age 19 nearly three-quarters of females have engaged in premarital sexual intercourse, a percentage matching that of adolescent males. And the increases have occurred at all the ages from 15 to 19. It is clear that adolescents generally are engaging in sex earlier than in previous generations, but the major changes have occurred for adolescent females.

Ethnic Group Differences.   Just as there are sex and age differences in the initiation of sexual behavior, there also are ethnic group differences. The cumulative percentages of male and female White, African American, and Hispanic adolescents who had engaged in premarital sexual intercourse at various age levels is shown in Table 8–3. At each age level African American adolescents, male and female, are more likely to have engaged in sexual intercourse than their White or Hispanic peers. The differences are larger at the younger age levels, and are somewhat larger for boys than girls. For example, at age 15 the difference in the percentage of White and African American boys having engaged in sexual intercourse was about 30%; at age 19 the difference was only about 3%. For girls, the differences were 5% and 17% for ages 15 and 19, respectively.

Hispanic youth also engage in sexual intercourse earlier than White youth (Table 8–3), although the differences are smaller than those between White and African American adolescents. Such ethnic group differences in sexual intercourse seem to reflect differences in sociocultural contexts of sexuality. Just as there are differences in the rates of sexual intercourse among unmarried adolescents in different countries, which reflects differing socialization of sexuality (Hyde, 1990), subcultural differences in sexual socialization within a country result in differing rates of sexual intercourse.

The increase over the past 25 years or so in the percentage of adolescent females who have engaged in sexual intercourse is primarily due to an increase for White females. Dryer (1982) reported an increase of over 300% in the percentage of college females who had engaged in premarital sex. Among younger adolescents the increase in the percentage of females who engaged in premarital sex is due much more to increases for White than for African American adolescents (Zelnick et al., 1981).

Table 8–2 Percentage of Females Who Have Engaged in Premarital Intercourse over Time

AGE	YEAR			
	1971	1976	1979	1982
15–19	31.7	39.0	43.4	45.2
19	54.0	65.8	64.8	73.4

Source: Hofferth, S. L., Kahn, J. R., & Baldwin, W. (1987). Premarital sexual activity among U.S.
teenage women over the past three decades. *Family Planning Perspectives, 19,* 46–53.

Table 8–3   Percentages of Sexually Active Adolescents in Three Ethnic Groups, for Age and Sex Subgroups

Age	Boys	Girls
White (*n* = 2,828 boys, 2,788 girls)		
15	12.1	4.7
16	23.3	11.3
17	42.8	25.2
18	60.1	41.6
19	75.0	60.8
20	81.1	72.0
Black (*n* = 1,146 boys, 1,157 girls)		
15	42.4	9.7
16	59.6	20.1
17	77.3	39.5
18	85.6	59.4
19	92.2	77.0
20	93.9	84.7
Hispanic (*n* = 683 boys, 703 girls)		
15	19.3	4.3
16	32.0	11.2
17	49.7	23.7
18	67.1	40.2
19	78.5	58.6
20	84.2	69.5

Source: Hayes, C.D. (Ed.). (1987). *Risking the future: Adolescent sexuality, pregnancy, and childbearing.* Washington, DC: National Academy Press.

Attitudes About Sex and Sexual Behavior.   Reiss (1967) was among the first to assess the degree of relationship between attitudes toward sexuality and actual sexual behavior. He studied 248 college juniors and seniors and found their current sexual behavior and their current attitudes were highly related. For example, of the 25 students who felt kissing was the acceptable standard, 64% engaged in kissing, 32% engaged in petting, and only 4% engaged in coitus. Of the 84 students who felt coitus was acceptable, 5% engaged only in kissing, 31% engaged in petting, and 64% engaged in coitus.

More recent evidence pertinent to the attitude–behavior relationship comes from a report by Shah and Zelnik (1981) who studied 15- to 19-year-old females. The girls were asked to indicate if premarital sexual intercourse was (1) acceptable even if there were no plans to marry, (2) acceptable only if there were plans to marry, or (3) never acceptable. The percentages of women in these three groups who engaged in sexual intercourse are presented in Table 8-4. As you can see, in general, attitudes and behavior were strongly related. Only 11% of those who said premarital intercourse was never acceptable had engaged in premarital sex, but 79% of those who felt premarital sex was acceptable even if marriage was not planned had engaged in premarital sex.

A second type of information, directly related to the issue of promiscuity, concerns the number of sexual partners the adolescent has had. The data generally support the notion that adolescents are not promiscuous. Over a quarter of a century ago Luckey and Nass (1969) reported that over 70% of both males and

Table 8–4 Percentage of 15- to 19-Year-Old Women with Premarital Sexual Experience, by Respondents' Opinion on Premarital Sex

Respondents' Opinion on Premarital Sex	Percentage
Acceptable	79.1
Acceptable if engaged	54.7
Never Acceptable	10.7

Source: Adapted from Shah, F., & Zelnik, M. (1981). Parent and peer influence on sexual behavior, contraceptive use, and pregnancy experience of young women. *Journal of Marriage and the Family, 43,* 339–348.

females engaged in premarital intercourse with one partner with whom they were deeply involved emotionally. Very few females engaged in one-night affairs (about 7%), although males did so to a somewhat higher degree (30%) (Luckey & Nass, 1969). R. Bell and Coughey (1980) reported that although substantial percentages of college women had sexual intercourse, there was no evidence of an increase in the number of partners they had. In 1968, 44% of college females surveyed had had sexual intercourse with only one partner, and only 22% had had sex with five or more partners. The comparable percentages for a 1978 sample from the same university were 37% and 23%, respectively.

More recently, McLaughlin, Biermeier, Chen, and Greenberger (1994) investigated the number of sexual partners that White and Asian American college males and females reported they had had overall and in the previous year. White males had the most overall (over 4) and in the past year (over $1\frac{1}{2}$). White females (about $2\frac{1}{2}$ overall and 1 in the past year) had more partners than either Asian males or females (less than 1 partner lifetime and in the past year). With the possible exception of White males, then, it does not appear from these data that adolescents are promiscuous.

A third type of evidence comes from information about the adolescent's initial sex partner. In a survey of college students, Faulkenberry and colleagues (1987) reported that females (about 21%) were much less likely than males (about 55%) to have a casual acquaintance, unknown partner, or relative as their initial sex partner. Females were much more likely than males to have their initial sexual experience within the context of an emotional relationship.

Hence, although more college women have engaged in sexual intercourse than previously, and although the first experience comes earlier, it is not casual. For college women, sexual attitudes and behaviors are more strongly related than they are for males.

Other Sexual Behaviors

Of course, premarital intercourse is not the only sexual behavior adolescents engage in. Petting and masturbation are the other two most frequently experienced sexual behaviors.

Petting. By age 16, over 90% of adolescent males and females have engaged in at least "light" petting, and before age 17 over 80% have engaged in "heavy" petting (DeLamater & MacCorquodale, 1979). Moreover, the evidence seems to verify the commonsense lore that there is a sequence in sexual behaviors leading to intercourse: necking, French kissing, petting, intercourse.

As with intercourse, petting is more prevalent and occurs at younger ages today. Robinson, King, and Balswick (1972) report that in 1965 71.3% of college males and 34.3% of college females had engaged in heavy petting. The comparable figures for students in the same college in 1970 were 79.3% for males and 59.7% for females. More recent data indicate a continued increase in heavy petting, and report it is occurring at younger ages (Haas, 1979). By age 17 over three-quarters of males and females had touched the genitals of the opposite sex (Haas, 1979).

Masturbation. Masturbation is a primary source of sexual gratification for adolescent males and for an increasing percentage of adolescent females (Haas, 1979; Hyde, 1990; Janus & Janus, 1993). In general, adolescents do not feel particularly guilty about masturbating (Sorensen, 1973). Masturbation may provide the opportunity to learn sexual responsiveness, and some of Sorensen's adolescents agreed. Although previous generations of adolescents may well have grown up with unnecessary guilt born of falsehoods about the consequences of masturbation, large percentages of today's adolescents do not have these feelings. At present, most adolescents (approximately 80%) feel that masturbation is an acceptable sexual behavior, and by age 21, 83% of men and 77% of women have masturbated (Janus & Janus, 1993).

Reasons for Not Engaging in Sex. Although most adolescents have engaged in sex by age 18, a substantially large minority have not. One reason for some adolescents is that they have yet to enter into a relationship with someone with whom they feel such strong attachment they will consider engaging in sex (Sorensen, 1973). Sorensen reports that about 55% of both male and female sexually inexperienced adolescents—those with no sexual contact other than kissing—said they were not ready for sex and that they had not yet found a person with whom they wanted to have sex.

College students cite a variety of reasons for not engaging in sex. Both males and females who do not engage in sex state they have moral concerns (65%) and fear pregnancy (63%). Females also state they fear parental disapproval (60%) and have concerns for their reputation (55%). Males cite an unwilling partner (55%) as a major reason for not engaging in sex, although 43% also note fear of parental disapproval and 40% fear for their reputation (Leigh, 1989; P. Miller & Simon, 1980).

INFLUENCES ON ADOLESCENT SEXUAL BEHAVIOR

Researchers have examined a number of social and interpersonal factors that might relate to adolescents engaging in sex or not.

Socioeconomic Status

Socioeconomic status largely reflects one's economic standing. One finding that has emerged in studies of the relation of social standing and adolescent sexuality is that regardless of ethnic group membership adolescents from more economically disadvantaged families engage in sexual intercourse earlier than their more economically advantaged peers (Furstenberg, Brooks-Gunn, & Morgan, 1987). This relation cannot, of course, be due simply to income. Income is an indicator of other factors—one's orientation to the future, for example—that likely are the reasons for the relationship that has been reported.

Income also is related to resolution of adolescent pregnancy. Adolescents from middle and upper social standing are more likely to terminate their pregnancies with abortions, in part because of their economic ability to do so.

Parent vs. Peer Influences and Family Composition

Much research has centered on the roles that parents and peers play in adolescents' initiation of sexual behavior. Some has been directed at the relative role of parental versus peer influence. Other research has examined the role of family composition.

Parent vs. Peer Influences.   The most extensive study of the relative influences of parents and peers on adolescent sexual behavior was reported by Shah and Zelnik (1981). The participants, 2,193 females aged 15 to 19, were asked whether their views about college, career plans, sex before marriage, making lots of money, and having an abortion were like those of their (1) parents, (2) friends, (3) both, or (4) neither. They also were asked their opinions about sex

Adolescents who feel they have views more similar to those of their parents than their peers are less likely to engage in premarital sexual intercourse. (*Shirley Zeiberg*)

prior to marriage, and indicated if it was (1) permissible even if the couple had no plans to marry, (2) permissible only if the couple had plans to marry, or (3) never permissible. These questions allowed the determination of the degree to which the adolescent's beliefs were like those of the parents, the peers, both or neither, and which exerted the greater influence on the adolescents' views of sex.

Of the females who believed premarital sex was acceptable, 64% felt their views about sex were like those of their friends and only 7% felt their views about sex were like those of their parents. In contrast, of those who felt premarital sex was never acceptable, only 33% felt their views were like their parents.

To understand these data more fully, it is helpful to look at the adolescent female's views of similarity to parents and friends on some of the other issues. The data for views about college, careers, and making money indicated the women felt their views were much like those of their parents or both their parents and friends. In other words, there was not simply a bias toward feeling one's views were more like those of friends than parents. Shah and Zelnik suggest these data indicate that, with regard to premarital sexual behavior, a substantial percentage of adolescent females face a real conflict between the values expressed by their parents and those of their peers.

This conflict is illustrated most clearly by the data presented in Table 8-5: Sexual experience is relatively highly related to perceptions of how one's views relate to those of the parents or the peers. Conflict in parent and peer values is demonstrated by the fact that the relationships are not perfect. For example, 26% of adolescent females who felt their perspectives were like those of their parents *had* engaged in premarital sexual intercourse. In turn, 41% of adolescent females who perceived their views were like those of their peers *had not* engaged in premarital sexual intercourse.

More current research (Casper, 1990; Moore, Peterson, & Furstenberg, 1986) confirms that parental influences on adolescent sexual behavior are minimal. Adolescents whose parents discuss sex with them, or whose parents keep a tight rein on their activities, are no more or less likely to engage in premarital sex, although some evidence indicates that greater maternal monitoring of activities is associated with reduced unprotected sex for females (O'Beirne, 1994).

Table 8–5 Percentage of 15- to 19-Year-Old Females with Premarital Sexual Experience, by Similarity of Views on Sex to Significant Others

Views on Sex Similar to	Percentage
Parents	26.0
Friends	59.4
Both	36.2
Neither	44.2
All	47.5

Source: Adapted from Shah, F., & Zelnik, M. (1981). Parent and peer influence on sexual behavior, contraceptive use, and pregnancy experience of young women. *Journal of Marriage and the Family, 43,* 339-348.

Adolescent girls who believe their friends or sisters are sexually active are more likely to become sexually active themselves. Deciding to become sexually active is strongly influenced by perceived social norms. (*Laima E. Druskis*)

Similarly (Eisen & Zellman, 1987), attending sex education classes does not promote or discourage adolescents from engaging in sexual intercourse.

Adolescents who have sexually active friends, or *believe* their friends are sexually active, are more likely to be sexually active themselves (Brooks-Gunn & Furstenberg, 1989; East et al., 1993; Udry, 1987). These factors are stronger for older than younger adolescents, and are more salient for females than males. For example, East et al. (1993) report that for sixth- through eigth-grade females, having a greater number of sexually active friends or sisters was related to more permissive sexual attitudes, greater intentions of becoming sexual if one was a virgin, and greater likelihood of being sexually active. The strength of these relations differed for Hispanic, Black, White, and Asian girls, indicating further the complexity of the contextual factors that relate to adolescent females becoming sexual. It seems reasonable to conclude that contextual factors—what one believes one's friends are doing and feels is "right" or the norm—are important determinants of adolescents' sexual behavior.

It appears, then, that adolescents may discuss aspects of sexuality with parents and learn their views. The same may be true for sex education classes. But the factors related to having sex are contextually and situationally driven. An examination of the reasons that adolescents give for having sex or not having sex supports this distinction. The feeling of wanting to please one's partner, for example, may be a stronger motivator for behavior than knowing that one's parents might disapprove.

Family Composition.   The possibility that family composition—living in a two-parent or one-parent family—might influence adolescent sexual behavior stems from the view that living in a single-parent household necessarily involves less parental supervision and control than living in a two-parent family. The evidence is that girls living in a single-parent household are more sexually active than their peers living in a two-parent home (Crockett & Bingham, 1994). Whether this is due to the disruption that might be caused by a (impending) divorce or due to living with a parent who is modeling dating and sexual behavior, or some other factor(s), remains an open question. For now, however, it is reasonable to conclude that family composition is an important contextual factor related to female adolescent sexual behavior.

CONTRACEPTION, PREGNANCY, AND SEXUALLY TRANSMITTED DISEASES

As the data just described demonstrate, substantial percentages of adolescents engage in premarital sexual intercourse. And the percentage of younger adolescents doing so is increasing. However, adolescents by and large do not guard against pregnancy with regularity, resulting in a large number of premarital pregnancies in the adolescent population.

Contraceptive Use

A well-established finding is that adolescents engage in sex without the benefit of contraception. Although one might expect that the initial sexual intercourse may occur without the benefit of contraception, subsequent intercourse, which may be more "planned" or "expected," could involve the use of contraception. An important question is whether the initial sexual intercourse really is spontaneous. Think about your own experience, if you have been sexually active, and that of your friends whom you know to have been sexually active. In all likelihood, the initial sexual intercourse was in fact "planned" if one considers planning as knowing it was going to occur. It may not have seemed planned if one views planning as admitting to the self that it was going to happen and that it was all right for it to happen. Because sexual intercourse is a new experience, and one our society makes adolescents feel uncomfortable about, it is difficult to integrate becoming sexual into our identity. Hence adolescents may rationalize that the first intercourse was unplanned when in reality they knew it was going to happen.

First Intercourse.   Sorensen (1973) reported that 55% of adolescents (49% of males and 63% of females) did not use contraception during their first intercourse. In 32% of the instances either the boy (28%) or the girl (37%) used some form of contraception. (In the remaining instances the boy did not, and he was unsure if the girl did or did not.) Use at first intercourse was higher for older (45%) than younger (26%) adolescent females. This was an interesting finding because about 86% of all the females felt that contraception was their responsibility.

Zelnik and Kantner (1980) report changes from the mid to late 1970s for adolescent women. In 1976 only 38% of adolescent women used some form of contraceptive the first time they engaged in sexual intercourse, but in 1979, 49% said they did. More recent evidence (see Davidson & Haviland, 1989b), however, indicates no further change during the 1980s for 15- to 19-year-olds in general, although older adolescents are increasingly using contraception at their first intercourse.

Like other aspects of sexual behavior, use of contraception during the first intercourse has a strong cultural component. I.M. Schwartz (1993) reported that 46% of the American females, compared to only 26% of Swedish females, reported using no contraception the first time they engaged in sex. Of those who used contraception, the condom was the most prevalent form: 40% of the American sample and 52% of the Swedish sample.

General Contraceptive Use.   Use of contraception at other than the first intercourse is increasing. Current estimates are that about 40% of sexually active adolescents use birth control some of the time, and about a third say they use it all the time. Unfortunately, about a sixth of sexually active adolescent women report never having used birth control (Hayes, 1987). Although effective methods of birth control, such as the pill and the condom, are used by high percentages of adolescents, too many rely on less effective means, such as withdrawal and the rhythm method. The changes in adolescent contraceptive use are a good sign and may ultimately result in a lowering of adolescent pregnancy rates, but unless condoms are used the rates of sexually transmitted diseases (discussed later), including AIDS, will remain high.

Reasons for Not Using Contraception.   Adolescents give a variety of reasons for not using contraception (Hayes, 1987; Shah & Zelnik, 1981; Sorensen, 1973; Zelnik & Kantner, 1980; Zelnik, Kim, & Kantner, 1979). Some adolescents indicate they do not know about contraceptive techniques or devices, and others indicate they want to get pregnant. In each case, however, the percentages are small, about 5% (Sorensen, 1973; Zelnik & Kantner, 1980). About 70% of adolescent males and females believe if the girl uses the pill or other birth control, it means she is planning on having sex, and that may make her feel guilty because being sexual is not yet integrated into her identity.

Because adolescents may have a somewhat romantic view of sex as being spontaneous, they do not wish to have it seem planned. I.M. Schwartz (1993), for example, reported that about two-thirds of both the American and Swedish

Although adolescents are knowledgeable about contraception, they often do not use it when engaging in sexual intercourse. (*Bebeto Matthews/AP/Wide World Photos*)

adolescent females interviewed indicated that their first sexual intercourse was spontaneous, not planned. In addition, to plan for sex requires admitting you are a sexual person, a task that is difficult for adolescents, and especially younger ones, who are at the greatest risk of pregnancy (Shah & Zelnik, 1981; Zelnik & Kantner, 1980). In support of this analysis, Davidson and Haviland (1989a, 1989b) noted that the ability to accept one's sexuality increases the probability that the adolescent female will use some form of contraception. This may be particularly difficult for adolescent females because of the way their sexual desires are socialized (Tolman, 1993). Although clearly acknowledging they feel sexual urges, many girls are socialized to believe that engaging in sexual behavior is something to be avoided, something to feel self-conscious about. This makes it difficult for them to integrate sexuality into their identity, to admit they have sexual feelings, are planning on having sex, and are sexual. Finally, females who are in love and who have some sex education are more likely to be consistent contraceptive users (Chilman, 1973; Zelnik & Kantner, 1977, 1978).

In part, adolescent females do not use contraception because they fear their parents will find out (Sorensen, 1973). Fifty-eight percent of Sorensen's females stated this reason. Health concerns, particularly with respect to the pill, are also stated as reasons for not using contraceptives (Sorensen, 1973; Zelnik & Kantner, 1980; Zelnik et al., 1979). In all likelihood, awareness of health concerns accounts for the decrease in adolescent females' use of the pill. As Rogel, Zuehlke, Petersen, Tobin-Richards, and Shelton (1980) note, there is a tendency to equate contraception with the pill, which may account for the failure of some adolescents to use any contraception.

Gerrard (1987) has suggested that part of the reason for college students' failure to use contraception is attributable to what he calls *sex guilt*. Adolescents who feel guilty about having sex are less likely to use contraception, perhaps because their guilt prevents them from planning to use it or perhaps because planning to use it increases their guilt. Some evidence (Davidson & Haviland, 1989a) indicates that when sexuality is integrated into one's identity, contraceptive use increases, perhaps by reducing guilt associated with being sexually active.

Some reasons for not using contraception seem to be very immature. For example, a substantial proportion of nonvirgin females (40%) agree that sometimes they don't care if they get pregnant, and a third of adolescents believe that if a girl doesn't want to get pregnant she won't, even if she has sex without contraception. And 30% to 40% believe they won't get pregnant because they don't have sex often enough (Zelnik & Kantner, 1980). Still others simply feel that pregnancy can't happen to them, a kind of egocentrism discussed in Chapter 4. Believing false notions such as these can lead the adolescent to suffer the consequences of premarital pregnancy.

Adolescent Pregnancy

Koenig and Zelnik (1982) reported that in 1976, 32% of sexually active urban adolescent females experienced a premarital pregnancy within 2 years of their first intercourse. This figure rose to 36% in 1979. The increase was due largely to the younger adolescents, those aged 15 or less. In 1976, 27% of sexually active females aged 15 or less had a premarital pregnancy within 2 years of their initial intercourse. In 1979, 41% of this group had a premarital pregnancy within 2 years of initiating sexual intercourse. There was little change from 1976 to 1979 for adolescent females older than 15. It is reasonable to conclude that if there is a continuation of the decline in average age of first intercourse, and if the frequency of engaging in sexual intercourse continues to increase, we shall see a continued increase in the percentage of adolescent females who experience a premarital pregnancy (Koenig & Zelnik, 1982).

Incidence of Premarital Pregnancy.   American adolescent pregnancy rates are among the highest in the industrialized world (Zabin & Hayward, 1993). Current estimates are that by age 18 about 25% of adolescent women will experience a pregnancy. About 40% of African American adolescents will have a pregnancy before age 18 (Hayes, 1987). Historically, more African American and Hispanic than White youth have chosen to remain single (Hayes, 1987). Increasingly, White adolescents now also are opting to remain single. Hence the increase in the number of White adolescents who elect to not marry is largely responsible for the increase in births to *single* adolescents.

It is important to distinguish between pregnancies and *birthrates*. Recent statistics indicate that the birthrate among adolescents actually is lower now than in previous decades (Hayes, 1987). The lower birthrate likely is due to the increase in adolescents choosing abortion as a means to terminate their pregnancy.

Not all adolescent females who are sexually active get pregnant. Some information (Crockett, 1994; Crockett & Bingham, 1994) sheds light on the risk factors for those who do become pregnant. Compared to sexually active peers who do not experience a pregnancy, those who do tend to come from the lower socioeconomic strata, live in families in which they have poor relations, have a sister who was pregnant in her teens (East, 1994), and are less involved in academic activities. Crockett suggests that this constellation of factors may reflect differing social-class values related to one's views of the future. Those from the lower social strata may encourage early marriage and adolescents in these families may be less concerned about avoiding pregnancy, or may even opt to get pregnant as a route of entrance into adulthood, because they do not see a future including further education and a career.

Pregnancy Resolution

There are several resolutions to an adolescent premarital pregnancy. Stillbirths and miscarriages account for about 10% of adolescent pregnancies. About 40% have abortions, 45% have the baby and keep it, and about 5% of adolescents have the baby and place it for adoption (Henshaw, 1987). In other words, about 90% of adolescents who give birth keep their child.

Adolescent Stillbirths and Miscarriages. During the 1970s there was an increase in adolescent stillbirths and miscarriages, from 10% in 1971 to about 14% in 1979 (Zelnik & Kantner, 1980). This increase is largely attributable to the increase in pregnancies for those under age 15. Researchers generally agree that these and other health risks faced by adolescent mothers are due largely to their behavior patterns (Hayes, 1987). Adolescent females generally neglect their health and have poor eating habits. When they discover they are pregnant they do not make the adjustments necessary to promote sound prenatal development. And they often do not obtain prenatal health care until well into the pregnancy. These failures may lead to increased risks for low birth weight babies, premature babies, and babies with higher risks of health problems as they develop (Hayes, 1987). Modifying one's daily health and nutritional habits would go far toward correcting these health risks to the mother and the fetus.

One means of modifying adolescents' prenatal health care is to provide ready access to sound health care in a comfortable atmosphere. Seitz and Apfel (1994) have shown that school-based health care programs that allow pregnant adolescents to receive continuous monitoring have a substantial effect on reducing premature births for a group of mostly Black, low social-class adolescents, a group at a high risk for premature births. They attribute the benefit to the medical, psychological, and educational support the future mothers receive.

Adolescent Abortions. During the 1970s the birthrate for unmarried adolescents declined, from 67% in 1971 to 49% in 1979. At the same time the percentage of adolescents having an abortion increased, from 23% in 1971 to 39% in 1979 (Zelnik & Kantner, 1980). The increase in abortions continued into the 1980s, and current estimates are that over 450,000 abortions per year are performed on unmarried women aged 19 or younger, with a substantial percentage of these (over 10%) for women younger than age 15 (Hayes, 1987; Henshaw, 1987). Statistics such as these have led to the idea that adolescents use abortion as a form of birth control. However, Hayes argues this is not the case. She points out that repeat abortions among adolescents are relatively rare, accounting for about 12% of abortions for those aged 15 to 17 and 22% of abortions for those aged 18 to 19.

Having an abortion involves a decision process affected by a number of personal factors. Girls who are doing well in school and who have a strong orientation to the future are more likely to choose abortion rather than have the baby (Hayes, 1987). White adolescents are more likely to choose abortion than are African Americans, as are those from higher socioeconomic statuses, those whose mothers have more liberal views about abortion, and those whose friends are more positively disposed toward abortion (Hayes, 1987).

All forms of abortion involve some health risks to the mother, including death—about .6 deaths occur for every 100,000 legal abortions (Centers for Disease Control, 1980). These risks increase when the abortion is performed later in the pregnancy. Because some adolescents, especially those who are younger, may not recognize the signs of pregnancy or may deny the pregnancy until they no longer can, the percentage of those aged 19 or less having an abortion after the first trimester is about twice that of women aged 20 or more (Centers for Disease Control, 1980). As a group, then, adolescents face greater health risks from abortion than do older women.

The Adolescent Mother and Father.   Although previous conceptualizations of being an adolescent mother were in some ways overly pessimistic (Furstenberg et al., 1987), it still is difficult and often results in a less bright future. Nor is it a particularly desirable situation for the adolescent father.

Part of the difficulty encountered by pregnant adolescents lies in their completing their education, which relates to their employability. Although the stereotype of the pregnant adolescent dropping out of school and never completing her high school education is true for some, it is untrue for others (Furstenberg et al., 1987; Linares, Leadbeater, Kato, & Jaffe, 1991; Scott-Jones, 1991a, 1991b). Those who remain in school throughout their pregnancies experience less delayed grade placement and fewer repeat pregnancies than those who drop out, drop out and then return, or drop out after they have the baby. Linares et al. suggest that what is needed are programs aimed at keeping pregnant adolescents in school. Scott-Jones further suggests that these programs should be instituted early in adolescence, for early adolescent childbearers are not behind national averages on measures of school performance. She further makes the important point that the mother's earlier school success and experience may be crucial to her decision to remain in school.

The educational attainment of adolescent mothers also depends on their ethnic group. Scott-Jones (1991a, 1991b) notes that the Hispanic adolescents in her study of adolescent mothers had lower educational levels than either the Black or White mothers. And Black mothers were nearer the average educational attainment level for their age than were White or Hispanic mothers. She suggests that familial and community support may play a stronger role for Black than Hispanic or White adolescent mothers, thereby allowing the greater opportunity to complete more education. Nonetheless, the average educational level for 19-year-old Black mothers was still less than graduation from high school.

An important part of remaining in school is delaying further pregnancies (Seitz & Apfel, 1993a, 1993b, 1994). Adolescent mothers who have a second child relatively soon after the first are much more likely to drop out of school, be economically dependent and on welfare, and subsequently have large families. The second and subsequent children overtax the child-rearing system and contribute to the mother deciding to put off further education until her children are in school. Home visit, clinic-based, and school-centered programs that provide prenatal care to poor African American and White adolescent mothers and continue to provide care postnatally have been shown to be effective in promoting delayed further childbearing and continuance in educational programs (Furstenberg et al., 1987; Horwitz, Klerman, Kuo, & Jekel, 1991; Olds, Henderson, Tatelbaum, & Chamberlin, 1988; Seitz & Apfel, 1993a, 1993b, 1994). The benefits have been shown to last for at least 6 years after the mother was no longer in the program.

Seitz and Apfel (1993a, 1993b) suggest that the success of the programs lies in their modifying the mothers' postnatal behavior, which sets a "trajectory" for their future life. Having contact with program staff (e.g., school nurse) increases the effective use of contraception and even results in increased avoidance of sexual behavior. Each of these decreases the likelihood of an early second pregnancy and sets the course for continued delay. Once the delay is under way it is more likely to be continued. The delay in subsequent childbearing contributes to continued education and reduced reliance on welfare.

What this suggests is that poverty conditions are an important factor in determining the effects of adolescent pregnancy on both the mother and the child. The concerns are complex. It turns out that babies born of nonpoverty adolescent mothers are very similar in their development to babies born of married mothers. The converse also is true. These data underscore the importance of economics in understanding the effects of adolescent pregnancy on the child.

Age at first birth is related to the ratio of income to the poverty level (needs) for African American, Hispanic, and White mothers (Moore et al., 1993). Those who have children at a younger age complete less school, earn less, have larger families (especially African Americans), and ultimately live in families that have lower total family income (especially Hispanics). Although subsequently marrying may benefit the White adolescent mother economically, it does not do so for African American mothers (Astone, 1993).

An important factor in the child's development is that adolescent mothers are not particularly skilled at mothering. Compared to older mothers they are less communicative with their babies and engage in less play and interaction with them (Culp, Culp, Osofsky, & Osofsky, 1989). They are less expressive, engage in poorer quality play, and generally interact at a qualitatively lower level with their infants than do other mothers. As a result, the child's development does not progress at an optimal level. In part, this stems from adolescent mothers, and particularly younger adolescent mothers, having poor knowledge of typical infant development (Karraker & Evans, 1993; Sommer, et al., 1993), which contributes to poor rearing skills (Sommer et al., 1993). In part, it stems from the infant's grandmother providing considerable infant care, especially early in infancy (Penny, Watson, Saunders, & Womble, 1993). This reduces the learning experience of the adolescent with her child.

The most basic difficulty for adolescent mothers is economics (Furstenberg et al., 1987). Adolescent mothers who can reenter the educational system fare well in the job market. Their children develop in a manner similar to children born of wedded mothers. In addition, maintaining an exclusive relationship with the child's father is desirable (C. Russell, 1980) because it stabilizes the relationship with the father and encourages the father's interactions with the child.

Much less is known about the fathers of the children born to adolescent mothers. Many are, in fact, not adolescents themselves, but are young adults. As adolescents, they are more likely to have had serious school problems (to have been expelled or suspended), to have engaged in antisocial aggression (fighting), to have used drugs, and to have had serious encounters with the law (Elster, Lamb, & Tavare, 1987). These findings, with few exceptions, held for African American, Hispanic, and non–African American/non-Hispanic groups that were representative of the population. About half are "atypical" in the sense of inability to assume adulthood roles and having emotional and social difficulties.

Most adolescent fathers are not in a position to provide child support. What is needed, some argue (Smollar & Ooms, 1987), are programs that allow adolescent fathers to complete school or to gain job training allowing them to enter the work force. By being steadily employed the father not only will be in a position to help support his child, but also will gain in self-esteem and adjust better to adulthood roles.

Part of the reason fewer adolescent mothers marry now than previously is they are aware that adolescent fathers are unable to support themselves let alone a family, and that adolescent fathers may be facing a bleak future in the world of work. Adolescent marriage is a very high-risk alternative for the adolescent mother. Moreover, adolescent marriages have a much higher likelihood of divorce than adulthood marriages.

The available evidence indicates that the best long-term option for the adolescent mother is not to marry. Those who live for a time with their parents enjoy greater opportunities to continue education as they adapt to motherhood; this enhances their opportunities for the future. School-based programs that are designed to allow adolescent mothers to continue their education, perhaps by bringing the child to school with them, and community-based or school-based

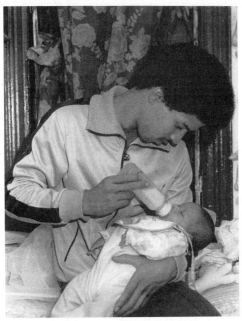

In order to allow adolescent fathers to be responsible for their children, we need programs to help them gain training, allowing them access to employment. (*Katherine McGlynn/The Image Works*)

programs aimed at helping the mother not become pregnant again make sound sense when one understands the problems and difficulties faced by the adolescent mother (Seitz & Apfel, 1994).

Adoption.   As Namerow, Kalmuss, and Cushman (1993) remind us, the group of adolescents that decides to have the child rather than abort it includes two subgroups, those who will keep the child and those who will place the child for adoption. Interest in adolescents selecting adoption has several bases, one of which is that putting the child up for adoption relieves the adolescent of the burdens faced by those who decide to keep their child.

Because there is no national agency responsible for collecting information on adoption, unlike there is for abortion, only estimates of adoption can be made. It appears that the percentage of adolescents having their baby and putting it up for adoption has been declining. Hayes (1987) reported that for 15- to 19-year-olds in 1982, 4.6% of unmarried mothers gave their babies up for adoption. White mothers did so to a greater extent (7.4%) than African American mothers (0.7%). In 1986 only 2.8% of babies born to unmarried mothers were placed for adoption (Namerow et al., 1993).

Although the research on the characteristics of those who select adoption is not extensive, some generalizations can be made. One important factor is what Namerow et al. (1983) call "adoption socialization," which involves exposure to adoption as a serious potential means of resolving the pregnancy. These researchers found that women who had prior exposure to adoption, for example, being adopted or having a sibling or friend who was adopted, related positively to seriously considering adoption and putting the child up for adoption. Women with no prior exposure to adoption do not seriously consider it—a woman cannot consider seriously *all* possible means of terminating a pregnancy without having a schema that includes adoption.

The decision to place the child for adoption also is influenced by the attitudes and views of others—the girl's mother, close relatives, boyfriend. Their support greatly enhanced the probability that the girl would place the child for adoption. These individuals function as agents of adoption socialization. Being able to *seriously* consider adoption allows for a more informed choice and, for those who decide against abortion, opens the door to an alternative that might not otherwise be chosen.

The Fundamental Problem

The information presented here indicates two major concerns: adolescent sexuality and adolescent pregnancy. Furstenberg et al. (1987) note that adolescent sexuality may not be the major problem. They point out that in Sweden the sexual behavior of adolescents is very similar to that of American youth yet the pregnancy rates are lower, largely due to the increased consistent use of effective contraception. They suggest that the real problem is not adolescent sexuality but rather adolescent pregnancy. It is adolescent childbearing that causes emotional, educational, and health concerns for the mother and the infant.

Adolescent sexuality has always occurred and no doubt always will. That the median age of first intercourse has been dropping certainly is not desirable. But attempts to encourage abstinence, especially for those who experience poverty, racism, or other conditions that make their futures look bleak, have not been shown to be effective (Bartels, Limber, O'Beirne, & Wilcox, 1994). What is needed are sound sex education programs that teach adolescents about contraception, sexually transmitted diseases, and especially how to behave in a sexually responsible manner.

Programs that teach expectant adolescent mothers *and* fathers about typical child development, child care, parenting skills, and the importance of prenatal care are sorely needed. We also need programs designed to allow adolescents to continue their education; these will benefit not only adolescents but also their children and the society. Such programs also will help adolescents who are sexual, or considering becoming sexual, integrate sexuality into their identity, which is related to increased sexual responsibility.

Sexually Transmitted Diseases

The term *sexually transmitted diseases* refers to a variety of diseases transmitted from one person to another through sexual intercourse, although it is

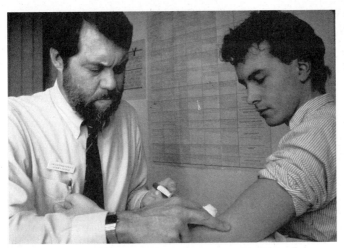

Sexually transmitted diseases are epidemic in the adolescent population because of adolescents' failure to engage in safe sex. (*Jim Wil-
son/Woodfin Camp & Association*)

known that one, **acquired immune deficiency syndrome (AIDS)** , can be
transmitted in other ways such as through shared use of needles used for intravenous drugs.

Although they are aware of the names of various sexually transmitted diseases, most adolescents do not know the symptoms of the diseases and, thus,
are unlikely to recognize them when they occur. This is especially unfortunate
because for some diseases, such as **syphilis** and *herpes*, the symptoms may
come and go, leading the adolescent to believe he or she is not suffering from a
very serious problem.

In general, sexually transmitted diseases are caused by bacteria or para-
sites. The most common among the adolescent population are **gonorrhea** and
herpes, which can lead to disorders of the reproductive system, sterility, and
other symptoms (headache, fever), including in the case of herpes increased
risk of cervical cancer and miscarriage.

Among the most serious sexually transmitted diseases is AIDS because it
has few if any initial symptoms. The adolescent population is at high risk because of increased sexual activity and intravenous (IV) drug use (Millstein,
1989). Indeed, adolescents have the highest age-adjusted sexually transmitted
disease rates of all age groups studied, which places them at an increased risk
for AIDS. It is estimated that every 14 months the number of adolescents diag-
nosed with AIDS doubles (Koniak-Griffin, 1993). Most of the young adults diag-
nosed with AIDS contracted the disease during their adolescent years, given the
8- to 10-year incubation period. AIDS has now become the leading cause of
death for those aged 25 to 45.

The high degree of sexuality among adolescents puts them at high risk for

AIDS because (1) sexual activity begins at a relatively early age, when individuals are likely limited in their ability to foresee realistic consequences of their activity, and (2) condoms are unlikely to be used (condoms provide some protection against AIDS infection; Koniak-Griffin, 1993; Rimberg & Lewis, 1994). In addition, adolescents represent a high-risk group if they fall into one or more of the following categories: being homeless, a runaway, an IV drug user, a person with multiple sexual partners, or gay. Because AIDS initially has no overt symptoms of infection, the individuals can become infected, infect others, and not know they need treatment. Thus AIDS may become a major epidemic among the adolescent population even though it is not detected (because of its long incubation period) until the adolescents are young adults.

Because of adolescents' heightened risk of contracting AIDS, health care professionals and others have tried to determine what factors are related to adolescents' increasing their use of safe sex practices. It is now clear that simply providing adolescents with information about contraception and AIDS is not sufficient (S.A. Johnson & Green, 1993; Rimberg & Lewis, 1994). Despite adequate knowledge, high percentages of adolescents and college students engage in unsafe sexual practices. In order to understand the failure of adolescents to use contraception and to increase safe sexual practices, then, we must look at the individual adolescent's beliefs about sexuality.

Accepting that one is sexual and therefore should plan for safe sex, becoming comfortable learning about a potential partner's sexual history, overcoming embarrassment at purchasing and using contraception are all related to increased safe sex practices, and understanding that engaging in unsafe sex practices puts you at risk for pregnancy and disease are all related to increases in safe sex practices (S.A. Johnson & Green, 1993; Rimberg & Lewis, 1994). These behaviors and realizations cannot occur until one has integrated sexuality into the identity, which is difficult for adolescents in our society. Unfortunately, then, we likely will continue to see large numbers of adolescent pregnancies and large numbers of adolescents contracting AIDS.

SEX EDUCATION

Sex education in the public schools is problematic for parents, educators, and adolescents. First, the need for sex education classes must be established. Second, the curriculum must be determined, including decisions about what should be taught at different age levels. Finally, the structure of the class must be decided, which involves concerns about who should teach it, whether it should be coed or sexually segregated, and whether it should be a separate class or part of some other class, such as biology or health.

What kind of sex education did you receive at your school? What made it valuable or lacking? What would you have changed? How did your parents react to your having sex education? Someday you will have children and adolescents. What kind of sex education do you want them to receive through the school system? How much will you communicate to them? The issues are not simple because they touch not only on sex but also on religious and moral values, the rearing "rights" of parents, and socially determined standards for acceptable conduct, including legal sanctions.

Considerable evidence supports the need for sex education in the public schools (DiClemente et al., 1989). Many advocates cite the incidence of premarital pregnancy. Others point to the serious problems of sexually transmitted diseases among adolescence. Still others suggest that proper sex education will help adolescents cope with the prevalence of sexuality in the media and the fact that, for the most part, the media does not place sex in a realistic light—issues of contraception, possible adolescent pregnancy, and sexually transmitted diseases are generally not portrayed. Finally, others believe sex education in the public schools is necessary to ensure that young people obtain accurate information about sexual matters.

Over the past 50 years or so, substantial research has examined sources of information about sex for adolescents. For the vast majority of adolescents, friends and reading material are the major sources (Andre, Frevert, & Schuchmann, 1989; Hayes, 1987). Mothers (especially for girls), courses at school, and personal experience were the next major sources of information. It is an unquestionable finding that peers are the major source of sexual information for most adolescents but unfortunately what peers "know" is often faulty and incomplete (Hayes, 1987). Although books or pamphlets may provide accurate information, one cannot hold a question-and-answer session with printed material. Hence it is often not the best resource for the adolescent interested in learning about sexual matters. Moreover, most written material focuses on physiological and biological information, and does not deal with other personal concerns, such as how to make the decision to become sexually active. Unfortunately, par-

Through sex education classes, adolescents gain significant amounts of accurate information about sexuality. (*Elizabeth Crews/Stock Boston*)

ents, teachers, and others who might be able to engage the adolescent in discussions of these issues are not widely utilized as sources of information.

Surveys indicate that the content of sex education classes fails when it comes to adolescents' personal concerns. Although most adolescents who are exposed to a sex education class learn about the biology of sex and reproduction, they do not learn how to engage in sex or have a forum to discuss their moral concerns about sex (Hayes, 1987). Programs that include such topics, along with information about decision-making skills and how to resist peer pressure, promise to help adolescents cope better with sexuality (Hayes, 1987). Improving sex education classes by including such information may even reduce the degree of adolescent courtship violence, including date rape (Box 8-3).

Sex education programs clearly teach facts, but the evidence shows they do not encourage adolescents to engage in sex or influence the frequency with which they do (Eisen & Zellman, 1987). Unfortunately, sex education classes also do not increase the likelihood of adolescents using contraception (Hayes, 1987). Hence, although existing sex education classes influence knowledge and attitudes, they have only a limited effect on behavior.

ADOLESCENCE AND HOMOSEXUALITY

It is important to distinguish between homosexual experience and homosexuality. Homosexual experience refers to sexual experiences in the company of same-sex peers or adults. **Homosexuality** refers to a sexual attraction and preference for those of one's own sex. Having a homosexual experience does not mean one is a homosexual.

Janus and Janus (1993) report that having a homosexual experience is not uncommon. In their representative national sample of over 2700 adult men and women, they found that 22% of the men and 17% of the women reported having had a homosexual experience. Of these, 39% of the men (about $8\frac{1}{2}$% of the men surveyed) and 27% of the women (about $4\frac{1}{2}$% of the women surveyed) reported frequent or ongoing homosexual experiences. When the adults were asked to identify their sexual orientation, 91% of the men and 95% of the women reported it was heterosexual, 4% of the men and 2% of the women reported it was homosexual, and 5% of the men and 3% of the women reported a bisexual orientation.

The factors determining any sexual orientation—homosexual, heterosexual, or bisexual—are not well understood. The prevalent view about the development of a homosexual orientation attributes it to an interaction between biological and social factors (Green, 1980, 1987; Savin-Williams, 1988). Savin-Williams suggests that prenatal exposure to certain hormones influences early brain organization and, thereby, sexual orientation. He also points out that twin studies, similar to those discussed for the inheritance of intelligence (Chapter 4), indicate greater similarity in sexual orientation among identical than fraternal twins. Biological predispositions for sexual orientation, then, may exist.

As we have noted previously, however, biological predispositions are car-

BOX 8–3   Violence and Date Rape in Adolescent Courtship Relationships

In recent years, researchers have become increasingly aware that adolescent courtship relationships may involve various aspects of abuse similar to that involved in spousal abuse. They have termed this type of abuse *courtship violence*. Although courtship violence may involve verbal or psychological abuse of varying types, its most serious form is **date rape** (B. Carlson, 1987), forcing a dating partner to have sexual intercourse against his or her will.

Courtship violence is more prevalent than most of us would guess. Between 20% and 36% of college students report having been physically violated—grabbed, shoved, or pushed—by a dating partner (Clark, Klein, & Beckett, 1992). Among adolescents, about 10% of White females and 5% of African American females report having been date raped (Moore, Nord, & Peterson, 1989). If one includes other forms of forced unwanted sexual behavior, the percentages of unwanted physical contact may approach a quarter of White adolescent females (Klingaman & Vicary, 1992). Several points need to be made. First, courtship violence involves more than date rape or other unwanted sexual behavior. It also involves verbal and physical aggression. Second, although the female in the dating partnership is much more prone to experience courtship violence, it does happen to some males (Camarena & Sarigiani, 1994). Third, courtship violence is not a new phenomenon; it likely has existed for generations. Our current concerns simply reflect a heightened awareness that courtship violence is a serious problem that begins during adolescence. Finally, sexual victimization has long-term negative effects on emotional well-being, especially for those who found the experience had a very negative impact on their lives.

Researchers who investigate the underlying causes of courtship violence, including date rape, have noted that both the child-rearing history of perpetrators and the personality and attitudes of aggressors and victims may be important factors (Clark et al., 1992; Klingaman & Vicary, 1992). In summarizing the literature, Clark and colleagues note that evidence indicates the importance of parents and parental rearing practices in understanding why some males engage in courtship violence. Males whose parents model violence in their interpersonal interactions are more likely to engage in courtship violence. Abusive males also tend to have a masculine sex-role orientation and to hold traditional views of the role of women in society.

Clark et al. found that males having a mother who was not particularly involved in the boy's life or who was not very child centered was predictive of the boy being verbally aggressive. For girls, verbal aggression was related to mother's use of firm discipline. Physical aggression by boys against the dating partner was associated with having a mother who was detached from the boy and who did not particularly enforce rules for behavior. Girls whose mothers were overly controlling were more prone to using physical aggression in their courtship relations.

In explaining their findings, Clark et al. take an interesting perspective. They note that parental rearing practices, personality traits of the individuals, and attitudes about the roles of women and men in society relate to how the couple deals with interpersonal conflict in their relationship. The most important factor, they argue, is how each person perceives the behavior of the other. Perceiving the partner as being verbally or physically aggressive seems to elevate the likelihood that one will behave in a similar manner.

In their study of date rape and sexual assault experienced by adolescent girls, Klingaman and Vicary (1992) investigated a variety of potential "risk factors." Risk factors are personal attributes or circumstances that increase the likelihood of the individual having a particular experience, in this case sexual assault. A total of 23% of the females in their study had experienced one or more types of unwanted sexual activity, and 15% had been date raped. Although family factors, such as structure or church attendance, and the use of alcohol were not related to the likelihood of experiencing sexual assault, being younger at menarche or when she first had intercourse were. Those who had been sexually assaulted also had poorer peer relations and reported having more friends who had experienced sexual intercourse than those who had not been sexually assaulted. Finally, the girls who were sexually assaulted felt more lonely, guilty, and "bad" about themselves.

It is apparent that explaining sexual assault by adolescents, including date rape, requires us to consider a variety of factors. We observed in Chapter 3 that girls mature earlier than boys, and we note in this chapter that girls tend to date somewhat older boys, at least initially. Klingaman and Vicary report that younger girls (14 and under) were victimized by males 4 or more years older, and that older girls (16 and up) by men in their 20s and 30s. Such information suggests that interactions between physical development and social expectations for behavior are significant. It also is clear that parental rearing techniques and models for male–female interaction are important considerations.

Sexual assault, including date rape, is an unacceptable form of behavior. What can we do about it? Klingaman and Vicary suggest developing training programs for adolescents to teach them about these concerns. Such training might well include conflict resolution, as investigated by Clark et al. By teaching adolescents how to resolve conflicts in couple relations it may be possible to reduce the incidence of adolescent sexual assault.

ried out in an environmental context, leading to an interaction between biological and social factors that determines our behavior. In this instance, it may be that biological factors related to sex-typed behavior (see Chapter 7) predispose the individual to play and social activities that ultimately result in a homosexual orientation. Recall that testosterone is related to behaving more aggressively and estrogen to acting more passively (Chapters 3 and 7). As an infant and child the individual may develop play preferences and ways of interacting socially that reflect behavioral expressions of biological predispositions. These, in turn, affect how others react to the individual.

This line of reasoning has led some researchers to examine parental rearing techniques that might relate to the child developing a homosexual orientation. In general, homosexual boys feel their mothers were domineering, overprotective, and made them feel dependent; they saw their fathers as presenting poor role images and as ignoring them and making them feel unwanted (A. P. Bell, Weinberg, & Hammersmith, 1981). Green (1987) suggests that these boys' preference for more feminine play and interaction may have alienated their fathers and their young male peers, causing them as they grew up to seek affection from males, those from whom they did not gain affection during their childhood and younger adolescent years. A similar argument is made for lesbians, who as a group perceive their mothers as cold and distant (A. P. Bell et al., 1981).

We need to make two points about this theorizing, however. First, not all children and adolescents who view their parents as cold or distant grow up with a homosexual orientation. This suggests there are factors involved about which we know nothing. It is likely that sexual orientation is determined by many highly individualistic factors. Different individuals may develop a particular sexual orientation through different means (Garnets & Kimmel, 1991). Much further research will need to be done before we can determine how sexual orientations are decided.

Second, contrary to what many believe, homosexuality is not a disease or considered a mental health problem. The American Psychiatric Association does not identify it as a mental disorder. Nonetheless, substantial percentages of the population do, which is a basis for **homophobia,** perhaps the most commonly experienced difficulty homosexuals encounter. Homophobia is an irrational fear and/or hatred of homosexuals. This most often is expressed as prejudice and discomfort among homosexuals.

Marsiglio (1993) surveyed a national sample of Black, Hispanic, and White adolescents about their attitudes toward homosexual behavior and homosexuals. Regardless of ethnic background, about 89% of the adolescents agreed "a lot" with the statement "The thought of men having sex with each other is disgusting." The majority (59%) "Disagreed a lot" or "Disagreed a little" with the statement "I could be friends with a gay person." Among black adolescents the percentage was 80; 53% of Hispanic and 59% of white adolescents also disagreed a lot or disagreed a little. Such evidence suggests that homophobic feelings are strong among adolescents.

Homosexual adolescents face other problems as well. They may experience peer rejection, the lack of role models, religious intolerance, and difficulties with family members. Homosexual adolescents may face identity development difficulties and feelings of being "different." Most do not incorporate homosexuality into their identity until young adulthood; as adolescents they remain confused and uncommitted about their sexual identity.

Because of the social stigma attached to the homosexual orientation in our society, the gay or lesbian adolescent may face a very difficult decision: Do I hide my sexual orientation or do I come out of the closet? Boxer, Cohler, Herdt, and Irvin (1993) note that the gay or lesbian adolescent often cannot find support from family or friends, must cope with religious beliefs that are opposed to homosexuality, and may face outright hostility. As a result, many gay and lesbian adolescents simply hide their sexual orientation, which may deter their identity development.

SUMMARY

During adolescence we experience an increase in the sex drive and an increase in interest in the opposite sex and sexuality. It also is the time when we begin to explore sex and integrate it into our identity. For these and other reasons, sexuality is linked to the adolescent years as an important developmental phenomenon that is a source of concern among adolescents, parents, and society.

Evidence shows that the increase in interest in sexuality is not an all-consuming one, as stereotypes would have us believe. Adolescents have many interests, sex being just one of them. Research also indicates that although biological factors may initiate an increased interest in sexuality, social factors are more instrumental in the actual engagment in sexual behaviors. This biosocial view of explaining sexuality allows us to better understand differences between males and females, ethnic groups, and cultures. For example, whereas boys are more likely to engage in sex with an initial partner for whom they don't necessarily feel strong emotions just a few times, girls are more apt to have sex with their initial partner over a more extended time period because they feel in love with him. These contrasting experiences reflect differing socialization of the sex drive for males and females. Current research, however, shows the attitudes of male and female adolescents are converging: Males are becoming more sensitive to sex within a close, loving relationship whereas females are becoming more liberal in their attitudes about when sex is appropriate.

Our culture is best described as semirestrictive regarding adolescent sexual behavior. Although the official standard is that premarital sex for adolescents is wrong, the restrictions are not very strongly enforced. This contrasts with other cultures, which are best characterized as restrictive or permissive. Hence adolescents generally feel sexual intercourse is allowable if the people are in love or engaged, or if they are older, but most also agree that casual sex is not appropriate. Most sexually active adolescents are monogamous: They have a single sexual partner. In general, the evidence indicates most adolescents are not promiscuous.

Adolescent sexuality is a developmental progression. It starts with auto-erotic behavior (fantasies about sexuality or masturbation) and progresses to sociosexual behavior (sexual behavior with another person). In addition, sexual intercourse is not the beginning of sexual behavior, but rather the culmination of a progression that starts with necking and petting. Males generally engage in sex earlier than do females, although there has been a convergence over the past several decades, resulting in a smaller gap between the percentage of males and females who have engaged in sexual intercourse at any given age during the adolescent years. Ethnic group differences also exist, with African American and Hispanic youth more likely to be sexually active than White adolescents, particularly younger adolescents. Although females who are sexually active are more likely to feel embarrassment, guilt, and anxiety, most male and female sexually active adolescents find their sexual experiences satisfying.

A number of factors influence adolescent sexual behavior. Those from more economically disadvantaged backgrounds, regardless of ethnic group membership, are more likely to be sexually active, as are those who perceive their general values to be more like those of their peers than their parents. In general, parents exert relatively little influence on whether or not their adolescents will become sexually active. Having or believing they have sexually active friends or siblings and wanting to please their partner are more potent influences than parental wishes or values in adolescents' becoming sexual.

Very large percentages of adolescents do not use contraception during their first intercourse or do not use it consistently thereafter. As a result, adolescent pregnancy and sexually transmitted diseases are at high levels. Although about 450,000 abortions are performed on adolescents each year, abortion is not a form of contraception: Few adolescents have a second abortion. In addition, only about 3% of adolescents place their babies for adoption. The majority of adolescents having a baby keep it, but relatively few get married because they know it is not the right thing to do at that point in their life.

Contrary to the stereotypes, the typical adolescent mother has no particularly distinguishing characteristics: She is a typical adolescent. The adolescent father, in contrast, has a high likelihood of having had serious problems in school and with the law, may come from a very poor family situation, and may have dropped out of school. Most are unable or unwilling to provide support for their child.

Sexually transmitted diseases are prevalent among adolescents, largely because they do not use effective means, such as condoms, for preventing them. Adolescents are among those at the highest risk for contracting the AIDS virus, both because of the lack of condom use and the high rates of intravenous drug use.

Although many adolescents are able to take a sex education class in school, for many it occurs too late and does not cover topics that adolescents want discussed. For example, adolescents want to learn more than simply the biology of reproduction, including values about sexuality, when it is right or wrong, and the like. Sex education programs clearly offer correct information—much more than peers—but taking a sex education class does not increase contraceptive use. However, it also does not increase the likelihood of adolescents engaging in sex, contrary to the fears of parents, for example.

Although only a small percentage of adolescents are homosexual, that is, have a primary sexual preference for someone their own sex, having a homosexual experience—a sexual experience in the company of same-sex peers or adults—is much more common. Having a homosexual experience does not mean one is homosexual. Although biological factors may predispose one toward a homosexual orientation, such as a preference for certain play and social activities, social factors, such as how others, especially parents, react to the individual are likely more important to developing a homosexual orientation. The most common difficulty experienced by homosexuals is homophobia, the irrational fear or hatred of homosexuals. This may result in adolescent homosexuals being rejected by their peers and facing identity problems.

GLOSSARY

acquired immune deficiency syndrome (AIDS): Fatal disease, most often sexually transmitted, that attacks the body's immune system and thereby reduces the individual's ability to fight diseases and infections. Also may be transmitted through the use of shared needles, as in drug use, or from mother to fetus in utero.

autoerotic behavior: Sexual behavior that is experienced alone, such as masturbation.

biosocial perspective: View that both biological and sociocultural factors are important in determining behavior.

date rape: Forcing a dating partner to engage in sexual intercourse against her or his will through physical or psychological (coercive) means.

gonorrhea: Sexually transmitted disease that may lead to heart problems, blindness, or other physical problems.

homophobia: Irrational fear and/or hatred of homosexuals.

homosexuality: Sexual attraction and orientation to those of one's own sex.

serial monogamy: Engaging in sexual intercourse with a single steady partner. The partner may change from time to time.

sexual adventurer: Adolescent who engages in sexual behavior for the pleasure of sex. Has multiple partners.

sociosexual behavior: Sexual behavior involving another person, such as necking, petting, and intercourse.

syphilis: Sexually transmitted disease that may lead to severe retardation, physical problems, or death.

DISCUSSION QUESTIONS

1. What factors have led to the lowering of the median age of first intercourse for females over the past two decades?

2. Why have there been only very small changes in the percentage of adolescent males who have engaged in sexual intercourse by age 18?

3. What attitudinal changes in society other than those dealing with sexuality may have contributed to the changes in adolescent sexual behavior over the past several decades?

4. Did you have a sex education program in your high school? If not, why? If you did, how would you evaluate it—what were its strengths and weaknesses? Did it change your attitudes, behaviors, or knowledge about sexuality?

5. What factors lead so many adolescent women to decide to keep their child as opposed to giving the baby up for adoption? Is this generally in the best interest of the girl? The child?

6. Some have suggested that for boys the rewards intrinsic to sex are more important than they are for girls in the decision to initiate sexual behavior. What are the rewards intrinsic to sex?

7. What are some of the conditions that might account for cultural, subcultural, and ethnic group differences in adolescents' becoming sexual?

8. Adolescents give many reasons for not always using the most effective means of contraception. Which of these do you view as valid? Why do you believe that? If there are valid reasons for not always using effective contraception, what should adolescents do in order not to become pregnant?

9. What programs existed in your school system to allow adolescents who were pregnant or who were mothers to complete their education? Were the programs effective?

10. What factors account for the very high rates of sexually transmitted diseases among adolescents?

11. In what ways is AIDS transmitted other than through sexual intercourse? Why are adolescents among those with the highest risk for contracting the disease?

12. Homophobia is perhaps the most prevalent form of discrimination faced by gay individuals. What causes people to be homophobic? How can we change these fears?

9

Adolescents and Work

Major Issues Addressed

Adolescent Interest in Work
The Benefits and Detriments of Part-Time Work
The Work Experiences of Adolescents
Employment Opportunities for Female Adolescents
Parental and Sibling Influences on Vocational Development
Ethnic Groups and Adolescent Vocational Decisions
Long-Range Vocational Planning
Individual Characteristics and Vocational Choice
Theories of Vocational Choice

Throughout his high school years he was enamored with becoming a business tycoon. He grew up in the times of big mergers, takeovers, and astounding amounts of dollars being made. He made up his mind he would go into business—that's where the action was and that's where the bucks were. He entered a business school curriculum as a college freshman. At break at the end of the first semester he was unhappy. "I can't take enough literature or philosophy," he lamented. We talked about his interests and he transferred into the College of Arts and Sciences. He now has a degree with a major in English and a minor in philosophy. With that, he teaches tennis. And he's happy! He discovered the most important rule of vocational decision making: In the long run try to get paid for doing what you enjoy, for doing what is a hobby.

◆   ◆   ◆

During adolescence we begin to explore career goals seriously. This starts with some set of values about what we want out of a career. It is likely most of us start out wanting to have a glamorous career. As we develop further, we expand our perspectives of what we wish to gain from a vocation—money, prestige, excitement—to how it fits our self-views and helps us express them. Optimally, we are able to come to a career choice that allows us to enjoy a happy and rewarding vocation. How do we do it? Why do we make the choice we do? We explore these issues in this chapter.

INTRODUCTION

Planning and preparing for a vocation is one of the major developmental tasks of the adolescent years. This was not always the case. Until the mid-1800s, children and adolescents often worked long hours on the family farm or in shops. Some, especially boys, were given as apprentices, for example, to blacksmiths, and worked for no money, the learning of the trade being their only reward (Kett, 1977). The learning of work skills occurred on the job, with increasing

Child labor laws took children and adolescents out of the workplace and thereby contributed to their segregation from adults. In this way they helped create the adolescence we have today. (*Lewis W. Hine/Library of Congress*)

demands placed on youngsters as they grew more capable of contributing to the family or as an apprentice or a worker. Adolescents had little or no say in their choice of a vocation.

After the passage of the first child labor laws (in Massachusetts in 1836), the nature of adolescent vocational training changed dramatically. The initial labor laws were protective, in that they defined working conditions and hours, set age limits for work in some areas, and later established job training programs for youth. Although passage of labor laws meant many adolescents did not experience too much work too soon, it also meant that acquiring vocational training outside working on the family farm or in the family business was much more difficult. Younger adolescents were now prevented from acquiring skills by working in many jobs. Society began to function under the assumption that adolescents were not necessary to the labor force. In Benedict's (1938) terms, vocational development became discontinuous, making vocational decisions and the transition into adulthood more difficult.

The institution of child labor laws, in conjunction with our increasing urbanization and the availability of free (and mandated) public education, signaled a change in adolescents' roles (Kett, 1977). Historically, children and adolescents were workers; later, children and adolescents were primarily students, usually until their early teens, after which they became workers. As the availability of free education grew and as mandated education to the age of 16 or so became prevalent, adolescents remained in the school environment longer before leaving it to become workers. Being both a worker and a student was very rare.

Since the 1920s and 1930s, however, we increasingly have seen a merging of the student and worker roles, such that by the time of high school graduation most students have had some experience as a part-time worker. The growth in adolescent part-time work was a result of changes in the nature of industry—the growth of businesses such as fast-food outlets needing low-cost, short-hour employees—and the adolescent's increased cost of living: CDs cost money. Adolescents, whose numbers were increasing and whose financial needs had grown, filled the bill. As a result, it has become the norm for adolescents to have work experience prior to graduating from high school. Hence we see adolescents spending large numbers of hours in two primary places, at school and at work.

The increased employment of adolescents points to several important concerns regarding the transition into adulthood. First, how does the adolescent develop a vocational identity? As noted by Erikson and Marcia (see Chapter 6), an important part of identity involves one's views of the self as a worker. Second, what are the typical experiences of adolescents in the workplace, and what are the positive and negative aspects of those experiences? Finally, how do adolescents go about making long-term vocational decisions and how can we facilitate that process? We explore these and other questions in this chapter.

To set the stage, consider your own vocational experiences. Have you ever worked? How did you view the experience? What did you do with your money—help support the family, save large percentages of it, or spend it in a discretionary manner? Were the jobs you held "training experiences" or simply a way to make money? How did your experiences affect your view of becoming an employee? If you worked during the school year, how did it affect the time you spent with family and friends, on extracurricular activities and homework, and on other leisure time activities? Did you ever get fired? If so, how did you feel; how did it impact on your views of being a worker?

DEVELOPING A VOCATIONAL IDENTITY

Forming a vocational identity is a developmental process that begins in childhood and continues through the adolescent and adulthood years (Vondracek, 1993). It includes a developing awareness that at some point in the future one must choose a vocation and become a "worker." It also entails the integration of work into the identity (Erikson, 1959, 1963). Each task involves complex interplays between characteristics of the individual, such as one's interests, and aspects of the environment, such as educational opportunities.

Adolescents' Awareness of Future Work

Interest in one's future vocation begins in childhood and grows throughout the adolescent years. By the high school and college years, it ranks among the top interests of adolescents (Dusek, 1978). The increasing interest in one's future vocation likely is spurred by a need to resolve the identity crisis (Chapter 6) because one's vocation is an important part of identity. It also reflects a developmental history of being a worker, which for most children in our society begins with doing chores around the house, progresses to doing odd jobs such as lawn mowing, baby-sitting, or delivering newspapers, proceeds to part-time work during the summer and/or school year, and culminates in becoming a full-time employee. Each of these experiences allows the individual to develop a sense of the self as a worker and emphasizes that one must make a vocational choice.

Despite this increasing awareness, most adolescents give relatively little organized thought to their vocational plans, and most go about making their choices haphazardly and randomly. How did you decide on your future vocation? Some always knew what they wanted to be, but how? Others simply fell into a vocational choice, perhaps because of an instructor or course they took in high school or college. Few of us go about this very important decision systematically. In general, as a society we do a very poor job of helping adolescents and young adults make informed vocational decisions.

Although vocational training programs may help those considering entering skilled occupations (Lambert & Mounce, 1987), help for the remainder is lacking. Career education programs, which allow students to have work experiences while still enrolled in school, and federally sponsored employment programs aimed at disadvantaged youth were instituted in part to help students make more informed vocational choices. Although such programs have been shown to have some limited success—participants have better job-hunting and job-getting skills and are less likely to drop out of school—they apparently do not increase one's employability (Steinberg, 1982, 1984).

Failures such as these, and the growing awareness of the importance of vocational identity development, have led some to suggest school-based intervention programs focused on helping the individual more smoothly and systematically explore vocational options within the context of identity development (Super, 1990; A. S. Waterman, 1989). By formalizing career exploration, it is argued, the child and adolescent may explore the many facets of career choice to help them make sounder choices and deal more effectively with the identity crisis and the formulation of a vocational identity. To date, few such programs have been instituted.

Forming a Vocational Identity

Some theorists (for example, Vandenberg, 1968) have argued that adolescence cannot end until the individual chooses a vocation and enters the adult work world. From Erikson's (1959, 1963; see also Marcia, 1980) perspective, developing a view of the self in a vocational setting is critical to forming a mature adult identity. Although adolescent work experiences may be beneficial to identity formation, too much pressure for vocational decisions too early may retard its development.

Because the role of work in one's life is closely related to one's gender, males and females may not develop **vocational identities** in the same manner. Occupational identity may be a more salient issue for males and a less pressing issue for females because of its relation to traditional sex roles. In addition,

During adolescence we begin to acquire work habits and to identify the self in work settings. Some have suggested that the poor quality of the jobs open to adolescents may result in poor vocational identity. (*Laima E. Druskis*)

males and females may have different career interests due to differences in traditional sex roles (Schulenberg, Goldstein, & Vondracek, 1991).

Despite the fact that more women than ever before are entering the job market and are employed in traditionally male occupations, many occupations remain sex typed. This sex typing of occupations begins in adolescence (Greenberger & Steinberg, 1983), with boys more predominantly employed in some jobs (e.g., manual labor, gardening) and girls more represented in others (e.g., baby-sitting, waiting tables). These differences seem to reflect differences in **career interests** (Schulenberg et al., 1991), which are preferences for work settings, activities, and responsibilities. Schulenberg and his colleagues reported that, consistent with sex-role stereotypes, male adolescents showed greater interest in science and technology and female adolescents in art and service-related activities. The divergence in career interests was especially marked for those who had lower educational aspirations and who decided on a career relatively early.

The determinants of vocational interests lie, in part, in the opportunities provided by parents and in parental expectations for their offspring's future. In a study of adolescents' occupational aspirations, Harold and Eccles (1990) reported that mothers provided more opportunities for their sons in traditionally male-dominated areas (computers, math, sports) and their daughters in traditionally female-dominated areas (music, art, dance). In addition, the mothers differentially stressed with their offspring, having a happy marriage, entering the military, and having a job that could support a family. At the same time, however, it appears the mothers were sensitive to the preferences of their children. For example, the mothers of nontraditional daughters (those who aspired to a traditionally male occupation) had higher expectations for math performance and were more upset if the daughters did not do well in math. Conversely, the mothers of traditional daughters emphasized the more traditional feminine roles, such as family care. Information such as this suggests identity development and vocational choice should be related, and that sex-role development may play a role in the relationship.

Patterns of relationships between vocational identity development and sex-role development were the subject of a study by Grotevant and Thornbecke (1982). They measured high school juniors' and seniors' identity status and sex-role orientation. Although the males and the females had progressed equivalently toward achieving a vocational identity, they did so by different paths. For males, viewing the self as masculine—having an instrumental orientation, enjoying acceptance of challenging tasks, and not being too concerned about the negative evaluations of others—was related to higher levels of occupational identity. Occupational identity development for females was related to a willingness to work hard and to the avoidance of competition. For males, sex-role concerns seemed intimately tied to vocational issues. For females, no such direct link was shown. The authors suggest, therefore, that adolescent work experiences may have different meanings for males and females.

Identity also is related to **work values,** those aspects of personality, motivation, and work ethic that one brings into the workplace. Junior and senior high school students who are identity achieved have a greater concern for (1) developing and using their abilities on the job, (2) assisting others, and (3) achievement status on the job (Vondracek & Galanopoulos, 1992). These data suggest that identity-achieved adolescents are more vocationally mature, personally mature, and advanced in their views of what they want to do vocationally.

Describing how we develop vocational identities, then, is a difficult task. It begins in childhood and extends into adulthood (Vondracek, 1993). The developmental process of forming a vocational identity is shown in Havighurst's (1972) developmental task approach (Table 9–1). The first step is integrating the concept of becoming a worker into the self (through identification with adults). During preadolescence and early adolescence the second step entails learning work habits, which become primary over play and leisure habits—when your chores are done you may do other things. The third stage involves becoming a worker, which is the first step in becoming economically independent. Finally, vocational identity becomes solidified as we enter the adult work force. From this perspective, adolescent work experiences play an important role in vocational identity formation.

Table 9–1   Tasks of Vocational Development

Age	Task
5–10	Identify with significant others, such as parents
10–15	Acquire work habits versus, other habits, such as play
15–25	Identify the self in work settings
25–40	Be a productive worker

ADOLESCENT WORK EXPERIENCES

In many ways, studying adolescent work experiences entails the same considerations as exploring adult work experiences. Unemployment rates, what is
looked for and seen as important in a job, job satisfaction, and the influence of
the job on development are important factors in understanding both adolescent
and adult employment. In addition, it is becoming increasingly evident that gender discrimination in employment begins in adolescence (see Box 9-1).

Early views held that adolescent employment would ease the transition to
adulthood. Hence the major questions asked centered on how working increased
responsibility, taught job-relevant skills, and fostered entrance into adulthood. We
now realize that working may also entail some costs, just as it does in adulthood.
Hence the questions asked concern the types of jobs adolescents hold, how adolescents react to job pressures, the degree to which working facilitates (or not)
the entrance into the adult job market, how the number of hours worked (**work
intensity**) impacts on the adolescent, and how working in different settings, not
just working per se, influences aspects of adolescent development (Bachman &
Schulenberg, 1993; Greenberger & Steinberg, Final Report; Mortimer, Finch,
Ryu, Shananhan, & Call, 1993; Mortimer, Finch, Shanahan, & Ryu, 1992a, 1992b).

Adolescent Presence in the Work Force

Before examining statistics on employment, we first must decide what we mean
by the term *work*. To provide a perspective on work, Steinberg (1984) suggests
we must look at the role the adolescent is playing. From this perspective, **work**
is any activity that places the individual, subjectively or objectively, in the role
of "worker" and takes the person out of the role of "student" or "family member." It makes no difference if the work is for pay or if it is voluntary. Hence
doing household chores is not considered work, for the role the adolescent is
playing is that of family member—all members of a family have chores to do.
However, working in a family business is not part of the family member role of
son or daughter and, therefore, is considered work.

Since 1940, when the U.S. Bureau of the Census first began reporting employment statistics for both in- and out-of-school teenagers, there has been a
steady increase in the proportion of adolescents in the part-time work force and
in the amount of time they work (Greenberger, Steinberg, Vaux, & McAuliffe,
1980; Steinberg, Greenberger, Garduque, & McAuliffe, 1982). In 1940 about 4%
of in-school male and 1% of in-school female 16-year-olds were employed. In
1970 these figures were 17% and 16%, respectively. Dramatic increases also occurred for younger (14- to 15-year-old) adolescents (Greenberger et al., 1980).
Employment rates based on census data (U. S. Bureau of the Census, 1987) for
the years 1970 to 1992 are shown in Table 9-2. As you will see, a substantial
proportion of adolescents work at least part time. Indeed, it is estimated that by
the time they graduate over 80% of high school students will have held a job
(Greenberger & Steinberg, Final Report).

BOX 9–1   Does Sex Discrimination in Employment Begin in Adolescence?

In recent years we all have been made aware of the problems of job discrimination on the basis of gender. It is well established that, on average, adult women earn less money than men, even within the same broad occupational category (for example, professional). Women are clustered in lower paying and lower prestige jobs. Indeed, until recently, some professions were virtually entirely closed to women.

Information based on data collected by the Bureau of Labor Statistics and by the U.S. Census for in-school adolescents aged 14 and above indicates that more boys than girls are employed and boys work longer hours than girls, although these differences are narrowing. There also is evidence of sex segregation in the adolescent workplace very similar to that experienced in the adult workplace. Boys are more likely to be employed as unskilled or skilled laborers; girls are more likely to be employed in child care or clerical jobs. In part as a result of this distribution of occupations, girls earn nearly a dollar less per hour than boys. Finally, even within the same job category, boys generally make more money than girls.

Although it is tempting to attribute differences in hours worked and money earned to sex discrimination, Greenberger and Steinberg (1983) point out that the differences may be attributable to differences in job histories rather than gender. For example, if boys enter the work force at an earlier age than girls and have more experience working, it would be reasonable and logical to attribute differences in hours worked and money earned to differential work histories and not gender.

To study the relation between adolescents' work histories and employment experiences, Greenberger and Steinberg (1983) surveyed nearly 1,900 adolescents, some of whom had had as many as three different part-time jobs. The questions asked concerned hours worked, hourly wage, how long the job had been held, and job history. They found that boys held their first job at a younger age than did girls. Age was clearly related to the job held, with older workers holding more formal jobs, such as working in a store or factory, and younger workers holding jobs similar to the chores they do at home, such as baby-sitting, house cleaning, and newspaper delivery. In their first jobs, boys are more likely to work as laborers or recreation aides and girls are more likely to work as sales clerks or in child care. Similar trends were observed for the adolescents' second and third jobs. Although girls worked fewer hours on their first job, there was no gender difference in hourly wage. Girls earned lower hourly wages than boys on their second and third jobs, however.

In interpreting their findings, Greenberger and Steinberg (1983) note that when they enter the labor force adolescents are exposed to the same sex discrimination which exists in the adult labor force. The type of work open to male and female adolescents is different, the hours worked different, and, to some degree, the wages different. They go on to suggest that adolescent work experiences socialize the adolescent to expect differential employment opportunities as a function of gender once they enter the adult work force. Indeed, they note that early work training through doing chores around the house reflects sex discrimination, with boys and girls having different chores that reflect sex roles.

It appears, then, that eliminating sex discrimination in the adult work force may be more difficult than imagined because of adolescents' socialization experiences at work. These experiences may cause adolescents to expect and accept job discrimination, and may relate to the different occupations they consider for adulthood. In order to expand the occupations considered by adolescents for their life's work, we may have to alter adolescent employment and adolescents' attitudes about part-time work.

Part-time work experiences help the adolescent learn the role of "worker." Volunteer work as well as work for pay can facilitate role learning. (*Lenox McLendon/AP/Wide World Photo*)

Of course, not all adolescents who wish to work are able to do so. Unemployment rates—the percentage of the population looking for a job—for adolescents are much higher than in the population at large. And they tend to be much higher for younger than older adolescents and for Black than for White adolescents (see Table 9-3). Unemployment rates for Hispanic youth are about midway between those for White and Black youth. Of interest, unemployment rates for males and females within each ethnic group are about equivalent. Finally, unemployment rates for school dropouts are about twice those of graduates (Bureau of Labor Statistics, 1986).

In part, these statistics reflect general labor trends—adolescents do not have the skills for some jobs and usually are unable to take full-time jobs. In part, they reflect socioeconomic background differences: Disadvantaged youth have fewer educational opportunities even when educational background is equivalent to that of nondisadvantaged youth (Schulenberg, Vondracek, & Crouter, 1984). In a response to these needs, the federal government sponsors

Table 9–2 Percentage of 16- to 19-Year-Old Adolescents in Civilian Work Force, 1970–1992

Sex	Age	1970	1975	1980	1985	1990	1992
Male	16–17	47.0	48.6	50.1	45.1	43.7	41.1
	18–19	66.7	70.6	71.3	68.9	67.0	66.0
Female	16–17	34.9	40.2	43.6	42.1	41.9	39.3
	18–19	53.5	58.1	61.9	61.7	60.5	59.0

Source: U.S. Bureau of the Census. (1987). *Statistical abstract of the U.S., 1987* (108th ed.). Washington, DC: U.S. Government Printing Office; U.S. Bureau of the Census. (1993). *Statistical abstract of the U.S., 1993* (113th ed.). Washington, DC: U.S. Government Printing Office.

Table 9–3   Adolescent (Ages 16–19) Unemployment Rates, 1980–1992

Group	1980	1985	1990	1991	1992
All workers	7.1	7.2	5.5	6.7	7.4
Ages 16–19	17.8	18.6	15.5	18.6	20.0
Male, 16–19	18.3	19.5	16.3	19.8	21.5
Female, 16–19	17.2	17.6	14.7	17.4	18.5
White, 16–19	15.5	15.7	13.4	16.4	17.1
Black, 16–19	38.5	40.2	31.1	36.3	39.8
Hispanic, 16–19	22.5	24.3	19.5	22.9	27.5

Source: U.S. Bureau of the Census (1993). *Statistical abstract of the U.S., 1993*
(113th ed.). Washington, DC: U.S. Government Printing Office.

several types of job programs aimed at helping disadvantaged youth better prepare for the workplace. However, the extent of these programs is not sufficient
to meet the employment needs of many minority or disadvantaged youths.

Not only are more adolescents working, but they are working longer. Recent data (Bachman & Schulenberg, 1993) for a national sample of about 26,000
male and 27,000 female high school seniors who work shows that whereas
about 20% of males and females work 10 hours per week or less, about 45% of
males and 38% of females work more than 20 hours per week. Because working
part time now is the norm, the focus of research has changed somewhat, and an
emphasis on how work intensity, as opposed to simply working or not, impacts
on the adolescent has emerged.

Given the numbers of adolescents in the work force, and the amount of
time they work, an interesting question is why so many choose to work as opposed to doing other things. The most prevalent reasons given, not surprisingly,
deal with making money, whether simply for spending or for saving, as for college expenses. Girls rate training and experience as somewhat more important
than boys, who rate automobile expenses as a more important reason to work.

This analysis is borne out by looking at the ways that adolescents spend
their money. Boys spend more money than girls in categories related to dating
(gasoline, entertainment) and girls spend more money on categories related to
femininity (grooming, cosmetics). The two sexes spend about equal amounts of
money on records, cigarettes, books, and other non-sex-typed categories. Adolescents save relatively small percentages of their earnings.

As adolescents mature in vocational identity they begin to consider work
values outside the realm of income. The most extensive research on older adolescents' work values was conducted by Bachman and his associates (Bachman
& Johnston, 1979; Bachman et al., 1980). One measure assessed what was
viewed as important in a job. Approximately 90% of the large national sample
listed having interesting work as important, approximately 75% wanted a job
that would allow them to use their skills and abilities, and over 60% indicated
they felt a job should allow you to see the results of what you do. Only about
50% of college bound and 60% of non-college-bound seniors listed making a lot

of money as important in a job (Bachman & Johnston, 1979). Similar results were found for a 1980 survey of high school seniors, who were asked to rank a variety of job characteristics from not important to important. Those characteristics that were ranked as "pretty important" or "very important" included seeing the results of one's work, having something interesting to do, good chances of advancement, the opportunity to help others, having a secure future, the chance to make friends, learning new skills, and not having to pretend to be someone you aren't. Those characteristics indicated as "not important" or only "a little important" included an easy pace of working, more than 2 weeks of vacation, and being free of supervision.

Although these older adolescents and young adults are interested in job security and income, they are also interested in the opportunity to make themselves better people and to develop as a person. They view a job as one type of experience that will make them well rounded and as a setting in which they can employ their skills and talents. One may conclude they are not interested in working at just any job, but rather want a job that will help them develop themselves. It is interesting to note that these values were shared nearly equally by those planning to attend college and by those with no college plans (or plans for less than 4 years of college). Concerns about quality of vocational experience, then, pervade the younger work force. Unfortunately, many find their jobs do not meet these needs (Schulenberg & Bachman, 1993).

The Positive and Negative Aspects of Adolescent Work Experiences

Adolescents' part-time work has always been viewed as beneficial (see Table 9-4). Until recently, concerns about negative influences of working were largely ignored, with the possible exception that working part time during the school year might harm school performance. Current studies of the influences of working on the adolescent's development are focused on both the positive and negative consequences of entering the work force.

Table 9–4   Presumed Benefits of Adolescent Work Experience

Increase self-reliance
Promote intergenerational harmony
Increase social responsibility
Teach personal autonomy
Increase employability
Increase feelings of integration into adulthood
Learn mature work attitudes
Learn role flexibility
Enhance and broaden the self-concept
Learn to live with boring routines
Obtain relevant vocational training
Enhance educational experiences
Smooth the transition to adulthood

Positive Aspects of Part-Time Work.   Adolescents who work part time do indeed experience an increased sense of autonomy and responsibility, particularly if they work in a sales position or other setting that places them in contact with other people (Mortimer et al., 1992a, 1992b, 1993; Schulenberg & Bachman, 1993; Steinberg, 1982). The majority of adolescents take job requirements such as punctuality quite seriously, and about half feel the way they do their job is important for the well-being of others (Steinberg et al., 1982).

The workplace also provides opportunities for some adolescents to acquire practical knowledge, such as dealing with consumer concerns and business practices (Schulenberg & Bachman, 1993) and some facility in coping with the needs of others, for example as might occur in retail sales jobs (Greenberger, Steinberg, & Ruggiero, 1982). These, and other skills that could be learned on the job, may well stand the adolescent in good stead in the long run, but few adolescents work in jobs teaching these skills (Mortimer et al., 1992a, 1992b; Schulenberg & Bachman, 1993). Most adolescents' work time is spent on tasks that have no particular cognitive component, for example, manual labor, cleaning, and other non-problem-solving activities (Table 9–5). Even adolescents who work in clerical jobs spend less than 10% of their time using school-taught skills. In part, these trends reflect the lack of on-the-job training in adolescent work activities, and in part they reflect the fact that most adolescents do not work in cooperative activities with other workers, especially adults, from whom learning could occur (Mortimer et al., 1992a, 1992b; Schulenberg & Bachman, 1993). Contact with adults is limited to very minimal instruction; adults in the workplace do not become the adolescent's friend or confidant (Greenberger et al., 1982). Few adolescents report a close relationship with an adult with whom they work.

Adolescents who work develop better skills in dealing with distraction, task persistence, and gaining pleasure from a job well done than do their non-working peers (Steinberg, Greenberger, Vaux, & Ruggiero, 1981). Boys become

Table 9–5   Job Types Held by Adolescents

Job	Percentage
Food Service	35
Manual labor	15
Retail sales	13
Cleaning	10
Clerical	19
Skilled labor and operatives	6
Recreation aides and ushers	3
Hucksters	3
Child care	2
Newspaper delivery	2
Health aides	1
Educational aides	1

Source: Derived from Greenberger, E., & Steinberg, L. (Final Report). *Part-time employment of in-school youth: An assessment of costs and benefits.* Washington, DC: National Institute of Education.

more interested in exercising authority in an adult job, girls become more interested in job security and making a good living, and both boys and girls indicate that being able to be creative is an important job criterion. Nonetheless, working does not alter adolescents' expectations for career attainment or occupational prestige. The effects of working on long-range career and educational planning are minimal.

Some researchers (Mortimer, Finch, Owens, & Shanahan, 1990; Mortimer, Finch, Shanahan, & Ryu, 1990, 1992a, 1992b; Schulenberg & Bachman, 1993) indicate that working may be beneficial to psychological adjustment. They note that when adolescents perceive their jobs teach skills that will be useful in the future, or when the job is seen as allowing them to use skills learned in school, working has positive effects on self-esteem and a sense of well-being. Those who feel their jobs use their talents and skills also are less likely to smoke cigarettes or use marijuana or report that work interferes with their family and social lives. Because girls are more likely to be employed in these types of jobs than boys, girls benefit developmentally from work more than boys.

Negative Aspects of Part-Time Work. Working part time during the school year has several detrimental effects on school performance (Greenberger et al., 1981; Steinberg et al., 1982; Wirtz, Rohrbeck, Charmer, & Fraser, 1988). Compared to their nonworking peers, working adolescents may spend less time on homework, are absent more, and say they enjoy school less. Many adolescents who work more than 15 to 20 hours per week also perform less well academically, probably because they simply are less involved in school (Steinberg, Fegley, & Dornbusch, 1993). Working adolescents also are less involved in extracurricular activities because they do not have the time for them. If you worked during the school year you likely found you spent less time on homework (but perhaps enhanced quality time) and may have had to give up some activity (sports, clubs,

Working aids personal growth but also carries some detriments, such as alcohol use, which is related to job stress and work intensity. (*Mary Levin/University Photography*)

band). Some evidence indicates these negative influences of work are positively related to work intensity, and may be due not so much to work as to the personality predispositions of those who work more. Students who are not doing particularly well in school and who are not especially committed to schooling may simply be more willing to spend more time at work (Bachman & Schulenberg, 1993; Schulenberg & Bachman, 1993; Steinberg et al., 1993) in anticipation of a quicker transition into adulthood, which has been called **precocious development**.

Researchers also have reported that part-time work entails some health costs associated with the added stress placed on the working adolescent. As work time increases adolescents are more prone to using cigarettes, alcohol, and marijuana, and those in more stressful working conditions use these more (Bachman & Schulenberg, 1993; Mortimer et al., 1993; Schulenberg & Bachman, 1993). These effects appear to be more closely associated with stress in the workplace—feeling one's job is meaningless, conflicts between the various roles one plays, and poor working conditions—than with simply working. These researchers also indicate that work intensity is related to other health concerns, such as lack of sleep and exercise, poor dietary habits, and feeling one has insufficient leisure time.

About 60% of working adolescents report they have engaged in some form of deviance on the job. You may have too. Did you ever give a discount to a friend, give someone free food, take a taste of food prior to serving it, or take home something you did not pay for? Did your co-workers? If you did, why? Because everyone did it? Common among the deviances documented by researchers were stealing goods, giving friends a monetary break, stealing from co-workers, or calling in sick when not ill (Greenberger & Steinberg, Final Report; Steinberg et al., 1981). Working adolescents also develop cynical attitudes about working, including feeling work is meaningless and gaining little satisfaction from working hard. How did (do) you feel about the jobs you have held? Is it simply something to do—you need the money to help pay tuition—or is it a career-enhancing opportunity? How have the jobs you have held influenced your views of becoming a worker and of work in general?

The research just described suggests that working, and especially the number of hours worked, might relate to adolescents' psychological adjustment. Some evidence suggests this is the case, but further research indicates that an important factor to consider is the nature of the job (Mortimer et al., 1992a, 1992b, 1993; Schulenberg & Bachman, 1993). The negative influences of work, and work intensity, are greatest for those who are working in jobs they describe as something one would do "just for the money." Working and work intensity in and of themselves are not related to psychological adjustment. In understanding this conclusion, keep in mind that these types of jobs also impact negatively on adults. That is, to understand the implications of working on the adolescent's development we must consider not only the job and work intensity, but also the degree to which the adolescent finds personal fulfillment in the job he or she is doing—that is the most important factor.

Are these negative aspects of adolescent part-time work due to working, or do they simply reflect differences in the general characteristics of adolescents who work and those who do not? This was the subject of a study by Steinberg and his colleagues (1993). They tested over 1,100 students in grades 10 and 11. At the first testing none of them were working. At the second testing some still were not working, some were working up to 20 hours per week, and some worked more than 20 hours per week. At the first testing, before they started to work, those who subsequently became workers already had lower grades, lower future educational aspirations, spent less time on homework, and were more disengaged from school than those who remained nonworkers. Once they started to work, these students spent even less time on homework, cut class more, and became more disengaged from school than those who remained out of the work force. Finally, those who were working at the first testing and who later stopped working, or reduced the number of hours they were working, showed improvements in school-related measures: They cut class less and had higher educational expectations.

What does all this mean? Steinberg and his colleagues make the following points. First, they note that, as a group, those who work part time during the school year already are disenchanted with the school setting—academic and extracurricular. Some of the poorer attitudes about school expressed by adolescents who work is not due to working, but rather to other factors that foster a negative view about school prior to their starting to work. Second, working itself also contributes to reduced commitment to school-related activities. The researchers conclude that for many adolescents going to work contributes to making a bad situation worse.

Adolescent Part-Time Work: Conclusions.   It is reasonable to conclude that adolescent work experiences provide some benefits aside from money and foster some types of psychological growth. But these benefits are most likely to be seen by those working in jobs that utilize their skills and talents. Those working in what might be called mindless jobs entailing repetitive and boring tasks seem to suffer from their work experiences.

These findings have led researchers to conclude that in order to enhance the benefits of working, the jobs adolescents perform should engage them in a number of ways that are not typical. One suggestion has been to increase the utilization of school-taught skills. Another has been to increase contact with adults, not in the sense of introducing adolescents into adult cultural leisure activity patterns, such as drinking, but by providing greater supervision and on-the-job contact with adults. Finally, some researchers (e.g., Schulenberg & Bachman, 1993) have suggested that a better match between the individual's characteristics and the job's demands would make adolescent work experiences a better introduction to the adult world of work. This latter point is at the heart of vocational decision making. Virtually every theorist has argued that the optimal vocation is the one which allows the individual to mesh competencies, interests, and talents with job demands. Next we review how we make vocational decisions.

THEORIES OF VOCATIONAL CHOICE

Theories of vocational choice outline the critical factors in vocational determination. The various theories that describe how people make vocational choices have diverse approaches and emphases, but the most productive share the view that a match between one's personal characteristics and job demands is a critical component of an optimal vocational choice.

You can get some idea of the various aspects of vocational decision making that the theorists attempt to explain by examining your own vocational decision making. If you have made a choice, how did you go about it and why did you pick it? If you "always knew" what your choice was going to be, how did you know? How do your personal characteristics—intellectual skills, interests, talents—mesh with the demands of the job? Concerns such as these are the focus of vocational theories.

Components of Vocational Theories

Vocational theories serve several functions. They not only describe the processes of vocational decision making, thereby allowing us to understand how one makes vocational decisions, but they also should have some practical value. They should allow us to provide vocational guidance to adolescents and adults (see Box 9–2) and help us develop vocational training programs.

Super (1953) has summarized the types of information any theory of vocational choice should include in order to accomplish these goals. First, people have different interests, abilities, and personalities, and jobs have different demands. A sound theory must account for an appropriate match between the individual difference characteristics of the person and the talents and skills required by the job. For example, someone interested in a career in medicine has a variety of choices, including being a general practitioner, a surgeon, a nurse, a technician, or a medical social worker. Not everyone is suited to the demands of each of these professions. Finding the right match between the characteristics of the person and the job demands will allow the person to enjoy the job more and gain greater satisfaction from it.

Second, sound theories should help us understand our personal vocational growth, including advancement within a vocation through promotion and the taking on of added responsibility, and changing jobs or careers. In other words, a useful theory would allow us to understand and provide guidance to the individual as the person grows and develops within the vocation.

Although current theories fall short in some ways, such as tending to take the male orientation of preparing for a vocation and entering it, with no consideration of possibly dropping out for a time to care for children (Osipow, 1987), several have proven useful and influential.

Trait Measurement Theory

The earliest systematic attempts to explain vocational choices used a **trait measurement** approach. The basic notion is that people seek occupations which fit their particular interests and abilities. Hence a popular approach to vocational

BOX 9–2   Career Counseling Methods

Brooks (1990a) has identified four aspects of the practice of career counseling: diagnosis, the counseling process, the expected outcomes, and using occupational information. She notes that the particular theory one holds influences each of these because it dictates how the career counselor approaches the issue of vocational decision making.

The most common form of career counseling to which adolescents are exposed comes from the trait measurement approach to vocational decision making. Most adolescents take one or another form of vocational inventory during their high school years, and many schools have computerized vocational guidance systems based on the trait measurement approach. Unfortunately, for most that is where the process stops. We draw on Brooks's descriptions to examine the process of career guidance from the trait measurement approach, such as Holland's, described in the text.

DIAGNOSIS

Diagnosis tries to determine why the adolescent is having a problem deciding on a vocation or, for college students, a major. From the trait measurement perspective, the problem lies in the individual's lack of information about personality types, job environments and requirements, and how they relate (Brooks, 1990a, 1990b). Of course, this diagnosis comes from the core tenets of the theory—the way to choose a vocation is to match traits of the individual to characteristics of the job. The indecision reflects an information problem.

THE COUNSELING PROCESS

To guide the individual, the counselor's job is to help the person gather and evaluate relevant information. This information is both about the self and about occupations and their characteristics and demands.

Through the use of standardized instruments that measure one's traits, values, and personality characteristics, and through the classification of occupational types, the individual is provided with an objective way to gather both the personal and occupational information that is lacking. As Brooks notes, however, this approach does not spell out clear decision rules for making choices, which is particularly problematic for those who have severe problems with vocational decision making.

EXPECTED OUTCOMES

The hoped for outcome, of course, is for the adolescent to make a career choice that will be optimal, provide satisfaction, and allow the individual to grow as a person. From Holland's perspective this is a simple issue: Help the adolescent make a specific career choice, or confirm one that has been made tentatively. The emphasis is on the choice, not on the process of making the choice.

OCCUPATIONAL INFORMATION USAGE

In the trait measurement approach, information about the self and about occupations are viewed as equally important to the selection of a vocation (Brooks, 1990a, 1990b). Holland, for example, would have adolescents gather information about the occupational environment—what the tasks of the job are, the nature of the daily routine, and the lifestyle associated with the job. The optimal vocational choice would be the one that best matches occupational information with personal information. Unfortunately, most descriptions of occupational requirements are rather mundane and standardized, and do not provide much detail.

Brooks (1990a, 1990b) concludes that, despite the shortcomings of the approach, theories such as Holland's have proven very useful in a variety of circumstances. She notes that the standardized instruments formulated to assess personal preferences and the classification of occupations into various types has proven of benefit to counselors.

Why, then, do many adolescents find the vocational inventories they took in high school were of little benefit? No doubt there are a variety of reasons. But one may well be that high school guidance counselors provide only part of the information needed, namely, that about student values and orientations. Few have the time to follow up with serious one-on-one counseling of students. Until we are better able to guide our students in a personal, intensive manner we likely will continue to see waves of students who make vocational decisions by simple happenstance—just as most of us did.

choice, best exemplified by use of vocational inventories such as the one you may have taken in high school, is to assess an individual's interests, vocation-related competencies, and personality characteristics, and then match those with similar measures on individuals successfully and happily engaged in various professions.

Holland (1985, 1987; Weinrach & Srebalus, 1990) extended and refined the trait measurement approach by identifying personality types and groups of vocations that would allow each type to be expressed. His approach has had the greatest impact on applying vocational theory to practical application. Indeed, it has had such a strong impact that an entire issue of the *Journal of Vocational Behavior* (1992) was devoted to his theory.

After examining large amounts of data, Holland identified six modal personal orientations: realistic, intellectual, social, conventional, enterprising, and artistic (see Table 9–6). Each orientation reflects a complex set of personality, ability, and aspirations. Corresponding to each personal orientation is a set of possible vocational environments requiring specific adjustments and skills. Choosing a suitable career involves seeking out vocational environments that mesh with one's personal orientation toward the world. Possible careers for each personal orientation are listed in Table 9–6.

Although the trait measurement approach has some practical value, it also has some limitations. First, there are few "pure" personality types. Each of us has some dominant characteristics and others that are of less importance to us. If you read the orientations in Table 9–6 you likely will identify several types to which your traits belong. If you took a vocational test in high school, this is why you probably received some vocational suggestions that seemed unlikely. Second, because an important part of adulthood personality is growth into the demands of a job, personality traits that initially may have been of lesser importance to our vocational decision making may become predominant, making what might have been an initially less desirable choice now one that is a good fit. Both of these limitations stem from the fact that this approach is not a developmental one. That we all grow and change is not part of the theory. Each of

Table 9–6   Holland's Modal Personal Orientations and Possible Vocations

Type	Orientation	Possible Vocation
Realistic	Concrete orientation toward physical skill and masculinity with a deemphasis on social, interpersonal, and verbal skills.	Mechanic, farming, construction, wildlife.
Intellectual	Orientation toward understanding and working with ideas rather than people.	Scientist, mathematician.
Social	Orientation toward working with people and avoidance of intellectual pursuits.	Teacher, social worker, counselor, therapist.
Conventional	Orientation toward a structured environment, following set regulations, and power and status identification.	Clerk, secretary, bank teller.
Enterprising	Orientation toward success through manipulation of others.	Salesperson, politician, manager.
Artistic	Orientation toward self and creative expression; avoidance of structure and social interaction; artistic expression predominates.	Artist, writer, composer, or musician.

Source: Adapted from Holland, J.L. (1964). Major programs of research on vocational behavior. In H. Borow (Ed.), *Man in a world at work*. Boston: Houghton Mifflin. Reprinted by permission of American Association for Counseling and Development.

these factors makes it very difficult to suggest vocations to individuals with a great deal of confidence.

An important omission in the trait measurement approach is that it does not take into account a number of influences which are very important to vocational decision making. Some, such as one's gender, social class, and ethnicity, are personal characteristics. Others, such as parental influences, the quality of education one receives, and the influences of siblings and friends, are social in nature. As we detail later, each of these is critical to the occupations one will consider or have the resources to enter. Taken as a group, they may be more important to the actual vocational decisions one makes than is one's personality.

Developmental Theories

Both Eli Ginzberg (1990) and Donald Super (1990) take a stage approach to vocational decision making. As a result, it is possible to examine vocational choices within various age groupings and discuss the important parameters of vocational choice and development in children, preadolescents, adolescents, and young adults. Both theorists argue that the individual is continually forced to make adjustments in vocation-related choices which to some degree limit future choices. Each takes a developmental approach to vocational decision making.

Ginzberg's Stage Theory.   Ginzberg and his associates (Ginzberg, 1990; Ginzberg, Ginzberg, Axelrod, & Herman, 1951) proposed that in each stage of vocational decision making people make choices based on their wishes and their assessment of the opportunities available to them. Ginzberg views vocational decision making as an adaptive process involving conflict resolution. For most individuals these decision processes take place during adolescence, over a 6- to 12-year span.

There are four stages in Ginzberg's theory. The first, fantasy, lasts until about age 10 or 11. The young person makes arbitrary vocational choices with no real consideration of realities of the situation. During this stage children want to be movie stars, astronauts, jet pilots, lawyers, doctors, rock musicians, or rappers, depending on what captures their fancy at any particular moment.

The second stage, labeled tentative, begins during early adolescence. We start to take into account our interests, values, and capabilities when thinking about future vocational choices. There are four substages. In the first, or interest, period, choices are made on the basis of personal likes and dislikes. This is a transition period between the fantasy and tentative stages. The second, or capacities, period begins at about age 13 or 14, coinciding with the onset of formal operational thinking; adolescents begin to assess their capabilities with respect to particular kinds of vocations, realizing that interest is not enough. At about 15 or 16, personal values, orientations, and goals become an important part of vocational considerations (the value substage). The individual begins to realize specific vocations have particular relationships to personal value structures, and that some vocations may be more suited to one's value structure than others. The fourth substage is a transition between the tentative period and the realistic stage. This transition period, which begins about age 17, is a period of consolidation during which interests, capabilities, and values are focused on particular vocational alternatives.

Ginzberg's third, or realistic, stage begins about age 18. It is during this time that reality testing becomes critically important as the individual tests the tentative vocational choices against the reality of vocational demands, and comes up with a vocational selection that satisfies both personal values and the demands of a particular occupation or group of occupations. These compromising aspects of vocational choice occur primarily during the exploration substage. During the crystallization substage, the individual develops a clear vocational goal with specific satisfactory occupations identified. A crystallization of the realities of vocational demands and the individual's personal capabilities, interests, and values has taken place.

The fourth stage is specification. It is reached when the individual makes a commitment to a specific vocation either by entering it or by beginning to train for it. Although there is considerable individual variation, most people enter this stage by the early 20s, at about the time their identity is solidifying (Chapter 6).

Ginzberg and his associates suggest that four specific psychological processes are essential to the vocational choice process. Reality testing involves coming to grips with one's ability to perform the vocation and a sound assessment of the likelihood one has the resources to enter it. *Ability to defer gratification* refers to working toward a goal without necessarily receiving immediate rewards. You do this when you work hard in order to receive a reward (a good grade in a course) later. Sensitivity to compromise involves the ability to make an alternative choice if that becomes necessary. Many who enter college to become engineers or architects find they cannot or do not wish to make the sacrifices necessary or do not have the talent required. They must make a compromise choice. Development of time perspective entails learning that one may have to engage in a period of preparation or apprenticeship before the desired vocation or level of vocation can be achieved. Development of each of these perspectives helps the individual make optimal vocational choices.

Although Ginzberg's theory was developed primarily from observations on boys, girls are assumed to progress through the fantasy and tentative periods of vocational choice in much the same way. During the reality stage, however, many girls also consider the vocational alternative of marriage and child rearing (Borow, 1976). And many more women than men take into account the desire to stay home with young children—they consider entering a vocation, leaving it for some period of time, and then reentering it. Hence their vocational decision process may be different.

Another important individual difference variable is social class. The same general progression of the stages is evident in both middle- and lower-class adolescents, although lower-class adolescents move through the realistic stage more quickly than middle-class adolescents. In large part this is because middle-class adolescents consider a wider variety of vocational alternatives than lower-class adolescents (Borow, 1976) and because middle-class adolescents take a longer educational preparation period than do their lower-class counterparts. Ethnicity, which is related to social class, apparently is ignored in Ginsberg's formulations.

Super's Vocational Self-Concept Theory.   Super (1990) has developed the most comprehensive life-span developmental theory of vocational choice. Super (1990) notes he has made a concerted effort to ensure the theory would be applicable to women as well as men, and to those coming from different social standings and ethnic groups. As a result, the applicability of the concepts to a number of different people and circumstances has been shown to be quite good (Osipow, 1983; Super, 1990; Wallace-Broscious, Serafica, & Osipow, 1994).

The basic concept in Super's theory is that vocational choices are made in such a way as to allow the greatest opportunity for the expression of the individual's developing self-concept. Individuals are viewed as continually developing their self-concept as related to both career choices and job performance, a form of reality testing. Vocational development, then, is a process involving changes in vocational choices that reflect changes in the individual's developing self-concept. From this perspective, the vocations picked are the ones that allow the greatest expression of the self-concept (Wallace-Broscius et al., 1994). As the self-concept changes, the adolescent's vocational choices become more narrowly defined. The adult's changing self may lead to a change in his or her vocation. Hence Super's theory truly is a life-span developmental theory of vocational development (see Figure 9–1).

Super also realizes that environmental factors affect vocational choices. For some, such as youth from poorer backgrounds, these limiting factors make

Figure 9–1   Life Stages and Substages Based on the Typical Development Tasks, with Focus on the
Maxicycle.   Note: Each transition, whether psychogenic, sociogenic, econogenic, or all of these,
has its own minicycle of growth, exploration, establishment, maintenance, and decline: its
recycling.

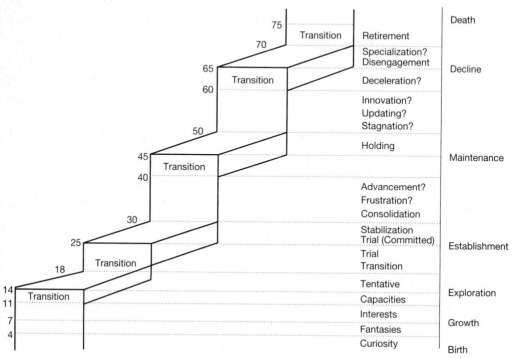

Source: Super, D.E. (1990). Career and life development. In D. Brown, & L. Brooks & Associates (Eds.). *Career choice and development.* San Francisco: Jossey-Bass.

some vocations extremely difficult to attain even though they might mesh well
with self-concept. Career choice and change, then, reflects a continual process
of adapting personal characteristics and one's own unique circumstances to occupational demands.

The first stage, *growth,* lasts until about the mid-teen years. From birth to
about age 14 the individual learns more about the self than about occupations.
This learning about the self is critical to the process of making serious investigations into possible vocations, which begins in the second stage, *exploration.*
The early adolescent begins to consider possible vocations based primarily on
interests—if a vocation captures the adolescent's interest it may be considered
as a possible choice. At the same time, the adolescent is learning about competencies and abilities, and possible vocational choices begin to reflect one's skills
and aptitudes. Finally, during the third substage the individual makes possible
choices based on a combination of interests and abilities. At the same time, the
adolescent begins to investigate and learn about various vocations, and to make
possible choices realistically given his or her circumstances.

Once the person has chosen a vocation, he or she enters the next stage, *establishment.* The emphasis is on learning the job, making the position secure, and fitting the self into the job. As you can see in Figure 9-1, this includes not only the learning of the job (termed trial) but also stabilization (making a commitment to the job—this is what I want to do) and then evaluation, which involves not only career advancement but one's view of the fit between the self and job demands.

The next stage is *maintenance.* The central task is maintaining quality of performance and proving one can compete successfully with others in similar positions. The last stage is labeled *decline.* During late adulthood most workers retire and must find other activities to occupy their time. Developing nonoccupational roles and doing things one has always wanted to do are the primary focuses of this stage.

Figure 9-1 illustrates that there are transitions between the stages. These may involve psychological, sociological, or economic changes that cause one to "recycle" through the stages. For example, winning a multimillion dollar lottery will cause anyone to rethink their position with regard to working. This will involve considerations of the self, exploring alternatives, and recycling the process in a manner analogous to the college student changing majors.

One obvious implication of Super's theory is that the adolescent is continually testing potential vocational choices. Courses studied in school, independent study programs, volunteering one's services, doing an internship, and work-study programs are all helpful as one tries out various work roles. When the person finds a work role that meshes with the self-concept (that is, one in harmony with one's abilities, interests, and personality), the individual is more likely to stay with it than with one in which the fit is not as good. A mismatch, that is, a poor fit, motivates the individual to repeat the vocational decision process in order to enter a new vocation, or make changes in the current one so a match exists.

Super's theory suggests that vocational guidance courses and counselors should help adolescents understand the self, particularly as it relates to the world of work. The better people understand themselves and how they will function in the vocational setting, the greater the likelihood the vocations chosen will satisfy them and benefit society as a whole.

Finally, Super's theory has a number of implications for exceptional adolescents. The retarded, the physically disabled, or the learning disabled adolescent is likely to have a different self-orientation and outlook on vocational and career opportunities than the nonexceptional adolescent. Different kinds of training programs and guidance procedures might be implemented to ensure these special students receive the right kind of vocational help.

Developmental theories focus on the processes underlying the development of vocational behavior. As a result, they play down the overstressed issue of specific vocational choice (Super, 1990). What is important is the process, which allows the individual to choose a vocation with demands that will mesh with the self. Because all of us could enter a variety of vocations and have rewarding and satisfying careers, the specific choice we make is not particularly important. How we do so is very important. In this regard, it has been shown that identity formation may be more predictive of vocational decision making than self-concept (Wallace-Broscious et al., 1994). High school seniors who are identity achieved are more able to define their occupational choices than those in the moratorium or diffusion statuses.

Implications of Theories of Vocational Choice

Although the vocational theories tell us something about how long-term vocational plans are (or should be) made, they tell us little about how adolescents choose part-time jobs. This is because adolescents' primary reason for working is to make money. Adolescents are not highly motivated to find a job that will satisfy self-concept needs or suit basic interests. They are willing to take jobs that they well might not consider for careers. This may in part explain why they state they rarely do more than expected on the job (Greenberger & Steinberg, Final Report). And it may explain their lack of satisfaction with becoming workers. You likely have worked on part-time jobs during the school year or worked during the summer. Although it is possible these were training experiences on jobs of high interest to you, it is more likely you worked in order to make money rather than for personal satisfaction gained from the job.

The theories are consistent with suggestions that advocate formalizing the career decision process, for example in school-based programs (Vondracek, 1993). Helping adolescents evaluate their self-needs, competencies, and interests *in the context of knowledge about various vocational demands* no doubt would facilitate the process of vocational decision making and enhance the likelihood of making an appropriate choice.

Because women and men make vocational decisions somewhat differently, and because minority students generally have educational and economic disadvantages, researchers such as Brooks (1990a, 1990b) have argued for special school-based programs targeting these groups. Specifically, Brooks recommends that school counselors exert special efforts to ensure these students and their parents are aware of all the vocational possibilities open to them and any means that may be available for them to obtain the training necessary. Because exploration is so critical to vocational choices, Brooks believes women and minority students should not short-circuit that process just because they may hold stereotyped beliefs of what is expected of them or "appropriate" for them.

INDIVIDUAL DIFFERENCES
AND VOCATIONAL CHOICE

As we noted earlier, a number of individual difference characteristics are important in the vocational decision-making process. Intellectual capabilities, socioeconomic background, ethnicity, gender, and one's particular interests all relate both to the processes underlying vocational decision making and to the actual vocational choice made.

Intellectual Capabilities

Intellectual ability relates to vocational concerns in several ways. First, although some vocations simply require high levels of intelligence, in general, those with higher intellectual capabilities have a greater chance of success in many different vocations (Borow, 1976), other factors being equal. What are the other factors? Examples include motivation to succeed, personality relative to job demands, social skills, and the opportunity to obtain necessary training. As we noted in Chapter 4, the range of intelligence of those in any given vocation is very wide because of the importance of these other factors.

Second, intellectual competence is related to educational attainment. Jobs that require high levels of formal training are more likely to be entered by those who are more intellectually competent. Of course, even if one possesses high intellectual ability, social factors, such as discrimination, poverty, and the like, may prevent one from even aspiring to such training.

Some evidence also suggests that intellectual capabilities are related to the manner in which decisions about vocations are made (Borow, 1976). Adolescents who are brighter make vocational decisions that are more in line with their capabilities, interests, and probabilities of employment than do less bright adolescents (Gribbons & Lohnes, 1966). The vocational choices of bright adolescents are more realistic than those of less bright adolescents, who tend to have vocational aspirations that are unrealistically high and require competencies and skills they do not possess. Brighter adolescents also tend to be somewhat less dependent on the opinions of family and peers and less susceptible to social pressure in general when they make occupational choices.

Role of Socioeconomic Status

A number of investigators (e.g., Sum, Harrington, & Goedicke, 1987) have researched and discussed the relationship of social class to vocational aspirations and attainment. Generally speaking, social class relates to vocations in three ways. First, to some degree it determines the occupations that will be familiar to, and therefore considered by, the individual. Because middle-class adolescents are aware of a wider variety of vocations than lower-class adolescents, they have a wider range from which to select. Second, to some degree social class determines the acceptability of a particular vocation for an individual. The lower-class adolescent who wants to become a doctor or the middle-class adolescent who wants to work on a production line is likely to meet with considerable criticism from parents, peers, and family members because the aspirations are considered too high in the one case and too low in the other. Third, social class determines in a very real way what jobs will be open to individuals. The bright, motivated lower-class adolescent may find that entering a high-prestige occupation is impossible because he or she does not have the money to go to school. A middle-class Black adolescent may have the money to attend college, but may find some professions are closed to him or her because of prejudice.

Generally speaking, lower-class adolescents have lower vocational aspirations than middle class adolescents (Sum et al., 1987). Some (see Hollingshead, 1949) have argued this is because lower-class adolescents have a "class horizon" view of occupational goals; that is, they aspire to the same occupational level held by their parents. Adolescents tend to choose jobs they know about, jobs in which their parents and parents' friends are employed, and those that are universally familiar, such as nurse, teacher, or police officer. As a result, the lower-class youth, who sees a great many people employed as unskilled or semiskilled workers, may set lower goals than the middle-class youth. Others have argued that lower-class youths view the opportunities for entering upper-status occupations as small, and as a result set lower vocational goals than middle-class adolescents. As we discover in our later discussion of gender and ethnic background, the restrictions of vocational choice resulting from social-class background no doubt result in losses of contributions these people might have made to society.

The Influence of Gender

One of the major social tragedies of our time has been the view that women should be housewives and mothers and only secondarily, if at all, be allowed to achieve personal satisfaction and growth through a career. This personal loss is only one aspect of the tragedy; the loss of the contribution these women could have made to science, business, and the professions is another. Although the value of women in the labor force was amply demonstrated during World War II (L. Hoffman, 1979, 1980), it is only in more recent times that women have been allowed to enter the labor force freely and in high-prestige, high-level occupations (Borow, 1976; L. Hoffman, 1980).

The percentage of women who work outside the home is increasing. In 1980, 45.1% of married women with children under the age of 6 were employed, and 61.7% of married women with children between the ages of 6 and 17 were employed (U. S. Bureau of the Census, 1987). The comparable percentages for separated and divorced women are even higher. At present, approximately 70% of women aged 18 to 64 work outside the home. And there is every reason to believe the percentage will increase in the future. In other words, as adolescent women leave secondary schools we can expect increasing proportions of them to enter the work force. It is important, therefore, to look at the vocational prospects for these women.

Although improvements in earnings have been made in recent years, women still earn substantially less than men (U. S. Bureau of the Census, 1987). In part, this occurs because women still tend to be employed in traditional female vocations, such as secretarial, clerical, and nursing jobs, and not employed in professions that pay more and are typically male dominated, such as legal, managerial, and medical. The future, however, looks bright. Substantial changes in the percentage of women employed in traditionally high-prestige, high-paying, male-dominated vocations have occurred. The trends toward greater employment opportunities for women, and toward equal pay for equal work,

The percentage of mothers who work outside the home has reached all-time highs. The daughters of these mothers have more nontraditional career plans. (*Rhoda Sidney*)

bode well for today's adolescent females. They will have more opportunities and career choices than previous generations had.

Evidence (see Chapter 10) suggests that girls whose mothers work have a less restricted view of the female sex role and are more career and achievement oriented. In part, this results from the mother providing a model of a female who can work outside the home. Working mothers provide a role model for their daughters that in many ways is comparable to that provided by fathers for their sons. Working mothers also may train their daughters to be more independent and may encourage that independence. As a result, the daughters of working mothers may grow up in an atmosphere in which independence is not sex typed male or sex typed at all, especially if the father accepts his daughter as feminine and expresses this while at the same time not limiting her independence.

Ethnic Group Membership

Ethnic background relates to vocations in a number of different ways (Hoyt, 1989). One involves educational attainment, including dropping out of high school and completing a college education. Black and Hispanic adolescents are much more likely than White adolescents to drop out of school; Asian adolescents complete high school at about the same rate as White adolescents. And a lower percentage of Black than White students complete a college education. Because educational attainment is related to the jobs one can obtain and thereby the income one earns, minority youth have fewer job opportunities available to them. As in the case of women, there no doubt is a loss to the society because of the contributions these people may have made but could not.

Minority youth are also more likely to have grown up poor and had an inferior education, again limiting job opportunities even if one completes high school. Whether from the dominant White culture or from a minority background, adolescents who come from poverty backgrounds are at a disadvantage, which means their children also will be. Because a higher proportion of Black than White adolescents come from such backgrounds, Black adolescents have fewer opportunities than their White counterparts when it comes to careers.

Finally, minority youth, and especially African Americans, face serious discrimination problems. Although both Black and Hispanic adolescents have career aspirations as high as those of White adolescents when social class is equated, they have lower expectations of achieving those aspirations. These feelings can impact on one's sense of accomplishment, job satisfaction, and general performance.

Minority adolescents and adults continue to face discrimination in the job market. As a result, fewer obtain jobs to which they aspire. (*M. Richards/ Photo Edit*)

INTERPERSONAL INFLUENCES ON VOCATIONAL ASPIRATIONS AND CHOICE

A number of interpersonal influences affect adolescent vocational choices and aspirations. Parents, peers, siblings, and teachers are among those socializing agents who significantly affect adolescents' career planning and decisions.

Parental Influences

One way parents influence the vocational aspirations and choices of their offspring is through modeling (Vangelisti, 1988). Boys who identify strongly with their fathers tend to have traditional sex-typed interests and tend to use the father as a role model for vocational expression.

Parents are especially important in females' development of interests in entering nontraditionally female careers (see Chapter 10). Girls whose parents support their interest in a nontraditional career are more likely to consider and enter such a career than are girls whose parents don't. These parents tend to be better educated and less sexist in their views (Hannah & Kahn, 1989).

In some ways, parental influences on adolescents' vocational choices are unfortunate. Few parents are capable of giving the right kind of vocational advice to their offspring, and those who do may often do so for the wrong reasons. Some parents wish to relive their own lives through their children. Clearly, this may not be best for the child. Also, parents are poor judges of the capabilities of their offspring and their offspring's interests. Overestimating the capabilities of the adolescent and recommending a vocation for which the individual is ill-suited can be devastating to career development.

Sibling Influences

Siblings, and their sex status relative to the adolescent, are also important influences on vocational aspirations and views (Vangelisti, 1988). Boys with all-male siblings hold highly masculine vocational interest patterns, and girls with all-female siblings hold highly feminine ones. But girls with older brothers have highly masculine vocational interests. One explanation of this finding is that older brothers act as significant role models. The older brother may encourage a lifestyle that is not traditionally feminine.

School Influences

Generally speaking, schools prepare students best for vocations that involve working with ideas, for that is largely what school is about (Vangelisti, 1988). In some ways, schools are getting away from this orientation and are becoming more interested in vocational training for specific occupations. This represents a shift from the philosophy of the 1960s, which was strongly influenced by industry's desire to have more highly educated employees. The school influences most directly affecting the vocational choices, aspirations, and training of the individual adolescent are the classroom teacher and the guidance counselor.

One way teachers affect their students' choices is by personal influence. The teacher's personality, warmth, knowledge, and advice are important and influential in students' vocational decision making. One study indicates that 39% of college students regard their high school teachers as the major influence in occupational choice. There are a number of other direct but less personal ways that teachers can influence vocational choice. The teacher who is ill-prepared or who denigrates students can damage the career plans of students, particularly marginal college-bound students, who may come to believe they are incapable of competing successfully at the college level.

Within the school setting, the guidance or vocational counselor is the person most directly responsible for helping students select appropriate vocations and curricula designed to prepare for the vocation. In effect, the vocational counselor's main job is to see that the student makes a realistic choice given the student's personal characteristics and the job demands, the projected employment possibilities in the chosen vocation, and the adequacy of the students' curriculum.

Some evidence indicates guidance counselors are not doing as good a job as desirable. Significant percentages of students say they get little or no help from their school's guidance counselors. In their study of 32,800 students in grades 8, 9, and 11, Noeth, Roth, and Prediger (1975) reported that 20% of 11th graders had only a low level of involvement in career planning and 50% indicated they got no help from their guidance counselors. In another large-scale study involving 5,225 males aged 14 to 24, Kohen and Breinich (1975) reported that degree of availability of guidance counselors did not relate to the student's knowledge of the work world, perhaps because contact of this sort is very limited for so many students. One hopes that new guidance techniques, such as courses in the "how to" of career planning and computerized vocational choice systems, will help students help themselves and will aid guidance counselors in their task.

Rural versus Urban Setting

Although most adolescents live in urban or suburban settings, many live in rural areas. Adolescents who grow up in rural areas have lower educational aspirations than those living in urban or suburban areas (Sarigiani, Wilson, Petersen, & Vicary, 1990). Hektner (1994) suggests that rural adolescents may experience a conflict, specifically between their desire to remain in the area and close to family on the one hand and occupational aspirations that would require they move away, likely to an urban area, on the other. Those who face such a conflict feel negatively about their future, are generally unhappy when engaged in activities related to their future roles, and more hesitant about continuing their education.

SUMMARY

In the early history of the United States, children and adolescents were expected to work and contribute to the welfare of the family. Hence adolescents worked on farms or as apprentices, and did not enjoy the freedom from work that most current-day adolescents have. With the passage of child labor laws and mandated education, the nature of adolescent vocational training and decision making changed. Adolescents no longer had to work, and the work they could do was limited by law. We began to view working, and vocational decision making, in a discontinuous manner.

Recent years have seen a change in this perspective. Emphasis has been placed on the benefits of employment to the adolescent and the society. It has been argued that working will build self-esteem, teach valuable skills, and help integrate the adolescent into adulthood, thereby alleviating the barriers between generations. Currently, about 80% of adolescents will work part time before they leave high school. The work experiences of adolescents do have some benefits: increases in personal responsibility; for some, the learning of valuable skills; and feeling that the work done is of benefit to others. However, there is no evidence that adolescents' working experiences make them more employable, consolidate school-taught skills, or teach other cognitive skills. Indeed, there is evidence to the contrary. Adolescents who work extensive hours per week spend less time with peers and family and on homework, enjoy school less, and may do less well in school. The stresses associated with working in conjunction with other pressures on the adolescent may result in increased use of alcohol, cigarettes, and marijuana, particularly for those in jobs that do not utilize their skills. These findings have renewed interest in the nature and importance of adolescent part-time work and are cause for concern.

Long-range vocational planning is an important task of adolescence. Theories of vocational development emphasize the important role played by personality characteristics, self-concept, interests, and abilities in career planning. In general, long-range career planning should take each of these factors into account and match the needs and abilities of the individual with job characteristics. The better the match, the more likely the individual will be successful and happy in the vocation.

A number of individual difference characteristics relate to vocational decision-making processes. Girls with working mothers tend to be more career oriented than girls whose mothers do not work. With the increased opportunities for vocations at all levels, and with the increasing percentage of working women with children, this is an important consideration. Parents act as vocational role models. Intellectual competence is another individual characteristic that relates positively to vocational satisfaction, although motivation and the willingness to work hard are important to vocational success. Ethnic group membership affects vocational aspirations and feelings that one can be successful in a vocation, even when social class is equated. Reducing poverty and eliminating barriers to minority group adolescents not only will increase their career opportunities but also will allow society to profit from their (currently lost) contributions. Peers, siblings, school personnel, and co-workers also are important in determining vocational attitudes and choices.

GLOSSARY

career interests: Preferences for work settings, activities, and responsibilities.

precocious development: Early transition into adulthood roles related to the work environment.

trait measurement: Approach to vocational decision making involving matching one's interests and traits to the demands of vocations.

vocational identity: One's identity as a worker and contributor to society; one's view of the self in a vocation.

work: Any activity that places the adolescent in the role of worker and removes the individual from student or family ties.

work intensity: Number of hours per week the adolescent works.

work values: Personality, motivation, and work ethic values that the individual brings to the work situation.

DISCUSSION QUESTIONS

1. Why did you decide on the major you chose? How does it relate to the vocation you wish to enter?

2. What *process* did you use to make your decision about your future vocation? How does it correspond to the theories of vocational choice discussed in the text?

3. Did you ever consider the possibility of leaving your job for some period of time and staying home with children? Why or why not? Did it influence your choice of careers?

4. If you are a minority student, how do you think that influenced your vocational choice? If you are not from an ethnic minority, how might your choice of a career have been different if you were?

5. Who were the most influential individuals regarding your choice of a vocation? Why?

6. What role did your high school guidance counselor play in your vocatonal planning?

7. What talents and skills do you feel you possess that relate to the vocation you have chosen?

8. In what ways did you try to seek information about vocations you were considering? Were these helpful?

9. If you have been a worker, what benefits did you gain from working? What detriments?

10. It has been argued that adolescents' part-time employment teaches them to accept unethical business practices. Did this happen to you?

11. How did you view your first job? What was exciting and for how long? How did you feel about being a worker? Has this had any long-term impact on your views of working?

12. Did you ever feel any discrimination or sexual harassment on the job? How did you handle it and why? Did you learn simply to put up with it?

13. Most adolescents view their earnings as discretionary money, funds they may spend in leisure/nonessential ways. What did you do with your money?

14. Did you experience "precocious development" when you went to work? If so, what were the behavioral manifestations? If not, did you know anyone who did? How did it manifest?

Parent and Family Influences

10

Major Issues Addressed

Changes in the Family Unit
Methods of Rearing and Disciplining Adolescents
Adolescents' Perceptions of Parental Rearing Practices
Growing up in a One-Parent Home
How Children and Adolescents Adapt to Parental Divorce
The Influence of the Working Mother
Adolescent Strivings for Independence and Autonomy
Siblings and the Adolescent
Lesbian and Gay Parents

I had shaving cream over half my face when he came into the house crying. He had a permit that allowed him to drive in daylight and was taking the car to school that day. While backing out of the driveway he "took out" the driver's side of the car when he hit the trees that line the driveway. Being very proud of his driving ability, he was very upset he had been in an accident. I went out to look at the car, opened and closed the driver's door to make sure it worked, patted him on the shoulder, and said simply, "Have a good day at school. I hope your friends don't make fun of you." We later discussed what he should do in the future to make certain this type of accident did not happen again.

◆   ◆   ◆

Parents often must discipline their children, and there are a variety of ways to do it. The research demonstrates that inductive discipline, discussing why something was wrong to do, and authoritative parenting, which includes inductive discipline and demanding age-appropriate behavior, are associated with the most positive outcomes. We look at the role of parenting practices and other parental and family influences in this chapter.

INTRODUCTION

Most adolescents grow up in families, although they vary widely in structure: two parent versus one parent, nuclear versus extended, small versus large, biological parents versus a stepparent. The most important impact of the family on the adolescent comes from the parents, largely due to their having a long developmental history with the adolescent. They have raised the adolescent from birth and have been central in shaping the adolescent into what he or she is today. Hence the impact of other family members such as siblings, although perhaps stronger in areas such as music or slang preferences, are not as great as those of the parents.

In addition to its members, families have structures and undergo transitions, such as a mother starting to work when children enter school, or parental divorce and remarriage. These transitions impact on the adolescent and require adjustment. They represent another, more global, way in which the family influences the adolescent's development.

CHANGES IN THE FAMILY UNIT
IN THE UNITED STATES

Changes in the structure of the family have occurred at an extremely rapid rate during this century. As a consequence, successive generations of adolescents have matured in circumstances often quite different from those of their parents' adolescence. Some of the important changes have been in the setting of the family and others have been in family composition.

Family Setting

Urban vs. Rural.   In 1900 approximately two-thirds of the American population lived in rural areas. Today only about a fifth does (U. S. Bureau of the Census, 1992a). The population shift has been mainly from the rural parts of the Midwest and the south to the large metropolitan areas on the Great Lakes and East and West coasts, and to the southwestern sunbelt. Over the course of this century successive generations of adolescents have grown up in environments very different from those of their parents, both with regard to the general setting (such as smaller towns versus increasingly larger metropolitan areas) and with respect to the demands placed on the adolescent (such as adapting to larger schools, increased crime, and drugs).

Mobility.   In addition, familiy mobility has increased. It is estimated that approximately 20% of the families in the United States changed residence each year during the past decade. With such movement comes the need to develop adaptation skills—to new schools, new towns and neighborhoods, making new friends, and the loss of old friends who may have been very dear.

Family Composition

The composition of the American family has changed substantially since the turn of the century (see Box 10-1). The changes have been in terms of size of the family and family type.

Family Size.   Two factors have contributed to a reduction in family size. First, there has been an increase in the percentage of families that are nuclear (parents and their offspring) as opposed to extended (families with more than two

BOX 10–1 Family Composition of the United States

Adolescents grow up in families that have diffferent structures and compositions. Changes that have occurred, especially over the past three decades, have resulted in large percentages of adolescents growing up in families of widely different types (U.S. Bureau of the Census, 1992a, 1992b).

The composition of the family unit is one major change that has occurred. The percentage of families with children composed of two parents has been declining in recent decades and the percentage of single-parent families has been increasing. These trends are more evident for Black than for White or Hispanic family groups.

Percentage of Two-Parent Families

RACE		YEAR	
	1970	1980	1990
All	87.1	78.5	71.9
White	89.9	82.9	77.4
Black	64.3	48.1	39.4
Hispanic	NA	74.1	66.8

This change in family composition has resulted in a decrease in the percentage of children and adolescents living with both biological parents and an increase in the percentage of those living with a stepparent. Again, the percentages are higher for Black than for White or Hispanic adolescents.

Percentage of Children Under 18 Living in Each Family Type

TYPE		YEAR	
	1970	1980	1990
Biological Parents			
All	83.7	82.1	81.5
White	84.7	83.1	83.0
Black	71.5	69.7	63.6
Hispanic	NA	NA	81.1
Stepparent Family			
All	12.8	14.9	15.9
White	11.9	14.0	14.6
Black	24.4	26.2	32.3
Hispanic	NA	NA	16.1

These changes also mean an increase in the percentages of children and adolescents living with a single parent. Typically this is the mother; very few fathers have custody of their children. As you will see here, over half of Black children and adolescents living in a single parent family live with their mother. The major reason for living with a single-parent is divorce. The divorce ratio—the number of divorced persons per 1,000 married persons living with their spouses—has increased rather dramatically. It was 79 for males and 120 for females in 1980; in 1987 it was 107 for males and 154 for females.

Percentage of Children and Adolescents Living with Mother Only Race

	YEAR		
	1970	1980	1990
All	10.8	18.0	21.6
White	7.8	13.5	16.2
Black	29.5	43.9	51.2
Hispanic	NA	19.6	27.1

Another salient factor is that when children become adolescents their parents are older than in previous generations. This is directly attributable to the increase in age of first marriage for both males and females. As you will see in the following table, between 1970 and 1988 the median age of first marriage for both males and females increased by about 3 years between 1970 and 1988, rsulting in parents being older now than previously when their children become adolescents.

Median Age of First Marriage for Males and Females

Year	Males	Females
1970	22.5	20.6
1980	23.6	21.8
1988	25.5	23.7

Finally, in 1985 it became the norm for children to grow up with mothers who worked outside the home. As shown in the next table, the large majority of divorced mothers typically has done so. But the percentage of married mothers working outside the home has increased by about 30% since 1970.

Percentage of Mothers Who Work Outside the Home

	CHILDREN (BIRTH—5)		CHILDREN (6—17)	
	Married	Divorced	Married	Divorced
1970	30.3	63.3	49.2	82.4
1980	45.1	68.3	61.7	82.3
1988	57.1	70.1	72.5	83.9

What do all these changes in family composition mean for the adolescent? Coupled with the changes discussed in the text, for the vast majority of adolescents the family unit now is very different than it was when their parents were adolescents. This contributes to a kind of generation gap—what it means to be an adolescent now is not always what it meant a generation ago.

Such changes emphasize the social nature of adolescence: As broad changes occur in the society, in family composition, for example, they signal changes in the nature of adolescence. They also point to the importance of studying practical questions, such as how adolescents adapt to parental divorce, the effects of growing up in a single-parent home, adaptation to stepparents, returning from school to a home with no adult supervision, and other such questions. We address such questions in this and the following chapters.

generations in residence). Second, the size of the nuclear family is shrinking as parents have fewer children.

The anthropologist Margaret Mead (1970) noted that this trend has taken away from today's adolescents the modeling of intergenerational interactions and has contributed to what she called a *cofigurative* culture, in which peers act as increasingly important models for its members. Although the influence of peers increases substantially during adolescence, we now know it remains secondary to that of parents.

The typical adolescent grows up in a nuclear family, which
limits the learning of intergenerational interaction patterns.
(*Steve Takatsuno*)

Family Type.   At the turn of the century, and until relatively recently, the modal
family (the most common type) involved only a single working parent, usually
the father. As illustrated in Box 10–1, this no longer is the case. Unlike their parents, today's adolescents are more likely to grow up in a family that has two parents, or a single parent, who work outside the home.

   The percentage of adolescents experiencing the divorce and subsequent
remarriage of their parents also has been increasing (see Box 10–1). Current estimates are that about a third of adolescents will spend some time in a single-
parent home, and that of those whose parents divorce, over half will experience
the remarriage of one or both of their parents, although this percentage is lower
for Black youngsters. Because divorce usually means a reduction in economic
resources, and remarriage an increase, a large percentage of adolescents, and especially Black adolescents, will be exposed to the consequences of living in
poverty or near poverty conditions (McLoyd, 1989a, 1989b), and for some this
will be for an extended period of time.

   These changes have several implications for understanding adolescent development. First, because of the different adolescent experience of parents and
their adolescents, parents will be somewhat out of touch with the stresses,
strains, and pressures faced by contemporary adolescents, which can lead to
parent–adolescent conflict. For example, what will it mean to be an adolescent
in the year 2015, when many of you reading this text will have your own adolescents? How will the adolescent experience be similar and different from yours?
How will you be "out of touch" or "in sync"? Second, the changes have contributed to a further reduction in the age at which some children must take on
substantial responsibility, further lowering the age at which adolescence begins.
Coming home from school to no adult supervision and being responsible for traditionally adult-defined chores such as meal preparation and caring for younger
siblings are examples of how we may now be making adolescence start at a
younger age than in previous generations.

THE PARENTAL ROLE
IN ADOLESCENT SOCIALIZATION

Parental influences on the adolescent are a continuation of their influences during childhood. One thrust of research on parent effects on adolescent development has been to study parental rearing styles, including disciplinary techniques. A second focus has been to relate the adolescent's *perceptions* of parental rearing to the adolescent's development. A third emphasis aimed at relating parental personality characteristics to adolescent behavior is emerging as an important field of study.

Parental Disciplinary Techniques and Rearing Styles

Research on the importance of parental disciplinary techniques was spurred by Sigmund Freud (1924, 1950, chap. 2), who suggested that children with extremely punishing parents may not identify with them, resulting in poor socialization. The social-learning theorists also emphasize the importance of parental disciplinary techniques in socialization. They note that parents teach children and adolescents how to behave appropriately through their disciplinary techniques. Hence the study of parental disciplinary techniques is important to understanding the adolescents' behavior in the same way it is for understanding why children behave as they do.

Types of Discipline and Parenting. Three types of frequently used disciplinary techniques have been identified (Maccoby & Martin, 1983). The first, **power assertion,** involves the use of physical punishment, the deprivation of privileges or possessions, or the threat of these. By showing the relative weakness of the child, the parent tries to control the child's behavior. Although we tend to associate this type of discipline with younger children, threatening to withdraw privileges from the adolescent (e.g., use of the car) is a form of power-assertive discipline. Ironically, this type of discipline may teach the adolescent that the use of power and physical abuse is a legitimate way to control the world. As a result, the parent may rear an adolescent who uses this form of discipline in future child rearing.

The second and third types of disciplinary techniques may be described as **non-power-assertive. Love withdrawal** refers to nonphysical expressions of parental anger or disapproval. Ignoring the child, isolating the child from friends or siblings, and verbally expressing dislike or disappointment are examples. Because these techniques involve implicit threats of abandonment and explicit expressions of disapproval that may undermine the child's feelings of self-worth, they may in fact be more punitive than physical abuse.

The other non-power-assertive technique is **induction**. It provides the adolescent with a reason for not behaving in some particular way—driving without a license or while intoxicated—and offers alternative ways to behave. Induction techniques attempt to alter behavior by appealing to the adolescent's ability to understand that certain situations require specific forms of behavior. Induction teaches desired behavior within the context of a punishment situation.

In general, parents use a variety of disciplinary techniques; few use exclusively one. Thus researchers have developed ways of classifying parents according to their modal discipline strategies and have related these to the adolescent's development.

One scheme for identifying different styles of parental rearing involves classifying parents as either high or low on two major dimensions of rearing: parental responsiveness and parental demandingness (Baumrind, 1991; Maccoby & Martin, 1983). **Parental responsiveness** refers to the degree to which the parent interacts with the adolescent in a warm, supportive, and accepting manner. **Parental demandingness** refers to the extent to which parents expect and demand mature and responsible behavior *consistent with the child's developmental level.* Four parent types can be identified by looking at the combinations of high and low for each dimension: authoritative, authoritarian, indulgent, and indifferent (see Table 10–1).

Authoritative parents are high in both warmth and demandingness. Although supportive and accepting, they expect their adolescents to behave in a mature and responsible manner consistent with their maturity level. They teach autonomy and self-directedness, but they do not abdicate their own responsibility for their offspring. Authoritative parents use high levels of inductive discipline and talk matters over with their adolescent.

Authoritarian parents use power-assertive discipline techniques to force conformity and obedience from their children. They believe adolescents should obey parents simply because they are parents, and therefore are unconditionally "right." They are intrusive and restrict their adolescent's autonomy.

Indulgent parents, although accepting, warm, and supportive, place few demands on their adolescents because they view such demands as intrusive. Their adolescents have a high degree of freedom—perhaps too much—and lack guidance.

Indifferent parents spend little time with their adolescents and minimize the time they must interact with them—they arrange their lives for their own benefit and not for that of their adolescents. They have little knowledge of their adolescent's interests or friends, and use power-assertive discipline.

Evidence indicates the authoritative parenting style is related to more positive outcomes in children and adolescents. Authoritative parents are viewed as more fair in rule making and enforcement, and as making their adolescents feel wanted and valuable, important components of identity development. Adolescents who see their parents as authoritative have higher self-esteem, are more intellectually curious and creative, and engage in less delinquent behavior than

Table 10–1   Types of Parental Disciplinary/Rearing Techniques

Parent Type	Demandingness	Responsiveness
Authoritative	High	High
Authoritarian	High	Low
Indulgent	Low	High
Indifferent	Low	Low

those who are reared by parents who use the other types of discipline (Maccoby & Martin, 1983). Authoritative parenting also is related to better school performance (Dornbusch, Ritter, Leiderman, Roberts, & Fraleigh, 1987; Steinberg, Lamborn, Dornbusch, & Darling, 1992); better psychological adjustment (Baumrind, 1991; Lamborn, Mounts, Steinberg, & Dornbusch, 1991); and better skills for coping with stress (Dusek & Danko, 1994; Guay & Dusek, 1992).

The parental rearing styles also are associated with changes in adjustment over a 1 year time period for African American, Hispanic, and White adolescents (Steinberg, Lamborn, Darling, Mounts, & Dornbusch, 1994). Adolescents reared by authoritative parents continue to have good psychological adjustment and school performance. In contrast, those reared by authoritarian parents experience increased levels of somatic distress such as headaches, stomachaches, and colds. Indulgently reared adolescents are well adjusted, but their school performance declines they engage in more school misconduct, and show increases in delinquency. Steinberg and his colleagues suggest that continued exposure to authoritarian parenting acts to maintain already healthy psychological adjustment and good school performance. Continual exposure to parents who use one of the other three rearing styles is associated with some increases in undesirable outcomes.

There are a number of reasons why authoritative parenting relates positively to school performance and psychosocial development (Guay & Dusek, 1992; Steinberg, Lamborn, Dornbusch, & Darling, 1992). First, authoritative parents engage in substantial amounts of inductive discipline. This entails a give-and-take that promotes reasoning about right and wrong, empathy, and identification with the parent in the context of a warm, affectionate relationship. The adolescent learns that mistakes are tolerable and feels freer to try new things and to explore competencies.

Authoritative parents also place limits that are appropriate to the adolescent's competencies, allowing rules to bend and change as situations dictate and as the adolescent matures. An example comes from the realm of independence and autonomy. Authoritative parents are more likely to grant increasing autonomy as the adolescent becomes capable of handling more independence. Making exceptions about staying out late on a school night for some special event or allowing an adolescent to take a part-time job on a trial basis lets the adolescent learn limits and competencies. Academic difficulties, poor social relationships with peers and adults, psychosomatic disorders, and delinquency are related to parental hostility and rejection (Kagan & Moss, 1962; Sears, Maccoby, & Levin, 1957; Weiner, 1970), aspects of the authoritarian and indifferent parent types. Parental rejection may make the adolescent feel unwanted and worthless, and may cause him or her to lash out in aggressive ways. Parental restrictiveness is related to offspring who are inhibited, less curious and creative, and less flexible in problem solving.

One widely studied aspect of child-rearing influences during the adolescent years has focused on the precursors of aggression and delinquency (B. Martin, 1975). The use of power-assertive disciplinary techniques is a correlate of aggression and delinquency. It appears that modeling of aggressive disciplinary

techniques outweigh the suppressive effects on the adolescent's aggressive behavior. The parent provides a model of control based on aggression and the adolescent learns to behave in a similar manner (Quiggle, Garber, Panak, & Dodge,
1992).

Perceptions of Child Rearing

The study of rearing effects on development focus on the *adolescent's perspective* of parental rearing techniques because it is the adolescent's perceptions,
called the **effective environment**, which influence his or her behavior. It is
the adolescent's interpretation (perception) of the parents' behavior that is important, not the behavior as seen by others or as reported by the parents.

In order to measure perceptions of parental childrearing techniques,
Schaefer (1965a, 1965b) developed the **Children s Report of Parental Behavior Inventory (CRPBI).** After reading a brief statement or question, the re-
spondent indicates whether it is like, somewhat like, or not like the parent. The
questionnaire is completed once for each parent in order to relate perceptions
of both the mother's and the father's rearing patterns to behavior. The CRPBI
measures perceptions on three dimensions of rearing (see Table 10-2 for example items). The first is labeled **acceptance versus rejection** and reflects the degree to which the parents' attitude toward the child is one of acceptance and
warmth or rejection and hostility. The second is called **psychological autonomy versus psychological control.** Scores on this dimension reflect the degree to which respondents feel their parents use psychological methods (e.g.,
guilt, hostility, and intrusiveness) to control behavior. The third dimension is labeled **firm control versus lax control** and reflects the degree to which parents limit activities by rigidly enforcing rules and regulations. It is similar to the
parental demandingness dimension.

Some research (e.g., Adams & Jones, 1983; Litovsky & Dusek, 1985, 1988;
Ziegler & Dusek, 1985) shows that adolescents who perceive their parents as
more warm and accepting and as using less psychological control (e.g., guilt) report higher self-esteem. Girls who perceive their mothers as encouraging of independence and as not being too controlling and regulating have advanced

Table 10-2   Example Items from the CRPBI

Acceptance vs. Rejection	Psychological Autonomy vs. Psychological Control	Firm Control vs. Lax Control
Enjoys talking things over with me	Feels hurt when I don't fol- low advice	Is easy with me
Is able to make me feel bet- ter when I am upset	Feels hurt by the things I do	Usually doesn't find out about my misbehavior
Makes me feel like the most important person in his (her) life	Tells me of all the things he (she) has done for me	Excuses my bad conduct
Comforts me when I'm afraid	Will talk to me again and again about anything bad I do	Can be talked into things eas- ily

Parental warmth, acceptance, and nurturance helps the adolescent gain a sense of worth and facilitates self-esteem and identity development. (*H. Hans/The Image Works*)

identity development relative to those who perceive their mothers as less warm and more controlling. The girls who held these latter perceptions were still largely identity diffuse. Of interest, girls in the foreclosed identity status (those who had made a commitment to an identity without a period of crisis [see Chapter 6]) felt their mothers were warm and supportive, but fairly controlling (Adams & Jones, 1983).

Although perceiving both parents as warm, supportive, and accepting is associated most strongly with positive adolescent psychological development, some evidence shows that perceptions of the mother's rearing may be more important to adolescent adjustment. Litovsky and Dusek (1988) reported that adolescents who perceived both parents, or their mother, as more warm, nurturing, and accepting had the best psychological adjustment. Perceiving the mother as accepting, warm, and nurturant could compensate for perceiving the father as less so. However, the reverse was not the case. It appears that mother can compensate for father in the adolescent's eyes, but not the reverse. In the case of perceptions of parental intrusiveness and use of guilt, however, no such compensatory effect existed. Adolescents who viewed either parent in this manner were less well adjusted.

The results of these studies point to the importance of feeling accepted and wanted as a significant aspect of adolescent development. Feeling accepted fosters a sense of self-worth and aids the development of a more flexible self-concept. It is also clear that feeling a degree of independence is necessary for optimal development, which is fostered by similar parental rearing practices.

Parent Personality and Adolescent Adjustment

One potentially productive type of research on the influence of parents on the adolescent's development focuses on the role played by the parent's personality, and how it and the adolescent's own characteristics relate to the adolescent's behavior. The general notion is that parental personality may be related to rearing practices that, in turn, impact on the personality and behavior of the adolescent. This research stems from the family-systems approach to development (see Box 10-2).

One line of research has focused on the role of parents on adolescent drug use (Brook, Whiteman, & Gordon, 1983; Brook, Whiteman, Gordon, & Brook, 1984; Brook, Whiteman, Gordon, & Cohen, 1986). Brook and her colleagues examined the role of the adolescent's personality, the parents' personality, and parental childrearing techniques in adolescent drug use. In general, it appears the adolescent's personality is the more important factor in drug use. Adolescents who have a high tolerance of deviancy, are rebellious, lack responsibility, and who have low expectations for academic achievement are prone to use drugs. These traits seem to result from parental childrearing techniques that cause an emotional detachment from the parents (Turner, Irwin, & Millstein, 1991). More specifically, adolescents reared by parents who are not child centered (the indifferent parents noted earlier) and who have difficulty granting autonomy are more prone to becoming drug users. Distant and cold relationships with the parents also contribute to drug use, as does having overly permissive parents. Having appropriately restrictive parents, and a father who is warm and accepting, seems to insulate adolescents from drug use. Having parents who are drug users and having one or both parents highly tolerant of drug use contributes to adolescent drug use.

Some research has focused on maternal personality, more specifically maternal acute depression (Dodge, 1990a, 1990b; Gondoli & Silverberg, 1994; Hops, Sherman, & Biglan, in press), and its relation to adolescent development. In comparison to adolescents of nondepressed mothers, those of depressed mothers are more irritable, depressed, prone to suicide, at an increased risk for emotional problems and school difficulties, and report their mothers use more psychological control in disciplining them. Girls growing up with a depressed single mother not only do poorer in school but also have lower educational aspirations (Silverberg, Marczak, & Gondoli, 1993). In addition, depressed mothers report more problems with their offspring, as do the teachers of these children (Richters &

BOX 10–2   Development in a Family with Lesbian and Gay Parents

Historically, developmental psychologists have been concerned with numerous issues related to how the home, and particularly how parents as primary caretakers, affect offspring development. Typically, this has meant the development of children growing up in homes with two heterosexual parents. The vast majority of this research was conducted in so-called traditional homes—White, middle class, having a father who works outside the home and a mother who does not. Because of cultural changes, views of what constitutes a family have changed and this model has been shown to be lacking. Researchers are now studying what it means to grow up in families that vary with regard to the number of parents, economic circumstances, ethnicity, the number of working parents, and a variety of other characteristics. A general conclusion from this research is that healthy psychological development clearly can take place in highly diverse home environments.

One family type that is increasing in numbers has gay and lesbian parents (C. J. Patterson, 1992). Charlotte Patterson, a developmental psychologist at the University of Virginia, has reviewed the relatively scant research findings concerning the development of children growing up with lesbian or gay parents. Although it is difficult to estimate the number of such families or the number of children in them, Patterson notes the number is substantial—conservatively, somewhere between 6 and 8 million. We draw on her review here.

One area of research has been concerned with sexual identity, which has three components: identification of the self as a male or female (gender identification); the degree to which the adolescent's behavior, occupatonal aspirations, and goals are sex typed male, female, or both (gen-der-role behavior); and the adolescent's sexual orientation. In each of these three areas of sexual identity no evidence shows that children and adolescents of gay and lesbian parents differ from those of heterosexual parents. For example, the percentage of adolescents and young adults who had gay or lesbian parents and who identified themselves as gay or lesbian was no greater than the percentage in the control group of adolescents or young adults whose parents were self-identified as heterosexual. Being reared by gay or lesbian parents, then, does not seem to result in any different sexual identity than being reared by heterosexual parents.

What about other areas of personality development, such as self-concept, moral development, and emotional development? And what about relations with peers, adults, and parents? Following her review of research in these and other areas, Patterson found no evidence that children or adolescents of gay or lesbian parents were any different than the children of heterosexual parents. Their status in the peer group, their relations with adults, and their risk of sexual abuse is no greater than that of children whose parents are heterosexual.

Although acknowledging that much more research is needed, Patterson concludes that at the present time no evidence suggests gay or lesbian parents put their adolescents at a developmental disadvantage. She suggests that there are constellations of parental behaviors and family life that promote healthy psychological development and one need not be heterosexual to provide them. As we note in the text, parental behavior, not family structure (single parent vs. two parent, for example), seems to be the critical feature that fosters sound growth.

Pellegrini, 1989). Hops et al. (in press) suggest that depressed mothers lack sound parenting skills, are less capable of taking care of their adolescents, tend to use physical punishment, and have a difficult time showing affection, warmth, and acceptance toward their adolescents. Having a father who is warm, accepting, and nurturant seems to counteract the negative influence of the depressed mother, perhaps because he makes the home atmosphere more like an authoritarian one.

Just as children grow into early, mid, and later adolescence, their parents grow through stages of adulthood. At about the time adolescents are striving for independence and dealing with the identity crisis, parents are going through similar changes. They must deal with the reality that their children will soon be leaving home and perhaps they have reached the limit of their parenting job. Some may reassess their lives and the choices they have made, and perhaps wish they had made different ones. In other words, at the same time that adolescents are dealing with major identity concerns, their parents may be going through a similar phase. In the extreme, a parent may face what we commonly call a midlife crisis.

Some researchers now have begun to examine the transition to adolescence in light of parental transitions into middle age (Montemayor, McKenry, & Julian, 1992; Silverberg, 1992). The very scant research shows that parental midlife concerns are related to the quality of interactions with adolescents. The intensity of fathers' midlife concerns relate negatively to the quality of interactions with their adolescents (Montemayor et al., 1992) and, more generally, parental midlife concerns may be more negatively related to interactions with female than male adolescents (Silverberg, 1992). These researchers suggest that parental preoccupations with their own life concerns detract from their ability to be involved with similar concerns of their adolescents. In other words, parental midlife concerns are important not only in themselves but also because they impact on the quality of parental rearing styles and interactions with their adolescents.

The research we have reviewed here shows a complex interplay between the characteristics of the parents, including personality and childrearing techniques, and the adolescent that we must consider when trying to understand adolescent development. An important component is the general predisposition (personality) of the parents. It is not so much the specific personality or crises being faced by the parents or adolescents that is important, but rather how the situation (personality, midlife concerns, or adjusting to becoming divorced, which we discuss later) relates to parental rearing techniques and parent–adolescent interactions. This type of research is another example of the family-systems approach to understanding development.

FAMILY COMPOSITION
AND ADOLESCENT SOCIALIZATION

Although examination of childrearing patterns helps us gain some understanding of parental influences on adolescent development, such research is only part of the picture. Other family factors also are important. In this section we examine two such factors: (1) parental divorce and living in a single-parent home, and (2) living in a home with two working parents.

Divorce and Living in a Single-Parent Family

There has been a steady increase during the last two decades in the number of children and adolescents affected by parental divorce (Box 10-1); over 1 million children are affected annually. It is estimated that during the 1990s about a third of all American children under the age of 18 will live some amount of time with a divorced parent.

Early research on adapting to parental divorce had a number of conceptual and methodological flaws (Hetherington, 1979). For example, early researchers focused on the negative influence of father absence (the **deficit model**) without considering the reason (death, divorce, military service) or permanency of the absence. In addition, the tendency was to attribute aberrant development directly to father absence—a single-variable, unidirectional causal approach. There was a general tendency to treat all father-absent families as homogeneous, regardless of other differences, such as social class, the reason for the absence, or the child's relationship to both parents and the parents' relationship to each other. In addition, the majority of the studies were not longitudinal. The study of children or adolescents only once, usually relatively soon after the divorce, precluded studying how they adapted as time passed. Finally, early researchers often failed to study or even consider the relationship between the divorced father and the child, a relationship which is very important to the child's adjustment to parental divorce. We now have longitudinal research findings, studies in which control groups of children in intact families are included, and research on the importance of the father after divorce. As a result, some myths about the influence of divorce on the development of children and adolescents have been dispelled.

Stress and Divorce. Historically, divorce was viewed as a unitary event that occurred relatively quickly and then was over. The stress of divorce was associated with the short time period involved when separation happened. Current conceptualizations view divorce as a sequence of events to which children—and adults—must adapt. There is the family situation prior to divorce, which may expose the child to conflicting loyalties, hostilities between the parents, and perhaps children's doubts about their feelings toward one or both parents. In addition, the home atmosphere may be conflict ridden (parents may argue and there even may be physical violence between them), which may retard development.

Despite evidence showing the difficulty offspring have dealing with parental divorce, it may ultimately be beneficial to the child. The preponderance of the evidence indicates that development may be better when living with one parent in a relatively harmonious home atmosphere, as opposed to living with two parents in a home characterized by fighting, hostility, bitterness, and all of the negative emotions associated with two adults who live together but are unhappy doing so. Children from single-parent homes have fewer psychosomatic illnesses, lower delinquency rates, and better emotional adjustment than do children from intact but unhappy homes. Research (Feldman, Wentzel, Weinberger, & Munson, 1989; Rossman & Rosenberg, 1989; Sarigiani, 1989) demonstrates that the quality of the marital relationship is generally more important than family structure in determining adolescent adjustment, and this is important both before and after parental separation (Hetherington, 1989). The detrimental effects of poor marital cohesion begin in childhood (Turturo, 1993), perhaps because life changes such as childbearing and rearing cause changes in selfviews (Hooker & Fiese, 1993), and continue through the adolescent years. Adolescents in relatively conflict-free homes, whether dual or single parent, show fewer behavioral, social, and cognitive problems in general and in coping with divorce.

A second period of stress is evidenced in the disorganization associated with parental separation. Adolescent stress associated with loss of a parent, change in family structure, and uncertainty about the future is greatest during the first year or so following separation. The change in the structure of the family has a number of consequences: living in a female-headed household, which may be more stressful than a dual-parent household (McLanahan, 1983); developing changing relationships to both parents; perhaps mother going to work for the first time and all that that entails (more responsibility, more time without parent supervision); and a changed economic situation.

This latter circumstance is especially critical. In general, lower social status, which is related to lower income, is associated with poorer psychological adjustment (Lempers, Clark-Lempers, & Simons, 1989) for both male and female adolescents (Flanagan, 1989). The median family income of female-headed divorced families is only about 50% that of two-parent, married families (U. S. Bureau of the Census, 1989). As a result, approximately four times as many divorced families as intact families are below the poverty level and are subject to the harmful effects of poverty and the stresses associated with it. The numbers are even larger for Black adolescents (McLoyd, 1989a, 1989b), who generally are not as well off as White adolescents.

Of course, the relation between poverty and adolescent adjustment is not a direct one. Poverty, in and of itself, does not cause developmental difficulties. Rather, research shows that poverty negatively influences marital quality, feelings of efficacy in the parenthood role, and parental emotional health (R.D. Conger, Conger, Elder et al., 1992; Elder, Eccles, Ardelt, & Lord, 1993; Ge et al., 1992). These lowered feelings of ability as a parent and of self-worth are related to poorer parenting skills which, in turn, are related to poorer childhood outcomes. The lowered economic standards and concurrent economic stresses that often occur when a parent leaves the home may result in poorer development because of their impact on the single parent's rearing skills.

Finally, within 5 years after the divorce, most children must adjust to living in a **reconstituted family** (Hetherington, Clingempeel, Colyar, Brand, &

Hetherington, 1992). Some research indicates that homes involving a stepparent may have more stress and lower cohesiveness than original homes, especially if the stepparent is a stepmother. Added stress comes from alterations to the family routine, which may have been established only recently, the addition (at times) of stepsiblings, and the disciplinary techniques of the stepparent. Relying on a large nationally representative sample of 8th graders living in a family without the natural mother, and especially in father-stepmother homes, some researchers (Lee, Burkam, Zimiles, & Ladewski, 1994) reported an increase in school-related emotional and behavioral problems among the young adolescents in such reconstituted families.

Coping with divorce, then, is a developmental process that requires resolving a series of six social and personal tasks (Wallerstein, 1983; see Table 10-3). Each requires adjustment, and readjustment, over an extended period of time, often with little help from the parents, who are going through their own period of adjusting to new relations with each other, their children, and their lives. Successful adaptation will depend on the age of the child, the nature of the parent–child interactions, and the coping skills and supports the child can muster. In this regard, researchers (e.g., P.A. Miller, Kliewer, & Burkeman, 1993) have begun to investigate the role of the custodial mother in the teaching and modeling of coping behaviors. These researchers report that maternal encouragement of problem- and emotion-focused support seeking was related to increased use of these means of coping, whereas the preadolescents of mothers

Table 10–3 Psychological Tasks in Adapting to Parental Divorce

1. *Acknowledging the reality of the marital rupture.* The child must come to grips with fears and fantasies about how difficult things will be and must learn that the parents will not live together again. This is especially difficult for young children.
2. *Disengaging from parental conflict and distress and resuming customary pursuits.* Children must learn to distance themselves from the parental difficulties, often with little help from the parents, and go about living a normal life conducive to healthy growth. Child also must not let the parental seperation be completely consuming. As children get older this task does not get easier.
3. *Resolution of loss.* The child, who at this point may feel "unlovable," must come to grips with feelings of rejection and worthlessness. This may be especially difficult to do if mother is the one who leaves the house. This task is the most difficult and may take many years to resolve.
4. *Resolving anger and self-blame.* The child must overcome anger over the parents' decision to separate rather than stay together as the child wishes. The younger child especially must come to realize that he or she was not responsible for the divorce.
5. *Accepting the permanence of the divorce.* Children must overcome fantasies and hopes about parental reconciliation. This may be more difficult for younger children because of their lack of mature understanding of the nature and meaning of divorce.
6. *Achieving realistic hope regarding relationships.* This is primarily a task of the adolescent years. The adolescent must learn to trust others in intimate relationships and to develop the capacity to love, and be loved, by others.

Source: Wallerstein, J.S. (1983). Children of divorce: The psychological tasks of the child. *American Journal of Orthopsychiatry, 53,* 230-243. Reprinted by permission of American Orthopsychiatric Association.

who modeled a "reactive" means of coping (e.g., high avoidance coping) were more likely to use these means for dealing with parental divorce.

For the adolescent, the sixth task is of special importance. It relates to resolution of the intimacy versus isolation crisis and has important consequences for the adolescent's views of marriage, friendships, trust, and intimacy. Successfully dealing with this crisis—developing hope, optimism, and trust in interpersonal relations—is critical to forming trusting adult relations. Some evidence (Guttman, 1988-1989) shows that boys who successfully resolve this conflict are as able to form strong, intimate relations with girlfriends as boys from intact families.

Reactions to Divorce.   Reactions to divorce vary with the age of the child. and are highly specific, but in general the younger the child, the more difficulty he or she has in adapting to parental divorce. There also are gender differences in coping with divorce and recovering from the trauma it causes; girls generally cope better than boys. Similarly, there are age and gender differences in adjusting to a stepparent—it is more difficult for adolescents than children, and more difficult for adolescent females than males.

The most extensive studies of adaptation to divorce involve preschoolers (Hetherington, 1989; Hetherington et al., 1992; Hetherington, Cox, & Cox, 1976, 1979; Wallerstein & Kelly, 1980). Preschool children have a very difficult time emotionally, socially, and psychologically when their parents divorce. They may regress (behave in ways characteristic of younger children), become more aggressive, show high dependency needs and disturbed play and social interaction patterns, and blame themselves for the divorce. Researchers report that the disturbances are more pervasive and last longer for boys than girls. Although both boys and girls show improvement 2 years after their parents divorce, boys lag far behind girls, who are nearly fully recovered.

Hetherington and her colleagues suggest these gender differences in adapting to parental divorce result from the mother–son relationship, which is a troubled one. Divorced mothers with sons are more negative and have less control over their son's behavior than nondivorced mothers (Hetherington et al., 1992) or divorced mothers of daughters. In part this is due to the general decline in parenting skills that accompanies divorce, which relates to the stress the mother is experiencing, the learning of how to be a single parent, and the fact that mothers of boys generally report that boys are harder to raise than girls. The lowered parenting skills, such as control and monitoring of the child's behavior (Smetana, 1993), is related to greater noncompliance by the child, and a vicious circle is started.

Although the mother–son relationship improves over time, it remains a troubled one. Hetherington (1989) reported that when the children were 10 (6 years after their parent's divorce), the mothers of boys still used less effective rearing techniques and did not show a great deal of warmth toward their sons. In contrast, there were few differences between divorced and married mothers' relationships with daughters. These preadolescents, who were preschoolers when their parents were divorced, also tended to grow up sooner than age-mates living in intact families because they had more responsibility, independence, and input into decision making. Although this was beneficial for some, it was detrimental to others, particularly those whose mothers had undue expectations of their offspring's competence.

Part of the difficulty seems to lie in how the mother and adolescent view rule and decision making. In contrast to married mothers and divorced mothers of girls, divorced mothers of boys seem to abdicate some of their responsibility as a parent. They have a tendency to view all rules as less subject to their authority; their sons feel more strongly that decision making is more their province than that of their mothers. It may be that the stresses of divorce compound the difficulties mothers generally have with rearing boys and this is reflected in lowered monitoring and acceptance of parental responsibility.

Other evidence (Wallerstein, 1984) shows that young adolescents who were preschoolers when their parents divorced have little memory of the divorce or their reactions at the time. Most wished they had an intact family, but indicated they had open and trusting relationships with their mothers and maintained strong emotional ties to their fathers, regardless of how frequently they saw them. Finally, most were optimistic about their own future marriages and family prospects.

The adjustment of children between the age of 5 and adolescence to parental divorce vary in predictable ways. With increasing age, children are better able to cope with parental divorce (Wallerstein & Kelly, 1980), and gender differences in coping dissipate. For example, by ages 5 and 6 some children do not particularly suffer in self-esteem or developmental progress, and by age 7 to 8 few children blame themselves for their parents' divorce. Although the precise reasons for these developmental changes are not known, they likely relate to increased ability to comprehend the reasons for divorce, and to better coping resources, such as the use of social support from relatives and friends that are unavailable to younger children.

In general, adolescents cope better with divorce than children, particularly if they disengage themselves from the divorce (Wallerstein & Kelly, 1980) and do not feel caught in the middle of their parents' disputes (Buchanan, Maccoby, & Dornbusch, 1991). Withdrawing from the situation—refusing to get involved in parental disputes and not allowing themselves to become allies of either parent—allows the adolescent to go about the business of dealing with other normative developmental tasks. Similarly, not feeling in the middle is associated with lowered depression and better psychological adjustment. Parents who use their adolescents to carry messages between them or who try to make their adolescents choose sides by relating the ways they have been "mistreated" place their adolescents in an unwanted and awkward position. Although some adolescents feel moral indignation, have school problems, and find parental divorce very difficult, they rebound in a reasonable time and go about the job of growing up.

Indeed, it now appears that parental divorce or family structure, in and of

288 Chapter 10 Parent and Family Influences

themselves, are of little importance to adolescent adjustment. The key factor seems to be parental discord (Kurdek, 1988; B. Long, 1986). Daughters' self-esteem is unaffected by *family* structure—those in single-parent and intact households have equivalent self-esteem. However, *parental conflict* is negatively related to self-esteem. Regardless of family structure, a daughter's self-esteem is lower if her parents have a discordant relationship. In a similar vein, a cooperative, working relationship not only helps the daughter—and likely the son—maintain a healthy self-esteem but also helps the child cope with divorce more successfully (Kurdek, 1988) and maintain cognitive and social competence (N. Long, Forehand, Fauber, & Brody, 1987). Some evidence (Kerig & Hutchinson, 1993) indicates these young adult daughters of divorce describe their gender role more negatively and are less trusting of men than daughters in intact families, and that sons of divorce describe their gender role more positively. Kerig and Hutchinson suggest these long-term effects of experiencing parental divorce are related to parental conflicts as just discussed. Parental conflict, then, may not only have an immediate negative impact on the adolescent's adjustment, but may result in the development of more long-term traits that influence social relationships.

Very little research has been aimed at the adjustment of college students to parental divorce (Grant, Smith, Sinclair, & Salts, 1993; Swartzman-Schatman & Schinke, 1993). Researchers have studied (1) how college students adapt if their parents divorce while they are in college, and (2) the adaptation of students to college in relation to how old they were when their parents divorced.

It appears that college student reactions to parental divorce are much like those of adolescents, but they generally receive less support from their parents in coping with divorce, likely because the parents feel college students are old enough to handle it more on their own (Swartzman-Schatman & Schinke, 1993). Of interest, college students face a difficulty that adolescents are less likely to face, namely, how to spend their vacation time. Unlike adolescents, college students live most of the time away from home—divorced parents seem to view them as fully grown adults who can choose who they wish to visit. Hence they may become pawns in their parents' lives, which can produce anxiety and guilt.

Adjustment to the college environment is more influenced by when the student's parents divorced than current living arrangements (Grant et al., 1993). Adjustment to college was more difficult if the student was in childhood as opposed to being a preschooler or adolescent when the parents divorced. Although it is likely that being a preschooler when the parents divorce may not lead to difficulty adjusting to college, given Wallerstein's findings cited earlier, it is not obvious why being a child when parents divorce makes adjustment to college more difficult. Perhaps the very young child, who remembers little of the actual experiences, and the adolescent, who generally adapts better, have a natural insulation for psychosocial adjustment that helps them in the long run. The child, who may well remember more of the difficulties encountered, a feeling of being caught in the middle, and the inability to "manage" the situation, may not have this protection.

Our review of adapting to divorce reveals the complexity of the issues. Divorce has negative influences, but these are less tied to family structure than to interpersonal relations between the child and both parents. Having an absent father need not be a negative influence on development; indeed, continued and sustained meaningful contact with the father can attenuate much of the negative impact of divorce. In turn, it is difficult to discern any real positive influences of divorce per se, other than the possible improvement of home atmosphere and subsequent increases in personal growth.

Of course, adjusting to divorce involves more than relations with parents. Adapting to new living arrangements, adjusting to stepparents, and changing relations with siblings and other family members occurs.

The Issue of Living Arrangements

Historically, the courts have awarded children's living arrangements to the mother. Recently, however, the notion of joint custody has gained in popularity, and researchers have begun to investigate how custody arrangements impact on the adolescent.

Proponents of joint custody note that it increases contact with the "other" parent (Kline, Tschann, Johnston, & Wallerstein, 1989), which allows the child the opportunity to maintain meaningful contact with both parents. Those who are opposed note that co-parenting entails some amount of moving, the possible uprooting of friendships, and confusion about having a "psychological parent," that is, a parent and caretaker to whom the child has constant access. There also is the risk of the child or adolescent being continually in the middle of parental conflict that, as we noted earlier, is detrimental to development (Buchanan et al., 1991). In their study of offspring aged 3 to 14 at the time of their parent's divorce, Kline and colleagues found that type of custody—sole versus joint—was unrelated to psychological or social/emotional adjustment several years after the divorce. What was important to healthy growth was parental discord: Parents who did not get along, who put their offspring in the middle of their disagreements, and who were hostile toward each other provided home atmospheres that were not conducive to healthy psychological growth. Of importance, the number of times the child or adolescent switched homes and lived with one parent and then the other was not related to how the child developed.

More recent research extends and elaborates these findings (Barber, Clark, Clossick, & Wamboldt, 1992; Buchanan, Maccoby, & Dornbusch, 1992). It now appears that the critical components of custody arrangements not only involve the degree of parental conflict and the extent to which the adolescent feels in the middle of parental difficulties, but also the relation with each parent. Some evidence (e.g., Buchanan et al., 1992) indicates that father custody can be more difficult because fathers do not monitor their adolescent's behavior as closely as mothers do, and because both males and females seem to feel less close to their fathers than their mothers. These difficulties were especially large when the par-

About one third of all adolescents will spend some time in a single-parent home, most often with the mother. Living in a happy home is better than living in a tension filled one. Sustained meaningful contact with the non-resident parent helps make living in a single parent home easier. (*Left: Ken Karp. Right: Page Poore Kidder*)

ents exhibited a high degree of discord. Other evidence (Barber et al., 1992) shows that when noncustodial fathers frequently visit their adolescents, differences in development between adolescents living with mothers and those living in intact families are very minimal. As we noted earlier, the involvement of the noncustodial parent is an important aspect of the adolescent's adjustment to divorce and to his or her general adjustment, particularly if the parent is the same gender as the child (Gunnoe, 1994).

Adjusting to Stepparents

Within 5 years of their parents' divorce, a substantial proportion of offspring must adapt to the remarriage of one or both of their parents. Some research has shown that this adaptation is more difficult for girls during childhood (Hetherington et al., 1992; Hetherington, Cox, & Cox, 1985), preadolescence (Santrock, Warshak, Lindbergh, & Meadows, 1982), and adolescence (Buchanan, Maccoby, & Dornbusch, 1994). Girls become more anxious, hostile, and cool emotionally as a result of mother's remarriage. Females also seem to have a more difficult time than males adapting to a stepmother (Buchanan et al., 1994). Although these effects may dissipate over time, residues may be present 2 years after the remarriage (Hetherington, 1989) for those who were children when their mother remarried.

In contrast, stepfathers seem to play a beneficial role vis-à-vis stepsons, both during childhood (Hetherington et al., 1985) and preadolescence (Santrock et al., 1982). Although some initial problems may occur, by 2 years after remarriage the boys did not show more aggressive or disruptive behavior than did boys in intact families. Parental remarriage during early adolescence, however, may be associated with sustained long-term behavior problems for both sons and daughters (Hetherington, 1989).

Other researchers have not found such strong gender differences in adjustment due to family structure or remarriage (Alliston & Furstenberg, 1989; Kurdek & Sinclair, 1988a). In these studies it was found that family structure was less important to adjustment, in general, and specifically adjustment to remarriage, than was the general interaction pattern in the family. Successful psychological adjustment in any family structure is associated with high family cohesion, a supportive family environment, and the use of positive coping skills such as strong social supports. The family atmosphere that is conducive to providing these characteristics will foster psychological adjustment (Kurdek & Sinclair, 1988a).

Hetherington (1989) and Hetherington et al., (1992) have described how the process may operate. For about the first 2 years after remarriage, stepfathers spend time trying to establish relationships with stepchildren, but they feel little affection for them. They tend to be somewhat distant, expressing neither positive nor negative feelings toward stepchildren. When they did use authoritative stepparenting, it resulted in increased behavior problems in both stepsons and stepdaughters during this time. Although these problems later diminished for stepsons, this was not the case for stepdaughters. Hetherington suggests that initially any attempt at control by the stepfather is viewed adversely. She suggests that the stepfather should not try to shape and mold the child's behavior at first, but should (1) support the mother's child rearing and (2) attempt to establish a meaningful and workable relationship with the child. Authoritative parenting may be introduced later, when stepfather and stepchildren know each other better.

The stepchild's reactions to the stepfather represent the other aspect of the interaction. Initially, stepfathers may be viewed as intruders who compete for time, care, and affection from mother. Stepchildren may feel their relationship with their mother is threatened; this may especially be the case for daughters. Hence initial reactions may be one of rejection and hostility, and of anger toward the mother for remarrying. It is as though no matter what the stepfather does, he can't win. These reactions may be greater during early adolescence owing to increased independence strivings and identity concerns.

These reactions on the part of the stepfather and stepchildren result in an interaction style that will have a degree of tension and could result in lower family cohesion, especially if there is a deterioration in the mother–child relationship. Hence initial adjustment to stepfathers may be difficult and these difficulties may carry over to other areas of daily behavior. One could expect that where these problems are less evident, adolescent adjustment will be easier and occur more quickly. The key to successful adolescent adjustment to remarriage, then, lies in family interactions that promote cohesion, warmth, and a supportive environment devoid of threats to the self and to the child's relations with the mother.

A critical component of the adolescent's acceptance of the custodial parent's new partner is marriage (as opposed to living with or apart from the custo-dial parent; Buchanan et al., 1994). Adolescents are more likely to accept the au-thority of a new marriage partner and to grant greater consideration and respect to that person—whether stepmother or stepfather. This greater acceptance of the stepparent is related to increased feelings of closeness to the stepparent, lowered engagement in deviant behavior, and reduced scores on measures of depression. Parental remarriage seems to confer a sort of legitimacy in the (now) stepparent (the legitimacy involving a sense of parenting rights for the new parental partner) and a sense that the relationship will be a lasting one (which may allow the formation of an attachment to the parent's partner).

Sibling Relations in Divorce.   The effect of divorce on sibling relations has not been the central focus of research efforts. This is surprising because siblings could act as significant buffers and social supports in dealing with the stress of divorce. Alternatively, there could be increased hostility and rivalry as siblings vie for decreased family resources in the spheres of parental attention, caregiv-ing, and affection. Unfortunately, the findings seem to indicate the latter is more common than the former.

Both Hetherington (1989; Hetherington et al., 1992) and MacKinnon (1989) report that sibling pairs involving a boy (boy-girl or boy-boy) showed greater hostility, aggression, and sibling rivalry than girl-girl pairs. This was espe-cially the case when there was an older brother and a younger sister. Siblings in stepfamilies, in general, also had more negative interactions.

There are two important exceptions to this general finding. First, although the relationships between siblings in stepfamilies improves over time, by 2 years after the divorce they are still not on a par with the interactions of siblings in in-tact families. Second, older daughters in stepfamilies engage in more caretaking, nurturing, and supportive interactions with their younger sisters, perhaps be-cause they have a more realistic understanding of divorce (Kurdek, 1989).

The bases of these findings are not well understood at this time. MacKin-non (1989) suggests that boys may be modeling an assertive father, a father in-volved in conflict with a spouse prior to divorce. It may be, too, that the girls in boy-girl dyads are modeling more submissive behavior because that is how the mother behaved prior to the divorce. In other words, it may be that siblings model the style of interaction of their parents prior to the divorce when they face the stress of the divorce situation.

The adolescent's perception of the family environment is highly individual-istic and, therefore, affects siblings differently (Monahan, Buchanan, Maccoby, & Dornbusch, 1993). Those adolescents who perceive their shared home differ-ently report different levels of adjustment, whether with regard to school per-formance, depression, or antisocial behavior. The better the perception of the home atmosphere, the better the adjustment. The critical features seem to be household organization, which relates to the regular following of household routines such as mealtime and knowing which chores are to be done by whom, and parent–adolescent conflict over concerns such as curfews and doing chores. Monahan and her colleagues suggest adolescents may be differently invested in the household and that this may lead to contrasting perceptions of household routines even when objectively siblings are held to the same expectations. Such findings highlight how important it is to study the adolescent's perceptions of the home environment when considering how adolescents adjust to divorce.

Other Potential Supports.   Other social and institutional supports are available to the child and adolescent coping with parental divorce. Hetherington (1989) mentions in this regard grandparents, schools, and peers.

Grandparents may play important social and emotional roles with their divorced or remarried children, but they have little control or influence on their grandchildren's adjustment unless they live in the home with them (Clingempeel, Colyar, Brand, & Hetherington, 1992). Although living in the same home with their divorced offspring and their grandchildren may benefit the grandchildren, it seems to produce a stifling effect on the grandparents' own children—the mothers felt like they were children again, as though they had lost independence by living with their own parents. In addition, conflicts between mother and grandparents arose over parenting issues, which made for difficulties. As Hetherington (1989) put it, grandparents are useful in emergencies, as with problem children, but otherwise provide little influence on the child's adjustment to divorce. In contrast, the loss of one parent from the household may cause adolescents to seek out others, such as grandparents, or cause grandparents to feel greater responsibilities and closeness, which can cause greater closeness of grandchildren to their grandparents (Clingempeel et al., 1992).

In contrast, the school environment seems to afford a much needed stable atmosphere of authoritativeness. Children in school when divorce occurred profited from the routine, regularized schedule. The structured school environment seemed a safe haven for the children and attenuated the adversity found at home. In addition, academic success was associated with enhanced coping, and for boys athletic achievement functioned similarly. It appears that the routine and structure found in the school environment can buffer the child and adolescent in much the same manner that a supportive home environment can.

With increasing age of the child experiencing the divorce, peers can play an increasingly important buffering role. Hetherington noted that a single close good friend was beneficial—children without such friendships had a more difficult time adjusting to divorce. This may be especially important for adolescents, who more readily disengage themselves from the divorce situation. Strong friendships and school affiliations provide support and structured activities that allow the adolescent to continue to deal in adaptive ways with not only the typical aspects of development faced by youngsters but also with the consuming aspects of parental divorce.

Maternal Employment and Adolescent Development

Along with the increase in single-parent families, one of the most widespread structural changes in the American family has been the increase in the employment of mothers. As we discuss in Box 10–1, there has been a steady increase since 1970 in the percentage of mothers who work outside the home. And the increase applies to both married and divorced mothers, although the latter already were highly represented in the work force in 1970. Whether the increases will continue is unknown. What is clear, however, is that the modal family in the United States involves a mother who works outside the home.

Mothers are increasingly entering the work force for a variety of reasons. For some it is an economic necessity. The increase in single-parent homes attests to this fact. For many women, working is seen as a form of achievement for which they were trained, just as is the case for men. The increase in educational level of women supports this argument (L. Hoffman, 1979, 1980, 1989). The greater efficiency of household management, including modern appliances and food processing techniques, has meant less time is needed to manage everyday household activities. Finally, working mothers seem generally to be more satisfied with their lives (D. Gold & Andres, 1978a, 1978b), which makes work and the feelings of achievement even more attractive. In sum, women work for the same basic reasons that men do.

Unraveling the precise effects of maternal employment on adolescent development is difficult for many of the same reasons that discovering the effects of divorce is problematic. When the mother begins to work outside the home, the nature of the family structure and responsibilities changes (L. Hoffman, 1989). Children take on more responsibility around the home, and husbands, at least in the middle classes, do more housework. Family income rises in two-parent families. Although mothers do not spend less time with their adolescents when they go to work, the adolescents of mothers who work full time spend more time alone with their fathers than do the adolescents whose mothers work part time or not at all (M.H. Richards & Duckett, 1994). And many women are happier because they are working outside the home.

One of the major concerns in the earlier research was the negative effects of maternal employment on the socialization of children and adolescents (L. Hoffman, 1980). A general rule that has emerged from research findings is that if appropriate care is provided for the child no particular socialization problems occur (L. Hoffman, 1979); the same general rule holds for adolescents during after-school hours (L. Hoffman, 1979). The critical feature is not that mothers spend less time with their children, but rather the time spent is of a higher quality, as measured, for example, by time spent in direct interaction with children (L. Hoffman, 1979, 1989). In this regard, M.H. Richards and Duckett's (1989) study of adolescents in grades 5 through 9 found that older adolescent females spent more time with the family and younger adolescents spent no less time with the family when mother worked. In addition, maternal employment does not affect adversely the quality of the time spent with the family and may lead to enhanced feelings of friendliness in the time spent with mother (M.H. Richards & Duckett, 1994). In part, this was because the adolescents spent more time with father when mother worked. Losses in time spent with the parents come from afternoon time; time spent with the parents during the evening and on weekends is unrelated to maternal employment status (M.H. Richards & Duckett, 1994).

Other major issues concern mother's reasons for working and her job satisfaction. Each is important because of its relationship to family harmony and the degree of conflict in the home. Mothers who are unhappy with their work have poorer relationships with their children than mothers who are happily employed (L. Hoffman, 1989). In addition, mothers who are ill-prepared for satisfying jobs may make inappropriate demands on their children with respect to accepting responsibility for home management and care, which may make maternal employment a difficult situation for the family. Working mothers who are happily employed and nonworking mothers who are content staying home use very similar child-rearing practices. However, mothers who want to work, but stay home because they feel it is their duty, report they have difficulty controlling their children and feel less confident about themselves as mothers (L. Hoffman, 1979). Moreover, mothers who are not working but wish to work report relatively poor marital adjustment, which may lead to an unhappy home atmosphere not conducive to good psychological growth for the child (L. Hoffman, 1989).

Adolescents' perceptions of their parents' childrearing methods also are related to maternal employment (Litovsky & Dusek, 1988). Up to about the 10th grade, adolescents perceive their parents as more warm and accepting when mother does not work, or works only part time. Older adolescents perceive their parents as more accepting and supportive when mother works full time. It may be that younger adolescents require (and want?) more parental contact than do older adolescents, who in turn have stronger independence needs and may find being around parents stifling and an infringement on their freedom. As L. Hoffman has argued, families in which both parents work may be especially conducive to meeting older adolescents' needs for developing autonomy because they are better able to relinquish tasks that promote the developing of autonomy and competence. When mother is home it may be more difficult to do so because a substantial component of mother's self-worth revolves around family care, the giving up of which could damage her own feelings of self-worth. These findings, then, point to the benefits for the adolescent when mother works, largely through family context conditions that allow the development of self-reliance.

One interesting area of research on maternal employment deals with the adolescent's conception of traditional sex roles. If both parents work, offspring develop a broader notion of sex roles. Adolescent daughters of working mothers have a less negative view of femininity than do daughters of nonworking mothers (Broverman et al., 1972). The adolescent daughters of working mothers are more independent, motivated, and do better on measures of achievement

(L. Hoffman, 1979). They also are better adjusted socially and personally. Maternal employment is related to better adjustment to social relations at school and better family relationships at home for both adolescent males and females (D. Gold & Andres, 1978a). The daughters of working mothers also are more career oriented and interested in less traditionally feminine careers. Sons of working mothers view women as more competent and see men as warmer than do sons of nonworking mothers (D. Gold & Andres, 1978a, 1978b).

Maternal employment, then, has both beneficial and detrimental effects on the adolescent, although the positive influences seem to far outweigh the negative effects. It is important to note that the difficulties involved with maternal employment should not be viewed as arguments against it (L. Hoffman, 1980). Rather, they simply indicate situations to which solutions must be found. In and of itself, maternal employment does not affect the adolescent's development (M.H. Richards & Duckett, 1991). It is what the family does to ensure quality supervision, increased interactions during the evening hours, mother's work satisfaction, and the other factors noted earlier that are critical to the adolescent's development.

PARENT–ADOLESCENT RELATIONS AND ADOLESCENT INDEPENDENCE STRIVINGS

The adolescent years are marked by increases in independence strivings and interest in gaining autonomy (J. Hill, 1980). The attainment of increased independence from parents is sometimes conflictual, particularly during the early part of the pubertal cycle. Later, conflict is at a lower level as the adolescent and parent adapt to the adolescent's independence attainment.

Steinberg and Hill (1978) and Steinberg (1981) studied parent–child interactions in families with 11- and 14-year-old sons. They were interested in both age and pubertal status as precursors of changes in parent–offspring interactions such as speech interruptions, dominance, aggression, and intrapsychic conflict. Each family was observed three times over 1.5 years. In general, conflict between the son and the mother increased during the early period of the growth spurt and then declined. During the early maturity period sons and mothers interrupted each other with increasing frequency, sons showed less deference to their mothers, both mothers and sons explained their views less frequently, and there were rigid patterns of family interaction best characterized as strained and tense. Fathers became more assertive with their sons, but sons generally showed increased deference toward their fathers. In general, mothers and fathers had approximately equal positions greater than sons in the dominance hierarchy during the early part of the maturity period. During the later part of the maturity cycle the son was more influential than the mother but less influential than the father. Steinberg (1981) suggests that both adolescents and parents respond to the son's physical development (pubertal status) as an indication of entrance into adulthood because these differences occur regardless of age; that is, they occur solely as a function of physical characteristics.

If conflict is defined more narrowly a different picture emerges. Brett Laursen (Laursen & Collins, in press; Laursen & Ferreira, 1994) and his colleagues examined developmental trends in two-person (dyadic) interpersonal conflict involving opposition (including quarrals and arguments). They argue that this definition of conflict is more in line with that used by scholars who study conflict than are definitions including speech interruptions and dominance. Following an exhaustive review (published and unpublished works from the years 1926 to 1992 were examined), they concluded there was no evidence that this type of parent–child conflict peaked during the mid-adolescent years or at the apex of pubertal development. The data indicated stability in conflict during early and mid adolescence with a small decline during the later adolescent years. Alterations in parent–adolescent relations occur slowly and gradually— they are not disjunctive.

Researchers have also examined the domains within which conflict is likely to occur (Smetana, in press; Smetana & Asquith, 1994). The general notion is that if parents and adolescents agree on who has the major authority over a domain of behavior, conflict for that domain should be low. If there is disagreement, conflict may occur. The premise underlying this approach to adolescent independence is that during adolescence there is a shift from unilateral parental jurisdiction over behavior to mutually agreed-upon authority. Identifying areas of agreement and disagreement about who has final authority for various domains of behavior gives insight into what is likely to result in adolescent-parent conflict.

Parents and adolescents generally agree that parental authority predominates for moral (for example, taking money from parents without permission, breaking promises to parents), conventional (cursing, not doing assigned chores), and prudential (smoking cigarettes, drinking alcohol) issues. They also agree that personal issues (what to watch on TV, choosing clothes) are the adolescents' choice. A major area of disagreement is in the realm of friendships. Adolescents feel this is their domain, but parents feel they should have greater influence, in part because of the influence of friends on the adolescent. This, then, is an area of potential parent–adolescent conflict.

In order to increase our understanding of how adolescent–parent interactions change during the adolescent years, researchers have begun to focus on the concept of *relationship closeness* (W. A. Collins & Repinski, 1994; Laursen & Collins, in press; Repinski & Collins, 1994). To assess relationship closeness, Repinski and Collins (1994) had students in grades 7, 9, and 11 indicate the amount of time they spent alone with each parent in the past week (a measure of frequency of interaction with the parent), the number of various activities they engaged in with each parent in the past week (a measure of diversity of interaction), and the degree to which each parent influenced them in various activities, decisions, and plans (a measure of strength of influence). The measures allowed the researchers to assess age differences in several aspects of adolescent–parent relationships which related to independence and autonomy.

With increasing grade, there was a decrease in both the mother's and father's influence. In addition, the older adolescents reported having fewer and less diverse interactions with their fathers. In general, then, younger adolescents have more interdependence in their parental relationships than do older adolescents. Although feelings of closeness to father decreased, feelings of closeness to mother did not, emphasizing a continuity in adolescent–parent relationships and underscoring the need to consider relations to each parent separately.

Adolescent independence strivings, then, do not necessarily signify a breaking away from the parents that results in increased conflict. Rather, they relate to changes in the role the adolescent plays in the family interaction system (J. Hill, 1980) and to the fact that the family is in general a secure base from which the adolescent explores the world. Adolescents must learn to rely less on the parents when making personal decisions and adopting values in order to become prepared for the adult world. In turn, parents must adapt by allowing their adolescents to gain independence. This may put a strain on parent–adolescent relations because just as the adolescent is undergoing developmental changes so too are the parents (Ryan & Lynch, 1989). Although some of the maturing adult's concerns overlap parallel concerns of the adolescent, for example, changing physical characteristics and occupational achievements, others, such as children leaving the home, are very different. During adolescence, then, we should expect changes in family interactions because both the parent and the adolescent are undergoing developmental changes that relate to their interpersonal interactions. To be sure, some degree of conflict will arise, but as Laursen and Ferreira (1994) point out, families still tend to be supportive atmospheres for the adolescent.

How do relations with parents relate to leaving home, perhaps the ultimate assertion of independence? Stattin and Magnusson (1994) have investigated this issue in a sample of Swedish adolescents and report that mother–daughter relations are an important predictor of how early the girl leaves the home. Those who left home early (younger than age 18) had a long history of a discordant relationship with their mother, lived in a home where the mother and father had a discordant relationship, and exhibited more externalizing behavior (violation of rules, aggression, acting out). They also adjusted less well to school, smoked and used alcohol more, engaged in sexual behavior at earlier ages and had more partners, and were more impulsive than those who left home later. As we have emphasized throughout this chapter, home harmony and parental relations are an important determinant of adolescent adjustment and behavior.

Theoretical Explanations of Independence Strivings

Ausubel (Ausubel, Montemayor, & Svajian, 1977) has presented the most comprehensive theoretical formulation of adolescent independence strivings. The theory is steeped in the nature of transitions in parent–offspring interactions across the childhood and adolescent years. Ausubel's general idea is that alterations in rearing patterns foster a change from the high dependency of infancy to the relative independence of late adolescence. The infant is completely dependent on the parents for care. As the infant grows into early childhood the realization of this dependency becomes evident. Children realize they need the parents and are dependent on them for their general well-being. As children mature they begin to take this dependency on their parents as a threat to their self-esteem, and this initiates a crisis that the child may solve in one of several ways.

One solution is **satellization**, which means the adolescent comes to accept dependency on the parents, being a satellite revolving around them. Both the child and the parent understand the parent is the power in the relationship and each is satisfied with the relationship. The parents value the child and treat the child with respect; the child, in turn, tries to live up to parental expectations. There is a sense of autonomy relatedness (Allen, Hauser, Bell, & O'Connor, 1994)—the adolescent gains in autonomy (appropriate assertiveness, decision making, and resistance to peer pressure) within the context of being attached (related) to the family (the home is a secure base from which to explore the world and one's competencies).

Not all offspring and parents establish a satellization relationship. There are two forms of nonsatellization: undervaluation and overvaluation. **Underval-**

During adolescence desatellization leads to greater autonomy as both parents and adolescents learn to deal with concerns of independence. (*John Coletti/Stock Boston*)

uation reflects a rejecting parental attitude toward the child. Although the parent meets the child's needs, it is done in a rather cold manner (like the indifferent parenting style) because the child is seen as a burden. Because the child comes to realize this, comformity to parental demands and wishes is done not out of a desire to please the parents but to avoid punishment.

Overvaluation may result when parents are highly accepting of the child out of a wish to vicariously relive their lives through their child's life. These parents often overindulge their child and spoil him or her because the child could become what they were not (like the indulgent parenting style). The parents plan the child's life so as to relive what they wished to be.

During adolescence desatellization occurs. It is evidenced by a severing of ties to the parents as independence strivings increase. Secure feelings about the self and the self's ability to cope develop. The desatellized adolescent is able to function autonomously, behaving in a way consistent with his or her own needs and values. Behaviors no longer necessarily reflect an attempt to please the parents.

Ausubel's theory suggests that satellization leads to optimal adolescent development because it allows the adolescent to develop feelings of self-worth based on feelings of competence and value. Nonsatellization threatens this aspect of development and may lead to difficulties during the adolescent years, such as insecurity in independence strivings.

Factors Affecting Independence Attainment

Age and Cognitive Development. Initially, adults extend adolescents independence and autonomy in a relatively haphazard and inconsistent manner; responsibilities and privileges are generally based on age. This is evidenced in a number of different ways, such as the age at which the adolescent is allowed to date, changes in the time when he or she is expected home, changes in the nature and number of chores he or she is expected to do (Jacobs & Osgood, 1994).

Physical development relates to age trends in granting independence (Steinberg, 1981). Adolescents become more influential in family decision making as they gain in physical maturity. And adolescents who are bigger or grow more rapidly than their peers are treated more like adults and are given more adultlike responsibilities than smaller or later-maturing adolescents.

Cognitive development (Chapter 4) also enters into adolescent independence strivings by allowing the adolescent to reevaluate social circumstances. Adolescents are capable of understanding that some social rules are flexible and, therefore, are also capable of demanding answers to questions about why they are treated the way they are. They demand that parents justify the way they treat them. If this justification seems rational and reasonable, the adolescent may accept it with relatively little debate. Conflict may arise, however, if the parent is autocratic and unreasonable (the authoritarian style we described earlier).

Child Rearing and Independence Attainment.   Parental child-rearing practices influence adolescent independence strivings in several ways. First, parents can help their adolescents learn independence by giving them privileges and responsibilities at the appropriate age (Allen et al., 1994). Indeed, the adolescent's age is among the most powerful predictors of parental curfew and time/distance limits (from adult supervision/home) parents allow. Second, adolescents can learn independent behaviors by observing the adults or parents who model these behaviors. In addition, certain parent types make adolescents feel they are wanted, which increases identification with, and modeling of, them. Baumrind (1978), particularly, has addressed this set of issues and has pointed out it is extremely important for the adolescent to be given models of independence behaviors, as well as age-graded experiences in behaving independently, in order for appropriate degrees of autonomous and independent behavior to develop.

The importance of appropriate parental involvement in the granting of autonomy in the realm of privileges (e.g., deciding how to spend money, dating, when to drink coffee, having no curfew when out at night) was shown by Feldman and Wood (1994). They reported that the sons of fathers who retained involvement and expected (when their sons were preadolescents) to grant these privileges later were better adjusted adolescents. They had better school grades, were more involved in school, reported less misconduct, and had fewer sex partners than the sons of fathers who expected to grant privileges sooner. Feldman and Wood suggest that the father's attitudes about granting privileges measured during their son's preadolescence shape the son's autonomy expectations and are reflected in his later behavior. The father's involvement and monitoring (as reflected by expected timetables for the granting of privileges) helps insulate the adolescent male from potential adverse influences of peers because it helps build regulatory mechanisms—the son learns to be autonomous from potentially negative peer influences.

SIBLING INFLUENCES

Although siblings grow up in the same family, they experience their shared environment very differently (Chipuer, 1992; Plomin & Daniels, 1987). Not only are siblings treated differently by parents and other family members, but they perceive these distinctions. The differences occur for a variety of reasons, including the fact that, except for twins, siblings are of different ages, and therefore are growing up in different stages of the family life cycle.

Sibling relationships undergo developmental changes. One way of characterizing these changes is through the concept of distancing (Anderson & Starcher, 1992). During early adolescence, there is an increase in distancing from siblings. At the same time, there is an increase in avoiding younger siblings and feeling they are embarrassing. As siblings grow through the adolescent years and into adulthood, there is an increase in sibling warmth, and conflict with siblings declines (Lanthier & Stocker, 1993).

Siblings often engage in self-disclosure, which
provides them with social and emotional support.
(*R. Sidney/The Image Works*)

Siblings hold a unique status with each other. In a sense they are peers,
but they are more than that. Whereas other friends may come and go, siblings
affect each other throughout their lives. They share a common developmental
history—same parents, same home, same schools and perhaps teachers, and
even shared friends. As a result, siblings have a unique relationship.

One consequence of this is that siblings likely know each other better
than anyone else. As a result, they are likely to share their most intimate feelings with each other, that is, they are likely to engage in **self-disclosure**
(Howe, Aquan-Assee, & Bukowski, in press). Same-sex siblings are more likely
to engage in self-disclosure such as confiding things they would not tell their
parents and sharing secrets and feelings. And self-disclosure is more likely to be
to a sister than a brother. Finally, self-disclosure is more likely to occur in families that encourage discussing how one feels and thinks. In this way, sibling relations may be important for developing intimate relations with others and may
facilitate the negotiation of the intimacy versus isolation crisis the older adolescent faces.

SUMMARY

The nature of the family has changed considerably during this century, with many of the major changes occurring during the past 30 years. Although the modal family is now urban, mobile, nuclear, smaller, and composed of two working parents, there has been an increase in the number of single-parent families and the emergence of the gay or lesbian family. In addition, the number of children and adolescents growing up in single-parent families, either by the choice of the mother or as a result of divorce, has been increasing. Although parents remain the single most important socialization influence on the adolescent, the changes in family living circumstances and in family composition mediate their influence.

Researchers have identified three major dimensions of child rearing that relate to various aspects of child and adolescent behavior. Parents who are rejecting (as opposed to accepting) frustrate adolescents' nurturance needs and feelings of being wanted. These children are more aggressive and engage in more delinquency. Lax and inconsistent discipline also is related to adolescent delinquency. In general, power-assertive disciplinary techniques teach the adolescent control through force and aggressive behavior. Parents who are accepting, who do not overly use psychological means of controlling the adolescent's behavior, and who do not try to rigidly control the adolescent, rear adolescents with more positive self-esteem and better identity development. This constellation of rearing techniques also leads to a more androgynous sex role and adaptive identity.

Researchers have identified four types of parents based on their predominant rearing styles: authoritative, authoritarian, indulgent, and indifferent. The evidence is convincing that the authoritative style of child rearing is more optimal than the others because it not only makes the adolescent feel wanted and loved but also provides for appropriate restrictions on behavior without ignoring the adolescent's input into decision making. Authoritative parents are accepting and warm but at the same time demand age-appropriate behavior.

Divorce is a disruptive event for the entire family, in part because of the emotional aspects of the circumstance and in part because of the disruption to family composition and daily routine. There are many factors to which the adolescent must adjust, including living with only one parent—usually the mother—and, perhaps, the remarriage of one or both of the parents. Adolescent reactions to parental divorce generally include anger and moral indignation. Many adolescents withdraw from both parents and only a few take sides with one parent. Some adolescents experience difficulty in school, but many do not. The more psychologically mature and independent adolescents adapt better to parental divorce. In general, it appears that although divorce is difficult for the adolescent it is easier for them than it is for preadolescents or preschool children.

It is now recognized that family structure in and of itself is not the critical feature in adolescent development. Whether growing up in a single-parent, stepparent, or intact family, or with parents who are lesbian, gay, or heterosexual, the adolescent's psychological health is most affected by family atmosphere. The freer from conflict, the more cohesive, and the warmer the family atmosphere, regardless of family structure, the happier and more psychologically healthy the adolescent will be.

The majority of mothers with children under 18 years of age now work. There are a number of benefits to the adolescent of a working mother. Both male and female adolescents of working mothers develop more flexible views of sex roles. Adolescent females have a less negative view of femininity, and they tend to be more independent, motivated, and career oriented. These aspects of maternal employment may be lost if the mother is unhappy because she is working or if her going to work disrupts the family routine too much.

Independence strivings increase during the adolescent years. In part, this reflects the physical development of the adolescent. More physically mature adolescent males tend to exert greater influence on family decision making. As secure feelings about the self develop, the adolescent becomes desatellized, that is, less reliant on the parents and more autonomous. Although some conflicts between parent and adolescent occur over independence strivings, these tend not to be particularly serious for most adolescents. Communication between parent and adolescent fosters better adjustment of both the parent and the adolescent to independence.

GLOSSARY

Children s Report of Parental Behavior Inventory (CRPBI): Questionnaire that assesses children's perceptions of their parent's rearing syles.

deficit model: Perspective that the important factor in parental divorce is the lack of a father in the home.

dimensions of child rearing:

  acceptance versus rejection (Schaefer): Dimension of the CRPBI that reflects how accepting, warm, and supportive—versus cold, hostile, and rejecting—the child perceives the parents to be.

  psychological autonomy versus psychological control (Schaefer): Dimension of the CRPBI reflecting the degree to which the child perceives the parents as using guilt and other psychological means to control his or her behavior.

  firm control versus lax control (Schaefer): On the CRPBI, the dimension of child rearing reflected by the making and enforcing of many rules and regulations as opposed to allowing greater freedom and spontaneity on the part of the child.

induction: Form of discipline involving explanations for why some behavior was wrong and providing alternative forms for behaving.

love withdrawal: Form of punishment involving ignoring or isolating the child and verbally expressing dislike and disappointment toward the child.

non-power-assertive: Form of discipline involving love withdrawal or induction.

overvaluation: Parental overacceptance and overindulgence of their offspring in a vicarious attempt to relive their own childhood.

parental demandingness: Extent to which parents expect and demand mature and responsible behavior.

parental responsiveness: Degree to which a parent is warm, supporting, and accepting.

parent types:

  authoritative: High-demanding, high-responsive parents.

  authoritarian: High-demanding, low-responsive parents.

  indifferent: Low-demanding, low-responsive parents.

indulgent: Low-demanding, high-responsive parents.

power assertion: Disciplinary technique involving the use of physical punishment or the threat of it.

reconstituted family: Family in which there is a stepparent.

satellization: Perception of children that they are not independent of their parents but are like satellites, revolving around their parents and dependent on them.

self-disclosure: Sharing innermost feelings.

undervaluation: Parental rejection of the child, causing the child to conform to parental wishes out of a fear of punishment.

DISCUSSION QUESTIONS

1. How would you define the term *family?* How does your family compare to your definition?

2. How do the characteristics of your family compare to those your parents grew up in? What caused the differences?

3. What changes were your parents experiencing while you were an adolescent? How do their concerns compare to the ones you had at that time?

4. In what ways did your parents understand what it meant for you to be an adolescent, and in what ways didn't they? How can you explain why or why not?

5. In what ways will you likely understand what it means for your adolescents to be an adolescent? In what ways might you not?

6. What was your parents' primary mode of disciplining you? Will you use the same with your children? Why or why not?

7. What is the deficit model? Why was it abandoned?

8. What are the typical reactions of adolescents to parental divorce? What modes of adapting help the adolescent cope best? Why?

9. What are the best ways for stepparents to interact with stepchildren in a reconstituted, or blended family?

10. Why might siblings react quite differently to the divorce of their parents?

11. What is the school's role in helping the adolescent cope with parental divorce?

12. Did your mother work while you were in school? If so, in what ways did that impact on you? Did you have added responsibilities? Did mother's working impact on your view of the female sex role?

13. How is pubertal status related to adolescent independence attainment? How can we explain that relationship?

14. What is the typical course of independence attainment? Does it match your experiences?

11

Peer Group Influences on Adolescent Development

Major Issues Addressed

Factors Related to Peer Group Formation
Ways That Peers Affect the Individual
The Role of Intimate Friends in Development
Variables Related to Peer Popularity
The Development of Heterosexual Friendships
Factors Involved in Dating
Adolescent Marriage
Peer vs. Parent Influences
Dating Infidelity

I thought I'd buy him a new shirt while I was at the mall. Then I had a second thought. I knew the size, but what about the color? Would it be the right insignia—polo player or crocodile? Would the style be right? I gave up and didn't buy anything. I wouldn't dare without him with me. If it wasn't just right he wouldn't wear it. Conforming to the dress code was very important to him.

◆   ◆   ◆

Adolescence is a time of increased conformity to peers. That includes the clothes one wears, but much more—language, music, leisure activities. During adolescence time spent with friends increases, as does the number of opposite-sex friends. Cliques form, dating begins, and friends influence a number of aspects of our development more than they did in childhood. We explore the broad-ranging influences of adolescents' peers in this chapter.

INTRODUCTION

It is important to make four points at the outset of our discussion of the many ways in which peers influence the adolescent. First, much of the research on peer group formation and function was done between the late 1920s and the early 1950s (B.B. Brown, 1992; Hartup, 1989). As Brown and Hartup point out, this does not mean the general findings no longer apply. Much of what was learned earlier still contributes to our understanding of peer group formation and function today. However, some types of peer activities may occur sooner now than they did for previous generations of adolescents. You may have joined heterosexual peer groups or cliques sooner or started dating earlier than the ages reported here, but the processes of group formation or entering the dating system likely are the same as those of earlier generations.

Second, the study of peer relations presents many complicated challenges. How do you study the processes involved in group formation, for example? You could devise a questionnaire and have adolescents complete it. You could ob-

serve adolescents in social situations. Or you could create groupings of adolescents in real-life settings (e.g., summer camp) by randomly assigning individuals
to different groups and then watch the process of group formation. All these approaches have been used and have provided valuable insights. But each has its
limitations: Responses to questionnaires promote responding in socially desirable ways, observations are of necessity limited to certain settings, and forcing
groups to form in a naturalistic but unusual setting may not reveal some of the
processes of spontaneous group formation. By considering evidence collected
by all these and other methods, researchers attempt to provide an accurate picture of peer influences.

Third, it often is not possible to determine the direction of causation when
studying peer influences. For example, you will read here that peer popularity is
positively correlated with school achievement—those who are more popular
also do a bit better in school than those who are less popular. Although it is
tempting to argue that achieving better in school makes one more popular, the
reverse argument is just as plausible—being popular may make one more comfortable in the school atmosphere. While you are reading the material here, take
care how you infer causation.

Finally, the study of group formation, the development of friendships, and
dating patterns is affected by a large number of individual difference and social
factors—age, social class, ethnicity, the school one attends (how integrated?).
Each of these may influence the psychological and social processes underlying
peer influences. Attending a racially segregated school or a single-sex school
will substantially impact on the nature of peer relations.

WHY STUDY PEER RELATIONS?

There are a number of reasons to study peer relations during the adolescent
years. As children gain emancipation from their parents, they spend increasing
amounts of time with their peers (B.B. Brown, 1992; Hartup & Laursen, 1989),
which serves a variety of functions. It is with peers that adolescents try out various roles, picking and choosing those that seem to fit, with few long-term negative consequences of failure. For example, if the role of leader does not fit, the
peer group is likely to make this obvious. This is one way peers facilitate learning about the self.

Peer interaction also allows contact with age-mates who share similar
problems, conflicts, likes, and dislikes. In this way, peers help each other adapt
to intergenerational conflict and to those with differing values (Armsden &
Greenberg, 1987; Berndt, 1989; Hartup & Laursen, 1989). However, because
adolescents' closest friends generally come from the same social class and ethnic background, this influence of peers is limited.

Studying peer relations allows us to assess the relative importance of peers
and parents on the adolescent's development. The evidence suggests that susceptibility to peer influence increases during adolescence (for example, Berndt,
1989; O'Brien & Bierman, 1988), but unlike the popular stereotype of an om-

nipotent peer group it does not surpass the impact of the parents (B. B. Brown, Mounts, Lamborn, & Steinberg, 1993; Buhrmester & Furman, 1987). The relative influence of peers and parents depends on the domain of behavior being studied (Reid, Landesman, Treder, & Jaccard, 1989). Peers exert stronger influences on music tastes and slang language whereas parents are more influential in career choice and moral values, for example.

In contrast to the largely unisexual childhood and early adolescent peer groups, the heterosexual nature of later adolescent peer groups provides training grounds for adult peer interactions that also are often heterosexually oriented. In this way adolescent peer groups provide a kind of practice for adulthood peer relations. Studying peer interactions in adolescence helps us better understand the social forces that promote growth toward adulthood roles.

PEER GROUP FORMATION AND FUNCTION

As we noted earlier, much of the research on peer influences was done a generation or more ago (Hartup, 1989). The establishment of university schools during the 1930s was largely responsible for these investigations. Major issues investigated included the formation of peer groups, developmental changes in the influence of peers on the child or adolescent, and the nature of social interactions with peers. More contemporary research has focused on the relative influence of parents versus peers, the factors influencing friendship choices, why isolation from peers occurs, the development of romantic peer relations, and peer abuse.

Defining Peer Groups

During the childhood and early adolescent years the term *peer* usually means an age-mate because children and younger adolescents typically associate with those who are of the same age (Hartup, 1989), largely because of the age structuring of schools (Shrum, Cheek, & Hunter, 1988). Older adolescents' peers may come from a relatively wide age range. For example, adolescent girls tend to date somewhat older boys, and earlier maturers tend to associate with somewhat older adolescents. Age, then, is not a good way to define an adolescent's peers. For adolescents, the term *peer* is best defined by commonality in interests and experiences much as is the case for adults.

The term *group* also is somewhat elusive. A group is not simply a crowd or group of individuals who happen to be in one place at the same time. Psychologists generally agree that groups are composed of *interacting individuals who possess a common goal and norm structure* (Sherif, Harvey, Hood, & Sherif, 1961; Sherif & Sherif, 1953). Groups have leaders and followers and usually a division of labor. They are formed for some purpose and generally have sets of rules—implicit or explicit—that govern the behavior of the members. This is true of long- or short-term groups and of spontaneous as well as ad hoc groups (those formed for some single purpose, such as organizing a dance).

The formation and influence of peer groups obviously does not begin in adolescence. Children are members of peer groups that influence age-appropriate norms and behaviors. These groups continue into early to mid-adolescence and slowly evolve into the groups to which older adolescents belong. The functions of childhood and adolescent groups are similar in some ways but differ in others (Box 11-1). The influence of the adolescent's peers, then, is an extension of

---

BOX 11–1   Peer Influences on Children and Adolescents

Some of the functions served by peer contact are similar during the childhood and adolescent years. Peer contact provides the opportunity to interact with age-mates and to develop age-appropriate social skills. One of the more important of such skills is simply how to get along with others in various situations, including cooperation and competition. In both childhood and adulthood, peers provide someone with whom to do things of mutual interest. Peers also provide the opportunity to develop age-related intellectual and physical skills.

In some ways, the role of peer contact during the adolescent years is more important than it is during the childhood years. Peer relations during adolescence become much more like adult peer relations. The peer group becomes heterosexual, for example (Connolly, 1989). Learning how to interact with peers of the opposite sex is an important aspect of adolescent, but not childhood, peer groups. Some adolescent peer groups (clubs, for example) are also very similar to adulthood groups, and give adolescents the chance to learn the social skills involved in being a member of a formal organization. Adolescent peer groups also provide the opportunity to share ideological values and ideals and help the adolescent develop a sustained sense of morality.

Another important aspect of adolescent, but not childhood, peer groups involves social comparison and self-evaluation. The peer group provides the adolescent with a natural environment for social comparison, particularly with respect to norms and values for appropriate appearance, likes and dislikes, and behavior (J. C. Coleman, 1980). In addition, adolescence is a time for self-evaluation as the self-concept and identity are being developed (Connolly, White, Stevens, & Burstein, 1987; Gavin & Furman, 1989). The commonsense view holds that social comparison with peer group norms and values leads to self-evaluation and attempts to change the self in ways deemed desirable (Ausubel et al., 1977). Eisert and Kahle (1982) suggest that the reverse causal direction may be more correct. They argue that self-evaluation provides a framework for assessing social information and, therefore, mediates social comparison. In their study, they had junior high school boys judge physical (strength, appearance) and role (being a friend, being liked) self-evaluation, and physical (strength) and role (getting along with teachers) status at the start of the junior year and then a year later. They reported that self-evaluation was causally predominant over social comparison. In other words, during late adolescence, self-attitudes temper the nature of social comparisons with the peer group. As a result, they conclude that adolescence is not a time of extreme dependence on the peer group for social comparison and, hence, self-evaluation.

Peer group influences show a continuity from childhood through adolescence, then, but there are important differences. Adolescent peer groups provide a model for adult peer relations that is not provided by childhood peer groups.

peer influences on children and a precursor of peer and group influences on the adult, another example of how adolescence is a transition between childhood and adulthood.

Characteristics of Childhood vs. Adolescent Peer Groups

From the preschool years to about seventh or eighth grade, three major factors determine peer group formation: gender, age, and neighborhood. During the childhood years boys and girls certainly play together. But the amount of time spent with opposite-sex peers and the number of close opposite-sex friendships is relatively limited, likely because of the largely sex-typed activities in which children engage (Hartup, 1989). This tendency continues into the mid-adolescent years and is stronger for White than Black adolescents (Hallinan, 1991). It is not until the later adolescent years that adolescents have more opposite-sex friends and peer groups are more heterosexual, akin to adult peer groups.

Children's peer groups tend to have a relatively narrow age range, which probably reflects age differences in interests and physical competencies related to the types of games and activities in which children engage (Connolly, 1989; O'Brien & Bierman, 1988). During adolescence age remains an important determinant of friendships and group membership largely because of the age group of the school system. When friends come from different schools it is as likely they will be either older or younger as the same age as the adolescent (Blyth, Hill, & Thiel, 1982).

Children associate more with those who live in the immediate vicinity. As children get older friends may live further away and groups may include individuals who do not all live on the same few blocks. With the adolescent's much greater mobility and independence, groups members and friends may live in widely separated areas. Athletic competitions can promote friendships across school district lines, and clubs within a school can result in groups that include adolescents who live far apart.

During adolescence two other factors become increasingly important to group memberships: social class and ethnic group membership. Hollingshead (1975) found that social class was a very important determinant of group membership. Although friendships and dating partners might cross a single social-class line (e.g., middle class and upper middle class), almost never did they cross two social-class lines (e.g., upper class and middle class).

During the adolescent years ethnic group becomes an increasingly important determinant of group membership (Shrum et al., 1988). In part this reflects social-class differences—minority youth are overrepresented in the lower social classes and, as we already noted, social class is associated with group membership. DuBois and Hirsch (1990) observe that even if an adolescent has a cross-ethnic friend in school, that person is not seen very often out of school, partly because of economic and social-class differences. In part, it reflects neighborhood differences, which are related to social-class membership and economic standing. In part, it reflects differences in school achievement (Hallinan & Williams, 1989) and may be one undesirable result of tracking. And in part it results from attitudinal differences and stereotypes (Schofield, 1981). Poor and perhaps unrealistic perceptions of those of different ethnic group membership (e.g., Whites seeing Blacks as threatening or hostile and Blacks seeing Whites as prejudiced and unwilling to be friends with them) can create alienation between the ethnic groups that limits peer group membership.

Adolescent Group Formation

Most adolescents belong to two basic groups: the **crowd** and the **clique**, the major distinction being size (B. B. Brown, 1992; Dunphy, 1963) and orientation. The crowd is the larger of the two and composed of a collection of cliques. In Dunphy's investigations, crowds contained from 15 to 30 members, with an average size of about 20. These crowds were roughly three times the size of cliques, which ranged from 3 to 9 members, with an average of about 6 members. The average crowd, then, was made up of 2 to 4 cliques.

Groups develop through a sequence of identifiable stages (Figure 11-1). The first is the precrowd stage, which describes the late childhood peer groups discussed earlier. The stage 2 unisexual cliques provide their members with support and security for the relatively new experience of increased and concentrated contact with members of the opposite sex. During stage 3, individual heterosexual interaction (dating) is begun by the upper-status members of the unisexual cliques. These adolescents maintain dual membership in a unisexual clique and a heterosexual clique. There is no longer the high level of support

The evolution of our educational system increasingly segregated adolescents from adults and contributed to the increased time adolescents spend with peers as opposed to adults. (*Ken Karp*)

Figure 11–1   Stages of Group Development in Adolescence

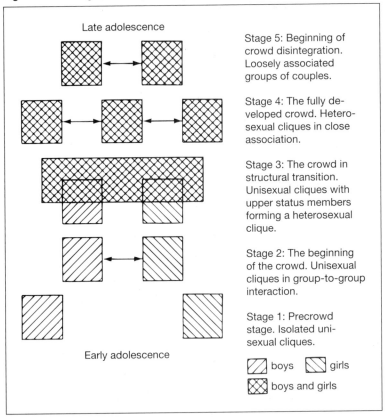

Late adolescence

Stage 5: Beginning of crowd disintegration. Loosely associated groups of couples.

Stage 4: The fully developed crowd. Heterosexual cliques in close association.

Stage 3: The crowd in structural transition. Unisexual cliques with upper status members forming a heterosexual clique.

Stage 2: The beginning of the crowd. Unisexual cliques in group-to-group interaction.

Stage 1: Precrowd stage. Isolated unisexual cliques.

Early adolescence

boys   girls
boys and girls

Souce: Dunphy, D.C. (1963). The social structure of urban adolescent peer groups. *Sociometry, 26*, 230–246.

provided by the stage 2 unisexual clique, but they still enjoy the security that comes from belonging to a unisexual clique.

Stage 4 involves fully developed heterosexual cliques that interact rather closely with each other. The cliques now form what Dunphy calls a fully developed crowd. From middle adolescence onward, the number of opposite-sex friends in the individual's network increases, as does the likelihood of having a romantic friend (Connolly, 1989).

During stage 5, the crowd begins to disintegrate, and cliques consisting primarily of couples emerge. Stage 5 represents the completion of the cycle from the precrowd, unisexual cliques of late childhood and early adolescence to cliques composed of heterosexual couples, a pattern typical of adulthood cliques. The need for emotional support and comfort from the unisexual clique no longer exists as strongly because individuals have developed the interpersonal skills necessary for heterosexual relationships.

Adolescent cliques are composed of a small number of individuals. Their major function is to plan and promote larger crowd activities. (*Ken Karp*)

Functions of the Clique.   The major functions of cliques are talking about and
planning crowd activities, the dissemination of information about crowd activities, and the evaluation of past activities (B. B. Brown, 1992; Dunphy, 1963)—
they are interaction based (B. B. Brown, Lohr, & Trujillo, 1990). The relatively
small number of members in a clique permits a high degree of cohesion, which
is reflected in the similar interests and backgrounds of its members. Cliques
function primarily during weekdays; only about a third of their activities occur
on the weekends. As with any group, cliques have leaders as well as followers.
The leaders often push the members into adultlike roles, such as forming heterosexual friendships sooner than others and thus by example encouraging others to do so.

   More so than crowds, which we discuss later, cliques may impact strongly
on psychosocial development (e.g., B. B. Brown, 1992; Savin-Williams & Berndt,
1990). As we noted, cliques provide a forum for trying out roles, which promotes identity development because the adolescent can get feedback from
friends that cannot be obtained from parents or other adults (B. B. Brown,
1992). Peers in the clique are important influences on autonomy and sexual socialization because they provide a forum for trying out new roles (Hartup,
1989). However, poor peer relations may cause psychological problems—dropping out of school, engaging in delinquency, and experiencing a variety of psychological problems (Savin-Williams & Berndt, 1990).

The Functions of the Crowd.   The crowd is the center of organized group activities, such as parties or other social activities, and serves the function of introducing adolescents to heterosexual interaction (B. B. Brown, 1992; Dunphy,
1963). Crowd activities take place primarily on weekends. All crowds are heterosexual. Not all members of a clique belong to a crowd, but everyone in a

crowd belongs to a clique. Because of its size and composition (a collection of cliques), a crowd is considerably less intimate than a clique, but still acts as a facilitator for the transition from same-sex to heterosexual cliques.

There is some debate about just what a crowd is and the number of crowds to which the adolescent may belong (B. B. Brown, 1992). Does one belong to a crowd only if one interacts with other members perceived to belong to the crowd? Or does one belong to a crowd by mere reputation? Sociologists and social psychologists prefer the interaction definition. The prevailing view of developmental psychologists is the latter definition, for it is the reputation one holds, and others hold for him or her, that is important to identity development—crowd membership is reputation based (B. B. Brown et al., 1990; Mory, 1994). For example, one does not have to be an athlete to belong to the so-called jock crowd, the crowd with the highest prestige in most high schools. If one has several jock friends, dresses like a jock, talks like a jock, and goes where jocks go, one may feel membership in that crowd and may be stereotyped as belonging to it. Moreover, one may be seen by others as belonging to more than one crowd. These "hybrids" belong to two crowds that share some characteristics (for example, involvement in school activities) but differ in others (e.g., peer status or popularity). Hence one may be seen as a member of the "prep" and "jock" crowd (jocks have higher peer popularity but both are involved in

Although cross ethnic friendships often exist in the school setting, such friends likely see each other rarely outside the school, in part because of social class differences, which are an important determinant of adolescent friendship development. (*Ken Karp*)

school activities). In contrast, one would not be identified as belonging to the "druggie" and "prep" crowds (Mory, 1994).

You probably were formally a member of some crowds (jocks, brains, normals) and an informal member of others. You may not have been a student athlete but may have been associated with the jock crowd because you had a girlfriend or boyfriend who was a formal member of that crowd and you spent time with the other members. Whether you viewed yourself as a jock or not, others may have. Although this may be a positive and even beneficial experience, it could be detrimental—if you associated with members of the drug or tough crowd your reputation might have suffered.

Aside from the typical crowds that exist in most high schools (jocks, nerds, brains, druggie, or whatever labels may exist in any given school), B.B. Brown (1992) has noted that in large racially or ethnically diverse schools it is necessary to include crowds based on ethnic group background. He suggests that in such schools one may be identified primarily by neighborhood, and hence be stereotyped as belonging to specific crowds.

The crowds to which one belongs also are a reflection of parenting practices and family circumstances (B.B. Brown et al., 1993). For example, adolescents from intact families are less likely to be associated with the drug crowd than are adolescents from stepparent families; the reverse is true for membership in the brain crowd. Similarly, parental emphasis on achievement acts to direct adolescents to achieve and, thereby, is a mediator of the adolescent belonging to the brain crowd. By belonging to such crowds, the crowd norms reinforce parental desires for their adolescent's behavior and in a sense act as "parent surrogates."

Crowds, like cliques, have advantages and disadvantages (B.B. Brown, 1992; Dunphy, 1963). Crowds provide opportunities to interact with, learn to understand, and adapt to others with differing values and backgrounds, and they promote heterosexual contact. Because they are larger than cliques they have a less strong impact on psychosocial development than cliques or individual friendships. For some adolescents, the crowd may have undesirable influences, such as encouraging snobbishness or neglect of school and home life.

The transitions in group formation and function just discussed culminate in the adolescent better understanding the nature of adulthood groups. Individual members become important for companionship and emotional support (Buhrmester & Furman, 1987; O'Brien & Bierman, 1988; Reid et al., 1989). The groups to which one belongs become important to feelings of self-worth and a feeling of connectedness. In turn, peer rejection can lead to social withdrawal (Connolly et al., 1987; Killeen & Frame, 1989) and poor adjustment.

Conceptualizing Adolescent Culture

One conclusion we can draw for the studies of adolescent crowds is that, unlike earlier suggestions (e.g., J.S. Coleman, 1961), there is no such thing as *the* adolescent culture. The variety of adolescent crowds reflects the diversity of adolescent cultures that exist. Popular stereotypes of adolescents all being the same—consumed with interest in sex, only moderately involved in school work, always interested in partying—or even of there being two types of adolescents—the good and the bad—simply is not supported by the research.

In studying how to conceptualize the various crowds and hence the adolescent cultures that exist, B. B. Brown et al. (1990) have outlined a scheme that applies not only to understanding crowd formation in the United States but also to other countries. He suggests that adolescent crowds reflect differing orientations to two dimensions of involvement in the school: the formal adult-controlled aspects (curriculum, extracurricular activities) and the informal peer-centered status system. More generally, we may expand Brown's definitions to include adult-structured aspects of society versus those built on the basis of peer influences.

As you can see in Table 11-1, adolescent crowds vary in the degree to which the members find important involvement in adult-defined and peer-defined aspects of the school atmosphere or the broader society in general. The party crowd most closely fits one of the stereotypes of the adolescent culture—the members of this crowd are highly involved in peer-defined aspects of what is important and not very engaged in academics or extracurricular activities in the school setting. At the opposite end of the two dimensions are the nerds—often seen as bookworms interested only in getting good grades. The rowdies might be considered asocial—they have low involvement in both the adult-dominated institutions or the peer-defined concepts of popularity and importance. The jock group may seem oddly placed, but you must remember that scholastic athletics is not only directed by adults, but success carries high prestige from both adults and peers.

Think about the crowds to which you belonged in your high school years

Table 11–1   Conceptualizing Adolescent Crowds

		IMPORTANCE OF PEERS		
		High	Medium	Low
S C H O O L I N V O L V E M E N T	High	Jocks		Nerds
	Medium		Normals	
	Low	Party		Rowdies

Source: Based on Brown, B. B. (1992). The meaning and measurement of adolescent crowd affiliation. *SRA, 6*, 6–8.

and to which you belong today. Step outside the crowd and see how you would assess the members' involvement in the two dimensions. How would you place them in the two-dimensional space? More importantly, how did the crowds influence your behavior? Brown makes the point that the behavior of the members of the various crowds depends on a number of individual difference factors—socioeconomic status, ethnicity, gender, community, and the nation in which one lives. He further notes that this means the impact of peer groups on the adolescent's life is constantly changing: It may be consistent with, antithetical to, or totally independent of the influences of adult culture.

Conformity to Peer Group Norms

Adolescents are often stereotyped as conformists. Whether this stereotype is used in connection with group preferences for certain tastes in music or clothing, or whether it relates to more global concepts, such as group togetherness, it suggests that adolescents do not think or act independently or autonomously.

Conformity refers to the degree to which the individual follows the behavior patterns deemed appropriate by the group, such as parents or peers. In general, there is an increase in *conformity to peers* (peer pressure) to mid-adolescence, followed by a decline through the later adolescent years (Berndt, 1989; B. B. Brown et al., 1990). This trend is especially true for antisocial behavior (delinquency, cheating) and for boys. Similarly, early and mid-adolescents *report* greater conformity to peers than do older adolescents (Gavin & Furman,

Conformity to peer group norms, as in hairstyles, increases from early to mid-adolescence and then declines, when the adolescent feels more comfortable with the identity he or she is developing. (*Shirley Zeiberg*)

1989; Urberg & Degirmencioglu, 1989), and younger adolescents report that peers exert a greater influence on them than do older adolescents.

The developmental trend in conformity is similar to that reported for egocentrism (Chapter 4). It may be that adolescents conform in order to avoid being different and "sticking out" in front of the imaginary audience. As egocentrism increases, then, it may contribute to increases in conformity. Both egocentrism and conformity may decline from mid to late adolescence as a result of the adolescent's developing identity. As the adolescent develops a set of personal values, there is less need to conform and an increase in the need to express unique aspects of the self.

Other researchers (e.g., B. B. Brown, Clasen, & Eicher, 1986; Gavin & Furman, 1989; Steinberg & Silverberg, 1986) have suggested that the increased susceptibility to peer pressure during mid-adolescence is related to the increases in autonomy that occur during adolescence. They suggest that as adolescents gain emotional autonomy from parents a void is created and increased susceptibility to peer influence results. Some evidence supports this view (Papini, 1994). Adolescents who are more strongly attached to their peers deal with the stresses of school transition better and are more self-reliant, comfortable in close relationships, and emotionally mature than those who are less closely attached to peers. As adolescents mature in their ability to deal with autonomy from the family unit, there is a reduced need to conform to peers.

Are adolescents more conforming in general than children or adults? That depends on the kind of conformity with which one is concerned. Children are quite conforming to their parents and other adults (teachers, baby-sitters, relatives). As children and younger adolescents gain autonomy from parents they become more susceptible to peer pressure—conformity to peers increases and there is some decline in susceptibility to adult pressure. To what do adults conform? Perhaps the most simple answer is adult-defined social roles such as worker, spouse, and parent. We all are conformists—to a greater or lesser degree—but we conform to different pressures.

We also conform to differing degrees. Just as some adults choose to not marry or not have children and thereby conform less to socially defined roles, some adolescents are less susceptible to peer pressure than others. Some children conform (obey) to parental pressures more than others. As always, stereotypes—for example, adolescents are highly conforming—paint a biased picture of reality.

FRIENDSHIPS AND POPULARITY

Friendships are a special kind of peer relation. Friends understand each other, learn from each other, and self-disclose to each other—they are more likely to "tell everything" to a friend than to a parent or other adult (Savin-Williams & Berndt, 1990). Stability and reciprocity of friendships increases during adolescence (Hartup, 1989; Savin-Williams & Berndt, 1990), perhaps because adolescents make friends who share similar values and attitudes. Adolescents with stable friendships do better in school, adjust better to the school setting, and exhibit fewer problem behaviors than those whose friendships are unstable (Berndt, 1992). Among African-American adolescents, higher quality friendships are related to better psychological adjustment, increased involvement of parents in the adolescent's life, and a better relationship with the mother (Tolson, Halliday-Scher, & Mack, 1994). These researchers suggest that for Black adolescents, similarity to peers is less important than it is for White adolescents in forming friendship patterns.

Roles Played by Friends

In childhood, friends are simply companions to play with. During early adolescence (ages 11–13), friendships are still focused on activities, with little notion of long-term mutuality (O'Brien & Bierman, 1988). From about age 14 to 16, friendships are based on the concepts of loyalty and security, more so for females than males (Berndt, 1992; Buhrmester & Furman, 1987; O'Brien & Bierman, 1988). Friends must be trustworthy and loyal, for the adolescent is highly dependent on friends for identity and value development. From age 17 onward, friendships are based on concepts of mutuality and shared experiences. Friends are chosen on the basis of personality and their contribution to a mutually rewarding relationship (Savin-Williams & Berndt, 1990).

Adolescent friendships play an important role in identity development (Gavin & Furman, 1989). By having loyal friends with whom to share one's innermost feelings and beliefs, the adolescent is able to come to a greater realization of who he or she is. Sharing ideas and opinions with a close friend helps the adolescent explore identity concerns and facilitates developing a concept of self (Savin-Williams & Berndt, 1990).

Another vital role played by friends during the adolescent (and adulthood) years is emotional support (Moran & Eckenrode, 1989; Reid et al., 1989). Friends not only can help the adolescent deal with daily ups and downs, but also are valuable resources when dealing with highly stressful situations, such as parental divorce or the death of someone. These benefits of stable, close friendships have been found for adolescents from different social classes and for both White and African American adolescents (Savin-Williams & Berndt, 1990).

Because of the intensity and intimacy involved in adolescent friendships, which is much higher than during childhood, a friend's betrayal can be devastating. To be put down or ridiculed by someone to whom you have revealed your innermost feelings may hurt a great deal. Adolescents may interpret such behavior as meaning their own self-worth has declined and may develop negative feelings about themselves (O'Brien & Bierman, 1988). In extreme instances, adolescents may become the object of peer abuse (Box 11–2).

The intensity and passion involved in adolescent friendships declines during the later adolescent years (O'Brien & Bierman, 1988), when friendships become based more on the compatibility of personal characteristics than on the need to have someone to share confidences with. In turn, there is an increasing tendency to appreciate and even seek out people with widely differing characteristics.

Because adolescent friendships are based on trust and loyalty, close friends can hurt the adolescent emotionally. (*Michal Heron/Woodfin Camp & Associates*)

Intimate Friendships

The most influential peers are intimate friends. **Intimate friendships** involve the sharing of personal and private thoughts and feelings (Berndt, 1982). Intimate friends know each other's feelings, worries, and personality.

Intimate friendships increase from the beginning to the end of adolescence, and this is true for both same-sex and opposite-sex relationships (Buhrmester & Furman, 1987). Females seek intimate friendships sooner than males, and their intimate friendships are more intense. Although opposite-sex friendships also increase during adolescence, these do not replace intimate friendships with same-sex peers. The development of opposite-sex intimate friendships continues to increase during the adulthood years (Reis, Lin, Bennett, & Nezlek, 1993), especially for males. It seems that females' intimacy development is more advanced during the adolescent and college years than it is for their male counterparts.

Not everyone has intimate friends, and not everyone can be a "good" intimate friend. A number of researchers have investigated the characteristics of adolescents who have intimate friendships. Adolescents with intimate friends

BOX 11–2   The Victims of Peer Abuse

The study of aggression during the childhood and adolescent years has focused on the nature of the aggressive individual and the circumstances that relate to that person behaving in an aggressive manner. It has been found that a vast majority of children and adolescents do not prefer an aggressive mode of interaction and that those who do become rejected by peers and may experience long-term adjustment problems. In contrast, there have been but few studies of the victims of peer aggression, particularly those who are chronically the target of peer abuse.

A number of interesting questions come to mind in this regard. Are some adolescents "picked out" to be victims? Do victims behave in ways, for example, aggressively, that prompt others to make them victims? Do victims provide reinforcement to those who are aggressive against them, thereby making themselves targets for aggression? Does being an adolescent victim mean one will be a victim during adulthood?

These and similar questions are behind the research of David Perry and his colleagues (Perry, Kusel, & Perry, 1988; Perry & Williard, 1989) on the dynamics of being a victim of peer abuse during the childhood and early adolescent years. In one study they developed a questionnaire to assess one's standing as a victim of peer physical and verbal abuse and used it to investigate victimization with students in grades 3 through 6. One finding was that victims tended to be rejected children, that is, children who had been rated by their peers as more frequently disliked than liked. In other words, a minority of children (about 10%; Olweus, in press) receive the bulk of peer aggression. Second, although being aggressive was related to being rejected and therefore increasing one's likelihood of being a victim, not all rejected children were highly aggressive.

Aggression and victimization are not related; they are independent.

In a second study, Perry and his colleagues (Perry & Williard, 1989) examined the consequences that victims were perceived to provide those who were aggressive against them. Possible consequences included tangible rewards (e.g., money), showing signs of pain and suffering, and retaliation. In addition, the researchers sought to determine whether the perceived rewards were different for children known to be high versus low in victimization.

The results indicated that children were more likely to expect tangible reinforcers and victim suffering, and less likely to expect retaliation, when aggressing against another child who was a typical target of peer abuse. In addition, they cared more about obtaining tangible rewards and were less concerned about victim suffering and the potential for retaliation.

Explaining why one becomes a peer victim is difficult, but some evidence (reviewed by Perry et al., 1988) suggests it may be related to the formation of insecure attachments to parents during the infancy years, resulting in the youngster behaving in a vulnerable manner and projecting a vulnerable personality. Part of this may be due to victims showing lower rates of assertive behavior and social initiatives, and higher levels of submissiveness (D. Schwartz, Dodge, & Coie, 1993). Because victims are rejected by their peers they are in a group of youngsters and adolescents who are more prone to dropping out of school, becoming delinquents, and experiencing psychological maladjustment, such as depression. Being able to determine those who are most prone to becoming victims of peer abuse early may allow remediation and improved peer relations. In this regard, Olweus (in press) suggests that the appropriate intervention should not be centered on changing the personality of the victim, but rather the behavior of the aggressors.

What of the long-term effects of having been an adolescent victim of peer abuse? In an extensive study, Olweus (in press) reported a discontinuity in victimization. Being an adolescent victim did not predict being an adulthood victim. Olweus suggests that in adulthood the previous victim has more freedom to choose social environments and escape those that could lead to victimization. Despite no longer being a victim, however, as adults the previous victims were more prone to depression and poor self-esteem, which Olweus attributes directly to having been a victim of peer abuse.

have the ability to be socially sensitive and infer others' feelings, and are highly altruistic—they share, show concern for others, and help others. They also base friendships on interpersonal understanding to a greater degree than do those who do not have intimate friendships. Intimate friends engage in more mutual interactions that are beneficial to each other and share similar views of schooling, music and clothes preferences, and interests (Savin-Williams & Berndt, 1990).

Peer Popularity in Adolescence

Considerable research has been directed toward discovering the characteristics of popular and less popular adolescents. Although a variety of means have been employed to determine the correlates of popularity, the general procedure is to obtain a measure of popularity (e.g., by peer nominations) and then correlate popularity ratings with other measures, such as IQ, social class, or information from personality tests. Those measures that correlate highly with the popularity scores indicate the characteristics associated positively or negatively with popularity.

Popularity in the peer group depends largely on having certain qualities and behaving in ways approved by the peer group (Hartup, 1989). Liked peers are good looking, well groomed, fun, and outgoing; they possess good social skills, act their age, are cooperative, are cheerful and happy, have a good sense of humor, are more self-confident, and are more committed to their own best friends (Clark & Ayers, 1988). Disliked peers are seen as homely, sloppy, shy and withdrawn, rude, childish, having a bad reputation, quarrelsome, inconsiderate, conceited, and irresponsible. Liked peers make others feel accepted and comfortable. Disliked peers have the opposite effect. In general, adolescents like peers who are similar to themselves and hold like values. They dislike peers with highly different values or those who have different backgrounds and personality characteristics. Adolescents also like peers who are bright and who come from the culturally dominant groups in society (Clark & Ayers, 1988). Intelligence and social class, then, are positively correlated with peer popularity and acceptance.

An important determinant of the adolescent's acceptance and popularity is physical attractiveness (Clark & Ayers, 1988). In general, adolescents who are

During adolescence physical attraction becomes
an important determinant of popularity, but only at
the extremes. (*Laima E. Druskis*)

seen as better looking are more popular and those who are seen as less attractive are less popular. However, this relationship is only of importance at the extremes of physical attractiveness. Because most adolescents are in the middle
ranges of physical attractiveness, their appearance is not especially related to
how popular they are.

During adolescence, personality characteristics and other individual difference traits become important to popularity, just as they do with friendships in
general. This shift no doubt has a number of causes, including changing concepts of social relations (Chapter 4) and the role that friends play.

Peer Rejection

A special case of unpopularity involves the rejected adolescent. Researchers
(Bierman, Smoot, & Aumiller, 1993; Rabiner & Gordon, 1992) have attempted to
identify the correlates of being a rejected peer. Although initial studies of rejection showed that behaving in a highly aggressive manner was related to becom-

ing rejected, they also showed that some who were highly aggressive were not rejected (Bierman et al., 1993). Hence researchers have attempted to identify the personality correlates of peer rejection other than behaving aggressively.

Current explanations of peer rejection focus on the rejected individual's inability to interact with others within the range of commonly accepted social behaviors. For example, boys who have severe conduct problems and poor **prosocial behavior** are more rejected than others, quite aside from how aggressive they are. Similarly, those who are more self-centered and interested in meeting their own needs as opposed to showing a concern for others are more rejected. Finally, those who are shy, withdrawn, and inhibited are among the rejected. Researchers argue that the failure to integrate personal needs with those of others, or with general social expectations for interpersonal interaction, reflects a lack in social cognition (Chapter 4) that places these individuals at risk for rejection.

HETEROSEXUAL PEER RELATIONS

The first heterosexual friendships are often awkward and sometimes even antagonistic relationships, but they are the first opportunity to learn to relate and adjust to opposite-sex peers. When the adolescent begins to take part in heterosexual group activities (look again at stage 3 in Figure 11-1), he or she still has the support of a same-sex peer group. As the adolescent becomes more comfortable with opposite-sex relationships (stage 4), he or she no longer needs the support of a same-sex peer group, and what we commonly call dating begins.

Developmental Sequences in Heterosexual Friendships

There is a developmental trend in the formation of opposite-sex friendships; the number of opposite-sex friends listed in the friendship network increases from middle to later adolescence (Connolly, 1989). Opposite-sex friends also become more important to the adolescent as opposite-sex intimate friendships are developed. Adolescent females seek out these types of intimate friendships at earlier ages than do adolescent males (Buhrmester & Furman, 1987).

Research on the development of cross-sex friendships has increased in recent years, but this topic remains one about which too little is known (Werking, 1994). Preference for same-gender friends begins in early childhood (perhaps as early as age 3 or 4; Howes & Philipsen, 1992) and peaks during the elementary school years. During adolescence the number of cross-gender friends increases, but they still account for only 8% to 13% of friendship choices during the middle school and high school years (Degirmencioglu & Urberg, 1994) and are unlikely to be the first friend an adolescent lists. Opposite-sex friends are also listed as less important than same-sex friends as sources of intimacy, social support, and companionship (Lempers & Clark-Lempers, 1993).

Some research aimed at identifying the factors related to the development of opposite-gender friendships has focused on the role played by social competence (Degirmencioglu & Urberg, 1994; Sroufe, Bennett, Egelund, Urban, & Shulman, 1993). Sroufe and his colleagues reported that during the preadolescent years those who were more socially competent were less likely to have opposite-sex friends but were more likely to test the gender boundaries, perhaps because of the importance of conforming to peer norms. The testing and even violation of gender boundaries may be a precursor for ultimately crossing them. During preadolescence, then, social competence is related to conforming to peer group norms while at the same time having the ability to test the boundaries in ways that do not cause the person to become isolated from same-gender peers.

During the adolescent years social competence seems to be related to having at least one opposite-gender friend (Degirmencioglu & Urberg, 1994). Adolescents who listed at least one opposite-gender friend not only indicated more friends but were listed by others as a friend (reciprocated friendship) more frequently than those who did not list an opposite-gender friend. They also were more likely to be a clique member and less likely to be isolates (those who were not listed as a friend by anybody).

These changing relations to peers are due to a variety of factors. Changes in the sex drive (Chapter 8) no doubt cause reevaluations of the appropriateness of opposite-sex friends for some. The modeling of adult peer relations and finding opposite-sex peers reinforcing and satisfying in many ways (Chapter 2) also contribute to increases in opposite-sex friendships. The changes in opposite-sex friendships lead to changes in the cliques and crowds to which the adolescent belongs, as we described earlier. They also reflect an as yet not well understood relation to social adjustment, peer acceptance, and psychosocial development.

Dating Patterns During Adolescence

Dating is the most common form of adolescent heterosexual relationships. For most adolescents, the first dates are in groups. As they become increasingly comfortable interacting with the opposite sex, adolescents begin to date outside a group context.

Today, adolescent girls begin to date by about age 12 or 13 and adolescent boys by about age 13 or 14 (McCabe, 1984), although early maturers begin dating earlier than late maturers (Simmons & Blyth, 1987). The earliest age at which dating begins is 10 or 11, when about 25% of both the boys and girls say they have had a date. In most instances, these dates occur less than once a month and with a very small number of partners. By 14 to 15 years of age, more than 80% of the adolescents are dating. And dating tends to increase in frequency, with about 25% of adolescents dating once a week. By 16 to 17 years of age, 95% or more of the boys and girls indicate they are dating. Both the frequency of dating, which is now typically once a week, as well as the number of dating partners, increased. These age trends seem not to have changed much, if at all, over the past 30 years (McCabe, 1984).

During adolescence opposite-gender friendships increase, dating begins, and adult forms of friendships develop. (*Laima E. Druskis*)

An interesting question, then, concerns why adolescents begin to date when they do. On the surface this seems simplistic: Dating begins because of biological and physiological changes (Dornbusch et al., 1981). The increase in the sex drive (see Chapter 3) and other biological changes (for example, physical maturity that makes one look like an adult) are given precedence in the initiation of dating. Others (for example, Ausubel et al., 1977) note the importance of social influences, such as peer group norms for when one should be dating, in the initiation of dating.

Dornbusch et al. (1981) conducted an investigation to determine the relative influence of biological or maturational and social influences on dating. Over 6,700 adolescents, representing a national probability sample of 12- to 17-year-olds, were subjects in the study. They were asked if they had ever had a date, their age was determined, and an examining physician indicated by reference to standardized pictures their degree of sexual development. The correlations between age and having had a date were .56 for males and .62 for females. The correlations between sexual maturity and having had a date were .49 for males and .38 for females. Other more sophisticated analyses also revealed stronger relationships between age and dating than between sexual maturity and dating. These authors, and others who have investigated the role of biological versus social factors in dating (e.g., Simmons & Blyth, 1987), concluded that, although biological maturity is an aspect of initiating dating, social factors, including peer pressure, institutionalized expectations, and social maturity are more important in determining when adolescents start to date.

Because the dating system is the primary vehicle for mate selection in the United States, and may be partly responsible for the high divorce rate, it is important to try to understand its nature, development, and function. Unfortunately, our understanding of the nature of dating is somewhat limited by the atheoretical and descriptive nature of research on dating.

Aspects of the Dating Process.   A number of researchers have investigated the values looked for in a dating partner. Social characteristics, for example, prestige (belonging to the "correct" group), popularity, personality characteristics, disposition, and manners are important in date selection. Although adolescents may say that personality characteristics outweigh prestige factors in date selection, in actual dating situations, prestige factors outweigh personality characteristics. This is, in part, a result of the artificial and superficial nature of the American dating system.

Both prestige and personality traits are important in date selection, but at different times in the relationship (Modell & Goodman, 1990). Prestige factors, especially physical appearance, are initially important in determining potential dating partners. Following an initial dating exposure, social sophistication factors become more important. Self-confidence, ease in meeting people, and being able to carry on a conversation are important determinants for the beginning of a long-term relationship. Personality traits become more important during the third stage of dating. Honesty, reliability, and the like, determine whether or not one will continue the relationship. At all stages of the dating process each partner must weigh the prestige and personality factors in determining the desire to continue the relationship.

Functions of Dating.   Dating serves a number of functions besides those of courtship and mate selection, especially during early and middle adolescence (Douvan & Adelson, 1966). Although dating may lead to courtship and mate selection, for most adolescents it is a social experience that serves other functions (see Table 11-2).

The socialization function of dating allows the adolescent to develop both

Table 11–2   Functions of Dating

1. Socialization	Dating allows one to get to know the opposite sex and learn how to interact with them.
2. Recreation	Dating is a source of fun and pleasure.
3. Participative eagerness	Dating helps one avoid boredom, loneliness, anxiety, or work.
4. Independence assertion	Dating allows independence from the family and its rules.
5. Status seeking	Dating allows one to associate with prestigious peers and the in-group, which enhances one's status.
6. Sexual gratification	Dating is an appropriate and acceptable means for sexual contact.
7. Courtship	Dating allows one to get to know members of the opposite sex and select a mate.

Source: Compiled from Grinder, R. E. (1966). Relations of social dating attractions to academic orientation and peer relations. *Journal of Educational Psychology, 57,* 27–34; Skipper, J. K., Jr., & Nass, G. (1966). Dating behavior: A framework for analysis and an illustration. *Journal of Marriage and the Family, 28,* 412–420.

personally and socially. By dating, adolescents learn a number of social skills related to interacting with persons of the opposite sex; they also get to know persons who, by virtue of their sex, are simply different from themselves. The value of the socialization function, of course, is that it helps the individual learn appropriate adult forms of behavior.

Dating also provides recreation and entertainment opportunities: "It's fun." Dating is and can be viewed as a form of diversion. In this sense, it is an end in itself.

Participative eagerness and independence assertion are closely allied functions of dating, in that they allow the adolescent to behave in ways that are independent of the adult world. *Participative eagerness* refers to dating in order to avoid boredom, responsibility, or doing things with the family. *Independence assertion* refers to the sometimes flagrant flouting of adult social norms, for example, using a false ID to obtain drinks in a bar or racing cars on public streets. In this sense, dating is an opportunity for the adolescent to strike out against adult authority with the support of a date and peers.

Dating can also be a way to achieve status. Being seen with highly desirable peers may help one achieve membership in the in-group or enhance one's own social standing. In this sense, dating is a mechanism for manipulating one's social status.

Dating is obviously a source of sexual gratification. In fact, for some, dating may be no more than an opportunity to engage in heterosexual behavior, with no intention of having any kind of a long-term relationship.

Of course, courtship and mate selection are an important part of dating. Through dating, individuals come to know each other and to respond as a pair, particularly if they date over a relatively long period of time. They learn to anticipate each other's behavior, and thereby to guide their own behavior. This function of dating involves a high degree of instrumental orientation and emotional involvement. In other words, in the instance of courtship and mate selection, dating involves a means to a larger goal (instrumental involvement) as well as a high degree of emotional involvement. When both dating partners feel this way the relationship is likely to continue.

Douvan and Adelson (1966) spelled out several consequences related to these functions of dating. First, they noted that for middle-class adolescents dating seems to fulfill many of these functions. The experience gained by interacting with a variety of opposite-sex peers tends to make the individual feel comfortable in heterosexual situations. However, they also pointed out that dating can lead to a series of superficial and empty relationships because of the role playing that goes on.

According to the dating code, a good date is one who is cheerful, well mannered, and fun, no matter what the situation. Certainly this is not how people are all the time, but if they act that way because it is expected of them, they may never get to the point where they can be completely honest with their dating partner. Douvan and Adelson note that this is particularly likely to occur if dating is begun too early. Perhaps this is because early dating cuts the individual off to a certain degree from same-sex relationships, which are helpful and perhaps necessary for developing self-identity.

Beginning to date too late may also be a problem. Adolescents who begin to date late lag behind their peers in social development and may become more dependent on adults and parents for security. They may feel cut off from their peers and develop into loners or isolates who become absorbed in themselves and do not learn how to rely on others for companionship, friendship, and self-assurance.

Husbands (1970) has criticized the dating system because of the superficiality of the relationships that develop. Multiple dating (dating a number of people at one time) entails a relatively low degree of involvement in a single relationship, which, on the one hand, makes it easier to terminate, but, on the other hand, impedes the development of meaningful emotional relationships. Playing the dating game leads to role playing and deemphasizes the importance of basic human values in interpersonal relationships. Making a good impression becomes the mode and motivation of behavior. It also makes it difficult for game players to make a commitment to a long-term relationship. Husbands suggests that this may produce conflict in the dating relationship and ultimately instability in marriage. Less superficial dating norms should be beneficial to the development of meaningful heterosexual relationships.

We do not wish to make it seem that adolescent dating in the United States is bad. Some evidence (R. Miller & Gordon, 1986) indicates a decline in some of the less desirable aspects of dating, such as sex-role stereotypes in expected behavior. As a result, dating may be more psychologically healthy now than previously, in that it allows greater time to learn to interact with opposite-sex peers, which may enhance the likelihood of developing intimate opposite-sex friendships.

Going Steady/Breaking Up

Going steady (going out with someone) involves a commitment to a single dating partner. Adolescents who go steady go on more dates than those who do not, but of course date fewer people. Going steady has the advantage of making one feel secure, popular, loved, and wanted. It also assures companionship. But these advantages come at some costs. Being cut off from making other close friends of the opposite sex, at times feeling tied down, perhaps conflicts with parents who do not approve of the steady or feel the relationship is too serious, and increased expectations for engaging in sexual behavior are among some of these (Reiss, 1967).

C. Hill, Rubin, and Peplau (1979) studied the effects of breaking up. They surveyed 231 college couples over a 2-year period, at the end of which 103 (45%) broke up. Those couples who remained together had higher levels of love and intimacy at the start of the relationship and had a relationship that involved equal commitment to each other, as opposed to one person being more committed to the other. Those couples that remained together also were more similar in age and educational plans than those who broke up.

Breaking up was clearly tied to the academic calendar—breakups were most likely during the summer (perhaps because the partners were apart), during the holiday break in December and January, and in September, at the start of the school year. The reasons for breaking up typically involved boredom, a growing difference in interests, and the female's desire for independence. One partner being romantically involved with someone else was not mentioned with a high frequency.

Breaking up was psychologically difficult for both partners. The one rejected, particularly if the male, showed more depression and difficulty adapting. Nonetheless, the one initiating the breakup remained somewhat lonely, guilty, and depressed even a year after the relationship ended.

Having a commitment to a single dating partner leads to the possibility of dating infidelity. In a survey of 247 undergraduates, Roscoe and his colleagues (1988) found that approximately half of both the males and females had been unfaithful to a steady dating partner. Those who had been unfaithful indicated dissatisfaction with the relationship, sexual incompatibility, and being insecure or unsure of the relationship as reasons for being unfaithful. Behaviors considered acts of unfaithfulness included dating others, sexual intercourse, flirting, and being emotionally involved with someone else. About 60% of the adolescents indicated they would terminate or consider terminating the relationship if their partner was unfaithful, and only about a third indicated they would try to find out the reason for a partner's infidelity. Roscoe and his colleagues noted the high degree of similarity between adolescents and adults in the acts considered to be unfaithful and the reasons for infidelity.

Adolescent Marriage

Marriage involves the formal acceptance of a number of responsibilities. It also implies a dramatic change from a previous lifestyle. For adolescents, adjustment to marriage is likely to be even more difficult than it is for adults because of the adolescent's relative immaturity, desire for postsecondary education, and the financial burdens. Coping with restrictions on personal freedom and learning to be considerate of the needs and desires of another person requires a degree of maturity and willingness to sacrifice that few adolescents possess. Entering marriage romantically and idealistically, as adolescents may do, makes adjustment difficult, if not impossible.

The most extensive study of the long-term consequences of adolescent marriage was conducted by Teti and Lamb (1989; Teti, Lamb, & Elster, 1987). They were interested in discovering the effects, in adulthood, of having been married, parented a child, or both during the adolescent years. They surveyed both males and females aged 30 to 55. Some had never married, some had married during adolescence, and some had married during adulthood. Within each of these three groups, some had never become parents, some had become parents during adolescence, and some had become parents during adulthood. This procedure allowed them to examine marriage, childbearing, or both, and relate

Those who marry during the adolescent years often feel deprived, unhappy, and dissatisfied. The likelihood of divorce is substantially increased if marriage occurs during adolescence. (*Sepp Seitz/Woodfin Camp & Associates*)

each factor to marital adjustment. The survey concerned schooling, employment and income, and marital stability.

For females, both adolescent marriage and having a child during adolescence were detrimental to socioeconomic status and marital stability. Females who had their first child during adolescence had lower educational levels and economic status than those who had their first child during adulthood or who never had a child. Women who married during adolescence were somewhat better off, but they still did not match the attainments of those who married during adulthood. Both adolescent marriage and adolescent childbirth were associated with lowered marital stability.

For males, the critical factor was not becoming a parent but rather whether or not they married during their adolescent years. Those who married during adolescence completed less schooling, had lower status occupations, and earned less money than those who married during adulthood. In addition, marriage during adolescence was associated with increased marital discord, divorce, and remarriage.

The consequences of adolescent marriage on employment and socioeconomic status for both males and females, and for adolescent childbirth for females, are relatively easy to understand. Marriage entails economic realities that may force adolescents to leave school. Lower educational levels result in lower paying jobs, which in turn results in lower socioeconomic status.

Teti and Lamb suggest that, for females, the relation of adolescent marriage and childbearing to marital stability may be a result of failure to resolve adequately the identity and intimacy crises adolescents face (Chapter 2). Because these crises are entered into, and resolved, during the adolescent and young adulthood years, early marriage may have a disruptive influence resulting from an inability to explore relationships with a variety of people. These researchers go on to suggest that failure to establish satisfying relations during adolescence results in a continued failure to do so during adulthood.

PEER VS. PARENT INFLUENCE

Generally speaking, differences between parents and their adolescent children tend to be rather superficial. Parents, more than anyone else, are responsible for their child's social values, morals, and codes of behavior. Although there is a heightened conformity to peer group values during early to mid-adolescence, the influences of the adolescent peer group tend to be much more superficial, narrowly defined, and short term than parental influences. In addition, as we pointed out earlier, adolescents collect in peer groups that are composed of individuals with backgrounds and values generally similar to their own. In effect, this means the peer group may act to reinforce the basic values the parents have taught the adolescent. As a result, the influences of parents and peers will more often be complementary than conflicting.

It should also be pointed out that neither the parent nor the peer group has an overriding influence on all aspects of the adolescent's life. The adolescent evaluates and weighs the opinions and beliefs of each group, and is influenced by each to a greater or lesser degree according to the content area. Peer influences and opinions dominate in the realms of fads, music, dress, language, and some aspects of social behavior. Parental influences predominate in basic social values and morals.

A study by Floyd and South (1972) specifically investigated the adolescent's orientation to parents and peers in a sample of 409 6th-, 8th-, 10th-, and 12th-grade males and females. One questionnaire assessed the degree to which the students were peer or parent oriented. The subjects indicated the degree to which they agreed or disagreed with statements such as, "I prefer to grow up to be more like my friends rather than my parents." The subjects were divided into peer (27%), parent (30%), and mixed orientation (43%) groups. They then indicated the degree to which parents, as opposed to peers, met their needs for a series of items previously rated as high, medium, or low in importance.

Generally speaking, the percentage classified as parent oriented decreased and peer oriented increased, though somewhat less, with increasing age. There was also an increase in the mixed orientation category over age. Males were slightly more peer oriented then females. When parents were viewed as the better source of need satisfaction, adolescents were parent as opposed to peer oriented. The reverse was also true. These results demonstrate developmental trends in parent and peer orientation and support the notion that each influence has its place in adolescent socialization. There are areas in which parents are seen as better able than peers to meet the adolescent's needs, and parents are sought out. The converse is also true. Neither parents nor peers are omnipotent influences in the adolescent's development.

Montemayor's (1982) study lends further insight into these issues. He studied the activities in which adolescents engage with parents and peers and when alone. He found that adolescents were equally involved with parents and peers, but in different activities. Time spent with parents was much more likely to be task oriented, time with peers, recreation oriented. Parents and peers satisfy differing needs—parents exerting necessary controls and teaching aspects of responsibility, and peers providing more personal need satisfaction and necessary recreational outlets. Later research (e.g., Connolly, 1989; Moran & Eckenrode, 1989; Reid et al., 1989) further clarified these differences. Adolescents seek *information* from parents but *social* and *emotional* support from peers, the latter showing increases with the age of the adolescent. These differences in the roles played by parents and peers are related to the types of conflicts—and conflict resolutions—that adolescents have with parents and peers.

Conflicts with parents typically involve issues of independence and autonomy (Laursen, 1992), and conflict resolution generally involves compromise that allows the relationship to continue (Rubenstein & Feldman, 1993). Conflicts with friends generally involve pesonal problems, such as being ignored or left out, and telling secrets (Hartup & Laursen, 1989). Resolution is done in a matter allowing the relationship to continue (Laursen, 1992; Raffaelli, 1989). Because sibling conflicts, which largely are over turf issues, may escalate to high levels, parental invervention is often how the conflict is resolved.

We also should keep in mind the role individuality plays in the adolescent's need to conform to either the parents or the peer group. Children and adolescents who are raised by democratic parents, and those who are more self-confident, need not be dominated by either group because they have learned the skills that are necessary for making appropriate decisions. In contrast, some parents use rearing styles that seem to "force" their adolescents to seek out peers more than parents (Fuligni & Eccles, 1993). Adolescents who perceive their parents as providing little opportunity for them to be involved in decision making or perceive their parents as authoritarian are much more peer than parent oriented. They are more likely to turn to peers for help in dealing with personal problems and concerns about the future, such as vocational plans. Indeed, they may become so peer oriented that they intentionally break parental rules, skip doing schoolwork, and the like, in order to maintain popularity with their friends.

Finally, real difficulties can arise when there is conflict between parental values and those of the peer group. This will occur primarily when there is a homogeneous peer group with a set of values that are quite different from those of the parent, and when there is a tendency on the part of the adolescent to be

Time spent with peers and parents entails different functions. Time with peers is largely for recreation; time with parents is largely task oriented. (*Left: Ellen Levine/Editorial Photocolor Archives, Inc. Right: Laima E. Druskis*)

highly conforming to the peer group. In such an instance, the adolescent is torn between two sets of values that may be at bipolar positions. Although rare, these occurrences are particularly likely when parent–adolescent relationships are poor because the parent shows a lack of interest in the adolescent and an unwillingness to become involved in his or her life. With an especially deviant peer group, it is critical that the parents provide appropriate models for the adult world and help the adolescent acquire a set of values that will stand the adolescent in good stead during adulthood.

What does all this mean about susceptibility to peer and parent pressure? It seems that as they mature adolescents become concerned with seeking out those most competent to help them both understand and deal with various issues they face. For concerns dealing with peer interactions, social problems, or personal difficulties involving peers they seek out friends. For matters of fact or importance to the long-term goals they have for the future they seek out other experts—parents, teachers, guidance counselors.

SUMMARY

In many ways, peer interactions serve the same functions for adolescents and children, including the teaching of age-appropriate skills. However, because of its heterosexual composition, the adolescent peer group setting provides a much better training ground for adult peer interactions. In adolescence, the peer group provides the opportunity for trying out various social roles and sets standards for adolescent behavior.

Adolescents typically belong to two types of groups, the clique and the crowd. The clique is a small group (3–9 members), serving the primary function of conversation and planning of group activities. Crowds are made up of cliques, and provide the initial opportunity for heterosexual interaction. The crowd is the center of organized social activities.

Adolescent crowds can be identified on the basis of how much their members are involved in the formal adult controlled and informal peer controlled aspects of the school environment. For example, the party crowd has a low involvement in academics and other adult controlled aspects of school and a high involvement in peer centered aspects. The nerds are at the opposite extreme.

During the earlier years of adolescence, there is an increase in conformity to peer group norms and standards, perhaps as a result of increasing egocentrism and the need to develop an identity. During the later high school years, conformity declines as egocentrism abates and identity develops.

Intimate friendships develop during the adolescent years. These friends tend to show high levels of empathy and social perspective-taking ability. Intimate friends must be loyal and trustworthy because of their very close ties. Of course, betrayal by an intimate friend can be devastating to the adolescent.

Popularity during the adolescent years largely depends on having acceptable social skills, behaving in accord with group norms, and the like. At the extremes of physical attractiveness, popularity and attractiveness are related. In addition, adolescents tend to like more those peers who are from their own social standing.

It is during adolescence that heterosexual peer relations begin. These intimate relations do not replace same-sex intimate relations, but supplement them. As adolescence progresses, the number of opposite-sex friends increases. This is most readily seen in the initiation of dating, which seems more closely tied to social expectations than to biological maturity. Through dating, adolescents acquire social skills for interacting with the opposite sex, are able to exert independence needs, achieve status, and, of course, engage in recreational activities. Although mate selection can occur via dating during the adolescent years, adolescent marriages are more prone to end in divorce than marriages occurring during the adulthood years.

Although adolescents spend more and more time with peers, resulting in an increase in the influence of peers, parents remain highly influential on the adolescent. This occurs because parents and peers fulfill different needs of the adolescent. Parents provide needed guidance and skill training, and peers provide recreational outlets. The peer group, then, does not become omnipotent for most adolescents.

GLOSSARY

clique: Small tightly knit group of people who share common interests.

conformity: Willingness to allow external events or people to govern one's behavior.

crowd: Collection of cliques. All who belong to a crowd belong to a clique.

intimate friendship: Friendship in which the individuals know the other's likes, dislikes, personality, and the sharing of private thoughts and feelings.

prosocial behavior: Moral behaviors involving helping, sharing, and other behaviors for which the individual expects no reward.

DISCUSSION QUESTIONS

1. Think about who you believe is your best friend. What are that person's values, ideals, goals, and the like? How similar are they to yours?
2. To which cliques do you belong? What are their characteristics? Do your best friends belong to the same cliques? Why?
3. Ask your best friend from high school to identify the crowds to which you belonged. Do you agree? Why or why not?
4. How well did your experience match that described by Dunphy for peer group formation and dissolution? Why does the progression exist?
5. What friend have you known the longest? Why do you suppose you have known this friend so long?
6. Think about your most intimate friend. What do you *not* know about him or her? What does he or she *not* know about you? How does this compare to others you know and who know you?
7. What is a date? If you and a friend meet for coffee after class, is that a date? If you call someone to go to a movie, is that a date? How do you know when you've had a date?
8. Do you remember your first date? Your tenth? Why do you remember the first, but not the tenth? A hint: Think of Coleman's focal theory (Chapter 2).
9. How old were you when you first started dating? What were the most important factors in your doing so?
10. Of the list of functions of dating (Table 11-2), which have you found most satisfying? Why?
11. If you ever broke up with someone or had someone break up with you, how did you handle the situation? Was it the "best" decision?
12. Think about your closest friends in high school. In what areas were they more influential on you than your parents? How about the reverse? Why the differences?
13. What is a peer? Are you and your siblings peers? Why are you and your parents not peers?
14. Are adolescents more conforming than children or adults? On what dimensions? Do we need to consider different types of conformity in judging the stereotype of adolescents being highly conforming?

12

School Influences on Adolescent Development

Major Issues Addressed

The Functions of Schooling
Adolescents' Views of Schools and Schooling
The Role of Athletics in the School Environment
Family Influences on School Performance
The Characteristics of Schools
Student Characteristics Related to Academic Success
Causes of Dropping Out of School
The Importance of School Transitions
Educating the Gifted and Learning Disabled Adolescent
Ethnicity and Schools

"So, how was school today?" The reply was a simple "OK." "What did you do?" I inquired. The reply again was simple: "Nothing." I used to receive excited and detailed answers about what was going on in the classroom, how his friends were, who got in trouble, and even details of a police drug raid at the middle school. This sharing of his school day slowly tapered off as he went through the middle school. Once he started high school it seemed the taxpayers were providing a lot of money for the adolescents in the district to spend their time doing nothing.

◆   ◆   ◆

Schools and the school atmosphere—teachers and administrators, peers, the curriculum, the feelings of safety—exert a strong influence on the child and adolescent. Adolescents view schools as their turf and as something their parents, and even their teachers, don't and can't really understand! It is the private world of the adolescent. In this chapter we discuss how the school atmosphere impacts on the adolescent's personal, social, and intellectual growth.

INTRODUCTION

The school is the one social institution to which virtually all adolescents are exposed. In the 1988–1989 school year there were over 83,000 public and private elementary and secondary schools in the United States (U.S. Bureau of the Census, 1992c). Approximately 49 million students were enrolled in these schools: 95.4% of 5- to 6-year-olds, 99.7% of 7- to 13-year-olds, 98.8% of 14- to 15-year-olds, 93.3% of 16- to 17-year-olds, and 59.6% of 18- to 19-year-olds in 1991, and the percentages were not very different for White, Black, Hispanic, or Mexican children (U.S. Bureau of the Census, 1992c). From the time the child begins school until the adolescent leaves, more time is spent in school and school-related activities than in any other single environment.

The school is the meeting ground for the peer group, the setting for many of its functions. As a result, schools have both formal and informal mechanisms that strongly influence the socialization of adolescents. The formal aspect of the school's socialization function is the transmission of the knowledge and skills that will enhance the likelihood of the individual becoming a successful member of society. The informal influence relates to the physical setting of the school, including the neighborhood, classmates' values, the influence of friends and peer groups, the qualities and attitudes of teachers, and general school climate.

THE FUNCTIONS OF SCHOOLS

The school serves two primary functions: maintenance-actualization is individual oriented and skills training/cultural transmission is community oriented (Linney & Seidman, 1989; Murphy, 1987). In general, the **maintenance-actualization function** aims to give the student an opportunity to grow socially, personally, and emotionally. Much has been written about the role of school in promoting high self-esteem, broadening students' interests, and fostering emotional growth. The **skills-training/cultural-transmission function** of schools provides the individual with the necessary skills and knowledge to become an economically independent and productive member of society. School success in the former function should enhance the adolescent's general psychological adjustment; success in the latter should facilitate the adolescent's ability to function optimally in our social system.

The Maintenance-Actualization Function

The maintenance-actualization function of schools is to enrich the individual's personal, psychological, and emotional development. Adolescents should come out of school feeling better about themselves than they did before, even if they were relatively secure already.

In some ways schools achieve this function, but in other ways they do not. For example, schools generally do relatively little with regard to the quality of the students' school experience, social or academic (Slavin, 1994). Although school counselors may attempt to help students function better in the school setting, they are overloaded with students and are typically more concerned with helping them gain entrance into college than with helping them cope with current problems. Furthermore, little is done to teach students how to identify and deal with problems. As a result, the student may continually fail and, ultimately, drop out of school—a loss both to the individual and society.

Schools fail in their self-actualization function in other ways. In fact, the school setting and atmosphere may in some ways be detrimental to maintenance-actualization (Slavin, 1994). The prolonged period of time spent in the school setting lengthens the adolescent's emotional and economic dependence on parents; and the school, as an agent of adult society, maintains control over the adolescent but at the same time tries to teach independence (Slavin, 1994). This is especially true for college students, who may remain more or less economically dependent and under parental control for a significant number of years.

Some researchers have argued that the basic Anglo "middle-class" values underlying our schooling system are partly responsible for the academic difficulties and poor attitudes toward school learning of some students (Slavin, 1994). Those who do not come from mainstream middle-class homes and backgrounds that emphasize academic competition, doing your own work, and working hard for the future are at a disadvantage in our educational system, which is built on these characteristics. Robert Slavin notes that students from lower socioeconomic strata and some minority students are taught different values—cooperation and joint work efforts—and may not have the opportunities to learn to pace their work to meet distant deadlines. As a result, students from cultural heritages different from the middle-class emphases of the schools may be at a disadvantage.

The Skills-Training/Cultural-Transmission Function

The training-acculturation function refers to the school's traditional role of teaching skills and imparting information. It is this function that has been most stressed, both historically and currently, in the American educational system. The school acts as a community organization that channels people into future educational and vocational arenas, and to a large degree determines the future of everyone. Completing school opens the door to other opportunities and greater economic potential; failure to do so results in fewer opportunities and lowered earning power.

Similarly, schools serve to pass on the beliefs, values, and traditions of a culture from generation to generation (Slavin, 1994). The basic middle-class value orientation of schools means transmitting middle-class, and usually Anglo middle-class, values, as we already noted. As the number of children from minority groups increases, this aspect of schooling is relevant to fewer students.

Factors Influencing Schools Meeting Their Goals

Researchers have investigated a number of broad-ranging factors that impact on the effectiveness of schools in meeting the two broad goals we just outlined. Among other factors, such as school size (discussed later), these include school atmosphere, the transition between elementary and junior high or middle school, and the effects of tracking.

School Atmosphere. Although curricular offerings, the availability of modern technology, and updated textbooks are clearly important to the success adolescents experience in school, we must also consider a number of more intangible factors. These generally fall into the category of **school atmosphere,** which includes the general climate and nature of classroom interaction, the relation between the administration and the teachers, the commitment of the teachers,

One function of schooling is skills training/cultural transmission. Schools are expected to provide students with the skills and knowledge they will need to help them become effective adults. (*Laima E. Druskis*)

and the general school environment. Some schools are more successful than others in optimizing these intangibles.

Effective schools are characterized by strong leadership, orderly and nonoppressive atmospheres for students and teachers, a high frequency of monitoring of student performance, and teacher input into decision making (Linney & Seidman, 1989). The roles, values, and commitment of the teachers are especially important (Rutter, 1983; Teddlie, Kirby, & Stringfield, 1989). How the school administration sets the tone for teachers translates into teacher behaviors in the classroom, which then affect student learning, student achievement, and student views of schooling.

For example, when teachers are allowed to have input into decisions they feel more a part of the system and more committed to the course of action chosen. In turn, these teachers provide a classroom atmosphere that is more conducive to learning—their classrooms are characterized as more friendly, they interact with and reward their students more, and their students have high involvement in learning. In effective classrooms, the climate fosters not only high standards and effective presentation of material, but also sound classroom management. The emphasis is one of neither extreme task orientation nor extreme control of student behavior, but rather a balance between the two. Effective teachers, like effective parents, use authoritative techniques (Chapter 10) in the classroom. They set high but appropriate standards, maintain an orderly classroom, treat students with respect, monitor their students' progress, and are committed to their students. Hence adolescents know the rules, come to respect the teacher, and put forth greater effort. In contrast, teachers who are authoritarian, indulgent, or neglecting overemphasize control or underemphasize the necessary organization related to successful teaching. These orientations impact negatively on the adolescents they teach.

The Effect of School Transitions.   The transition from elementary to middle or junior high school is another important facet of the adolescent's school experience. Because it occurs at a time when adolescents are experiencing other changes—such as physical growth, evolving parent and peer relationships, and other potential life transitions, such as divorce of the parents—changing schools may add more stress to the adolescent's life and may have deleterious effects on both personal growth and academic performance (Seidman, Allen, Aber, Mitchell, & Feinman, 1994; Simmons & Blyth, 1987; Simmons, Burgeson, Carlton-Ford, & Blyth, 1987). Researchers have examined school transitions both with respect to the general development of the adolescent and with regard to academic performance. In addition, researchers have examined whether the transitions are easier or more difficult if they occur in a system involving a middle or junior high school as opposed to one involving only one transition, usually after the eighth grade.

It now is clear that school transitions cause substantial changes in personal development. Girls evidence increases in depressive symptomatology (Hirsch & Rapkin, 1987), for example. In general, students suffer from declines in self-esteem and motivation (e.g., confidence in one's academic ability, general interest in school; Eccles, Midgley, et al., 1989b; Wigfield, Eccles, MacIver, Reuman, & Midgley, 1991), and these transitions may be more difficult in school systems employing a junior or middle school (Simmons & Blyth, 1987; Simmons et al., 1987). In addition, transitions from supportive to nonsupportive teachers, and vice versa, result in decreases or increases, respectively, in performance in mathematics (Midgley, Feldlaufer, & Eccles, 1989a, 1989b).

The shifts in general self-esteem between the sixth and seventh grade are not long lasting. Wigfield et al. (1991) reported that the drop experienced at the start of the seventh grade was temporary—self-esteem increased throughout the seventh-grade school year. The researchers suggest that the initial decline reflects adapting to a new social and academic environment, one in which students no longer are the oldest. They go on to note that the school transition results in a disruption of the social network, which may contribute to some of the changes in self-views. As the social network is strengthened, self-esteem increases. The same increase in self-esteem following the transition from middle school to high school has been documented (Kinney, 1993). When those labeled as "nerds" in middle school entered high school, with its more diverse population and less rigid social structure, their self-esteem levels increased. Finding more students like them allowed the development of friendship patterns and group structures that enhanced their self-image.

For poor urban Black, Latino, and White youth, it has been shown that school transitions are also associated with changes in peer relations and involvement in extracurricular activities (Seidman et al., 1994). For all three groups, daily hassles with schools increased and involvement in extracurricular activities decreased following the school transition. In addition, these poor youth perceived less social support from school personnel. The researchers suggest that such changes may place these adolescents at increased risks for undesirable outcomes, such as delinquency, academic failure, and dropping out.

Researchers suggest that easing the transition by employing team teaching—which allows for smaller classes and closer contact between students and teachers, structuring the middle school or junior high school around subunits, called "houses," which results in a smaller reference group—can do much to reduce the strain of the transition and its negative impact on personal growth (Fenzel, 1989a, 1989b). Although such procedures may facilitate the transition in some ways, they do not address other factors that make the transition stressful. For example, self-concept of math ability declined from sixth to seventh grade and continued to decline in the Wigfield et al. (1991) study. The researchers suggest that differences in the classroom climate generated by mathematics teachers in the two grades are an important factor. Teacher–student relations in seventh-grade math classes are less warm and positive than they are in sixth grade, for example. And the grading procedures are more stringent in seventh grade. In order to ease the transition, it is necessary to better prepare students for the changes in both the social and academic atmosphere of the junior high school.

Tracking.   The large diversity of students with differing academic needs, interests, and goals has led to the common practice of **tracking,** placing students into different levels of classes within the same school. Although the classes may have the same labels, some are designed for advanced students, others for the so-called average student, and others for students in need of remedial work. Formal tracking is most prevalent in junior high and high school, but it may begin as early as elementary school, when students may be placed in different levels of reading groups, for example.

The practice of tracking students has been a very controversial one (Hallinan, 1991). Those who favor it claim tracking allows the homogeneous grouping of students, which can be a strong advantage in large schools with many students of widely diverse abilities. By grouping students, it is argued, teachers are better able to move through the curriculum and, at the same time, provide for the learning needs of students who differ in academic ability.

Those who question the value of grouping point to the potential inequities that may result. They note that tracking could result in fewer learning opportunities for those not in the top track (Oakes, 1985). This could result from differences in the quality of teachers assigned to different tracks, the quality of the instruction in different tracks, and to misassignment of students to tracks. In addition, students in different tracks might develop different self-views regarding education and their abilities, and thereby progress differently in school. This could be detrimental to those in the lower tracks. Those opposed to tracking also point out that performance on the measures used to assign students to tracks, such as previous school achievement or scores from achievement tests, is related to social class and ethnicity. Hence tracking may result in continuing educational inequity. Finally, early tracking, as in middle school or even in the freshman year of high school, may have long-term serious consequences for those in the lower tracks because of the course selection open to them. They may not be able to prepare optimally for college because they may not be academically prepared to change tracks.

Tracking relates to both the maintenance-actualization and skills-training functions of schools. If tracking negatively influences self-perceptions and the interactions of students across various tracks, it could be detrimental to the maintenance-actualization function. If it results in poorer learning opportunities for some students it could be detrimental to the skills-training function. Of course, if tracking allows students to learn more because they are being taught with others of similar ability and skills it may enhance senses of self-worth and achievement. In this case, tracking may facilitate the two major functions of schools. What does the evidence suggest?

Researchers have identified a number of disadvantages for students in the lower or lowest tracks (Gamoran, 1987; Gamoran & Mare, 1989; Hallinan, 1991; Oakes, 1985). In contrast to students in the advanced track, who received a high-quality education that was academically challenging, those in the lower tracks received a lower quality of instruction and, even after initial ability was taken into account, learned less. Those in lower tracks have lower educational aspirations, are more likely to drop out of school, and generally receive a lower quality of education. Such evidence has led some educational psychologists to argue that tracking as a means of educating students should be avoided (Slavin, 1994).

Tracking may impact on the skills-training function of schools in two ways. For those in the upper or college-oriented track it is a benefit—they get the best instruction from better teachers. Their teachers spend less time on classroom discipline and more time on instruction. Their curriculum is designed to prepare them optimally for future education. For those in the lower tracks, however, the picture is less bright. They receive a lower quality of instruction and the classroom climate is not as conducive to learning. They achieve less, expect to achieve less, and are more prone to drop out.

Similar conclusions may be drawn about the impact of tracking on the maintenance-actualization function. Those in the lower track develop a sense of alienation and poor self-esteem—at least as related to schooling. The maintenance-actualization function of schools is undermined for these students.

These, and other factors we discuss later, affect the ability of the school to meet the actualization and skills/cultural-transmission functions of the educational system. Adolescents who attend schools and classes that have an atmosphere conducive to learning and personal growth, institute procedures to ease transitions between schools, and provide high-quality education for all students will achieve better, learn more, and grow personally in positive ways.

THE CHARACTERISTICS OF SCHOOLS

We have been talking about schools in a rather general way. It is time to be more specific. The public school is a community organization. But free public education was not always available; it took a large number of court cases to establish our current concept of community-financed, community-run primary and secondary schools.

Initially, educational systems were privately financed by wealthy backers interested in keeping "young hoodlums" off the streets. With time, efforts to provide tax monies to support public education arose and, around 1850, began to become accepted. The large influx of immigrants was a major factor in the final approval of taxation for the support of public education for the masses. In 1851 compulsory education laws began to be considered, debated, and passed. This was the beginning of the establishment of childhood and, as the school years slowly were lengthened, adolescence (Kett, 1977). Today, compulsory attendance at school extends to at least the age of 16 in most states.

As with any social institution, it was necessary for the public school to establish a series of goals. Historically, the public high schools' primary goal was to provide instruction for students who wished to go to college (Murphy, 1987). Slowly, however, this concept changed, and is still changing, toward the goal of providing an education for all young people, not just those who want a college education. More and more, the public is demanding that high schools, in particular, teach a variety of skills to adolescents of differing abilities and interests. That demand led to the notion of the *comprehensive high school,* a school that could serve the diverse needs of a variety of groups. In a comprehensive high school there are special programs for the retarded, for the gifted, for the learning disabled, for those who wish to enter college, and for those who want job-specific skills (Box 12–1).

Along with the various curricular options that may be offered, additional characteristics of schools are important for understanding how they impact on the adolescent: social and academic orientations, emphasis on sports, and different sizes.

Social vs. Academic Orientation

The evidence clearly indicates that students view the school primarily as a social rather than an academic setting (see Johnston & Bachman, 1976; Linney & Seidman, 1989). This is a somewhat disheartening but hardly surprising conclusion given that the school is the center of peer group activity.

J. S. Coleman (1961, 1965) conducted the initial extensive studies on the social nature of schools over 30 years ago, but the conclusions apply today (Slavin, 1994). After interviewing students in midwestern high schools ranging in size from 100 to about 2,000 students, he concluded that adolescents received greater reinforcement for being athletic or popular than for academic achievement. Although about 30% of males and females mentioned wanting to

BOX 12–1   Educating the Gifted and Learning Disabled Adolescent

Historically, the U.S. educational system treated all students in basically the same learning atmosphere. Aside from the mentally retarded or the physically disabled, little attention was paid to the possibility that other identifiable groups of students might require or benefit from special treatment. Hence if a student was not doing well in school it was presumed he or she simply did not have the ability or motivation to do better. Or if a student did not pay attention in class the difficulty was attributed to a poor attitude. During the 1980s, however, two other groups of students in need of special services were identified: the learning disabled and the gifted.

The term **learning disability** is defined by reference to three criteria (Singh & Beale, 1992). A student is learning disabled if he or she (1) is not performing up to expectations, if the difficulty (2) is not attributable to emotional problems, such as dealing with parental divorce or sensory deficits (e.g., poor vision) and (3) if there is some evidence of neurological impairment. For example, some students suffer from **dyslexia**; they see letters on the printed page upside down, rotated, or jumbled. They not only have trouble reading, perhaps taking many hours to read a short story, but may also have difficulty completing homework on time because it takes them so long to read and comprehend the assignment. They also may have difficulty taking tests, paying attention in the classroom, or keeping track of where they are in an assignment. As a result of the learning disability, the student may become an underachiever, perhaps falling several grade levels behind.

What can be done to help the learning disabled adolescent cope with school and learn better? A number of suggestions have been made (Singh & Beale, 1992). One common technique to help the learning disabled adolescent perform more closely to his or her ability level is to provide extra time to complete tests or assignments. In cases of extreme disability it may be appropriate to give an alternative type of test— an oral examination instead of a written one. At the college level it sometimes is justified to alter requirements or allow substitutions for required courses, for example, an added math or science course in place of a required literature course.

A second group of adolescents who can profit from specialized programs are the **gifted** and talented. Although we generally associate the term *gifted* with intelligence, which generally is the way students are assigned to this group (an IQ of 130 or above; Bireley & Genshaft, 1991; Horowitz & O'Brien, 1986), it actually includes more than simply intellectual competence. According to the Education Consolidation and Improvement Act of 1981, it includes all those who show exceptional ability in creativity, specific academic fields, and artistic areas as well. Giftedness, then, entails more than intellect, and it may be limited to a single area.

Generally speaking, educational programs for the gifted and talented adolescent fall into two categories (Bireley & Genshaft, 1991). *Enrichment* programs provide these students with opportunities for added learning by including experiences they normally would not get until they reached a higher grade level. For example, providing further training in chemistry or literature along with the regular class or the use of honors classes provides these students with added opportunities to develop their analytical skills as well as their knowledge. An alternative approach is to provide *accelerated* programs that allow students to attend classes above their grade level and progress (accelerate) at a faster pace than otherwise would be possible. For example, allowing junior high school students to attend mathematics classes in the high school or high school students, college mathematics classes lets these students develop their specialized skills at a faster pace.

Although we generally consider gifted-ness in a positive light, this is not always the case. Gifted adolescents may encounter social and emotional difficulties. For exam-ple, we all have heard of early adolescents who enroll in college. They may excel in the classroom, but their social life may suf-fer—who will date them or allow them to join their fraternity or sorority? Some have used this type of argument to bolster the view that enrichment programs are more optimal than acceleration programs.

Specialized programs for the learning disabled and the gifted are attempts to pro-vide optimal learning atmospheres for ado-lescents with special needs. They are one way in which the educational system has tried to adjust to the needs of students and provide for their intellectual and personal growth.

be remembered as good students, 45% of boys wanted to be remembered for athletic prowess and over 70% of girls wanted to be remembered for their popu-larity. Academic success was less important to the legacy the student body wished to leave than the social aspects of the school experience. Coleman con-cluded that peers, teachers, school administrators, and the general community rewarded the nonacademic aspects of schooling more than they did the acade-mic.

Other researchers (Johnston & Bachman, 1976) have shown that high school boys and teachers agree that athletics receives more emphasis than acad-emics, although both groups concur that academic matters, such as motivating students to learn and preventing dropping out of school, *should* be among the major emphases of schools. Why aren't they? Being an athlete brings prestige and popularity with peers (Chapter 11), and athletic competition can enhance community and school pride. In other words, adolescents receive greater satis-faction from the nonacademic aspects of the school than they do from academic success.

Athletics and the School

The preceding discussion established the strong influence of athletics in the school setting. This is not to say that stressing athletics is all bad. Athletics can play a positive role. As we noted earlier, athletes tend to be popular among their peers (Watkins, 1989; Watkins & Montgomery, in press). As a result, the suc-cessful athlete is likely to be looked up to and emulated more than the nonath-lete. Hence the successful athlete can become a model for other students, which, in turn, should enhance his or her self-esteem and self-confidence, and perhaps force the athlete to live up to the expectations of others by learning more mature behavior patterns than fellow classmates (Watkins & Montgomery, in press). Participation in interscholastic athletics, then, may contribute to fur-thering one's socialization. This may translate to increased self-confidence and a higher level of academic achievement.

A second way academics and athletics are positively related is that athletes may receive a greater degree and higher quality of counseling from career counselors and teachers than other students do. As a result, they may be able to crystallize future goals and deal with current academic problems more successfully than nonathletes. Although this benefit may be more subtle at the high school level, at the college level athletes have ready access to tutors, greater contact with academic advisors, and other resources that can aid academic achievement.

Third, achievement in athletics and achievement in academics are positively related. The same qualities that lead to success in the athletic arena may also bring success in the classroom. Wishing to excel, being competitive, and being willing to work hard will bring the adolescent success both academically and athletically.

Fourth, participation in athletics with other achievement-oriented peers may reinforce the athlete's high aspirations and may act as a cohesive influence to push him or her to higher levels of academic performance. The team provides a peer group with similar interests, and participation facilitates a sense of belongingness.

Finally, the athlete may try hard to perform well in the classroom in order to present a consistent picture of the self, one of an individual who is successful in a number of different endeavors. To be known as the proverbial "dumb jock" may be extremely damaging to the adolescent's self-concept. As a result, striving toward high academic achievements often goes hand in hand with success in athletics.

The Role of School Size

In the United States, bigness often is equated with goodness. Applying this to schools, we might say bigger schools must be better because they are able to offer students significantly more curricular and extracurricular opportunities than are smaller schools. On the one hand, these advantages may outweigh the criticism that large schools are cold and impersonal. On the other hand, some claim small schools are better because they give each student more individual attention and a greater sense of belonging (Linney & Seidman, 1989).

Some researchers who study the impact of school size have focused on the students' opportunities to participate in various extracurricular settings, such as sports, language clubs, and student councils. One of the major findings is that students in small schools engage in a greater number of activities than do students in large schools (Barker, 1964; Goodlad, 1984). In fact, students in small schools participate in more than twice the number of activities, although there are only about a quarter of the number of different activities available. Students spend more time and effort in school-related activities in the small school in part because they are pressured to do so to maintain these activities in the school (Grabe, 1981). They have a sense of obligation to the school and community. This pressure to maintain activities leads to a somewhat lower criterion for en-

Although athletic competition has many positive benefits for the athlete and the community, many argue that it has become too emphasized. (*Laime E. Druskis*)

trance into certain activities (for example, sports) because the group from which students can be selected is more limited than it is in larger schools.

Students from small schools feel their involvement in school activities has helped them develop skills and self-confidence (Grabe, 1981). Students in small schools received a greater degree of satisfaction and feeling of accomplishment from their involvement, regardless of the activity, than students from larger schools (Table 12–1). Although students from large and small schools who participate in school activities report greater satisfaction and feelings of accomplishment than those who do not, these feelings are greater for those in small schools.

What this demonstrates, then, is that smaller schools do a better job of translating opportunities into engagement because being able to join a sport, club, or other activity is greater. Because students who participate derive a high degree of satisfaction from their participation (Linney & Seidman, 1989), smaller

Table 12–1   Examples of Activities That Affected Students in Small Schools More Positively Than Students in Large Schools

Attribute Affected	Activity
Skill development	Games, play, dances
Build confidence	Games, play, projects
Test one's abilities	Play, dances, projects
Feel needed by others	Games, play
Feeling of accomplishment	Play
Work closely with others	Games, play, projects

Source: Derived from Wicker, A.W. (1968). Undermanning, performance, and students' subjective experience in behavioral settings of large and small high schools. *Journal of Personality and Social Psychology, 10,* 255–261.

Although larger schools offer more academic and extracurricular opportunities to their students, a larger percentage of students avail themselves of these opportunities in smaller schools. (*Laime E. Druskis*)

schools—those with 500 to 1,000 students—(Entwisle, 1990) may do a better job of meeting the maintenance-actualization function of schools. In larger schools, students tend to receive more satisfaction from observing the participation of others and from feelings of school spirit that are built up through association and identification with the success of the smaller percentage who participate. This vicarious participation does not lead to the individual satisfaction that is gained from actual participation. Sheer school size may make it more difficult for larger schools to do as good a job of enhancing student self-esteem and teaching the skills of participation. Nonetheless, when degree of participation is equated, students from large and small schools do not differ in satisfaction. The key, then, is not so much school size as it is participation, and smaller schools provide opportunities for a higher percentage of the student body.

When speaking of large and small schools, the issues of teacher quality and responsibilities and curricular offerings inevitably arise. Are there differences in the quality of instruction and teacher responsibilities? Do curricular offerings differ substantially as a function of school size? These concerns are directly related to the skills-training function of schools. Do larger schools perform better?

In large schools, the teachers tend to be better qualified academically, are required to teach fewer courses outside of their major area of interest or expertise, and are better at preparing students to go on to college. The advantage of smaller schools seems to lie in the greater degree to which teachers cooperate with each other, which may lead to a greater degree of student confidence in the teacher.

However, bigness does not substantially increase the variety of academic offerings (Monk & Haller, 1993). Generally speaking, a 100% increase in the size of the school produces only a small increase in the variety of the curriculum. And after some size is reached, curricular offerings do not further diversify. Although both large and small schools offer the same core curriculum in order to meet state requirements, adolescents attending larger schools have a greater number of electives and curricular variety, including vocational courses, from which to choose than do students from smaller schools. It is this fact, along with the slightly better academic qualifications of the teachers, that allows larger schools to better prepare students for college.

What are the specific curricular advantages and disadvantages of attending large versus small schools? This was the question addressed by Monk and Haller (1993), who looked at the impact of high school size on the curricular opportunities offered students. They investigated curricular offerings in schools with small (25), medium (300), and large (600) graduating classes. Although the number of classes in English and science did not differ appreciably among large, medium, and small schools, the larger schools had increased offerings in foreign languages and the visual and performing arts, more remedial classes in mathematics, and increased vocational education opportunities. The larger schools also had more of the advanced English and science classes, but fewer remedial science classes.

These researchers draw several important conclusions. First, increases in school size do not impact evenly across the academic curriculum. Larger schools provide selective opportunities, enhancing those interested in vocational studies and some "academic" areas, but perhaps at the expense of those in need of remedial work in some areas. Second, the special education student is not necessarily served better in larger high schools. Although some added remedial classes are offered, others are not.

We can summarize the research in the following way. Larger schools do, indeed, offer both a greater variety of courses and more extracurricular activities. However, the percentage of students who participate in outside activities is smaller in large schools. In smaller schools, nearly everyone is expected to participate in one or more of the social and extracurricular activities of the school, and in fact does so. Given the benefits of participation (that is, gains in self-confidence and feelings of self-worth), small schools certainly offer one advantage that larger schools do not, albeit to a smaller percentage of their students. Indeed, even the potential dropout is less likely to become a real dropout in the smaller school because of pressure exerted by peers, teachers, and others for completing the school curriculum. In turn, in some academic areas, such as advanced English and science, larger schools may better prepare students for furthering their education.

Thus far, we have emphasized the benefits of participation, but there are potential drawbacks as well. Grabe (1981) studied the detrimental and beneficial effects of participation in high school activities, such as clubs, athletics, fine arts, and social situations, on students in grades 9 to 12. He found that in both small and large schools, poor participative performance led to feelings of alienation, but these negative feelings were much stronger in small schools.

What, then, might we do to try to capture the best of both worlds for the adolescent? Linney and Seidman (1989) suggest that dividing large schools into "houses" or "schools within schools" can reduce deviancy, help develop a sense of identity, and provide greater opportunities for student involvement. Providing a small school atmosphere in the large school can help the adolescent prosper personally and intellectually.

The Role of School Curricula

Larger schools do a better job academically of preparing their students for college. This is true for at least two reasons. First, the teachers are better qualified in larger schools. Second, the curriculum offers the students a wider variety of academic experiences. Next to the influence of the teacher, the curriculum has the greatest impact on the adolescent's academic development.

Havighurst (1978) analyzed the content of school curricula from 1955 and pointed out some of the major changes that occurred. During the decade from 1955 to 1965, schools flourished, with wide-ranging support from parents, the community, and government officials. There was a change in perspective, and programs aimed at a variety of students with differing characteristics were instituted. In addition, a strong emphasis on science and mathematics education prospered as the space race made its impact on those responsible for educating youth. The decade from 1965 to 1975 witnessed a change in the philosophy of education. Educators and curriculum experts became more concerned with the educational needs of low-income and minority students. Alternative curricula, including a decrease in required courses, sprang up. And there was an emphasis on educating students to understand their history, role, and identity as members of a pluralistic society (Linney & Seidman, 1989). Hence, for example, courses on Black studies or women's studies became popular and replaced other elective or required courses.

As you are aware, there have been numerous recent criticisms of the nature of the educational system and a concomitant move to return "to the basics" (Murphy, 1987). Citing declining average scores on standardized tests such as the Scholastic Aptitude Test (SAT), critics argue that schools are not educating youngsters adequately. As a result, we hear much of lengthening school days or the school year, adding requirements for graduation, increasing homework assignments, which increases learning (Chen & Stevenson, 1989; Keith, 1982), and competence learning.

One result of the historical changes we have described is that many high schools today offer three major curricula. The *college preparatory* curriculum prepares students for college work. The *vocational* curriculum is employment oriented. In addition to studying basic subjects such as English and mathematics, students enroll in specialized courses teaching specific vocational skills and, in some instances, engage in on-the-job training. Finally, there is the *general* curriculum, usually a less stringent form of the college preparatory curriculum aimed at providing a general education for students not interested in attending college or making a commitment to a vocational training program. By offering these alternative curricula schools attempt to provide educational opportunities to the majority of their students.

Increasing percentages of students feel the need and have the desire to gain further education upon graduation from high school. (*Laima E. Druskis*)

How do students view their school academic experience? They find the best things about school involve factors such as being with friends and meeting people (B. Brown, Lamborn, & Newmann, 1992). The worst? Doing homework, taking tests, and the restrictive and regimented nature of schools. Thus, even in the 1990s, students have much the same complaints about schools that they did in previous decades (Hurrelman, 1987; D. Miller, 1976).

FACTORS INFLUENCING SCHOOL PERFORMANCE

Through teaching methods, curriculum development and implementation, grading procedures, and personal characteristics, the teacher exerts a very large influence on adolescent attitudes about schooling, learning, and school success. But a number of other factors also are important.

The Role of Parents

Parental influences on school performance begin long before the adolescent years and include parental views about education, parental involvement in their child's education, family structure (see Box 12-2), and child-rearing techniques. Moreover, as parents make changes in these areas their influences on school performance change (Bradley, Caldwell, & Rock, 1988). Hence it is the parents' *current* attitudes and behaviors, not those of the past, that are most important to the adolescent's school achievement. And research demonstrates it is equally important for the father and the mother to provide an atmosphere conducive to educational attainment (Melby, 1993; Paulson, in press).

Parental educational attainment is highly related to the aspirations and success of adolescents in the school setting (Sewell & Shah, 1968a, 1968b). For ex-

BOX 12–2   Family Structure and Adolescent School Achievement

Researchers have become interested in studying family structure as it relates to adolescents' school achievement (see Kurdek & Sinclair, 1988b; Zimiles & Lee, 1991). This is an important subject because of the large number of adolescents who will live for some period of time in a single-parent or stepparent family. Researchers have been concerned not only about school performance, such as grades earned, but also school behavior, such as absences and misconduct. Research with children has shown that those from intact families not only perform somewhat better academically but have fewer behavioral problems related to school, although the differences between the groups diminish when social class is controlled (see Kurdek & Sinclair, 1988b). Does family structure relate to adolescent school achievement and behavior?

Kurdek and Sinclair (1988b) studied eighth-grade males and females from each family structure. They found that students from intact families had higher year-end grades than students in the other two family structures. In addition, those from intact families had higher quantitative achievement test scores than those from stepfather families and fewer absences than those from where the mother had custody. Amount of contact with the noncustodial father was not related to school achievement for those students not living with their biological father. This finding indicates that the differences in school grades are not the result of the lack of a male model.

Zimiles and Lee (1991) studied over 13,000 high school sophomores from intact, single-parent, and stepparent families.

Those from intact families had higher grades than those from the other two groups, both as sophomores and as seniors. In general, students from intact families were less likely to drop out of school. Males from single-parent families were more likely to drop out than males from stepfamilies. The reverse was true for the females. The differential dropping out of school by students in the three family types seemed not to be a result of differential levels of achievement, as assessed by either achievement tests or school grades.

Several points should be noted. First, the differences in grades and achievement test scores, although statistically reliable, are not large. As a group, students from single-parent and stepparent families are not failing school. Second, the group differences, as is always the case, mask individual differences among students. Just as some students from intact families are excellent and others are not, some students from single-parent and stepparent families are excellent and others are not. These differences among students seem more related to other factors, such as parental involvement in school and an authoritative parenting style (see text), than to the type of family structure.

Finally, these differences are unrelated to social class; that is, the differences are not simply a result of reduced economic circumstances. The causes of these differences, then, lie in how the adolescent adjusts to parental divorce, in general, and in the nature of family interaction patterns. At present, we know virtually nothing of the specific nature of the causes of the differences.

ample, adolescents who come from families with highly educated parents are more likely to attend college. Generally speaking, the educational level reached by the father has a more significant influence on adolescents of both sexes than the educational level of the mother. Partially, this is because educated parents stress the importance of education (Steinberg, Lamborn et al., 1992).

Parental encouragement to do well in school and parental involvement in schooling are related to better adolescent
school achievement. (*Michelle Bridwell/Photo Edit*)

Similarly, parental encouragement and rewards generally lead to better
school performance (Rosenthal & Feldman, 1991; D.L. Stevenson & Baker,
1987). Parental encouragement reflects attempts to develop mature behavior in
their adolescents. When parents spell out a definable set of expected behaviors
in a demanding but nonconflictual manner, adolescents know what is expected
of them in school and attempt to perform at this level, particularly when they
have rewarding parents who are actively involved in their education (see Table
12-2). For example, Connell, Spencer, and Aber (1994) reported that for
African-American adolescents, family support and involvement in schooling was
a substantial predictor of involvement in school over and above economic level.

These data suggest that parental child-rearing techniques may be related to
school performance (see Chapter 10; Slavin, 1994). For a wide variety of social
classes and ethnic groups, authoritarian and permissive parenting styles are negatively related to the adolescent's academic achievement (Dornbusch et al., 1987;
Paulson, in press; Pratt et al., 1989; Steinberg, Lamborn et al., 1992). In turn, an
authoritative parenting style is associated positively with school achievement.

Table 12–2   Examples of Parent and Family Behaviors That Distinguish High- and
Low-Achieving Boys

Parent/Family Activity Positively Related to High Achievement
More family recreation
Family sharing of confidences
Parental approval
Family morale
Parental appropriate restrictiveness
Reasonable parental discipline
Having trusting parents
Respect and affection for one's parents

Source: Based on Morrow, W.R., & Wilson, R.C. (1961). Family relations of bright high achieving
and underachieving high school boys. *Child Development, 32,* 501–510.

Authoritative parents engage in a variety of behaviors that promote school success (Steinberg, Lamborn et al., 1992). They have more contact with the school and teachers and more positive attitudes about homework. They also promote autonomy and independence, both of which are positively related to school success (Grolnick & Ryan, 1989; D. L. Stevenson & Baker, 1987; Wentzel, 1989).

Finally, adolescents who come from homes that provide a supportive environment conducive to inquisitiveness and learning generally perform better in school. Having newspapers, magazines, a quiet place to study, and being exposed to art, music, and literature emphasize an appreciation of the value of education.

Peer Influences on School Achievement

In Chapter 11 we outlined a number of important peer group influences on the adolescent's development. These influences clearly carry over into the realm of academic achievement, with those who are well liked by their peers being scholastically more successful than those who are less well liked or rejected by their peers. Peers can provide an environment conducive to academic competence in which the individual is expected to conform to the norms and expectations of others. Given this conformity, those who are able to succeed in school are more likely to hold similar views and higher aspirations than those who are not able to be successful. The influence of the peer group, then, is mediated by mutual reinforcement of a relatively common basic set of notions about the value of education.

The role of peers, however, is not always so positive, particularly for African American students (Fordham, 1988; Fordham & Ogbu, 1986). Black students who excel academically may develop feelings of not belonging to the peer group of other Black students. As a result, they may feel less pride in their individual accomplishments, and may in fact reduce their efforts to do well so they may better fit in and maintain a sense of belonging. Their pride in achievement may come more from a sense of group success than individual accomplishment.

Part of the reason for these feelings stems from the "burden of acting white" (Fordham & Ogbu, 1986). Black peers who are not achieving as well may withdraw support, and may even make up nicknames for the Black students who are high achievers and who are seen as acting white. These students must find means of coping with a peer group that may be hostile while at the same time satisfying themselves and their parents, a difficult task.

Socioeconomic Status and Educational Aspirations and Success

Social class is a global variable that includes a number of different dimensions: the neighborhood in which one lives, the income level of the family, the child-rearing practices of the parents, and the attitudes of family members and friends toward education. As a result of these and other differences, middle-class students start school with an advantage over lower-class students, but the exact reasons remain unclear. Therefore, making broad generalizations about social-class differences related to educational aspirations or achievements is very difficult.

The complexity of the issues was shown clearly by K. White (1982), who reviewed the findings of 101 studies that related various measures of social class to school achievement. The strongest correlations between social class and achievement occurred for differences in home atmosphere. Those children and adolescents whose parents encouraged them to complete homework, modeled the value of education, and provided educational opportunities outside the school setting achieved at higher levels. Measures such as social-class rating of the school, the value of the parents' house, and the resources available to the school were less strongly related to student achievement. In order to be as precise as possible in our presentation of social class and its relationship to school achievement and aspirations, we have broken the discussion down into several subcategories.

Neighborhood characteristics are strongly related to social class as well as to academic aspirations and achievement. Students from more prosperous areas have higher educational aspirations and do better in school than students from poorer neighborhoods, even when we adjust for age, measurement procedures, intellectual levels, and family background factors. The neighborhood is an important factor in school achievement because the schools students attend are generally determined by the neighborhood in which they live (Slavin, 1994). As a result, the students in a school tend to be of relatively homogeneous backgrounds. In fact, if high schools are classified according to the socioeconomic status of the majority of individuals in the school, the aspirations of any one student will lie in the direction of the aspirations of the majority of the students in the school. For example, middle-class students attending a school in a lower-class neighborhood have lower educational aspirations than do middle-class students attending a middle-class school. The reverse is also the case, with lower-class students who attend middle-class schools having higher educational aspirations than lower-class students who attend lower-class schools.

Parental views of the value of school also differ across social classes. Middle-class parents tend to value school and promote school success to a greater degree than lower-class parents, and they are more involved in their adolescent's education (D.L. Stevenson & Baker, 1987). Lower-class parents tend to be less involved in the schooling of their children and tend to view it more as a vocational than an academic experience. These views of parents, in some ways, are not unrealistic. Schools are geared to the needs and desires of middle-class students and are aimed primarily at preparing people for middle-class society.

Ethnicity and School Achievement

It is well established that there are substantial ethnic group differences in school achievement (e.g., Slavin, 1994). In general, African American and Hispanic youth do not perform as well as White adolescents, and all three groups perform less well than Asian American adolescents (Slavin, 1994; Steinberg,

Dornbusch, & Brown, 1992). But there is little agreement on why these differences exist. From a historical perspective, the concept of "separate but equal" schools—school segregation—has been blamed. There is no doubt today that school desegregation has worked to the advantage of the minority group student (Box 12-3).

Steinberg and his colleagues note several other possible explanations. First, families from different ethnic groups may socialize achievement-related values differently, which may then cause differences in school achievement. Second, families from different ethnic groups may place different values on education. Third, discrimination in educational settings, whether simply perceived or real, may result in differences in achievement.

BOX 12–3   School Desegregation and Minority Student Achievement

Until 1954 Black, Hispanic, and White students in 20 states and the District of Columbia were legally required to attend separate schools (Slavin, 1994), which often meant students were bused many miles. In 1954 the Supreme Court struck down previous decisions upholding the "separate but equal" concept of education in the *Brown v. Board of Education of Topeka* case. Nonetheless, school segregation continued well into the 1970s, forcing a series of Supreme Court decisions that required districts to establish and maintain standards for the proportion of minority students in schools. In some large urban areas this meant substantial numbers of students were bused to schools in order to achieve racial balance. In others it resulted in the development of magnet schools—specialized schools for those with particular talents in the arts or for gifted students—in attempts to entice students outside their own segregated neighborhood district.

One intent of school desegregation was to promote the academic progress of minority group students and thereby in the long run their economic circumstances. How good a job has desegregation done? The evidence depends on the measure used—school achievement or more long-term benefits. In general, school desegregation has had a minimal impact on overall school achievement of Black students (Entwisle, 1990) unless it is begun in elementary school with minority group students being bused to high-quality schools with a largely middle-class student body (Slavin, 1994). By attending a better school than they might otherwise, minority students reap long-term benefits: They are more likely to graduate, work in integrated settings, continue their education, and enter occupations that afford greater earnings. The benefits of school desegregation, then, may not be evident until after the adolescent has completed the formal educational system. And the benefits of desegregation lie not so much in the racial composition of the school—mixing students from differing ethnic groups but from the same lower social-class background does not result in the same benefits—but rather in the provision of a higher quality education (Braddock, 1985).

The beneficial effects of school desegregation lie in the quality of education received. Those from inner-city areas, from economically depressed communities, and those who attend schools that are inferior—and minority students are overrepresented in each of these groups—receive a lower quality of education. Desegregation can work only if a high-quality education is provided.

In order to begin to understand how these factors produce ethnic group differences in achievement, Steinberg and colleagues administered an extensive questionnaire to 15,000 African American, Asian American, Hispanic, and White high school students. The students came from inner-city as well as rural settings, and were from a variety of social classes. The researchers measured adjustment (work orientation, self-esteem); schooling (time spent in school activities, school performance, educational aspiration); behavioral problems (drug and alcohol use, delinquency); and psychological distress (anxiety, depression). They also obtained information about parental rearing techniques, peer group norms, engagement in extracurricular activities, classes enrolled in, and classroom atmosphere.

The researchers found that authoritative parenting (see Chapter 10) was related to greater school success, but the degree to which this was true depended on a number of other factors. For example, White and Hispanic adolescents benefited more from authoritative rearing practices than did the African American or Asian American students. One reason for these differences is the student's belief about the consequences of *not* getting a good education. More than those in the other groups, the Asian Americans believed not getting a good education would have serious negative consequences. Hispanic and African American students were more optimistic, which Steinberg et al. suggest may limit their achievement because they may expend less effort in attempts to do well. Other research (Taylor, Casten, Flickinger, Roberts, & Fulmore, 1994) indicates that for both lower- and middle-class African American adolescents, feelings of racial discrimination relate to perceived importance of schooling. The greater the view that discrimination in the job market occurs, the lower the view that schooling is important and, for public school adolescents, the lower the involvement in school work.

Researchers also have examined ethnic group differences in the role of peers in school achievement (Steinberg, Dornbusch, & Brown, 1992). White adolescents from authoritative rearing environments tended to have friends from similar environments, and all valued education. Their peers reinforced the value of education and the behaviors that lead to success. The relation between parental rearing style and friends did not occur for the African American and Asian American adolescents. But those minority youth who belonged to a crowd that did not emphasize achievement in school performed less well even if their parents were authoritative. For Asian American students, having peers who valued school success offset the detrimental effects of nonauthoritative parenting practices.

How can we begin to sort out these complex findings? First, parental rearing practices are clearly important to school success regardless of ethnic group. Authoritative parenting practices, as we discussed in Chapter 10, foster a sense of self-determination and provide a home atmosphere conducive to achieving near one's potential. However, the peer group's values, parental values aside from rearing techniques, and the feeling that schooling will allow an equal entrance into the job market all *interact* to influence the adolescent's attitudes and values related to educational achievement.

THE SCHOOL DROPOUT

We typically think about the dropout as an individual who leaves school and does not graduate with his or her class. This is only one measure, called the **cohort dropout** rate (Carson, Huelskamp, & Woodall, 1993). Because students move, change schools for other reasons (like entering a private school), or are retained in a grade, for example, it is difficult to obtain accurate information on the cohort dropout rate. Hence those concerned with studying dropping out of school have developed two other measures.

The **event dropout** measure is simply the proportion of students who drop out of school in a given year, regardless of their cohort. For your high school, for example, it would be the proportion of students who left school prior to the end of the school year, whether they returned the next year or not. Because laws set lower limits on the age at which one may dropout, event drop out rates are usually calculated for grades 10 through 12. A difficulty with this measure is that it makes it sound like the person will never complete graduation requirements, either by returning to school or by obtaining a GED (General Education Diploma). A person enrolled in high school or a GED program after leaving school is different from one who leaves and does not attempt to complete diploma requirements.

The **status dropout** rate is the proportion of the population who have not completed high school and are not enrolled regardless of when they dropped out. Because one may reenroll in school at any age, status dropout rates usually are calculated for an age range, such as 16 to 24. In Table 12-3, the status dropout rates are for those aged 16 to 24—they dropped out of school at some age and, as of the various age levels in the table, were not currently enrolled in a

Those who drop out of high school often are from poorer neighborhoods, feel they cannot do well in school, have difficulties with authority, and feel their teachers are not interested in them. (*Marc Anderson*)

Table 12–3   Percentage of Population Not Having Completed High School

Group	1975	1980	1985	1990
		YEAR		
EVENT DROPOUTS				
Total	5.9	6.2	5.3	4.1
White	5.0	5.3	4.4	3.4
Male	4.6	5.7	4.6	3.6
Female	5.4	4.9	4.1	3.2
Black	8.5	8.4	8.1	5.1
Male	8.4	7.8	8.5	4.3
Female	8.7	8.9	7.7	5.8
Hispanic	11.1	11.8	9.9	8.1
Male	10.4	17.7	9.5	8.9
Female	11.8	6.8	10.3	7.4
STATUS DROPOUTS				
Total	13.9	14.1	12.6	12.1
White	11.4	11.3	10.4	9.0
Male	10.9	12.2	11.0	9.3
Female	11.8	10.5	9.9	8.7
Black	22.8	19.2	15.2	13.2
Male	22.9	20.8	16.1	11.9
Female	22.8	17.8	14.4	14.4
Hispanic	29.2	35.2	27.6	32.4
Male	26.7	37.2	29.9	34.3
Female	31.6	33.2	25.2	30.3

Source: U.S. Bureau of the Census (1992c). Status dropouts are for persons aged 16 to 24.

program to complete their diploma requirements. The percentage of event and status dropouts for various years, ethnic groups, and males and females is shown in Table 12-3. Several trends are obvious.

On both measures the percentage of the population dropping out declined from 1975 to 1990. Currently, then, when one examines measures of total dropouts across ethnic groups, only about 12% of students have not completed high school requirements by age 24. Second, the event dropout rate is about the same for Black and White students, but is much higher for Hispanic students, perhaps because of a poor facility with the English language, which is a strong predictor of dropping out (Steinberg, Blinn, & Chan, 1984). Finally, the status dropout rate is higher for Black adolescents and much higher for Hispanic adolescents than it is for White adolescents.

The disadvantages to the high school dropout are many. There are few job opportunities for the dropout. In 1990 the unemployment rate for dropouts was 34.1%; for graduates it was only 15.1% (U.S. Bureau of the Census, 1992c). Although many jobs do not require a high school diploma, these jobs nevertheless often go to those with a high school diploma or even more education, which puts the high school dropout at the bottom of the economic ladder. This is particularly a problem for those who come from minority group backgrounds. There are large numbers of young nonwhite dropouts who have very bleak employment prospects. These individuals make up a disproportionate share of those who engage in socially unapproved behaviors, and at present little has been done to help them.

Many believe the primary reason for dropping out of high school is economic. Although dropping out is more prevalent among adolescents from poorer backgrounds (Zimiles & Lee, 1991), only a very small small percentage leave school for financial reasons. The vast majority leave for other reasons. Some adolescents leave school because they cannot perform at a satisfactory level. Others who are capable of dealing with the school curriculum leave because the curriculum is boring or otherwise distasteful to them, or because they cannot compete successfully in a middle-class school system.

Because both Black and Hispanic parents hold high expectations for their adolescents' school grades—at least as high or higher than the expectations of White parents (H. W. Stevenson, Chen, & Uttal, 1990)—it must be that other factors account for the higher status dropout rates for these two groups of students. We noted one possible cause earlier, namely differential facility with the English language (Steinberg et al., 1984). At present, researchers have not identified other specific reasons for the higher dropout rate of Hispanic youth. The strong links between social class and dropping out suggest that the overrepresentation of minority groups in the lower social strata may contribute to differential status dropout rates for these adolescents, perhaps because of social-class differences in views of schooling and the relevance of schooling already discussed.

It may also be that the school climate, which we noted earlier is poorer in the general track, is a critical factor (Pittman & Haughwout, 1987; Schneider, Stevenson, & Link, 1994). Although dropout rates are higher in larger than smaller schools this is less tied to school size than it is to school atmosphere. An impersonal atmosphere, in which regimentation is emphasized, coupled with a classroom climate involving substantial amounts of time devoted to classroom management and discipline, will contribute to some marginal students finally deciding to drop out. This is especially true in larger schools that employ tracking (Bryk & Thum, 1989). Students who feel their teachers are uninterested in them, who have disrupted social ties due to grade-level retention, and who feel the school environment is not one that encourages learning are more likely to drop out (Schneider et al., 1994).

Thus dropping out of school clearly has a number of antecedents. Parental and family influences are certainly important. All adolescents need support and encouragement for continuing and performing well in the school setting. Parents who do not provide this kind of support may be encouraging their sons and daughters to view school negatively. Peers, too, play an important role. To the degree the individual feels accepted by peers, he or she is more likely to remain in school. The school, however, also plays an important role. School curricula that reflect and foster middle-class values do not meet the needs of a relatively large segment of the population, with the result that adolescents from that segment tend to think of themselves as inadequate and school as irrelevant. All these factors combine and contribute to the decision of the individual to leave school. Dropping out, then, is the end point of a developmental history that includes difficulty dealing with the school curriculum, seeing opportunities in other outlets, feeling school is irrelevant, and ultimately deciding to leave school. Unfortunately, the outlook for dropouts is not very good. Their lower level of academic competencies and lack of a high school diploma leave these individuals with an uncertain occupational future and a poor outlook for advancement. Dropouts come to realize this (Tidwell, 1988), the large majority saying they would not recommend dropping out to a friend.

One may well ask what can be done to help alleviate the dropout situation. Unfortunately, it appears that current efforts are not very helpful. As you might suspect from our previous discussions, work on reducing the number of dropouts must begin at the elementary school level. The dropout has a tendency to fall behind at that level and continues to fall further behind as school progresses. In other words, dropping out is not a onetime event that occurs at a single point. As we noted, it is a developmental phenomenon involving increasing failure and alienation and decreasing self-esteem. By introducing remedial treatment early, and perhaps even altering the curriculum to reflect the needs of these students, it may be possible to keep substantial numbers of potential dropouts in school. However, simply keeping students in school is no guarantee they will learn, or profit, from their education.

Furthermore, keeping them in school may be forcing them to remain in an environment that is relatively unrewarding. Therefore, it will be necessary to program the environment in such a way as to provide the rewards necessary to maintain an appropriate level of interest in school. In all likelihood, this will have to be accomplished through curriculum revisions aimed at making education more relevant for these students. Bachman suggests that dropping out is not a problem but only a symptom of previously existing problems. In that case, we must alter the family behaviors and attitudes that are presumably at the root of these problems. Unfortunately, this is much easier said than done.

SUMMARY

Broadly speaking, schools serve two functions for the 49 million children and adolescents enrolled in them. The maintenance-actualization function aims to enrich the individual's personal life, psychological well-being, and emotional development. In general, schools do not meet this function very well. The second major goal of schools involves skills-training/cultural transmission. This function, which involves imparting information and teaching skills, is met relatively well by the public and private school system.

Schools are characterized by a middle-class orientation. Teachers and administrators largely come from middle-class backgrounds, and schools promote and teach middle-class values. Hence the school system succeeds best with students who hold these values. Those from different cultural or ethnic backgrounds may find this orientation adverse and contradictory to their heritage, and as a result may not profit as much from their school experience. Schools also have a strong social orientation. Students view the social and athletic activities of the school as the primary way to gain acceptance, leadership, and popularity. They downplay the importance of academic excellence, and relatively few wish to be remembered as outstanding students. Boys generally wish to be remembered as good athletes, and girls as being popular.

One concern that has stimulated considerable research is school size. Small schools allow a greater percentage of students to participate in various extracurricular activities. Large schools offer greater academic opportunities. In both large and small schools, participation in extracurricular activities facilitates self-concept and self-confidence development. And, in both types of schools, failure in activities chosen for participation leads to some feelings of alienation. Because smaller schools provide extracurricular opportunities for a higher percentage of students, they perform this function better than larger schools. Although larger schools offer greater curricular opportunities, the benefits to students is minimal.

A very important concern is how well schools meet their functions. This is an especially salient issue today, given the criticisms of the school system and the declining mean SAT scores of students. One way of examining this problem is to look at dropout rates. These are declining for both Black and White students, but remain very high for Hispanic students. A greater percentage of students are completing high school, and they are learning more by staying in school longer. Although there are problems with the schooling of children and adolescents, adjustments made within the schools seem to have resulted in a lowering of dropout rates.

School atmosphere, which involves the administration, the teachers, and the students and how these three groups interact, in very important to student success. When teachers are involved in decision making, committed to all students learning, and involved in helping students learn, the atmosphere is conducive to meeting the two primary functions of schools.

A variety of other factors influence school success. Parental influences are important, particularly with respect to the attitudes they espouse toward schooling. Parents who encourage academic excellence, who are not authoritarian in their child rearing practices, and who encourage autonomy and independence have children who perform better in school. Peers also exert important influences on school achievement. Adolescents who are generally liked and accepted by their peers do better. In addition, if the peer group and close friends have strong academic orientations, the individual adolescent is likely to hold a similar perspective of schooling and do better.

Another important factor is the socioeconomic background of the student. The important issue here is general home atmosphere. Students from backgrounds in which education is encouraged, in which parents provide a suitable atmosphere for learning, and in which the student is allowed to pursue education do better. Similarly, school desegregation that places minority students in schools that are more populated with middle-class students and provide a better quality of education promotes greater educational and occupatonal achievement.

Despite the general feelings about the value of schooling, some adolescents still choose to drop out of school. Few do so because they need to help support the family. In addition, most dropouts have the intellectual competence to complete a high school curriculum. These data suggest that, although some students drop out because of lack of ability, many others do so for a variety of other reasons. Many dropouts tend to be insecure and lack self-confidence. Finally, some drop out because they feel the curriculum simply is irrelevant to them. Unfortunately, at the present time, there appears to be little we can do to keep some students from dropping out of school.

GLOSSARY

cohort dropout: Proportion of a cohort, those who entered school at the same time, who drop out.

dyslexia: An impairment in reading ability often due to seeing letters upside down, rotated, or jumbled.

event dropout: Proportion of students who drop out of school in any given year.

gifted: Those adolescents who are exceptionally talented intellectually, creatively, or artistically.

learning disabled: Those adolescents who suffer from neurological damage that interferes with learning.

maintenance-actualization function: Func-

tion provided by schools to enhance students' social and emotional growth.

school atmosphere: General atmosphere pervading the school and classroom, including relations between teachers and administrators and students and teachers.

skill-straining/cultural-transmission function: Function of schools involving transmission of the skills and knowledge allowing the individual to become an economically independent and productive member of society.

status dropout: Proportion of the population who dropped out of school and are not enrolled, regardless of when they dropped out.

tracking: Placing students into different levels of classes in the same school.

DISCUSSION QUESTIONS

1. What are the major maintenance-actualization functions of schools? How well did your high school meet them?
2. Did your high school use a tracking system? What were the advantages to you? Were there any disadvantages?
3. Have you ever talked with anyone who dropped out of school? What were his or her reasons? Would the person do the same now?
4. How do small schools operate differently than large schools to perform the two major functions of schools?
5. How can schools provide for the gifted and the learning disabled? Did your school make these adaptations?
6. What are the dimensions of school atmosphere, and how can it impact on the adolescent within each of the two major functions of schools?
7. How did you deal with the transition from one school to the other? What was easy and what most difficult? Why?
8. Did you and your friends view high school as primarily a social gathering place or an institution for learning? Why might adolescents take either view?
9. What are the benefits and detriments of participation in extracurricular activities? Did you experience any of these?

10. How big a variety of elective courses did your school have? How many did you take advantage of?

11. What criticisms do adolescents generally have of their school experience? Did these apply to you? Why or why not?

12. How influential were your parents and peers in your views about school and schooling? Did the areas in which they influenced you overlap, or were they different? How does this relate to the parent versus peer influences discussed in Chapter 11?

13. What are the specific factors that connect socioeconomic status to successful school experiences?

14. What factors other than your intellectual ability influenced your school performance?

15. What teacher characteristics did you find most helpful in your schooling; which were detrimental? Why did these influence you?

13

Deviant Behavior During Adolescence

> Major Issues Addressed
>
> The Definition of Deviant Behavior
> The Incidence of Delinquent Behavior
> The Causes of Delinquent Behavior
> Adolescent Suicide
> Eating Disorders During the Adolescent Years
> Adolescent Drug Use—What and Why?
> Psychological Disorders of Adolescence
> Parental Influences on Delinquency and Other Disorders
> Medical vs. Preventive Models of Treatment

Parents worry about their adolescents for many reasons. Will they get in trouble? How do they feel about their appearance? Are they happy? Are they normal? They want to help their children, but often their help is not requested. What are they to do?

◆   ◆   ◆

Although most traverse the adolescent years in seeming quiescence, a substantial percentage do not. Some engage in one form or another of deviant behavior. For some it may be a conduct disorder, such as delinquency or running away from home. For others it may be an eating disorder. Still others may suffer from depression or another psychological disorder. And, sadly, some take their own lives. These difficulties in developmental experiences are the focus of this chapter.

INTRODUCTION

The focus of the previous chapters was on typical, or normative aspects of adolescent development. The intent was to provide information about the many facets of development experienced by most adolescents and the psychological and social processes underlying them. In a sense, we described the adolescent experience with which most adolescents are familiar. In the attempt to dispel the myths of adolescence we focused on the development of the typical adolescent.

A review of the material presented earlier demonstrates that most adolescents traverse this developmental epoch and emerge in a manner that stands them well in adulthood. Although some get pregnant, most do not. Although some drop out of school, most do not. Although some have enduring difficulties with their parents, most do not. The list could go on and on. The point is that for most adolescents the transition to adulthood has strains and stresses but is not an especially difficult time.

However, as we noted in Chapter 2, adolescence is in fact a particularly stressful period of development for some. For some, chronic difficulties are the norm in their lives. They may show an inability to cope with common stressors. They may become delinquents, drug users, runaways, or dropouts. Although the conditions leading to these outcomes likely begin in childhood, they are manifested in adolescence. In this chapter we focus on the most prevalent types of serious difficulties that occur during the adolescent years, including conduct disorders, such as delinquency and drug use, and disorders of social functioning, such as eating disorders, suicide, and mental disturbances.

One purpose here is to provide some foundations for understanding deviant behavior and its causes. Deviant behavior is not specific to the adolescent years; its causes have a foundation in childhood. A second purpose is to put aspects of deviant behavior into a perspective, notably one that demonstrates it is part of so-called normal development. Most of you reading this text have engaged in a delinquent act (have you ever stolen anything or given a friend your discount?), engaged in premarital sexual intercourse, had an argument with your parents, experienced extremely stressful events, and felt depressed. What is it that separates you from those who experience an alternative developmental track leading to one or another chronic disorder? We hope to answer that question as the chapter unfolds.

We all experiment with deviant forms of behavior; however, only for relatively few of us do these become enduring lifestyles. Along with the facts presented in the chapter we demonstrate that in some ways what we call deviant behavior is, in fact, common. In turn, we also show that for some it is a way of life. There are juvenile delinquents, those who have severe eating disorders, adolescents who are drug addicts, and many adolescents who are depressed to some degree. This does not mean these are either disorders of adolescence—they have their roots much earlier—or that they are normative. But for some they are real.

DEFINING DEVIANCY

In everyday usage, deviancy usually implies behaving in an abnormal or unacceptable way. We immediately place a value judgment, typically negative, on deviant behavior. In addition, for most of us deviancy usually refers to some aspect of social behavior. However, deviancy may be of several sorts (Box 13-1).

Intellectual deviance exists in the form of mental retardation or extremely high IQ scores; it also exists when a child is very precocious cognitively (see Chapter 4). We discussed physical growth deviance, specifically with regard to being an extremely early or extremely late maturer, in Chapter 3. Other forms of deviancy are evidenced by behaviors that are considered illegal; these may be termed *socially deviant behaviors*.

Two aspects of deviancy are illustrated by these examples. First, our general tendency to place a negative connotation on the term deviant is not justi-

BOX 13–1 The Diagnostic and Statistical Manual of Mental Disorders

Defining the symptoms of various mental disorders is perhaps even more difficult than defining deviance. Because the American Psychiatric Association recognized both the theoretical and applied/practical importance of being able to define mental disorders in an accurate, appropriate manner, the Task Force on Nomenclature and Statistics was established in 1974 to wrestle with the issues. The task force was charged with developing a set of diagnostic criteria—a glossary of terms—and a well-articulated classification scheme of mental disorders. The result of the effort is now *The Diagnostic and Statistical Manual of Mental Disorders-IV.*

Early in the planning and writing of *DSM-IV* and earlier versions, it was recognized that no simple, acceptable definition of mental disorder existed. Therefore, it was decided that behavioral descriptions of symptoms would provide the most useful guide. As a result, in *DSM-IV* mental disorders are considered to be clinical syndromes with either a painful symptom, such as distress, or as involving an interruption of normal functioning, that is, a disability or impairment.

The purpose of the *DSM-IV* is to facilitate identification and treatment of clinical disorders. In order to accomplish this goal, the task force established a reliable set of diagnostic criteria for 16 different broad categories of disorders and numerous subcategories. The use of commonly accepted and standardized criteria, and the clear definition of terms, is of benefit to patients, to those who train health-care professionals, to those who administer treatment, and to researchers.

As an example, consider the eating disorder anorexia nervosa. The defining characteristics of the disorder include a disturbance of body image, a weight loss of at least 25%, an intense fear of becoming obese, a refusal to maintain a normal body weight, and no physical illness causing the weight loss (that is, the weight loss is not a result of organic circumstances). This set of symptoms (behaviors) defines the disorder. Other constellations of symptoms define other disorders.

The task force took great care to classify disorders, not people. In *DSM-IV* people are not classified as schizophrenic or depressed; rather, a set of behavioral symptoms is identified as schizophrenia or depression. Although this is a subtle point for the layperson, it is an important one because all individuals with a similar disorder may differ in ways important for their treatment. Labeling the disorder and not the person helps maintain the individuality of the disorder that any given patient may exhibit.

---

fied. Indeed, at times there are advantages to being deviant—consider the early-maturing male we discussed in Chapter 3. The advantages of being deviant far outweigh the disadvantages in this case. Second, deviancy is defined with respect to some concept of a norm or average. The norm may be stated in terms of theoretical averages, as is the case of IQ; cultural standards, such as expressed in the legal code; or general averages, such as found in growth rates. Nonetheless, in each instance, deviance is considered within the context of a norm. An individual's behavior is considered deviant if it departs in a substantial way from the norm.

The term deviance is a normative judgment. Just as the hard-core delinquent is deviant, so too is the extremely tall person. Deviance is neither good nor bad; it is just being different. The specific form of deviance is what determines its virtue. (*Ken Karp*)

JUVENILE DELINQUENCY

Defining Delinquency

Juvenile delinquency is the term typically applied to the criminal behavior of those who are under 16 or 18 years of age, depending on state laws. Delinquency is a legal term denoting law-breaking by those who are not considered adults (G. R. Patterson, DeBaryshe, & Ramsey, 1989).

The term *juvenile delinquency* was developed to protect young offenders from being labeled criminals with police records and to allow them to be treated differently from adults by the legal system (Binder, 1988). Hence juvenile courts were established and laws were passed prohibiting the publication of juvenile offenders' names. All this was done with the hope of rehabilitating young offenders and reducing the risk of social stigma that might contribute to their becoming adult criminals.

Delinquent acts include all the crimes that apply to adults: burglary, robbery, car theft, murder, and sexual offenses. These are called **index offenses.** Delinquency also includes behaviors that if performed by adults would not be considered illegal: truancy, running away from home (Box 13-2), and violating a curfew. These are called **status offenses.** Because laws about these offenses vary from state to state, what is delinquent in one community may not be considered delinquent in another. Similarly, some communities enforce the laws more vigorously than others. Finally, many juvenile delinquent acts are never discovered, or illegal acts are not known to be done by delinquents. For all these reasons, official statistics on delinquency are likely underestimates of its occurrence.

BOX 13-2   Running Away: Its Causes and Consequences

Despite the attention in the popular press and the other media, surprisingly little research has been directed at understanding the causes and consequences of running away, and even less has been done on the utility of possible intervention strategies (Cairns, 1989). Although the precise definition of running away has been the subject of some debate, it generally involves three factors: age (under the age of majority), being absent without the consent of the parent or guardian, and the amount of time one is away. It is the latter that has led to debate, the upshot of which is that being away for more than 24 hours or overnight is the criterion (Young, Godfrey, Matthews, & Adams, 1983).

Each year over 700,000 adolescents run away from home. About 60% are females, and they stay away from home longer than males do (Cairns, 1989). About twice as many boys think about running away as do it; about as many girls run away as think about doing it. The most common reason for running away is to get out of an undesirable home situation, often characterized by arguing with parents over friends or school problems, fear of being punished or abused, and poor communication (Young et al., 1983). Some runaways may better be characterized as "throwaways"—they are asked to leave by their parents or guardian or have been abandoned. Poor school performance may cause some adolescents, es-

pecially males, to run, although it may simply reflect an inability to cope with a poor home life (Young et al., 1983). Finally, having delinquent peers may contribute to running away.

Runaways are at a high risk for many problem behaviors (Rosario & Rotheram-Borus, 1993; Young et al., 1983). Runaways are at increased risk for alcohol and drug use, particularly males, and increased emotional distress, especially females. About a third report having attempted suicide at one time or another. Both male and female runaways report increased sexual behavior with multiple partners, which enhances risks of contracting sexually transmitted diseases, and many female runaways become prostitutes. Finally, upon returning home runaways generally do not find a better home environment. Many parents severely discipline the returned runaway, and if a reconciliation is reached it often is very strained and tense, which may increase the predisposition to run away again.

The causes and consequences of running away are similar to those involved in other disorders. A key to understanding adolescent conduct disorders in general is examining the home environment. Poor relations with parents—however that may be defined by the adolescent—is a risk factor that predisposes the adolescent to engage in risky behavior.

Incidence of Juvenile Delinquency

Studying the incidence of juvenile delinquency is difficult because most of the information comes from recorded incidences of delinquency as opposed to actual rates of occurrence, which may be much higher (M. Gold & Petronio, 1980). Moreover, there are multiple measures of incidence—**adjudicated** cases, number of arrests, the percentage of adolescents who engage in delinquency, types of crimes committed, and self-reports of delinquency.

Despite the difficulties caused by these vagaries, it is clear the incidence of juvenile delinquency increased into the mid-1970s. It then leveled off and began to decrease. The increase in delinquency occurred at a greater rate than the increase in the juvenile population. Hence, not only was there more delinquency, but apparently more adolescents were engaging in delinquency and were doing so at higher rates than previously.

The percentage of persons arrested who were under age 18 is shown in Table 13-1. Since 1974 this percentage has progressively declined, and the de-

One measure of delinquency rate is adjudication—bringing a minor before a judge. This measure likely underestimates delinquency rates because much delinquency is never reported. (*Eugene Gordon*)

Table 13–1 Percentage of Those Arrested Who Were Under Age 18, by Year

1974	1976	1978	1980	1982	1990
27.2	24.9	23.3	20.9	17.9	15.6

Source: Adapted from U.S. Bureau of the Census (1989 & 1992C). *Statistical abstract of the United States: 1989 & 1992.* Washington, DC: U.S. Government Printing Office.

cline applies to both males and females for both serious crimes (e.g., murder, forcible rape) and nonserious crimes (e.g., vandalism, running away from home). Despite the decline in the percentage of arrestees who were juveniles, the number of cases disposed by juvenile courts (Table 13-2) and the number of juveniles residing in various facilities (Table 13-3) generally has been increasing. So, too, has the cost of keeping these juveniles in various facilities; in 1989 it cost about $2.86 billion.

Gender Differences in Juvenile Delinquency

As you can see in Table 13-3, more males than females reside in facilities for juveniles. This reflects the general finding that males engage in more delinquency than females, even when self-report data, which likely are more accurate than arrest records, are used to make the comparison (Huizinga & Elliott, 1987; Yoshikawa, 1994). It also is a result of differences in the types of delinquent behaviors done by males and females. Females are much more likely to engage in status offenses, whereas males are much more likely to engage in criminal behavior, such as theft and robbery. As a result, males are more likely than females to be incarcerated.

Table 13–2 Delinquency Cases Disposed by Juvenile Courts

REASON FOR REFERRAL	YEAR			
	1983	1985	1987	1989
ALL DELINQUENCY OFFENSES	1,030	1,112	1,145	1,189
Violent offenses	55	67	65	77
Criminal homocide	1	1	2	2
Forcible rape	3	4	4	4
Robbery	24	26	22	23
Aggravated assault	27	36	38	48
Property offenses	451	489	500	514
Burglary	145	139	134	131
Larceny	270	307	313	309
Motor vehicle theft	31	36	48	67
Arson	5	7	6	7
Delinquency offenses	524	555	580	599
Simple assault	81	92	100	108
Vandalism	64	84	84	83
Drug law violations	57	76	73	78
Obstruction of justice	55	68	79	82
Other	268	235	245	248

Source: U.S. Bureau of the Census (1992c). Note: The number of cases is in thousands. The Other category includes stolen property, trespassing, weapons offenses, other sex offenses, liquor law violations, disorderly conduct, and others.

Table 13–3   Juveniles Held in Custody in Detention Centers, Shelters, Training
Schools, and Other Placements

	YEAR		
	1985	1987	1989
Total	83,402	91,648	93,945
Male	66,393	72,611	76,045
Female	17,009	19,035	17,900
White	53,968	57,942	56,401
Black	27,473	31,414	35,079
Per resident cost (in $1,000)	24.75	27.4	30.45

Source: U.S. Bureau of the Census (1992c).

Social Class and Delinquency

In general, official rates of delinquency are higher for lower socioeconomic status adolescents than for those from the middle classes (M. Gold & Petronio, 1980; Mc-Cord, 1990), partly because lower-class adolescents are more likely to get caught and prosecuted (see M. Gold & Petronio, 1980). Some researchers (Braithwaite, 1981; Elliott & Ageton, 1980) also suggest that social-class differences reflect inaccuracies in reporting of juvenile delinquency data. They note that when self-report data are used there are virtually no social-class differences in delinquency.

A most carefully conducted study of self-reported delinquency was done by Elliott and Ageton (1980). They surveyed 1,726 adolescents aged 11 to 17. The sample was a representative national probability sample composed of proportionate numbers of males and females, Blacks and Whites, and social-class levels. The interview contained 47 items assessing a variety of categories of criminal behavior (e.g., crimes against people, hard drug use, crimes against property). The respondents indicated how many times during the past year they had committed each of the behaviors and, if more than 10, the frequency (once a week, once a month, etc.). All respondents were assured of confidentiality and protection from legal subpoena by the U.S. Department of Health, Education, and Welfare.

The findings indicated social-class differences in delinquency for crimes against people (sexual assault, aggravated assault robbery); there were no differences for the other categories. Lower-class adolescents engaged in over 3.5 times the crimes against people as did middle-class adolescents, but only at the extreme level of delinquency. For those who reported engaging in low levels of delinquency there was no difference between the social classes. Because the odds of getting caught and prosecuted are higher for those who engage in more delinquency, these data are consistent with official statistics, such as arrest records, showing social-class differences in delinquency.

Ethnicity and Delinquency

The available evidence indicates that once social class is taken into account, racial differences in levels of delinquency are very small (Henggeler, 1989; Krisberg et al., 1987). In addition, Krisberg et al. report no substantial racial differences in repeat offenders, those whose life is built around engaging in delinquent or criminal behavior. Yet minority adolescents are more likely to be arrested for both minor and serious crimes and to be incarcerated in one or another type of facility than White adolescents engaging in the same offenses.

Clearly, these data support the contention that there is a racial bias in the justice system. They also are consistent with the information relating social class to delinquency because a higher proportion of minority than White youth live in poverty conditions and areas with higher concentrations of police. These seem to be the keys to understanding ethnic group differences in official statistics showing differences between minority and majority youth because the reports of the youth themselves do not show substantial differences in engaging in delinquency—including engaging in violent crimes.

Developmental Trends in Delinquency

There are developmental trends in delinquency. M. Gold and Reimer (1975) collected self-report data from a representative sample of 1,395 adolescents aged 11 to 18. For both males and females, frequency of nontrivial delinquent acts increased from age 11 to age 18. For boys, the increase was from 2.25 to 10.5; for girls it was from 1.25 to 6.5. In each case, there was an approximate fivefold increase. Males showed an increase in serious crimes from age 11 (2.25) to age 15 (8.25), after which there was little change. Incidence of serious crimes by females remained relatively low (1 to 2) at all age levels.

Other data (see O'Malley, Bachman, & Johnston, 1977) demonstrate that relatively serious crimes against people and property decline from age 16 to age 18, but rise again at age 19 before declining into early adulthood (age 23). The general trend is for delinquent behaviors to be associated most strongly with the mid-adolescent years, especially about age 15, and to decline thereafter, although it is unclear it reaches zero for any representative group thus far tested.

Stattin and Magnusson (1993) examined age of onset of delinquency and subsequent delinquent and adult criminal behavior in a sample of Swedish boys studied from age 10 into adulthood (age 30). They reported that those with the earliest age (up to age 14) of onset of delinquency (as measured by official records) accounted for 59% of delinquent acts up to age 14, 63% of adolescent (ages 15–20) delinquency, and 62% of adult (ages 21–29) criminal behavior. In other words, the vast majority of delinquent and adult criminal behavior is accounted for by a very small percentage of youth who engage in antisocial behavior early and continue to do so. These boys did less well in school, did not get along well with their peers, lacked motivation and interest in school, and engaged in more antisocial behavior than boys not engaging in delinquent behavior. In contrast, those boys who initiated delinquency during adolescence were popular with their school peers, although they also were not particularly good students. The researchers suggest that different developmental experiences are important in determining different groups of delinquents. Poor home environment, inadequate parental monitoring, and a history of antisocial behavior characterizes the early delinquent. This developmental history seems to breed individuals who generally are antisocial. They might be labeled "aggressive" delinquents. Those who initiate delinquency later seem more to be those who associate with peers who endorse norm breaking. They were more peer than parent oriented and were more likely to belong to gangs. They might be labeled "socialized" delinquents.

The Causes of Delinquency

There is no simple way to determine the causes of delinquency; many factors determine whether or not a given adolescent will engage in delinquent behavior. For any single causal factor, one can find some adolescents who possess that characteristic and who are delinquent and others who possess it and are not. Delinquency is caused by *multiple determinants*.

The Peer Group and Delinquency.   Studies of peer group effects on delinquency have centered on the adolescent's susceptibility to peer pressure, which is one way adolescents are socialized into delinquent behavior (G. R. Patterson et al., 1989). Fear of being rejected by peers—an indirect peer group influence—is related to alcohol and drug use but direct social pressure is much less important.

The role of peers in adolescent delinquency cannot be considered outside the role of parental rearing techniques (Dishion, Patterson, Stoolmiller, & Skinner, 1991). Early harsh discipline is related to greater susceptibility to peer pressure (Chapter 10) and to the development of an aggressive interpersonal interaction style that can lead to peer rejection (Chapter 11). The child and

Engaging in delinquent behavior can improve self-esteem for those who have very low self-esteem, but only temporarily. (*Julie Markes/AP/Wide World Photos*)

adolescent may have little choice of friendships outside those who also are equally disliked and prone to aggressive behavior. It is not surprising to find that adolescents whose friends are delinquent are more likely to be delinquent themselves (M. Gold & Petronio, 1980).

Do strong peer relationships lead to delinquency, or vice versa? Does associating with delinquents cause one to become delinquent, or do delinquents seek out each other for companionship? Perhaps each direction is true to some degree, as we suggested earlier. Developing friendships with others who come from equally undesirable homes may be reinforcing and may lead to delinquency. In turn, being a delinquent may cause one to seek out other delinquents for companionship.

Child Rearing and Delinquency. Delinquents describe their parents' disciplinary techniques as erratic, overly strict, and involving both physical punishment and a high degree of hostility (G. R. Patterson et al., 1989). The home atmosphere of delinquents is characterized by a greater degree of parental rejection and a lower degree of cohesiveness than that of nondelinquents. It is not surprising that parents of delinquents have minimal aspirations for their offspring. They also express little interest in their child's school performance and may have a host of personality and adjustment problems of their own (G. R. Patterson et al., 1989).

Paternal absence is one aspect of the father–son relationship that is related to delinquency (Farnworth, 1984; Kopera-Frye, Ager, Saltz, Poindexter, & Lee, 1993). Paternal absence may produce an overcompensating masculine personality in the adolescent male, particularly if the father leaves home before the child is about 5 years of age (Lynn & Saurey, 1959). In addition, paternal absence is related to recidivism rates for males. Kelly and Baer (1969) reported recidivism rates for juvenile delinquents whose fathers were in the home as well as for a group coming from mother-only homes. The recidivism rate was 12% for those adolescents coming from intact homes. Among those coming from nonintact homes, however, the recidivism rate was 39% if the father left home before the child was 7 years old but dropped to 10% if the father left after the child was 7. As we noted earlier, the effects of a one-parent home are most dramatic if the father leaves when the child is very young.

The critical feature of paternal absence is its relation to maternal parenting skills and family functioning, as we pointed out in Chapter 10. Following divorce, for example, parenting skills of both the custodial parent and noncustodial parent decline. Disruptions in home atmosphere and routine and in monitoring of the adolescent's behavior can lead the adolescent to engage in problem behavior and make him or her more vulnerable to engaging in delinquent acts (G. R. Patterson et al., 1989), particularly if the child is young when the father leaves. It is well documented that the younger the child is when first arrested, the greater the recidivism rate. These "early starters" average about twice the convictions as those who are "late starters," perhaps because the late starters have had a longer period of more adequate child rearing and a happier home life that teaches the importance of prosocial behavior.

Recent research on parental influences on delinquency has taken a systematic approach to analyzing family interaction patterns that may predispose the child toward antisocial behavior in general (G. R. Patterson et al., 1989; Yoshikawa, 1994). As we already noted, delinquents describe their family atmosphere as harsh, with the parents having little positive involvement with them. In addition, the parents do not monitor the child's behavior or supervise youngsters' activities (Forgatch, DeGarmo, & Knutson, 1994; Forgatch & Stoolmiller, 1994). The interaction between parent and child is one of continually intensifying coercion, which may result in the child employing antisocial behaviors to escape unpleasant interactions with family members. When successful, the coercive means of controlling social interactions through antisocial behavior is reinforced. G. R. Patterson and colleagues (1989) suggest that parents teach their children to behave in antisocial ways in social interactions; they train their children for deviant behavior. This is often accompanied by little training for prosocial behavior, the child's positive social behaviors often being ignored or responded to inappropriately. In addition, children in homes such as these often do not learn proper social skills—they don't know the right way to behave in a variety of social situations.

Other evidence suggests that delinquents perceive and define social situations differently from nondelinquents (see M. Lee & Prentice, 1988; Slaby & Guerra, 1988). Compared to nondelinquents, delinquents have relatively immature role-taking and moral-reasoning ability. They define social problems in hostile ways and see few consequences for behaving aggressively. Moreover, they believe aggression is a legitimate means for dealing with social problems and do not see suffering to others resulting from their actions. It seems reasonable to presume this is the result of a long developmental history of learning poor interpersonal skills as a result of poor family interactions. A significant component of this learning may involve peer interactions. Bank, Reid, and Greenley (1994) provide evidence that "practicing" negative interpersonal interactions with siblings predicted not only adult arrests but also hostility toward women, perhaps because the opportunities to do so lead to a lowered concern for victims. Finally, some evidence (Feldman & Weinberger, 1994) of parenting practices that do not promote internalization of self-regulatory skills (in general, considering the consequences of one's actions) are related to elevated levels of delinquency. The authors suggest parenting practices result in personality characteristics. Those who are better able to monitor the consequences of their behavior, a personality characteristic, are less likely to engage in delinquency.

The chain of events leading to delinquency is illustrated in Figure 13–1. As you can see, the key is the nature of parental child rearing and the home environment, including parent–child interactions. And the process begins with the home environment of the parents when they were themselves children.

Figure 13–1 The Roots and Consequences of Antisocial and Delinquent Behavior

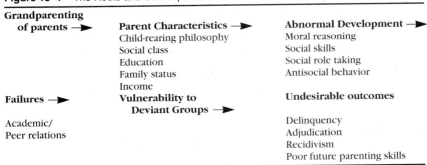

Grandparenting of parents ➤	Parent Characteristics ➤	Abnormal Development ➤
	Child-rearing philosophy	Moral reasoning
	Social class	Social skills
	Education	Social role taking
	Family status	Antisocial behavior
	Income	
Failures ➤	Vulnerability to Deviant Groups ➤	Undesirable outcomes
Academic/ Peer relations		Delinquency
		Adjudication
		Recidivism
		Poor future parenting skills

Correlates of Delinquency

Because juvenile delinquency is a form of deviancy one would expect that a number of aspects of the behavior as well as personality formation of juvenile delinquents will be different from those of adolescents who are not delinquent.

Self-Esteem and Delinquency. Generally speaking, delinquents have poor self-esteem (Bynner et al., 1981). They view themselves negatively and feel undesirable. They have little self-respect and place little value on their own contributions to society. In general, they feel society views them in this way. Thus self-esteem of delinquent adolescents may be characterized as uncertain, confused, and quite variable. This contrasts sharply with the self-concepts of nondelinquent adolescents, who have positive and much more stable self-views.

Some evidence indicates that delinquents may enhance their self-esteem by engaging in delinquent behavior (Wells, 1989). Those who engage in serious crimes, and those with the lowest self-esteem initially, enhance self-esteem by behaving in a delinquent manner. For those who engage in nonserious crimes or who do not have very low self-esteem, engaging in delinquent acts does not enhance self-esteem. Self-esteem enhancement through delinquency is limited to those delinquents with pathologically poor self-esteem.

Personality Correlates. Researchers have compared a number of personality characteristics of delinquents and nondelinquents in an attempt to elucidate the personal consequences of delinquency. Although no single personality type can be associated with delinquency, delinquents tend to be defiant, resentful, hostile, and lacking in self-control. They also lean toward an external locus of control (Parrott & Strongman, 1984), which leads them into feeling they are at the mercy of forces outside their sphere of influence.

Moral development is another area of psychological functioning in which delinquents and nondelinquents have been compared. Generally speaking, delinquents score lower than nondelinquents on tests of moral development (M. Lee & Prentice, 1988; Slaby & Guerra, 1988). Delinquent boys apparently see the world as an amoral jungle in which everyone is a potential victim, and they seem to feel they must grab whatever they can before someone else gets it or gets them. In addition, they express little guilt over what they have done because they feel that people deserve what they get. Juvenile delinquents lack inner controls or a highly developed superego, and have their behaviors guided more by social or external controls (Slaby & Guerra, 1988) than by more generally accepted principles for appropriate interpersonal interaction.

The complexity of the relation between personality factors and delinquency was shown in a study by Feldman and Weinberger (1994). They studied boys' self-restraint (the ability to inhibit immediate behavior in the interest of achieving long-term goals) as a result of parental rearing practices and a precursor of delinquent behavior. Parental rearing practices during preadolescence were related to boys' restraint: Child-centered, consistent, nonabusive rearing practices were related to increased self-restraint. Preadolescent self-restraint was related positively to restraint 4 years later. The latter measure of restraint related negatively to the amount of delinquency in which the boys engaged at that time. The role of parenting practices in delinquency, discussed earlier, may be indirect, the relation being mediated by the impact of parenting practices on personality development. As Feldman and Weinberger note, then, what the parents do early in the child's life may be more important than what they do when the child begins to get into trouble.

Delinquency and School Performance.   As assessed both by teacher ratings and by achievement measures (G. R. Patterson et al., 1989; Yoshikawa, 1994), juvenile delinquents perform poorly in school. Some have suggested that doing poorly in school is a cause of delinquency because the adolescent then drops out of school and takes up delinquent behaviors. Alternatively, G. R. Patterson and colleagues (1989) suggest it is the child's learning of antisocial behavior and difficulty with following rules and dealing with authority that results in poor school performance. Antisocial children have poor attentional skills and, perhaps because of poor monitoring by the parents, do not complete homework assignments. They lack those basic skills necessary to compete successfully in an academic environment. For example, McGee, Williams, Share, Anderson, and Silva (1986) reported that specific reading disability predicted parent- and teacher-assessed boys' behavior problems from ages 5 to 11 in a New Zealand study.

Prevention and Treatment

The data presented here are rather depressing. First, the crimes of the delinquent are often serious. Assault, theft, vandalism, and the time consumed in dealing with such problems all represent losses of human and material resources. But most important is the loss of thousands of young people who might have made substantial contributions to the growth and development of the social order. The delinquent adolescent, especially if put away in an institution, is probably lost forever. Unfortunately, the incarceration of delinquents has done little to lower delinquency rates (note the recidivism rates discussed earlier). Adolescents themselves believe that frustrating experiences with their parents, poor home atmospheres, and boredom are the major contributors to delinquent behavior, and it is these factors that must be changed if their lives are going to change.

Treatment for juvenile delinquents has typically fallen into two categories: psychoanalytic and related kinds of therapy and behavior modification programs. Therapy is viewed as a way to help individual adolescents deal with the specific problems confronting them. For example, teaching acceptance of responsibility and self-monitoring might be necessary for some delinquents; teaching higher levels of moral thinking and the building of a strong superego might be necessary for others. In addition, different forms of treatment are very likely necessary to deal with individuals with different personalities or with differing needs (McCord, 1990). Although these arguments appear rational and reasonable, the success of various therapeutic programs has not been very great. There is evidence (G. R. Patterson et al. 1989) that adolescents in therapy have lower recidivism rates, but when the therapy sessions are stopped, recidivism rates increase. Hence therapy helps reduce delinquent behaviors, but only for a short time after it is completed. Permanent changes in behavior are much more difficult to obtain. At present, there is no especially successful treatment that reduces recidivism more than any other kind (McCord, 1990; Whitehead & Lab, 1989).

As we note in Box 13–3, the traditional method of treating delinquency and other behavioral and social problems has been to wait until they occur and then treat the symptoms—the undesirable behaviors. An alternative to this approach is a preventative model. As applied to delinquency, G. R. Patterson and others (1989) note that a key is to teach parents better family management techniques that will help the child and adolescent learn more socially appropriate behaviors. When this type of intervention is done with preadolescents it has proved successful in reducing antisocial and delinquent behavior. In addition, teaching the child sound academic and social relationship skills is beneficial. Patterson and colleagues now believe we are able to identify children at risk for antisocial behavior sufficiently early in the school years to institute intervention techniques aimed at preventing delinquency.

In a similar vein, Yoshikawa (1994) has noted that some programs focused on the multiple risk factors related to delinquency have proven to be effective in preventing delinquency. Programs focused on early intervention and not only on the child but the parent and family unit as well have been shown to influence multiple outcomes in a variety of settings. Providing emotional and informational support to parents, including the teaching of parenting skills and values clarification, and early educational interventions with children at risk seems to reduce the likelihood the child will become chronically delinquent.

BOX 13–3   Treatment vs. Prevention of Behavioral
           and Psychological Disorders

The way we deal with behavioral and psychological disorders is to treat them after the fact. In other words, when a behavioral or psychological problem is evidenced by certain symptoms, we identify the nature of the disorder and then prescribe some means of treatment aimed at reducing the symptoms. When the symptoms disappear we presume the problem is gone. Rarely do we go to the causes of the symptoms and alter the situation. Moreover, we do not engage in preventative care, dealing with the underlying causes of the problem before the problem emerges.

This way of dealing with psychological disorders is based on the medical model of treatment for physical disorders: The patient exhibits certain symptoms that lead to a diagnosis which results in some form of treatment for the symptoms. Consider the following example:

Antecedents	Symptoms	Treatment
In the rain	Sniffles	Rest
Get wet	Cough	Aspirin
Cold	Sore throat	Decongestant
Exposure to someone with the flu	Aches and pains	Take liquids

Certain antecedent conditions lead to specific symptoms calling for a standard treatment. The person has contracted a cold or the flu and takes drugs and other treatment that basically alleviate the symptoms until they are gone. None of the treatment is aimed at altering the antecedent conditions. Admittedly, this is an oversimplified example, but it represents the typical means of dealing with common medical disorders.

We treat psychological disorders in much the same manner. Consider the following example for delinquency:

Antecedents	Symptoms	Treatment
Poor family relations	Learned antisocial behavior	Incarceration
Academic failure	Aggressiveness	Work program
Poor self-esteem	Gang membership	Therapy

Again, albeit a simplified version of the material presented in the text, the example makes the point that we deal with the symptoms rather than the causes of psychological problems. Hence when the individual reenters the environment that caused the problem, the treatment's successful effects are eroded, just as reinstituting contact with those with the flu can cause a recurrence of respiratory symptoms.

An alternative model focuses on prevention rather than treatment. In the field of medicine preventative care is popular and the public is encouraged to use it. Maintaining a diet low in fat, not smoking, not drinking if one is pregnant, and similar health measures are examples of preventative medicine aimed at lowering cholesterol, reducing the risk of lung cancer and heart disease, and improving the prenatal environment. The intent is to eliminate the antecedents of disease.

G. R. Patterson et al. (1989) suggest that preventative measures might be used to help children at risk for delinquency. Such measures would include forms of parental training with regard to child management, teaching children appropriate social relationship and academic skills, and teaching the parent about childrearing techniques. By making the early home atmosphere conducive to proper prosocial development, it may be possible to reduce delinquency and criminal activity when the adolescent becomes an adult.

EATING DISORDERS

Three eating disorders are of concern in discussions of adolescent health: obesity, anorexia nervosa, and bulimia. Obesity may begin during childhood; anorexia nervosa and bulimia generally begin during the adolescent years. Each has serious health risks associated with it.

Obesity

Maintenance of normal body weight for the adolescent's height and bone structure is very difficult for some. During the growth spurt years there is a reduction in **basal metabolism rate**, the minimum number of calories burned in a resting state. Adolescents who continue to take in large amounts of calories (needed caloric intake decreases during the later adolescent years) and who do not exercise more in order to compensate may become **obese.** Approximately 10% to 15% of all adolescents are truly obese as defined by skin fold measures of the fat layer underneath the skin (subcutaneous fat) measured by calipers applied to the triceps, the muscle on the underside of the upper arm. More gener-

Obesity is not necessarily related to poor eating habits, but it may be related to biological conditions.
(*Esaias Baitel/Photo Researchers, Inc.*)

ally, obesity is defined as weighing 20% or more over recommended body weight for one's age, gender, and height.

Obesity is classified into two types. Simple, or exogenous, obesity is due to eating too much food, getting too little exercise, or both. Endocrine, or endogenous, obesity is due to irregularities of glandular secretions, such as in diabetes. Both these forms of obesity show similar symptoms, including excessive perspiration, irritation of the skin, joint discomforts, menstrual disorders, and reduced physical ability.

Obesity is more prevalent in girls than in boys, probably because boys are generally more active than girls. In addition, the increased estrogen output of puberty fosters an increase in the size rather than the number of fat cells. This makes a transient plumpness an invariable part of adolescence for adolescent girls as well as boys. Obesity in adolescence presents current and future problems for the obese individuals. It can affect social relationships, school performance, and emotional adjustment in such diverse areas as dependency and sex identification.

Obesity entails future health hazards. It is related to cardiovascular disease, hypertension, joint disease, and gynecological disorders. Even during adolescence, a certain amount of abnormality exists in obese youngsters in terms of timing of growth. They are taller and their skeletal development and urinary steroid output corresponds to those a year or so older. In other words, obese children tend to demonstrate an accelerated growth trend over their normal weight peers. Obesity tends to be chronic—most obese adolescents become obese adults. If an individual has not reduced his or her weight to the norm by the end of adolescence the odds are 28 to 1 against that individual's *ever* attaining a normal adult weight (L. H. Epstein, 1987).

The roots of obesity are complex and may include both biological and psychological factors. It is the latter that present the greatest problem for treatment. The specific problem seems to be the obese adolescent's view that his or her life is directed by others, perhaps through extreme dependence on parents. As a result, they feel they do not or cannot control their own eating urges. Although behavioral training, such as teaching eating patterns, can be effective in altering eating behavior (L. H. Epstein, 1987), the long-term prognosis is not good until the individual is brought to realize his or her own competency and separateness as a human being and develops a self-directed view of life. Hence treatment of obesity involves both alteration of eating patterns and the alleviation of psychological symptoms.

Anorexia Nervosa

Anorexia nervosa is characterized by a relentless pursuit of a thin body despite hunger, help from others, and threat of starvation (Halmi, 1987). The defining criteria are: A weight loss of 15% or more, or for those who are still growing, a weight of 85% or less of that expected for the person's age, gender, and height; an intense fear of gaining weight or getting fat; a disturbed body image; in females, missing three consecutive menstrual cycles (amenorrhea).

Most anorexics are females (90% to 95%), come from the upper-middle and upper social classes, and are highly preoccupied with thoughts of food (Howat & Saxton, 1988). Available evidence suggests that anorexics tend to be rather model children and adolescents, experiencing few if any developmental difficulties. Although in the past anorexia could lead to death due to starvation (in about 10% of anorexics), that is rare today.

Examination of the family background and precipitating conditions of anorexics leads to some similarities with the obese individual (see Hood, Moore, & Garner, 1982). Parents of anorexics often do not allow the development of independence and a sense of self-determined identity. Rather, they try to control the adolescent's life and encourage dependence, both of the adolescent on them and of them on the adolescent. As a result, the adolescent prone to become anorexic, like the obese adolescent, comes to feel that outside forces are in control of his or her life.

Anorexics also have a disturbed body image. They tend to overestimate

Anorexics have a poor body image and see themselves as fat even when they are severely underweight. (*Susan Rosenberg/Science Photo Library/Photo Researchers, Inc.*)

body size and individual body parts. They see themselves as fat even when they are nearly emaciated. They tend to deny, or not recognize, hunger pangs, and feel full after very meager meals. As a result, they keep dieting, inducing vomiting, and engaging in other attempts to lose yet more weight (Koff & Rierdan, 1993; Striegel-Moore, Schrieber, Pike, Vilfley, & Rodin, in press).

The syndrome may have roots in an inability, or unwillingness, to grow up. The extreme dependence sought by the parents, and especially the mother, may get transmitted into an inability to handle sexual maturity, a fear of becoming independent, just generally growing up. Some have interpreted anorexia as an attempt to reverse the growth process.

Because of the physical as well as psychological factors involved in anorexia, treatment is two-pronged. One aspect is aimed at coping with the physical stress on the individual. Dealing with the physical consequences helps ensure survival. Behavior modification programs aimed at increasing food intake have proven somewhat useful (Halmi, 1987). The second aspect of treatment focuses on the psychological causes underlying the anorexia. This includes developing a personality that feels in control, a strong self-concept, appropriate relationships with family members, who may also be involved in treatment, and a sense of being able to take responsibility for one's life. About two-thirds of anorexics get better or are cured; the remaining one-third remain chronically ill (Coupey, 1992).

Bulimia

Bulimia is characterized by periods of binge eating—eating as much as 4,800 calories in one sitting, mostly in the form of sweets—and purging, through self-induced vomiting, the use of laxatives, or both (American Psychiatric Association, 1987).

Bulimics are nearly exclusively females (99%), many of whom have difficulty relating to, and communicating with, their mothers. For most, binge eating begins at about 18 years of age. Because most bulimics have had some college, which begins at about 18, it has been speculated that one factor in bulimia is a lack of ability to adapt to living away from home.

Johnson, Lewis, Love, and Stuckey (1984) surveyed 1,268 high school females and found that nearly 5% met the criteria for bulimia. Other estimates of incidence put it at between 3% and 9% (Halmi, 1987). Some interesting contrasts between the bulimic and nonbulimic women were observed. Even though the weight of the two groups was equal, the bulimics were prone to view themselves as overweight. They also showed less satisfaction with their body image and were more frequent dieters. Sixty-eight percent of the bulimics but only 35% of the nonbulimics were on diets.

Aside from the demographic characteristics of bulimics, little is known of the nature of the disorder. Treatment involves therapy and behavior modification (Agras, Schneider, Arnow, Raeburn, & Telch, 1989), and is about 50% successful.

SUICIDE

Suicide is the taking of one's own life. One of the more difficult issues involved is identifying it when no objective evidence of suicide (such as a note) is present. Failure to report a death as a suicide also can occur because of religious reasons, economic concerns due to life insurance policy exemption clauses for suicide, and sensitivity to the impact of suicide on the family. For these and other reasons, estimates of the number of adolescent suicides vary widely. The numbers and percentages reported here come from those reported in U.S. government publications, and likely are on the conservative side. Regardless of the reporting criteria used, however, it is clear that in the past three to four decades the incidence of adolescent suicide has been on the rise, which has caused increased and justified concern.

Incidence of Suicide

In absolute terms, adolescent suicide does not account for a large number of deaths; about 2,300 people under age 19 committed suicide in 1988 (Garland & Zigler, 1993). However, it is the second leading cause of death among adolescents, outranked only by deaths due to accidents (except for African American males whose primary cause of death is homocide). Although adolescents account for only about 7% of suicides, they account for about 12% of attempts; between 6% and 13% of adolescents report they have attempted suicide.

In general, suicide is the fifth leading cause of death for those under age 15 (accidents, heart disease, cancer, and pneumonia head the list) and the second leading cause of death for those ages 15 to 24 (accidents are first). The most recently available prevalence rates for the adolescent years are presented in Table 13-4. Regardless of gender or ethnic group there was nearly a doubling of the

Suicide, the second leading cause of death among adolescents, claims about 5,000 young people each year. (*George Rizer/AP/Wide World Photos*)

Table 13–4   Rate of Suicide per 100,000 for Early and Late Adolescents,
Males and Females, and Black and White Adolescents, 1970–1989

	YEAR		
Group	1970	1980	1989
All			
Age 10-14	0.6	0.8	1.4
Age 15-19	5.9	8.5	11.3
White males			
Age 10-14	1.1	1.4	2.2
Age 15-19	9.4	15.0	19.4
Black males			
Age 10-14	0.3	0.5	1.7
Age 15-19	4.7	5.6	10.3
White females			
Age 10-14	0.3	0.3	0.7
Age 15-19	2.9	3.3	4.5
Black females			
Age 10-14	0.4	0.1	NA
Age 15-19	2.9	1.6	2.3

Source: U.S. Bureau of the Census (1992c). NA = not available.

rate from 1970 to 1989 for both males and females. The suicide rate among Native Americans is higher than that of any other ethnic group, as high as 43 per 100,000 in some Apache groups. Garland and Zigler report that the suicide rate of incarcerated youth may be as high as 2,041 per 100,000.

Classifying attempted suicide is an even bigger challenge than confirming a suicide has occurred. Ratios of attempted to successful suicides range from 50 to 1 to 200 to 1 (Garland & Zigler, 1993). Females attempt suicide at higher rates than males; males succeed at higher rates than females, largely because males are much more likely than females to use aggressive and violent means (stabbing, hanging, and shooting) to take their lives. Females are more likely than males to use passive means to commit suicide: poisons, drugs, or gassing. These less violent means leave more time for medical intervention and treatment, thereby lowering the likelihood of success. For both sexes, however, the use of violent means of attempting suicide is more likely to result in a successful attempt.

In addition to suicide and suicide attempts, researchers have studied **suicide ideation,** which means thinking about committing suicide. Research shows suicide ideation is a common event among adolescents, with nearly two-thirds of high school students and over half of college students reporting they had thought about committing suicide (Garland & Zigler, 1993). Feelings of self-derogation (feeling useless, no good, and a failure), feeling parents are not particularly accepting (believing they don't enjoy doing things with you, not being very praising, not giving much care and attention), and viewing the parents as psychologically controlling (being strict, using guilt) are associated with increased suicidal ideation (Shagle & Barber, 1994).

Warning Signs and What to Do

Adolescents may exhibit a number of warning signs indicating they are contemplating suicide (Blumenthal & Kupfer, 1988). Some of these are listed in Table 13-5. Although any of us might evidence some of these symptoms, such as sleep disturbances or eating problems, adolescents who are vulnerable to attempting suicide will generally show more than one or two at a time, and the intensity and duration of the symptoms will be greater.

At one time or another many adolescents come into contact with others who are contemplating suicide, and they often are at a loss about what to do. The first rule is to take seriously any comment the person might make about committing suicide. Calling a suicide hot line or obtaining some other form of help such as calling 911 is important. If the person has a means and method in mind it is vital to try to get him or her help and to stay until help is obtained. Often the initial crisis can be reduced by talking seriously with the person and by avoiding empty assurances such as "things can't be that bad" or "everything will be all right." Finally, it is important to realize that unless you have had specific crisis intervention training, you should not attempt to deal with the situation by yourself. Even if you manage to help your friend over the initial hump, you should report the incident to a responsible person who can then see to follow-up measures. In this instance, breaking a confidence is justified.

The Causes of Suicide

Two components are important in discussions of the causes of suicide. One involves identifying the precipitating event that caused the individual to attempt suicide. What finally led the person to attempt to take his or her own life? The second involves identifying the conditions that predisposed the individual to develop a suicidal orientation. In this regard, researchers have examined child-rearing practices, the relation of suicide to psychological disorders such as depression, and the development of coping skills.

Precipitating Events.   In general, precipitating events cause shame or humiliation that is "the last straw" (Garland & Zigler, 1993). High on the list is breaking

---

Table 13–5   Warning Signs for Possible Adolescent Suicide

1. Expressing that one is considering suicide.
2. Feelings of hopelessness or helplessness.
3. Eating and sleeping disturbances.
4. Becoming socially isolated from friends and family.
5. A previous suicide attempt.
6. Giving away personal possessions.
7. Drug or alcohol abuse.
8. Loss of interest in school and hobbies.
9. Sudden changes in behavior.
10. Preoccupation with death.

Source: Derived from Blumenthal and Kupfer (1988) and Garland and Zigler (1993).

up with a boyfriend or girlfriend or serious arguments with parents (Marttunen, Aro, & Lonnqvist, 1993, 1994). Interpersonal conflicts may make the person feel a sense of worthlessness and hopelessness from which he or she cannot recover. Doing poorly in school and not meeting one's own and other's (probably unrealistically high) expectations is also a significant event that precipitates suicide. Sexual or physical abuse is a common factor in the adolescent girl's suicide. Finally, contagion has been shown to precipitate suicide. It is well documented that a suicide in a school may lead others to commit suicide, and as recent events have demonstrated this *contagion effect* (sometimes called cluster suicide) may range from coast to coast. A result of this finding has been serious concern about publicity in cases of suicide (D.P. Phillips & Carstensen, 1986).

Although it is tempting to say breaking up with a boyfriend or girlfriend "caused" the individual to commit suicide, that is not the case. Adolescent suicide is rarely an act of impulse; it is the culmination of a developmental process with the precipitating event simply being one contributor (Marttunen, Aro, & Lonnqvist, 1992). In their studies of Finnish youth who committed suicide, Marttunen and his colleagues (1992, 1993, 1994) reported that about a third had previously attempted suicide, 60% had talked about committing suicide, and the majority experienced weakened parental support during the year prior to suicide.

Predisposing Factors.   The factors that predispose the adolescent to consider suicide are difficult to determine (Halmi, 1987). One clearly is poor family relationships (Blumenthal & Kupfer, 1988; Marttunen et al., 1994; Rubenstein, Heren, Housman, Rubin, & Stechler, 1989). A large majority of adolescent suicide attempters come from families in which home harmony is lacking. The parents may be fighting, a divorce may be impending or apparently impending, and the parents and the adolescent may not get along well. The major disciplinary mode is power assertive; physical abuse is associated with adolescent suicide (Summerville & Kaslow, 1993; B.M. Wagner, Cole, & Schwartzman, 1993). As a result, the adolescent often feels neglected, unwanted, and alienated from the family. And communication between the parents and the adolescent is poor at best. The adolescent may come to feel socially isolated, the single most important factor in decisions to attempt suicide. As relations with parents deteriorate, then, there is an increase in suicidal ideation (Mayhue, 1992) and possibly suicide attempts.

These difficulties with parents are involved in suicide for both Black and White adolescents, but there are some interesting differences in background factors. White adolescents who were suicidal reported a greater amount of physical and sexual abuse than Black suicidal adolescents; Black suicidal adolescents were more likely to manifest delinquency and aggression than White suicidal adolescents (Summerville & Kaslow, 1993). At present, it is not possible to determine why these differences exist.

Suffering from a psychological disorder is a common underlying factor in adolescent suicide (Garland & Zigler, 1993). Psychological disorders related to suicide include the following: depression (Borst & Noam, 1993; Brent et al., 1993), substance use and abuse (especially in conjunction with depression), and the various eating disorders. Other important underlying factors include a previous suicide attempt, a family history of suicide, the availability of firearms, and increases in stressful life events. The increase in the past several decades in adolescent suicide is related to increase in adolescent alcohol use, the increased divorce rate, and the greater availability of firearms (Garland & Zigler, 1993).

In part, the picture one gets is that those who attempt suicide—both adolescents and others—have insufficiently developed coping skills (Halmi, 1987). They may be isolated from other people, an important social support system, and may not have effective means of coping with daily hassles and important but stressful life events. As a result, they see suicide as the only way out.

Researchers have found that depression, particularly in the extreme and in the first serious episode (Brent et al., 1993), is a very important factor in adolescent suicide, and highlights the importance of early identification and treatment of adolescents who are depressed. Although substance abuse is clearly implicated in the increase in adolescent suicide in recent years, it is not a leading cause of suicide by itself. When it occurs in conjunction with depressive symptomatology it increases the risk the adolescent may attempt suicide. Previous suicide attempts are the most significant predictor of suicide after depression (Brent et al., 1993).

Researchers also have identified subgroups of adolescents who commit suicide (Borst & Noam, 1993). Some may be characterized as angry-defiant types. They direct aggression at others and at the self and are impulsive in their suicide attempts. Others experience extreme guilt and are highly sensitive to the feelings of others, and they tend to feel hopeless about the future. Given there are different paths to suicide attempts, treatment efforts must be tailored to the adolescent's specific needs.

Garrison et al. (1993) suggest that engaging in physically self-damaging but not suicidal behaviors also is a risk factor for suicide. They found that about 2.5% of males and 2.75% of females of the 3,283 12- to 14-year-olds they interviewed had engaged in self-damaging acts (skin cutting or burning, self-hitting, hair pulling, bone breaking). Depression, suicidal ideation, perceived family cohesion, and undesirable life events were associated with self-damaging behavior, as is the case with suicide. They reported that engaging in self-damaging acts was a risk factor for suicide.

Treatment of Potential Suicides

There can be no treatment for the individual who has successfully committed suicide. However, treatment for those who are suicide prone or those who have attempted suicide is possible. And prevention programs can be instituted in an effort to reduce the likelihood that adolescents will attempt suicide.

Garland and Zigler (1993) have discussed and evaluated the effectiveness of the various types of prevention programs and have made suggestions for improvement. We summarize their work. The most prevalent suicide prevention programs involve hot lines for crisis intervention. The purpose of these programs is to help the person deal with a crisis situation that involves ambivalence about continuing to live. Talking with the trained personnel on the hot line may provide the interpersonal contact necessary not only to deal with the immediate situation but to motivate the individual to seek professional help. In reviewing the literature on the effectiveness of hot lines, Garland and Zigler conclude that hot lines do not appreciably reduce suicides, except for White women, who are the most frequent callers.

School-based prevention programs also have become increasingly popular. They involve attempts to train students about the warning signs of suicide and inform them of how to deal with the immediate situation and the resources available in the community. Often the programs involve modules about how to cope with stress and stress reduction. Although evaluation of these programs is not conclusive, Garland and Zigler note there is little evidence that the programs reduce suicidal ideation or suicide attempts. And some evidence shows that those who had previously attempted suicide and were enrolled in one of these classes found them upsetting.

Virtually all treatment programs involve therapy for both the long-term problems making one prone to suicide attempts and for the immediate situation. In order to be maximally successful, especially with adolescent suicide attempters, the therapy should involve not only the adolescent but the parents as well. Relationships with parents must be changed in order to make the adolescent feel less alienated and estranged. In addition, skills necessary for coping with frustrations and depression must be taught. A difficulty with therapy is that a high percentage of adolescents drop out relatively early, and therefore do not get exposed to the value of the experience and do not learn the skills necessary to deal with a crisis situation (Garland & Zigler, 1993).

DRUG USE

In this section we focus on adolescent drug use, including adolescent use of cigarettes (nicotine) and alcohol. Although in everyday discourse we may not consider these latter two drugs to be in the same category as the **illicit** (illegal) **drugs** adolescents use, they are the two **licit** (legal) **drugs** adolescents most frequently use (Johnston, O'Malley, & Bachman, 1989). Adolescents may develop both physical and psychological addiction to these drugs, just as they do to illicit drugs, and these drugs also present health hazards to the adolescent.

Prevalence of Drug Use

The most comprehensive studies of adolescent licit and illicit drug use have been conducted by Johnston and his associates (1989). Each year since 1975 these researchers have surveyed very large national samples of high school seniors about their drug use and about a variety of values and goals. Because of the size of the samples and the manner in which they were chosen—namely, to reflect the larger population of graduating high school students—it is a valuable source of information about how seniors generally behave and feel about a variety of topics.

One measure of drug use the researchers employed was whether or not the individual had ever tried each of a variety of drugs. Alcohol (tried by 92%) and cigarettes (tried by 66%) were the most prevalently tried. Among the illicit drugs only marijuana (47% had tried it) was ever tried by any substantial percentage of graduating seniors. The more exotic illicit drugs such as heroin (1.1%), crack (5%), and cocaine (12%) were used by only small percentages of the sample. Regular use—use during the past month—was much lower in all cases.

What do these data tell us about adolescent drug use? First, the stereotype of adolescents being immersed in a drug culture simply is not true. Trying a drug is very different from being a regular user. Few adolescents have a serious drug problem or use hard drugs. Most have not even tried the hard drugs. Extensive drug use by adolescents cannot account for the difficulties in growing up that most adolescents face.

Although these findings may be encouraging, it is important to exercise caution in generalizing the results. Those who completed the questionnaire were seniors—they had not dropped out of school or otherwise been prevented from graduating. Hence they are a select sample. Drug use among dropouts, those who have been expelled, or delinquents who have been incarcerated may be different from that for the general sample.

Gender Differences in Drug Use

Adolescent males admit to more drug use than adolescent females, and they admit to more regular (daily) use of drugs. However, these gender differences are related more strongly to illicit drugs, such as marijuana, heroin, and cocaine, than licit drugs. A greater percentage of females have used, or are using, stimulants and tobacco (Newcomb & Bentler, 1989). The percentage of males and females admitting to alcohol use is nearly equal (93.4% of males and 91.8% of females in 1981 and declined to 88.5% and 85.3% in 1982); males are more likely to have used alcohol recently.

Developmental Trends in Drug Use

The use of drugs must be considered from the standpoint of their legality. As we noted, some drugs, such as alcohol and cigarettes, are licit. Others, such as marijuana and cocaine, are illicit. Substantial evidence shows that, although about a third of adolescents have tried at least one illicit drug, most drug use involves licit drugs (Newcomb & Bentler, 1989).

Some examples of both licit and illicit drug use are shown in Table 13-6 for both adolescents and young adults. As you can see, use of illicit drugs increased from the mid-1970s to the mid-1980s. The same was true for alcohol,

Table 13–6   Drug Use Statistics

| | PERCENTAGE OF THOSE AGED 12–17 | | | | PERCENTAGE OF THOSE AGED 18–25 | | | |
| | *EVER USED* | | *CURRENT USER* | | *EVER USED* | | *CURRENT USER* | |
	1974	1985	1974	1985	1974	1985	1974	1985
Marijuana	23.4	23.7	12.0	12.3	52.7	60.5	25.2	21.9
Cocaine	3.6	5.2	1.0	1.8	12.7	25.2	3.1	7.7
Alcohol	54.0	55.9	34.0	31.5	81.6	92.8	69.3	71.5
Cigarettes	52.0	45.3	25.0	15.6	68.8	76.0	48.8	37.2

Source: U.S. Bureau of the Census (1989). *Statistical abstract of the United States: 1989.* Washington, DC: U.S. Government Printing Office.

but a reverse occurred for cigarettes. In general, there was a decline in drug use
across the 1980s (Newcomb & Bentler, 1989), although that decline seems to
have stopped.

Etiology of Drug Use and Abuse

Newcomb and Bentler (1989) distinguish between drug *use* and drug *abuse.*
Abuse involves negative consequences to the self, others, and property. Abuse
also involves using drugs known to have a high probability of dependence. Oc-
casional use of a drug, such as alcohol or tobacco, is simply use. Although a
fuzzy distinction, it is an important one because it helps us distinguish levels of
drug users.

Drug use is closely tied to social influences, such as peer pressure and social class, and psychological factors, such as family relations, poor self-esteem,
and stressful life events. These factors may cause the adolescent to on occasion
use various drugs in order to gain acceptance, to relieve stress (see Box 13-4),
or to escape unpleasant feelings. Drug abuse, as with alcohol, may have a genetic basis (Newcomb & Bentler, 1989).

Adolescent drug use, including cigarette smoking, is on the
decline. (*Laima E. Druskis*)

BOX 13–4 Psychosocial Development and Adolescent Coping Styles

One focus of research on coping with stress has been the investigation of the relation between coping styles and psychological adjustment. Some research demonstrates that general psychological adjustment is related to coping styles. More well-adjusted adults employ coping strategies aimed at changing the stressful event, whereas less well-adjusted adults tend to employ avoidant, or emotion-focused, coping styles (e.g., Holahan & Moos, 1987; McCrae & Costa, 1986). Among adolescents, those with better self-esteem are more likely to use active as opposed to avoidant coping strategies (Compas, 1987; Compass & Phares, 1991; Ebata & Moos, 1989, 1994).

Jorgensen and Dusek (1990) investigated the relation between resolution of Erikson's psychosocial crises and the use of various coping strategies in a group of college students. Those students who were more psychosocially well adjusted (they resolved the crises more optimally) reported that when stressed they were more likely to employ strategies aimed at altering the stressful event. They were more likely to seek information and advice, talk to friends, and try to do something to alter the stressful situation than those who were less well adjusted. The latter group was more likely to use avoidant coping strategies; they would vent their frustration through blaming others or becoming belligerent, avoiding doing things to alter the stressful situation, and sleeping more. Of course, the difference between the two groups of students is relative; everyone may cry or avoid dealing with stressful events, and everyone may tackle stressful events. The differences that Jorgensen and Dusek found were, first, that by late adolescence general coping styles develop. Second, there are clear preferences for the modal manner of dealing with stress that relate to psychological adjustment.

It appears, then, that adolescents and adults have general styles of coping with stress. Jorgensen and Dusek suggest that these general styles may develop during infancy and childhood as the individual resolves the various crises discussed by Erikson (1968). For example, optimal resolution of the basic trust versus mistrust and intimacy versus isolation crises may result in the individual trusting his or her own judgment and feeling comfortable seeking social support from others when under stress.

Successful resolution of the autonomy versus shame and doubt, initiative versus guilt, industry versus inferiority, and identity versus identity diffusion crises generally results in the acquisition of instrumental traits—having the confidence in one's ability and desire to make choices, having a sense of the ability to achieve through self-initiated plans and actions, and viewing the self as active and as taking charge of one's life. Those who more successfully resolve these crises seem to have developed the psychological resources necessary to confront stressful situations actively, and they seem to have the feeling they can deal with those situations successfully. Hence they are more prone to employ active coping strategies.

What fosters the nature of the coping strategies we use? This is a question that is just beginning to be answered. Some research points to the role of parental rearing practices (Danko & Dusek, in press; Guay & Dusek, 1992; Hardy, Power, & Jaedicke, 1993). Adolescents who report their parents used authoritative rearing (see Chapter 10) also reported they were more likely to use problem-focused coping strategies and less likely to use emotion-focused coping when facing a stressful situation. Those who reported their parents used other rearing styles were more inclined to use less effective means of coping. How do parental rearing styles affect the means by which one copes? The answer seems to lie in the influence of rearing styles on general psychosocial adjustment and the development of identity and self-esteem (Chapter 10). Adolescents who feel confident in their abilities, who know who they are, and who are given the opportunity to explore their competencies are more self-assured in their ability to cope effectively with stressful events.

As further research is conducted on the determinants of coping strategies we no doubt will be able to fill in the picture of how we develop coping styles. Research on the importance of learning coping strategies from parents, siblings, peers, and the role of child-rearing practices in coping will be important in this regard.

The nature of family and parental influences are clearly implicated in adolescent drug usage. Having a sibling who exhibits frequent and problematic drinking is predictive of the adolescent engaging in alcohol use (R. D. Conger, 1994). Having a sibling who drinks puts the adolescent at risk for drinking. It also relates to the adolescent subsequently seeking out friends who drink. Conger suggests this may result from the drinking sibling in a sense legitimizing drinking.

Parental drinking is both directly (R. D. Conger, 1994) and indirectly (R. D. Conger, Conger, & Simons, 1992; Dishion, Ray, & Capaldi, 1992; Hops, 1994) related to adolescent alcohol and other drug use. Mother's substance use and abuse is related directly to adolescent drug use. Both mother's and father's substance use relates indirectly to adolescent substance use and abuse through the use of harsh and inconsistent discipline. R. D. Conger (1994) suggests that parental substance use is a source of added stress, disrupting parenting practices such as monitoring and demanding age-appropriate behavior (a protective factor in adolescent substance use). Moreover, maternal substance use and problems represent an extreme form of deviant behavior—because they are less common than paternal use—and thereby legitimize substance use.

Prevention and Treatment

Although the current trend is to educate adolescents about the problems that can arise from drug use and abuse, the evidence such programs are successful is mixed (Newcomb & Bentler, 1989). Attempts to prevent the availability of drugs also do not solve the problem. The upshot of these efforts is that for drug use there are some benefits, but for drug abuse there are none. The latter situation involves strong feelings of unhappiness, limited life opportunities, and psychological distress not addressed by current prevention programs. Helping those who are at risk for drug abuse will require much more extensive and personally tailored programs. Successful programs focus on improving social functioning, eliminating drug use, continuing school enrollment, and staying in treatment. These procedures help the individual integrate the self into the social fabric of those who are more well adjusted and help the individual improve self-esteem.

SCHIZOPHRENIA AND DEPRESSION

Adolescence is a time of relatively rapid change in biological, cognitive, social, peer, and parent relationships. All increase stress on the adolescent (see Chapter 2; Weiner, 1980). Although most adolescents cope with the changes in an adaptive manner, for some the added stress may lead to one or another psychological disorder. We review here two of the more common psychological disorders affecting adolescents: schizophrenia and depression.

Schizophrenia

Those who experience schizophrenia are most likely to exhibit the symptoms initially during the adolescent or early adulthood years (Weiner, 1980, 1992). Weiner notes that about a quarter to a third of adolescents *seeking professional help for psychological problems* exhibit schizophrenic symptoms. The symptoms of the disorder include a reduced ability to think logically and coherently, variability in moods, hallucinations (visual and aural), deteriorating social relationships, decreases in energy, withdrawal, and hostile or impulsive behavior.

Researchers (e.g., Pogue-Geile & Harrow, 1987) have identified several means of distinguishing adolescent schizophrenia from other adolescent disorders such as depression. First, a key is the persistence and pervasiveness of exhibiting the symptomatology. An adolescent who may experience depression but who, when not depressed, still shows symptoms of schizophrenia is a likely candidate for actually having the disorder. Second, adolescents who exhibit little concern for normal development in peer and other social relations may be exhibiting schizophrenic symptoms. Immaturity of interests and attitudes may reflect a lack of interest in the typical aspects of adolescent life and be indicators of withdrawal. Finally, the pervasiveness of showing the symptoms is a key. For example, the inability to deal with ordinary thoughts in logical and nonambiguous ways may indicate schizophrenic symptomatology.

Treatment of schizophrenia during adolescence is difficult, as it is during any other part of the life span. More importantly, the earlier the disorder occurs the less successful treatment tends to be, which means that when it occurs during adolescence as opposed to adulthood, the prognosis is mediocre at best. Only about 23% of adolescents showing schizophrenic symptoms recover completely (Weiner, 1992), and about half permanently display schizophrenic tendencies.

Treatment of schizophrenic symptoms varies a great deal. Hospitalization is common, at least for short periods of time. Individual, family, or group therapy is aimed at building social relationships in an attempt to build self-esteem and reduce withdrawal. In some instances, drug therapy is used to reduce the hallucinogenic features of schizophrenia. This apparently has the benefit of facilitating the effectiveness of other forms of therapy (Siris, Van Kammen, & Docherty, 1978).

Depression

Depression, in varying degrees, has been experienced by virtually all of us; it is called **depressed mood** (Petersen et al., 1993). It usually occurs when we feel a loss of some type, for example, through death, a broken relationship with someone important to us, or through separation (Halmi, 1987). Although we all have felt this way on one occasion or another, we have adapted well. For some adolescents, or adults, the adaptation is not effective. Weiner (1980, 1992) estimates that about 10% of adolescents may at one time or another exhibit symptoms of primary depression (**clinical depression**), including self-deprecation, crying spells, and suicidal thoughts. Indeed, being clinically depressed is a risk factor for attempting suicide. As many as 60% of adolescents at times feel sad and hopeless (**depressive syndrome**) (Gans, 1990).

The symptoms of depression depend on age. Younger adolescents, up to about age 16 or 17, do not exhibit the same signs of depression as older adolescents or adults (Weiner, 1980, 1982). The reasons for this are related to the developmental tasks (see Chapters 1 and 2) faced by adolescents of different ages. Younger adolescents face tasks that challenge self-esteem (for example, independence from parents, heterosexual friendship patterns), which make them less likely to admit self-critical attitudes and feelings of helplessness. Second, they are more likely to express feelings and emotions through doing rather than thinking. Hence they are much less likely than older adolescents or adults to express and feel the brunt of depression through cognitive functions such as introspective preoccupation.

During adolescence there are some other symptoms of depression. Extreme fatigue, even after adequate rest, difficulty in concentrating, on schoolwork for example, and extreme occupation with physical development may be signals of impending or existent depression (Weiner, 1980, 1992). Older adolescents and adults may manifest depression through drug abuse, alienation from others, or other means of cutting the self off from the social world. This seems to reflect a view that there is little point in doing anything constructive.

As with other disorders, identifying depression in adolescents is difficult because of stereotypes about typical adolescent development. Adolescents are "supposed" to be moody, tired all the time, aloof, unpredictable, and flighty. Hence it is easy to miss the signs of what in actuality is depression. And, as with many stereotypes, there is truth in this one. How, then, can one identify the normal alterations in moods and other behaviors from the possibility that an adolescent is depressed? According to the criteria listed in the *DSM-IV,* an adolescent demonstrating several of the symptoms concurrently for a 2-week period, when the symptoms represent a change from normal behavior, may be suffering from depression and should seek professional help.

Depressive disorders are more common for girls than boys (Petersen et al., 1993). This difference, which is evident by age 14 or 15, continues through the adulthood years. The exact bases of this difference are not known, but there is speculation that it relates to sex-role differences in socialization and to the fact that girls enter the growth spurt at about the same time they must adjust to other substantial changes, such as moving into a new school, which may heighten the stresses they undergo. At present, there appears to be no clear indications that adolescent depression is more prevalent in any particular ethnic group (Petersen et al., 1993).

Depression is caused by many factors and it is unclear which are most important. Seligman (1975) argues that learned helplessness—the feeling one has very little control over life events and that they are determined by others or by forces outside one's control—is a key to depression. Others argue that depression results from poor self-esteem and a negative view of the self resulting from earlier poor rearing and experiences. Some evidence points to the importance of biological and genetic factors. Identical twins are much more likely than fraternal twins to each experience depression (Petersen et al., 1993). Growing up with a depressed mother also places the adolescent female especially at risk for depression (Chapter 10), as does feeling distant from mothers and fathers (Gouws & Huffman, 1994). Conflictual relations with the parent of the same sex is predictive of developing depressive symptomatology. More positive relations with parents seem to insulate the adolescent from depression (Herman-Stahl, 1994), especially for girls.

Each of these beliefs about the etiology of depression is tied to various therapeutic approaches, including individual, family, group, drug, and behavior therapy. Which, if any, is most successful is completely open to debate (Petersen et al., 1993; Weiner, 1992). The best hope may lie in prevention programs, particularly aimed at adolescents in high-risk categories, such as those with a depressed parent.

SUMMARY

Deviancy refers to development, or behavior, outside some norm. Hence one may be deviant in terms of biological growth, intellectual development, or social behavior. The most prevalent forms of deviancy in adolescence are juvenile delinquency, various eating disorders, suicide, drug use and abuse, and other psychological disorders such as schizophrenia and depression.

Juvenile delinquency is the term used to describe illegal behaviors of those who are minors (usually those under 16 or 18 years of age, depending on the state of residence). The incidence of delinquency increased until the mid-1970s and then leveled off. Boys engage in more delinquency than girls; boys also engage in more violent forms of delinquency. The incidence of delinquency peaks at about 15 years of age and then levels off.

A number of factors presumably fostering delinquency have been investigated. One of the more salient characteristics is social class. Whether working with official police and court records or with adolescent self-reports, it is clear there is a social-class difference in delinquency. Adolescents from poorer socioeconomic backgrounds engage in more delinquency than their middle-class peers but only at the extreme of engaging in delinquency. The social-class differences in delinquency are small to nonexistent for those who engage in low to moderate levels of delinquency.

Other factors involved in socializing an adolescent into delinquency are the peer group and the relationship with the parents. Peers not only teach delinquent behavior but also reinforce it. This might be especially true in some types of adolescent gangs. For boys, the single most important factor involved in delinquency is the relationship with the parents. Delinquents, both boys and girls, view their relationships with their parents very negatively. They see their fathers as neglecting, hostile, and rejecting. In addition, the parents of delinquents tend to use considerable physical punishment and to be erratic and overly strict in child rearing.

In general, delinquents develop poor self-concepts and see themselves as cut off from society. In part, then, they view society in a hostile manner. Delinquent adolescents also have an external locus of control, which means they see things as happening to them rather than seeing themselves in control of their own destiny. Delinquents also tend to do poorly in school, which may lead to their engaging in some specific forms of delinquency, such as truancy, and to their dropping out of school.

At the present time, no evidence suggests one form or another of treatment is best to use with delinquents. Because we identify delinquents after the fact, that is, after they already have engaged in delinquent behavior, we seem to treat the symptom and not the cause.

Three main eating disorders occur with high frequency in the adolescent population. Obesity, the most common, may result from eating too much or from metabolic disorders. However, obese adolescents tend to be more sedentary than their leaner peers. Obesity is a serious problem because of the health hazards it poses, including hypertension, heart disease, and joint disease. Treatment usually involves changing eating patterns and dealing with psychological factors predisposing one to obesity.

Anorexia nervosa is also a health hazard. The anorexic tends to eat very little, despite hunger, and to lose considerable body weight. Most anorexics are females and most become anorexic during the adolescent years. One factor that seems to predispose the adolescent to anorexia nervosa is the failure of parents to allow the individual to become independent. Anorexics also have a poor body image, seeing themselves as fat even though they are emaciated. Treatment often involves behavior modification to increase food intake and therapy to deal with psychological problems.

Bulimics eat huge amounts of food (up to nearly 5,000 calories) and then purge their systems through the use of laxatives, induced vomiting, or both. Bulimics are nearly all females, the disorder appearing usually around 18 years of age or so. The causes of the disorder and the best treatment are not yet determined.

Although the absolute number of adolescents who commit suicide is not large, it is a tragedy. Nearly 7% of all suicides are adolescents, and estimates are that 1 in 1,000 adolescents tries to commit suicide. The one factor clearly associated with suicide is poor family relations, which make the adolescent feel neglected and isolated. These feelings lead to depression, which may predispose the adolescent to suicide. Treatment typically involves building better family and peer relationships.

Drug use by high school adolescents seems to have peaked in the late 1970s. Since then, there has been a slight decline in the use of most drugs. Nonetheless, high percentages of adolescents admit to having tried various licit (alcohol, cigarettes) and illicit (marijuana) drugs. Males admit to using more drugs more regularly. Whether it be marijuana, nicotine, or alcohol, the most frequently used drugs, serious physical effects are associated with their use. In addition, some drugs, such as nicotine, are physically addicting.

An important factor in drug use is parental behavior and parental attitudes about drug use. Adolescents whose parents model drug use are more likely to use drugs, as are adolescents whose parents do not convey messages about the dangers of drug use. In addition, feelings of isolation and alienation from parents contribute to drug use. Finally, peer drug use is related to the adolescent's use of various drugs.

Schizophrenia and depression are the two most prevalent psychological disorders during the adolescent years. At the present time, we know little of the precipitating causes for these disorders. Treatment usually involves dealing both with the symptoms, perhaps through drug therapy, and with family relationships, which seem to be primary causes in the disorders.

GLOSSARY

adjudicate: To bring a case before a judge or a jury.

anorexia nervosa: Psychological eating disorder characterized by a failure to eat, causing a dangerous drop in body weight.

basal metabolism rate: Amount of energy (calories) burned during a resting state.

bulimia: Psychological eating disorder characterized by binge eating and then purging.

clinical depression: Extended and severe demonstration of a number of depressive symptoms.

depression: Psychological disorder characterized by lowered self-esteem, feelings of inferiority, and sadness.

depressed mood: Feelings of sadness or unhappiness, often due to a loss of some type.

depressive syndrome: Constellation of behaviors and cognitions indicative of depression, including feeling lonely, unloved, nervous, guilty, sad, and worried.

DSM-IV (Diagnostic and Statistical Manual-IV): Manual listing the psychological and behavioral criteria for the classification of psychological disorders.

illicit drugs: Drugs that are illegal, such as crack or marijuana.

index offenses: Acts that are illegal at all age levels.

juvenile delinquency: Illegal acts performed by juveniles.

licit drugs: Drugs that are legal, such as alcohol.

obesity: Overweight condition characterized by high levels of subcutaneous fatty tissue.

suicide ideation: Thinking about committing suicide.

status offense: Delinquent act, such as underage drinking, that would not be considered a crime if committed by an adult.

DISCUSSION QUESTIONS

1. What acts of juvenile delinquency did you engage in? Why did you stop?
2. What factors might account for the gender differences in types and frequency of delinquent behavior?
3. Have you known any hard-core delinquents? How did they feel about school, their family, and themselves? Why?
4. How did your weight fluctuate during your early to mid-adolescent years? Did it cause you to diet? Why were you concerned?
5. Have you ever lost your appetite? Were you suffering from anorexia nervosa?
6. Have you ever binged while eating, devouring much more than you should have? Were you suffering from bulimia?
7. How can you tell adolescent depression from the normal mood swings and other behavioral changes we all experience?
8. What are the defining characteristics of schizophrenia? Have you ever had any of them? Does that mean you are schizophrenic?
9. What drugs have you experimented with? Why did you and other adolescents do so? What drugs did you not try, and why?
10. Did you ever think about committing suicide? Is that normal?
11. What school programs might help students cope with the suicide of their friends? Did your school have such a program? Was it helpful? Why or why not?
12. How can we distinguish deviant from so-called normal behavior?

Appendix: Methods of Research in the Study of Adolescence

MAJOR ISSUES ADDRESSED

Why We Do Research with Adolescents
The Nature of Research Designs
The Importance of Statistical Evaluation
Important Types of Statistics
Problems in Conducting and Interpreting Research
What We Can Determine from Doing Research
Inferential and Descriptive Statistics

INTRODUCTION

The intent of this appendix is not to make a researcher or statistician out of you, but rather to give you some idea of how research studies are designed and conducted. We also want you to become familiar with some of the terms used in discussing research projects. In order to accomplish these goals, you must understand the relation of research to theory. Theories generate hypotheses that we test through research.

The product of every research study is some form of data that must be evaluated. In psychology, the data typically are in the form of numbers, and evaluation involves the use of statistics. In order to understand and fully appreciate the findings presented in the text, it is useful to have a basic understanding of some statistical concepts. Although you surely understand the concept of the mean, or average, of a group of scores—one of the most basic statistics psychologists employ—you may not know what a correlation is or what it means. In the second section of this appendix we present some very basic statistical concepts that will help you better understand the material in the chapters.

Another issue involves problems in conducting research and in evaluating the findings. The especially critical concerns are how subjects are selected, how particular questionnaires or inventories are constructed, and the generalizability of the findings. These are important issues because of the diversity of the adolescent population and the widely different experiences that adolescents have.

THE FUNCTION OF RESEARCH

A theory is a model of reality, an attempt to explain why events occur as they do. Regardless of the area of study—physical sciences, social sciences—theories serve the same functions. Researchers derive hypotheses—best guesses about the causes of some behavior—from theories and test these hypotheses by doing research. If the research findings support the hypothesis, we gain confidence in the theory. If the research does not support the hypothesis, we have a right to question the theory, the design of the research, or the appropriateness of that kind of research as a test of the hypothesis. In this sense, research acts to help develop and define the limits of a theory. Research may produce new constructs that relate to the theory being tested. In this way, research is a critical tool for pointing directions in which theories may be developed or expanded.

Although this process may sound esoteric and the province of the laboratory scientist, it is not. You formulate theories—best guesses as to what may happen in some circumstance—very often. Consider the first time you attend a class. You have a set of expectations (hypotheses) about what will occur—how the instructor will behave, the content of the class, the format of instruction. These expectations are based on previous experience—your "theory" about why things will occur—of attending classes, what you have heard about the instructor, and what you believe the class content will be. As the class progresses you collect data by experiencing what is going on—the instructor's mannerisms, the course syllabus, how the instructor conducts the class. You are testing your hypotheses. This is analogous to the researcher collecting data by doing a research project to test hypotheses. You may find your hypotheses confirmed: Class goes exactly as you predicted. Or you may find you have to modify your theory: It's a lecture course but you will not have multiple-choice exams, the instructor is very staid and speaks in a monotone as opposed to being more relaxed and animated, the course content is not what you expected. Your best guesses likely will be more accurate as you gain experience in the college atmosphere. You continually modify your theory to make it a better model of reality. In many ways you are behaving like the scientist attempting to explain why some behavior occurs.

With particular reference to adolescent psychology, research must be focused in several directions; it must address itself to the biological, cultural, and intellectual factors underlying adolescent development. Because adolescence is a time of change and transition, the research must be developmental in nature, that is, it must focus on changes in behavior.

Dimensions of Research

Psychological research projects vary in a number of ways. In Table A-1 we list four dimensions of research projects and summarize the major aspects of each. Although these dimensions are not all-inclusive, they will serve to demonstrate the different focuses an investigation may have. The end points of these four dimensions are not necessarily mutually exclusive either: A single research design may contain elements from both end points of a single dimension.

Laboratory vs. Naturalistic. Laboratory research is typically conducted in an artificial situation, and the tasks presented are usually unfamiliar to the subject. This is done because it is necessary to control extraneous variables in order to assess the effects of the particular variable under study. The artificial situation eliminates distracting and extraneous influences on performance, and unfamiliar tasks are chosen because they are equally novel to all those tested. Some people will not do better because they have had practice. Thus, in studies of memory

Table A–1   Dimensions of Research Projects

1. Laboratory	versus	Naturalistic
artificial situation;		natural environment
control of extraneous variables		loose control of extraneous variables
2. Manipulative	versus	Nonmanipulative
cause and effect oriented		discover relationships among variables—not cause and effect
usually experimental		usually correlational
3. Theoretical	versus	Atheoretical
test theories		answer immediate questions of applied nature
laboratory/manipulative		naturalistic/observational
4. Age change	versus	Age difference
longitudinal		cross-sectional
growth oriented		behavior-difference oriented

the subject is not studied in his or her own living room, but is more likely to be placed in a quiet and unfamiliar room. Rather than be exposed to everyday, familiar material, the subject is more likely to be exposed to unfamiliar material that is novel to all those involved.

Naturalistic observation is conducted in the field, and usually entails simply observing and recording what people do in certain kinds of real-life circumstances, for example, how people behave after or while viewing an automobile accident or at the dinner table. Another example of naturalistic observation is the kind of research done in astronomy. It is not possible to create a functional replica of the universe in the laboratory. Therefore, the astronomer's only laboratory is a post from which he or she can observe the kinds of behaviors that go on in the heavens. Other examples of observational research include assessments of social behaviors, for example, the behaviors of street gangs, and unobtrusive observations of individuals in any kind of a naturalistic situation. A special form of the latter involves the participant observer, a person who becomes part of some group setting and observes how the group functions.

Manipulative vs. Nonmanipulative.   Manipulative research involves a manipulation of some variable by the experimenter in an attempt to determine whether or not that variable will produce differences in the behavior of the subjects in an experiment. The variable manipulated is called the **independent variable.** The behavior measured is called the **dependent variable.** The logic of the manipulative strategy states that subjects receiving one level (manipulation) of the independent variable should perform better (or worse) than subjects receiving a different level. For example, subjects drinking 4 oz. of alcohol immediately before a driving test should perform more poorly than subjects taking no alcohol before the test. The independent variable is the amount of alcohol consumed; the dependent variable is some measure of driving performance, such as crossing lines on a driving range. Typically, manipulative research is conducted in the laboratory, although it may be done in a real-life setting such as a summer camp—randomly assigning students to different groups in order to study group formation and function. In nonmanipulative research, the experimenter simply observes and records the behavior of the subjects—naturally occurring groups in the school setting.

The advantage of the manipulative research approach is that it is a very reliable way to discover how a variable relates to behavior because cause-and-effect relationships may be determined. One might, for example, manipulate the amount of practice that people have in some particular situation, and then assess their performance on a related task. In this way it is possible to determine the degree to which practice relates to performance. Alternatively, one may go into naturalistic settings and find people who in the normal course of events have varying degrees of practice at some particular skill and assess their performance on some criterion task. In this case, the experimenter is not performing any particular manipulation. Observational research of this sort is particularly necessary when it is not feasible to use manipulation; for example, in many instances it would not be ethical (or legal) to conduct manipulative research on hormonal factors relating to human behavior because of potential adverse effects. Relating hormones to the adolescent's behavior is done by measuring differences in naturally occurring levels of hormones.

Theoretical vs. Atheoretical.   The third dimension listed in Table A–1 is labeled *theoretical* versus *atheoretical*. A good deal of research is conducted to test theories for the reasons just noted. However, some research is conducted to collect data to begin to formulate a theory. The latter kinds of research studies are atheoretical in the sense no particular theory is being tested.

Most developmental psychologists, including those who are interested in adolescent development, primarily do theory-oriented research. However, atheoretical research is often conducted in order to answer questions of immediate concern. For example, much of the research on adolescent sexual behavior is not particularly theory guided; it is aimed at assessing adolescent's attitudes about contraception and its use, when adolescents feel it is right to have sex, and what adolescents know about sexually transmitted diseases.

Age Change vs. Age Difference.   The fourth dimension is a very important one for developmental psychologists who are typically interested in changes in behavior. This kind of research is represented by the longitudinal research strategy we discuss later. Age-change research is truly developmental because it produces growth curves of behavior in a single group of subjects retested over a period of time. In other words, repeated measurements on a group of subjects as they mature permit direct developmental assessments.

Age-difference research refers to research in which data on age-related differences in behavior are obtained from subjects of different ages in a single experiment. Because the subjects in age-difference research studies are of different ages, and because they are tested only one time, it is impossible to demonstrate *change* in behavior. It is possible to examine age differences, however.

A good deal of developmental research, including that in adolescent psychology, is of the age-difference sort, partly because it is cheap to do in terms of time, personnel, and money, whereas age-change research presents a number of problems that are sometimes extremely difficult to solve. The studies of early versus late maturity described in Chapter 3 started with the birth of the child and continued into adulthood. Keeping track of the participants, finding them in adulthood, subject attrition, and the commitment of the researchers to continue the project are but some of the difficulties encountered in longitudinal research.

Research Designs in Adolescent Psychology

Four research designs are commonly employed in developmental psychology. Each has limitations, advantages, and disadvantages.

Cross-Sectional Research.   **Cross-sectional design** (research) is defined as the systematic assessment of several groups of people at approximately the same point in time. One major characteristic of a cross-sectional study is that all groups of subjects involved in the study are tested only once, and all the participants are tested within a relatively short period of time. Cross-sectional research is often age-difference oriented, that is, adolescents of different ages are involved and age differences in the results are examined.

The major advantage is that it is relatively economical in terms of time, money, and personnel. Research involving many hundreds of people might be conducted in only a few days. Much of the research on the development of sexuality during the adolescent years involved asking adolescents of different ages about their sexual experiences and examining age differences in these experiences. These studies typically are carried out on large numbers of adolescents and the data are collected in a very short period of time. From this research investigators have learned about the percentages of adolescents of different ages who have experienced various levels of sexual involvement, and they have done so very efficiently and economically.

Longitudinal Studies.   **Longitudinal design** (research) is defined as the systematic study of the same group or groups of individuals at regular intervals over time. Because the behaviors of the same group of subjects are assessed at different points, the longitudinal study is truly developmental. It permits the assessment of uniformity and diversity in patterns of *change* (age changes in behavior).

The classic studies on how being an early or late maturer is related to psychological development (Chapter 3) were done by measuring the development of large groups of children from birth through the high school years, an 18-year longitudinal study. By taking measures of physical growth at regular (6-month) intervals, the researchers were able to determine who was an early and who a late maturer. They then were able to examine how physical growth related to other measures of development, such as self-esteem, peer relations, and behavior in school.

The major advantage of the longitudinal study is that it can measure age changes. However, this benefit comes at some costs and difficulties. A longitudinal study is expensive in terms of time, money, and personnel. The commitment of the researchers and subjects must be extraordinary or the study will fail. There also is the problem of subject attrition: Subjects may, move, die, or decide to cease participation, which reduces the size of the sample and may result in a biased sample and a lack of generalizability of the findings. It is difficult to replicate longitudinal research. The Berkeley Growth Studies of human growth and development are unlikely to be replicated due to the high costs involved.

Combined Longitudinal and Cross-Sectional Designs.   Cross-sectional and longitudinal designs have certain drawbacks that make them at times inadequate for assessing developmental phenomena. In the traditional cross-sectional design, in which several different age groups are tested at the same time, age effects may be **confounded** with **cohort** effects. In other words, subjects of different ages may respond differently *not* because they are at different developmental levels but *because* they had different experiences due to growing up at different times. What may appear to be an age difference in performance may in reality be a cohort (time of birth) difference. Because the two effects (age and cohort) are perfectly confounded, we cannot logically conclude that one and not the other is responsible for the observed differences. It is particularly difficult to assess cohort effects in cases where a significant cultural factor might have influenced development. For example, some differences in the attitudes of adolescents and their parents are due not to the fact that they are at different developmental levels, but result from their growing up in different social times. One need only think about music preferences to see that *when* one is developing is as important as one's level of development.

In a longitudinal study, age and time of measurement are confounded. In other words, the age of the subjects is related directly to the time at which measurements are taken. To the extent that significant cultural events intervene between one testing and another, the changes that one observes might or might not be due to the intervening cultural events. For example, Glen Elder has shown that those who were adolescents during the Great Depression hold different values than those who were not. Their trust in banks and attitudes about money in general, for example, reflect the severe economic conditions under which many of them grew up. As with the confoundings in the crosssectional study, only rarely can the effects be separated. You can discover this yourself simply by thinking about the differences in attitudes you, your parents, and your grandparents or even great-grandparents have about money, wasting food, and trusting banks.

By using a **cross-sequential design** it is possible to separate age changes from cohort and time of measurement effects. An example comes from Dusek's (Dusek & Flaherty, 1981) study of self-esteem during the adolescent years. These researchers tested about 100 students in each of the grades 6 through 12 once a year for 3 consecutive years. Taken separately, each year is a cross-sectional study. Hence there were three cross-sectional studies. Taken separately, the data for each of the original grades 6 through 10 represent a 3-year longitudinal study. Hence there were six 3-year longitudinal studies, one for each of six cohorts. By examining the results for both the cross-sectional and longitudinal studies, the researchers were able to determine that self-esteem did not change dramatically during the adolescent years, and that this was true for all six cohorts.

Case Study Design. The **case study design** is defined as the systematic assessment of a single individual at regular intervals over time. It is a special case of longitudinal assessment.

There are several benefits to the case study approach, including the fact that it is inexpensive in terms of the amount of data collected, and it is quite practical for assessing treatment practices. In fact, case studies are most common in therapy situations. Case studies allow the examination of **intraindividual** (within a person) **changes** in behavior. By studying stability of performance in a single individual we gain some notion about the stability of psychological traits. For example, case studies of IQ development reveal wide variations in the tested IQ, leading to the conclusion that IQ test performance is not very stable (Chapter 4).

There are some disadvantages to case studies, however. First, the data are not very generalizable because they represent growth and development for one individual. As a result, the information obtained cannot (usually) be generalized to other cases and usually do not lead to the formulation of general laws of development and behavior. A second problem is that it is quite difficult, although not impossible, to manipulate variables and make clear interpretations of the results. For instance, an individual cannot be both low and high anxious, or low and high IQ, or male and female.

Although case studies are popular for demonstrating and illustrating certain aspects of development, psychologists are more concerned with general laws of development derived from research on groups of adolescents than with the particular development of a single adolescent. This is not to deny the importance of individual differences, but rather to emphasize the more general aspects of adolescent development.

Interview-Survey Research. The most frequently used research technique in the study of adolescence is the survey or questionnaire approach. When the questionnaire asks the adolescent to state views about some topic, for example, political or moral behavior, the questionnaire is called an *opinionnaire* because the subjects are expected to respond on the basis of their own feelings and opinions. When a questionnaire is administered in person by an examiner, it is an **interview.** When it is sent through the mail or administered to a large group of people at once, it is a *survey.*

There are a number of advantages to this approach, which is why it has become so popular. First, a great deal of information may be collected from large numbers of people in a very short period of time. For example, the author and his assistants have administered as many as 800 questionnaires to large groups of adolescents in just a few days. In that time, approximately 30,000 pieces of data were collected. In addition, adolescents may give more honest answers on sensitive items (for example, those dealing with sexual behavior and feelings about parents) when they can respond anonymously to a written questionnaire.

The most serious limitation of the questionnaire method is that it is descriptive in nature. Hence it reveals no information about cause-and-effect relationships. Issues dealing with whether or not subjects are lying when they respond to the questionnaire, whether the interviewer is somehow biasing the subjects' responses, and the reliability of retrospective reports (how accurately one is reporting what happened in the past) are other problems that enter into an evaluation of the utility of data collected by the questionnaire method.

STATISTICAL CONCEPTS

All observations, whether made in the laboratory or in a naturalistic setting, must be organized, categorized, and summarized before any meaning can be attributed to them. This process of data compression (reduction) produces numerical measures, for example, scores on a performance measure such as IQ or a listing of heights and weights for the sample studied. These numerical measures describe the data collected; therefore they belong in the realm of **descriptive statistics.** Testing of hypotheses is done through the use of **inferential statistics.**

Descriptive Statistics

Descriptive statistics are used to summarize the data that are collected and to communicate the findings to the scientific community. A listing of various descriptive statistics is given in Table A-2. Because many of these terms are probably familiar to you, we review them only briefly.

Measures of Central Tendency. One way to summarize data is through various measures of central tendency, each of which reflects a "typical" score. There are several such measures, including the mean, the median, and the mode. The *mean* is commonly employed to communicate differences between groups of subjects who vary according to age, gender, or experimental treatment. Hence by looking at the mean we are able to speak of scores increasing or decreasing as a function of age level or differing according to gender or some other variable of interest.

The median and the mode are less frequently employed. The *median*, which is used for dividing a distribution of scores into two groups with equal numbers of scores, is most frequently used to separate subjects into two groups that differ on some trait. For example, by dividing a group of adolescents into those who are above and below the median on a measure of peer popularity

Table A–2   Statistical Concepts

Descriptive Statistics summarize and describe data.
    Measures of central tendency:
        mean—average of the scores
        median—the middle score (50% of the scores are higher and 50% are lower)
        mode—the most frequently occurring score
    Measures of variability:
        range—the difference between the lowest and the highest score
        standard deviation—square root of the variance
        variance—the sum of the squared deviations of the scores from the mean divided by the
            number of scores
    Measures of association:
        correlation coefficient—a measure of association between two variables
        a factor—a cluster of test scores or items that are highly related to each other and not
            related to scores or items in other factors
Inferential Statistics are used to test hypotheses.
    Random sample: a sample drawn from a population in such a way that every member of
        the population has an equal chance of being picked
    Experimental group: the subjects receiving the experimental treatment
    Control group: the subjects receiving no experimental treatment
    Significance level: the probability that differences between the experimental and control
        groups at the end of the experiment are due to chance
    t-test: technique used to assess differences between experimental and control groups in a
        two-group experiment
    F-test: technique used to assess differences when more than two groups are tested or more
        than one variable is manipulated
    Independent variable(s): the variable(s) manipulated in the experiment
    Dependent variable(s): the variable(s) measured in the experiment

---

one can examine how high or low popularity relates to self-esteem, participation in group activities, and involvement in school activities.

The mode is used primarily to describe a distribution of scores in order to highlight scores that are obtained relatively frequently. It is the most frequently occurring score.

The grades you and your fellow students receive in your class represent one example. The entire distribution of scores is a frequency distribution—the number of students who received each score. The mean is the average score for all the students. The median is the score that divides the group in half. The mode is the score that has the most number of students.

Measures of Variability.   Just as there are measures of central tendencies, or similarities, in scores, there also are measures of variability, or difference. One measure of variability is simply the range of the scores, the highest to the lowest score. In your classes there is a top and bottom score.

To describe more completely the nature of the distribution of scores, psychologists use two measures: the *standard deviation* and the *variance* (the square of the standard deviation). Each is a measure of the variability of the scores within the distribution from the mean score. The smaller the standard deviation or variance, the more compact (closer to the mean) the distribution of scores; the larger the standard deviation or variance, the more disparate the scores. In a bell-shaped (normal) distribution, 68% of the scores fall within plus or minus one standard deviation from the mean. For example, IQ tests are designed to have a mean score of 100, and a standard deviation of either 15 or 16. By knowing this information we know a score of 116 is one standard deviation above, and a score of 84 one standard deviation below, the mean IQ. By knowing the mean of the distribution and the standard deviation of the scores, then, we are able to discern the relative position of any given score within the distribution.

The final descriptive statistic we discuss is the *correlation coefficient,* denoted by *r,* which is a measure of the relationship between two scores derived from each subject. For example, we might wish to know the relationship between intelligence and school performance. In order to calculate this relationship we would need to have an IQ score on each subject as well as some measure of school performance. The correlation coefficient allows us to determine how related the two sets of scores are.

The correlation coefficient may take on any value from −1 to +1. The larger the absolute value of the number, the number irrespective of the sign attached to it, the stronger the relationship. The smaller the absolute value of the number, the weaker the relationship. A correlation of 0 demonstrates that there is no relationship between the two sets of scores. A correlation of +1 indicates a perfect positive relationship between the scores. In our example of IQ scores, this means the highest score on IQ is matched with the highest score on the school measure, and the lowest score on IQ is matched with the lowest score on the school measure, with all the intermediate scores falling in a perfect rank ordering. A correlation of −1 indicates the highest IQ score goes with the lowest school performance score and the lowest IQ score with the highest school performance score, with all of the other intervening scores having the same perfect *inverse* relationship. In psychology, it is extremely rare to find correlations that are + 1.0 or −1.0. We are much more used to dealing with correlations on the order of .5 or .6. These correlations indicate there is some degree of relationship between the two scores but also that the two scores are not perfectly related.

We must caution you about interpreting correlation coefficients. First, do *not* infer that simply because two variables are related (correlated), one somehow causes the other. Correlations are not measures of causation; they are simply measures of relationship. For example, if we give the same group of adolescents an IQ test at the age of 12 and then again at 18, we will find a correlation of about .76 (Chapter 4). None of us would suggest the IQ test given at 18 *caused* the performance at age 12. Nor is the reverse the case. Rather a certain set of abilities, motivating conditions, and other factors, perhaps unknown, cause the correlation.

Second, the absolute value of the correlation coefficient, not its sign, determines its strength. The sign attached to the correlation coefficient simply tells the direction of the relationship. Correlations of −.6 and +.6 are equally strong, but in opposite directions.

Finally, one must take care in interpreting the correlation coefficient in terms of its "realness." To clarify this point, let us take up again our example of IQ and school achievement. If we square the correlation coefficient, we have an estimate of the variability in school performance that is accounted for by IQ test performance. In our example, this variability will range somewhere between .36 (.6 x .6 = .36) and .49 (.7 x .7 = .49). In other words, only 36% to 49% of school performance can be accounted for by knowledge of the IQ. The remainder of the variability in school performance must be accounted for by other factors—home environment, school climate, interactions with teachers, peer group views. Although knowing the adolescent's IQ test score will help us deal with issues about the ability to handle school tasks, it is not a perfect predictor of performance. Unless the correlation is extremely high, for example, .90 to 1.0, one should look for other factors that might be related to the adolescent's ability to perform some task.

Factor Analysis. **Factor analysis** is a tool frequently employed by investigators who want to describe a large number of measures by a smaller number of factors. Suppose we administer a test containing nine items. We tabulate the scores and compute the correlations shown in part *a* of Table A–3. The entries in the main diagonal are all 1.0 because scores correlated with themselves always produce a perfect positive correlation. Examination of the remaining correlations indicates the items show a high correlation in some instances and a low or zero correlation in others. In part *b* of Table A–3 we have listed three factors for the matrix in part *a*. As you can see by looking in part *a*, the items in each cluster show high intercorrelations among themselves and low intercorrelations with items from the other clusters. By examining the contents of the items included in each factor we can often label the factor.

This technique is used in many aspects of test development. The SATs, for

Table A–3   Item Intercorrelation Matrix

	a. INTERCORRELATIONS FOR THE NINE ITEMS								
	1	2	3	4	5	6	7	8	9
1	1.0	.1	.8	.2	.9	.2	.0	.1	.0
2		1.0	.1	.7	.1	.2	.8	.0	.1
3			1.0	.0	.1	.2	.1	.0	.1
4				1.0	.1	.0	.0	.1	.2
5					1.0	.1	.1	.3	.2
6						1.0	.0	.8	.7
7							1.0	.3	.2
8								1.0	.8
9									1.0

b. FACTORS PRODUCED BY GROUPING RELATED CORRELATIONS		
I	II	III
1	2	6
3	4	8
5	7	9

example, are composed of two factors: verbal and mathematical. Each factor is measured by a number of subtests, such as vocabulary, punctuation, algebra, and calculus. Each measures a different aspect of verbal or mathematical ability, and within each grouping scores on the subtests will be highly correlated. The correlations between subtests for the two different factors will be much lower. By examining the scores for the two factors we have to deal with less information than if we had to consider all the individual subscores. Factor analysis is a useful technique for summarizing large amounts of information and reducing it to a manageable size.

Inferential Statistics

Although the techniques of descriptive statistics are useful for categorizing and summarizing the data collected, they are not particularly helpful for testing hypotheses about the causes of behavior. For example, suppose we expose one group of ninth graders to a standard algebra curriculum and a second, comparable, group to a new and presumably better curriculum. Is a difference of 3 points favoring the new curriculum on the year-end achievement test a meaningful one? Should we switch all the students to the new curriculum? These are the questions that inferential statistics (see Table A-2) were designed to answer.

Inferential statistics permit us to go beyond a mere description of data and infer cause-and-effect relationships between the dependent variables we measure and the independent variables we manipulate. Consider, for example, a simple experimental design that involves only two groups of subjects. One group will be the experimental group, the group that will be subject to some kind of manipulation (the new algebra curriculum). The other group will be a control group, the group that will receive no manipulation (they receive the old curriculum). We go to a large school, take the names of all the 10th graders in the school, put them in a hat, and then randomly draw 50 names for each of our two groups.

We have now selected a *random sample* of subjects—a sample of subjects picked from a given population in such a way that everyone in the population has an equal chance of being selected. The population we are talking about is the population of 10th graders in a single school; it is not the population of all 10th graders in the United States.

When we pick two random samples in this fashion, we may assume logically that if we were to measure them at the start of the experiment on any of a number of variables the two groups would be very similar. For example, each group will have about the same number of males and females, each should have the same number of good and poor students, and each should have roughly equivalent intelligence levels. The larger the random sample, the more likely this is to be the case. Moreover, each random sample drawn from a given population will be representative of the larger population from which it is drawn, again with the proviso that the larger the random sample the greater the degree to which it will reflect characteristics of the larger group.

Because we have two comparable random samples at the start of the experiment, we may assume any differences in their performance at the conclusion of the experiment must be due to our experimental manipulation and nothing else. To the extent our random samples accurately reflect the larger population, we may generalize the results of the experiment to the larger population.

As we noted earlier, the factor we manipulate is called the independent variable. The measure that we take is on the dependent variable. Our interest, then, is in the performance of the experimental group and the control group on the dependent variable. Do they perform similarly or differently?

Following the completion of the experiment (the teaching of algebra by the two different curricula), inferential statistical techniques are used to evaluate the difference between the experimental and the control group. The logic of inferential statistics says that if the results of our experiment demonstrate a difference in performance between the experimental and control groups, we may assume a true cause-and-effect relationship exists between the independent and dependent variables. Also inherent in the logic of inferential statistics is the concept of error—that because of chance factors, the samples we have selected are not exactly representative of the larger population, and therefore will yield erroneous data. In general, we are willing to accept the results obtained if we can prove (mathematically) that there is only a 5% chance the independent variable had no effect. We do this by calculating a statistic that will tell us if the difference between the two groups is so large it is unlikely to be due to chance and more likely due to our manipulation (the use of two different algebra curricula). Obviously, with a probability of error of 5 in 100, we may be incorrect in our assumption. However, because we have conducted only one experiment, we accept this error level and rely on replication of the results to demonstrate if we are wrong.

When we talk about significant differences, or levels of significance, we are talking of differences that would occur by chance only 5% of the time. Sometimes the mathematical formula reveals an even smaller probability-of-error statistic. You will see such statistics on the tables in this text ($p = .01$, $p = .02$). This means there is only an even smaller probability (1 out of 100 or 2 out of 100) that the results are erroneous.

The important point to understand is that by manipulating potential causes of behavior (independent variables) in an experiment and then demonstrating that the manipulation produced differences in performance (dependent variable) of the experimental and control groups, we are able to determine the causes of behavior. The same statistics can be applied when no manipulation is done. For example, we might measure the proportion of opposite-sex friends for adolescents of different age levels and apply inferential statistics to see if the difference in number of opposite-sex friends is significantly different.

Typically, you will not read about p levels in the text. You will see statements that older adolescents were more likely than younger adolescents to have opposite-sex friends, be more involved in gaining independence, or be more likely to use contraception. When these statements are made they reflect differences that have been shown to be large, that is, important or statistically significant. When you read there were no differences it means the differences were too small to be statistically different.

PROBLEMS IN EVALUATING AND CONDUCTING RESEARCH

Thus far we have talked about research in a fairly simple way. In reality, however, there are a number of potential pitfalls in any research project, some obvious and some not so obvious, and you should be aware of these when evaluating research results. In this final section, we discuss some of these issues.

Problems of Sampling

A number of problems are encountered in obtaining samples of adolescents. One is simply the practical difficulty of obtaining random groups of adolescents for experiments or for filling out questionnaires. The problem here is one of generalizability, about which we have more to say later.

Another problem, somewhat peculiar to studies of adolescent development, is how to define or measure adolescence. In Chapter 1 we noted that adolescence begins with the onset of puberty and ends with maturity, a socially defined measure. We also noted that there is some discussion about the validity of that particular definition because it is somewhat arbitrary. By using a simple age criterion we will certainly make some errors, classifying some potential subjects as adolescents when in fact they are not, particularly at the younger age levels. However, classifying adolescents on measures other than age is extremely difficult. One can hardly imagine a school allowing an investigator to ask girls if they have reached menarche or to ask boys to reveal their secondary sex characteristics. Clearly this problem of measurement will cause us to have some random error in our research findings. In turn, this will mean our results will be somewhat limited. Although in some research this may not be a serious problem, in normative studies (those that attempt to detail typical or usual development) it is an important issue.

In a similar vein, any sample we take from a normal school classroom will necessarily leave out some types of adolescents. For example, adolescents who are chronically ill or who are severely disabled are unlikely to be found in a typical classroom. To the extent our sample does not reflect students in these special categories, it will limit the generalizability of our research findings. Research conducted with samples of adolescents drawn from suburban schools, inner-city schools, or rural schools have similar limitations because they represent select subgroups of adolescents. By employing samples from a variety of subgroups, or by replicating the research with a number of different subgroups, researchers are able to determine if social class, ethnicity, or other factors must be taken into account when interpreting the findings.

A third sampling problem arises when one uses volunteers or paid subjects as opposed to a captive population. There are data indicating that volunteer subjects differ in a number of personality dimensions from nonvolunteer subjects. To the extent a sample is composed entirely of volunteer subjects it will be biased and will not allow us to make general statements about the adolescent population with as much certainty as we would have with a completely random sample. The most obvious way in which volunteer subjects differ is in terms of their cooperativeness, which means they may be more willing to discuss certain matters (such as drug use, sexual behavior, parental childrearing techniques) or to reveal certain kinds of behavior about themselves than nonvolunteer subjects. Therefore, by using only volunteer subjects, we obtain inflated values on certain kinds of information and, perhaps, deflated values on others. Obviously, such a bias will influence the conclusions we derive about adolescent development. Replication of an experiment with nonvolunteer subjects is of some help in determining whether or not our results are biased.

Problems of Reliability and Validity of Measuring Instruments

A common problem encountered in psychological research deals with the reliability and validity of measuring instruments, whether IQ tests, questionnaires of moral development, or scales that measure self-esteem or attitudes. **Reliability** is the degree to which the instrument measures whatever it measures in consistent ways. In other words, if I were to give you IQ tests today and tomorrow, the reliability of the test would be indicated by the closeness of your scores. **Validity** is the degree to which the test measures what it purports to measure. If a test is both reliable and valid, our confidence in the results of research employing the test is increased because we know the test consistently measures what it claims to measure.

Generalization of Research Findings

There are a number of problems related to the generalization of research findings. One is the tendency to regard research findings as more significant or clear cut than they actually are. Our discussion of the use of the correlation between IQ and school achievement falls within this category. Too often teachers, parents, or counselors interpret a correlation between IQ and achievement as much stronger and more important than it actually is. Many children have been victimized by this kind of misuse or misinterpretation of the correlation coefficient.

A second problem, more important for our understanding of adolescent development generally, is to apply research findings gathered in one situation and under one set of circumstances to another situation that differs from the original in one or more critical characteristics. For example, a primarily Catholic population might give a very different set of responses in a research study about attitudes on birth control, abortion, and sexual behavior than another religious population. Generalizing experimental results from one sample to the larger population requires great care, as we noted earlier.

Inappropriate generalization also occurs in case studies. As we noted, case studies are popular in adolescent development, and indeed are useful for highlighting certain aspects of development. Naive readers too often generalize from a given case study to the adolescent population in general or to themselves. However, because a case study involves a single individual, it is unlikely to reflect general laws of development. Furthermore, most, but certainly not all, case studies evolve from the study or treatment of some form of abnormal behavior. The bulk of the published case studies in adolescent psychology deals with adolescents who have had some sort of personality disorder or problem. To derive general laws of adolescent development from them is unfair both to the individual involved in the case study and to those who wish to discover general laws of development. This is not to say there is no value in case studies or in intensive studies of a single individual. However, caution is necessary in reading case studies and generalizing them to yourself or to your friends. Like you, the individual in the case study has a unique developmental history. Therefore, the developmental influences which shaped that particular individual may or may not accurately reflect the influences that were a part of your particular development.

It is, of course, perfectly legitimate to generalize research results, but one must first consider the population on which the study was done and the characteristics of the population to which one wishes to generalize. The closer the characteristics of the two groups, the more reasonable the generalization. In addition, if experimental findings are replicated with different samples of people having different characteristics, we can generalize those results to broader spectrums of the adolescent population.

Special Problems in Studying Adolescents

Researchers have become increasingly aware that it is a subject's right to refuse to participate in an experiment. Therefore, we are faced with a dilemma: On the one hand, we must recognize the rights of the individual; on the other hand, we wish to advance science. Jeopardizing one value for the other is not beneficial to either. Moreover, the ethical guidelines of the American Psychological Association insist that before a subject participates, he or she be informed of the nature of the experiment, the uses to which the information will be put, and any kinds of stress under which the subject may be placed. The subject may refuse to participate at any time and not be penalized for not participating.

Because of the nature of many areas of interest in the study of adolescence, this issue is an extremely important one. Adolescents may not want to discuss aspects of their sexual behavior, sexual development, relationships with their parents and siblings, or a host of other factors of interest to those of us who study adolescent development. This is not so much a problem with adults because adults are generally more aware of the value of research. It is also not so much an issue with children because teachers and principals and others in the school organization are capable of reviewing the research and making judgments on participation based on the value of the research. And often parental consent is obtained along with that of school officials. Adolescents, however, are old enough to make the decision for themselves. Their right to information about the study and their right to refuse to participate must be guaranteed. In adolescent research, then, it is common to obtain not only school and parental permission for participation, but also that of the adolescent.

Another issue, related more to the study of adolescent development than to the study of development in childhood or adulthood, is the notion of frankness. There are a number of studies of adolescent development in which aspects of sexual behavior (see Chapter 8) have been investigated with adolescents who were quite candid and open in their responses to the questionnaires. A guarantee of anonymity helps one gain the confidence of adolescent subjects. However, more often than not, it is probable this degree of frankness occurs only in a select group of adolescents, and we may not know the exact characteristics of that group. In this case, the generalizability of the research findings is difficult and problematical.

Special Problems in Studying Minority Adolescents

Researchers who study minority adolescents face a number of special difficulties (Spencer & Dornbusch, 1990). Although we cannot go into great detail, we summarize some of the points noted in Spender and Dornbusch's excellent discussion.

One is the same as that faced by those involved in cross-cultural research. Researchers bring their own values and ideals to the research setting—how they identify and frame the important questions to be asked, their definitions of optimal and poor development, and their interpretations of the findings. Moreover, the theories that guide the research endeavor are largely based on White middle-class concepts. For these reasons it is important for researchers to constantly be aware that their biases may distort what they "see" and how they interpret it. As Spencer and Dornbusch note, it may not be possible to conduct completely value-free research, but it is incumbent on the researcher to reduce the possibility of bias in research design, instrument selection, and interpretation of the data.

In much of the early research comparing development of minority and White adolescents differences were attributed to racial or ethnic group membership. These researchers failed to take into account the fact that minority status and social class are confounded: Minority youth are overrepresented in the lower social strata. The reported differences in development may reflect social-class differences—poverty, quality of education, living conditions—and not minority group membership. Spencer and Dornbusch further note that even if one assesses development for middle-class White and minority youth it may be an unfair comparison because middle-class minority adolescents still are subject to prejudice and discrimination not experienced by majority adolescents.

Finally, the majority of research has been directed at identifying the negative as opposed to positive aspects of minority group membership. Hence the literature is filled with studies that show poorer development—poorer school performance, greater adolescent pregnancy rates, higher unemployment—attributed to "deficits" in the minority adolescent's home background. Little research has centered on identifying the successes.

Dealing with these difficulties is problematic. Spencer and Dornbusch argue that research dealing with minority youth development must be concerned not only with psychological variables but also sociohistorical contexts. For example, in the study of identity development researchers have now begun to examine the emergence of ethnic identity (Chapter 6)—the degree to which one identifies with one's ethnic group values, ideals, and history. To understand ethnic identity development one must consider not only the processes of identity development (psychological variables) but also the historical and social aspects of being a member of an ethnic minority (sociohistorical factors).

SUMMARY

In this appendix on statistics and design we have tried to make you aware of a number of issues that are involved in conducting research projects so you may become a more sophisticated and knowledgeable student of adolescent development. The various research designs we have discussed, and the problems associated with them, are common in all areas of developmental psychology.

The information on statistics is important because some rudimentary understanding of statistics is necessary for reading and understanding psychological, and any other, research. We do not want you to be handicapped by lack of relevant knowledge as you read through the text, but we also do not want you to become so involved with statistics that you lose sight of the fact we are talking about people.

As with any endeavor, there are problems involved in using research to understand behavior. We discussed a number of these in the final section. In spite of these drawbacks, there have been a substantial number of useful research projects in the field of adolescent development. We should be able to gain considerable information from these projects as we go through the text. You, as a more sophisticated reader, should also be able to profit from your increased understanding of the role of research and theory in explaining behavior.

GLOSSARY

case study design: Systematic study of a single individual at regular intervals over time.

cohort: Group of individuals born in the same year.

confound: Two (or more) measures that are perfectly related, as age and time of measurement or age and cohort.

cross-sectional design: Systematic study of different age groups at about the same point in time.

cross-sequential design: Combined cross-sectional and longitudinal design.

dependent variable: Measure taken in the research.

descriptive statistics: Statistics used to describe the scores obtained (see Table A-2).

factor analysis: Statistical technique for combining scores that are highly related to each other in order to reduce the amount of information one must deal with.

independent variable: Variable that is manipulated in an experiment.

inferential statistics: Techniques used to determine if scores for different groups are statistically meaningful (see Table A-2).

interview: Questionnaire administered in person (or over the phone) by the researcher.

intraindividual change: Change measured for a single individual.

longitudinal design: Systematic assessment of a group of individuals at regular intervals over time.

reliability: How consistently some measure assesses what it is supposed to assess.

validity: How accurately some measure assesses what it is supposed to assess.

References

ABSI-SEMAAN, N., CROMBIE, G., & FREEMAN, C. (1993). Masculinity and femininity in middle childhood: Developmental and factor analyses. *Sex Roles, 28,* 187-206.

ADAMS, G., & FITCH, S. (1982). Ego stage and identity status development: A cross-sequential analysis. *Journal of Personality and Social Psychology, 43,* 574-583.

ADAMS, G., & JONES, R. (1983). Female adolescents' identity development: Age comparisons and perceived childrearing experience. *Developmental Psychology, 19,* 249-256.

ADAMS, G. R. (1992). Introduction and overview. In G. R. Adams, T. P. Gullotta, & R. Montemayor (Eds.), *Adolescent identity formation.* Newbury Park, CA: Sage.

ADELSON, J. (1971, Fall). The political imagination of the young adolescent. *Daedalus,* 1013-1050.

ADELSON, J., & DOEHRMAN, M. (1980). The psychodynamic approach to adolescence. In J. Adelson (Ed.), *Handbook of adolescent psychology.* New York: Wiley.

AGRAS, W. S., SCHNEIDER, J., ARNOW, B., RAEBURN, S., & TELCH, C. (1989). Cognitive-behavioral and response-prevention treatments for bulimia nervosa. *Journal of Consulting and Clinical Psychology, 57,* 215-221.

AHLSTRÖM, W. M., & HAVIGHURST, R. J. (1971). *400 losers.* San Francisco: Jossey-Bass.

AIKEN, L. R. (1987). *Assessment of intellectual functioning.* Boston: Allyn & Bacon.

ALBRECHT, S., BAHR, H., & CHADWICK, B. (1979). Changing family and sex roles: An assessment of age differences. *Journal of Marriage and the Family, 41,* 41-50.

ALLEN, J. P., HAUSER, S. T., BELL, K. L., & O'CONNOR, T. G. (1994). Longitudinal assessment of autonomy and relatedness in adolescent-family interactions as predictors of adolescent ego development and self-esteem. *Child Development, 65,* 179-194.

ALLISTON, P. D., & FURSTENBERG, F. F., JR. (1989). How marital dissolution affects children: Variations by age and sex. *Developmental Psychology, 25,* 540-549.

ALSAKER, F. D., & OLWEUS, D. (1992). Stability of global self-evaluations in early adolescence: A cohort longitudinal study. *Journal of Research on Adolescence, 2,* 123-145.

AMERICAN PSYCHIATRIC ASSOCIATION. (1994). *Diagnostic and statistical manual of mental disorders.* (4th ed.). Washington, D.C.

ANDERSON, E. R., & STARCHER, L. D. (1992, March). *Transformations in sibling relationships during adolescence.* Poster presented at the biennial meetings of the Society for Research on Adolescence, Washington, DC.

ANDERSSON, T., & MAGNUSSON, D. (1990). Biological maturation in adolescence and the development of drinking habits and alcohol abuse among young males: A prospective longitudinal study. *Journal of Youth and Adolescence, 19,* 33-42.

ANDRE, T., FREVERT, R. L., & SCHUCHMANN, D. (1989). From whom have college students learned what about sex? *Youth and Society, 20,* 241-268.

ANTILL, J. (1983). Sex-role complementarity versus similarity in married couples. *Journal of Personality and Social Psychology, 45,* 145-155.

ARBUTHNOT, J. (1975). Modification of moral judgment through role playing. *Developmental Psychology, 11,* 319-324.

ARCHER, S. (1982). The lower age boundaries of identity development. *Child Development, 53,* 1551-1556.

ARCHER, S. A. (1992). Identity as an aspect of optimal psychological functioning. In G. R. Adams, T. P. Gullotta, & R. Montemayor (Eds.), *Adolescent identity formation.* Newbury Park, CA: Sage.

ARLIN, P. K. (1975). Cognitive development in adulthood: A fifth stage? *Developmental Psychology, 11,* 602-606.

ARMSDEN, G. C., & GREENBERG, M. T. (1987). The inventory of parent and peer attachment: Individual differences and their relationship to psychological well-being in adolescence. *Journal of Youth and Adolescence, 16,* 427-454.

ARO, H., & TAIPALE, V. (1987). The impact of timing of puberty on psychosomatic symptoms among fourteen- to sixteen-year-old Finnish girls. *Child Development, 58,* 261-268.

ASTONE, N. M. (1993). Are adolescent mothers just single mothers? *Journal of Research on Adolescence, 3,* 353-371.

AUSUBEL, D. P. (1954). *Theory and problems of adolescent development.* New York: Grune & Stratton.

AUSUBEL, D. P., MONTEMAYOR, R., & SVAJIAN, P. (1977). *Theory and problems of adolescent development* (2nd ed.). New York: Grune & Stratton.

BABER, K. M., & MONAGHAN, P. (1988). College women's career and motherhood expectations; New opinions, old dilemmas. *Sex Roles, 19,* 189-203.

BACHMAN, J. G., & JOHNSTON, L. D. (1979). *Fewer rebels, fewer causes: A profile of today's college freshmen.* Ann Arbor, MI: Institute for Social Research.

BACHMAN, J. G., JOHNSTON, L. D., & O'MALLEY, P. M. (1980). *Monitoring the future: Questionnaire responses from the nation's high school seniors, 1980.* Ann Arbor, MI: Institute for Social Research.

BACHMAN, J. G., & O'MALLEY, P. (1977). Self-esteem in young men: A longitudinal analysis of the impact of educational and occupational attainment. *Journal of Personality and Social Psychology, 35,* 365-380.

BACHMAN, J. G., & O'MALLEY, P. (1986). Self-concepts, self-esteem, and educational experiences: The frog pond revisited (again). *Journal of Personality and Social Psychology, 50,* 35-46.

BACHMAN, J. G., & SCHULENBERG, J. (1993). How part-time work intensity relates to drug use, problem behavior, time use, and satisfaction among high school seniors: Are these consequences or merely correlates? *Developmental Psychology, 29,* 220-235.

BANDURA, A. (1964). The stormy decade: Fact or fiction? *Psychology in the Schools, 1,* 224-231.

BANDURA, A. (1969). Social-learning theory of identificatory processes. In D. A. Goslin (Ed.), *Handbook of socialization: Theory and research*. Chicago: Rand McNally.

BANDURA, A. (1973). *Aggression: A social learning analysis*. Englewood Cliffs, NJ: Prentice-Hall.

BANDURA, A., & MacDONALD, F. J. (1963). Influence of social reinforcement and the behavior of models in shaping children's moral judgments. *Journal of Abnormal and Social Psychology, 67*, 274-281.

BANDURA, A., & WALTERS, R. H. (1959). *Adolescent agression*. New York: Ronald Press.

BANDURA, A., & WALTERS, R. H. (1963). *Social learning and personality development*. New York: Holt, Rinehart & Winston.

BANK, L., REID, J., & GREENLEY, K. (1994, February). *Middle childhood predictors of adolescent and early adult agression*. Poster presented at the biennial meetings of the Society for Research on Adolescence, San Diego, CA.

BARBER, B. K., OLSEN, J. E., & SHAGLE, S. C. (1994). Association between parental psychological and behavioral control and youth internalized and externalized behaviors. *Child Development, 65*, 1120-1136.

BARBER, B. L., CLARK, J. J., CLOSSICK, M. L., & WAMBOLDT, P. (1992, March). *The effects of parent-adolescent communication on adjustment: Variations across divorced and intact families*. Paper presented at the biennial meetings of the Society for Research in Child Development, Washington, DC.

BARDWICK, J. M. (1971). *The psychology of women: A study of biocultural conflicts*. New York: Harper & Row.

BARKER, R. G. (1964). Ecological units. In R. G. Barker & P. V. Gump (Eds.), *Big school, small school*. Stanford, CA: Stanford University Press.

BARTELS, C. L., LIMBER, S. P., O'BEIRNE, H., & WILCOX, B. L. (February, 1994). *Federally funded abstinence-only sex education programs: A meta-evaluation*. Paper presented at the biennial meetings of the Society for Research on Adolescence, San Diego, CA.

BAUCOM, D. H., BESCH, P. K., & CALLAHAN, S. (1985). Relation between testosterone concentration, sex role identity, and personality among females. *Journal of Personality and Social Psychology, 48*, 1218-1226.

BAUMRIND, D. (1978). Parental disciplinary patterns and social competence in children. *Youth and Society, 9*, 239-276.

BAUMRIND, D. (1986). Sex differences in moral reasoning: Response to Walker's (1984) conclusion that there are none. *Child Development, 57*, 511-521.

BAUMRIND, D. (1991). Parenting styles and adolescent development. In J. Brooks-Gunn, R. Lerner, & A. C. Petersen (Eds.), *The encyclopedia of adolescence* (pp. 746-758). New York: Garland.

BELL, A. P., WEINBERG, M., & HAMMERSMITH, S. (1981). *Sexual preference: Its development in men and women*. Bloomington: Indiana University Press.

BELL, R., & COUGHEY, K. (1980). Premarital sexual experience among college females, 1958, 1968, 1978. *Family Relations, 29*, 353-357.

BELL, R. Q. (1968). A reinterpretation of the direction of effects in studies of socialization. *Psychological Review, 75*, 84-88.

BEM, S. (1974). The measurement of psychological androgyny. *Journal of Consulting and Clinical Psychology, 42*, 155-162.

BEM, S. (1975). Sex role adaptability: One consequence of psychological androgyny. *Journal of Personality and Social Psychology, 31*, 634-643.

BEM, S. (1977). On the utility of alternative procedures for assessing psychological androgyny. *Journal of Consulting and Clinical Psychology, 45*, 196-205.

BEM, S. (1981). Gender schema theory: A cognitive account of sex typing. *Psychological Review, 88*, 354-364.

BENEDICT, R. (1938). Continuities and discontinuities in cultural conditioning. *Psychiatry, 1*, 161-167.

BERNDT, T. (1979). Developmental changes in conformity to peers and parents. *Developmental Psychology, 15*, 608-616.

BERNDT, T. (1982). The features and effects of friendship in early adolescence. *Child Development, 53*, 1447-1460.

BERNDT, T. J. (1989, April). *The pathways of friends' influence: Description and developmental change*. Paper presented at the biennial meetings of the Society for Research in Child Development, Kansas City, MO.

BERNDT, T. J. (1992, March). *Stability in friendships: How much, for which adolescents, and why does it matter?* Paper presented at the biennial meetings of the Society for Research in Child Development, Washington, DC.

BERNSTEIN, R. (1980). The development of the self-system during adolescence. *Journal of Genetic Psychology, 136*, 231-245.

BERTI, A. M. (1988). The development of political understanding in children between 6-15 years old. *Human Relations, 41*, 437-466.

BIERMAN, K. L., SMOOT, D. L., & AUMILLER, K. (1993). Characteristics of aggressive-rejected, aggressive (nonrejected), and rejected (nonaggressive) boys. *Child Development, 64*, 139-151.

BINDER, A. (1988). Juvenile delinquency. In M. R. Rosenzweig & L. W. Porter (Eds.), *Annual review of psychology* (Vol. 40). Palo Alto, CA: Annual Reviews.

BIRELEY, M., & GENSHAFT, J. (Eds.) (1991). *Understanding the gifted adolescent: Educational, developmental, and multicultural issues*. New York: Teachers College Press.

BLOCK, J. (1973). Conceptions of sex role: Some cross-cultural and longitudinal perspectives. *American Psychologist, 28*. 512-527.

BLOCK, J., & ROBINS, R. W. (1993). A longitudinal study of consistency and change in self-esteem from early adolescence to early adulthood. *Child Development, 64*, 909-923.

BLOS, P. (1962). *On adolescence*. New York: Free Press.

BLOS, P. (1967). The second individuation process of adolescence. In R. Eissler, A. Freud, H. Hartman, & M. Kris (Eds.), *Psychoanalytic study of the child* (Vol. 22). New York: International Universities Press.

BLOS, P. (1972). The function of the ego ideal in late adolescence. In R. Eissler, A. Freud, M. Kris, & A. J. Solnit (Eds.), *Psychoanalytic study of the child* (Vol. 27). New York: International Universities Press.

BLOS, P. (1974). The genealogy of the ego ideal. In R. Eissler (Ed.), *Psychoanalytic study of the child* (Vol. 29). New Haven, CT: Yale University Press.

BLUMENTHAL, S. J., & KUPFER, D. G. (1988). Overview of early detection and treatment strategies for suicidal behavior in young people. *Journal of Youth and Adolescence, 17*, 1-23.

BLYTH, D., HILL, J., & THIEL, K. (1982). Early adolescents' significant others: Grade and gender differences in perceived relationships with familial and non-familial adults and young people. *Journal of Youth and Adolescence, 11*, 425-450.

BOLDIZAR, J. P., WILSON, K. L., & DEEMER, D. K. (1989). Gender, life experiences, and moral judgment development: A process-oriented approach. *Journal of Personality and Social Psychology, 57*, 229-238.

BOROW, H. (1976). Career development. In J. F. Adams (Ed.), *Understanding adolescence: Current developments in adolescent psychology*. Boston: Allyn & Bacon.

BORST, S. R., & NOAM, G. G. (1993). Developmental psychopathology in suicidal and nonsuicidal adolescent girls.

Journal of the American Academy of Child and Adolescent Psychiatry, 32, 501-508.

BOXER, A. M., COHLER, B. J., HERDT, G., & IRVIN, F. (1993). Gay and lesbian youth. In P. H. Tolan, & B. J. Cohler (Eds.), *Handbook of clinical research and practice with adolescents.* New York: Wiley.

BOYES, M. C., & WALKER, L. J. (1988). Implications of cultural diversity for the universality claims of Kohlberg's theory of moral reasoning. *Human Development, 31,* 44-59.

BRADDOCK, J. H. (1985). School desegregation and black assimilation. *Journal of Social Issues, 41,* 9-22.

BRADLEY, R. H., CALDWELL, B. M., & ROCK, S. L. (1988). Home environment and school performance: A ten-year follow-up and examination of three models of environmental action. *Child Development, 59,* 852-867.

BRAITHWAITE, J. (1981). The myth of social class and criminality reconsidered. *American Sociological Review, 46,* 36-57.

BRENT, D. A., PERPER, J. A., MORITZ, G., ALLMAN, C., FRIEND, A., ROTH, C., SCHWEERS, J., BALACH, L., & BAUGHER, M. (1993). Psychiatric risk factors for adolescent suicide: A case-control study. *Journal of the American Academy of Child and Adolescent Psychiatry, 32,* 521-528.

BROOK, J., WHITEMAN, M., & GORDON, A. (1983). Stages of drug use in adolescence: Personality, peer, and family correlates. *Developmental Psychology, 19,* 269-277.

BROOK, J., WHITEMAN, M., GORDON, A., & BROOK, D. (1984). Paternal determinants of female adolescent's marijuana use. *Developmental Psychology, 20,* 1032-1043.

BROOK, J., WHITEMAN, M., GORDON, A., & COHEN, P. (1986). Dynamics of childhood and adolescent personality traits and adolescent drug use. *Developmental Psychology, 22,* 403-414.

BROOKS, L. (1990a). Career counseling methods and practice. In D. Brown, L. Brooks, & Associates (Eds.), *Career choice and development.* San Francisco: Jossey-Bass.

BROOKS, L. (1990b). Counseling special groups: Women and ethnic minorities. In D. Brown, L. Brooks, & Associates (Eds.), *Career choice and development.* San Francisco: Jossey-Bass.

BROOKS-GUNN, J., & FURSTENBERG, F., JR. (1989). Adolescent sexual behavior. *American Psychologist, 44,* 249-257.

BROOKS-GUNN, J., & REITER, E. (1990). The role of pubertal processes. In S. Feldman & G. Elliott (Eds.), *At the threshold: The developing adolescent.* Cambridge, MA: Harvard University Press.

BROOKS-GUNN, J., & RUBLE, D. (1982). The development of menstrual-related beliefs and behaviors during early adolescence. *Child Development, 53,* 1567-1577.

BROOKS-GUNN, J., & WARREN, M. P. (1989). Biological and social contributors to negative affect in young adolescent girls. *Child Development, 60,* 40-55.

BROVERMAN, I., VOGEL, S., BROVERMAN, D., CLARKSON, F., & ROSENKRANTZ, P. (1972). Sex-role stereotypes: A current appraisal. *Journal of Social Issues, 28,* 59-78.

BROWN, B. B., CLASEN, D., & EICHER, S. (1986). Perceptions of peer pressure, peer conformity dispositions, and self-reported behavior among adolescents. *Developmental Psychology, 22,* 521-530.

BROWN, B. B., LAMBORN, S., & NEWMANN, F. (1992). "You live and you learn": The place of school engagement in the lives of teenagers. In F. Newmann (Ed.), *Student engagement and achievement in American high schools.* New York: Teachers College Press.

BROWN, B. B. (1992). The meaning and measurement of adolescent crowd affiliation. *SRA, 6,* 6-8.

BROWN, B. B., LOHR, M. J., & TRUJILLO, C. M. (1990). Multiple crowds and multiple lifestyles: Adolescents' perceptions of peer group characteristics. In R. E. Muuss (Ed.), *Adolescent behavior and society: A handbook of readings* (4th ed.). New York: Random House.

BROWN, B. B., MOUNTS, N., LAMBORN, S. D., & STEINBERG, L. (1993). Parenting practices and peer group affiliation in adolescence. *Child Development, 64,* 467-482.

BRYK, A., & THUM, Y. (1989). The effects of high school organization on dropping out: An exploratory investigation. *American Educational Research Journal, 26,* 353-383.

BUCHANAN, C. M., MACCOBY, E. E., & DORNBUSCH, S. M. (1991). Caught between parents: Adolescents' experience in divorced homes. *Child Development, 62,* 1008-1029.

BUCHANAN, C. M., MACCOBY, E. E., & DORNBUSCH, S. M. (1992). Adolescents and their families after divorce: Three residential arrangements compared. *Journal of Research on Adolescence, 2,* 261-291.

BUCHANAN, C. M., MACCOBY, E. E., & DORNBUSCH, S. M. (1994, February). *Relationships between adolescents and their parent's new partners.* Paper presented at the biennial meetings of the Society for Research on Adolescence, San Diego, CA.

BUHRMESTER, D., & FURMAN, W. (1987). The development of companionship and intimacy. *Child Development, 58,* 1101-1113.

BULLOUGH, V. L. (1981). Age at menarche: A misunderstanding. *Science, 213,* 365-366.

BUREAU OF LABOR STATISTICS. (1986). *Employment and earnings.* Washington, D.C.

BURTON, R. V. (1963). The generality of honesty reconsidered. *Psychological Review, 70,* 481-499.

BYNNER, J., O'MALLEY, P., & BACHMAN, J. (1981). Self-esteem and delinquency revisited. *Journal of Youth and Adolescence, 10,* 407-441.

CAIRNS, B. D. (1989, April). *Emancipation, abdication, and running away: A longitudinal perspective.* Paper presented at the Biennial Meetings of the Society for Research in Child Development. Kansas City, MO.

CALSYN, R., & KENNY, D. (1977). Self-concept of ability and perceived evaluation of others: Cause or effect of academic achievement? *Journal of Educational Psychology, 69,* 136-145.

CAMARENA, P. M., & SARIGIANI, P. A. (February, 1994). *Sexual victimization and psychological adjustment across adolescence.* Poster presented at the biennial meetings of the Society for Research on Adolescence, San Diego, CA.

CAMPBELL, E. Q. (1969). Adolescent socialization. In D. A. Goslin (Ed.), *Handbook of socialization theory and research.* Chicago: Rand McNally.

CAPLOW, T., & BAHR, H. (1979). Half a century of change in adolescent attitudes: Replication of a Middletown survey by Lynds. *Public Opinion Quarterly, 43,* 1-17.

CARLSON, B. (1987). Dating violence: A research review. *Social Casework, 68,* 16-23.

CARLSON, R. (1965). Stability and change in the adolescent's self-image. *Child Development, 36,* 659-666.

CARSON, C. C., HUELSKAMP, R. M., & WOODALL, T. D. (1993). Perspectives on education in America: An annotated briefing. *Journal of Educational Research, 86,* 259-310.

CARTER, D. B. (1987). The roles of peers in sex role acquisition. In D. B. Carter (Ed.), *Current conceptions of sex roles and sex typing.* New York: Praeger.

CARTER, D. B., & PATTERSON, C. (1982). Sex roles as social conventions: The development of children's conceptions of sex-role stereotypes. *Developmental Psychology, 18,* 812-824.

CASPER, L. (1990). Does family interaction prevent adolescent pregnancy? *Family Planning Perspectives, 22,* 109-114.

CATTELL, R. B. (1941). Some theoretical issues in adult intelligence testing. *Psychological Bulletin, 38*, 592.

CATTELL, R. B. (1963). Theory of fluid and crystallized intelligence: An initial experiment. *Journal of Educational Psychology, 105*, 105–111.

CECI, S. J. (1991). How much does schooling influence general intelligence and its cognitive components? A reassessment of the evidence. *Developmental Psychology, 27*, 703–722.

CENTERS FOR DISEASE CONTROL. (1980). *Abortion survival.* Washington, D.C.: Department of Health, Education, and Welfare (Centers for Disease Control).

CHEN, C., & STEVENSON, H. W. (1989). Homework: A cross-cultural examination. *Child Development, 60*, 551–561.

CHILMAN, C. (1986). Some psychosocial aspects of adolescent sexual and contraceptive behaviors in a changing American society. In J. Lancaster & B. Hamburg (Eds.), *School-age pregnancy and parenthood: Biosocial dimensions.* New York: Aldine/de Gruyter.

CHIPUER, H. M. (1992, March). *Sibling's differential experiences: A within-family analysis.* Poster presented at the biennial meetings of the Society for Research on Adolescence, Washington, D.C.

CLARK, M. L., & AYERS, M. (1988). The role of reciprocity and proximity in junior high school friendships. *Journal of Youth and Adolescence, 17*, 403–411.

CLARK, M. L., KLEIN, J., & BECKETT, J. (1992, March). *Correlates of courtship violence.* Paper presented at the biennial meetings of the Society for Research on Adolescence, Washington, D.C.

CLAUSEN, J. A. (1975). The social meaning of differential physical and sexual maturation. In S. E. Dragastin & G. H. Elder, Jr. (Eds.), *Adolescence in the life cycle.* New York: Halsted.

CLINGEMPEEL, W. G., COLYAR, J. J., BRAND, E., & HETHERINGTON, E. M. (1992). Children's relationships with maternal grandparents: A longitudinal study of family structure and pubertal status effect. *Child Development, 63*, 1404–1422.

COADY, H., & SAWYER, D. (1986). Moral judgment, sex, and level of temptation as determinants of resistance to temptation. *Journal of Psychology, 120*, 177–181.

COLBY, A., KOHLBERG, L., GIBBS, J., & LIEBERMAN, M. (1983). A longitudinal study of moral judgment. *Monographs of the Society for Research in Child Development, 48* (Serial No. 200).

COLEMAN, J. C. (1978). Current contradictions in adolescent theory. *Journal of Youth and Adolescence, 7*, 1–11.

COLEMAN, J. C. (1980). Friendship and the peer group in adolescence. In J. Adelson (Ed.), *Handbook of adolescent psychology.* New York: John Wiley & Sons.

COLEMAN, J. S. (1961). *The adolescent society.* New York: Free Press.

COLEMAN, J. S. (1965). *Adolescents and the schools.* New York: Basic Books.

COLLINS, W. A., & REPINSKI, D. J. (1994). Relationships during adolescence: Continuity and change in interpersonal perspective. In R. Montemayor, G. Adams, & T. Gullotta (Eds.), *Advances in adolescent development: Personal relationships during adolescence.* Beverly Hill, CA: Sage.

COMMONS, M. L., RICHARDS, F. A., & ARMON, S. (1982). *Beyond formal operations: Late adolescent and adult cognitive development.* New York: Praeger.

COMPAS, B. E. (1987). Coping with stress during childhood and adolescence. *Psychological Bulletin, 101*, 393–403.

COMPAS, B. E., & PHARES, V. (1991). Stress during childhood and adolescence: Sources of risk and vulnerability. In E. M. Cummings, A. L. Green, & K. H. Karraker (Eds.), *Life-span developmental psychology: Perspectives on stress and coping.* Hillsdale, NJ: Erlbaum.

CONGER, J. J., & MILLER, W. C. (1966). *Personality, social class, and delinquency.* New York: Wiley.

CONGER, R. D. (1994, February). *Family risks and resilience for adolescent alcohol abuse.* Paper presented at the biennial meetings of the Society for Research on Adolescence, San Diego, CA.

CONGER, R. D., CONGER, K. J., ELDER, G. H., JR., LORENZ, F. O., SIMONS, R. L., & WHITBECK, L. B. (1992). A family process model of economic hardship and adjustment of early adolescent boys. *Child Development, 63*, 526–541.

CONGER, R. D., CONGER, K. J., & SIMONS, R. L. (1992, March). *Family economic stress, parenting behavior, and adolescent drinking.* Paper presented at the biennial meeting of the Society for Research on Adolescence, Washington, D.C.

CONNELL, E. B., DAVIS, J. E., GOLDZIEHER, J. W., & WALLACE, E. Z. (1971). *Hormones, sex, and happiness.* Chicago: Cowles.

CONNELL, J. P., SPENCER, M. B., & ABER, J. L. (1994). Educational risk and resilience in African-American youth: Context, self, action, and outcomes in school. *Child Development, 65*, 493–506.

CONNOLLY, J. (1989, April). *The adolescent peer group: Age-related changes in size, membership, and context.* Paper presented at the biennial meetings of the Society for Research in Child Development, Kansas City, MO.

CONNOLLY, J., WHITE, D., STEVENS, R., & BURSTEIN, S. (1987). Adolescent self-reports of social activity: Assessment of stability and relations to social adjustment. *Journal of Adolescence, 10*, 83–95.

CONSTANTINOPLE, A. (1969). An Eriksonian measure of personality development in college students. *Developmental Psychology, 1*, 357–372.

COOLEY, C. H. (1902). *Human nature and the social order.* New York: Scribner's.

COOPERSMITH, S. (1967). *The antecedents of self-esteem.* San Francisco: Freeman.

COUPEY, S. M. (1992). Anorexia nervosa. In S. B. Friedman, M. Fisher, & S. K. Schonberg (Eds.), *Comprehensive adolescent health care.* St. Louis, MO: Quality Medical Publishing.

CRNIC, L. S., & PENNINGTON, B. F. (1987). Developmental psychology and the neurosciences: An introduction. *Child Development, 58*, 533–538.

CROCKETT, L. J. (1994, February). *Antecedents of adolescent pregnancy: A person centered approach.* Poster presented at the biennial meeting of the Society for Research on Adolescence, San Diego, CA.

CROCKETT, L. J., & BINGHAM, C. R. (1994, February). *Family influences on girls' sexual experience and pregnancy risk.* Paper presented at the biennial meeting of the Society for Research on Adolescence, San Diego, CA.

CULP, R. E., CULP, A. M., OSOFSKY, J. D., & OSOFSKY, H. J. (1989, April). *Adolescent and older mothers: Comparison of their interaction with their six-month-old infants.* Paper presented at the biennial meetings of the Society for Research in Child Development, Kansas City, MO.

CUNNINGHAM, M., & SWANSON, P. (1993, March). *African American adolescent male coping strategies: Expressions of manhood.* Paper presented at the biennial meetings of the Society for Research in Child Development, New Orleans, LA.

DACEY, J. (1989). *Fundamentals of creative thinking.* Lexington, MA: D. C. Heath.

DAMON, W. (1988). *The moral child.* New York: Macmillan.

DAMON, W., & HART, D. (1988). *Self-understanding in childhood and adolescence.* New York: Cambridge University Press.

DAMON, W., & KILLEN, M. (1982). Peer interaction and the process of change in children's moral reasoning. *Merrill Palmer Quarterly, 28*, 347–367.

DARWIN, C. R. (1859). *On the origin of the species by means of natural selection.* London: J. Murray.

DAVIDSON, R. B., & HAVILAND, J. M. (1989a, April). *A developmental approach to understanding and predicting adolescent contraception.* Paper presented at the biennial meetings of the Society for Research in Child Development, Kansas City, MO.

DAVIDSON, R. B., & HAVILAND, J. M. (1989b). *A review of the adolescent contraception literature: A developmental perspective on age and gender.* Unpublished manuscript, Rutgers University, New Brunswick, NJ.

DEGIRMENCIOGLU, S. M., & URBERG, K. A. (1994, February). *Cross-gender friendships in adolescence: Who chooses the "other"?* Poster presented at the biennial meeting of the Society for Research on Adolescence, San Diego, CA.

DELAMATER, J., & MACCORQUODALE, P. (1979). *Premarital sexuality: Attitudes, relationships, behavior.* Madison: University of Wisconsin Press.

DELANEY, J., LUPTON, M., & TOTH, E. (1988). *The curse: A cultural history of menstruation.* Urbana: University of Illinois Press.

DELLA SELVA, P., & DUSEK, J. B. (1984). Sex role orientation and resolution of Eriksonian crises during the late adolescent years. *Journal of Personality and Social Psychology, 14,* 204-212.

DEMO, D., & SAVIN-WILLIAMS, R. (1983). Early adolescent self-esteem as a function of social class: Rosenberg and Pearlin revisited. *American Journal of Sociology, 88,* 763-774.

DICLEMENTE, R. J., PIES, C. A., STOLLER, E. J., STRAITS, C., OLIVIA, G. E., HASKIN, J., & RUTHERFORD, G. W. (1989). Evaluation of school-based AIDS education curricula in San Francisco. *Journal of Sex Research, 26,* 188-198.

DISHION, T. J., PATTERSON, G., STOOLMILLER, M., & SKINNER, M. (1991). Family, school, and behavioral antecedents to early adolescent involvement with antisocial peers. *Developmental Psychology, 27,* 172-180.

DISHION, T. J., RAY, J., & CAPALDI, D. (1992, March). *Parenting precursors to male adolescent substance use.* Paper presented at the biennial meeting of the Society for Research on Adolescence, Washington, DC.

DODGE, K. A. (1990a). Developmental psychopathology in children of depressed mothers. *Developmental Psychology, 26,* 3-6.

DODGE, K. A. (1990b). Special section: Developmental psychopathology in children of depressed mothers. *Developmental Psychology, 26,* 3-67.

DONENBERG, G. R., & HOFFMAN, L. (1988). Gender differences in moral development. *Sex Roles, 18,* 701-717.

DORNBUSCH, S. M., CARLSMITH, J., GROSS, R., MARTIN, J., JENNINGS, D., ROSENBERG, A., & DUKE, P. (1981). Sexual development, age, and dating: A comparison of biological and social influences upon one set of behaviors. *Child Development, 52,* 179-185.

DORNBUSCH, S. M., RITTER, P. L., LEIDERMAN, P. H., ROBERTS, D. F., & FRALEIGH, M. J. (1987). The relation of parenting style to adolescent school performance. *Child Development, 58,* 1244-1257.

DRAGASTIN, S. E., & ELDER, G. H. (Eds.). (1975). *Adolescence in the life cycle.* New York: Wiley.

DRYER, P. (1982). Sexuality during adolescence. In B. Wolman (Ed.), *Handbook of developmental psychology.* Englewood Cliffs, NJ: Prentice-Hall.

DUBOIS, D., & HIRSCH, B. (1990). School and neighborhood friendship patterns of blacks and whites in early adolescence. *Child Development, 61,* 524-536.

DUDGEON, J. A. (1973). Breakdown in maternal protection: Infections. In L. J. Stone, H. T. Smith, & L. B. Murphy (Eds.), *The competent infant.* New York: Basic Books.

DUNCAN, P., RITTER, P., DORNBUSCH, S., GROSS, R., & CARLSMITH, J. (1985). The effects of pubertal timing on body image, school behavior, and deviance. *Journal of Youth and Adolescence, 14,* 227-236.

DUNPHY, D. C. (1963). The social structure of urban adolescent peer groups. *Sociometry, 26,* 230-246.

DUSEK, J. B. (1978). *The development of the self-concept in adolescents.* (Final Report, Contract No. HD-09094). Washington, DC: National Institute of Education.

DUSEK, J. B. (1987a). *Adolescent development and behavior.* Englewood Cliffs, NJ: Prentice-Hall.

DUSEK, J. B., CARTER, D. B., & LEVY, G. (1986). The relationship between identity development and self-esteem during the late adolescent years: Sex differences. *Journal of Adolescent Research, 1,* 251-265.

DUSEK, J. B., & DANKO, M. (1994). Adolescent coping styles and perceptions of parental child rearing. *Journal of Adolescent Research, 9,* 412-426.

DUSEK, J. B., & FLAHERTY, J. (1981). The development of the self-concept during the adolescent years. *Monographs of the Society for Research in Child Development, 46* (4, Whole No. 191), 1-61.

DUSEK, J. B., KERMIS, M., & MONGE, R. H. (1979). The hierarchy of adolescent interests: A social-cognitive approach. *Genetic Psychology Monographs, 100,* 41-72.

DUSEK, J. B., & MONGE, R. H. (1974). *Communicating population control facts to adolescents* (Final Report, Contract No. R01-HD 06724). Washington DC: National Institute of Child Health and Human Development, U. S. Department of Health, Education, and Welfare.

DYKE, P. A., & ADAMS, G. R. (1987). The association between identity development and intimacy during adolescence: A theoretical treatise. *Journal of Adolescent Research, 2,* 223-235.

EAST, P. L. (1994, February). *The younger sisters of childbearing adolescents: Their sexual and childbearing attitudes, expectations, and behaviors.* Paper presented at the biennial meetings of the Society for Research on Adolescence, San Diego, CA.

EAST, P. L., MORGAN, M., FELICE, M. ET AL. (1993, March). *The influence of girlfriends and sisters on girls' sexual behavior, intentions, and attitudes.* Poster presented at the biennial meetings of the Society for Research in Child Development, New Orleans, LA.

EBATA, A. T., & MOOS, R. H. (1989, April). *Coping and adjustment in distressed and healthy adolescents.* Paper presented at the biennial meetings of the Society for Research in Child Development, Kansas City, MO.

EBATA, A. T., & MOOS, R. H. (1994). Personal, situational, and contextual correlates of coping in adolescence. *Journal of Research on Adolescence, 4,* 99-125.

ECCLES, J. S. (1987). Adolescence: Gateway to gender-role transcendence. In D. B. Carter (Ed.), *Current conceptions of sex roles and sex typing.* New York: Praeger.

ECCLES, J. S., JACOBS, J., HAROLD-GOLDSMITH, R., JAYARATNE, T., & YEE, D. (1989, April). *The relations between parents' category-based and target-based beliefs: Gender roles and biological influences.* Paper presented at the biennial meetings of the Society for Research in Child Development, Kansas City, MO.

ECCLES, J. S., MIDGLEY, C., FELDLAUFER, H., WIGFIELD, A., REUMAN, D., & MACIVER, D. (1989, April). *Student and classroom environment mismatch: Junior high school transition effects.* Paper presented at the biennial meetings of the Society for Research in Child Development, Kansas City, MO.

ECCLES, J. S., ET AL. (1993). Developing during adolescence: The impact of stage-environment fit on young adolescent's experiences in schools and families. *Ameican Psychologist, 48,* 90-101.

ECCLES, J. S., & WIGFIELD, A. (1985). Teacher expectations and student motivation. In J. B. Dusek (Ed.), *Teacher expectancies* (pp. 185-226). Hillsdale, NJ: Erlbaum.

EHRHARDT, A., & BAKER, S. (1973). *Hormonal aberrations and their implications for the understanding of normal sex differentiation.* Paper presented at the biennial meetings of the Society for Research in Child Develoment, Philadelphia.

EHRHARDT, A., & BAKER, S. (1974). Fetal androgens, human central nervous system differences, and behavior sex differences. In R. C. Friedman, R. M. Richart, & R. Vande Weile (Eds.), *Sex differences in behavior.* New York: Wiley.

EISEN, M., & ZELLMAN, G. L. (1987). Changes in incidence of sexual intercourse of unmarried teenagers following a community-based sex education program. *Journal of Sex Research, 23,* 527-533.

EISERT, D., & KAHLE, L. (1982). Self-evaluation and social comparison of physical and role change during adolescence: A longitudinal analysis. *Child Development, 53,* 98-104.

ELDER, G. H., JR. (1974). *Children of the great depression.* Chicago: University of Chicago Press.

ELDER, G. H., JR. (1980). Adolescence in historical perspective. In J. Adelson (Ed.), *Handbook of adolescent psychology.* New York: Wiley.

ELDER, G. H., JR., ECCLES, J. S., ARDELT, M., & LORD, S. (1993, March). *Inner city parents under economic pressure: Perspectives on the strategies of parenting.* Paper presented at the biennial meetings of the Society for Research in Child Development, New Orleans, LA.

ELKIND, D. (1967b). Egocentrism in adolescence. *Child Development, 38,* 1025-1034.

ELKIND, D. (1970). *Children and adolescents: Interpretive essays on Jean Piaget.* New York: Oxford University Press.

ELKIND, D. (1978a). *The child's reality: Three developmental themes.* NJ: Erlbaum.

ELKIND, D. (1978b). Understanding the young adolescent. *Adolescence, 13,* 127-134.

ELKIND, D., & BOWEN, R. (1979). Imaginary audience behavior in children and adolescents. *Developmental Psychology, 15,* 38-44.

ELLIOTT, D. S., & AGETON, S. S. (1980). Reconciling race and class differences in self-reported and official estimates of delinquency. *American Sociological Review, 45,* 95-110.

ELLIOTT, D. S., VOSS, H. L., & WENDLING, A. (1966). Capable dropouts and the social milieu of the high school. *Journal of Educational Rsearch, 60,* 180-186.

ELSTER, A. B., LAMB, M. E., & TAVARE, J. (1987). Association between behavioral and school problems and fatherhood in a national sample of adolescent youths. *Journal of Pediatrics, 111,* 932-936.

ENGEL, M. (1959). The stability of the self-concept in adolescence. *Journal of Abnormal and Social Psychology, 58,* 211-215.

ENRIGHT, R., LAPSLEY, D., & SHUKLA, D. (1979). Adolescent egocentrism in early and late adolescence. *Adolescence, 14,* 687-695.

ENRIGHT, R., & SUTTERFIELD, S. (1980). An ecological validation of social cognition development. *Child Development, 51,* 156-161.

ENTWISLE, D. (1990). Schools and the adolescent. In S. Feldman & G. Elliott (Eds.), *At the threshold: The developing adolescent.* Cambridge, MA: Harvard University Press.

EPSTEIN, L. H. (1987). Behavioral treatment of childhood obesity. *Psychological Bulletin, 101,* 331-342.

ERIKSON, E. (1959). Identity and the life cycle. *Psychological Issues, 1,* 1-71.

ERIKSON, E. (1963). *Childhood and society* (2nd ed.). New York: Norton.

ERIKSON, E. (1968). *Identity, youth, and crisis.* New York: Norton.

EVELETH, P., & TANNER, J. (1976). *Worldwide variation in human growth.* New York: Cambridge University Press.

FAGOT, B. I., & LEINBACH, M. D. (1987). Socialization of sex roles within the family. In D. B. Carter (Ed.), *Current conceptions of sex roles and sex typing.* New York: Praeger.

FAGOT, B. I., & LEINBACH, M. D. (1989). The young child's gender schema: Environmental input, internal organization. *Child Development, 60,* 663-672.

FARNWORTH, M. (1984). Family structure, family attributes, and delinquency in a sample of low-income, minority males and females. *Journal of Youth and Adolescence, 13,* 349-364.

FAULKENBERRY, J. R., VINCENT, M., JAMES A., & JOHNSON, W. (1987). Coital behaviors, attitudes, and knowledge of students who experience early coitus. *Adolescence, 22,* 321-332.

FAUST, M. S. (1977). Somatic development of adolescent girls. *Monographs of the Society for Research in Child Development, 42* (Whole No. 169).

FEATHER, N. (1975). *Values in education and society.* New York: Free Press.

FEATHER, N. (1980). Values in adolescence. In J. Adelson (Ed.), *Handbook of adolescent psychology* (pp. 247-294). New York: Wiley.

FEINGOLD, A. (1988). Cognitive gender differences are disappearing. *American Psychologist, 43,* 95-103.

FEIRING, C. (1993, March). *Developing concepts of romance from 15 to 18 years.* Paper presented at the biennial meeting of the Society for Research in Child Development, New Orleans, LA.

FELDMAN, S. S., & WEINBERGER, D. A. (1994). Self-restraint as a mediator of family influences on boys' delinquent behavior: A longitudinal study. *Child Development, 65,* 195-211.

FELDMAN, S. S., WENTZEL, K. R., WEINBERGER, D., & MUNSON, J. A. (1989, April). *Marital satisfaction of parents of preadolescent boys and its relationship to family and child functioning.* Paper presented at the biennial meetings of the Society for Research in Child Development, Kansas City, MO.

FELDMAN, S. S., & WOOD, D. N. (1994). Parents' expectations for preadolescent sons' behavioral autonomy: A longitudinal study of correlates and outcomes. *Journal of Research on Adolescence, 4,* 45-70.

FELSON, R., & ZIELINSKI, M. (1989). Children's self-esteem and parental support. *Journal of Marriage and the Family, 51,* 727-735.

FENZEL, L. M. (1989a, April). *An ecological study of changes in student role strains during the transitions to middle school.* Paper presented at the biennial meetings of the Society for Research in Child Development, Kansas City, MO.

FENZEL, L. M. (1989b, April). *The transition to middle school: Longitudinal trends and sex differences in student role strains.* Paper presented at the biennial meetings of the Society for Research in Child Development, Kansas City, MO.

FILSINGER, E. (1980). Difference between own and friend's social status as a predictor of psychological differentiation. *Psychological Reports, 45,* 187-195.

FILSINGER, E., & ANDERSON, C. (1982). Social class and self-esteem in late adolescence: Dissonant context or self-efficacy? *Developmental Psychology, 18,* 380-384.

FINE, G., MORTIMER, J., & ROBERTS, D. (1990). Leisure, work, and the mass media. In S. Feldman & G. Elliott (Eds.), *At the threshold: The developing adolescent.* Cambridge: Harvard University Press.

FLAHERTY, J., & DUSEK, J. (1980). An investigation of the relationship between psychological androgyny and components of self-concept. *Journal of Personality and Social Psychology, 38,* 984–992.

FLANAGAN, C. (1989, April). *Economic stress in the family: Do the effects for daughters and sons differ?* Paper presented at the biennial meetings of the Society for Research in Child Development, Kansas City, MO.

FLAVELL, J. H. (1985). *Cognitive development.* Englewood Cliffs, NJ: Prentice-Hall.

FLOYD, H. H., JR., & SOUTH, D. R. (1972). Dilemma of youth: The choice of parents or peers as a frame of reference for behavior. *Journal of Marriage and the Family, 34,* 627–634.

FORD, M. (1982). Social cognition and social competence in adolescence. *Developmental Psychology, 18,* 323–340.

FORD, M., WENTZEL, K. R., WOOD, D., STEVENS, E., & SIESFELD, G. A. (1989). Processes associated with integrative social competence: Emotional and contextual influences on adolescent social responsibility. *Journal of Adolescent Research, 4,* 405–425.

FORDHAM, S. (1988). Racelessness as a factor in black students' school success: Pragmatic strategy or pyrrhic victory? *Harvard Educational Review, 58,* 54–84.

FORDHAM, S., & OGBU, J. U. (1986). Black students' school success: Coping with the "burden of 'acting white.'" *Urban Review, 18,* 176–206.

FORGATCH, M. S., DEGARMO, D. S., & KNUTSON, N. M. (1994, February). *Transitions within transitions: The impact of adolescence and family structure on boys' antisocial behavior.* Paper presented at the biennial meetings of the Society for Research on Adolescence, San Diego, CA.

FORGATCH, M. S., & STOOLMILLER, M. (1994). Emotions as contexts for adolescent delinquency. *Journal of Research on Adolescence, 4,* 601–614.

FOWLER, J. (1981). *Signs of faith.* New York: Harper & Row.

FREUD, A. (1948). *The ego and the mechanisms of defense* (C. Baines, Trans.). New York: International Universities Press.

FREUD, A. (1958). Adolescence. In R. Eissler, A. Freud, H. Hartman, & M. Kris (Eds.), *Psychoanalytic study of the child* (Vol. 13). New York: International Universities Press.

FREUD, S. (1924). The passing of the Oedipal complex. In *Collected papers* (Vol. 2). London: Hogarth Press.

FREUD, S. (1950). *The ego and the id.* London: Hogarth Press. (Original work published 1923)

FRIEDMAN, W. J., ROBINSON, A. B., & FRIEDMAN, B. L. (1987). Sex differences in moral judgments? A test of Gilligan's theory. *Psychology of Women Quarterly, 11,* 37–46.

FRISH, R. E. (1974). Critical weight at menarche, initiation of the adolescent growth spurt, and control of puberty. In M. M. Grumbach, G. D. Grave, & F. E. Mayer (Eds.), *Control of the onset of puberty.* New York: Wiley.

FRISH, R. E. (1983). Fatness, puberty, and fertility: The effects of nutrition and physical training on menarche and ovulation. In J. Brooks-Gunn & A. C. Petersen (Eds.), *Girls at puberty.* New York: Plenum Press.

FRISK, M., TENHUNEN, T., WIDHOLM, O., & HORTLING, H. (1966). Psychological problems in adolescents showing advanced or delayed physical maturation. *Adolescence, 1,* 126–140.

FULIGNI, A. J., & ECCLES, J. S. (1993). Perceived parent-child relationships and early adolescents' orientation toward peers. *Developmental Psychology, 29,* 622–632.

FURMAN, W., & WEHNER, E. A. (in press). Romantic views: Toward a theory of adolescent romantic relationships. In R. Montemayor (Ed.), *Advances in adolescent developm*

Relationships in adolescence (Vol. 3). Beverly Hills, CA: Sage.

FURSTENBERG, F., JR., BROOKS-GUNN, J., & MORGAN, S. (1987). *Adolescent mothers in later life.* New York: Cambridge University Press.

FURTH, H., & MCCONVILLE, K. (1981). Adolescent understanding of compromise in political and social arenas. *Merrill Palmer Quarterly, 27,* 413–427.

GADDIS, A., & BROOKS-GUNN, J. (1985). The male experience of pubertal change. *Journal of Youth and Adolescence, 14,* 61–70.

GALLUP, G., & POLING, D. (1980). *The search for America's faith.* New York: Abington.

GALTON, F. (1883). *Inquiries into human faculty and its development.* London: Macmillan.

GAMORAN, A. (1987). The stratification of high school learning opportunities. *Sociology of Education, 60,* 135–155.

GAMORAN, A., & MARE, R. (1989). Secondary school tracking and educational inequality: Compensation, reinforcement, or neutrality? *American Journal of Sociology, 94,* 1146–1183.

GANS, J. (1990). *America's adolescents: How healthy are they?* Chicago: American Medical Association.

GARDNER, H. (1983). *Frames of mind.* New York: Basic Books.

GARDNER, W. M., ROPER, J. T., & GONZALEZ, C. C., (1988). Analysis of cheating on academic assignments. *Psychological Record, 38,* 543–555.

GARLAND, A. F., & ZIGLER, E. (1993). Adolescent suicide prevention. *American Psychologist, 48,* 169–182.

GARNETS, L. D., & KIMMEL, D. C. (1991). Lesbian and gay male dimensions in the psychological study of human diversity. In J. Goodchilds (Ed.), *Psychological perspectives on human diversity in America.* Washington, DC: American Psychological Association.

GARNETS, L. D., & KIMMEL, D. C. (Eds.). (1993). *Psychological perspectives on lesbian and gay male experiences.* New York: Columbia University Press.

GARRISON, C. Z., ADDY, C. L., MCKEOWN, R. E., CUFFE, S. P., JACKSON, K. L., & WALLER, J. L. (1993). Nonsuicidal physically self-damaging acts in adolescents. *Journal of Child and Family Studies, 2,* 339–352.

GAVIN, L. A., & FURMAN, W. (1989). Age differences in adolescents' perceptions of their peer groups. *Developmental Psychology, 25,* 827–834.

GE, X., CONGER, R. D., LORENZ, F. O., ELDER, G. H., JR., MONTAGUE, R. B., & SIMONS, R. L. (1992). Linking family economic hardship to adolescent distress. *Journal of Research on Adolescence, 2,* 351–378.

GERRARD, M. (1987). Sex, sex guilt, and contraceptive use revisited: The 1980s. *Journal of Personality and Social Psychology, 52,* 975–980.

GEWIRTZ, J. L. (1969). Mechanisms of social learning: Some roles of stimulation and behavior in early human development. In D. A. Goslin (Ed.), *Handbook of socialization theory and research.* Chicago: Rand McNally.

GIBBS, J. (Ed.) (1988) *Young, black and male in America: An endangered species.* Dover, MA: Auburn House.

GILLIGAN, C. (1982). *In a different voice.* Cambridge, MA: Harvard University Press.

GILLIGAN, C., & ATTANUCCI, J. (1988). Much ado about . . . knowing? Noting? Nothing? A reply to Vasudev concerning sex differences and moral development. *Merrill Palmer Quarterly, 34,* 451–456.

GINZBERG, E. (1990). Career development. In D. Brown, L. Brooks, & Associates (Eds.), *Career choice and development.* San Francisco: Jossey-Bass.

GINZBERG, E., GINZBERG, S. W., AXELROD, S., & HERMAN, S. L.

(1951). *Occupational choice.* New York: Columbia University Press.

GLAZER, C., & DUSEK, J. B. (1985). The relationship between sex-role orientation and resolution of Eriksonian developmental crises. *Sex Roles, 13,* 653-661.

GOLD, D., & ANDRES, D. (1978a). Developmental comparisons between adolescent children with employed and nonemployed mothers. *Merrill Palmer Quarterly, 24,* 243-254.

GOLD, D., & ANDRES, D. (1978b). Developmental comparisons between 10-year-old children with employed and nonemployed mothers. *Child Development, 49,* 75-84.

GOLD, M., & PETRONIO, R. J. (1980). Delinquent behavior in adolescence. In J. Adelson (Ed.), *Handbook of adolescent psychology* (pp. 495-535). New York: Wiley.

GOLD, M., & REIMER, D. J. (1975). Changing patterns of delinquent behavior among American 13 through 16 year olds: 1967-1972. *Crime and Delinquency Literature, 7,* 483-517.

GONDOLI, D. M., & SILVERBERG, S. B. (February, 1994). *Use of psychological control by mothers of early adolescents: The role of maternal depressive symptoms.* Poster presented at the biennial meetings of the Society for Research on Adolescence, San Diego, CA.

GOODLAD, J. (1984). *A place called school.* New York: McGraw-Hill.

GOOSSENS, L. (1994, February). *Separation-individuation and the "new look" at adolescent egocentrism.* Poster presented at the biennial meetings of the Society for Research on Adolescent Development, San Diego, CA.

GOUWS, K. R., & HUFFMAN, A. (1994, February). *Depressive symptomatology and quality of relationships with family and friends.* Poster presented at the biennial meetings of the Society for Research on Adolescence, San Diego, CA.

GRABE, M. (1981). School size and the importance of school activities. *Adolescence, 16,* 21-31.

GRANT, L. S., SMITH, T. A., SINCLAIR, J. J., & SALTS, C. J. (1993). The impact of parental divorce on college adjustment. *Journal of Divorce and Remarriage, 19,* 183-193.

GREEN, R. (1980). Homosexuality. In H. Kaplan, A. Freedman, & B. Sadock (Eds.), *Comprehensive textbook of psychiatry* (3rd ed., Vol. 2). Baltimore: Williams & Wilkins.

GREEN, R. (1987). *The 'sissy boy' syndrome and the development of homosexuality.* New Haven, CT: Yale University Press.

GREENBERGER, E., & STEINBERG, L. D. (Final Report). *Part-time employment of in-school youth: An assessment of costs and benefits.* Washington, DC: National Institute of Education.

GREENBERGER, E., & STEINBERG, L. D. (1983). Sex differences in early labor force experience: Harbinger of things to come. *Social Forces, 10,* 467-486.

GREENBERGER, E., STEINBERG, L. D., & RUGGIERO, M. A. (1982). A job is a job is a job . . . or is it? *Work and Occupation, 9,* 79-96.

GREENBERGER, E., STEINBERG, L., VAUX, A., & MCAULIFFE, S. (1980). Adolescents who work: Effects of part-time employment on family and peer relations. *Journal of Youth and Adolescents, 9,* 189-202.

GREIF, E., & ULMAN, K. (1982). The psychological impact of menarche on early adolescent females: A review of the literature. *Child Development, 53,* 1413-1430.

GRIBBONS, W. D., & LOHNES, P. R. (1966). Occupational preferences and measured intelligence. *Vocational Guidance Quarterly, 14,* 211-214.

GROLNICK, W. S., & RYAN, R. M. (1989). Parent styles associated with children's self-regulation and competence in school. *Journal of Educational Psychology, 81,* 143-154.

GROTEVANT, H. D. (1986). Assessment of identity development: Current issues and future directions. *Journal of Adolescent Research, 1,* 175-182.

GROTEVANT, H. D. (1987). Toward a process model of identity formation. *Journal of Adolescent Research, 2,* 203-222.

GROTEVANT, H. D. (1992). Assigned and chosen identity components: A process perspective on their integration. In G. R. Adams, T. P. Gullotta, & R. Montemayor (Eds.), *Adolescent identity formation.* Newbury Park, CA: Sage.

GROTEVANT, H. D., SCARR, S., & WEINBERG, R. (1977). Patterns of interest similarity in adoptive and biological families. *Journal of Personality and Social Psychology, 35,* 667-676.

GROTEVANT, H. D., & THORNBECKE, W. (1982). Sex differences in styles of occupational identity formation in late adolescence. *Developmental Psychology, 18,* 396-405.

GROTEVANT, H. D., THORNBECKE, W., & MEYER, M. (1982). An extension of Marcia's identity status interview into the interpersonal domain. *Journal of Youth and Adolescence, 11,* 33-47.

GRUMBACH, M. M., GRAVE, G. D., & MAYER, F. E. (Eds.), (1974). *Control of the onset of puberty.* New York: Wiley.

GUAY, J. A., & DUSEK, J. B. (1992, March). *Perceived childrearing practices and styles of coping.* Poster presented at the biennial meetings of the Society for Research in Child Development, New Orleans, LA.

GUILFORD, J. P. (1988). Some changes in the Structure-of-Intellect model. *Educational and Psychological Measurement, 48,* 1-4.

GUMP, P. V. (1966). *Big schools, small schools.* Moravia, NY: Chronicle Guidance Publications.

GUNNOE, M. L. (1994, February). *Noncustodial mothers' and fathers' contributions to the adjustment of adolescents in stabilized stepfamilies.* Paper presented at the biennial meetings of the Society for Research in Adolescence, San Diego, CA.

GUTTMAN, J. (1988-1989). Intimacy in young adult males' relationships as a function of divorced and non-divorced family of origin status. *Journal of Divorce, 12,* 253-261.

HAAS, A. (1979). *Teenage sexuality.* New York: Macmillan.

HALL, G. S. (1904). *Adolescence* (2 vols.). New York: Appleton.

HALLINAN, M. T. (1991). School differences in tracking structures and tract assignments. *Journal of Research on Adolescence, 1,* 251-175.

HALLINAN, M. T., & WILLIAMS, R. (1989). Interracial friendship choices in secondary schools. *American Sociological Review, 54,* 67-78.

HALMI, K. A. (1987). Anorexia nervosa and bulimia. In V. B. Van Hasselt & M. Hersen (Eds.), *Handbook of adolescent psychology.* New York: Pergamon Press.

HALPERN, C. T., & UDRY, J. R. (1992). Variation in adolescent hormone measures and implications for behavioral research. *Journal of Research on Adolescence, 2,* 103-122.

HALPERN, C. T., UDRY, J. R., CAMPBELL, B., & SUCHINDRAN, C. (1992, March). *Hormonal influences on adolescent male sexual activity.* Paper presented at the biennial meetings of the Society for Research on Adolescence, Washington, DC.

HANNAH, J., & KAHN, S. (1989). The relationship of socioeconomic status and gender to occupational choices of twelfth grade students. *Journal of Vocational Behavior, 34,* 161-178.

HARDY, D. F., POWER, T. G., & JAEDICKE, S. (1993). Examining the relation of parenting to children's coping. *Child Development, 64,* 1829-1841.

HAROLD, R. D., & ECCLES, J. S. (1990, March). *Maternal expectations, advice, and provision of opportunities: Their relationships to boys' and girls' occupational aspirations.*

Paper presented at the biennial meetings of the Society for Research on Adolescence, Atlanta, GA.

HARTER, S. (1986). Processes underlying the construction, maintenance, and enhancement of the self-concept in children. In J. Suls & A. G. Greenwald (Eds.), *Psychological perspectives on the self* (Vol. 3). Hillsdale, NJ: Erlbaum.

HARTER, S. (1989). Processes underlying adolescent self-concept formation. In R. Montemayor (Ed.), *Advances in adolescent development: Vol. 2. The transition from childhood to adolescence.* New York: Russel Sage Foundation.

HARTER, S. (1990). Identity and self development. In S. Feldman & G. Elliott (Eds.), *At the threshold: The developing adolescent* (pp. 352-387). Cambridge, MA: Harvard University Press.

HARTUP, W. W. (1989). Social relationships and their developmental significance. *American Psychologist, 44,* 120-126.

HARTUP, W. W., & LAURSEN, B. (1989, April). *Contextual constraints and children's friendship relations.* Paper presented at the biennial meetings of the Society for Research in Child Development, Kansas City, MO.

HAVIGHURST, R. J. (1951). *Developmental tasks and education.* New York: Longmans, Green.

HAVIGHURST, R. J. (1972). *Developmental tasks and education* (3rd ed.). New York: David McKay.

HAVIGHURST, R. J. (1978). Common experience versus diversity in the curriculum. *Educational Leadership, 36,* 118-121.

HAYES, C. D. (ED.). (1987). *Risking the future: Adolescent sexuality, pregnancy, and childbearing* (Vol. 1). Washington, DC: National Academy Press.

HAYWARD, C., KILLEN, J., & TAYLOR, C. B. (1994, February). *Timing of puberty and the onset of psychiatric symptoms.* Paper presented at the biennial meetings of the Society for Research on Adolescence, San Diego, CA.

HEKTNER, J. (February, 1994). *How talented rural adolescents think about their future careers: Questions of geographic and social mobility.* Poster presented at the biennial meeting of the Society for Research on Adolescence, San Diego, CA.

HELLER, K., & PARSONS, J. (1981). Sex differences in teachers' evaluative feedback and students' expectancies for success in mathematics. *Child Development, 52,* 1015-1019.

HENGGELER, S. W. (1989). *Delinquency in adolescence.* Newbury Park, CA: Sage.

HENSHAW, S. K. (1987). Characteristics of U. S. women having abortions, 1982-1983. *Family Planning Perspectives, 19,* 5-9.

HERDT, G. (1990). Developmental discontinuities and sexual orientation across cultures. In D. P. McWhirter, S. A. Sanders, & J. M. Reinish (Eds.), *Homosexuality/heterosexuality: Concepts of sexual orientation.* New York: Oxford University Press.

HERMAN-STAHL, M. (1994, February). *Individual differences in the relationship between stress and adjustment during early adolescence.* Poster presented at the biennial meeting of the Society for Research in Adolescence, San Diego, CA.

HERRNSTEIN, R. J., & MURRAY, C. A. (1994). *The bell curve: Intelligence and class structure in American life.* New York: Free Press.

HETHERINGTON, E. M. (1979). Divorce: A child's perspective. *American Psychologist, 34,* 851-858.

HETHERINGTON, E. M. (1989). Coping with family transitions: Winners, losers, and survivors. *Child Development, 60,* 1-14.

HETHERINGTON, E. M., CLINGEMPEEL, W. G., ET AL. (1992). Coping with marital transitions. *Monographs of the Society for Research in Child Development, 57* (Serial No. 227).

HETHERINGTON, E. M., COX, M., & COX, R. (1976). Divorced fathers. *Family Coordinator, 25,* 417-428.

HETHERINGTON, E. M., COX, M., & COX, R. (1979). Family interactions and the social, emotional and cognitive development of children following divorce. In V. C. Vaughan & T. B. Brazelton (Eds.), *The family: Setting priorities.* New York: Science and Medicine.

HETHERINGTON, E. M., COX, M., & COX, R. (1985). Long-term effects of divorce and remarriage on the adjustment of children. *Journal of the American Academy of Child Psychiatry, 24,* 518-530.

HIGHAM, E. (1980). Variations in adolescent psychohormonal development. In J. Adelson (Ed.), *HAndbook of adolescent psychology.* New York: Wiley.

HILL, C., RUBIN, Z., & PEPLAU, L. (1979). Breakups before marriage: The end of 103 affairs. In G. Levinger & O. Moles (Eds.), *Divorce and separation.* New York: Basic Books.

HILL, J. (1980). The family. In M. Johnson (Ed.), *Toward adolescence: The middle school years. The 79th yearbook of the National Society for the Study of Educaton: Part I.* Chicago: University of Chicago Press.

HILL, J., & MONKS, F. (1977). *Adolescence and youth in prospect.* Surrey, England: IPC Science and Technology Press.

HILL, J., HOLMBECK, G., MARLOW, L., GREEN, T., & LYNCH, M. (1985a). Pubertal status and parent-child relations in families of seventh-grade boys. *Journal of Youth and Adolescence, 5,* 31-44.

HILL, J., HOLMBECK, G., MARLOW, L., GREEN, T., & LYNCH, M. (1985b). Mencheal status and parent-child relations in families of seventh-grade girls. *Journal of Youth and Adolescence, 14,* 301-316.

HIRAGA, Y., CAUCE, A. M., MASON, C., & ORDONEZ, N. (1993, March). *Ethnic identity and the social adjustment of biracial youth.* Paper presented at the biennial meetings of the Society for Research in Child Development, New Orleans, LA.

HIRSCH, B. J., & RAPKIN, B. D. (1987). The transition to junior high school: A longitudinal study of self-esteem, psychological symptomatology, school life, and social support. *Child Development, 58,* 1235-1243.

HODGSON, J., & FISCHER, J. (1979). Sex differences in identity and intimacy development in college youth. *Journal of Youth and Adolescence, 8,* 37-50.

HOFFERTH, S. L., KAHN, J. R., & BALDWIN, W. (1987). Premarital sexual activity among U. S. Teenage women over the past three decades. *Family Planning Perspectives, 19,* 46-53.

HOFFMAN, L. (1977). Changes in family roles, socialization, and sex differences. *American Psychologist, 32,* 644-657.

HOFFMAN, L. (1979). Maternal employment: 1979. *American Psychologist, 34,* 859-865.

HOFFMAN, L. (1980). The effects of maternal employment on the academic attitudes and performance of school-aged children. *School Psychology Review, 9,* 319-335.

HOFFMAN, L. (1989). Effects of maternal employment in the two-parent family. *American Psychologist, 44,* 283-292.

HOFFMAN, M. L. (1970). Moral development. In P. H. Mussen (Ed.), *Carmichael's manual of child psychology* (3rd ed., Vol. 2). New York: Wiley.

HOFFMAN, M. L. (1980). Moral development in adolescence. In J. Adelson (Ed.), *Handbook of adolescent psychology.* New York: Wiley.

HOLAHAN, C. J., & MOOS, R. H. (1987). Personal and contextual determinants of coping strategies. *Journal of Personality and Social Psychology, 52,* 946-955.

HOLLAND, J. L. (1985). *Making vocational choices: A theory of vocational personalities and work environments* (2nd ed.). Englewood Cliffs, NJ: Prentice-Hall.

HOLLAND, J. L. (1987). Current status of Holland's theory of careers: Another perspective. *Career Development Quarterly, 36,* 24–30.

HOLLINGSHEAD, A. B. (1949). *Elmstown youth.* New York: Wiley.

HOLLINGSHEAD, A. B. (1975). *Elmtown's youth and Elmtown revisited.* New York: Wiley.

HOOD, J., MOORE, T. E., & GARNER, D. (1982). Locus of control as a measure of ineffectiveness in anorexia nervosa. *Journal of Consulting and Clinical Psychology, 50,* 3–13.

HOOKER, K., & FIESE, B. H. (1993, March). *Temporal perspectives on changes in self related to parenting.* Paper presented at the biennial meetings of the Society for Research in Child Development, New Orleans, LA.

HOPS, H. (1994, February). *Adolescent-mother interactions as predictors of substance use.* Paper presented at the biennial meetings of the Society for Research on Adolescent Development, San Diego, CA.

HOPS, H., SHERMAN, L., & BIGLAN, A. (in press). Maternal depression, marital discord, and children's behavior: A developmental perspective. In G. R. Patterson (Ed.), *Depression and aggression in family interactions.* New York: Erlbaum.

HORN, J. L. (1968). Organization of abilities and the development of intelligence. *Psychological Review, 75,* 242–259.

HOROWITZ, F. D., & O'BRIEN, M. (1986). Gifted and talented children. *American Psychologist, 41,* 1147–1152.

HORWITZ, S. M., KLERMAN, L. V., KUO, H. S., & JEKEL, J. F. (1991). School-age mothers: Predictors of long-term educational and economic outcomes. *Pediatrics, 87,* 862–868.

HOWAT, P. M., & SAXTON, A. M. (1988). The incidence of bulimic behavior in a secondary and university school population. *Journal of Youth and Adolescence, 17,* 221–231.

HOWE, N., AQUAN-ASSEE, J., & BUKOWSKI, W. M. (in press). Self-disclosure and the sibling relationship: What did Romulus tell Remus? In K. J. Rotenberg (Ed.), *Disclosure processes in children and adolescents.* New York: Springer-Verlag.

HOWES, C., & PHILIPSEN, L. (1992). Gender and friendship: Relationships within peer groups of young children. *Social Development, 1,* 2–242.

HOYT, K. B. (1989). The career status of women and minority persons: A 20-year retrospective. *Career Development Quarterly, 37,* 202–212.

HUDAK, M. A. (1993). Gender schema theory revisited: Men's stereotypes of American women. *Sex Roles, 28,* 279–293.

HUDSON, L., & GRAY, W. (1986). Formal operations, the imaginary audience and the personal fable. *Adolescence, 21,* 751–765.

HUIZINGA, D., & ELLIOTT, D. S. (1987). Juvenile offenders: Prevalence, offender incidence, and arrest rates by race. *Crime and Delinquency, 33,* 206–223.

HURRELMAN, K. (1987). The importance of school in the life course: Results from the Bielefeld study on school-related problems in adolescence. *Journal of Adolescent Research, 2,* 111–125.

HUSBANDS, C. T. (1970). Some social and psychological consequences of the American dating system. *Adolescence, 5,* 451–462.

HYDE, J. S. (1990). *Understanding human sexuality* (4th ed.). San Francisco: McGraw-Hill.

HYDE, J. S., & PHILLIS, D. (1979). Androgyny across the life-span. *Developmental Psychology, 15,* 334–336.

INHELDER, B., & PIAGET, J. (1958). *The growth of logical thinking from childhood to adolescence.* New York: Basic Books.

JACOBS, J. E., & OSGOOD, D. W. (1994, February). *Parental limits on adolescent autonomy.* Poster presented at the biennial meetings of the Society for Research on Adolescence, San Diego, CA.

JAMES, W. (1890). *The principles of psychology.* New York: Holt.

JANUS, S. S., & JANUS, C. L. (1993). *The Janus report on sexual behavior.* New York: Wiley.

JESSOR, R. (1993). Successful adolescent development among youth in high-risk settings. *American Psychologist, 48,* 117–126.

JOHNSON, C., LEWIS, C., LOVE, S., & STUCKEY, M. (1984). Incidence and correlates of bulimic behavior in a female high school population. *Journal of Youth and Adolescence, 13,* 15–26.

JOHNSON, S. A., & GREEN, V. (1993). Female adolescent contraceptive decision making and risk taking. *Adolescence, 28,* 81–96.

JOHNSTON, L. D., & BACHMAN, J. G. (1976). Educational institutions. In J. F. Adams (Ed.), *Understanding adolescence.* Boston: Allyn & Bacon.

JOHNSTON, L. D., BACHMAN, J. G., & O'MALLEY, P. (1986). *Monitoring the future: Questionnaire responses from the nation's high school seniors.* Ann Arbor: University of Michigan, Institute for Social Research.

JOHNSTON, L. D., O'MALLEY, P., & BACHMAN, J. G. (1989). *Drug use, drinking, and smoking: National survey results from high school, college, and young adult populations 1975–1988* (DHHS Publication No. ADM 891638). Washington, DC: U. S. Government Printing Office.

JONES, M. C. (1965). Psychological correlates of somatic development. *Child Development, 36,* 899–911.

JONES, M. C., & BAYLEY, N. (1950). Physical maturing among boys as related to behavior. *Journal of Educational Psychology, 41,* 129–148.

JONES, M. C., & MUSSEN, P. H. (1958). Self-conceptions, motivations and interpersonal attitudes of early and late maturing girls. *Child Development, 29,* 491–501.

JORGENSEN, R. S., & DUSEK, J. B. (1990). Adolescent adjustment and coping strategies. *Journal of Personality, 58,* 503–513.

JOSSELSON, R. (1988). The embedded self: I and thou revisited. In D. K. Lapsley & F. C. Power (Eds.), *Self, ego, and identity.* New York: Springer-Verlag.

JOVANOVIĆ, J. (March, 1993). *A longitudinal assessment of variables influencing young adolescent boys' and girls' mathematics performance.* Paper presented at the biennial meetings of the Society for Research on Child Development, New Orleans, LA.

JURKOVIĆ, G. J. (1980). The juvenile delinquent as a moral philosopher: A structural-developmental perspective. *Psychological Bulletin, 88,* 709–727.

KACERGUIS, M., & ADAMS, L. G. (1980). Erikson stage resolution: The relationship between identity and intimacy. *Journal of Youth and Adolescence, 9,* 117–126.

KAGAN, J., & MOSS, H. A. (1962). *Birth to maturity: The Fels study of psychological development.* New York: Wiley.

KALLEN, D., & STEPHENSON, J. (1982). Talking about sex revisited. *Journal of Youth and Adolescence, 11,* 11–23.

KANDEL, D. B., & LESSER, G. S. (1969). Parental and peer influences on educational plans of adolescents. *American Sociological Review, 34,* 213–223.

KAPLAN, H. (1975). *Self-attitudes and deviant behavior.* Pacific Palisades, CA: Goodyear.

KARRAKER, K. H., & EVANS, S. (1993, March). *Adolescent mothers' knowledge of infant development and expectations for their own infants.* Poster presented at the biennial meetings of the Society for Research in Child Development, New Orleans, LA.

KATCHADOURIAN, H. (1977). *The biology of adolescence.* San Francisco: Freeman.

KATCHADOURIAN, H. (1990). Sexuality. In S. Feldman & G. Elliot (Eds.), *At the threshold: The developing adolescent.* Cambridge, MA: Harvard University Press.

KEASEY, C. B. (1971). Social participation as a factor in the moral development of preadolescents. *Developmental Psychology, 5,* 216–220.

KEATING, D. (1980). Thinking processes in adolescence. In J. Adelson (Ed.), *Handbook of adolescent psychology.* New York: Wiley.

KEITH, T. (1982). Time spent on homework and high school grades: A large-sample path analysis. *Journal of Educational Psychology, 74,* 248–253.

KELLY, F. J., & BAER, D. J. (1969). Age of male delinquents when father left home and recidivism. *Psychological Reports, 25,* 383–388.

KERIG, P. K., & HUTCHINSON, S. R. (1993, March). *Children of divorce in young adulthood: Gender differences in self esteem and heterosexual trust.* Paper presented at the biennial meeting of the Society for Research in Child Development, New Orleans, LA.

KESSEN, W. (1965). *The child.* New York: Wiley.

KETT, J. (1977). *Rites of passage.* New York: Basic Books.

KILLEEN, M. R., & FRAME, C. L. (1989, April). *Peer relations and social self-concept.* Paper presented at the biennial meetings of the Society for Research in Child Development, Kansas City, MO.

KINNEY, D. A. (1993). From nerds to normals: The recovery of identity among adolescents from middle school to high school. *Sociology of Education, 66,* 21–40.

KLINE, M., TSCHANN, J. M., JOHNSTON, J. R., & WALLERSTEIN, J. S. (1989). Children's adjustment in joint and sole physical custody families. *Developmental Psychology, 25,* 430–438.

KLINGAMAN, L., & VICARY, J. R. (1992, March). *Risk factors associated with date rape and sexual assault of adolescent girls.* Poster presented at the biennial meetings of the Society for Research on Adolescence, Washington, DC.

KOCH, P. B. (1988). The relationship of first intercourse to later sexual functioning concerns of adolescents. *Journal of Adolescent Research, 3,* 345–362.

KOENIG, M., & ZELNIK, M. (1982). The risk of premarital first pregnancy among metropolitan-area teenagers: 1976–1979. *Family Planning Perspectives, 14,* 239–241, 243–247.

KOFF, E. (1993, March). *Impact of early pubertal timing for eating disturbance in early and mid-adolescent girls.* Paper presented at the biennial meetings of the Society for Research in Child Development, New Orleans, LA.

KOFF, E., & RIERDAN, J. (1993). Advanced pubertal development and eating disturbance in early adolescent girls. *Journal of Adolescent Health, 14,* 433–439.

KOHEN, A. I., & BREINICH, S. C. (1975). Knowledge of the world of work: A test of occupational information for young men. *Journal of Vocational Behavior, 6,* 133–144.

KOHLBERG, L. (1963). The development of children's orientations toward a moral order: I. Sequence in the development of moral thought. *Vita Humana, 6,* 11–33.

KOHLBERG, L. (1969). Stage and sequence: The cognitive-developmental approach to socialization. In D. A. Goslin (Ed.), *Handbook of socialization theory and research.* Chicago: Rand McNally.

KOHLBERG, L. (1976). Moral stages and moralization. In T. Lickona (Ed.), *Moral development and behavior: Theory, research, and social issues.* New York: Holt, Rinehart & Winston.

KOHLBERG, L. (1980). *Recent research in moral development.* New York: Holt.

KOHLBERG, L. (1984). *The psychology of moral development.* New York: Harper & Row.

KOHLBERG, L., & ZIGLER, E. (1967). The impact of cognitive maturity on sex-role attitudes in the years four to eight. *Genetic Psychology Monographs, 75,* 89–165.

KONIAK-GRIFFIN, D. (1993, March). *A qualitative technique for comprehensive assessment of childbearing/childrearing minority adolescents at risk for AIDS.* Paper presented at the biennial meetings of the Society for Research in Child Development, New Orleans, LA.

KOPERA-FRYE, K., AGER, J., SALTZ, E., POINDEXTER, J., & LEE, S. (1993, March). *Predictors of adolescent delinquency.* Paper presented at the biennial meetings of the Society for Research in Child Development, New Orleans, LA.

KRACKE, B., & SILBEREISEN, R. K. (1992, March). *Behavioral autonomy and pubertal maturation.* Poster presented at the fourth biennial meetings of the Society for Research on Adolscence, Washington, DC.

KREBS, D., & GILLMORE, J. (1982). The relationship among the first stages of cognitive development, role-taking abilities, and moral development. *Child Development, 53,* 877–886.

KRISBERG, B., SCHWARTZ, I., FISHMAN, G., EISILOITS, Z., GUTTMAN, E., & JOE, J. (1987). The incarceration of minority youth. *Crime and Delinquency, 29,* 333–364.

KUPFERSMID, J., & WONDERLY, D. (1980). Moral maturity and behavior: Failure to find a link. *Journal of Youth and Adolescence, 9,* 249–261.

KURDEK, L. A. (1988). A 1-year follow-up study of children's divorce adjustment, custodial mother's divorce adjustment, and post-divorce parenting. *Journal of Applied Developmental Psychology, 9,* 315–318.

KURDEK, L. A. (1989). Siblings' reactions to parental divorce. *Journal of Divorce, 12,* 203–219.

KURDEK, L. A., & SINCLAIR, R. J. (1988a). Adjustment of young adolescents in two-parent nuclear, stepfather, and mother-custody families. *Journal of Consulting and Clinical Psychology, 56,* 91–96.

KURDEK, L. A., & SINCLAIR, R. J. (1988b). Relation of eighth graders' family structure, gender, and family environment with academic performance and school behavior. *Journal of Educational Psychology, 80,* 90–94.

KURTINESS, W., & GEWIRTZ, J. (Eds.). (1987). *Moral development through social interaction.* New York: Wiley.

LAMBERT, B. G., & MOUNCE, N. B. (1987). Career planning. In V. B. VanHasselt & M. Hersen (Eds.), *Handbook of adolescent psychology.* New York: Pergamon Press.

LAMBORN, S. D., MOUNTS, N. S., STEINBERG, L., & DORNBUSCH, S. M. (1991). Patterns of competence and adjustment among adolescents from authoritative, authoritarian, indulgent, and neglectful families. *Child Development, 62,* 1049–1065.

LANTHIER, R. P., & STOCKER, C. (1993, March). *Sibling relationships: Development from childhood to early adulthood.* Poster presented at the biennial meetings of the Society for Research in Child Development, New Orleans, LA.

LAPSLEY, D. K. (1985). Elkind on egocentrism. *Developmental Review, 5,* 227–236.

LAPSLEY, D. K., JACKSON, S., RICE, K., & SHADID, G. E. (1988). Self-monitoring and the "new look" at the imaginary audience and personal fable: An ego developmental analysis. *Journal of Adolescent Research, 3,* 17–31.

LAPSLEY, D. K., MILSTEAD, M., QUINTANA, S. M., FLANNERY, D., & BUSS, R. (1986). Adolescent egocentrism and formal operations: Tests of a theoretical assumption. *Developmental Psychology, 22,* 800–807.

LAURSEN, B. (1992, March). *Conflict management among close friends.* Paper presented at the biennial meetings of the Society for Research in Child Development, Washington, DC.

LAURSEN, B., & COLLINS, W. A. (in press). Interpersonal conflict during adolescence. *Psychological Bulletin.*

LAURSEN, B., & FERREIRA, M. (1994, February). *Does parent-child conflict peak at mid-adolescence?* Paper presented at the biennial meetings of the Society for Research on Adolescence, San Diego, CA.

LAZAR, I., & DARLINGTON, R. (1982). Lasting effects of early education: A report from the consortium for longitudinal studies. *Monographs of the Society for Research in Child Development, 47* (Whole No. 195).

LEARY, M. R., & SNELL, W. E., JR. (1988). The relationship of instrumentality and expressiveness to sexual behavior in males and females. *Sex Roles, 18,* 509-594.

LEE, L. C. (1971). The conformitant development of cognitive and moral modes of thought: A test of selected deductions from Piaget's theory. *Genetic Psychology Monographs, 83,* 93-146.

LEE, M., & PRENTICE, N. M. (1988). Interrelations of empathy, cognition, and moral reasoning with dimensions of juvenile delinquency. *Journal of Abnormal Child Psychology, 16,* 127-139.

LEE, V. E., BURKAM, D. T., ZIMILES, H., & LADEWSKI, B. (1994). Family structure and its effect on behavioral and emotional problems in young adolescents. *Journal of Research on Adolescents, 4,* 405-437.

LEFURGY, W. G., & WOLOSHIN, G. W. (1969). Immediate and long-term effects of experimentally induced social influence in the modification of adolescents' moral judgments. *Journal of Abnormal and Social Psychology, 12,* 104-110.

LEIDERMAN, P. H., MELDMAN, M. A., & RITTER, P. L. (1989, March). *Parent and peer influences on adolescent self-esteem in a multiethnic high school population.* Paper presented at the biennial meetings of the Society for Research in Child Development, Kansas City, MO.

LEIGH, B. C. (1989). Reasons for having sex: Gender, sexual orientation, and relationship to sexual behavior. *Journal of Sex Research, 26,* 199-209.

LEMPERS, J. D., & CLARK-LEMPERS, D. S. (1993). A functional comparison of same-sex and opposite-sex friendships during adolescence. *Journal of Adolescent Research, 8,* 89-108.

LEMPERS, J. D., CLARK-LEMPERS, D., & SIMONS, R. L. (1989). Economic hardship, parenting, and distress in adolescence. *Child Development, 60,* 25-39.

LEVY, G. D., & CARTER, D. B. (1989). Gender schema, gender constancy, and gender-role knowledge: The roles of cognitive factors in preschoolers' gender-role stereotype attributions. *Developmental Psychology, 25,* 444-449.

LINARES, L. O., LEADBEATER, B. J., KATO, P. M., & JAFFE, L. (1991). Predicting school outcomes for minority group adolescent mothers: Can subgroups be identified? *Journal of Research on Adolescence, 1,* 379-400.

LINDZEY, G. (1965). Morphology and behavior. In G. Lindzey & C. S. Hall (Eds.). *Theories of personality.* New York: Wiley.

LINN, M. C., & PETERSEN, A. C. (1985). Emergence of characterization of sex differences in spatial ability: A meta-analytic analysis. *Child Development, 56,* 1479-1498.

LINNEY, J. A., & SEIDMAN, E. (1989). The future of schooling. *American Psychologist, 44,* 336-340.

LITOVSKY, V. G., & DUSEK, J. B. (1985). Perceptions of child rearing and self-concept development during the early adolescent years. *Journal of Youth and Adolescence, 14,* 373-387.

LITOVSKY, V. G., & DUSEK, J. B. (1988). Maternal employment and adolescent adjustment and perceptions of child rearing. *International Journal of Family Psychiatry, 9,* 153-167.

LIVSON, N., & PESKIN, H. (1980). Perspectives on adolescence from longitudinal research. In J. Adelson (Ed.), *Handbook of adolescent psychology.* New York: Wiley.

LONG, B. (1986). Parental discord vs. family structure: Effects of divorce on the self-esteem of daughters. *Journal of Youth and Adolescence, 15,* 19-27.

LONG, N., FOREHAND, R., FAUBER, R., & BRODY, G. (1987). Self-perceived and independently observed competence of young adolescents as a function of parental marital conflict and recent divorce. *Journal of Abnormal Child Psychology, 15,* 15-27.

LONKY, E., REIHMAN, J., & SERLIN, R. (1981). Political values and moral judgments in adolescence. *Youth and Society, 12,* 423-431.

LONKY, E., ROODIN, P. A., & RYBASCH, J. M. (1988). Moral judgment and sex-role orientation as a function of self and other presentation modes. *Journal of Youth and Adolescence, 17,* 189-195.

LOZOFF, B. (1989). Nutrition and behavior. *American Psychologist, 44,* 231-236.

LUCKEY, E., & NASS, G. (1969). A comparison of sexual attitudes and behavior in an international sample. *Journal of Marriage and the Family, 31,* 364-379.

LUTWAK, N. (1984). The interrelationship of ego, moral, and conceptual development in a college group. *Adolescence, 19,* 675-688.

LYNN, D., & SAUREY, W. L. (1959). The effects of father-absence on Norwegian boys and girls. *Journal of Abnormal and Social Psychology, 59,* 258-262.

MA, H. K. (1988). Objective moral judgment in Hong Kong, mainland China, and England. *Journal of Cross Cultural Psychology, 19,* 78-95.

MACCOBY, E. E., & JACKLIN, C. (1980). Sex differences in aggression: A rejoinder and reprise. *Child Development, 51,* 964-980.

MACCOBY, E. E., & MARTIN, J. (1983). Socialization in the context of the family: Parent-child interaction. In E. M. Hetherington (Ed.), *Handbook of child psychology: Socialization, personality, and social development* (Vol. 4). New York: Wiley.

MACKINNON, C. E. (1989). An observational investigation of sibling interactions in married and divorced families. *Developmental Psychology, 25,* 36-44.

MAGNUSSON, D., SATTIN, H., & ALLEN, V. (1986). Differential maturation among girls and its relation to social adjustment in a longitudinal perspective. In P. Baltes, D. Featherman, & R. Lerner (Eds.), *Life-span development and behavior* (Vol. 7). Hillsdale, NJ: Erlbaum.

MARCIA, J. (1966). Development and validation of ego identity status. *Journal of Personality and Social Psychology, 3,* 551-558.

MARCIA, J. (1976). Identity six years after: A follow-up study. *Journal of Youth and Adolescence, 5,* 145-160.

MARKUS, H., & NURIUS, P. (1986). Possible selves. *American Psychologist, 41,* 954-969.

MARSH, H. W. (1987). The big-fish—little pond effect on academic self-concept. *Journal of Educational Psychology, 79,* 280-295.

MARSH, H. W., BYRNE, B. M., & SHAVELSON, R. J. (1988). A multifaceted academic self-concept: Its hierarchical structure and its relation to academic achievement. *Journal of Educational Psychology, 80,* 366-380.

MARSIGLIO, W. (1993). Attitudes toward homosexual activity and gays as friends: A national survey of heterosexual 15- to 19-year-old males. *Journal of Sex Research, 30,* 12-17.

MARTIN, B. (1975). Parent-child relations. In F. D. Horowitz (Ed.), *Review of child development research* (Vol. 4). Chicago: University of Chicago Press.

MARTIN, C. L., & HALVERSON, C. F. (1981). A schematic processing model of sex typing and stereotyping in children. *Child Development, 52,* 1119-1134.

MARTIN, C. L., & HALVERSON, C. F. (1987). The roles of cognition in sex role acquisition. In D. B. Carter (Ed.), *Current conceptions of sex roles and sex typing.* New York: Praeger.

MARTTUNEN, M. J., ARO, H. M., & LONNQVIST, J. K. (1992). Adolescent suicide: Endpoint of long-term difficulties. *Journal of the American Academy of Child and Adolescent Psychiatry, 31,* 649-654.

MARTTUNEN, M. J., ARO, H. M., & LONNQVIST, J. K. (1993). Precipitant stressors in adolescent suicide. *Journal of the American Academy of Child and Adolescent Psychiatry, 32,* 1178-1183.

MARTTUNEN, M. J., ARO, H. M., & LONNQVIST, J. K. (1994, February). *Participant stressors in adolescent suicide.* Poster presented at the biennial meetings of the Society for Research on Adolescence, San Diego, CA.

MAYHUE, L. K. (1992, March). *The association between adolescent suicidal ideation and family relationships in a general population.* Poster presented at the biennial meetings of the Society for Research on Adolescence, Washington, DC.

MCADAMS, D., BOOTH, L., & SELVIK, R. (1981). Religious identity among students at a private college: Social motives, ego stage, and development. *Merrill Palmer Quarterly, 27,* 219-239.

MCADOO, H. (Ed.). 1981. *Black families.* Beverly Hills, CA: Sage.

MCCABE, M. (1984). Toward a theory of adolescent dating. *Adolescence, 19,* 159-169.

MCCALL, R., APPLEBAUM, M., & HOGARTY, P. (1973). Developmental changes in mental performance. *Monographs of the Society for Research in Child Development, 38* (Whole No. 150).

MCCARTHY, J., & HOGE, D. (1982). Analysis of age effects in longitudinal studies of adolescent self-esteem. *Developmental Psychology, 18,* 372-379.

MCCORD, J. (1990). Problem behaviors. In S. Feldman & G. Elliot (Eds.), *At the threshold: The developing adolescent* (pp. 414-430). Cambridge, MA: Harvard University Press.

MCCRAE, R. R., & COSTA, P. T., JR. (1986). Personality, coping, and coping effectiveness in an adult sample. *Journal of Personality, 54,* 385-405.

MCGEE, R., WILLIAMS, S., SHARE, D. L., ANDERSON, J., & SILVA, P. A. (1986). The relationship between specific reading retardation, general reading backwardness and behavioural problems in a large sample of Dunedin boys: A longitudinal study from five to eleven years. *Journal of Child Psychology and Psychiatry, 27,* 597-610.

MCLANAHAN, S. (1983). Family structure and stress: A longitudinal comparison of two-parent and female-headed families. *Journal of Marriage and the Family, 45,* 347-357.

MCLAUGHLIN, C., BIERMEIER, C., CHEN, C., & GREENBERGER, E. (February, 1994). *Family and attitudinal predictors of sexual experience in Asian-American and Caucasian-American college students.* Poster presented at the biennial meetings of the Society for Research in Child Development, San Diego, CA.

MCLOYD, V. C. (1989a, April). *Facing the future in hard times: Choices, perceptions, and behavior of black adolescents.* Paper presented at the biennial meetings of the Society for Research in Child Development, Kansas City, MO.

MCLOYD, V. C. (1989b, April). *Individual, familial, and external factors influencing the mental health of children in low-income female-headed families.* Paper presented at the biennial meetings of the Society for Research in Child Development, Kansas City, MO.

MEAD, G. H. (1934). *Mind, self, and society.* Chicago: University of Chicago Press.

MEAD, M. (1975). *Coming of age in Samoa.* New York: Morrow.

MEAD, M. (1953). *Growing up in New Guinea.* New York: Mentor Books.

MEAD, M. (1970). *Culture and commitment: A study of the generation gap.* New York: Doubleday.

MEILMAN, P. (1979). Cross-sectional age changes in ego identity status during adolescence. *Developmental Psychology, 15,* 230-231.

MELBY, J. N. (1993, March). *Family context of adolescent academic competence.* Poster presented at the biennial meetings of the Society for Research in Child Development, New Orleans, LA.

MELGES, F. T., & HAMBURG, D. A. (1977). Psychological effects of hormonal changes in women. In F. A. Beach (Ed.), *Human sexuality in four perspectives.* Baltimore: Johns Hopkins University Press.

MEREDITH, H. V. (1963). Change in the stature and body weight of North American boys during the last 80 years. In L. Lipsitt & C. C. Spiker (Eds.), *Advances in child development and behavior* (Vol. 1). New York: Academic Press.

MIDGLEY, C., FELDLAUFER, H., & ECCLES, J. S. (1989a). Change in teacher efficacy and student self- and task-related beliefs in mathematics during the transition to junior high school. *Journal of Educational Psychology, 81,* 247-258.

MIDGLEY, C., FELDLAUFER, H., & ECCLES, J. S. (1989b). Student/teacher relations and attitudes toward mathematics before and after the transition to junior high school. *Child Development, 60,* 981-992.

MILLER, D. (1976). What do high school students think of their schools? *Phi Delta Kappan, 57,* 700-702.

MILLER, P., & SIMON, W. (1980). The development of sexuality in adolescence. In J. Adelson (Ed.), *Handbook of adolescent psychology* (pp. 383-407). New York: Wiley.

MILLER, P. A., KLIEWER, W., & BURKEMAN, D. (1993, March). *Coaching and modeling influences on children's coping with divorce.* Poster presented at the biennial meeting of the Society for Research in Child Development, New Orleans, LA.

MILLER, P. H. (1993). *Theories of developmental psychology* (3rd ed.). New York: Freeman.

MILLER, R., & GORDON, M. (1986). The decline in formal dating: A study in six Connecticut high schools. *Marriage and Family Review, 10,* 139-156.

MILLSTEIN, S. G. (1989, April). *Behavioral risk factors for AIDS among adolescents.* Paper presented at the biennial meetings of the Society for Research in Child Development, Kansas City, MO.

MINUCHIN, P., & SHAPIRO, E. K. (1983). The school as a context for social development. In P. H. Mussen & E. M. Hetherington (Eds.), *Handbook of child psychology* (4th ed.). New York: Wiley.

MITCHELL, J. E., BAKER, L. A., & JACKLIN, C. N. (1989). Masculinity and femininity in twin children: Genetic and environmental factors. *Child Development, 60,* 1475-1485.

MODELL, J., & GOODMAN, M. (1990). Historical perspectives. In S. Feldman & G. Elliott (Eds.), *At the threshold: The developing adolescent.* Cambridge: Harvard University Press.

MOIR, D. J. (1974). Egocentrism and the emergence of conventional morality in preadolescent girls. *Child Development, 45,* 229-304.

MONAHAN, S. C., BUCHANAN, C. M., MACCOBY, E. E., & DORNBUSCH, S. M. (1993). Sibling differences in divorced families. *Child Development, 64,* 152-168.

MONEY, J., & EHRHARDT, A. (1972). *Man and woman, boy and girl.* New York: Mentor.

MONEY, J., HAMPSON, J. G., & HAMPSON, J. L. (1955). An examination of some basic sexual concepts: The evidence of human hermaphroditism. *Bulletin of Johns Hopkins Hospital, 97,* 301-319.

MONIQUE, W. L. (1994, February). *The nature and prevalence of sexual messages in the television programs adolescents view most.* Poster presented at the biennial meeting of the Society for Research on Adolescence, San Diego, CA.

MONK, D. H., & HALLER, E. J. (1993). Predictors of high school academic offerings: The role of school size. *American Educational Research Journal, 30,* 3-21.

MONTEMAYOR, R. (1982). The relationship between parent adolescent conflict and the amount of time adolescents spend alone and with parents and peers. *Child Development, 53,* 1512-1519.

MONTEMAYOR, R., BROWN, B., & ADAMS, G. (1985). *Changes in identity status and psychological adjustment after leaving home and entering college.* Paper presented at the biennial meetings of the Society for Research in Child Develoment, Toronto, Canada.

MONTEMAYOR, R., & EISEN, M. (1977). The development of self-conceptions from childhood to adolescence. *Developmental Psychology, 13,* 314-319.

MONTEMAYOR, R., MCKENRY, P., & JULIAN, T. (1992, March). *Psychological and physiological predictors of relationship quality in middle-aged fathers and their adolescents.* Paper presented at the biennial meetings of the Society for Research on Adolescence, Washington, DC.

MOORE, K. A., MYERS, D. E., MORRISON, D. R., NORD, C. W., BROWN, B., & EDMONSTON, B. (1993). Age at first childbirth and later poverty. *Journal of Research on Adolescence, 3,* 393-422.

MOORE, K. A., NORD, C. W., & PETERSON, J. (1989). Non-voluntary sexual activity among adolescents. *Family Planning Perspectives, 21,* 110-114.

MOORE, K. A., PETERSON, J., & FURSTENBERG, F., JR., (1986). Parental attitudes and the occurrence of early sexual activity. *Journal of Marriage and the Family, 48,* 777-782.

MORAN, P., & ECKENRODE, J. (1989, April). *Gender differences in the costs and benefits of social relationships among adolescents.* Paper presented at the biennial meetings of the Society for Research in Child Development, Kansas City, MO.

MORROW, W. R., & WILSON, R. C. (1961). Family relations of bright high-achieving and under-achieving high school boys. *Child Development, 32,* 501-510.

MORTIMER, J. T., FINCH, M. D., OWENS, T. J., & SHANAHAN, M. J. (1990). Gender and work in adolescence. *Youth and Society, 22,* 201-224.

MORTIMER, J. T., FINCH, M. D., RYU, S., SHANAHAN, M. J., & CALL, K. T. (1993, March). *The effects of work intensity on adolescent mental health, achievement and behavioral adjustment: New evidence from a prospective study.* Paper presented at the biennial meetings of the Society for Research on Child Development, New Orleans, LA.

MORTIMER, J. T., FINCH, M., SHANAHAN, M., & RYU, S. (1990, March). *Work experience, mental health, and behavioral adjustment in adolescence.* Paper presented at the biennial meetings of the Society for Research on Adolescence, Atlanta, GA.

MORTIMER, J. T., FINCH, M., SHANAHAN, M., & RYU, S. (1992a). Work experience, mental health, and behavioral adjustment in adolescence. *Journal of Research on Adolescence, 2,* 25-57.

MORTIMER, J. T., FINCH, M., SHANAHAN, M., & RYU, S. (1992b). Adolescent work history and behavioral adjustment. *Journal of Research on Adolescence, 2,* 59-80.

MORY, M. S. (1994, February). *When people form or perceive sets, they tend to be fuzzy: The case of adolescent crowds.* Poster presented at the biennial meetings of the Society for Research on Adolescence, San Diego, CA.

MUNRO, G., & ADAMS, G. (1977). Ego-identity formation in college students and working youth. *Developmental Psychology, 13,* 523-524.

MURPHY, J. (1987). Educational influences. In V. B. Van Hasselt & M. Hersen (Eds.), *Handbook of adolescent psychology.* New York: Pergamon Press.

MUSSEN, P. H., & JONES, M. C. (1957). Self-concepts, motivations, and interpersonal attitudes of late and early maturing boys. *Child Development, 28,* 243-256.

MUUSS, R. E. (1988). *Theories of adolescence* (5th ed.). New York: Random House.

NAMEROW, P. B., KALMUSS, D. S., & CUSHMAN, L. F. (1993). The determinants of young women's pregnancy-resolution choices. *Journal of Research on Adolescence, 3,* 193-215.

NEWCOMB, M. D., & BENTLER, P. M. (1989). Substance use and abuse among children and teenagers. *American Psychologist, 44,* 242-248.

NILES, W. (1986). Effects of a moral development discussion group on delinquent and predelinquent boys. *Journal of Counseling Psychology, 33,* 45-51.

NOETH, R. J., ROTH, J. D., & PREDIGER, D. J. (1975). Student career development. Where do we stand? *Vocational Guidance Quarterly, 23,* 210-218.

NUNN, G. D., & PARISH, T. S. (1987). An investigation of the relationships between children's self-concepts and evaluations of parent figures: Do they vary as a function of family structure? *Journal of Psychology, 121,* 563-566.

OAKES, J. (1985). *Keeping track: How schools structure inequality.* New Haven, CT: Yale University Press.

O'BEIRNE, H. A. (1994, February). *Differential correlates of male and female adolescents' sexual activity.* Poster presented at the biennial meetings of the Society for Research on Adolescence, San Diego, CA.

O'BRIEN, S. F., & BIERMAN, K. L. (1988). Conceptions and perceived influence of peer groups: Interviews with preadolescents and adolescents. *Child Development, 59,* 1360-1365.

O'CONNELL, L., BETZ, M., & KURTH, S. (1989). Plans for balancing work and family life: Do women pursuing nontraditional and traditional occupations differ? *Sex Roles, 20,* 35-45.

OLDS, D. L., HENDERSON, C. R., JR., TATELBAUM, R., & CHAMBERLIN, R. (1988). Improving the life-course development of socially disadvantaged mothers: A randomized trial of nurse home visitation. *American Journal of Public Health, 78,* 1436-1445.

OLEJNIK, A. (1980). Adult's moral reasoning with children. *Child Development, 51,* 1285-1288.

OLWEUS, D. (in press). Victimization by peers: Antecedents and long-term outcomes. In K. H. Rubin & J. B. Asendorf (Eds.), *Social withdrawal, inhibition, and shyness in childhood.* Hillsdale, NJ: Erlbaum.

O'MALLEY, P. M., & BACHMAN, J. G. (1983). Self-esteem: Change and stability between ages 13 and 23. *Developmental Psychology, 19,* 257-268.

O'MALLEY, P. M., BACHMAN, J. G., & JOHNSTON, J. (1977). *Youth in transition. Final report: Five years beyond high school: Causes and consequences of educational attainment.* Ann Arbor, MI: Institute for Social Research.

ORLOFSKY, J., MARCIA, J., & LESSER, I. (1973). Ego identity status and the intimacy vs. isolation crisis of young adulthood. *Journal of Personality and Social Psychology, 27,* 211-219.

OSIPOW, S. H. (1983). *Theories of career development* (3rd ed.). Englewood Cliffs, NJ: Prentice-Hall.

OSIPOW, S. H. (1987). *Theories of career development* (3rd ed.). Englewood Cliffs, NJ: Prentice-Hall.

PAPINI, D. R. (1994, February). *Early adolescent attachment to peers and psychosocial development: A longitudinal study.* Paper presented at the biennial meeting of the Society for Research on Adolescence, San Diego, CA.

PARIKH, B. (1980). Development of moral judgment and its relation to family environmental factors in Indian and American families. *Child Development, 51,* 1030-1039.

PARISH, T., & TAYLOR, J. (1979). The impact of divorce and subsequent father absence on children's and adolescents' self-concepts. *Journal of Youth and Adolescence, 8,* 427-432.

PARROTT, C. A., & STRONGMAN, K. T. (1984). Locus of control and delinquency. *Adolescence, 19,* 459-471.

PARSONS, J., KACZALA, C., & MEECE, J. (1982). Socialization of achievement attitudes and beliefs: Classroom influences. *Child Development, 53,* 322-339.

PATTERSON, C. J. (1992). Children of lesbian and gay parents. *Child Development, 63,* 1025-1042.

PATTERSON, G. R., DEBARYSHE, B. D., & RAMSEY, E. (1989). A developmental perspective on antisocial behavior. *American Psychologist, 44,* 329-335.

PATTERSON, S. J., SOCHTING, I., & MARCIA, J. E. (1992). The inner space and beyond: Women and identity. In G. R. Adams, T. P. Gullotta, & R. Montemayor (Eds.), *Adolescent identity formation.* Newbury Park, CA: Sage.

PAULSON, S. E. (in press). Relations of parenting style and parental involvement with ninth grade students' achievement. *Journal of Early Adolescence.*

PECK, R. F., & HAVIGHURST, R. J. (1960). *The psychology of character development.* New York: Wiley.

PENNY, J. M., WATSON, J. A., SAUNDERS, R. B., & WOMBLE, C. D. (1993, March). *Early and later maternal-infant interactions in adolescent mothers: A comparison study.* Poster presented at the biennial meetings of the Society for Research in Child Development, New Orleans, LA.

PERLMUTTER, R., & SHAPIRO, E. R. (1987). Morals and values in adolescence. In V. B. Van Hasselt & M. Hersen (Eds.), *Handbook of adolescent psychology.* New York: Pergamon Press.

PERRY, D. G., KUSEL, S. J., & PERRY, L. C. (1988). Victims of peer aggression. Developmental Psychology, 24, 807-814.

PERRY, D. G., & WILLIARD, J. C. (1989, April). *Victims of peer abuse.* Paper presented at the Biennial Meetings of the Society for Research in Child Development, Kansas City, MO.

PESKIN, H. (1967). Pubertal onset and ego functioning. *Journal of Abnormal Psychology, 72,* 1-15.

PESKIN, H. (1973). Influence of the developmental schedule of puberty on learning and ego development. *Journal of Youth and Adolescence, 2,* 273-290.

PETERSEN, A. C. (1985). Pubertal development as a cause of disturbance: Myths, realities, and unanswered questions. *Genetic, Social, and General Psychology Monographs, 111,* 205-232.

PETERSEN, A. C. (1988). Adolescent development. In M. R. Rosenzweig & L. W. Porter (Eds.), *Annual review of psychology.* Palo Alto, CA: Annual Reviews.

PETERSEN, A. C., COMPAS, B. E., BROOKS-GUNN, J., STEMMLER, M., EY, S., & GRANT, K. E. (1993). Depression in adolescence. *American Psychologist, 48,* 155-168.

PETERSEN, A. C., GRABER, J., & SULLIVAN, P. (1990, March). *Pubertal timing and problem behavior: Variations in effects.* Paper presented at the biennial meetings of the Society for Research on Adolescence, Atlanta, GA.

PETERSEN, A. C., LEFFERT, N., & GRAHAM, B. (1994, February). *Effects of puberty on adolescent development.* Paper presented at the biennial meetings of the Society for Research in Adolescence, San Diego, CA.

PETERSEN, A. C., & TAYLOR, B. (1980). The biological approach to adolescence: Biological change and psychological adaptation. In J. Adelson (Ed.), *Handbook of adolescent psychology.* New York: Wiley.

PETRONIO, R. (1980). The moral maturity of repeater delinquents. *Youth and Society, 12,* 51-59.

PFEFFER, C. (1986). *The suicidal child.* New York: Guilford Press.

PHILLIPS, D. P., & CARSTENSEN, L. L. (1986). Clustering of teenage suicides after television news stories about suicide. *New England Journal of Medicine, 315,* 93-115.

PHILLIPS, L. D. (1992, March). *Ethnic identity and the biracial adolescent.* Paper presented at the biennial meetings of the Society for Research in Child Development, Washington, DC.

PHINNEY, J. (1989). Stages of ethnic identity development in minority group adolescents. *Journal of Early Adolescence, 9,* 34-49.

PHINNEY, J. (1990). Ethnic identity in adolescents and adults: A review of research. *Psychological Bulletin, 180,* 499-514.

PHINNEY, J., & ALIPURIA, L. (1987, March). *Ethnic identity in older adolescents from four ethnic groups.* Paper presented at the biennial meetings of the Society for Research in Child Development, Baltimore.

PHINNEY, J. S., DEVICH-NAVARRO, M., DUPONT, S., & ESTRADA, A. (1994, February). *Bicultural identity orientations of African American and Mexican American adolescents.* Paper presented at the biennial meetings of the Society for Research on Adolescence, San Diego, CA.

PHINNEY, J. S., & ROSENTHAL, D. A. (1992). Ethnic identity in adolescence: Process, context, and outcome. In G. R. Adams, T. P. Gullotta, & R. Montemayor (Eds.), *Adolescent identity formation.* Newbury Park, CA: Sage.

PIAGET, J. (1932). *The moral judgment of the child.* Glencoe, IL: The Free Press.

PIAGET, J. (1952). *The origins of intelligence in children.* New York: International Press.

PIAGET, J. (1970). Piaget's theory. In P. H. Mussen (Ed.), *Carmichael's manual of child psychology* (Vol. 1, 3rd. ed.). New York: Basic Books.

PIAGET, J. (1980). Intellectual evolution from adolescence to adulthood. In R. E. Muuss (Ed.), *Adolescent behavior and society: A book of readings* (3rd ed.). New York: Random House.

PITTMAN, R. B., & HAUGHWOUT, P. (1987). Influence of high school size on dropout rate. *Educational Evaluation and Policy Analysis, 9,* 337-343.

PLOMIN, R., & DANIELS, D. (1987). Why are children in the same family so different from one another? *Behavioral and Brain Sciences, 10,* 1-60.

POGUE-GEILE, M. F., & HARROW, M. (1987). Schizophrenia: An evolving concept. In V. B. Van Hasselt & M. Hersen (Eds.), *Handbook of adolescent psychology.* New York: Pergamon Press.

PRATT, M. W., SEBASTIAN, T., & BOUNTROGIANNI, M. (1989, April). *Parenting beliefs and practices regarding school and homework: Parenting styles and ethnic differences at the junior high level.* Paper presented at the biennial meetings of the Society for Research in Child Development, Kansas City, MO.

PRINSKY, L., & ROSENBAYM, J. (1987). Leer-ics or lyrics? *Youth and Society, 18,* 384-394.

QUADAGNO, D., BRISCOE, R., & QUADAGNO, J. (1977). Effect of perinatal gonadal hormones on selected nonsexual behavior patterns: A critical assessment of the nonhuman and human literature. *Psychological Bulletin, 84,* 62-80.

QUIGGLE, N. L., GARBER, J., PANAK, W. F., & DODGE, K. A. (1992). Social information processing in aggressive and depressed children. *Child Development, 63,* 1035-1320.

RABIN, J. S. (1987). Two-paycheck families: Psychological responses to social change. In D. B. Carter (Ed.), *Current conceptions of sex roles and sex typing.* New York: Praeger.

RABINER, D. L., & GORDON, L. V. (1992). The coordination of conflicting social goals: Differences between rejected and nonrejected boys. *Child Development, 63,* 1340-1350.

RAFFAELLI, M. (1989, April). *Conflict with siblings and friends in late childhood and early adolescence.* Paper presented at the biennial meetings of the Society for Research in Child Development, Kansas City, MO.

RAYMOND, C. L., & BENBOW, C. P. (1986). Gender differences in mathematics: A function of parental support and student sex typing? *Developmental Psychology, 22,* 808-819.

REID, M., LANDESMAN, S., TREDER, R., & JACCARD, J. (1989). "My family and friends": Six- to twelve-year-old children's perceptions of social support. *Child Development, 60,* 896-910.

REIS, H. T., LIN, Y., BENNETT, M. E., & NEZLEK, J. B. (1993). Change and consistency in social participation during early adulthood. *Developmental Psychology, 29,* 633-645.

REISS, I. L. (1967). *The social context of premarital sexual permissiveness.* New York: Holt, Rinehart & Winston.

REPINSKI, D. J., & COLLINS, W. A. (February, 1994). *Relationship transformation during adolescence: Processes of parent-child adaptation.* Paper presented at the biennial meeting of the Society for Research in Adolescence, San Diego, CA.

REST, J. R. (1976). New approaches in the assessment of moral judgment. In T. Lickona (Ed.), *Moral development and behavior: Theory, research, and social issues.* New York: Holt, Rinehart & Winston.

REST, J. R. (1983). Morality. In J. Flavell & E. Markman (Eds.), *Handbook of child psychology: Vol. 3. Cognitive development.* New York: Wiley.

RHEINGOLD, H. L. (1969). The social and socializing infant. In D. A. Goslin (Ed.), *Handbook of socialization theory and research.* Chicago: Rand McNally.

RICHARDS, M. H., & DUCKETT, E. (1989, April). *Maternal employment and young adolescents' daily experience with family.* Paper presented at the biennial meetings of the Society for Research in Child Development, Kansas City, MO.

RICHARDS, M. H., & DUCKETT, E. (1991). Maternal employment and adolescents. In J. V. Lerner & N. Galambos (Eds.), *Employed mothers and their children.* New York: Garland.

RICHARDS, M. H., & DUCKETT, E. (1994). The relationship of maternal employment to early adolescent daily experience with and without parents. *Child Development, 65,* 225-236.

RICHARDS, M., & PETERSEN, A. C. (1987). Biological theoretical models of adolescent development. In V. B. Van Hasselt & M. Hersen (Eds.), *Handbook of adolescent psychology.* New York: Pergamon Press.

RICHTERS, J., & PELLEGRINI, D. (1989). Depressed mothers' judgments about their children: An examination of the depression-distortion hypothesis. *Child Development, 60,* 1068-1075.

RIERDAN, J., KOFF, E., & STUBBS, M. (1989). Timing of menarche, preparation, and initial menstrual experience: Replication and further analyses in prospective study. *Journal of Youth and Adolescence, 18,* 413-426.

RIMBERG, H. M., & LEWIS, R. J. (1994). Older adolescents and AIDS: Correlates of self-reported safer sex practices. *Journal of Research on Adolescence, 4,* 453-464.

ROBINSON, I. E., KING, K., & BALSWICK, J. O. (1972). The premarital sexual revolution among college females. *Family Coordinator, 21,* 189-194.

ROCHE, A. F. (1979). Secular trends in human growth, maturation, and development. *Monographs of the Society for Research in Child Development, 44* (Whole No. 179).

ROGEL, M., ZUEHLKE, M., PETERSEN, A., TOBIN-RICHARDS, M., & SHELTON, M. (1980). Contraceptive behavior in adolescnece: A decision-making perspective. *Journal of Youth and Adolescence, 9,* 491-506.

ROKEACH, M. (1973). *The nature of human values.* New York: Free Press.

ROSARIO, M., & ROTHERAM-BORUS, J. (1993, March). *Interrelationships of problem behaviors among runaways: Gender, ethnic and age differences.* Paper presented at the bi-

ennial meeting of the Society for Research on Child Development, New Orleans, LA.

ROSCOE, B., CAVANAUGH, L. E., & KENNEDY, D. R. (1988). Dating infidelity: Behaviors, reasons and consequences. *Adolescence, 23,* 35-43.

ROSENBERG, F., & ROSENBERG, M. (1978). Self-esteem and delinquency. *Journal of Youth and Adolescence, 7,* 279-291.

ROSENBERG, M. (1985). *Society and the adolescent self image.* Princeton, NJ: Princeton University Press.

ROSENBERG, M. (1986). Self-concept from middle childhood through adolescence. In J. Suls & A. G. Greenwald (Eds.), *Psychological perspectives of the self* (Vol. 3). Hillsdale, NJ: Erlbaum.

ROSENTHAL, D. A., & FELDMAN, S. S. (1991). The influence of perceived family and personal factors on self-reported school performance of Chinese and western high school students. *Journal of Research on Adolescence, 1,* 135-154.

ROSSMAN, B. B. R., & ROSENBERG, M. S. (1989, April). *Children in violent and discordant families: Coping, conflict control beliefs, and outcome.* Paper presented at the biennial meetings of the Society for Research in Child Development, Kansas City, MO.

ROWE, J., & MARCIA, J. (1980). Ego identity status, formal operations, and moral development. *Journal of Youth and Adolescence, 9,* 87-99.

RUBENSTEIN, J. L., & FELDMAN, S. S. (1993). Conflict-resolution behavior in adolescent boys: Antecedents and adaptational correlates. *Journal of Research on Adolescence, 3,* 41-66.

RUBENSTEIN, J. L., HEREN, T., HOUSMAN, D., RUBIN, C., & STECHLER, G. (1989). Suicidal behavior in "normal" adolescents: Risk and protective factors. *American Journal of Orthopsychiatry, 59,* 59-71.

RUBLE, D., & BROOKS-GUNN, J. (1982). The experience of menarche. *Child Development, 53,* 1557-1566.

RUSSELL, C. (1980). Unscheduled parenthood: Transition to 'parent' for the teenager. *Journal of Social Issues, 36,* 45-63.

RUSSELL, G. (1978). The father role and its relation to masculinity, femininity, and androgyny. *Child Development, 49,* 1174-1181.

RUTTER, M. (1983). School effects on pupil progress: Research findings and policy implications. *Child Development, 54,* 1-29.

RYAN, R. M., & LYNCH, J. H. (1989). Emotional autonomy versus detachment. Revisiting the vicissitudes of adolescence and young adulthood. *Child Development, 60,* 340-356.

SAMEROFF, A. J., SEIFER, R., BALDWIN, A., & BALDWIN, C. (1993). Stability of intelligence from preschool to adolescence: The influence of social and family risk factors. *Child Development, 64,* 80-97.

SANTROCK, J., WARSHAK, R., LINDBERGH, C., & MEADOWS, L. (1982). Children's and parents' observed social behavior in stepfather families. *Child Development, 53,* 472-480.

SARIGIANI, P. A. (1989, April). *Ratings of the marital relationship and parent and adolescent adjustment.* Paper presented at the biennial meeting of the Society for Research in Child Development, Kansas City, MO.

SARIGIANI, P. A., WILSON, J. L., PETERSEN, A. C., & VICARY, J. R. (1990). Self-image and educational plans of adolescents from two contrasting communities. *Journal of Early Adolescence, 10,* 37-55.

SAVIN-WILLIAMS, R., & BERNDT, T. (1990). Friendship and peer relations. In S. Feldman & G. Elliott (Eds.), *At the threshold: The developing adolescent.* Cambridge: Harvard University Press.

SAVIN-WILLIAMS, R. C. (1988). Theoretical perspectives accounting for adolescent homosexuality. *Journal of Adolescent Health Care, 9,* 95-105.

SAVIN-WILLIAMS, R. C., & SMALL, S. A. (1986). The timing of puberty and its relationship to adolescent and parent perceptions of family interactions. *Developmental Psychology, 22,* 342–347.

SCARR, S. (1992). Developmental theories for the 1990s: Development and individual differences. *Child Development, 63,* 1–19.

SCARR, S. (1993). Biological and cultural diversity: the legacy of Darwin for development. *Child Development, 64,* 1333–1353.

SCARR, S., WEBBER, P., WEINBERG, R., & WITTIG, M. (1981). Personality resemblance among adolescents and their parents in biologically-related and adoptive families. *Journal of Personality and Social Psychology, 40,* 885–898.

SCARR, S., & WEINBERG, R. (1983). The Minnesota adoption studies: Genetic differences and malleability. *Child Development, 54,* 260–267.

SCHAEFER, E. S. (1965a). Children's reports of parental behavior: An inventory. *Child Development, 36,* 413–424.

SCHAEFER, E. S. (1965b). A configurational analysis of children's reports of parent behavior. *Journal of Consulting Psychology, 29,* 552–557.

SCHNEIDER, B., STEVENSON, D., & LINK, J. (1994, February). *Leaving school early: Psychological and social characteristics of early school leavers.* Paper presented at the biennial meeting of the Society for Research on Adolescence, San Diego, CA.

SCHOFIELD, J. (1981). Complementary and conflicting identities: Images and interaction in an interracial school. In S. Asher & J. Gottman (Eds.), *The development of children's friendships.* Cambridge: Cambridge University Press.

SCHULENBERG, J., & BACHMAN, J. G. (1993, March). *Long hours on the job? Not so bad for some adolescents in some types of jobs: The quality of work and substance use, affect, and stress.* Paper presented at the biennial meetings of the Society for Research on Child Development, New Orleans, LA.

SCHULENBERG, J., GOLDSTEIN, A. E., & VONDRACEK, F. W. (1991). Gender differences in adolescents' career interests: Beyond main effects. *Journal of Research on Adolescence, 1,* 37–61.

SCHULENBERG, J., VONDRACEK, F. W., & CROUTER, A. (1984). The influence of the family on vocational development. *Journal of Marriage and the Family, 46,* 129–143.

SCHWARTZ, D., DODGE, K. A., & COIE, J. D. (1993). The emergence of chronic peer victimization in boy's play groups. *Child Development, 64,* 1755–1772.

SCHWARTZ, I. M. (1993). Affective reactions of American and Swedish women to their first prematrital coitus: A cross-cultural comparison. *Journal of Sex Research, 30,* 18–26.

SCOTT-JONES, D. (1991a). Adolescent childbearing: Risks and resilience. *Education and Urban Scoiety, 24,* 53–64.

SCOTT-JONES, D. (1991b). Educational levels of adolescent childbearers at first and second births. *American Journal of Education, 99,* 461–480.

SEARS, R. R. (1950). Personality. *Annual Review of Psychology, 1,* 105–118.

SEARS, R. R., MACCOBY, E. E., & LEVIN, H. (1957). *Patterns of child rearing.* Evanston, IL: Row, Peterson.

SEIDMAN, E., ALLEN, L., ABER, J. L. MITCHELL, C., & FEINMAN, J. (1994). The impact of school transitions in early adolescence on the self-system and perceived social context of poor urban youth. *Child Development, 65,* 507–522.

SEITZ, V., & APFEL, N. H. (1993a). Adolescent mothers and repeated childrearing: Effects of a school-based intervention program. *Child Development, 65,* 572–581.

SEITZ, V., & APFEL, N. H. (1993b). Adolescent mothers and repeated childrearing: Effects of a school-based intervention

program. *American Journal of Orthopsychiatry, 65,* 572–581.

SEITZ, V., & APFEL, N. H. (1994). Effects of a school for pregnant students on the incidence of low-birthweight deliveries. *Child Development, 65,* 666–676.

SELIGMAN, M. E. (1975). *Helplessness: On depression, development, and death.* San Francisco: Freeman.

SELMAN, R. (1976). Social-cognitive understanding: A guide to educational and clinical practice. In T. Lickona (Ed.), *Moral development and behavior: Theory, research, and social issues.* New York: Holt, Rinehart & Winston.

SELMAN, R. (1980). *The growth of interpersonal understanding.* New York: Academic Press.

SELMAN, R., & BYRNE, D. (1974). A structural-developmental analysis of levels of role taking in middle childhood. *Child Development, 45,* 803–806.

SERBIN, L. A., POWLISHTA, K. K., & GULKO, J. (1993). The development of sex typing in middle childhood. *Monographs of the Society for Research in Child Development, 58* (Serial No. 232).

SEWELL, W. H., & SHAH, V. P. (1968a). Parents' education and children's educational aspirations and achievements. *American Sociological Review, 33,* 191–209.

SEWELL, W. H., & SHAH, V. P. (1968b). Social class, parental encouragement, and educational aspirations. *American Journal of Sociology, 33,* 559–572.

SHAGLE, S. C., & BARBER, B. K. (1994, February). *Family and individual predictors of youth suicidal ideation.* Poster presented at the biennial meeting of the Society for Research on Adolescence, San Diego, CA.

SHAH, F., & ZELNIK, M. (1981). Parent and peer influence on sexual behavior, contraceptive use, and pregnancy experience of young women. *Journal of Marriage and the Family, 43,* 339–348.

SHAVELSON, R., & BOLUS, R. (1982). Self-concept: The interplay of theory and methods. *Journal of Educational Psychology, 74,* 3–17.

SHELDON, W. H. (1940). *The varieties of human physique.* New York: Harper & Row.

SHERIF, M., HARVEY, O. J., HOOD, W. R., & SHERIF, C. W. (1961). *Intergroup conflict and cooperation: The robbers cave experiment.* Norman: University of Oklahoma Press.

SHERIF, M., & SHERIF, C. W. (1953). *Groups in harmony and tension.* New York: Harper & Row.

SHERMAN, J., & FENNEMA, E. (1977). The study of mathematics by high school girls and boys: Related variables. *American Educational Research Journal, 14,* 159–168.

SHERMAN, S. J., JUDD, C. M., & PARK, B. (1988). Social cognition. In M. R. Rosenzweig & L. W. Porter, (Eds.), *Annual review of psychology* (Vol. 40). Palo Alto, CA: Annual Reviews.

SHIFFLER, N., LYNCH-SAUER, J., & NADELMAN, L. (1977). Relationship between self-concept and classroom behavior in two informal elementary classrooms. *Journal of Educational Psychology, 69,* 349–359.

SHRUM, W., CHEEK, N., JR., & HUNTER, S. (1988). Friendship in school: Gender and racial homophily. *Sociology of Education, 61,* 227–239.

SILVERBERG, S. B. (1992, March). *Parental well-being and the transition to adolescence.* Paper presented at the biennial meetings of the Society for Research on Adolescence, Washington, DC.

SILVERBERG, S. B., MARCZAK, M. S., & GONDOLI, D. M. (1993, March). *Maternal depressive symptoms and early adolescent females' academic achievement, expectations, and aspirations.* Paper presented at the biennial meetings of the Society for Research in Child Development, New Orleans, LA.

SIMMONS, R. G., & BLYTH, D. A. (1987). *Moving into adoles-*

cence: The impact of pubertal change and school context. New York: Aldine/de Gruyter.

SIMMONS, R. G., BLYTH, D. A., & McKINNEY, K. L. (1983). The social and psychological effects of puberty on white females. In J. Brooks-Gunn & A. C. Petersen (Eds.), *Girls at puberty.* New York: Plenum Press.

SIMMONS, R. G., BURGESON, R., CARLTON-FORD, S., & BLYTH, D. A. (1987). The impact of cumulative change in early adolescence. *Child Development, 58,* 1220-1234.

SIMPSON, E. (1987). The development of political reasoning. *Human Development, 30,* 268-281.

SINGH, N. N., & BEALE, I. L. (Eds.) (1992). *Learning disabilities: Nature, theory, and treatment.* New York: Springer-Verlag.

SIRIS, S. G., VAN KAMMEN, D. P., & DOCHERTY, J. P. (1978). Use of anti-depressant drugs in schizophrenia. *Archives of General Psychiatry, 35,* 1368-1377.

SLABY, R. G., & GUERRA, N. G. (1988). Cognitive mediators of aggression in adolescent offenders: I. Assessment. *Developmental Psychology, 24,* 580-588.

SLAVIN, R. E. (1994). *Educational psychology: Theory and practice.* Boston: Allyn and Bacon.

SMETANA, J. G. (in press). Conflict and coordination in adolescent-parent relationships. In S. Shulman (Ed.), *Close relationships and socioemotional development.* Norwood, NJ: Ablex.

SMETANA, J. G. (1993). Conceptions of parental authority in divorced and married mothers and their adolescents. *Journal of Research on Adolescence, 3,* 19-39.

SMETANA, J. G., & ASQUITH, P. (1994). Adolescents' and parents' conceptions of parental authority and personal autonomy. *Child Development, 65,* 1147-1162.

SMITH, E., UDRY, J., & MORRIS, N. (1985). Pubertal development and friends: A biosocial explanation of adolescent sexual behavior. *Journal of Health and Social Behavior, 26,* 183-192.

SMOLLAR, J., & OOMS, T. (1987). *Young unwed fathers: Research review, policy dilemmas and options* (Summary Report). Washington, DC.

SNAREY, J. R., REIMER, J., & KOHLBERG, L. (1985). Development of social-moral reasoning among Kibbutz adolescents. A longitudinal cross-cultural study. *Developmental Psychology, 21,* 3-17.

SOARES, A. T., & SOARES, L. M. (1972). The self-concept differential in disadvantaged and advantaged students. *Proceedings of the Annual Convention of the American Psychological Association, 7* (Pt. 1), 195-196.

SOBESKY, W. (1983). The effects of situational factors on moral judgments. *Child Development, 54,* 575-584.

SOMMER, K., ET AL. (1993). Cognitive readiness and adolescent parenting. *Developmental Psychology, 29,* 389-398.

SORENSEN, R. C. (1973). *Adolescent sexuality in contemporary America.* New York: World.

SPEARMAN, C. (1927). *The abilities of man.* New York: Macmillan.

SPENCE, J. T., & HELMREICH, R. (1979). Comparison of masculine and feminine personality attributes and sex-role attitudes across age groups. *Developmental Psychology, 15,* 583-584.

SPENCE, J. T., & HELMREICH, R. (1981). Androgyny versus gender schema: A comment on Bem's gender schema theory. *Psychological Review, 88,* 365-368.

SPENCE, J. T., HELMREICH, R., & STAPP, J. (1974). The Personal Attributes Questionnaire: A measure of sex role stereotypes and masculinity-femininity. *JSAS: Catalog of Selected Documents in Psychology, 4,* 43.

SPENCER, M., & DORNBUSCH, S. (1990). Challenges in studying minority youth. In S. Feldman & G. Elliot (Eds.), *At the thresh-*

old: The developing adolescent (pp. 123-146). Cambridge, MA: Harvard University Press.

SROUFE, L. A., BENNETT, C., EGELUND, M., URBAN, J., & SHULMAN, S. (1993). The significance of gender boundaries in pre-adolescence: Contemporary correlates and antecedents of boundary violation maintenance. *Child Development, 64,* 455-466.

STAGER, J. M., RITCHIE, B. A., & ROBERTSHAW, D. (1984). Reversal of Oligo/Amenorrhea in collegiate distance runner. *New England Journal of Medicine, 310,* 51.

STATTIN, H., & MAGNUSSON, D. (1993, March). *Convergence in time of age at onset of official delinquency and educational and behavioral problems.* Paper presented at the biennial meetings of the Society for Research in Child Development, New Orleans, LA.

STATTIN, H., & MAGNUSSON, C. (1994, February). *Behavioral and interpersonal antecedents behind the age at leaving home, and the future consequences for parent-child relations.* Paper presented at the biennial meetings of the Society for Research on Adolescence, San Diego, CA.

STEINBERG, L. D., LAMBORN, S. D., DARLING, N., MOUNTS, N. S., & DORNBUSCH, S. M. (1994). Over-time changes in adjustment and competence among adolescents from authoritative, authoritarian, indulgent, and neglectful families. *Child Development, 65,* 754-770.

STEINBERG, L. D., & SILVERBERG, S. (1986). The vicissitudes of autonomy in early adolescence. *Child Development, 57,* 841-851.

STEINBERG, L. D. (1981). Transformation in family relations at puberty. *Developmental Psychology, 17,* 833-840.

STEINBERG, L. D. (1982). Jumping off the work experience bandwagon. *Journal of Youth and Adolescence, 11,* 183-205.

STEINBERG, L. D. (1984). The varieties and effects of work during adolescence. In M. Lamb (Ed.), *Advances in developmental psychology* (Vol. 3). Hillsdale, NJ: Erlbaum.

STEINBERG, L. D. (1989). Pubertal maturation and parent-adolescent distance: An evolutionary perspective. In G. R. Adams, R. Montemayor, & T. P. Gullotta (Eds.), *Biology of adolescent behavior and development.* Newbury Park, CA: Sage.

STEINBERG, L. D., BLINN, P., & CHAN, K. (1984). Dropping out among language minority youth. *Review of Educational Research, 54,* 113-132.

STEINBERG, L.D. , DORNBUSCH, S. M., & BROWN, B. B. (1992). Ethnic differences in adolescent achievement. *American Psychologist, 47,* 723-729.

STEINBERG, L. D., FEGLEY, S., & DORNBUSCH, S. M. (1993). Negative impact of part-time work on adolescent adjustment: Evidence from a longitudinal study. *Developmental Psychology, 29,* 171-180.

STEINBERG, L. D., GREENBERGER, E., GARDUQUE, L., & McAULLIFFE, S. (1982). High school students in the labor force: Some costs and benefits to schooling and learning. *Educational Evaluation and Policy Analysis, 4,* 363-372.

STEINBERG, L. D., GREENBERGER, E., VAUX, A., & RUGGIERO, M. (1981). Early work experience: Effects on adolescent occupational socialization. *Youth and Society, 12,* 403-422.

STEINBERG, L. D., & HILL, J. (1978). Patterns of family interaction as a function of age, the onset of puberty, and formal thinking. *Developmental Psychology, 14,* 683-684.

STEINBERG, L. D., LAMBORN, S. D., DORNBUSCH, S. M., & DARLING, N. (1992). Impact of parenting practices on adolescent achievement: Authoritative parenting, school involvement, and encouragement to succeed. *Child Development, 63,* 1266-1281.

STERNBERG, R. (1988). *The triarchic mind.* New York: Viking Penguin.

STEVENSON, D. L., & BAKER, D. P. (1987). The family-school relation and the child's school performance. *Child Development, 58,* 1348-1357.

STEVENSON, H. W., CHEN, C., & UTTAL, D. H. (1990). Beliefs and achievement: A study of black, white, and Hispanic children. *Child Development, 61,* 508-523.

STILES, D. A., GIBBONS, J. L., HARDARDOTTIR, S., & SCHNELLMANN, J. (1987). The ideal man or woman as described by young adolescents in Iceland and the United States. *Sex Roles, 17,* 313-320.

STRIEGEL-MOORE, R., SCHREIBER, D., PIKE, K. M., VILFLEY, D. E., & RODIN, J. (in press). Drive for thinness in black and white preadolescent girls. *International Journal of Eating Disorders.*

SULLIVAN, E. V. (1970). Political development during the adolescent years. In E. D. Evans (Ed.), *Adolescents: Readings in behavior and development.* Hinsdale, IL: Dryden.

SULLIVAN, H. S. (1953). *Interpersonal theory of psychiatry.* New York: Norton.

SUM, A. M., HARRINGTON, P. E., & GOEDICKE, W. (1987). One-fifth of the nation's teenagers: Employment problems of poor youth in America, 1981-1985. *Youth and Society, 18,* 195-237.

SUMMERVILLE, M. B., & KASLOW, N. J. (1993, March). *Racial differences in psychological symptoms, cognitive style, and family functioning in suicidal adolescents.* Paper presented at the biennial meetings of the Society for Research on Child Development, New Orleans, LA.

SUPER, D. E. (1953). A theory of vocational development. *American Psychologist, 8,* 185-190.

SUPER, D. E. (1985). Coming of age in Middletown. *American Psychologist, 40,* 405-414.

SUPER, D. E. (1990). Career and life development. In D. Brown, L. Brooks, & Associates (Eds.), *Career choice and development.* San Francisco: Jossey-Bass.

SUPER, D. E., CRITES, J., HUMMEL, R., MOSER, H., OVERSTREET, P., & WARNATH, C. (1957). *Vocational development: A framework for research.* New York: Teachers College, Columbia University.

SWARTZMAN-SCHATMAN, B., & SCHINKE, S. P. (1993). The effect of mid life divorce on late adolescent and young adult children. *Journal of Divorce & Remarriage, 19,* 209-218.

TANNER, J. M. (1970). Physical growth. In P. H. Mussen (Ed.), *Carmichael's manual of child psychology* (3rd ed., Vol. 1). New York: Wiley.

TAYLOR, R. D., CASTEN, R., FLICKINGER, S. M., ROBERTS, D., & FULMORE, C. D. (1994). Explaining the school performance of African-American adolescents. *Journal of Research on Adolescence, 4,* 21-44.

TEDDLIE, C., KIRBY, P. C., & STRINGFIELD, S. (1989). Effective vs. ineffective schools: Observable differences in the classroom. *American Journal of Education, 97,* 221-236.

TETI, D. M., & LAMB, M. E. (1989). Socioeconomic and marital outcomes of adolescent marriage, adolescent childbirth, and their co-occurrence. *Journal of Marriage and the Family, 51,* 203-212.

TETI, D. M., LAMB, M. E., & ELSTER, A. B. (1987). Long-range socioeconomic and marital consequences of adolescent marriage in three cohorts of adult males. *Journal of Marriage and the Family, 49,* 499-506.

THOMA, S. J., & LADEWIG, B. H. (1993, March). *Close friendships, friendship networks, and moral judgment development during the college years.* Paper presented at the biennial meetings of the Society for Research in Child Development, New Orleans, LA.

THORNBURG, H. (1970-1971). Adolescence: A reinterpretation. *Adolescence, 5,* 463-484.

TIDWELL, R. (1988). Dropouts speak out: Qualitative data on early school departures. *Adolescence, 23,* 939-954.

TIEGER, T. (1980). On the biological basis of sex differences in aggression. *Child Development, 51,* 943-963.

TOBIN-RICHARDS, M. H., BOXER, A. M., & PETERSEN, A. C. (1983). The psychological significance of pubertal change: Sex differences in perceptions of self during early adolescence. In J. Brooks-Gunn & A. C. Petersen (Eds.), *Girls at puberty.* New York: Plenum Press.

TOLMAN, D. L. (1993, March). *"When my body says yes:" Adolescent girls' experiences of sexual desire.* Paper presented at the biennial meetings of the Society for Research in Child Development, New Orleans, LA.

TOLSON, J. M., HALLIDAY-SCHER, K., & MACK, V. (February, 1994). *Similarity and friendship quality in African-American adolescents.* Paper presented at the biennial meeting of the Society for Research on Adolescence, San Diego, CA.

TOMLINSON-KEASEY, C., & KEASEY, C. B. (1974). The mediating role of cognitive development in moral judgment. *Child Development, 45,* 291-298.

TORRANCE, P. (1966). *Torrance tests of creative thinking.* Princeton, NJ: Personnel Press.

TRACY, D. M. (1987). Toys, spatial ability, and science and mathematics achievement: Are they related? *Sex Roles, 17,* 115-138.

TROWBRIDGE, N. (1972). Self-concept and socio-economic status in elementary school children. *American Educational Research Journal, 9,* 525-537.

TRUGLIO, R. (1993, March). *Sex in the 90's: What are the lessons from prime-time TV?* Poster presented at the biennial meeting of the Society for Research in Child Development, New Orleans, LA.

TURNER, R. A., & FELDMAN, S. S. (1993, March). *Distance regulation in adolescent romantic relationships: An attachment approach.* Paper presented at the biennial meetings of the Society for Research in Child Development, New Orleans, LA.

TURNER, R. A., & FELDMAN, S. S. (1994, February). *The functions of sex in everyday life.* Paper presented at the biennial meeting of the Society for Research on Adolescence, San Diego, CA.

TURNER, R. A., IRWIN, C. E., JR., & MILLSTEIN, S. G. (1991). Family structure, family processes, and experimenting with substances during adolescence. *Journal of Research on Adolescence, 1,* 93-106.

TURTURO, K. A. (1993, March). *An investigation into the relation between marital quality and parenting style.* Poster presented at the biennial meetings of the Society for Research on Child Development, New Orleans, LA.

UDRY, J. (1987). Hormonal and social determinants of adolescent sexual initiation. In J. Bancroft (Ed.), *Adolescence and puberty.* New York: Oxford University Press.

UDRY, J., TALBERT, L., & MORRIS, N. (1986). Biosocial foundations for adolescent female sexuality. *Demography, 23,* 217-230.

UNGER, R. (1979). Toward a redefinition of sex and gender. *American Psychologist, 34,* 1085-1094.

U. S. BUREAU OF THE CENSUS (1987). *Statistical abstract of the U.S., 1987* (108th ed.). Washington, DC: U.S. Government Printing Office.

U. S. BUREAU OF THE CENSUS. (1989). *Statistical abstract of the U. S., 1989* (110th ed.). Washington, DC: U.S. Government Printing Office.

U. S. BUREAU OF THE CENSUS. (1992a). *1990 Census of Population and Housing.* Washington, DC: U.S. Government Printing Office.

U. S. BUREAU OF THE CENSUS. (1992b). *Marriage, divorce, and remarriage in the 1990s.* (Current Population Reports, P23-P180). Washington, DC: U. S. Government Printing Office.

U.S. BUREAU OF THE CENSUS. (1992c). *Statistical abstract of the U. S.: 1992* (112th ed.). Washington, DC: U.S. Government Printing Office.

U.S. BUREAU OF THE CENSUS. (1993). *Statistical abstract of the U.S.: 1993.* (113th ed.). Washington, DC: U.S. Government Printing Office.

URBERG, K. A. (1979). Sex role conceptualizations in adolescents and adults. *Developmental Psychology, 15,* 90–92.

URBERG, K. A., & DEGIRMENCIOGLU, S. (1989, April). *Peer influence on adolescent values.* Paper presented at the biennial meetings of the Society for Research in Child Development, Kansas City, MO.

VANDENBERG, D. (1968). Life-phases and values. *Education Forum, 32,* 293–302.

VANGELISTI, A. L. (1988). Adolescent socialization into the workplace: A synthesis and critique of current literature. *Youth and Society, 19,* 460–484.

VONDRACEK, F. W. (1993). Promoting vocational development in early adolescence. In R. M. Lerner (Ed.), *Early adolescence: Perspectives on research, policy, and intervention.* Englewood Cliffs, NJ: Erlbaum.

VONDRACEK, F. W., & GALANOPOULOS, A. (1992, March). *Identity status and work values in adolescence.* Paper presented at the biennial meetings of the Society for Research on Adolescence, Washington, DC.

WAGNER, B. M., COLE, R. E., & SCHWARTZMAN, P. (1993, March). *Prediction of suicide attempts among junior and senior high school youth.* Poster presented at the biennial meetings of the Society for Research in Child Development, New Orleans, LA.

WALKER, L. J. (1980). Cognitive and perspective-taking prerequisites for moral development. *Child Development, 51,* 131–139.

WALKER, L. J. (1983). Sources of cognitive conflict for stage transition in moral development. *Developmental Psychology, 19,* 103–110.

WALKER, L. J. (1986). Sex differences in the development of moral reasoning: A rejoinder to Baumrind. *Child Development, 57,* 522–526.

WALKER, L. J. (1989). A longitudinal study of moral reasoning. *Child Development, 60,* 157–166.

WALKER, L. J., DEVRIES, B., & TREVETHAN, S. D. (1987). Moral stages and moral orientations in real-life and hypothetical dilemmas. *Child Development, 58,* 842–858.

WALKER, L. J., & TAYLOR, J. H. (1991). Family interactions and the development of moral reasoning. *Child Development, 62,* 264–283.

WALLACE-BROSCIOUS, A., SERAFICA, F. C., & OSIPOW, S. H. (1994). Adolescent career development: Relationships to self-concept and identity status. *Journal of Research on Adolescence, 4,* 127–149.

WALLERSTEIN, J. S. (1983). Children of divorce: The psychological tasks of the child. *American Journal of Orthopsychiatry, 53,* 230–243.

WALLERSTEIN, J. S. (1984). Children of divorce: Preliminary report of a ten-year follow-up of young children. *American Journal of Orthopsychiatry, 54,* 444–458.

WALLERSTEIN, J. S., & KELLY, J. (1980). *Surviving the breakup: How children and parents cope with divorce.* New York: Basic Books.

WALTERS, J. M., & GARDNER, H. (1986). The theory of multiple intelligences: Some issues and answers. In R. Sternberg & R. Wagner (Eds.), *Practical intelligence: Nature and origins of competence in the everyday world.* New York: Cambridge University Press.

WATERMAN, A. S. (1982). Identity development from adolescence to adulthood: An extension of theory and a review of research. *Developmental Psychology, 18,* 341–358.

WATERMAN, A. S. (1989). Curricula interventions for identity change: Substantive and ethical considerations. *Journal of Adolescence, 12,* 389–400.

WATERMAN, A. S. (1992). Assigned and chosen identity components: A process perspective on their integration. In G. R. Adams, T. P. Gullotta, & R. Montemayor (Eds.), *Adolescent identity formation.* Newbury Park, CA: Sage.

WATERMAN, A. S., GEARY, P., & WATERMAN, C. (1974). A longitudinal study of change in ego identity status from the freshman to senior year at college. *Developmental Psychology, 10,* 387–392.

WATERMAN, A. S., & GOLDMAN, J. (1976). A longitudinal study of ego identity development at a liberal arts college. *Journal of Youth and Adolescence, 5,* 361–369.

WATERMAN, A. S., & WATERMAN, C. (1971). A longitudinal study of changes in ego identity status during the freshman year at college. *Developmental Psychology, 5,* 167–173.

WATERMAN, A. S., & WHITBOURNE, S. (1982). Androgyny and psychological development among college students and adults. *Journal of Personality, 50,* 121–133.

WATKINS, B. (1989, April). *Conceptions of athletic excellence among children and adolescents.* Paper presented at the biennial meetings of the Society for Research in Child Development, Kansas City, MO.

WATKINS, B., & MONTGOMERY, A. B. (in press). Conceptions of athletic excellence among children and adolescents. *Child Development.*

WEHNER, E. A. (1993, March). *The structure of adolescent romantic relationships.* Paper presented at the biennial meetings of the Society for Research on Child Development, New Orleans, LA.

WEINER, I. B. (1992). *Psychological disturbance in adolescence.* (2nd ed.). New York: Wiley.

WEINER, I. B. (1980). Psycopathology in adolescence. In J. Adelson (Ed.), *Handbook of adolescent psychology.* New York: Wiley.

WEINRACH, S. G., & SREBALUS, D. J. (1990). Holland's theory of careers. In D. Brown & L. Brooks, & Associates (Eds.). *Career choice and development.* San Francisco: Jossey-Bass.

WEISS, R. (1982). Understanding moral thought: Effects on moral reasoning and decision making. *Developmental Psychology, 18,* 852–861.

WELLS, L. E. (1989). Self-enhancement through delinquency: A conditional test of self-derogation theory. *Journal of Research in Crime and Delinquency, 26,* 226–252.

WENTZEL, K. R. (1988). Gender differences in math and English achievement: A longitudinal study. *Sex Roles, 18,* 691–699.

WENTZEL, K. R. (1989). Adolescent classroom goals, standards for performance, and academic achievement: An interactionist perspective. *Journal of Educational Psychology, 81,* 131–142.

WERKING, K. (1994). Cross-sex friendships: Introduction. *Personal Relationship Issues, 2,* 1.

WHITE, C. B. (1975). Moral development in Bahamian school children: A cross-cultured examination of Kohlberg's stages of moral reasoning. *Developmental Psychology, 11,* 535–536.

WHITE, K. (1982). The relation between socioeconomic status and academic achievement. *Psychological Bulletin, 91,* 461–481.

WHITEHEAD, J. T., & LAB, S. (1989). A meta-analysis of juvenile correctional treatment. *Journal of Research in Crime and Delinquency, 26,* 276–295.

WHITLEY, B. E., JR. (1988). The relation of gender-role orientation to sexual experience among college students. *Sex Roles, 19,* 619-638.

WHITLEY, B. E., JR. (1989, August). *College students' reasons for sexual intercourse: A sex role perspective.* Paper presented at the annual meetings of the American Psychological Association, Atlanta, GA.

WIGFIELD, A., ECCLES, J. S., MacIVER, D., REUMAN, D. A., & MIDGLEY, C. (1991). Transitions during early adolescence: Changes in children's domain-specific self-perceptions and general self-esteem across the transition to junior high school. *Developmental Psychology, 27,* 552-565.

WILLIAMS, F. S. (1993, March). *Familial antecedents of adolescent identity exploration.* Poster presented at the biennial meetings of the Society for Research in Child Development, New Orleans, LA.

WIRTZ, P. W., ROHRBECK, C. A., CHARMER, I., & FRASER, B. S. (1988). Employment of adolescents while in high school: Employment intensity, interference with schoolwork, and normative approval. *Journal of Adolescent Research, 3,* 97-105.

WYLIE, R. C. (1979). *The self-concept* (Vol. 2). Lincoln: University of Nebraska Press.

YALOM, I., GREEN, R., & FISK, M. (1973). Prenatal exposure to famale hormones: Effects on psychosexual development in boys. *Archives of General Psychiatry, 28,* 554-561.

YEE, D. K., & ECCLES, J. S. (1988). Parent perceptions and attributions for children's math achievement. *Sex Roles, 19,* 317-333.

YOSHIKAWA, H. (1994). Prevention as cumulative protection: Effects of early family support and education on chronic delinquency and its risks. *Psychological Bulletin, 115,* 28-54.

YOUNG, E., & PARISH, T. (1977). Impact of father absence during childhood on the psychological adjustment of college females. *Sex Roles, 3,* 217-227.

YOUNG, R. L., GODFREY, W., MATTHEWS, B., & ADAMS, G. R. (1983). Runaways: A review of negative consequences. *Family Relations, 32,* 275-281.

YOUNISS, J., & YATES, M. (1994, February). *Community service and political-moral awakening.* Paper presented at the biennial meetings of the Society for Research in Adolescence, San Diego, CA.

YOUTH INDICATORS. (1988). *Trends in the well-being of American youth.* Washington, D.C: U. S. Government Printing Office.

ZABIN, L. S., & HAYWARD, S. C. (1993). *Adolescent sexual behavior and childbearing.* Newbury Park, CA: Sage.

ZELKOWITZ, P. (1987). Social support and aggressive behavior in young children. *Family Relations Journal of Applied Family and Child Studies, 36,* 129-134.

ZELNIK, M., & KANTNER, J. (1977). Sexual and contraceptive experience of young unmarried women in the United States, 1976, 1971. *Family Planning Perspectives, 9,* 55-71.

ZELNIK, M., & KANTNER, J. (1978). First pregnancies to women aged 15-19: 1976 and 1971. *Family Planning Perspectives, 10,* 11-20.

ZELNIK, M., & KANTNER, J. (1980). Sexual activity, contraceptive use and pregnancy among metropolitan-area teenagers: 1971-1979. *Family Planning Perspectives, 12,* 230-237.

ZELNIK, M., KANTNER, J., & FORD, K. (1981). *Sex and pregnancy in adolescence.* Beverly Hills, CA: Sage.

ZIEGLER, C., & DUSEK, J. B. (1985). Perceptions of child rearing and adolescent sex role development. *Journal of Early Adolescence, 5,* 215-227.

ZIEGLER, C., DUSEK, J. B., & CARTER, D. (1984). Self-concept and sex-role orientation: An investigation of multidimensional aspects of personality development in adolescence. *Journal of Early Adolescence, 4,* 25-39.

ZIMILES, H., & LEE, V. (1991). Adolescent family structure and educational progress. *Developmental Psychology, 27,* 314-320.

ZUMPF, C. L. (1989). *Mirror, mirror on the wall: Gender differences in the link between appearance and self-worth in early adolescence.* Paper presented at the biennial meetings of the Society for Research in Child Development, Kansas City, MO.

Name Index

Subject Index